Visualizing
Theory

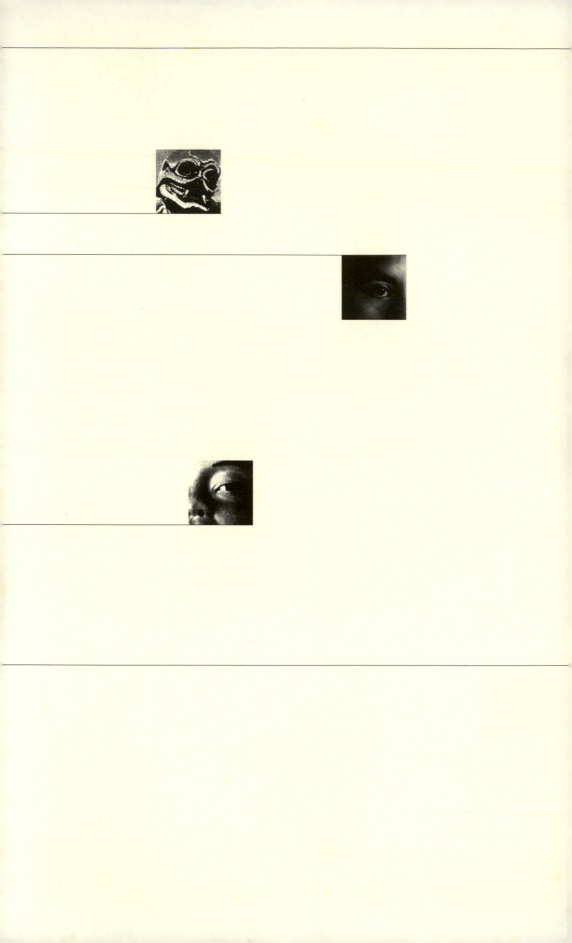

Visualizing
Theory

Selected Essays from V.A.R.
1990–1994

Edited by
Lucien Taylor

ROUTLEDGE   NEW YORK AND LONDON

Published in 1994 by

Routledge
29 West 35th Street
New York, NY 10001

Published in Great Britain by

Routledge
11 New Fetter Lane
London EC4P 4EE

Library of Congress Cataloging-in-Publication Data

  Visualizing theory: selected essays from V.A.R., 1990–1994 / edited by Lucien Taylor.
      p. cm.
    Includes bibliographical references.
    ISBN 0-415-90842-6. ISBN 0-415-90843-4 (pbk.)
    1. Visual anthropology. I. Taylor, Lucien.
III. Visual anthropology review.
GN347.V575 1993
301—dc20   93-31997
CIP

British Library Cataloguing-in-Publication Data also available

Book design, type and imaging by Leslie Sharpe

Set in Spectrum by Monotype, heads in Modula and Birch

Eliot Weinberger, "The Camera People," originally published in *Transition* 55 (1992), pp. 24–54. © Oxford University Press. Used with permission. The following articles have been reproduced by permission of the American Anthropological Association: David MacDougall, "Whose Story Is It?," from *Visual Anthropology Review* 7:2, Fall 1991. George Marcus, "The Modernist Sensibility in Recent Ethnographic Writing and the Cinematic Metaphor of Montage," from *S.V.A. Review* 6:1, Spring 1990. Annette Weiner, "Trobrianders on Camera and Off," from *V.A.R.* 8:1, Spring 1992. Bill Nichols, "The Ethnographer's Tale," from *V.A.R.* 7:2, Fall 1992. Paul Stoller, "Artaud, Rouch and the Cinema of Cruelty," from *V.A.R.* 8:2, Fall 1992. Dean MacCannell, "Cannibal Tours," from *V.A.R.* 6:2, Fall 1990. Henrietta Moore, "Trinh T. Minh-ha Observed: Anthropology and Others," from *V.A.R.* 6:2, Fall 1990. Rachel Moore, "Marketing Alterity," from *V.A.R.* 8:2, Fall 1992. Susan Suleiman, "Between the Street and the *Salon:* The Dilemma of Surrealist Politics in the 1930s," from *V.A.R.* 7:1, Spring 1991. Hal Foster, "Exquisite Corpses," from *V.A.R.* 7:1, Spring 1991. Martin Jay, "The Disenchantment of the Eye: Surrealism and the Crisis of Ocularcentrism," from *V.A.R.* 7:1, Spring 1991. Michael Taussig, "Physiognomic Aspects of Visual Worlds," from *V.A.R.* 8:1, Spring 1992. C. Nadia Seremetakis, "The Memory of the Senses," from *V.A.R.* 9:2, Fall 1993. Victor Burgin, "Paranoiac Space," from *V.A.R.* 7:2, Fall 1991. Marilyn Strathern, "One-Legged Gender," from *V.A.R.* 9:1, Spring 1993. Ludmilla Jordanova, "The Hand," from *V.A.R.* 8:2, Fall 1992. David MacDougall, "Films of Memory," from *V.A.R.* 8:1, Spring 1992. David Tomas, "Manufacturing Vision," from *V.A.R.* 8:2, Fall 1992. Marc Blanchard, "Post-Bourgeois Tattoo: Reflections on Skin Writing in Late Capitalist Societies," from *V.A.R.* 7:2, Fall 1991. Elizabeth Traube, "Family Matters: Postfeminist Constructions of a Contested Site," from *V.A.R.* 9:1, Spring 1993. Peter Redfield, "Remembering the Revolution, Forgetting the Empire: Notes After the French Bicentennial," from *V.A.R.* 8:2, Fall 1992. Bennetta Jules-Rosette, "Simulations of Postmodernity: Images of Technology in African Tourist and Popular Art," from *S.V.A. Review* 6:1, Spring 1990. Catherine Lutz & J. Collins, "The Photograph as an Intersection of Gazes: The Example of *National Geographic*," from *V.A.R.* 7:1, Spring 1991. Alan Macfarlane, "BBC Domesday: The Social Construction of Britain on Videodisc," from *V.A.R.* 6:2, Fall 1990. Christopher Pinney, "Future Travel," from *V.A.R.* 8:1, Spring 1992. Nancy Chen & Trinh T. Minh-ha, "Speaking Nearby," from *V.A.R.* 8:1, Spring 1992. Homi Bhabha & Victor Burgin, "Visualizing Theory," from *V.A.R.* 8:1, Spring 1992.

Acknowledgements

This volume displays the traces of many people to whom I am considerably indebted—Ilisa Barbash, an inimitable editorial colloquist, for her generous criticism every step of the way; Jean Rouch, whose example provided the initial inspiration for my interest in ethnographic film and visual anthropology; Timothy Asch and Daniel Marks for editing *V.A.R.*'s predecessors (*SVA Newsletter* and *SVA Review*); Francisco Ferrandiz, Faye Ginsburg, Nancy Lutkehaus, Bill Nichols, Chris Pinney, Peter Redfield, Jay Ruby, Christopher Steiner, Paul Stoller, and Sarah Williams, for their editorial input and willingness to review innumerable manuscripts beyond the call of duty; and Joseph Cerny, Meg Conkey, Nelson Graburn, Aihwa Ong, Jack Potter, and Paul Rabinow, for local support and furtherance at the University of California, Berkeley. *Visualizing Theory* would not have appeared without the original proposition and subsequent support of Max Zutty at Routledge, and it has been ably nurtured into being by Stewart Cauley, Production Editor, and Leslie Sharpe, the book's designer. I should like also to acknowledge the generous institutional support for *V.A.R.* provided by both the University of Southern California's Center for Visual Anthropology, and, since 1991, the Anthropological Film Program, Department of Anthropology, and Graduate Division of UC Berkeley.

Contents

Sight and Might, by Lucien Taylor (1984)

Visualizing Theory
Foreword

Lucien Taylor

Aㅣㅣ the essays here, bar one, originally appeared in *V.A.R.* (*VISUAL ANTHROPOLOGY REVIEW*) between 1990 and 1994.[1] Written by filmmakers and photographers, anthropologists and historians, and literary, cultural, and film critics, they may at first glance appear to have little in common over and above their attention to the visual. Being neither an individually authored monograph nor an edited volume stemming from a conference, with its inbuilt focus and coherence, *Visualizing Theory* is more heterogeneous than many academic tomes, addressing topics that range from the significance of mass-produced tourist art in Africa, and the panoply of chiasmic gazes in *National Geographic* photographs, to the "fractalization" of gender identity in Melanesia.

Still, it bears saying that while the essays encompass a variety of subjects and styles, most authors share the desire to clear a space for the theoretical analysis of the ocular, and indeed, of visuality in general. Many implicitly make a case for the *analytic* potential of visual media themselves, and thus try to further our understanding of modes of (non-linguistic) visual analysis. To non-anthropologists this last venture may seem faintly gratuitous, at any rate for the visual arts, since they should of course illuminate or demystify the critics, and not the critics the artworks, but it is perhaps an inevitable response to the scopophobia of the logocratic anthropological academy.

Without making a fetish of either theory or experience, many of the contributors to *Visualizing Theory* hope to counter both the disembodied abstraction of much social theory and the theoretical hypertrophy of the visual in the modern world. If few seem to be explicitly "visualizing" theory, this volume does yet signal a return to the etymological equivalence between theorizing and gazing (*theorèin*, to gaze upon). It engages with their reciprocities— the visual-sensual in the theoretical no less than the theoretical in the visual—after which, in short, the configuration of vision either as constitutive and corporeal or else as a reflective "mirror" of nature ceases to be a simple dichotomy. The lived-bodies of those cine-cephalous anthropologists known as ethnographic filmmakers surely knew this all along, as in the end must all spectators of film—that liminal medium hovering unsteadily, as Arnheim famously put it, somewhere between two- and three-dimensionality. Indeed, haven't the films of Jean Rouch, perhaps the one surrealist ethnographic filmmaker, succeeded—however awkwardly, however partially, however problematically—in reassociating the viewer with the viewed (as Merleau-Ponty might say) in the phenomenological flesh of the world? Has not Rouch, and in a very different register the MacDougalls too, done more than anyone else to de-pathologize ethnographic film spectatorship, to de-fetishize ethnographic film itself, to restore a reciprocity between spectator and subject—not simply in the labored fashion of Vertov to call intellectual attention to the mediation of the apparatus or *trucage* that is constructing the *vérité* of the *cinéma,* but to explode altogether the rupture between the pro-filmic and the filmic, the diegetic and the extra-diegetic? Or, in other words still, to restore Benveniste's absent discourse to the narratorless documentary story, and thereby re-enchant ethnographic cinema, or at the very least enable a healthy, participatory, and non-voyeuristic ethno-cinephilia?[2]

While few of the essays have to do with ethnographic cinema directly, they nonetheless are concerned with the effects of the disembodiment of other looks, and with the possibility of their reincarnation. This synaesthetic identification of seeing and touching—or surface and depth—seems also to be at the heart of so much recent criticism of the privilege accorded by modernism to the "purely" optical, and its so-called prison house of visuality. However, some commentaries on "visualism"—visualist logic, and the ontological foundationalism of opticality more generally—rely on an attenuated conception of the visual, and deploy an artificial antinomy between the optical and the haptic. Moreover, criticisms of the radical differentiation of the specular, and more broadly of the valorization of an (Always, Already) ahistorical subject situated outside the world (and itself), with its transcendental view from no-where, conjoined with contrary celebrations of the subjectivities of corporeality, the embodiment of space, the tactility of vision and so on— these seem at times to elide underlying experiential commonalities which will always constrain the proliferation of particular subjectivities, as well as the variation of cultural construction. Furthermore, it is one thing to criticize the disincarnated look, but quite another to celebrate the desirous body in all its manifestations. And advocates of the lusty appetite of the incarnated eye *tout court* appear at times to forget, as Martin Jay insists, that "[g]lancing is not somehow innately superior to gazing, vision hostage to desire is not necessarily always better than casting a cold eye, a sight from the situated context of a body in the world may not always see things that are visible to a 'high-altitude' or 'God's eye' view."[3] Thus this multifarious volume makes no concerted claim in favor of any particular order of visuality, or indeed any one hierarchy of visual or sensuous knowledge. Rather, it recognizes and embraces the plurality of modes of experience and cognition by which we may both visualize theory and theorize visuality.

•   •   •

The first section, "The Ethnographic & the Ipsographic," contains various essays on ethnographic film, seeking to revise and broaden the canon. An unabashedly unsympathetic outsider, Eliot Weinberger offers an amused reading of the genre's history, from Regnault and Flaherty to the present-day. He focuses on ethnographic film's "impossibly sloppy" attempts to comply with the conventions of realism, as well as the scientism of its very conception of the "Real" and its presumption of an unmediated and mimetic relation thereto. David MacDougall then argues that although ethnographic filmmakers are suddenly aware of the politico-epistemological quandaries of representation, and in particular the inescapable conjunction of author and authority, they must also recognize that films can have multiple identities, as compound artifacts variously structured (and so, in a sense, authored) by their subjects. Moreover, he suggests that ethnographic films should be made not to communicate prefabricated (anthropological) knowledge, but rather in order to *provoke* new knowledge through the very circumstances of their making. Thus conceived, ethnographic filmmaking becomes in itself less an instrument of communication than an activity of discovery, of *truth-making*.

In a more theoretical essay, George Marcus seeks to stimulate a new relationship between ethnographic writing and ethnographic film, one based on intellectual parity and a shared agenda. He argues that ethnographic writing is now resuscitating its "repressed" dimension of narrativity, by borrowing essentially cinematic techniques of montage, both in order to represent novel social subjects and in redefining the space-time identities of its customary ones (not, of course, that the two can be easily distinguished). Although much recent psychoanalytic and feminist film criticism has rightly problematized narrativity, attending as much to the stories that are *excluded* as to those getting told, Marcus views it as a space of hitherto ignored representational possibilities for anthropologists. But while montage might seem ideally suited to the contrapuntal representation of what Ernst Bloch called the synchronicity of the non-synchronous—the coevality of otherwise distinct historical moments, surely one of the core characteristics of modernity[4]—Marcus nonetheless laments that ethnographic film (and here he clearly has neither Rouch nor the MacDougalls in mind) has in fact been relatively "tame" in revising its methods of confronting the countervailing conditions of homogenization and fragmentation that constitute our world today.

Annette Weiner, who acted as the anthropologist for the Disappearing World documentary *The Trobriand Islanders of Papua New Guinea*, follows up on MacDougall's suggestion that ethnographic films should themselves "embody"—enact, so to speak, rather that simply report on—cultural encounters, by urging anthropologists to transcend the hoary old binarism between "us" and "them," and its corollary of an unidirectional oppositional gaze (underpinned, I might add, by an essentialist topology of nativism that would ineluctably counterpose indigene to alien). In turn, she insists, we need to fashion films (and texts) that recognize the multiple authorial and spectatorial imbrications between filmmakers, subjects, and audience. Such films, in her view, "must encompass the filmmaker and audience within the same processes of discovering . . . the powerful ways that global agencies are an intimate part of local encounters." Bill Nichols, on the other hand, coming to ethnographic film as a film critic, proposes that in fact those erstwhile objects (and blindspots) of ethnographic discourse—"women/natives/others," as Trinh's refrain goes—are now representing themselves in what he calls "auto-ethnographic" films which are more sophisticated and engaging than those produced by self-identified and self-addressed ethnographic filmmakers. Marilu Mallet's *Unfinished Diary*, John Akomfrah's *Handsworth Songs*, Christine Choy and Renée Tajima's

Who Killed Vincent Chin?, and Trinh T. Minh-ha's *Sur Name Viet Given Name Nam* are among Nichols' examples of films *not* inscribed in a discourse of sobriety, films which don't presume to have an unmediated relation to the Real, films which transgress the demarcations of "here" and "there," ineluctably homologized with Us and Them, and which celebrate the personal, the subjective, and the reflexive—films, in a word, which mark the cine-enunciation of identities hitherto marginalized and objectified by vococentric, ventriloquial anthropologists arrogating to themselves the media to "give voice" to those they would define as voiceless.[5]

Paul Stoller then suggests certain affinities between the anti-bourgeois, revelatory "theater of cruelty" of Antonin Artaud—who himself became of course profoundly disillusioned with the cinema—and the ethnographic films of Rouch. Stoller illustrates his argument with four of Rouch's "ethno-fictions," *Jaguar, Moi, un Noir!, La Pyramide Humaine*, and *Petit à Petit*, the last three of which have received little attention in the anglophone literature on Rouch's work. Dean MacCannell uses Dennis O'Rourke's 1987 film following tourists up the Sepik, *Cannibal Tours*, to meditate on the tourist/Other encounter in New Guinea, arguing counterintuitively that there is no real sociological difference between the performative primitives, those "ex-primitives" as he calls them, still obliged to play their part, and the "moderns." Anthropology's self-image, a growing slice of tourism, documentary filmmaking, and the economies of the "ex-primitives" themselves, are all implicated by MacCannell in the implosive construction of primitivism exacted by the old imperial centers of modernity. Henrietta Moore discusses the first two of Trinh T. Minh-ha's films, *Reassamblage* (1982) and *Naked Spaces: Living is Round* (1985), as well as her book *Woman, Native, Other* (1989). She appreciates how Trinh is able to eschew essentialism yet retain politics in her construal of the inscription of differences in the identity-formation of the "ethnic female subject," but Moore finds the multiple mediations of Trinh's films potentially undiscriminating. Certainly Trinh's almost fetishistic fascination with the representations she wishes to impugn is (deliberately) evident for all to see.[6] And finally, in "Marketing Alterity" Rachel Moore criticizes anthropology's virtually soteriologic embrace of "Indigenous Media"—a response of "savage empiricism," she suggests, to the crisis of ethnographic authority. She is interested here not so much in the perpetuation and transformation of indigenous identities in such media as in the uses made of them by the First World academy. As she argues, "To annex our academic/artistic discipline's redemption to that of indigenous peoples without allowing their work to prompt self-conscious and daring exploration of our politics of theory, our politics of style, furthers neither the projects of Ethnography nor Filmmaking."

•   •   •

The second section, "Surrealism, Vision, and Cultural Criticism," shifts attention from ethnographic film and its appendices, and offers a reconsideration of the politics of surrealism—of where to locate the political in surrealism—and of the surrealists' complicated and ambiguous relation to the dominant "scopic regime" of modernity, which Jay has dubbed Cartesian perspectivalism. Susan Suleiman describes how the street politics of the surrealists were gradually coopted by the *grands bourgeois salons* during the 1930s—a disarming canonization of the oppositional which, of course, resonates far beyond its historical occasion. Hal Foster, on the other hand, concentrates on surrealist photographic figures of automata and mannequins. He proposes that the political in Surrealism should be seen, not in its obstreperous party affiliations, but in its unsettling the instrumental logic of capitalism by highlighting modern rationalization's uncanny "other face": the normalization of fragmented perceptual shock in urban life, and the increasing inertia of capitalist bodies. Finally, Martin Jay concentrates on the denigration of the eye in Georges Bataille's anthropology as he traverses the tension between the surrealists' notion of an innocent form of vision and the various ways that they simultaneously called it into question. In view of the oft-asserted equivalence between the filmic and the oneiric, it is remarkable just how few films the surrealists managed to produce. Jay's story—ending with a perfectly absurd contrast between Descartes' dissection of the *oeil de boeuf* in the *Dioptrique* and Buñuel's slitting of the eye in *Un chien andalou*—tells of the ways the surrealists sought to topple the hierarchy of sight in the scopic regime of Cartesian perspectivalism: scenographic (post-)Quattrocento space, with the monocular spectator-subject sutured by an *aperta finestra* into the geometricalized center of things. Surrealism thus paradoxically emerges in Jay's analysis to be situated within a much longer and larger counter-tradition of anti-ocularcentrism.

L. Taylor

•   •   •

The third section "The Scopic and the Haptic," continues some of the above themes in a very varied consideration of some of the multiple "mediations" of modernity. In "Physiognomic Aspects of Visual Worlds," Michael Taussig ponders the "mimetic faculty"— our cultural capacity to create "second" nature out of nature, to imitate and to duplicate—and specifically defends its resurgence in the modern world in the form of the mimetically capacious technology that is film. Pace Walter Benjamin, he argues that films and advertisements are media as much of distracting tactility as they are of disincarnated visuality. Exposing the corporeal gnosis of the "optical unconscious," to use Benjamin's odd concept,[7] unremittingly penetrating your body as much as your mind's eye, they substitute cinematic distraction for disenchanted contemplation, refiguring your powers of mimesis, indeed your very sensorium. Thus, he suggests, is born a new mode of knowledge production, *corporeal* knowledge, reconfiguring science and art alike. Rather wistfully, Taussig casts modern-day mimesis—sensuously dissolving images into the body—as "sympathetic magic in a modernist, marxist revolutionary key," and in a willful leap of faith, he underscores Benjamin's embrace of the commodity form, no less than the advertisement which fetishizes the commodity, as containing within its phantasmagoric self the literally excessive possibility of its own supersession. If Taussig's concept of the mimetic is almost omnisubsumptive, what he yet unpacks so suggestively are the politics and poetics—in miming, in mimicry, in being similar but becoming other—masked by that very term, "mimesis." And if it would be too paradoxical to argue for the originality of imitation, what he still insists on is the infinitely imitable creativity of the copy.

"Modernity" in Nadia Seremetakis' scheme of things is something quite different, an abstract chronotope she deploys to critique a state of peculiar alienation, in which any mimetic or iconic commensality between copy and contact, or between self and other is strikingly absent. In her essay, itself a performative instance of promiscuous synaesthesia, urging and exemplifying a theoretical return to the senses, modernity is figured as the space-time for the museification and mummification of alterity, in which difference is domesticated as "dust," in which the past is petrified in the parlor, in which vision is voided of tactility. It is a time which has no space for colporteurs and their stories, coupling the past with the present, the historical with the biographical, the here with the there, the self with the other. And it is a space which has no time for a memory which is social and sensory.

Victor Burgin then takes his cue from a question posed by Edward Said, whether the nationalistic and the exilic may be two conflicting (but structurally complementary) configurations of paranoia, and from Julia Kristeva's apprehension that exilic experience is a key ingredient of modern life, "the cosmopolitalism of the excoriated." He makes heuristic use of psychoanalytic theory (from Klein and Lacan as well as Freud) in a wide-ranging survey of instances of nationalism and racism, conceiving of them "as if" they indeed were structures of paranoia.

Marilyn Strathern continues her on-going exploration into fractal identity in "One-Legged Gender," in which she cautions against some arguments for the embodiment of vision as vitiated still by their metaphorization of "greater awareness." For in those cases, as in her Melanesian instance, where the body itself acts as—*is*—the medium, incarnation in and of itself obviously uncovers nothing further. Moreover, in seeking to de-naturalize the body, and in particular its gender, she suggests that we would do well also to attend to its *composition*. Strathern suggests that genitalicentric Euro-Americans, while quite able to recognize almost any body part as a sexual symbol, are blind to other (Melanesian) re-figurations of the body, which not only might not privilege genitalia, but can also be created as relationships *between* people, rather than within one. In Melanesian imagining, this relational constitution of identity-formation results in the production of "fractal" subjects—subjects with relations integral to them—and, suggests Strathern, they act accordingly. Relations may thus be instantiated, and completed, if they are *seen* by others. Thus, as she puts it, "the person is only ever 'seen' as a (partible) extension of itself . . . [furthermore] it is only ever 'seen' from one side, for the other side of the (one) person is the (other person of the) elicitor who evokes and completes the relation . . . [thus] everything one 'sees' oneself is one's own other side. In this world, persons eye the effects of their own extensions." In "The Hand," Ludmilla Jordanova gives a brief but fascinating reading of *The Hand*, a treatise by the nineteenth century anatomist-artist (and theorist of vision) Charles Bell. His particular intermingling of natural theology with medicine legitimated and naturalized a certain sense of order—"man's" hands, needless to say, demonstrating his superiority—but as she insists, these hands were in fact the effect, not the cause, of such a hierarchy. For the eloquence and ingenuity of hands were but a reflex of their sacredness, as part of God's creative design.

David MacDougall addresses affinities between the filmic and the mnemonic, their fragmentary and multidimensional nature, in "Films of Memory," a meditation on filmic signs that translate and represent memory. He suggests that films have frequently conflated memory with its sources, and that in particular archival images, both still and moving, are used for their illusory verisimilitude to the past itself. But he also considers such films as *Sans Soleil* which problematize the translation of memory, or at least do not suppose it to be unmediated, or its mediations insignificant, and he reflects on filmic signs of "absence," signs that foreground the process of forgetting and the irrevocable rupture between the past and present. In the end, however, he concludes that the "unalterable record of appearance and place in [films] may ultimately prove to have a more profound effect upon our 'memory' of history than the interpretations we attach to them."

David Tomas undertakes an original analysis of Dziga Vertov's classic 1929 film *The Man with a Movie Camera*—structured, he discerns, in the form of a classic rite of passage, and inducing a crisis in habitual ocular mimesis—both for its documentation of an emergent industrial society, with its giddy post-Euclidian perceptual fields, but also as a product of new technologies of looking (cinema) and seeing (montage), and in particular for the *dialectical* attempt of Vertov's Kino-Eye project to engineer a new form of vision in concert with sociopolitical transformation. This Kinomatic "biocinematic" technology constituted, suggests Tomas, a veritably protocyborgian consciousness, and he makes a direct comparison to contemporary imaging technologies such as virtual reality, which he sees as re-schooling the human sensorium.

In a discursive essay on what he calls "post-bourgeois tattoos"—*tatus*, that is, that are no longer *tabu*—Marc Blanchard undertakes a cross-cultural and historical analysis of the functions of tattooing. He notes that the Polynesian hierarchy of hieratic tattoos was inverted when tattooing caught on in Europe and America, being confined in large part to the travelling lower classes, such as sailors, soldiers, and merchants—because, he suggests, tattoos were the sign of the colonized other. But he discerns that even while they remain artisanal, tattoos are today achieving a certain legitimacy, and popularity among the American middle classes, celebrating (and thereby deprived of) their former oppositionality.

In "Family Matters," Elizabeth Traube responds to the American New Right neoconservative assault on the "immorality" of the mass media, in particular the entertainment industry, which it perceives as undermining traditional American family values, above all of patriarchy. Taking "postfeminism" as indexing a hybrid and ambiguous gender consciousness and politics, Traube analyzes recent filmic fantasies of women's domestic autonomy—

notably, of single white mothers—and their identifications with women of subordinated social classes and ethnic groups, which she suggests are being deployed to reconfigure notions of middle-class femininity.

In "Remembering the Revolution, Forgetting the Empire," Peter Redfield reflects on the French Bicentennial celebrations he witnessed in Paris during the summer of 1989, in particular their representation of postmodern society, human nature, and that peculiarly French dialectic between the different and the universal, the *divers* and the *Même*. In so doing he seeks to reinvigorate anthropological concepts of political ritual so that they do not simply project back their fictions of "traditional" society onto the public spectacles of the present— the festivals of an epoch denuded of historical depth, an era that has forgotten, in Fredric Jameson's memorable words, how "to think historically in the first place." Bennetta Jules-Rosette then argues that African tourist art makes commodities out of indigenous cultural categories in order to create a new image of the continent. She suggests that tourist art is a symptom of a postmodern condition of global interconnectedness, characterized by industrial, high-technology production, the distancing of the artist's identity from the artifact, and the manufacture of "idyllic" images of a time-that-never-was. In respect to the tourist artists themselves, she reverses Valentin Mudimbe's classification of African "art" as a categorical invention of the West—a historical product of "the metamorphosis of concrete realities into abstract categories"—by suggesting that *they* transform abstract categories into concrete objects for display and trade. In analyzing "tourist art" as a form of inter-cultural communication, rather than fretting over its status as a category of objects whose commodification is at their core, she thereby insists that it must be accessible to anthropological inquiry.

The last three articles in this section are all about different kinds and directions of looking at, and through, visual media. Catherine Lutz and Jane Collins examine the intersection of a multiplicity of "gazes" in photographs of non-Westerners in the *National Geographic* magazine. Going beyond formal approaches to photographs, their analysis foregrounds both history and culture in showing how the complexity and instability of this intersecting site contains narratives of contemporary (but contestable) power, and enables viewers to negotiate various identities—identities for both themselves and those in the photographs. The social historian, anthropologist, and filmmaker, Alan Macfarlane provides a detailed description of the Domesday interactive videodiscs made by the British Broadcasting Corporation in 1984–6, probably still the most ambitious project of its kind ever attempted. Since they combine the technologies of the computer and television, videodiscs may hold not only text and statistics but also still photographs, moving film and graphics, and sound recordings. Macfarlane describes the contents of both the "Community Disc" (which gives a social portrait "from below") and the "National Disc" (containing mainly official statistics and national sources). He explains in turn the different forms of data searching, the interactive possibilities permitted by the microcomputer, and the limitations of the software (the discs do not, for example, incorporate either structured Boolean or "likelihood" searching—features, incidentally, that he has since developed on his Naga Videodisc). The discs involved more than a million "authors" and Macfarlane articulates the tension between, on the one hand, the aim to democratize information and encourage epistemological reflection about latent as well as surface meanings, and on the other, the authority conferred on the final product by the name of the BBC. And finally, taking off into the future, Christopher Pinney casts his disquisition on the possible anthropological applications of virtual reality in the form of an anthropologist's retirement lecture in the year 2029. Pace Virilio, he argues that cyberspace permits travelling without moving, as the ultimate technology of space-time compression. As such, he suggests it represents a rupture with the Heideggerian modern "age of the world picture" and a "de-framing" both of the journey (framed as it was by its tropes of departure and return), and hence of the Other visited in the journey—thereby blurring the distinction between Self and Other. "What we have learned," he concludes (in 2029, if perhaps not yet in

L.
Taylor

1994), "is that if I can arrive without ever having to set out, that self-same 'I' ceases to exist."

•   •   •

The concluding section, "Visualizing Theory" contains two selections from *V.A.R.*'s section "In Dialogue." The first is a photo-montage from *Shoot for the Contents*, by Trinh T. Minh-ha, interspersed with a conversation with Nancy N. Chen, in which they discuss Trinh's work and its reception, as well as her ambiguous and ambivalent relationship to anthropology. The last contains a conversation between Victor Burgin and Homi Bhabha, as well as a talk by Burgin on his 1989 "Minnesota Abstract." Burgin's work, as no other I know, at once theorizes visuality and visualizes theory. The narrativity and *mise-en-scène* of his work, in the juxtaposition of his images both with themselves and often with fragments of text (aiming at a kind of non-holistic contextualization), literally cites/sights the theory that informs it. Their discussion of "betweenness," of the interruption of gazes and of the interdisciplinarity of practices, raises themes that clearly lie at the heart of *Visualizing Theory* as a whole, and whose open-ended "inter-space" appropriately bring this volume to a close.

Notes

1   They comprise obviously only a small selection of all those published in *V.A.R.* during my tenure as Editor (1990–1994). *V.A.R.* (*Visual Anthropology Review*) is a journal of the Society for Visual Anthropology, and is published by the American Anthropological Association. Eliot Weinberger's "The Camera People" originally appeared in *Transition*. Written as it is by a self-professed "outsider," it has certain advantages to short histories by visual anthropologists themselves, not least its infidelity to ethnographic film's official version of itself (though there are, needless to say, more than one . . .).

2.   Metz has of course insisted that, in distinction to the still/dead photograph, moving/quick film, while it will perpetually play on fetishism, is at once too sensuous (through its simulation of lived experience) and intangible to submit to being a fetish itself. However the correlative concept of disavowal is still pertinent here, for it is precisely disavowal—which is to say, the film's pretense that it is not being viewed—which militates against any reciprocity between spectator and subject. The kinds of reflexivity at play, however differently, in both Rouch's and the MacDougalls' oeuvres, precisely disavow the illusion of disavowal.

3   Martin Jay, *Force Fields* (Routledge, 1993), 124.

4.   In *Postmodernism, or, The Cultural Logic of Late Capitalism* (Durham: Duke University Press, 1989), 310. Fredric Jameson perhaps too hastily proclaims that such signs of the past—"nature," peasants, their crafts and so on—have been transmogrified into organized simulacra in today's postmodern world. "Ours," as he puts it, that in-group oscillating unsurely between a universal inclusivity and a narrower North American reference, "is a more homogeneously modernized condition; we are no longer encumbered with the embarrassment of non-simultaneities and non-synchronicities."

5.   The paternalistic conceit of giving voice has a long history in anthropological apologetics. It is of course inherently problematic, for it ties the anthropological enterprise to those without voice; seeking to monopolize the expression of that voice paradoxically associates the discipline to a will to deny the subjects their own voice—representation by substitution—for in such an eventuality one would be out of business. Thus it also partakes of a narrowly mimetic conception of the work of anthropology.

6.   As Trinh mentioned in one interview, she has often caught herself filming "in conformity with anthropological preoccupations." In *Reassamblage*, Trinh abjures the conceit of speaking for, or even "about" another, but it is interesting that she still feels the need to legitimate her voice as situated "near by."

7.   Photography's revelations—through enlargement, slow motion, and so on—are hardly Freudian slips, after all, even if the mind's eye of the camera, particularly the motion picture camera, seems at times (as in Rouch's *Chronique d'un Eté*) to assume the appetite of the analyst.

L.
Taylor

one

The Ethnographic and the Ipsographic

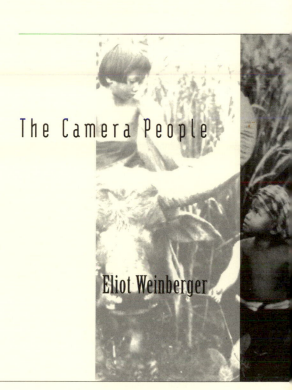

The Camera People

Eliot Weinberger

THERE IS A TRIBE, KNOWN AS THE ETHNOGRAPHIC FILMMAKERS, WHO BELIEVE THEY ARE invisible. They enter a room where a feast is being celebrated, or the sick cured, or the dead mourned, and, though weighted down with odd machines entangled with wires, imagine they are unnoticed—or, at most, merely glanced at, quickly ignored, later forgotten.

Outsiders know little of them, for their homes are hidden in the partially uncharted rain forests of the Documentary. Like other Documentarians, they survive by hunting and gathering information. Unlike others of their filmic group, most prefer to consume it raw.

Their culture is unique in that wisdom, among them, is not passed down from generation to generation: they must discover for themselves what their ancestors knew. They have little communication with the rest of the forest, and are slow to adapt to technical innovations. Their handicrafts are rarely traded, and are used almost exclusively among themselves. Produced in great quantities, the excess must be stored in large archives.

They worship a terrifying deity known as Reality, whose eternal enemy is its evil twin, Art. They believe that to remain vigilant against this evil, one must devote oneself to a set of practices known as Science. Their cosmology, however, is unstable: for decades they have fought bitterly among themselves as to the nature of their god and how best to serve him. They accuse each other of being secret followers of Art; the worst insult in their language is "aesthete."

•　　　•　　　•

Ethnos, "a people"; *graphe,* "a writing, a drawing, a representation." Ethnographic film, then: "a representation of a people on film." A definition without limit, a process with unlimited possibility, an artifact with unlimited variation. But nearly a hundred years of practice have considerably narrowed the range of subjects and the forms of representation. Depending on one's perspective, ethnographic film has become either a subgenre of the documentary or a specialized branch of anthropology, and it teems with contention at the margins of both.

•　　　•　　　•

Cinema, like photography sixty years before, begins by making the familiar strange: In 1895 the citizens of La Ciotat observed the arrival of a train with indifference, but those who watched Louis Lumière's version of the event, *L'Arivèe d'un Train en Gare* reportedly dove under their seats in terror. In one sense, this was the purest non-fiction film, the least compromised representation of "reality": the passengers walking blankly by Lumière's camera, not knowing that they are being filmed—how could they know?—are the first and, with a few exceptions, the last filmed people who were not actors, self-conscious participants in the filmmaking. In another sense, the film was pure fiction: like Magritte's pipe, the audience in their panic had intuitively grasped that *This is not a train*.

Recapitulating photography, film's second act was to make the strange familiar. In the same year as Lumière's thrilling train, Félix-Louis Regnault went to the West Africa Exposition in Paris to film a Wolof woman making a ceramic pot. It is Regnault however, not Lumière, who is considered the first ethnographic filmmaker. The reason is obvious: the "people" represented by ethnography are always somebody else. We, the urban white people, held, until recently, the film technology and the "scientific" methodology to record and analyze *them*: the non-Westerners and a few remote white groups. Moreover, according to our myth of the Golden Age, *they* lived in societies which had evolved untold ages ago and had remained in suspended animation until their contact with, and contamination by *us*. Ethnographic filmmaking began, and continues as, a salvage operation, as Franz Boas described anthropology. Film, said Regnault, "preserves forever all human behaviors for the needs of our studies." Oblivious to such hyperbole (and formaldehyde), Emilie de Brigard, an historian of the genre, writes that this is the "essential function" of ethnographic film, that it remains "unchanged today."

Where travelers had gone to collect adventures, missionaries to collect souls, anthropologists to collect data, and settlers to collect riches, filmmakers were soon setting out to collect and preserve human behaviors: the only good Indian was a filmed Indian. Within a few years of Regnault's first effort, anthropologists were taking film cameras into the field for their studies, and movie companies were sending crews to strange locales for popular entertainment. It is a curiosity of that era that the two polar allegorical figures in the history of early cinema, the Lumières ("Realism") and the Méliès ("Fantasy") were both engaged in shooting such exotica.

By the mid-1920s the representation of other people had evolved into three genres. At one extreme, the anthropological film, largely concerned, as it is today, with recording a single aspect of a culture (a ritual, the preparation of a food, the making of a utilitarian or sacred object) or attempting some sort of inventory. At the other, the fictional romance featuring indigenous people, such as the Méliès *Loved by a Maori Chieftainess* (1913), shot in New Zealand and now lost, or Edward Curtis's *In the Land of the Head-Hunters* (1914), made among the Kwakiutl. Somewhere in-between was a genre inadvertently named by John Grierson in a 1926 review of Robert Flaherty's second film: "Of course, *Moana*, being a visual account of events in the daily life of a Polynesian youth and his family, has documentary value."

E. Weinberger

•   •   •

Documentum, "an example, a proof, a lesson." Grierson's comment was not inaccurate, but there are few cases where it would not be applicable. Fiction, non-fiction, highbrow and low: much of what any of us know of much of the world comes from film: the daily operations of institutions like the police or the army or the prisons or the courts, life on board on a submarine, how pickpockets work the Paris mètro, how Southern California teenagers mate. Filling the frame of every film, no matter how "fictional," is an endless documentation of its contemporary life: a documentation that becomes most apparent with geographical or chronological distance. A Mack Sennett two-reeler is, for us now, much more than a pie in the face: it is long johns and cranked autos, plump women in impossible bathing costumes and the implicit Middle American xenophobia in the figure of the crazed mustachioed immigrant anarchist. The ditziest Hollywood production bears a subversive documentary message for viewers in China or Chad: this is what ordinary people in the U.S. have in their house, this is what they have in their refrigerator. Even the most fantastical films "document" their cultures: *Nosferatu* and *The Cabinet of Dr. Caligari* are inextricable from Weimar Germany, Steven Spielberg from Reagan America. Above all—and particularly in the United States— many of the greatest works of the imagination begin with the premise that a universe is revealed in the luminous facts of ordinary life. The most extreme case is America's greatest novel: a cosmology derived from the meticulous details, framed in a slight narrative, of an unheroic, low-caste profession that was considered disgusting at the time: the sea-going blubber-renderers of *Moby Dick*.

But in film it is precisely the fuzzy border between "documentary value" and "documentation" (a proof that is independently verifiable) that has led so many filmmakers and critics into acrimonious philosophical debate and methodological civil wars. *Moana* (1926) is a case in point: the work of a revered totemic ancestor in both the documentary and ethnographic lineages. Shot on the Samoan island of Savaii—"the one island where the people still retain the spirit and nobility of their race"—the film is subtitled *A Romance of the Golden Age*. Moana is played by a Samoan named Ta'avale; his "family" was cast from villagers, based on their looks. They are dressed in costumes that had long since been replaced by Western clothes, their hair is done in similarly archaic, "authentic" styles, and the women, almost needless to say, have been returned to their bare-breasted beauty.

There are scenes of "documentary value": gathering taro roots, setting a trap for a wild boar, fishing with spears in the incredibly limpid water, making a dress from mulberry bark. *Moana* also features what is probably the first boy-climbs-coconut-tree scene—though when the boy reaches the top, Flaherty, long before telephoto lenses, is somehow next to him for a closeup. [Superhuman tree-climbing abilities are a trademark of ethnographic filmmakers. Sixty years later, in *Baka: People of the Rain Forest* (1987), Phil Agland has a long shot of a Baka man gathering honey as he spectacularly climbs a 170-foot tree which stands alone and towers over the rest of the forest. In the next shot, he is seen from *above*, climbing up toward the camera. As he reaches camera eye level, where the hives are, the narrator intones "80,000 stinging bees pose a serious threat to his life." Evidently the crew brought along their insect repellent.]

To introduce what he called "conflict" into this portrayal of an utterly idyllic life, Flaherty paid Ta'avale to undergo a painful ritual tattooing which had dropped out of practice a few generations before. (The titles read: "There is a rite through which every Polynesian must pass to win the right to call himself a man. Through this pattern of the flesh, to you perhaps no more than cruel, useless ornament, the Samoan wins the dignity, the character and the fiber which keeps his race alive.") It is the conceit of the film that all we have seen so far "has been preparation for the great event": the climatic scene that intercuts the tattooing, frenetic dancing, and an otherwise unexplained "witch woman." (Moana's tattoo, unfortunately, is visible in the first minute of the film.)

In *Nanook of the North: A Story of Life and Love in the Actual Arctic* (1922) the "chief of the Itiumuits, the great hunter Nanook, famous through all Ungara" is played by an Eskimo named Allakariallak. (The character's name seems to be all-purpose: Flaherty planned to make a movie of the Acoma Indians of the Southwest called *Nanook of the Desert*.) The film is also set in the past, without noting the fact. The harpoons with which these "fearless, lovable, happy-go-lucky Eskimos" hunt walruses had long given way to rifles, and, in that crowd-pleasing scene, the gramophone record which Nanook bites was already a familiar item. Other scenes are transparently staged: the seal with which Nanook struggles (and pulls out of the ice-hole twice) in the famous sequence is obviously Dead on Arrival; the unmenacing "wild wolf" is tugging at a leash; and Nanook's family looks pretty chilly pretending to sleep in the half-igloo Flaherty had ordered constructed for sufficient light and his bulky camera. [Another trope of the genre: Agland—to take him again as a recent example—has his family woken by the rain coming through the leaky roof of their hut.] Again, in *Man of Aran* (1934), Flaherty revived customs extinct for as much as a hundred years, including the shark hunts that are the heart of the film. And again, he was sloppy with details: the cottages, lit by shark-oil lamps, clearly have electric wires running from roof to roof.

Flaherty is well-known for the remark, "Sometimes you have to lie. One often has to distort a thing to catch its true spirit." And his long-time assistant, Helen Van Dongen, wrote: "To me Flaherty is *not* a documentarian; he makes it all up." [It would be interesting to compare the "documentary value" of *Nanook* with a film the professionals would surely dismiss as Hollywood trash, Nicholas Ray's *The Savage Innocents* (1960), which is explicitly set in the 19th century, filmed partially on location, tells the story of a great hunter, Inuk (played by Anthony Quinn—a role that would recycle into Bob Dylan's song, "Quinn the Eskimo") and is full of ethnographic information, including culinary preferences and sexual mores, not found in *Nanook*.]

But he didn't have to make it up: the struggle against hunger in the Arctic persisted whether the Eskimos carried harpoons or rifles ("Nanook" later died of starvation on a hunt); the Aran Islanders continued to confront a raging sea even if electricity had replaced shark oil as their source of light; and "conflict" in idyllic Samoa was plain enough at the time in the social tensions caused by the missionaries, merchants, and British colonial administrators—which is the theme of an on-location, though strictly Hollywood, romance only two years later, W.S. Van Dyke's *White Shadows in the South Seas* (1928), where "the last remnants of an earthly paradise . . . from the morning of civilization" is turned into a squalid honkey-tonk.

The essential and largely hidden "conflict," of course, of any ethnographic film—one that, over the decades, was long denied and then debated—is between the filmmaker and the subject matter. It is curious that, a few years later, in a two-part fictional tale of "Paradise" and "Paradise Lost," F.W. Murnau's exquisite *Tabu* (1931)—a project Flaherty dropped out of—the ship that dooms the lovers' fate, a ship so eerily reminiscent of the plague ship of *Nosferatu*, is named "Moana."

Flaherty, unlike many others to come, spent long periods of time living in the communities he was planning to film. (After ten years in the Arctic, exploring for mineral ore deposits and making home movies, he persuaded the fur company Revillon Frères to finance Nanook as a kind of feature-length commercial.) He was the first to screen the daily rushes for the principals for their comments—a participatory filmmaking that would be abandoned until Jean Rouch revived the practice in the 1950s. Many of his scenes remain astonishingly beautiful, particularly the still unparalleled shots of the sea crashing against the cliffs, bouncing the canoes and kayaks, exploding through blow-holes (perhaps Flaherty was greater as an oceanographic filmmaker

Grass, Merian Cooper and Ernest Schoedsack.

fictionalizing reality?

than as an ethnographic one). And, above all, his image of humanness, particularly in *Nanook* and *Man of Aran*—the lone individual and the small community valiantly overcoming the brutalities of their environment—has had universal appeal in a century most notable for the victimization of its masses. [An appeal that even extended to the victimizers: Mussolini gave *Man of Aran* a prize, and Goebbels declared that it exemplified the virtue and spirit of fortitude that Hitler wanted the German people to possess. (Churchill's favorite films were the Marx Brothers', which may have affected the outcome of the war.) It must be recognized, however, that in certain ethnographic films, the emphasis on the courageous individual, the "wisdom of the folk," and the eroticization of the pure "savage" human body is equally characteristic of Fascist art. It's a small leap from Leni Riefenstahl's *Olympia* to her *Last of the Nuba*, particularly in the former's portrayal of Jesse Owens.] But in the end, Flaherty belongs most exactly to the popular travelogues and "romances" of the silent era, shot on location with native actors— though his films were less stylized, less narrative, and more naturalistic.

With the advent of sound, the expense and the size of the equipment forced most film-makers to move the exotic to the backlot, and, far more than Flaherty, make it all up. [Richard Leacock was fond of quoting an old Hollywood manual on lighting: "When shooting Westerns, use real Indians if possible; but if Indians are not available, use Hungarians."] The career of Merian Cooper and Ernest Schoedsack is exemplary: They began with *Grass* (1925) a stirring account of the annual migration by 50,000 Bakhtyari shepherds across the Zardeh Kuh mountains of Turkey and Persia. [It is, by the way, probably the only documentary film to end with an actual document: a notarized letter by the British consul in Teheran stating that the filmmakers were indeed the first foreigners to make the journey.] From Persia they went to Siam to film *Chang* (1927), an action-adventure featuring Lao hill people "who have never seen a motion picture" and "wild beasts who have never feared a rifle." By 1933, Cooper and Schoedsack were directing black-faced extras in their ritual worship of King Kong.

•   •   •

The Depression and the Second World War effectively stopped most ethnographic film production. In 1958, the genre revived with the most successful film of its kind since *Nanook*, and one cast strictly in the Flaherty mold: John Marshall's *The Hunters*. Like Flaherty, Marshall had not been trained as an ethnographer, but had spent years living with the people he filmed, the !Kung Bushmen of the Kalahari Desert in southern Africa. Like *Nanook* and *Man of Aran*, the film portrays courageous men—it is always men in these films—surviving in a harsh environment: the !Kung are a "quiet people" engaged in a "ceaseless struggle" for food in a "bitter land indeed where all the trees have thorns." Rather than one great hunter, *The Hunters* has four, whom it follows on a hunt that ends with the killing of a giraffe. One is "a man of many words and a lively mind," the "perfect man" for the job of headman; another is "the beautiful," "something of a dreamer" and "a natural hunter"; the third is "a simple kindly man, an optimist": and the fourth "forthright and humble." These are types rather than personalities, and we must take the narrator's characterizations on faith: in the film the four are indistinguishable.

Like Flaherty, Marshall is impossibly sloppy. Though the hunt, for some reason, is supposed to take place over thirteen consecutive days, it is clearly a pastiche of footage taken over many years. Not only does the number of giraffes in the herd they are tracking (seen in long shots) keep changing, the protagonists themselves are not always the same. And, as anthropologists have pointed out, !Kung subsistence was based more on gathering than hunting and, at the time, they had plenty of food. (They began to face starvation when the South African government put them on reservations.)

The film is sustained by continual narration. At times the narrator is a crafty insider ("Kaycho water is always brackish this time of year"; the kudus—a kind of antelope—are "more restless than usual"; and so on). At other times, Marshall takes the "Voice of God," familiar in most documentaries since the invention of sound, to new heights. Not only does he tell us what the men are thinking—what one critic has wittily called the telepathic fallacy—we even learn the thoughts and feelings of the wounded giraffe. ("She traveled in an open country with a singleness of mind." Later, she is "troubled," "too dazed to care," and "no longer has her predicament clearly in mind.") Worst of all, God has been reading Hemingway: "He found the dung of a kudu. A kudu is a big animal. A kudu would be ample meat to bring home." The machismo of such spoken prose becomes manifest when the final killing of the female giraffe is described in terms of gang-rape: The men "exhausted their spears and spent their strength upon her."

The film ends elevating this false narrative into myth: "And old men remembered. And young men listened. And so the story of the hunt was told." But the heroic exploits incessantly emphasized by the narrator are contradicted by what we are actually seeing in the film. They really are lousy hunters. The one kudu they manage to kill (with an utterly unheroic steel trap) is eaten by vultures and hyenas; only the bones are left for the men to rapaciously gnaw. (What, meanwhile, was the film crew eating?) And when the giraffe (also wounded by a trap) is finally cornered and dying, the men keep throwing their spears and missing. No doubt this is what hunting is actually like: Why then should Marshall insist, in his narration, that these "real" people are as unerring as some Hollywood white rajah of the jungle?

Filmmaker David MacDougall, normally quite strict about these matters, has written that *The Hunters* is "one of the few true ethnographic films we have," "a case of synthesis put to the service of truth." Marshall apparently did not agree. In his later films he abandoned the all-seeing eye of traditional fiction film (when the hunters have supposedly lost the track, for example, the film cuts to a shot that lets us know what the giraffe is up to); filmed single events as they occurred, and most important of all, let his subject matter do most of the talking.

• • •

E. Weinberger

The other celebrated ethnographic film of the era, Robert Gardner's *Dead Birds* (1963) employs many of Flaherty's conventions to produce a kind of anti-*Nanook*: a film that, perhaps inadvertently, is far from ennobling. Shot among the Dani, a previously little-documented group in Western New Guinea, the film is a narrative—based, like Flaherty, on a series of archetypal anecdotes rather than the full-blown dramatic structure and developed characterizations of a "plot"—about a warrior, Weyak, and a small boy, Pua. (The boy-figure in *Moana* is named Pe'a.) The characters do not speak; their actions (and, like *The Hunters*, thoughts) are conveyed to us by a continual narration, spoken by Gardner. Perhaps uniquely in ethnographic films, the narration is delivered in a nervous, unnaturally rapid speech: an edginess that considerably adds to the film's dramatic tensions.

Its unforgettable opening clearly announces some sort of allegory: a very long pan of a hawk flying over the treetops, and the spoken words: "There is a fable told by a mountain people living in the ancient highlands of New Guinea . . ." [It is a convention of the genre: the people are remote and as timeless as geography, but will be revealed to be, in some way, just like us. *Grass* opens by promising us the "Forgotten People" who will unlock the "secrets of our own past." *Nanook* opens by taking us to "mysterious barren lands" that, conversely, are "a little kingdom—nearly as large as England."] The fable is the story of the origin of human mortality: a race between a bird and a snake to determine whether people would die like birds or

Chang, Merian Cooper and Ernest Schoedsack.

shed their skins and live forever like snakes. Needless to say, the bird won, and *Dead Birds,* in the Flaherty tradition of portraying man against the odds, was apparently intended as a portrayal of one culture's response to the universal destiny. Gardner writes: "I saw the Dani People, feathered and fluttering men and women, as enjoying the fate of all men and women. They dressed their lives with plumage, but faced as certain death as the rest of us drabber souls. The film attempts to say something about how we all, as humans, meet our animal fate."

What the film actually shows is something quite different. With the exception of one quite powerful funeral scene, *Dead Birds* is not concerned with the effects of human destiny—rites, mourning, grief—but rather its provocation. The Dani were among the last people on earth to engage in a rigidly codified ritual war. (One which finally was ended by the local "authorities" shortly after the film was made.) The men of neighboring villages, separated only by their gardens and a strip of no man's land, would regularly adorn themselves and gather on a battlefield, fighting (theoretically) until there was one fatal casualty. Revenge for that death would provoke the next battle, and so on forever. An endless vendetta war in a land with plenty of food and no particular differences between the villages; where no territory or plunder was captured; with no mass killings and no deviation from the rules.

In fact—or at least according to the film—revenge was rarely achieved on the battlefield. In the battles themselves there is a great deal of back and forth feints and threats, but no hand-to-hand combat; wounds are mainly inflicted haphazardly in the shower of arrows. The two murders in the film, one for each side, occur when a group of men accidentally comes across someone from the other side: a small boy who wandered off, a man trying to steal a pig at night.

A continual, seemingly senseless war; battles where the two sides engage in menacing rhetoric but do relatively little harm; covert killings; a no man's land lined with tall watchtowers; daily life in a state of permanent dread. The allegorical import of *Dead Birds* must have been obvious to its viewers in 1963, when the Berlin Wall was still new. The film is hardly a meditation on death at all: if it were it would have presented Dani who had died from childbirth, sickness, accidents, age. Rather it is a feathered and fluttering reenactment of the Cold War that was being prolonged and endured by the drab souls of East and West.

The battle sequences in the film are extraordinary. Gardner was especially fortunate to have a mountainous terrain where he could get the aerial perspective to lay out what was, quite literally, the theater of war. A brief telephoto shot of the enemy wildly celebrating the death of the small boy becomes particularly unsettling following the moving, rapidly edited sequence of the child's funeral. (The narrator, as throughout the film, fortunately resists the usual temptation to editorialize.)

The film, in Flaherty style, occasionally concocts an artificial narrative structure: one set of battle scenes, for example, are intercut with shots of women gathering brine who are supposedly waiting for news of casualties, though there was obviously no second unit on the film. (The battles themselves are pastiches, though this is neither apparent nor explained.) And it is the Flaherty "hook"—the focus on the warrior and the boy—that seems misplaced in the film. We learn next to nothing about Weyak, and Pua, who is presented as a pathetic kid, is essentially irrelevant. Once again, women are far in the background. The cruel Dani practice of cutting off the fingers of young girls when there is a death in the village is mentioned only in passing twice. And Gardner, whose films are full of hands—(Flaherty: "Simply in the beautiful movement of a hand the whole story of a race can be revealed . . .")—only gives us a split-second glimpse of the mutilated fingers of Weyak's wife.

After this, his first film, Gardner would abandon the Flaherty anecdotal narrative of the hunter/warrior, both epitome and paragon of his people, the boy who wishes to emulate him, and the Western bard who sings his praises. In *Dead Birds*, Weyak is introduced by a shot of his hands, Pua by his reflection in a puddle. In the later films, Gardner would devolve an ethnographic cinema based entirely on such telling details and oblique images, films that would pose little difficulty to general audiences accustomed to foreign imports, but which the scientists would find incomprehensible.

•   •   •

In the 1950s ethnographic film became an academic discipline with the usual array of specialist practitioners, pedagogues and critics. It has always seen itself as besieged on two sides. On one flank, the anthropologists, whose conception of a representation of a people has always emphasized the written meaning of *graphe*—and moreover the fixed singularity of the

"Dani victory celebration," *Dead Birds*, Robert Gardner.

mono-graph. (As recently as 1988, filmmaker Timothy Asch was complaining that they "have shown little interest in the potential use of ethnographic film.") On the other flank, the aesthetes, or, as Margaret Mead put it: "There's a bunch of filmmakers now that are saying 'It should be art' and wrecking everything we're trying to do."

To prove their mettle to the anthropologists, ethnographic filmmakers have tended to adopt a more-scientific-than-thou attitude. Asch, in a scary comment, writes, "The camera can be to the anthropologist what the telescope is to the astronomer or what the microscope is to the biologist"—which assumes that the matter on the other side of the ethnographic lens is as imperturbable as galaxies or amoebae. Mead, who shot a great deal of footage in Bali in the 1930s with Gregory Bateson, believed that "objective" filming would replace "subjective" field notes, an idea picked up by David MacDougall who, speaking for the reception side, writes that film speaks "directly to the audience, without the coding and decoding inevitable with written language," a notion disproved by the second screening of Lumière's train. And the main textbook in the field, Karl Heider's *Ethnographic Film* (1976), is an attempt to set "standards" and create a "rational, explicit methodology" for the discipline.

Just what some of them have in mind was first articulated by Mead:

> Finally, the oft-repeated argument that all recording and filming is selective, that none of it is objective, has to be dealt with summarily. If tape recorder, camera, or video is set up and left in the same place, large batches of material can be collected without the intervention of the filmmaker or ethnographer and without the continuous self-consciousness of those who are being observed. The camera or tape recorder that stays in one spot, that is not tuned [*sic*], wound, refocused, or visibly loaded, does become part of the background scene, and what it records *did* happen.

Such a utopian mechanism—a panopticon with limitless film—has been extrapolated by critic Walter Goldschmidt into a definition of the genre:

> Ethnographic film is film which endeavors to interpret the behavior of people of one culture to persons of another culture by using shots of people doing precisely what they would have been doing if the camera were not there.

"New Guinea warrior shouts at enemy," *Dead Birds*, Robert Gardner.

The ideal, then, is either a dream of invisibility, or worse, the practice of the surveillance camera. Leaving aside the obvious moral and political questions of surveillance—white folks, as usual, playing God, albeit an immobile one with a single fixed stare—the value of such information could be nothing more than slight. The simplest human events unfold in a tangle of attendant activities, emotions, motivations, responses and thoughts. One can imagine a !Kung anthropologist attempting to interpret the practices and effects of the American cash economy from footage obtained with the cameras in the local bank.

Such films, amazingly, exist. Among them is *Microcultural Incidents at 10 Zoos* (1971) by Ray Birdwhistell, the inventor of *kinesics*, an analysis of body language. Birdwhistell, who might be one of the dotty anthropologists in Barbara Pym's novels, placed hidden cameras in front of the elephant cages in the zoos of ten countries to discover the national traits of behavior revealed by the way families feed the pachyderms. The resulting film is an illustrated lecture with frame numbers running along the top of screen, instant replays and freeze frames (including one of a kid being slobbered on by Jumbo), and phrases like "for those interested in proximics" or "note how the father places the peanut in the child's hand." Birdwhistell maintains that "there is enough information in one 4-second loop for a day's class in anthropology." His film—which is based on the assumption that a nation can be represented by a few members—demonstrates that Italians feed themselves while feeding elephants, the British give a slight formal bow, the Japanese keep a respectful distance, the Americans are easily distracted, and so forth—in other words, the kind of ethnographic information we get from television comedians. Birdwhistell, most tellingly, becomes completely flustered when he gets to India: there are too many people milling around to sort out, and they don't seem terribly interested. Despite his expertise of "organized patterning" and "gambits of caretaking," it apparently doesn't occur to him that in many parts of India an elephant is far less exotic than a cocker spaniel.

E. Weinberger

Birdwhistell may be an extreme case, but there are thousands of hours of such "scientific" ethnographic film, stored in archives like the Encyclopedia Cinematographica in Göttingen, covering probably every remaining tribe on earth, and devoted, in David MacDougall's words, to "rendering faithfully the natural sounds, structure and duration of events" —a description best applied to Andy Warhol's *Sleep*. [A recent two-hour Dutch film opened with a five-minute fixed shot of a man hacking away with his machete, and these four sentences of narration, with minute-long pauses between them: "Here is Ano. Here is his wife." (Nameless, of course.) "They are planting manioc. They live in a hut near their garden patch." I confess I never found out what happened next.]

In many other disciplines— including, recently, anthropology itself—a "faithful rendering" is recognized as being entirely subject to the vagaries of current style and individual taste. (As fiction and documentary films forever demonstrate, there is nothing

"An arrow is removed from a wounded warrior," *Dead Birds*, Robert Gardner.

more unreal than yesterday's realism.) But ethnographic film, unlike other filmmaking, thinks of itself as science, and a set of rules has been laid out in a series of charts by Heider. The ethnographic filmic representation of reality is based on:

1) "Basic technical competence."

2) "Minimal inadvertent distortion of behavior" (that is, interaction with the camera crew).

3) "Minimal intentional distortion of behavior" (staging or reconstructing events).

4) "Ethnographic presence." (Actually, Heider's most radical dictum: an acknowledgment that there's a filmmaker lurking on the premises.)

5) Minimal "time distortion" and "continuity distortion." Events must be presented in the order they occurred, and ideally in the same duration.

6) "Fully adequate explanation and evaluation of the various distortions" in accompanying printed material.

7) "Natural synchronous sound" (as opposed to soundtrack music).

8) "Optimally demystifying" narration, "relevant to the visual materials."

9) "Cultural and physical contextualizaton of behavior."

10) "Whole bodies." ("Long camera shots which include whole bodies of people are preferable . . . to close-ups of faces and other body parts.")

11) "Whole acts" (beginning, middle and end).

12) "Whole people" (emphasis on one or two individuals rather than "faceless masses").

13) "Ethnographic understanding" (made by/with a professional).

14) "Full integration with printed materials."

Adhering to most, but not all, of these dicta is Timothy Asch, one of the most respected of the "scientific" filmmakers. Asch, whose writings display unusual candor, has written: "I was ambitious. I wanted to take film that would be valuable for research as well as for instruction and curriculum development." [Clearly not a dream of making *Citizen Kane*, but then ethnographic filmmakers, with the exceptions of Rouch and Gardner, notably rarely or never, in their voluminous writings, mention any films outside of the genre. Apparently they don't go to the movies like the rest of us.] The kind of film he wants is spelled out elsewhere: a scholarly pill capable of being semi-sweetened for the masses:

> By focusing on the actions of a few people engaged in activities relevant to the research of the anthropologist, and by leaving the camera running for long uninterrupted periods, the resulting footage is likely to be valuable for research. With the addition of a few distant location shots and some cut-aways, as well as a few rolls of film related to a script, the footage should be equally valuable as a resource for editing film for instruction or for television.

His best-known project, a series of twenty-one films of the Yanomamö people of the Upper Orinoco, made with the anthropologist Napoleon Chagnon, comes with a "Utilization Chart" which divides cultural research into ten categories and checks off the applicability of each film. It's a grim taxonomy, and weirdly incomplete: Social Organization, Kinship, Political Organization, Conflict, Socialization, Women, Field Work, Ecology & Subsistence, Cosmology & Religion, and Acculturation. [A world, in other words, without Gastronomy, Music, Stories, Sex, Leisure, Dreams, Gossip, Body Ornamentation & Dress, Strange Occurrences, Petty Annoyances . . . or another ten after that.]

The chart's assumption that human life can be contained by such cubby holes is identical to the belief that any human activity is most fully represented by long takes, long shots, and "whole bodies." Worse, it assumes an existing structure to which all data must be applied; that which does not is simply excluded:

> Chagnon took a 2 1/2 minute sequence of a Yanomamö man beating his wife over the head with a piece of firewood. We looked at it together with James V. Neal and his wife, thinking we might include it in our film on genetics [!]. We three men agreed it was too

disturbing to show. Mrs. Neel saw this as a typically protective male view and argued that the beating was no worse than the experience of many wives in America. We agree; but we still decided not to use the footage.

Asch and Chagnon's *The Ax Fight* (1975) is an example of messy human life reduced to chunks of explainable phenomena. The film is in five parts. Part One is the unedited footage of a fight that suddenly erupts in a Yanomamö village; the violence of the scene is matched by the frantic quality of the film, as the hand-held camera wobbles, zooms in, and pans rapidly back and forth to keep up with the action. In Part Two, the screen is black as the filmmakers discuss what happened; Chagnon speculates that it is the reaction to a case of incest. In Part Three, text scrolls up the screen informing us, refreshingly, that the anthropologist was wrong: the fight was the result of a kinship conflict provoked when a woman was ill-treated in a neighboring village; the inevitable kinship charts are then shown. Part Four replays the original footage with a narrator and pointers identifying the players and their relation to one another. Part Five presents a polished version of the original, without commentary but edited for narrative continuity. The editing tellingly violates Heider's dictum that events must be presented in the order in which they occurred: as the critic Bill Nichols has pointed out, the original (sequential) footage ends with the wronged woman insulting the men; the narrative version both begins and ends with her, transforming her into a provocateur. (Nichols comments sarcastically, "That's the way women are.")

E.
Weinberger

The opening minutes are an indelible image of community violence, full of unclassifiable data—what filmmaker Jorge Preloran has called the "feel" for a people—a vision of the Yanomamö elsewhere unavailable on film. And it is obvious that the sudden outburst and equally sudden resolution of the fight cannot be explained by pointers and kinship charts. One can only imagine the untidy human narrative that would have emerged if the principals and other villagers—who don't speak in the film—were asked to give their versions; if we learned some of their previous history and what happened after the fight. One of the curiosities of ethnographic film, evident to any outsider, is that the strictly scientific films often provide far less information than their reviled "artistic" cousins, which tend to spill over the utilization charts.

Or, more damningly, they provide the same information. There are so many films of the Yanomamö that, in Paris in 1978, they could hold a festival of them. These included a number of the Asch-Chagnon films; a French TV

The Nuer, Hilary Harris and George Breidenbach.

documentary; two films from a Yugoslavian TV series on the rain forest; a Canadian film from the TV series *Full Speed to Adventure*, focusing on two Canadian missionaries living with the community; a Japanese TV film; three videos by New York avant-gardist Juan Downey; and unedited footage shot in the early 1960s by a woman gold prospector. The range of what Heider calls "ethnographic understanding" was obviously great: from experienced scientists to newly arrived television crews (only some of whom were accompanied by anthropologists) to the home movies of a passer-by.

There is an account of the festival in *Film Library Quarterly*, written by Jan Sloan. She points out that, despite the diversity of sources, "the actual images were surprisingly similar . . . It is also surprising to note the similarity of information presented in these documentaries. The same limited material is covered in many of the films over and over again . . ."

The recent literary dismantling of written anthropology (by Clifford Geertz, James Clifford, and others) has tried to demonstrate how the sober scientific professionals are no less prone to dubious generalization, manipulation of data, partial explanation, and prevailing ethnocentrism than the enthusiastic amateurs who write accounts of their travels. Similarly, the moment one erases the stylistic differences, the ethnographic differences between a research film and an episode of *Full Speed to Adventure* are less than meets the eye.

•　　　•　　　•

The amateurs, in fact, often turn out to be ethnographically richer. Consider the case of an utterly "unscientific" film: *The Nuer* (1970) by Hilary Harris and George Breidenbach, with the assistance of Robert Gardner. Until Gardner's *Forest of Bliss* (1986) this was probably the film most loathed by the professionals. Heider writes: "It is one of the most visually beautiful films ever made . . . But the film is almost without ethnographic integrity. By this I mean that its principles are cinema aesthetic; its framing, cutting, and juxtaposition of images are done without regard for any ethnographic reality." Throughout his book, Heider uses *The Nuet* as the classic example of how not to make an ethnographic film.

The film has no story, little narration, only one brief interview with an individual, no time frame and no events unfolded in their entirety. Most of it consists of rapidly edited shots of extraordinary beauty, accompanied by a soundtrack of local music and sounds and untranslated speech. There are galleries of close-ups—faces, tobacco pipes, jewelry, houses, corrals—and unforgettable sequences of these astonishingly elongated people simply walking through the dust and mist. Much of the film simply looks at the cows

Lorang's Way, David and Judith MacDougall.

The Wedding Camels, David and Judith MacDougall.

that are central to Nuer life: close-ups of cow legs and cow flanks and cow nostrils and cow horns.

Though this is one of the most "aesthetic" films in the genre, it is full of ethnographic information—far more, ironically, than something like *The Ax Fight*. We see what the Nuer look like, what they make, what they eat, what their music sounds like, their leisure activities, body art, architecture, fishing and cattle-herding, local fauna, diseases, rites of exorcism, spiritual possession, and so on. Most of all, as a study of a community based on cattle, it is a startling revelation of the cow. Even an untrained urban eye finds itself immediately differentiating the cows as individuals—much as the Nuer know the personal history of each; a history which, through bride-prices and ritual exchange, is inextricably tangled with their own histories. Moreover, it becomes evident in the course of the film how an entire aesthetic could be derived from the close observation of cattle; how the shapes and textures of the herds are recapitulated in so much of what the Nuer make.

"The final goal, of which an Ethnographer should never lose sight," wrote Malinowski sixty years ago in a famous dictum, now outdated only in its gender specificity, "is, briefly, to grasp the native's point of view, his relation to life, to realize *his* vision of *his* world." (*his* emphasis.) Of course the ideal is impossible—who can ever see with another's eyes, even within one's own culture? Yet *The Nuer*, rare among ethnographic films, lets us look closely at that which the Nuer look at, but which most of us do not—moreover seeing, as any of us see anything, not the "whole bodies" but the telling details that set each one apart. It is one of the few instances where ethnographic film presents information that is beyond the capabilities of the written monograph. Not observed and analyzed data: it is a physical and intellectual act of seeing. Neither a recapitulation of a foreign vision nor the first-person expression of the filmmakers, it is, most exactly, an act of translation: a reading of their sensibility, recoded into our (film) language. *The Nuer*, like any film, is a metaphor for the Nuer. Its difference is that it does not pretend to be a mirror.

•   •   •

Bill Nichols has written that the central question of ethnographic film is what to do with the people. This is true enough, but it is a center that must be shared by a parallel question: What to do with the filmmaker. Nanook mugged shamelessly for the camera; such footage ever since has tended to be scissored away, to preserve the illusion that the filmed events are being lived as they're always lived, and not being acted out.

David and Judith MacDougall are notable among the ethnographic filmmakers for making their own presence a central feature of their films. Moreover, they have effectively subverted the authority of the all-knowing narrator not only by allowing the subjects to speak—in the late 1960s they introduced subtitled dialogue to the genre—but also by basing their films on conversation. These take three forms: ordinary conversation among the people as observed and recorded by the filmmakers; conversation among the people on topics initiated by the filmmakers; and dialogue between the filmmakers and the people. That the MacDougalls are talking to their subject matter is radical enough in this corner of the film forest; they also allow themselves to be occasionally glimpsed and, in one startling moment, even show us where they're living during the making of the film. (An anthropologist's house is normally more taboo than the interior of a kiva.) They introduce topics with intertitles written in the first person ("We put the following to Lorang . . ."), and their intermittent voice-overs are subjective ("I was sure Lorang's wives were happy together . . .") and sometimes even confessional ("It doesn't feel like we're making progress . . ."). When they don't have certain information or footage, they readily admit it, rather than attempt to patch it over. Most impressively, the films are a *visual* dialogue between the filmmakers and their subjects: at every moment we know exactly where David MacDougall (the cameraman) is standing. And, thanks no doubt to the presence of Judith MacDougall, their films are full of women talking, and talking freely.

In short, they have found seemingly effortless solutions to most of the political and moral dilemmas of ethnographic film. Contrary to Goldschmidt's definition of the genre, the MacDougalls are shooting people doing precisely what they would have been doing with a camera crew there. The procedure, however, does have its limitations: what they are doing is often not terribly interesting.

Their trilogy—*Lorang's Way*, *A Wife Among Wives*, and *The Wedding Camels* (1978–81)—shot among the Turkana of northern Kenya is a case in point. The films focus on the family of a wealthy man: the first is a portrait of the patriarch, Lorang; the second talks to his wives; the third concerns the negotiations for the marriage of his daughter. The film rarely leaves the family compound, and for nearly six hours we watch and listen to people largely talking about money and complaining. [Rouch has remarked: "Many recent films of the direct-cinema type are thus spoiled by an incredible regard for the chatting of the people filmed."] Lorang is an Arthur Miller character: the self-made man disgusted by his good-for-nothing sons. But, in the absence of any dramatic catalyst—this being life and not theater—he's a character who goes nowhere: after the first half-hour or so, we only get more of the same. (The wives mainly repeat everything their husband says.) And the film gives us no way to evaluate whether Lorang is more representative of the Turkana or of the universal *nouveau riche*.

In many ways, the trilogy is like an excruciating evening with one's least favorite relatives. There's no doubt it is a precise representation of this particular family, but can it be considered ethnographic, a representation of a people? We actually learn very little about the Turkana besides work, money, and marriage procedures. No one is born, gets sick, or

"Bororo maiden choosing the most perfect male dancer at the Garawal ceremony,"
Deep Hearts, Robert Gardner.

dies in the films; there are no religious ceremonies; very little singing or eating; conflict with the outside world is alluded to, but not shown; although we come to know the compound well, we are never clear where it is or what its neighbors are up to. The family talks and talks . . . As a record, its style is unusually inventive; but it never solves the perennial questions of the genre: When there are no individuals, who speaks for the people? (Usually the wrong man: the narrator). When there is an individual, to what extent can she or he represent the group?

One answer is a multiplicity of voices—voices that echo, enlarge, and especially contradict one another. Certainly it would be possible in six hours of film, but it would undermine the premises of the genre: *They* have typical members. *We* do not. *They* are unusual, but can be comprehended. *We* are usual, but ultimately incomprehensible. *They* are somewhat like us. *We* are not like us. *They* must be represented in the simplest possible way. *We* must be represented with subtle complexity.

•   •   •

Most ethnographic films document a single event—perhaps, as Rouch has suggested, because such events come with their own ready-made mise-en-scène. Such documentation poses a dilemma for the scientists. Written ethnography is based on generalization: the ethnographer's description of, say, how a basket is woven is an amalgam based on watching a hundred baskets being made. Filmed ethnography cannot help but be specific: a unique and idiosyncratic instance of basket-weaving. (Often, the differences between what is seen and what is "usual" will be noted by filmmakers in interviews; but never, as far as I know, in the

"Boatman, the Ganges; Benares, India," *Forest of Bliss*, Robert Gardner. Photo: Jane Tuckerman.

film itself.) Moreover, the filmed event unravels the image of the "traditional" society on which ethnographic film is based, in a way that a written monograph does not: The endlessly repeated becomes the unrepeatable moment; the timeless is suddenly inserted into history; representation of a people becomes representation of a person; ethnography biography, archetype individual. (And a pastiche, like *The Hunters*, is no way out: it cannot help but be subverted by the expectation of a continuity based on matching shots.)

One solution, not so strangely, is surrealism: a superficial discontinuity revelatory of a profound unity. There are films to be imagined that would self-consciously (unlike *The Hunters*) feature different protagonists at different stages of an event, or the same protagonist in different versions, or one where the protagonists perform in a stylized, "unnatural" reenactment. Films that, to represent a people, would attempt to subvert film's natural tendency to specify individuals. (Would a *Discrete Charm of the Bourgeoisie* or a *Heart of Glass* of ethnographic films be any less stylized, or carry less information, than the currently prevailing modes of realism?)

Surrealism moreover introduced an aesthetic based on chance, improvisation, and the found object—an aesthetic which would seem tailored to the actual conditions of a Westerner making an ethnographic film. Yet the genre has had only one surrealist: ironically, the founder of *cinema verité*, Jean Rouch. (And there's a parallel to be drawn with another surrealist, the master of photojournalism, Henri Cartier-Bresson.) *Jaguar* (shot in the 1950s and released in 1967), to briefly take one example from a massive amount of work, has the improvisatory exuberance of the 1960s French New Wave—it even includes clips from other Rouch films. One can't anticipate what will happen next, as the film follows its three protagonists traveling from Niger to Ghana to find work; some of the adventures— as when one of the men becomes an official photographer for Kwame Nkrumah—even veer into fantasy. Most important, *Jaguar* is the only inventive exploration of non-synch sound in the genre. [Baldwin Spencer had taken an Edison cylinder recorder to Australia in 1901, but these possibilities remained unexplored for fifty years.] Shot silently, the soundtrack (recorded ten years later) features the three men commenting on the action: a non-stop patter of jokes, insults, commentary and light-hearted disagreements that effectively break down the normally unchallenged authority of the single narrator/outsider. *dialogue of their filmed*

·   ·   ·

Robert Gardner, in *Deep Hearts* (1978) and *Forest of Bliss* (1987), has adapted another aspect of surrealism to transform the idiosyncratic into the archetypal: he explodes time. By employing the simultaneous time of modern physics, he transforms the linear time of the unrepeatable into the cyclical time of the endlessly repeated. This has been, of course, one of the main projects of the century: through simultaneity—montage, collage, Pound's ideogrammic method—all ages become contemporaneous. It is both a criticism of Western linear time and a bridge to the mythic time which rules most traditional societies. But where the modernists sought to recapture both the formal aspects and the sheer power of so-called "primitive" art and oral epics, Gardner, uniquely, has employed the techniques of modernism to *represent* the tribal other. A cycle has been completed: with Gardner, James Joyce is our entry into Homer.

Deep Hearts is concerned with the annual Garawal ceremony of the Bororo Fulani of Niger. The nomadic groups converge at one spot in the desert, where the young men elaborately make themselves up and, wearing women's dresses, dance for eight days in the sun as the marriageable young women look them over, until one man is selected as the most virtuous and beautiful. According to the few lines of narration in the film, the Bororo consider themselves to be "chosen people" (who doesn't?) but they are threatened by "neighbors, new ideas, disease and drought." Their combination of "excessive self-regard" and "a fear of losing what they have" makes them "easily prey to envy." So they must bury their hearts within them, for "if a heart is deep no one can see what it contains."

If this group psychological analysis is correct, then the Bororo must remain, particularly to an outsider, unreadable. Everything will remain on the surface, only, at best, inadvertently revealing what is beneath. Gardner's response to this impermeability is to turn it into a dream, a shimmering mirage. Time is scrambled and events keep repeating themselves: men dancing, people arriving, men dancing, preparations for the dance, and so on. Shots of the farewell ceremony, near the end of the film, are followed by a scene we've already seen, near the beginning, of a woman washing her enormous leg bracelets before the dance. Sounds recorded at the dance are played over scenes of preparation for it. There are strange sideways shots of milk being poured from huge bowls that recall the abstract geometries of Moholy-Nagy's films. There are freeze frames and, in one sequence, slow-motion and distortion of the sound. [Though documentary was born out of slow-motion—Edward Muybridge's magic lantern studies of animal locomotion—it remains taboo for ethnographic film, being counter to prevailing notions of realism. Maya Deren's 1947–1951 study of voodoo in Haiti, *Divine Horsemen*, exploits both the hallucinatory quality of slow motion—which rhymes perfectly with the dance and trance possession she is filming—and its ability to let us see details we would otherwise miss in the frenetic action.]

Deep Hearts is a dream of the Garawal ceremony, stolen from the sleep of an anthropologist; the woozy memory of events one has witnessed in eight days of desert sun. (Its nearest cousin is the flashbacks to Guinea-Bissau in Chris Marker's *Sans Soleil*.) As science, it is probably as accurate a description as a more linear recreation. But, unlike science, it leaves its enigmas unsolved. Its last lines of narration are among the most abstract in the genre:

> The visitors leave as suddenly as they appeared, and, with the diminishing rains, they will resume their nomadic lives. They go knowing what they would hope to be, an ideal example having been selected from their midst. But this may only serve to remind them of the desires that cannot be met, and which, with the uncertainty of whether choices are really theirs, still lie at the bottom of their deep hearts.

This dream, then, becomes an expression of unfulfilled desire in an unstable society. It is interesting that we barely glimpse, and only from afar, the winner of the contest: this is a study of longing, not achievement. And, uniquely in ethnographic film—which seems to cover everything except what people really think about (other than money)—*Deep Hearts* is a study of erotic longing: the young women posed in tableaux of virginal meekness facing the men (we watch the dancers over the shoulder of one of them); the auto-eroticism of these dancing men dressed as women; the old women who, no longer in the courtship game, must ritually insult them; and the old men who, from the image of their past selves, select the most beautiful.

The film underscores what is obvious elsewhere: there are vast areas of human life to which scientific methodology is inapt; to which ethnographic description must give way to the ethnopoetic: a series of concrete and luminous images, arranged by intuition rather than prescription, and whose shifting configurations—like the points of and between the constellations—map out a piece of a world.

• • •

Simultaneous time, the babble of voices overlapping and interrupting each other, the rapid succession of images, the cacophony of programmed and random sounds: all modern art is urban art, and all film—being born with this century—is an image of the city. What then does one do with the subjects of ethnography who, with few exceptions, lead rural lives? The anthropological monograph is, as James Clifford has pointed out, this century's version of the pastoral, and its writing can and does draw on its literary antecedents. Film, however, with its short takes, shifting camera angles and multiple viewpoints is as intrinsically antipastoral as its filmmakers themselves. To take it (and oneself) into the countryside of the tribe, one may either deny its (and one's own) nature—as most ethnographic filmmakers have done—or somehow discover a way into one's subject.

Trinh T. Minh-ha's *Naked Spaces: Living is Round* (1985) returns ethnography to its origins: the observations of a perceptive and intelligent cosmopolitan traveler. Her ostensible subject is Bachelard's "poetics of space," as exemplified by a dozen ethnic groups in western Africa. The film leisurely shifts from village to village, sound to silence, staring—there is no other word for it—at the people, their dances, and endless architectural details. The soundtrack is local music and the fragmented speech of three women narrators who, at a given moment, may represent different perspectives, but elsewhere in the film exchange roles and even repeat each other's words. Little of what is seen is explained: the voices mention some African beliefs and stories, quote a five-foot shelf of Western literature and philosophy from Heidegger to Novalis to Shakespeare to Eluard, and utter gnomic statements written by the filmmaker herself. (The three narrators, according to Minh-ha, are an attempt to subvert the patriarchy of the single voice, but it is curious, given her political stance, that no Africans speak in the film.) Contrary to the hardliners—(Walter Goldschmidt: "The ethnographic filmmaker is not engaged in expressing himself")—what holds the film together is precisely its utter subjectivity: these extraordinarily beautiful images of Africa as filtered through the bric-a-brac-cluttered mind of a brilliant academic. And along the way, one *sees* more than in a hundred "scientific" films.

With *Forest of Bliss*, Robert Gardner has taken his modernist sensibility into an urban setting, however one that is uniquely archaic. The result is a panoramic "city" film in the tradition that begins with Paul Strand and Charles Sheeler's *Mannahatta* (1921) and Walther Ruttmann's *Berlin: Symphony of the City* (1927), and whose latest incarnation is the first half of Wim Wender's *Wings of Desire* (1987). And yet the nature of his subject, Benares, India, cannot help but insert the film into myth.

Benares is at least three thousand years old, and the oldest continually inhabited city on earth. Moreover, it always has had the same primary function, as the place where each day the countless dead are burned or dropped into the Ganges, and the living purified. To visit the sacred zones of the city, along the river, is like finding priests of Isis still practicing in Luxor. No other living city exists so purely in mythic time.

Similarly, the city itself is an iconographic representation of the passage from this world to the next: a labyrinth of bazaars, temples and houses for the dying opens out onto steps that lead down to the river (at one section of steps the dead are burned); the wide river itself, cleansing all, and beyond, distantly visible, the other shore.

These are universally recognizable symbols, from which— with a host of others: the kite perched between heaven and earth, the scavenging dogs, the boats that carry the dead to the other side, the purifying fire, the flowers of veneration —Gardner has constructed a montage of the eternally

"Boatman with dead child; Benares, India," *Forest of Bliss*, Robert Gardner. Photo: Christopher James.

repeatable. It is both a study of the mechanics of death (the organization of Benares's cremation industry) and a map of the Hindu cosmology of death—almost entirely presented
through iconic images. It is surely the most tightly edited film in the genre, truly a fugue
of reiterated elements, and one whose astonishing use of sound sustains the cyclical structure
by carrying over the natural sounds of one scene into the next —Godard's technique adapted
to a completely different purpose.

Most radically, Gardner has eliminated all verbal explanations. There is no narration,
the dialogue is not subtitled, and there is only one intertitle, a single line from the Yeats
translations of the Upanishads. *Forest of Bliss*, more than any other film, reinforces the
outsider status of both the filmmaker and the viewer: we must look, listen, remain alert,
accept confusion, draw our own tentative conclusions, find parallels from within our own
experiences. Travelers confronting the exotic, we are also the living standing before the dead.

I have spent time in Benares on three separate occasions: it is curious that this, the most
artistically crafted of all ethnographic films has approached the utopian mimesis of
the scientists: for me, at least, it is, as no other film I know, like being there—though there

Zulay, Facing the 21st Century, Jorge Mabel Preloran.

of course in a two-dimensional space with only two of the senses intact. This is because the
film takes as its center an ultimate incomprehension: of the gods by man, of the dead by the
living, of the blissful by the unenlightened, of the East by the West, of any culture by
another. In Hinduism, one attempts to bridge the gap through the primary form of worship,
darshana, the act of seeing—the eyes literally going out to touch the gods. Though I hesitate
to call *Forest of Bliss* a religious experience, it too is dependent on a similar contemplation of
iconic signs: it is an outsider's (refusing to be an insider's) seeing through Benares into the
cycles of life and death.

Needless to say, the film has driven the scientists mad. The newsletter of the Society
of Visual Anthropologists ran a series of polemics against it, filled with lines like "Technology
has left pure imagery behind, and anthropologists ought to do so too." (The same writer
commenting that, given the sanitary problems of disposing corpses in the river, an interview
with a public health official would have been informative.)

These are the people who prefer a kinship chart to *Anna Karenina*, but their project is intrinsically doomed: the specificity of their brand of linear film will always subvert their attempts to generalize human behavior. It is only elaborated metaphor and complex aesthetic structures that are capable of even beginning to represent human nature and events: configurations of pure imagery will always leave technology behind.

•   •   •

E.
Weinberger

Nearly all ethnographic filmmakers, in interviews, have remarked that the genre is, so many decades later, still in its infancy. It is difficult to disagree. The latest films selected for a recent Margaret Mead Film Festival in New York were generally more of the same: Every film had a narrator, many of them still speaking to a room full of slow children: "This is rice cooking. Rice is grown in their fields." Films still open with lines like, "This is the heart of Africa." There are still moments of incredible chauvinism, as when a narrator explains, "These village children have few toys, yet they are happy," or when, in a British film on the huge Kumbh Mela festival in India, the spiritual leaders of various temples are called bishops, abbots and deacons, as though this were a tea party in Canterbury.

A few things had changed: thanks to new high-speed films, many featured extraordinary night scenes, lit only by fires or candles. The effects of the West are no longer kept hidden: in one scene, a shaman in a trance stopped chanting to change the cassette in his tape recorder; and it was remarkable how many of the people, from scattered corners of the world, were wearing the same t-shirts with goofy slogans in English. Nearly every film featured synch sound and subtitled dialogue; the films were full of local speech.

•   •   •

The most interesting film I saw at the Festival was *Zulay, Facing the 21st Century* (1989) by Jorge and Mabel Preloran. Feature-length, the entire film is a dialogue between the filmmakers and Zulay, a woman from Otavalo, Ecuador, who comes to Los Angeles to live with them and help in the editing of a film on her community. (The Otavaleños stubbornly retain their traditions and dress, while simultaneously traveling all over the world to sell weavings most charitably described as tourist art.) The film cuts back and forth between the two places: Zulay's family speaking into the camera to give her messages; her reaction as she screens it in L.A; Zulay in traditional dress posing with Fred Flintstone at Marineland; Otavaleños dressing up as Mexican *charros* with huge sombreros for a local dance; Zulay operating a movieola with the same precise gestures and impassive face as the weavers in the footage she is editing; her family back home reading her letters out loud; Zulay's return to Otavalo and the local gossip that ultimately drives her back to L.A. (men or married couples may go everywhere, but single women do not leave the village), and so on. Most startlingly for ethnographic film and yet with absolute naturalness, the filmmakers discuss their own lives with Zulay: as expatriate Argentines who still do much of their work in Argentina, they too are adrift between cultures. The film is pure Rouch, and something more: the subject is interacting with the filmmakers not as a recording cultural presence, but as another human. The interview format finally reaches the condition of dialogue. And, in passing, we learn a great deal about Otavalo, all of it presented through the casual conversation.

The films ends with a complex metaphor: Zulay in Los Angeles, wearing traditional dress, screens yet another message from her mother, wearing the same clothes, in Otavalo. Her mother tells her it would be best if she did not come back; Zulay bursts into tears. The filmmakers ask her what she is going to do. Zulay, weeping, says, "I don't know." Film has both erased and created distances: it is Zulay's means of communication with her mother, and yet it is the cause of her expulsion from paradise: going to L.A. to work on the film, she has crossed to the other side of the camera, and though she is the mirror image of what the camera sees, she can't cross back.

It is impossible to separate what may be the next stage of ethnographic film from the fate of its subjects: extinction for some and tremendous cultural change for the rest. But there was an instant in a recent film, Howard Reid's *The Shaman and His Apprentice* (1989), that was, for me, a sudden glimpse into how much has been missing in the genre, and what its future may bring: when film technology is no longer a Western domain; when the observed become the observers; when ethnography becomes a communal self-portraiture, as complex as any representation of *us*; when the erotic can enter in as expression, not voyeurism; when *they*, at last, do all the talking.

The film follows a healer named José, of the Yamunawa people of the Peruvian Amazon, as he educates and initiates a young disciple, Caraca. In one scene José takes Caraca for his first visit to the nearest large town. The trip has only one purpose: to go to the local movie house, where there is an important lesson about healing to be learned:

"Cinema," José explains, "is exactly like the visions sick people have when they are dying."

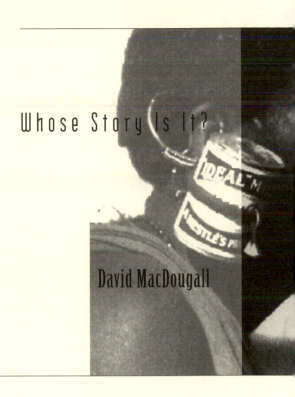

Whose Story Is It?

David MacDougall

ABOUT TWENTY YEARS AGO ANTHROPOLOGISTS AND ETHNOGRAPHIC FILMMAKERS BEGAN to feel uneasy about the unchallenged dominance of the author's voice in ethnographic descriptions. Both began to open their work more fully to the voices of their indigenous subjects. The intervening years have seen a tendency towards dialogic and polyphonic construction in ethnography. More recently some observers have argued that the indigenous voices in these works remain as subjugated as before, always appropriated in some discreditable way to what are, in the end, *our* projects. This has engendered a new round of self-criticism, sometimes resulting in fundamental doubts about the possibility of cultural description, sometimes in a paralyzing and, at times, proselytizing sense of guilt. If we keep writing anthropology or making films today, we do so with a greater awareness of the politics and ethics of representation. But this awareness can also lead to a decidedly condescending and moralistic strain of ethnocentrism. In our preoccupation with the part others play in our cultural affairs we may be less likely to pay attention to the part we play in theirs.

Films are objects, and like many objects may have multiple identities. An axe-head to you may be merely a paperweight to me. Films which are inwardly dialogic, juxtaposing the voices of author and subject, may also be outwardly so, by appearing as something quite different to each of them. I have a photographic postcard made in the 1930s which shows a Maasai man with a spear in one hand, a herdsman's stick in the other and a Nestlé's condensed milk tin stuck through the lobe of one ear (Fig. 1). This photograph and its connotations can be read on a variety of levels, from that of the original joke (a "savage," making a mistake about an object familiar to us) to what we now know of the impact of Nestlés infant formulas on the Third World. But what I see in it at this moment is the appropriation of one culture's product to another's use.

Such an image is paradoxical and surreal, like Max Ernst's zoomorphic landscapes, or a funerary jar used as an umbrella stand.[1] Its humor lies in incongruity, in the simultaneous perception of two different frames of reference, in boundaries crossed. In a certain group of ethnographic films we are presented with the similar paradox of two separate cultural meanings embodied in one image, like the well-known visual pun of the duck which is also a rabbit (Fig. 2). Indeed such films can be said to exist as two quite separate cultural objects, each appropriating certain features of the other.

Anthropology, in its traversing of cultural realities, is always on the verge of the surreal, but it endeavors to neutralize what Malinowski called the "coefficient of weirdness" through the rationale of cultural translation (Clifford 1988: 151). The lesson of surrealism, however, is that the experience of paradox is in itself significant and must be grasped to generate new perceptions. Thus, if these films have special value, anthropologically or more broadly, it is that they enable us somehow to confront the intersecting of the worlds they describe.

These worlds sometimes exert contradictory and disturbing gravitational forces on the ethnographic materials we create. Photographs and films, perhaps more than written descriptions, seem liable to distortion in this way, because of the continuity they share with the physical and sensory life of their referents. Such ties to another existence, at once subversive and at odds with the intentions of the maker, and yet also frequently in collusion with them, can become the strength or the demise of many an ethnographic film. I will give one instance of what must, for fieldworkers, be a fairly common but perhaps underdescribed phenomenon: that of feeling one's work disintegrating and being pulled back and reclaimed by the lives which generated it.

In October 1978 we filmed at an Aboriginal outstation in northern Australia, where a small group of people were attempting to resettle their traditional clan land.[2] Their plans hinged on a few old cattle yards left over from missionary days, which they hoped to turn into an economic base by mustering the wild cattle that roamed the surrounding bush.

What should be understood is how precarious the survival of such small Aboriginal groups is, both culturally and economically. In the settlement these people had left, fifty kilometers to the north, the 800 inhabitants spoke seven different Aboriginal languages. Some clans consisted of only a handful of people, and their future as autonomous groups depended upon the strength and ambitions of a few active family members.

Living at the outstation were about thirty people, many of them young and inexperienced at cattle work. They were led by an old Aboriginal man who had been a drover and stockman all his life. He was no longer physically strong, and what was clear from fairly early on was that most of the work of the station was in fact being done by his nephew's son, a thirteen-year-old boy named Ian Pootchemunka. Ian worked hard, set an example for others, and saw himself as eventually taking over from the old man. As in much of Aboriginal life, the group's prospects seemed here to depend crucially upon the strength and survival of one person.

Our filming, rather like this account of it, began by concentrating on the old man and ended on the boy. And not long after we finished filming we heard that the boy had died of an illness.

At this stage my perception of the material shifted quite radically. In some unaccountable way I felt that the film footage was now bound up with the boy and belonged to him, not in a proprietory way but existentially. It seemed like a physical piece of his life, his hopes and his death, and inseparable too from the community to which he belonged. Although this changed perspective was occasioned by his death, I believe it was always an inherently available one. When we heard of the death we felt that the film, as a film, had also died. We only returned to it some time later when the boy's parents asked us to complete it in his memory.

D. MacDougall

The point of recounting this is to ask: whose story was it? Was the film our story or his? By what means can we distinguish the structures we inscribe in films from the structures that are inscribed upon them, often without our knowing, by their subjects? And is a film in any sense the same object for those who made it, for whom it may have the status of discourse, and for those who in passing have left their physical traces upon it? The question of "whose story?" thus has both an ontological and moral dimension.

Some films construct narratives out of other peoples' lives, as I think Flaherty's often did.[3] One could say that John Marshall's *The Hunters* (1958) does this too in its creation of the story of a long hunt out of several shorter hunting expeditions. But many other films, including Marshall's *An Argument About a Marriage*, *A Joking Relationship* and *The Meat Fight*, take their structures from the events they record. They become stories in the Western sense by their framing of these events, although the participants would perhaps neither frame them that way nor recognize them as stories in their own narrative tradition.

Still other films attempt to accommodate indigenous narrative forms, either by mimicking them in their own structures (*The Hunters* is, arguably, conceived as a San hunting tale) or by utilizing the narratives of indigenous speakers. Roger Sandall's *Coniston Muster* (1972) is built around a group of stories told by Aboriginal stockmen, and many recent ethnographic films incorporate interview material and stories addressed to the filmmaker and the camera.

But the inclusion of indigenous narrative always raises the question of whether the film is making indigenous statements or merely absorbing a device into its own narrative strategies. Inevitably a method which purports to disperse some of its authority to its subjects is also capable of using this to reinforce its own. This has long been a critical issue in interview-based documentaries. As Bill Nichols has noted, in many of these films "a gap remains between the voice of a social actor recruited to the film and the voice *of* the film" [my emphasis] (1983: 23).

Sometimes this problem is avoided by clearly marking the use of indigenous narrative as a literary device, inviting us to read it in a complex way as the author's perception of another narrative mode. Rouch's film *The Lion Hunters* (1957/65) begins with a Gao storyteller's epic tale of lion hunting, setting the stage for Rouch's own epic treatment of the hunt for a lion called "The American." In a similar way, Robert Gardner borrows the Dani fable of a snake and a bird at the beginning of *Dead Birds* (1963) to lend mythic resonance to his own story of ritual warfare, and to offer a paradigm for it.[4]

In another Rouch film, *Jaguar* (1954/67), this overlapping of voices is more complex. To make the film, Rouch invited three young men to enact the sort of adventure that was common for just such young men to undertake in the 1950s. This is their story, and yet

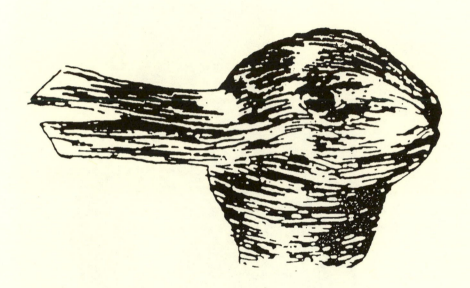

through the strange circumstances of filmmaking here they are, *playing* their story. They also recount it on the soundtrack in a mixture of improvised dialogue, jokes and reminiscence. As in *The Lion Hunters*, we feel we are witnessing the genesis of an epic tale, which will be elaborated over the years to eager youths in the village. And this aspect of the film soon becomes recognizable as the distinctive voice of Rouch, for whom the story is not just of a single African journey but a celebration of the collective experience of a generation of young Africans. Anecdote is here transformed into legend. By the end of the film it is this second narrative voice that is dominant. The story is now Rouch's and its subjects have become mythic figures. "These young men," he tells us on the soundtrack, "are heroes of the modern world."

Anthropology in recent years has been questioning its earlier aspirations towards scientific positivism and many of the conceptual categories through which it has described life in other societies. Recent ethnographies acknowledge in their own design what anthropologists have posited for years—that constructions of the world are dependent upon language, in the broadest sense. This challenge is not necessarily met by modest inclusions of quotations. And the language of the classical ethnographies has been found inadequate for reaching broader understandings of certain cultures, particularly those involving variant notions of the self, which previous invocations of the "native point of view" tended to take as unproblematic.

Recognition of this inadequacy has led to approaches oscillating between critical introspection on the one hand and a search for new formal and multivocal strategies on the other. Anthropologists are now more conscious that they too are telling stories. But curiously, although ethnographic filmmaking has followed a parallel course, it does not seem to have done so notably under the inspiration of anthropology. The challenging of authorial certainties, of received stylistic conventions, the introduction of self-reflexivity, the moves towards subtitling indigenous speech (allowing the inclusion of indigenous texts) all appear to have emerged from ethical and epistemological questions which documentary filmmakers began asking themselves thirty years ago. It is probably true to say that ethnographic filmmakers became sensitive to some of these textual implications independently of ethnographic writers.

D. MacDougall

If anthropologists once resisted the idea that they were telling stories, they have now certainly made up for it. Modern ethnographies are often extremely complex stories of other lives, or stories of anthropological encounters in the field. They are often manifold constructions, juxtaposing indigenous texts with anthropological reflections and analysis.[5] By using the words of their informants, anthropologists (and ethnographic filmmakers) bring into their work the narrative forms and cultural assumptions embedded in speech. Wherever "quotation" occurs, an indigenous narrative model is possible.

For all that, there are persisting doubts about this form of representation. If ethnographies now incorporate other voices, what textual independence do these voices actually have? In an absolute sense, all texts used in this way are subordinated to the text of the author. This may be more true of written ethnography than film, in which more unencoded information can be said to "leak" from the images, but in both cases the author decides what texts to include or exclude.

It can be argued that where we are allowed to hear other voices, it is only at the author's will, by a process of "transmission." But the question of how other voices can be transmitted is really preempted by another question: how the materials out of which a work is made act themselves to define and control its meaning. If a film is a reflection of an encounter between filmmaker and subject, it must be seen to some degree as produced by the subject. It is a rare book or film that emerges at the end of the process as the author preconceived it. The shape of the text may be said to take on characteristics of the subject by virtue of "exposure" to it, like a photographic plate.

This, of course, is the specific aim of certain films. Observational filmmaking was founded on the assumption that things happen in the world which are worth watching, and that their own distinctive spacial and temporal configurations are part of what is worth watching about them. Observational films are frequently analytical, but they also make a point of being open to categories of meaning that might transcend the filmmaker's analysis. This stance of humility before the world can of course be self-deceiving and self-serving, but it also implicitly acknowledges that the subject's story is often more important than the filmmaker's. And this can be seen as a necessary first step towards a more participatory cinema.

Sometimes there is no question whose story dominates. Karel Reisz and Tony Richardson's *Momma Don't Allow* (1956), for example, is a rough and ready reply to all those films about adolescence which purport to explain it or cloak it in romanticism. As in this case, the most explicitly observational films are usually fragments, or fragmentary. This is true of many of Timothy Asch's Yanomamö films. It is also true of most of John Marshall's African films as well as his series on the Pittsburgh police, which have titles like *Three Domestics*, *Henry is Drunk* and *You Wasn't Loitering*. Longer observational films are more often patterned on the narratives of realist fiction—for example, the Maysles brothers' *Salesman* (1969) and Gary Kildea's *Celso and Cora* (1983).[6]

Short observational films often come about accidentally, since the observational method entails shooting things without generally knowing how they will turn out. An instance is a film we made which began with rather straightforward coverage of a group of Jie men making leather straps and spear covers. A conversation started up, in the casual way these things do, and evolved into a discussion and then an argument about the behavior of motor cars and their drivers. The resulting film (*Under the Men's Tree* [1974]) is really no more than this fragment, surrounded by a few other sequences of talk and cattle herding. Its primary logic is the logic of the conversation.[7] This essential shape is sometimes blurred, and framed by other material, but it remains the dominant structure.

Other films "belong" to their subjects in a different sense. I mean here films that revolve around a single person. Often they are planned in this way, but occasionally someone emerges unexpectedly from the background and lays claim to them, as happened in Tanya Ballantyne's film *The Things I Cannot Change* (1966) and the Aboriginal outstation film *Three Horsemen* (1980).

One is always aware of this possibility in a negative sense when making films. There are people in any group who will be drawn to the film or the filmmakers, just as there are people who will volunteer to be an anthropologist's informants. Sometimes it is simply because they are intelligent and enquiring of mind. Sometimes they are marginal people, attracted to the outsider from a sense of their own awkward status, or in search of fulfillment. Many view themselves as brokers, experts or intermediaries. They can pose a challenge to the filmmaker's carefully-guarded sense of control, for they are inclined to put themselves at the center of any enterprise. One can resist them or be drawn to the complexities in them. The opposite case also occurs. On one occasion we were drawn to a person who at the beginning wanted to have nothing to do with us or the film, and we ended by making an entire film about him.[8]

There are many instances in documentary of the physical and spiritual being of a person seeming to overflow the film that sets out to contain it. The film "transmits" the presence, but it is as though the film is then consumed by it. Bob Dylan looks out from the film *Don't Look Back* (1966) as if to say, "This isn't much, and I will do what I like with it."

But the presence need not be so canny or assertive. Sometimes there is a gradual shift in the orientation of a film towards a particular narrative voice. In a series of films we made on an Aboriginal stockman, it was only in the third film that we finally recognized the links between his personal style and a much broader narrative tradition.[9] I think this was a case, more common than one perhaps supposes, of a local culture slowly gaining an influence over the filmmakers and the film. There are many variations on this theme, one of which is Rouch's films made under what he calls "cine-trance," such as *Tourou et Bitti* (1971).

Some films aim at just such an overflowing. The filmmaker Jorge Preloran has created a sub-genre of ethnobiographical films centered around extensive sound-recordings of his subjects recounting their lives. It began with Hermogenes Cayo, a religious painter and wood carver from the high plateau of Argentina. The fullness of a single life is the overriding quality of this film, *Imaginero* (1969), and other films like *Cochengo Miranda* (1974) and *Zerda's Children* (1978). To Preloran the film is, in certain essentials, the work of the subject himself—his voice, his words, the images of him, and the images he himself has made. Preloran has created the film, but then (to quote Preloran),

> . . . one day the film is completed . . . And suddenly the film is not mine anymore . . . It
> has a life of its own; suddenly Hermogenes is there in direct communication with the
> audience, and you are left out in the cold. (Sherman 1985: 37)

I need not defend Preloran here on charges of naiveté. He is as aware as anyone of how a filmmaker analyses, selects and finally constructs. His point is, I think, a more sophisticated one which goes beyond the assumption that filmmakers, or any other makers of cultural artifacts, exert total control over them. Just as we see that the maker is the locus of a set of cultural and historical forces, so too we must see the film in the same light, and acknowledge the maker as but one aspect of its coming into being. Here I side with Roland Barthes in holding that a film or a photograph is both analogical and coded, and that it can never be wholly the maker's fabrication.

I now turn to a rather different way in which films are impressed and, indeed, possessed by their subjects: when they become bound into a relationship with the subject as part of a larger set of cultural meanings. Some films are of little interest or immediate consequence to those who appear in them. They belong to a discourse to which they are largely indifferent. That famous remark of Sam Yazzie, the Navajo elder, to John Adair and Sol Worth—"Will making movies do the sheep good?"—is not some sage indictment of exploitative academic practices but an acknowledgement of differing cultural priorities.

D.
MacDougall

Clearly, films matter to their subjects when they have practical or symbolic implications for them. Films are shaped as much by the structures into which they are placed as by their avowed form and intention. The making of some films is thus part of a social process larger than the film itself. This can be said of many films in the abstract—commercial films are part of a social process too—but I am concerned here with films which are explicitly structured by what their subjects expect of them.

The Aranda of Central Australia can have expected little from the films of Walter Baldwin Spencer when he made them in 1901, nor can the Dani have expected much from Robert Gardner's sixty years later, especially as in Gardner's view "one essential advantage lay in the fact that the Dugum Dani did not know what a camera was" (1969: 30). One might look for more precise expectations among people more knowledgeable about the media, except that many apparently sophisticated people are merely flattered or intimidated when a camera is turned in their direction. Americans and Europeans are all too ready to put themselves unquestioningly in the hands of "media professionals." Perhaps, then, one should look to films of advocacy—except that many of these are made on behalf of people who are never consulted. I know of no easy way of identifying such films, except to say that they tend to be films in which the makers were to some degree under the direction of the subjects. One might include here the more improvisational passages in Flaherty or Rouch, where scenes were constructed for the film. But here I would like to look at another group of films in which rituals or ritualized relationships impose a signifying structure.

Australian ethnographic filmmaking has been concerned with Aboriginal ritual performance from the very beginning and there is a large body of work devoted to it. It includes an important series of films made by Roger Sandall with the anthropologist Nicolas Peterson in the 1960s and other films made by Ian Dunlop with the anthropologist Howard Morphy more recently. In both cases it is fair to say (and they have said it themselves) that often neither filmmaker nor anthropologist had a very clear idea of what was going on until after the fact.

Sandall's work tends to emphasize the spacial relationships and choreography of the rituals. Dunlop's looks more closely at the role of ritual leaders and translates more of the conversations and song texts. But at the time of filming, both filmmakers had to follow the course of events and take advice as best they could. The organizers of the rituals, for their own prestige, had an interest in conducting them properly under the eye of the camera, but they also had an interest in how the films would be used. The most secret rituals could only be shown to the legitimate owners or certain permitted outsiders. In more public rituals, certain meanings—in song texts, for example—could not be disclosed because they belonged to a particular clan or smaller kin group. In these films the actual words may be recorded and translated literally, but their significance often may not. The filmmaker is always under instruction, and the ultimate meaning of the film remains with the film's subjects.

This sense of ownership is strongly articulated at the end of Kim McKenzie's film, *Waiting for Harry* (1980), when the ritual's organizer, Frank Gurrmanamana, tells the assembled participants:

> This film is mine . . . Now men everywhere will see my sacred emblems, just as, in many places, I have seen theirs. So. The emblems I hold so dear are now on a film, so the film is also dear to me.

These films serve political and ritual purposes. Even if it is not always evident to the outside viewer, they are part of a continuing process of cultural reinforcement and contestation. They have themselves become emblems.

I shall attempt to describe from my own perspective while making it, the cultural and political circumstances of one such film, *Familiar Places* (1980), shot in Australia in 1977. It does not concern ritual as such, but ritual is never far in the background. What may be of interest is the way in which it enters into a complex network of relationships intersecting what film theorists like to call the "profilmic event."

The film was made near Cape Keerweer on the coast of the Gulf of Carpentaria in northern Queensland. It was made at a time of considerable pressure on Aboriginal communities by mining interests and State government authorities. The film records part of a journey made with a group of Aborigines and a young anthropologist to map sites in traditional clan country. This is a complex landscape of salt pans and estuaries, filled with places of significance, both secular and sacred. It is an area of increase centers, secret wells, cremation grounds and sites where totemic ancestors are said to have carved out the inlets and sandhills. Different parts of the land belong to different clans, but few people have visited it for thirty or forty years. Almost everyone lives at the old mission settlement of Aurukun 100 kilometers to the north. The young people have never been here, and for older people, returning means reorienting themselves to a terrain they may have last seen when they were themselves young.

The film concerns a dozen or so people but focuses primarily on an old man, Jack Spear Karntin, a younger couple (Angus and Chrissie Namponan, who are bringing their children to see their traditional land), and the anthropologist Peter Sutton. On the soundtrack Sutton gives a rough chronology of the journey and his views on the significance of the mapping process.

Looking at this casually, Western viewers might suppose they were in familiar narrative territory. Sutton appears to be in charge of the story as well as the expedition. Old Jack Spear appears to be making nostalgic visits to places of his youth. The couple, the Namponans, appear to be so-called "half primitives," caught between two worlds and somewhat uncertain of their own culture. The children look like any children enjoying a holiday.

A different perception of these relationships, and of the film as a whole, first requires recognizing that although Sutton is the voice "in the film" he is not necessarily the voice "of the film"—indeed he is only one of a set of players in a complex cultural drama. The film attempts to reveal certain aspects of this drama and Sutton's role in it. In one scene Angus Namponan puts pressure on Sutton to map his country rather than other people's, because time is running out before the Australian "wet" sets in. This is one of the points at which the political significance of the mapping, and Sutton's involvement as an agent of Aboriginal interests, is evident. People speak to one another in the film, but they are also speaking for other audiences. And they are aware of the film itself as a channel of communication.

When we came to analyze this situation we could point to more than a dozen separate "voices" or directions of discourse represented in the film. For example, although Aborigines may be speaking to Sutton, they are also addressing one another, and through the film other audiences, both Aboriginal and non-Aboriginal.[10] However, such an analysis focuses on speaking and telling, and in an important sense this misses the point, for films are also about *showing*. In Aboriginal terms this may be culturally of far greater consequence than it is for us. If we ask, "Whose story is it?" in Aboriginal terms, we may have to enlarge considerably our conception of what is *narrative*.

Aborigines in this part of Australia commonly speak of "story places" when referring to totemic sites, for these are places which were discovered and left for future generations when the spirit ancestors moved over the land. Such events can of course be recounted as "stories," but more importantly they form points in a larger narrative of travel through the country. The concept of totem, as an emblem of clan identity, is thus intimately bound up with the idea of story or narrative. A spoken reference, or the showing of a totemic object, conjure up both one's clan identity and the narrative which is associated with it. Thus, as Peter Sutton noted himself soon after the filming, a film can be conceived of by Aborigines as one more medium of reference, for ritually *showing* and thus giving recognition to objects and places. And in doing so it takes on all the accompanying connotations of "story" and narrative. If this happens, the film itself becomes a new story and object of totemic significance. It is not perceived merely as the filmmaker's story; it becomes, in effect, Aboriginal cultural property (Sutton 1978: 1).

When the Namponan children are being introduced to their country for the first time, the showing is not only to familiarize them with it. It is an act of investiture, a formal endorsement of their rights to the country. The showing, and their seeing, stand in place of what we might consider a formal statement or delineation of rights. Showing here constitutes a kind of charter. It demonstrates the crucial importance of the visual in Aboriginal affairs.

As we were filming we became aware that the perception which Aborigines had of the mapping, as a recognition (or "*registration*") of their clan territories, extended to the film itself. There are many expressions of this in the film, as when Jack Spear formally addresses the camera and sound recorder; but simply by the act of participating in the film people are appropriating it for an Aboriginal purpose. Sutton has written that "when filming is 'permitted', it is a mistake to see this permission as a passive acquiescence out of mere politeness, cooperativeness or desire for money. In a great many cases, film is being actively *used*" (Sutton: 6). Moreover, it may be essential that the filming be done by an outsider, who fulfils the traditional role of *pant*, or disinterested adjudicator, since a local person would clearly be placed in an equivocal position if asked to witness another person's claims. (Sutton: 3–4)

Here it becomes possible to say that the film is no longer outside the situation it describes, nor has it merely been expanded through self-reflexivity or acknowledgement of its fuller meanings. It is inside someone else's story. And if one seeks to define its shape at this level of interpretation, one may say that the film not only reflects Aboriginal narrative by moving physically over the country, but has become formally part of an implicit Aboriginal narrative of ritual display.

Whenever cultural forces within a subject act upon the structure of a film in the ways I have described—through the patterning of an event, a personal narrative, appropriation to a local function, or in some other way—the film can be read as a compound work, representing a crossing of cultural perspectives. Sometimes the process goes no further. We are familiar with films in which we "see through" the assumptions of the maker to those of the subjects, and are aware of their mutual illegibility.

Whether a film is capable of generating more complex statements seems to depend upon the filmmaker's ability to make the film more than merely a report on a cultural encounter and, instead, embody it. Rouch, for example, comes upon his subjects in the act of self-discovery, in the borderlands between cultures or in the liminal zones of ritual and possession. He sees liberation in the crossing of boundaries, which finds its metaphor in the scene in *Jaguar* where Lam, Illo and Damouré slip behind the police post to enter the unknown land of the Gold Coast. Rouch is a kind of cultural gun-runner. A different filmmaker (a Kim McKenzie or Marc Piault, for example) might make films which express the constant testing and reinvention of culture, or which (in the case of Jorge Preloran) represent the emergence in his subjects of an historical consciousness. But this kind of film can only exist when filmmakers regard their work as more than a transmission of prior knowledge. They need to approach filming instead as a way of creating the circumstances in which new knowledge can take us by surprise.

Notes

This paper was presented in a slightly different version on May 23, 1991 at the 1991 NAFA (Nordic Anthropological Film Association) Conference in Oslo. I am grateful to several of the NAFA participants for their comments, and I am particularly indebted to Peter Sutton (1978) and Fred Myers (1988) for their earlier discussions of Familiar Places (see below).

1. Buñuel's *Las Hurdes* (*Land Without Bread*, 1932) is provocatively surrealist in its presentation of European squalor and misery in the guise of a travelogue, accompanied by the "high art" of European classical music, in this case the Brahms Fourth Symphony.

2.   The film was released as *Three Horsemen* (1980).

3.   In making *Nanook of the North* (1922), however, Flaherty's relationship with the Inuit seems to have permitted a more open approach. A number of scenes were suggested and then enacted by Nanook himself.

4.   I use the recounting of a myth at the opening of *Good-bye Old Man* (1977) as a way of linking the events surrounding the *pukumani* ritual to Tiwi ideas of death.

5.   See, for example, Walter Goldschmidt's *Kambuya's Cattle* (1969), Paul Rabinow's *Reflections on Fieldwork in Morocco* (1977), and Peter Loizos' *The Heart Grown Bitter* (1981). The latter is structurally very innovative and brings to mind A.J.A. Symons' seminal biography of the 1930s, *The Quest for Corvo*.

6.   An exception is the work of Fred Wiseman. His films on American public institutions follow a theme-and-variations structure in which the fragments are subsumed by a discourse on regimentation and the fallibility of all such institutions.

7.   The film perhaps contains a further ironic narrative line, but it remains implicit: "Here are a remote people talking about their world. But no, you are mistaken, they are talking about yours."

8.   *Lorang's Way* (1974/79).

9.   This film is *Sunny and the Dark Horse* (1986). The first two were *Collum Calling Canberra* (1984) and *Stockman's Strategy* (1984).

10. These variously-directed discourses may be described as follows. To begin with:
     1) Sutton is speaking to the audience.
     2) The film, or filmmaker, is also speaking to the audience.
     3) The Aborigines are speaking to one another.
     4) The Aborigines are speaking to Sutton.
     5) Sutton is speaking to the Aborigines.
     6) Occasionally the Aborigines speak to the filmmaker.
     7) Occasionally, too, the filmmaker speaks to the Aborigines.
     8) One might also guess that during the filming, the filmmaker spoke to the Aborigines through Sutton, which in fact was the case. But here things become more complicated, because:
     9) The Aborigines are speaking to the audience through the film.
     10) The Aborigines are speaking to one another through the film.
     11) The Aborigines are speaking to Sutton through the film.
     12) The Aborigines are speaking to the audience through Sutton.
     And finally:
     13) The film, or filmmaker, is speaking to the Aborigines through the film.
     14) The film, or filmmaker, is speaking to Sutton through the film.
     15) Sutton is speaking to the filmmaker, through the film; and
     16) Sutton is speaking to the Aborigines, through the film.

References

Clifford, James. 1988. "On Ethnographic Surrealism." In *The Predicament of Culture*, 117–51. Cambridge: Harvard University Press.

Gardner, Robert. 1969. "Chronicles of the Human Experience: Dead Birds." *Film Library Quarterly* (Fall): 25–34.

Myers, Fred R. 1988. "From Ethnography to Metaphor: Recent Films from David and Judith MacDougall." *Cultural Anthropology* 3 (2): 205–20.

Nichols, Bill. 1983. "The Voice of Documentary." *Film Quarterly* 36 (3): 17–30.

Sherman, Sharon R. 1985. "Human Documents: Folklore and the Films of Jorge Preloran." *Southwest Folklore* 6 (1): 17–61.

Sutton, Peter. 1978. "Some Observations on Aboriginal Use of Filming at Cape Keerweer, 1977." Paper presented at Ethnographic Film Conference, Australian Institute of Aboriginal Studies, Canberra, May 13, 1978.

The Modernist Sensibility in Recent Ethnographic Writing and the Cinematic Metaphor of Montage

George E. Marcus

THIS ESSAY OBLIQUELY COMMENTS ON ETHNOGRAPHIC *FILM* THROUGH AN ARGUMENT about the cinematic imagination at work in contemporary experiments in ethnographic *writing*. Its offstage agenda is to stimulate a different relationship than has existed in the past between these two media of ethnographic representation in anthropology, given my perception of particularly favorable current conditions for so doing.

I want to begin with a highly impressionistic observation about the reception of ethnographic film among its predominant community of anthropologists. Mostly oriented to writing, anthropologists have been satisfied to be nothing more than the equivalent of scriveners, but we now understand text making straight through from fieldwork to publication as something much more complex. For most anthropologists, films have been primarily supplemental and naturalistic. That is, they can supplement the knowledge of a subject created through other modes of textualization—films can vividly confirm an insight, argument, or ethnographic common sense that has been established through writing and discussion—but they cannot create such intellectual capital. In short, ethnographic films have not yet in themselves served as arguments about established ethnographic representations of a particular subject so as to alter fundamentally the way anthropologists see or think about their objects of study.

Further, in watching colleagues watch ethnographic films, I have been struck by how similar their responses are to those of zoologists commenting on nature films. The latter often read behavioral scenarios on film with an essentially classificatory framework in mind. Certain actions are understood as registers or tokens of ways a particular species has been represented through classification. While ethnographic films have always been inherently narratives or stories, written ethnographies have not been, at least until recently. As Robert Thornton has shown (1988), classic ethnography has not created a sense of the real and a sense of totality (a whole culture, a people, etc.) through narrative techniques, but through the trope of classification (fixing subjects in space, primarily, and then treating by chapter and verse their religion, politics, kinship, etc.). Most theory in anthropology has indeed been the development of the detailed classificatory schemes to assimilate and constitute the description of "the real." As such, the stories of ethnographic film have been largely received and appreciated by anthropological scriveners, not for themselves, but as kinds of case studies of "nature" (messier and truer than writing) to be assimilated by the prior and essentially classificatory knowledge developed by written ethnography. For the realist ethnographic writer, then, ethnographic films are somehow more natural than written texts, and their appreciation lies in the confirmation and enrichment they provide for the local and global classifications by which anthropologists have created knowledge of others.

Both to contemporary ethnographic filmmakers, who, while they may still identify with the classic project of ethnography at the heart of modern anthropology, have joined their work to the broader discourse about film itself, with its own theories, problems, and interests, and to contemporary writers and theorists of ethnography, who, in a mood of experimentation with form, have made a fundamental break with the classificatory realism that has shaped the genre, this state of the just posited reception of ethnographic film in anthropology is highly regrettable. A new arena of debate is needed in which the differences between these two media of representation and their relative possibilities in reconstituting the idea of what anthropological knowledge is, or should be, can be discussed from a starting position which recognizes a certain identity between them as well as an equality of intellectual standing.

Of course, once this arena, based on identity, is opened, one would not expect, or even hope, that the new dialogue between the two media would be harmonious. But first, the task is to open it by insisting on common potentials at this moment of a self-critical mood about ethnography through appreciating it as a special kind of text-making activity regardless of medium. I do not think this opening can be made by any argument that attempts to demote writing in relation to film, or by one that makes greater claims for film than one should. Indeed, despite its keen sensitivity to issues of representation and reflexivity in textmaking, I have found ethnographic film rather tame in its will to rethink the project of ethnography itself. Yet, those who have done the work of critiquing ethnographic rhetoric, mainly with written texts in mind, either have operated from a cinematic imagination, or are dealing with experiments in form that could as easily if not more conveniently be handled in a film medium. In speaking to many anthropologists about the critique of ethnography over the past few years, I have been impressed by how much more comfortably it has been embraced by filmmakers, but also by how reticent or indifferent filmmakers are to opening new discussions with those the weight of whose voices and writing still define the project of ethnography itself—that is, the typically scrivening anthropologist.

As written ethnography moves more toward its repressed narrative dimension, it is more likely to appreciate new links with film. This shift toward constructing the real through narrative rather than classification is stimulated, I believe, not by some aesthetic preference, but rather by a shift in the historic conditions in terms of which anthropology must identify itself if it can be done at all—e.g., how it constructs its object (certainly no longer the primitive outside a modern world system), how it argues for the authority of its own representations of otherness in a much more complex field of such representations occupied by diverse others who aggressively and eloquently "speak for themselves" in the same media and to the same publics in terms of which anthropologists once felt themselves to occupy a secure position.

I want to pursue in this paper the potential change in relationship between film and writing in ethnography by making a strong claim about the cinematic basis of contemporary experiments in ethnographic writing. To do so, I want to report on three related lines of thinking in my recent work. These are directions in which I have gone since the early to mid-1980s critique of ethnographic rhetoric and representation in which I participated and are reflected in books such as *Writing Culture* (Clifford and Marcus 1986) and *Anthropology As Cultural Critique* (Marcus and Fischer 1986). I am strongly committed to sustaining the empirical nature of the practice of ethnography as well as the claims to knowledge for its representations, consistent with the way anthropologists currently invent their disciplinary tradition, while incorporating what may be viewed as the threatening (narcissistic, nihilistic, and thus socially irresponsible) aspects of a form which, although representing others, now critically requires a calling of attention to itself. This is of course not the only position that can be argued from the critique of ethnography, and it may be viewed as a conservative (as well as an optimistic) position in thinking about the implications of the critique for the practice of ethnography.

First, I have been trying to translate some of the critiques of ethnographic representation into a set of strategems for producing an alternative, or at least, a modified kind of ethnography. Anthropology is both addressing subjects new to it and recasting the space-time identity of its conventional ones. This is in response, I believe, to a *fin de siècle* phenomenon marked by a sense of an exhaustion of concepts and frameworks, or at least, to an inability to choose critically and decisively among them. Thus, witness the symptomatic loss of authority of metanarratives, working paradigms, and foundations in most disciplines, and the consequent inability to make the kinds of ethical judgements which have always policed the boundaries of knowledge to be pursued by discrete disciplinary communities of scholars. Contextualization, historicization, probing local variation, fragments, indeterminacies—these are the styles of inquiry generally in play. Thus, it is indeed a very appropriate time for the jeweller's-eye gaze of ethnography. Yet the conceptual capital of ethnography is very much the realism of nineteenth century social theory. While thus focussed appropriately, ethnography operates with concepts that cannot comprehend subtly enough the historic present of its subjects.

Since I am interested in "modernizing," so to speak, ethnography's apparatus of representation, I could do no other than to relate myself to the complex and at times hopelessly obscure realm of debate over the nature of late twentieth century aesthetics and culture as postmodernism. In this discursive space, I side with those who seek to show that postmodernism is best understood as another moment of modernism, and who attempt to rethink or revise the history of this signature Western movement in line with certain global changes and repositionings of the West in a world that is decidedly not *only* Western. Whatever postmodernity may mean for artistic production, I make the claim that the critiques of the rhetorical and conceptual apparatus of ethnography are leading finally to the introduction of some of the problems and techniques of classic (primarily literary) modernism, but very much for anthropology's own present purposes and predicaments. The nature of an essentially nineteenth century derived social realism in anthropology (that it shares with other disciplines of the humanities and social sciences) is being modified through the influence of aspects of a classic modernist sensibility toward redefining the real, particularly when the prestige and sovereignty of Western cognitive frameworks of representation are diminished. It is thus no accident that a renewed affinity between the tribal (or the cross-cultural) and the modern should be so profoundly marked in the turbulence about anthropology's methods and practices of representing its "others."

Second, I have been noting that the self-conscious experimental moves away from realist representation in both history and anthropology have been undertaken in the name of montage. Montage lends technique to the desire to break with existing rhetorical conventions and narrative modes through exposing their artificiality and arbitrariness. How montage techniques in themselves establish an alternative coherence, or whether they can, is a major issue in experimentation.

Montage is of course the key theoretical concept of cinema, and I began to examine the influence of cinema after its appearance in the late nineteenth century upon classic literary modernism. This development seems to me to offer the originary precedent for the emergence of a kind of modernist sensibility in ethnography. Reference to how cinema establishes narrative through montage is the way this writerly sensibility explicitly advertises itself. Keith Cohen's important study (1979) of the historic relation of film to fiction has been an important frame of reference for me in thinking about this cinematic basis of the changes in ethnography. As he concludes (219), "The cinematic precedence for the classic modern novel, therefore, deserves prominence as a primary example of one art technologically ahead of its time that shocked another art into the realization of how it could align itself with the times." Roughly, I see the same kind of event in the emergence of a modernist sensibility in ethnographic writing that ethnographic film itself has not exhibited. I want to suggest the potential of a modernist ethnography in writing, sensitive to its own cinematic basis, for sparking a different sort of relationship to ethnographic film that has little exploited the aspects of the film medium which experimental ethnographic writing has embraced ideologically, if not in practice.

Third, in working with my own ethnographic materials, I have been thinking through a specific problem that is relevant to the two concerns just introduced. Initially, in studying the Tongan diaspora during the 1970s, then in studying contemporary dynastic family fortunes in the United States, and now in pursuing the related topic of the emergence of great public cultural institutions in the West, I came to focus upon the increasingly deterritorialized nature of cultural process and the implications of this for the practice of ethnography. If ethnographic description can no longer be circumscribed by the situated locale or community, the place where cultural process manifests itself and can be captured in the ethnographic present, what then? How to render a description of cultural process that occurs in transcultural space, in different locales at once, in parallel, separate, but simultaneous worlds? This recalls a defining problem of literary modernism concerning the representation in a linear form of simultaneity. So, I have been experimenting with form under the influence of this modernist problematic to reconstitute the sense of the object of study and the practices for representing it. And I would argue that this sort of concern does not arise from an aesthetic concern to humanize the social sciences, but instead has the greatest importance for the latters' tradition of theory construction. The relevance of film enters here in adapting the concept of parallel editing as the basis for a solution in writing to achieve an effect of simultaneity. Further (and beyond my competence here), this modernist problem of ethnographic writing suggests a treatment in film itself. It is in extending the cinematic metaphor in experimental writing to filmmaking that a new relationship between ethnographic writing and film might be forged.

In the following sections, I want to explore in more or less elaborate detail each of these strains of thought coming out of the mid-1980s critique of ethnography. In the end, I return briefly to the possibility of an ethnographics dependent upon stimulating underdeveloped tendencies in ethnographic film and a revision of its relationship to ethnographic writing by showing how much proposed shifts in conventions of ethnographic writing rely on essentially filmic concepts.

The Emergence of a Modernist Sensibility in Late Twentieth Century Ethnographic Writing

G. Marcus

Why there should be a so-called crisis of representation that has called theoretical and critical attention to the form and rhetoric of textmaking in so many disciplines of the human sciences has yet to be fully addressed or explained, and how, or whether, such disciplines will find their way back to reasonably settled paradigms or working theories, away from the mood of self-critical reflexivity, is quite uncertain. One might argue, however, that the self-critical mood itself, in its most productive aspects, is evolving a working paradigm quite different from previous objectivist master frameworks which limit or exclude the possibility of calling critical attention to the ways that they stimulate the production of knowledge. In the internal discussions and activities of the increasingly institutionalizing interdisciplinary spaces of largely English-speaking academia (cultural studies centers, humanities research centers, etc.) that are constructing this alternative working paradigm, what is at stake is the late twentieth century understanding of modernity through a re-evaluation of the contemporary intellectual fecundity of the various European and American modernisms of the past century and a half. The specific intellectual capital for this re-evaluation, which has seeded the growth of the current interdisciplinary movement, has been the diffusion of the ideas of French poststructuralism through English-speaking countries along with the development of feminism as both a site of theory construction and social movement itself. There seems to be a parallel between the keenly critical and modernist nature of the signature deconstructive mood of this interdisciplinary movement (and here I associate deconstruction as a more general intellectual phenomenon than the practice specifically of Derrida) and a *fin de siècle* sense of the decline of the West, or at least of its social, political, and economic dissemination into a global order which it no longer can perceive itself as commanding.

Anthropology's own specific version of the more general crisis of representation might be more keenly felt. By the nature of its enterprise it has always been more or less explicitly deconstructing the West, yet its means of continuing to do so now have to some degree been trumped. On the one hand, more powerful and complex notions of anthropology's key concepts of culture and society are coming out of literature, despite how frustratingly ethnocentric many of these might be, and on the other, anthropological representations as claims to knowledge now exist in a complex matrix of dialogic engagement with diverse other representations, interests, and claims to knowledge concerning the same objects of study. The critiques that anthropological knowledge has offered in the past of the West must now reposition themselves in a much more complex space in which critical ideas generally are produced. This makes it essential to relate anthropology to the current debate over modernity/postmodernity through giving its central practice of ethnography a genealogy and context in intellectual history beyond anthropology's own disciplinary history. To this purpose, I proffer two positions that place the current experimental mood in ethnographic writing at the intersection of the debate about postmodernism/modernism and changes in the world which most powerfully stimulate this mood and sensitivity to its own descriptive practices.

A core notion in the contemporary debates about postmodernism, which manifest the continuing effort of the West to redefine its recent cultural past in the midst of an emergent world that is generating powerful and palpable effects of change without being well understood or described, is the idea that the creative possibilities of modernism are exhausted, assimilated by popular culture, that the distinction between high and popular culture no longer holds, that the new can no longer be constituted by or recognized in avant-gardes. In this context, I appreciate most those who, like Marshall Berman (1982), try to reread classic modernism and reinterpret it for the present and the emergent. In this reading, modernism rather than being a rejection of nineteenth century literary realism was a recasting of it in response to perceived changes in the conditions of society. Anthropology shares the intellectual capital of nineteenth century social theory which facilitated the objectification of such concepts as culture, society, community, and tradition. With reflexive issues absent or in the background, classifications and narrative frameworks of dispassionate observation produced representations of others with a distanced gaze. Literary modernism was a profound complication of the production of these modes of realism. Far from being exhausted, as appears to be the case for contemporary artists and aesthetic theorists, modernist techniques of representation, in the ways that they problematically construct "the real," seem fresh and compelling in a discipline like anthropology, with the act of realist description at its core. While postmodernism may be a proper subject of anthropological (or sociological) study as an techno-aesthetic movement in society, anthropology itself as a practice is merely becoming modernist in the classic literary sense.

Now, what stimulates this shift in cognitive/perceptual terms is an understanding that while the conceptual, rhetorical apparatus of producing ethnography may still do within the classic discursive frames for constituting theory in seminar rooms and the like, it will no longer do in most field situations—the other we study is as modern, or as embedded in conditions of modernity, as we are. The acknowledgment of this has profound implications for the current formulation of anthropology's core puzzle of the relationship between similarity and difference and its differential attribution to peoples of the world. Positing the global pervasiveness of modernity undercuts the ability of anthropologists to tell stories of isolated settled communities, worlds unto themselves, both by establishing and then problematizing global homogenization processes, and by denying the possibility of the distanced gaze on which the otherness of others depends for its construction. The relationship, thus, between deeply entwined simultaneous processes of homogenization and heterogeneity anywhere on the globe is what has most strongly disrupted the business-as-usual of the tradition of ethnographic representation. This is what requires an ethnography with an historic sense of the present to move toward modernist techniques/strategies of representation.

Such a move rests on a premise of shrewd anti-localism that derives from the perception of a profound late twentieth century globalism, yet without the naive assumptions of universalism that accompanied similar perceptions at the end of the last century. The world in a cultural or humanistic sense is not becoming "one," although it might be becoming more dialogic. Rather, difference, diversity, is generated not from the integrity and authenticity of the local community, rooted in tradition, resisting and accommodating a modern world system every more powerful in its force, but paradoxically from the very conditions of globalizing change themselves. To show the entanglement of homogenization and diversity without reliance on the positing of purer cultural states "before the deluge" of an exogenous modernity requires a shift in the conventions for establishing the space-time in which ethnography can be narrated, a fundamental change in the allegory of the pastoral—capturing worlds on the wane, endlessly studying them before their demise—on which most of its framing has depended.

In a recent paper, "Requirements for Ethnographics of Late Twentieth Century Modernity Worldwide" (1991), I attempted to evoke a set of strategies at the level of description that would constitute a modernist response to the homogeneity-diversity problematic that faces contemporary fieldworkers. The idea was to not assume a stance of pronouncing new methodology, but to sketch how older conventions of writing ethnography might be disqualified for the sake of meeting a different and more sophisticated sense of representing the real in the late twentieth century. There is no point here in going over that paper in detail, but I might briefly list and describe the strategems because, for me, they are the reference points for the translation and use of cinematic techniques like montage in experimental writing, to be discussed in the next section.

In that paper, I suggested that a key ethnographic analytic problem and aim was to explain the process of how cultural identity was constituted among peoples (virtually all peoples now) hyperaware of their own history and situation in a world system. Once irony is introduced as a factor in cultural analysis, then the process of identity formation against and in line with homogenizing technologies becomes the focal problem not only for the subjects of ethnography, but for the ethnographer too in producing knowledge of others. The problem of constituting identity thus becomes one for the observer as he or she attempts to account for this very same process among the observed. This is the theoretically important and indispensable aspect of reflexivity in any contemporary modernist ethnography.

I will briefly and schematically lay out a set of requirements for shifting the space-time framework of ethnography toward modernist assumptions about the organization of contemporary social reality. This will involve both changing certain parameters in the way that ethnographic subjects are analytically constructed as subjects as well as altering the nature of the theoretical intervention of the ethnographer in the text he or she creates. This duality of alteration, encompassing both the observer and the observed, is fully consistent with the simultaneous levels on which modernist perspectives work—the writer shares conditions of modernity, and at least some identities, with his or her subjects, and no text can be developed without some registering of this.

Thus, three requirements deal with the construction of the subjects of ethnography through problematizing the construction of the spatial, of the temporal, and of perspective or voice in realist ethnography. And three requirements will concern strategies for establishing the analytic presence of the ethnographer in his or her text: the dialogic appropriation of analytic concepts, bifocality, and the critical juxtaposition of possibilities. These requirements are by no means exhaustive, nor are there necessarily any existing ethnographies that satisfactorily enact any or all of them. I am particularly interested in how a distinctly modernist text is created in each work where it is shown how distinctive identities are created from turbulence, fragments, intercultural reference, and the localized intensification of global possibilities and associations.

I can do no more here than to give a thumbnail characterization of each characteristic:

1. Problematizing the spatial—a break with the trope of settled community in realist ethnography. A recognition of the contemporary deterritorialization of culture: Its production in many different locales at the same time, each of differing character. Thus, the disseminating character of cultural identities, and the need for the effect of simultaneity in ethnographic representation.

2. Problematizing the temporal—a break with the trope of history in realist ethnography. Not a break with historical consciousness or sensitivity in sites of ethnographic probing, but the escape from explanatory attachment to historical meta-narratives that weaken the ability of ethnography to probe the present moving toward the future in particular sites. Against historical narrative, the modernist ethnography is interested in the constitution of collective memory and its expressions, remembering that discourses are critical and responses to emergent, not yet fully articulated conditions in a way that the assimilation of ethnography to historical narrative is not.

3. Problematizing perspective/voice—a break with the trope of structure in realist ethnography. Ethnography has opened to the understanding of perspective as voice or polyphony, just as the distinctly visual, controlling metaphor of structure has come into question. The modernist text is open to the registering of indigenous voices without preemptive assumptions about how they might be located in terms of the conventional correlates by which structure is constituted in realist descriptions, through notions of class, gender, or hierarchy.

4. The dialogic appropriation of concepts and narrative devices—this replaces exegesis as the acknowledgment of the intellectual worth or equivalence of the other in standard ethnography. The realist ethnography has often been built around the intensive exegesis of a key indigenous symbol or concept pulled from its contexts of discourse to be reinserted in them but according to the dictates of the ethnographer's authoritative analytic scheme. In one sense, exegesis at the center of ethnography is a gesture toward recognizing and

privileging indigenous concepts over anthropology's own. Replacing this in the modernist ethnography is the reshaping of the usually authoritative structure of narrative and concepts of the analytic account by the anthropologist's incorporation of the other's discursive framework into his or her own. Short of some idyllic collaboration, this is done through the undeniably colonial discourse character of ethnography whereby the ethnographer uses her power to speak for the other to do so partly in the other's terms by a therapeutic and imaginative appropriation of the other's concepts into one's own framework.

5.   Bifocality—this involves effacing the distance of "otherness" which has been so important in constituting the ethnographic gaze. One assumes and demonstrates an always already connectedness of the observer to the observed, and thus works against exoticism based on us-them distance, on which much ethnography is predicated. The most defensible and necessary justification of a display of reflexivity in the modernist text is provided by this requirement, bifocality demands looking for the kinds of connections that allow one to construct difference in full recognition of the already constituted relationship that exists between observer and observed and that historically or personally precedes the moment of fieldwork and ethnography.

6.   Critical juxtapositions and contemplation of alternative possibilities—the function of modernist ethnography is primarily one of cultural critique, not only of one's disciplinary apparatus through an intellectual alliance with the alternative cosmologies and practices of one's subject, or of one's own society (à la Margaret Mead), but also of conditions within the site of ethnographic focus itself—the local world which it treats. This involves critical thought experiments whereby the ethnographer poses possibilities—the roads not taken, repressed possibilities documentable on the margins of cultures studied—to those that seem to be dominant, and explores their implications in dialogue with one's subjects. Indeed, this kind of critical thought experiment incorporated within ethnography in which juxtaposed actualities and possibilities are put analytically in dialogue with one another might be thought to border on the Utopian or the nostalgic if if were not dependent, first of all, on a documentation that these traces do have a life of their own, so to speak. Such clarification of possibilities, against the objective, defining conditions within the limits of discourse "that matter" in any setting, is the one critical intervention and contribution that the ethnographer can make that is uniquely his or her own.

Now, what I want to argue is that each of the above stratagems are more easily achieved in a cinematic medium than in a written one, and that indeed their realization in written texts involves the quite difficult translation of essentially cinematic narrative techniques—especially montage—into the linearity of the written text. I will only pursue this connection between the modernist and the cinematic in written ethnography in terms of the first of the requirements—the problematization of the spatial and the achievement of an effect of simultaneity. But an interesting exercise would be to think of a montage resolution of each of the modernist requirements that I have discussed, first in writing and then in film. Works such as Michael Taussig's *Colonialism, Shamanism, and the Wild Man* (1987), for example, would serve as an interesting vehicle for such an experiment.

Before treating in the next section the prominence of a cinematic imagination behind the transformation of ethnography, I want to conclude this section by making a point about how the modernist revision of ethnography changes the understanding of the general character of what ethnography is about. In the past, ethnography has been associated with discovery, i.e., describing specific groups of people who had not been treated before. Restudies have been oddities in anthropology, and the full matrix of existing representations (missionaries, travellers, journalists, the people's own, etc.) in which an ethnographer produces his or her own text has always been downplayed. Still holding is "one tribe, one ethnographer" as the persisting romantic ethic and ethics of the way research is organized long after the European age of exploration and discovery has ended. And there is a careful and sensitive etiquette in force about not working on another anthropologist's people, or at least on his or her specific group. In contrast, the kind of ethnography I have outlined above is supremely aware that it operates in a complex matrix of already existing alternative representations, and indeed derives it critical power and insight from this awareness. Of a deconstructive bent, modernist ethnography counts on not being first, on not discovering. It remakes, re-presents other representations. Experimental ethnography thus depends on preexisting, more conventional narrative treatments and is parasitic of them. Such ethnography is a comment, a remaking of a more standard realist account. Therefore, I would suggest the best subjects of modernist ethnography are those which have been heavily represented, narrated, and made mythic by the conventions of previous discourse. Part of the experimentation is in revealing the intertextual nature of any contemporary ethnography—it works through already constituted representations by both the observed and previous observers. So, there is no sense of discovery in the classic sense in modernist ethnography—it forgoes the romantic and nostalgic idea in anthropology that there are literally completely unknown worlds to be discovered. Rather, in full awareness of the historical connections that constitute bifocality it makes historically sensitive revisions of the ethnographic archive with eyes fully open to the present and the emergent in any context of work.

For example, what is innovative in the attempt to achieve the modernist effect of simultaneity in ethnographic description, as I will discuss, is not its discovery of unknown subjects or cultural worlds, but its appropriate complexification of what we understood the dimensions of our already known subjects to be. It creates a new vision and ear against the existing narrative myths in our analytic discourses. In my work with dynastic families (Marcus 1988), for example, I found that to understand these organizations only as families, in the way that family stories are pervasively narrated in our culture, by my dynastic informants as well as by my own family, in the popular media, and by scholars, for that matter, was very inadequate. Such families are produced by many different agencies, differently located in spatial and social categorization. What I needed to see this, and to contemplate the possibility of an alternative representation of these dynastic entities against their domestication in standard stories of family, was a sort of cinematic imagination geared to writing, a discussion of which I now turn to.

The Emblematic Use of Montage to Signal Self-Conscious Breaks with Past Practices in Historic and Ethnographic Narrative

Mundane montage—the technical condition of the juxtaposition of images in the production of film and the associated task of editing—is of course at the heart of the possibility of narrative in film. It is in the complex theorization of the concept of montage by Eisenstein, and others since, that the potential for its development as an aesthetic and critical technique of communication still remains undeveloped. In particular, the notion of an intellectual montage that Eisenstein distinguished from mundane montage and exemplified daringly, but by contemporary standards, crudely in certain sequences of *October* and *Potemkin*, is a possibility that is only now being literally explored in the writing of social scientists and historians responding to the crisis of representation to which I referred, and who frequently refer to their manipulations and ruptures of conventional forms of exposition as montage. Before actually addressing the character of this self-attributed use of montage in contemporary experimental ethnographies of a modernist bent, I want to establish the very important precedent for such a borrowing from film to writing in the history of modernism. Keith Cohen, in the work to which I previously referred, *Film and Fiction*, makes a very sophisticated case for the influence of a cinematic imagination on the work of classic modern novelists in the first quarter of the twentieth century. Cohen is particularly good in his discussion of the technical aspects of the transfer, and it is worth quoting him at length (1979: 208–209):

> For the cinematic experience included, among its most significant effects for the
> novelists, a spatial configuration of the flow of time, an innate relativity and perpetual

shifting of point of view, and a vivid discontinuity of the narrating material by means of montage.

Consequently, the most dynamic aspects of the new novel form were simultaneity, or the depiction of two separate points in space at a single instant of time, multiperspectivism, or the depiction of a single event from radically distinct points of view, and montage, or the discontinuous disposition in the narrative of diverse story elements.

It is important to note that in each case the novelist has been obliged to strain the limits of his art in order to come to grips with the new vision. Simultaneity and multiperspectivism, the temporal and perceptual aspects of roughly the same sort of experimentation, are fundamentally at odds with the consecutiveness and single-effectiveness of language. In both cases, the novelist exploits the inherent sequentiality of the novel but arranges the material in a stop-start, discontinuous manner so as to suggest ubiquity and co-existence. This new disposition, in turn, by gathering together the concurrent fragments, works against the overriding continuity of language and linguistic expression as a whole.

The straining of the limits of literary expression is a sign of the indelible mark left by the cinema's spatial narration. No other art had ever before been capable of narrating so completely through images, and never before had these images corresponded so completely to the mimetic objects they were modeled on. It is this narrative space, intrinsically discontinuous yet externally timed with electric regularity, constantly in development yet essentially no more of a "procession" than a three-ring circus, that determines a pronounced tendency in the early twentieth century toward the image and elicits in the novel a decidedly visual response.

Something very similar to this is now occurring in experiments with modernist ethnography. Indeed, the defining aspects of the classic modernist novel that can be traced to cinematic influence—simultaneity, multiperspectivism, and discontinuous narrative—are precisely the defining moves announced and practiced by experimental ethnography in the name of polyphony, fragmentation, and reflexivity. Of course the attempt to operate with and through intellectual montage has been repeated many times in the history of modernism. One thinks, for example, of between-the-wars modernism and the explicit embracing of montage by Walter Benjamin and Thomas Mann (in his *Story of the Novel*, an account of the construction of *Doctor Faustus*, he announced his method as a montage effect). All of these subsequent ideological and pragmatic uses of montage were attempts to edit written narrative for a critical effect, to make an argument through manipulations of given forms, at a time when theoretical and descriptive conventions were exhausted or called attention to themselves as inadequate. Rupturing linear narrative set in, and disciplined by, genre conventions thus becomes the means to cultural critique.

Usually, a critical intellectual montage becomes, in the contemporary idiom, a deconstruction in action, and its aim is to decompose categories that construct basic ideological concepts of common sense such as the individual, gender, or class. As Teresa de Lauretis has written (1987: 122), "The usual view of the political or aesthetic import of subverting narrative, that is to say, of anti-narrative or abstract film practices, is to decenter the individualist or bourgeois subject, to work against or to destroy the coherence of narrativity which both constructs and confirms the coherence of that subject in its imaginary unity." Interestingly, in the same paper (on strategies of coherence in feminist cinema), de Lauretis questions the value of extreme montage as a critical form, for what it loses in coherence, and thus audience. Feminist cinema, like modernist ethnography, works by retextualizing existing cultural images and narratives, doing so by rupturing the strategies of coherence—usually linearity—by which these analytic or cultural myths have been achieved. But perhaps the sacrifice of coherence in the alternative is too great, especially given her argument for feminist poetics. So the larger problem becomes how to retain the equivalent of a storytelling coherence while retaining the powerful critical advantages of montage.

In work on the cross-cultural, the critical use of montage in ethnography or historical writing is somewhat different from its use in the subversion of ideology realized through conventions of form in its own society. Montage calls attention, I would suggest, to the essentially oral conventions and techniques of other cultures, or to the different ways that literacy has established itself elsewhere, as a protest against what Jack Goody has called the domestication of the savage mind (1976) by the conventions of Western literacy and narrative production. Not to crack, by schematic representation of its structure, another culture's cognitive or symbolic code, but to give voice to the qualities of oral genres of communication in performance through the visual medium of film or writing is perhaps the main purpose of the resort to montage techniques in ethnography that seeks to represent otherness. Perhaps the most explicit example of this in recent ethnography is Michael Taussig's *Colonialism, Shamanism, and the Wild Man* (1978). While he makes no claim to a montage structure to the work itself (although it often does work cinematically) he does claim that the indigenous discourse of shamanism must be understood as montage. He makes quite explicit the connection between montage as the key form of modernist critical discourse in the West and also the form of shamanic discourse (1987: 444–45):

> As a form of epic theater these yage nights succeed not by suffusing the participants in relived fantasies. Instead their effect lies in juxtaposing to a heightened sense of reality, one of fantasy—thereby encouraging among the participants speculation into the whys and wherefores of representation itself. In a similar vein Stanley Mitchell (introduction to *Understanding Brecht*) delineates Benjamin's preoccupation with montage:
> "For fruitful antecedents, he looked back beyond German baroque to those forms of drama where the montage principle first made its appearance. He finds it wherever a critical intelligence intervenes to comment upon the representation. In other words where the representation is never complete in itself, but is openly and continually compared with the life represented, where the actors can at any moment stand outside themselves and show themselves to be actors."
> The technique of criticism and of discovery imputed here is not bound to an image of truth as something deep and general hidden under layers of superficial and perhaps illusory particulars. Rather, what is at work here is an image of truth as experiment, laden with particularity, now in this guise, now in that one, stalking the stage whose shadowy light conjures only to deconjure. It is this image of truth that flickers through the yage nights of which I write . . ."

In his interest to see the critical (against the grain of history) sides of discourses in other cultures that anthropologists have usually probed antiseptically and apolitically through one form or another of structural(ist) analysis, Taussig might be fairly criticized for trying to make modernists out of shamans and peasants. Yet, in the concern not to domesticate the savage mind to our literacy, there is something exciting in introducing the notion of montage as an analytic characterization of voice in non-Western cultural settings. For Taussig, montage is the ultimate reflexive operation that ruptures the narrative of straight, monological storytelling. The operation of reflexivity and disorderly, thus critical, narrative are bound together. Further, the appeal of montage for Taussig is both in its capacity to disrupt the orderly narrative of social science writing and in its critical capacity among his subjects as a performative discourse of healing in response to the history of terror and genocide as the present legacy of a colonial past in Columbia. Montage thus works as counter-discourse on two parallel levels at once, and unites the ethnographer with those he studies. As I noted, this parallelism is one of the key marks of the modernist ethnography.

I would argue that the complexity of an essentially cinematic imagination at work in Taussig's written ethnography—the toying with intellectual montage on dual levels—could have been more economically and clearly achieved in film. In a sense, his book is a scenario for such an experimental film in ethnography. Here I am reminded of Eisenstein's famous characterization of montage as a special form of emotional speech that operates through the imagistic value of words. This well suits both Taussig's own discourse and that of his subjects. The Conradian horror of which he writes and which his contemporary subjects address is not communicable otherwise, except in what would be the parodic form of dispassionate classic ethnographic narrative with which his work is a sharp break.

In the contemporary experimental efforts in ethnographic writing, there are two broad uses of montage. There is the use of montage in the alternative representation of discourse, consciousness, and memory of which Taussig's text is a rich and key exemplar. And there is the use of montage to radically disrupt and reconceive the way social and cultural process as action is represented in ethnography—how milieu, or the space-time framework, is constructed. The kind of experimental thinking about ethnographic form that I personally have been doing focuses on the latter use of montage to revise the representation of process, but ultimately it also becomes concerned with the montage of consciousness. Admittedly, it is this latter kind of montage that has become the hallmark of what experimental ethnography is supposed to be about—reflexivity, intertextuality, and the like—but I would argue that the need to rethink the realist representation of social action—problematizing the spatial in the construction of modernist ethnography, as I discussed—is just as important.

Objectification in ethnographic representation has been effectively critiqued, but the need for setting the scene objectively even in the most radical attempts to use a montage of consciousness requires some revision, but also a preservation, of an objectifying discourse about process and structure. This is what the use of montage technique in the service of representing the simultaneity and spatial dispersion of the contemporary production of cultural identity achieves.

Experiments in the Representation of the Simultaneity of Complexly Connected Knowable Locales

David Lodge's popular and very clever recent academic novel *Small World* (1985) is a good introduction to the problem of simultaneity in the contemporary representation of process within ethnography. It touches on the deterritorialization of culture and the adjustments that ethnographic description must make to it. The world to which the title refers is the peculiarly late twentieth century one in which academic gamesmanship must play out. As Morris Zapp, leading professor of English, and master of the game, describes it (74):

> Information is much more portable in the modern world than it used to be. So are people. Ergo, it's no longer necessary to hoard your information in one building, or keep your top scholars corralled in one campus. There are three things which have revolutionized academic life in the last twenty years, though very few people have woken up to the fact. Jet travel, direct dialling telephones, and the xerox machine (*obviously Lodge was a bit behind the computer revolution when he wrote this*). Scholars don't have to work in the same institution to interact, nowadays. They call each other up, or they meet at international conferences. And they don't have to grub about in library stacks for data: any book or article that sounds interesting they have xeroxed and read it at home. Or on the plane going to the next conference. I work mostly at home or on the planes these days. I seldom go into the university except to teach my course.

Lodge makes brilliant, but straightforward use of montage and cross-cutting to represent this world in the novel's action, focussed on the preparation of academics in several different places around the globe for a conference at which they all come together at the end of the novel. Part II of the novel (83–113) is a tour de force in the creation of the effect of simultaneity. It is anchored to Morris Zapp and his watch and a very limited set of actions as he awakens and prepares to leave for the airport:

At 5 a.m., precisely, Morris Zapp is woken by the bleeping of his digital wristwatch, a sophisticated piece of miniaturized technology which can inform him, at the touch of a button, of the exact time anywhere in the world. In Cooktown, Queensland, Australia, for instance, it is 3 p.m., a fact of no interest to Morris Zapp, as he yawns and gropes for the bedside lamp switch—though as it happens, at this very moment in Cooktown, Queensland, Rodney Wainwright, of the University of North Queensland, is laboring over a paper for Morris Zapp's Jerusalem conference on the Future of Criticism.

The rest of the chapter introduces new characters in simultaneity with Zapp's commonplace temporally compressed movements of awakening and preparing to leave the apartment to catch a plane. We have the global in the very specific and we see their intimate, necessary connection. The chapter ends in a crescendo of montage:

Big Ben strikes one o'clock. Other clocks, in other parts of the world, strike ten, eleven, four, seven, two," *(and then one long paragraph cascading to conclusion)*:
  Morris Zapp belches, Rodney Wainwright sighs, Desiree Zapp snores. Fulvia Morgana yawns . . . Arthur Kingfisher mutters German in his sleep . . . Michel Tardieu sits at his desk and resumes work on a complex equation representing in algebraic terms the plot of *War and Peace* . . . Ronald Frobisher looks up "spare" in the *Oxford English Dictionary* . . . and Joy Simpson, who Philip thinks is dead, but who is alive, somewhere on the spinning globe, stands at an open window, and draws the air deep into her lungs, and shades her eyes against the sun, and smiles.

The historic background for this virtuoso cinematic performance in literature is once again provided by Cohen in his discussion of the cinematic influence on literary modernism. As he says and demonstrates with interesting commentaries on *Ulysses* and *To the Lighthouse* (1979: 1141):

Simultaneity embraces both time and space: temporal coincidence and spatial disjunction. In so doing, it poses many problems at once: the nature of present time in narrative, priority of point of view, and textual decoupage. Cinema presents an image that is plastic, mobile, and perceivable at a glance. Consequently, a single shot can conglomerate two or more separate actions taking place at the same time. This generalized effect of simultaneity may be seen to earmark cinema as an essential precedent to colliding narratives and multiple presentations attempted in the novel, which is strictly speaking, confined to a single focus, a single effect at a time.
  Parallel editing or cross-cutting refers to the juxtaposition of two or more spatially noncontiguous sequences by alternating segments cut from each one. (the most celebrated example of parallel editing is Griffith's *Intolerance* of 1916). Under ordinary circumstances, cinema cannot, any more than literature, present simultaneously two noncontiguous, noncoterminous events. Parallel editing, however, is the technique that most nearly achieves this effect (most dissimilar from literature, where narrativity was for ages considered in mainly linear terms, the cinema seems to have arrived at narrativity through the concept of simultaneity).

It is in realizing such parallel editing so natural to film in the novel of which Lodge's is a model, especially in the passages quoted, that writing can produce cinematic effects. Yet there is an irony that should be well marked for the argument in this paper. *Small World* was made into a Granada Television film, but as the TLS reviewer of it noted (Zachary Leader, March 1988), it failed to capture any of the cinematic qualities of the novel.

The novel employs a variety of cinematic techniques (cross-cutting, montage, the rapid succession of vignette-like scenes) to create an impression of hectic simultaneity. The filmed version is much less inventive, full of plodding and mechanical flashbacks, voice-overs, and dream sequences. What is missing, for all the excellence of individual performance, is precisely that sense of forward movement, of a rush of convergence and interlacings, which is the novel's distinguishing narrative feature.

The film version seems to have substituted apparently more conventional aspects of a montage of consciousness (flashbacks, dream sequences) for a much more cogent montage of action, and lost what I see as the broader import of the novel for ethnographic representations of cultural and social process in the late twentieth century. Tellingly, film in this case has failed to accomplish what the novel has been able to accomplish cinematically, not because it is not able to do so (in fact it probably could have done what the novel did more easily), but because it did not appreciate the central problem of realist representations in late modernity which the novel raises.

Shifting ground a bit, what indeed is this problem of representation in terms of the framework of ethnography, for which experimentation with creating the effect of real time or simultaneity through montage, cross-cutting, and the like, is, if not a solution, as least a response? One might present the argument point by point.

1. Let us begin with the proposition that in the late twentieth century world, cultural events/processes anywhere cannot be comprehended as primarily localized phenomena, or are only superficially so. In the full mapping of a cultural identity, its production, and variant representations, one must come to terms with multiple agencies in varying locales the connections among which are sometimes apparent, sometimes not, and a matter for ethnographic discovery and argument. In short, culture is increasingly deterritorialized, and is the product of parallel diverse and simultaneous worlds operating consciously and blindly with regard to each other. What "relationship" is in this configuration becomes a matter of focal interest for ethnography, which presents itself initially as a problem of form, of representation. The "Small World" of peripatetic academics that Lodge evokes is paradigmatic of one sort of such production of culture, of which there are diverse examples.

A life goes on in place A and place B, for example. In the more difficult case, there is very little contact between the two in everyday life, yet they are intimately or powerfully related to one another in that they have mutual unintended consequences for each other. How does one explore this kind of complex relationship without dramatic resolutions, how to give a cultural account of this structure, how to represent it ethnographically?

2. The ethnographic grasp of many cultural phenomena and processes can no longer be contained by the conventions that fix place as the most distinctive dimension of culture. Merely historicizing local culture—connecting the village community to a particular historical narration—or describing the depth and richness of tradition fails to capture the side of culture that travels, its production in multiple, parallel, and simultaneous worlds of variant connection.

3. This problem of description and theoretical construction is nothing new in anthropology. In the 1960s, anthropologists came to terms with the forms of social/cultural organization of modernity (so called nongroups) through formalist techniques of modeling and the imagery of network and systems analysis from cybernetics. Models of course had their advantages, in dealing abstractly and linearly with relationships, but for the kinds of contemporary questions being asked about distinctly cultural processes within social organizations or as social organizations, they are descriptively impoverished. Models of networks, for example, are linear spatially and temporally: A moves to B, A causes B. There is no sense of the simultaneity of process and action which provides a profoundly different and more ambiguous sort of analytic experience of organization that allows one to understand content as well as form or rather form as content and vice versa.

I see the attempt to achieve the effect of simultaneity as a revision of the spatial-temporal plane on which ethnography has worked. Experiments with it posit three kinds of organizational situations:

a. Simultaneous operations, spatially dispersed within a conventional single institutional frame as a representation of process within it—academic small worlds is an example.

b. The operation of institutionally diverse agencies to constitute an entity and organization which they all fragmentally share—the dynastic family, an object of interest to me, is an example.

c. Independent worlds, operating blindly in relationships of unintended consequences in terms of one another. These are the most exciting, in terms of the discovery of nonobvious relationships, and controversial objects for this kind of experiment in anthropology. The kind of relationships posited in the 1960s project of cultural ecology in anthropology would offer examples. So would the ethnographic study of markets, especially highly speculative commodity markets (see, for example, Stephen Fay's account, 1981, of the attempt of the Hunt brothers to corner the world silver market in *Beyond Greed*).

The capacity, indeed the necessity, to deal ethnographically with the operation of complex systems in a world where cultural process is deterritorialized requires a replacement of the old social structural imageries, through models of network and system, with something equivalent to modernist literary techniques for the representation of simultaneity in social process and action.

4. In my own research projects, I have time and again come upon the multilocale determination of the identity of subjects upon whom I at first focussed as occupying a situated place. This necessitated for me a reconceptualization toward, in each case, a broader and more complex understanding of what the dimensions of the phenomena were that I was addressing. Often this shift has occurred in the middle or at the end of work that had operated through the conventional ways of representing my subjects whose lives seemed to be encompassed in knowable communities (to use Raymond Williams' term for the space-time framework of the pre-industrial revolution English novel). My realization of the partiality of this kind of knowledge stimulated me to look for an ethnography of different horizons.

My original work in the Polynesian Kingdom of Tonga during the 1970s was located in a number of different Tongan villages. This was a time of massive migration internally and overseas. Virtually nothing that happened in a village from kava ceremonies to church collections could be understood only in terms of the life of the village. What was happening in the village was always being experienced vicariously elsewhere—for example, in San Francisco, Sydney, Auckland, Honolulu— and vice versa. I tried to follow and map migration networks as an understanding of this internationalized dimension of Tongan culture, in which the home islands were becoming just one site, among others, in which contemporary Tongan identity was being constructed. From a cultural perspective, network/systems modeling takes one only so far; rather, one needs a sense of parallel existences through juxtapositions of everyday life in different locales. Models, perhaps too literally and linearly, imaging the connecting lines between such locales without fully describing life in the latter. Cultural description demands an account of ongoing, simultaneous activity in locales for which connections are posited (that is, the linkages are secondary to a description of life in the locales linked). This line of thinking in my Tongan work stopped here in the early 1980s without a clear sense at the time that the problem was one of technique of representation rather than being purely theoretical and methodological (now I understand problems of representation as the distinctive medium of theoretical and methodological discourse in contemporary anthropology).

This sense came through to me in the other project with which I was concerned and which I have pursued with more energy, especially as a vehicle for enacting some of the experimental strategies and problems that have derived from the critique of ethnographic conventions of the early to mid 1980s. This is the project on American dynastic families of the late twentieth century—how self-involved individualists sustain themselves as lineages in capitalist society. Eventually, I broke with the family narrative in terms of which accounts of such organizations have been pervasively recounted in Western societies (see Marcus 1988). I found that a particular family was the complex construction of a number of different kinds of agencies—lawyers, bankers, politicians, scholars, servants, workers, journalists, and family members themselves who were only one such agency. I confronted myself with diverse parallel worlds that must be accommodated by my account. Otherwise, my ethnography would just be repeating the mythic narrative of the family in the guise of scholarly production. But I had no model for representing such multiple and diverse representations of a phenomenon that I at first thought commonsensically was quite unified and localized. Also, as regards the current life of the family, in its disseminated representations, I found it difficult to deal linearly or in cause-and-effect terms with the various agencies that create it. I am now working on a completely different framework for describing this organization for which modernist experiments are a source of ideas.

Since I have come to see this configuration in my dynasty project, I have expanded my interests to include various other organizations which link the creation of great wealth and the production of culture together, such as operating foundations, like the J. Paul Getty Trust and its humanities research center where I spent the past year as a visiting scholar. I have also begun to think of my Tongan material again in these terms.

5. In a sense, I have returned to very old issues in anthropology in pursuing this modernist response to the critique of conventional ethnographic rhetoric—those that are at the foundations of the subject such as questions of social structure and organization. Touched by the sensibility and problematics of modernism, they become among the most pressing theoretical topics in contemporary anthropology on which its continuing relevance and vitality depends. The so-called "new" ethnography does not necessarily rely on storytelling, but on constructions that share with narrative similar problems of representation, which in modernism concerned how to bring a different sort of visual sensibility to classic realism. In this, the appearance of film was an important stimulus, as Cohen has demonstrated. I would suggest that it is productive to think of the present juncture or break with the past in ethnography in roughly the same terms. The aims here remain primarily those of analytic reason rather than of narrative, but the kind of theoretical exposition incorporated within the frame of ethnographic conventions cannot remain unchanged now that the problem of representation in ethnography has been effectively articulated. This paper has been an attempt to acknowledge this in seeking pragmatically a fulfillment of the classic aims of ethnography in anthropology. Minimally, a new sense of structure and the nature of relationship itself, on which ethnographic analytic discourse is so dependent, is at stake. Outcomes require more fertile interchanges between film and writing within single projects of research or across them. In other words, an ethnographics is needed, the point on which I want to, and in fact must conclude.

The Possibility of Ethnographics:
A New Relationship Between Anthropological Writing and Film

The argument of this paper is that an ethnographics, involving integrations of visual and written media in common projects, on the initiative of either writers or filmmakers but ideally in close cooperation and exchange, is not just a good idea, but a necessity given the problems of ethnographic text-making shaped by modernist requirements. Film of course has its own special domain of interest different from writing, but what they potentially share are projects that take full responsibility for mimetically confronting difference in a powerfully homogenizing world. Clear visions concerning how such difference emerges are needed more than ever. The route to these is through the complex problems of representing the real that modernism has developed for us, and through a response to these which lies in the hand extended by the cinematically sensitive ethnographic writer to the one that controls the camera. Textmaking in the face of the complex realities of late modernity and modernism is what the ethnographic writer and filmmaker share in common—a recognition on which they might base a collaboration that would have regard for past genre boundaries as starting points for conversation, but would not submit to their policings.

References

Berman, Marshall. 1982. *All That is Solid Melts Into Air: The Experience of Modernity*. New York: Simon and Schuster.

Clifford, James and George Marcus, eds. 1986. *Writing Culture: The Poetics and Politics of Ethnography*. Berkeley: University of California Press.

Cohen, Keith. 1979. *Film and Fiction: The Dynamics of Exchange*. New Haven: Yale University Press.

De Lauretis, Teresa. 1987. "Strategies of Coherence: Narrative Cinema, Feminist, Poetics, and Yvonne Rainer." In *Technologies of Gender: Essays on Theory, Film and Fiction*. Bloomington: Indiana University Press.

Fay, Stephen. 1981. *Beyond Greed*. New York: Random House.

Goody, Jack. 1977. *The Domestication of the Savage Mind*. Cambridge: Cambridge University Press.

Leader, Zachary. 1988. Review of the Granada TV production of *Small World*. *Times Literary Supplement*, March.

Lodge, David. 1985. *Small World*. New York: Random House.

Marcus, George E. and Michael Fischer. 1986. *Anthropology As Cultural Critique: An Experimental Moment In the Human Sciences*. Chicago: University of Chicago Press.

Marcus, George E. 1991. "Requirements for Ethnographies of Late Twentieth Century Modernity Worldwide." In *Modernity and Identity*, ed. Jonathan Friedman and Scott Lash. London: Blackwell.

————. 1988. "The Constructive Uses of Deconstruction in the Ethnographic Study of Notable American Families." *Anthropological Quarterly* 68: 3–16.

Taussig, Michael. 1987. *Colonialism, Shamanism and the Wild Man: A Study in Terror and Healing*. Chicago: University of Chicago Press.

Thornton, Robert. 1988. "The Rhetoric of Ethnographic Holism." *Cultural Anthropology* 3: 285–303.

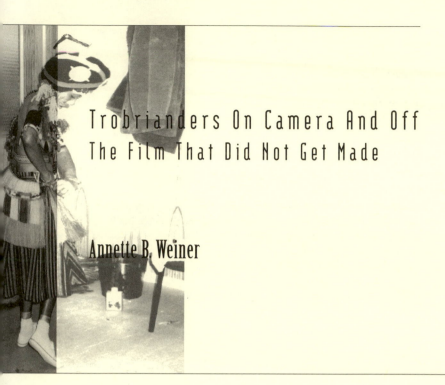

Trobrianders On Camera And Off
The Film That Did Not Get Made

Annette B. Weiner

David MacDougall RECENTLY REMARKED THAT FOR A FILM TO GENERATE MORE COMPLEX statements depends upon "the filmmaker's ability to make the film more than merely a report on a cultural encounter and, instead, embody it" (1991). In this essay, I want to raise this complex issue of how to prevent an audience from seeing a film merely as a window on an ethnographic world, especially when that audience is television's "prime time" public. In general, television's power lies in its ability to ground its discourse in "'the real'—in the evidence of one's eyes" while as Stuart Hall (1982: 75) points out, television dramatically limits our gaze, even when we view our own society's actions and events on "prime time." For anthropologists and ethnographic filmmakers the problem intensifies because often, in explaining cultural differences, the effects of these representations make the encounter appear unidirectional.

The challenge is how to represent images that convey multiple ways of seeing, making it difficult to perceive an encounter as merely an opposition between "us" and "them." Until the interactions between audience and film texts are taken seriously, television films will continue to reproduce a dominant ideology that has a long tradition in the public's response to representations of "exotic" peoples. When sixteenth and seventeenth century exhibitions of "primitive" peoples and their possessions filled the streets and fairs of European cities, Enlightenment thinkers, calling these events "rational amusement" (Altick 1978: 4), saw their value in providing an alternative media to print. Even with the advent of printing presses, Bacon's advocacy of the primacy of things over words as the most important instruments of knowledge only enhanced these exhibitions as "surrogates for books" (Altick 1978: 1). Just as the symbolism of the Medieval power of the Catholic Church was conveyed to the masses through icons and paintings covering cathedral ceilings and walls, the masses were educated about other cultures in frames that recreated "primitive" life before their eyes, yet firmly differentiated them from it.

Unthought of in these encounters were processes that would enable the discovery of the self in the Other and the Other in the self, a theme that pervades the historian Stephen Greenblatt's new book, *Marvelous Possessions: The Wonder of the New World* (1991). In an early part of the Introduction not focused on Columbus's colonial appropriation, Greenblatt recounts his own experience when he explored a tiny Balinese village. Entering along the village path, Greenblatt followed the source of a bright light coming from the pavilion where Balinese traditionally gather. There he found villagers huddled around a television set, excitedly watching a video of their own elaborate temple ceremony (1991: 4). For Greenblatt, this brief encounter revealed the multiple, interconnected sites of representation, "the mobility of spectacle and spectator alike . . . [the complexity] of images paradoxically linked to the dazzling power of display" (1991: 6–7). As Greenblatt points out, the issue is not simply the assimilation of the Other but rather who is assimilating whom.

Greenblatt's Balinese example shows how indigenous media brilliantly collapses traditional oppositions of spectator and spectacle, of Western and "primitive" ideologies and possessions, thereby accentuating the cultural complexities and political relevance of who is assimilating whom. Faye Ginsburg's (1990) recent essay on indigenous media importantly emphasizes how these modes of self-representation have theoretical and practical significance for all ethnographic film projects. For indigenous media can reveal the multiple directions and fragilities of assimilation, creating a new kind of educational process that alters the traditional relationship between the viewer and the film. By acknowledging the way representations circulate, the way they are exchanged, recombined

"Buying film before the next cricket performance."

"Time out at a cricket performance at Gateshead."

and reinvented, we see that individuals and cultures have powerful assimilative talents that they use, not only to participate in, but to radically alter Western ideologies and technologies. The question I pose is whether these multiple facets of representation and meaning so vitally exposed in indigenous media can be used in equally powerful ways in broadcast media to make audiences learn about an Other by seeing their own representations framed within an Other culture.

Having recently had the experience of collaborating (as anthropologist) with David Wason (producer and director) to make *The Trobriand Islanders of Papua New Guinea*, for Granada's *Disappearing World* Series, I want to examine these issues in light of Trobrianders' responses to the making of the film. As an ethnographer, I still feel great satisfaction with the Trobriand film for it conveys my ethnographic interpretations of Trobriand society (e.g., Weiner 1976, 1988) that I have explored and studied over many years. Further, its focus on women as well as the incorporation of reflexive elements set new standards for films in this Series. I also want to emphasize that from its beginning in the early 1970s, the *Disappearing World* Series promoted the important and highly original idea in which anthropologists and filmmakers collaborated to bring ethnography to British television's prime-time general viewers. Yet as we face the next century, I believe it is important to rethink the Series format in light of the vast interconnections between local cultures and global events that demand the representation of multiple perspectives. Therefore, my comments are not an elaborate critique of the Trobriand film but are presented as a challenge to shift directions in the format of these broadcast films so that the complex politics of assimilation are encompassed.

In the Granada case, authorship is the long-term relationship between the ethnographer and those who are being filmed. But still some would question, whose voice speaks for whom? As Ginsburg notes, "much of current postmodern theory, while raising important points about the politics of representation, is so critical of all 'gazes' at the so-called 'other' that to follow the program set forth by some, we would all be paralyzed into an alienated universe with no engagement across the boundaries of difference that for better or worse exist"(1990; 103). These multiple representations through which local and global ideologies and metaphors are recombined enable an audience to recognize how much they themselves are party to the lives of others.

For example, in the Trobriand film the visit by a chief in his Toyota pick-up truck to a higher ranking but clearly less powerful chief was as emblematic of Trobrianders' resiliency to capitalist markets and western representations as Greenblatt's Balinese example. Given my long experience in the Trobriands, I could easily situate this event in a history of tangled political power plays that reached from the Trobriands to the national capital of Papua New Guinea. Instead the delayed arrival of the Toyota truck, with the chief's nephew as chauffeur, and the chief stepping out of the vehicle and looking through his sunglasses jauntily at the camera, was compressed into an amusing moment for a television audience. There was no way to show the ease with which the chief and his relatives not only appropriated the filmmakers' presence but how they long had adapted capitalist ideologies and technologies to their own advantages. With all these circulating representations exposed, whose cultural possessions are disclosed?

My style of interviewing raised similar issues. The questions I asked my Trobriand colleagues on camera were pointedly simplistic as I wanted to elicit their views about information I thought we should have in the film. Many Trobrianders recognized this simplicity, even commenting on it in the interviews by saying to me, "you already know this." But what amazed me in these interviews was how quickly villagers assimilated the presence of the camera into their own thoughtful answers. As the interviews progressed they spoke to larger audiences than the members of the film crew as their words captured and exposed their own moving dilemmas. When Bunimega, a village leader I had known for twenty years, commented that

"Leaving Gateshead fairgrounds for their hotel after a long day of cricket playing and dancing."

he was politically "weak," I was amazed—not because I did not know that his father had been a chief and, because of matrilineal descent he could never become one, but because in the twenty years that I have known Bunimega, his actions were always centered on showing his strength to me and other villagers. The admission that he was "weak" was powerful, something he and I knew but something he would only say to an audience far beyond the Trobriand Islands.

Yet in the film there is no way to capture how novel and unexpected these and other similar moments were, no way to reveal how the presence of the camera recording a long conversation between the two of us suddenly elicits new experiences and comprehensions. Twenty minutes of an interview are compressed into two minutes of film, leaving little space to underscore the significance of what was truly happening in front of the camera as, for example, Bunimega altered this contact into something new for himself, for me and for the film. Whereas self-exposure dramatically occurs, the ethnographic surprise of new knowledge (what many of Jean Rouch's films portray) is lost to the audience.

A year after we filmed in the Trobriands, 27 Trobrianders along with a group of Sepik and Melpa peoples, arrived at Heathrow Airport. They were chosen to participate in a tour organized by a cultural exchange group based in London. Trobrianders were to dance and play cricket; the others would dance and apply face make-up for crowds gathered at Oxford, London, and Gateshead in England and for spectators in Amsterdam and Paris. Although admittedly there was not much advance notice of this trip, I searched in vain for a British television crew that would film these events. This film—not made—could have broken that traditional format of other worlds seemingly remote and "exotic." For this film would have had to cope with the multiple linkages and recombinations that question again and again whose possessions are assimilating whom. Picture, for example, the arrival in London of the Sepik group who brought few personal possessions but shipped huge wooden crates filled with their carvings. While the tourists came to watch them perform, like talented entrepreneurs, they capitalized on the audience by, in turn, selling them the carvings. At other times, Trobrianders dressed in their pandanus penis coverings were busy photographing the audience assembled to watch them

"Dressing for a dance performance, Flora Gardette fastens her Trobriand skirt before removing her Western skirt."

play cricket. Imagine this scene at Gateshead or Oxford cut to the representation in the film *Trobriand Cricket* (Leach and Kildea 1974) of a villager dressed as a European, mimicking a tourist filming Trobrianders playing cricket. What we see in *Trobriand Cricket* and in the film not made are Trobrianders making fun of us, assimilating us to them and them to us as evidence of that encounter. Such a film would take us far from those early exhibitions of "rational amusement" and far from the traditional ways of reducing cultural experience to a conservative representation. Thinking about this film not made enables us to grapple with the myriad ways in which the representations of our own cultural identities are deeply intertwined with those of "others" because the historical experiences of encounters have multiple points of authorship, exchange and control.

As we look to the 21st Century and to the emergence of a new world order, it is imperative that audiences continue to be educated about the kinds of global connections and assimilations they know little about. But the didactics of such instruction must shift from that of "rational amusement"—with assumptions that television audiences are incapable of learning—to more complex films. Such films must encompass the filmmaker and audience within the same processes of discovering not new or disappearing worlds but the powerful ways that global agencies are an intimate part of local encounters.

Acknowledgements

I thank Faye Ginsburg for her efforts as co-organizer with me of the session at the American Anthropological Association Annual Meetings, Chicago, 1991, where this paper was first presented. I also am grateful to Faye for her encouragement and helpful critiques of earlier drafts. Above all, I am indebted to David Wason and the other members of the film crew, to Modiyala Elliot, Chief Puliyasi and the many other Trobrianders who made the Granada film possible.

References

Altick, Richard D. 1978. *Shows of London*. Cambridge, Mass.: Belknap Press.

Ginsburg, Faye. 1990. "Indigenous Media: Faustian Contract or Global Village?" In *Cultural Anthropology*, 93–112.

Greenblatt, Stephen. 1991. *Marvelous Possessions: The Wonder of the New World*. Chicago: University of Chicago Press.

Hall, Stuart. 1982. "The Rediscovery of 'Ideology': Return of the Repressed in Media Studies." In *Culture, Society and the Media*, 56–90.

MacDougall, David. 1991. "Whose Story Is It?" In *Visual Anthropology Review* 7 (2).

Weiner, Annette B. 1976. *Women of Value, Men of Renown: New Perspectives in Trobriand Exchange*. Austin: University of Texas Press.

———. 1988. *The Trobianders of Papua New Guinea*. New York: Holt, Rinehart and Winston, Inc.

Filmography

Leach, Jerry W. & Kildea, Gary. 1974. *Trobriand Cricket: An Ingenious Response to Colonialism*. Distributed by University of California Extension Media Center, Berkeley, CA.

Wason, David (Director and Producer) with Weiner, Annette B. (Anthropologist). 1990. *The Trobriand Islanders of Papua, New Guinea*. Manchester: Granada Television, Inc. Distributed by Films Incorporated Video, Chicago, IL.

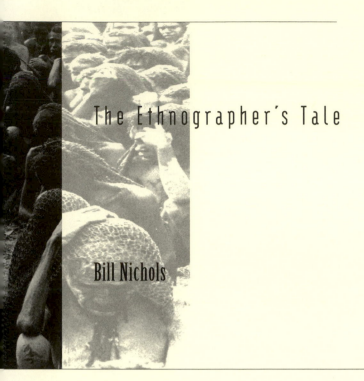

The Ethnographer's Tale

Bill Nichols

Preamble

Ethnographic film is in trouble. Not entirely due to what ethnographic filmmakers have done, or failed to do, but also because of the nature of the institutional discourse that continues to surround this mode of documentary representation. And not entirely due to either of these factors, but also because of the ground-breaking, convention-altering forms of self-representation by those who have traditionally been objects (and blindspots) of anthropological study: women/natives/others. For over ten years a significant body of work has been accumulating that comes from elsewhere, telling stories and representing experiences in different voices and different styles.

Ethnographic film has represented a concerted and valuable effort by those concerned with the principles and objectives of anthropology to represent other cultures to members of our own. Ten years or more ago, to explore other cultures on film meant exploring the fictional works of celebrated filmmakers like Satyajit Ray, Yasujiro Ozu or Glauber Rocha; openly political documentaries of national liberation struggles (*79 Springtimes* [Alvarez 1969], *Last Grave at Dimbaza* [Mahamos 1975]) or ethnographic films (*Kenya Boran* [MacDougall and Blue 1974], *Dead Birds* [Gardner 1963], *Jaguar* [Rouch 1967], and so on). Each of these three choices had value. Each expanded our horizons and our collective sense of the possible. As we move toward the present, however, the choices are far less clear cut. (This "we" is not universal; ten years ago or more the collectivity it referred to was predominantly white, male, and strongly university-based with minimal inclusion of those who now represent themselves. Given the contestation over and erosion of this traditional "we," though hardly its supplantation, I have used quotations marks around this particular "we" to indicate its lack of normative authority.)

Ethnographic film no longer occupies a singular niche. Other voices call to us in forms and modes that blur the boundaries and genres that represent distinctions between fiction and documentary, politics and culture, here and there. For those situated in the larger, non-specialist audience outside of anthropology per se, these other voices often seem more incisive, informative and engaging. The opportunity exists to learn from and engage with the ways in which others choose to represent themselves in "auto-ethnographies" from *Speak Body* (Armatage 1979) and *Unfinished Diary* (Mallet 1983) to *Handsworth Songs* (Akomfrah 1986), *Who Killed Vincent Chin?* (Choy and Tajima 1988), and *I'm British But* (Chadha 1989), and from *Surname Viet Given Name Nam* (Trinh 1989) to *Films Are Dreams* (Sensiper 1989). The voice of the traditional ethnographic filmmaker has become one voice among many. Dialogue, debate and a fundamental reconceptualization of visual anthropology in light of these transformations is, quite simply, essential.

All the better to vex you with, my dear

Clifford Geertz has described as well as anyone the finely honed interpretive skills required of the anthropologist, or ethnographer (1973). His account of the subtleties, and subtle misunderstandings, arising from the conflicting worldviews of a Berber tribe, a Jewish trader and a French colonial officer in the Morocco of 1912 captures well the "thickness" to which description might aspire—though it may be "thick" in an unintended sense as well. Following Geertz, "anthropology" becomes an institutional discourse which has assigned itself the challenge of representing others. Like the truth of "indefinite approximation" championed by Sartre (1965: 19), Geertz prefers refinement to perfection: "What gets better is the precision with which we vex each other" (29).

Both anthropology and documentary have caused themselves considerable vexation debating the issue of representation as a process of rendering likenesses effectively, according to criteria of realism, objectivity, accuracy or ethnographicness. Neither discipline has vexed itself quite as much with the realization that Geertz's model creates, but does not acknowledge, representation as trouble for the Other. Who has the responsibility and legitimacy (or power and authority) to represent, not only in the sense of rendering likenesses but also in the sense of "stand for" and "prepare an argument about," others? Evaluating the degree of difficulty attempted and level of sophistication attained is how "we" (objective, professional, "disciplined") vex each other more precisely at the expense of others. The unasked question is, In what way does this representation matter to those it represents?

Anthropology: Behind the Scenes

If only he (the anthropologist) could provide us with correct, consistent accounts of himself, his gossiping organization, and the specific instances of discourse that constitute his very accounts, then there would be no need for us to carry out an ongoing critique of ethnographic ideology and its claims to represent other cultures. (Trinh, 1989: 74)

Anthropological representation addresses the problems of being "on the scene" and of getting "behind the scenes" of other cultures. It has proven less adept at looking behind its own scenes, at the staging of its own representations and in debating what this activity represents as a symptom of our own cultural situation (the mythologies of travel, the valorization of experimental knowledge over experiential or tacit knowledge, and the prevalence of scientism: the regulation of institutionally legitimized discourse and authority).

From this perspective, the location of anthropology's Other may reside less in another culture than in the anthropological unconscious, as it were. Among other things, this anthropological unconscious might contain: whiteness and maleness, and, consequently, the body of the observer; the experiential; the narrative conventions and forms of other cultures; the canonical conventions of western narrative; the full indexical particularity of the image and its emotional impact; the erotics of the gaze; textual theory and interpretation; the actual workings of the institutional procedures that determine what counts as anthropological knowledge, and the viewer or audience for ethnographic film (a group that has been largely unseen, unknown and unexamined).

Looking at others in order to represent them may not be so easily rationalized by strictly scientific motives as some anthropologists believe. Long takes and minimal editing do not eliminate, though they may disguise, the psychodynamics that Malinowski reserved for his diary. Many different ways of seeing surround the use of a camera. As long as human agency comes into play it will do so in relation to desire and the unconscious as well as reason and science. In film study, a considerable body of work has argued that the ways and means of cinematic representation often gain motivation from narcissistic, voyeuristic, sadistic and fetishistic mechanisms.[1] Power, knowledge, hierarchy and scopophilic pleasure entail one another in ways that cannot be easily avoided. As Laura Mulvey argues, scopophilic identification and desire are "formative structures, mechanisms not meaning. In themselves they have no signification, they have to be attached to an idealisation [like the cinema's ability to re-present reality]. Both pursue aims in indifference to perceptual reality, creating the imagised, eroticised concept of the world that forms the perception of the subject and makes a mockery of empirical objectivity" (1985: 308). I wish to look behind the scenes of anthropology's representational mechanisms to examine its unconscious assumptions, or habits, and their implications. The purpose of this examination is to see in greater detail how the ethnographic film stages its representations, whether these representations can withstand the fundamental rebuke of usefulness to Others, and of then looking beyond as well as behind ethnography to other scenes of increasing interest.

The Ethnographer's Tale: Making Representations

I have felt that my own projects vis-à-vis the Other, as representations of my own processes of self-discovery, carry with them, as the other is there as an actual person, actual other place, the questions of potential dangers that arise from the inability to do anything but misrepresent that other person. (Feingold 1988: 21)

As used here, ethnographic film will refer to films that are extra-institutional, that address an audience larger than anthropologists per se, that may be made by individuals more trained in filmmaking than in anthropology, and that accept as a primary task the representation, or self-representation, of one culture for another. What characterizes ethnographic film as we have known it from *Nanook of the North* (Flaherty 1922) to *First Contact* (Connelly and Anderson 1984), from *Bitter Melons* (Marshall 1971) to *Forest of Bliss* (Gardner 1985), and from *Moi, un noir* (Rouch 1957) to *I'm British But?*.

Dead Birds, Robert Gardner.

Binarqism: If veni, vidi, can vici be far behind?

The separation of Us from Them is inscribed into the very institution of anthropology and into the structure of most ethnographic film. They occupy a time and space which We must recreate, stage or represent. Once upon a time, it was easy to say, "There is no one else to do it." Under the aegis of scientific responsibility (and power), this is a sober enterprise. Ethnographic film, in fact, belongs squarely among what I have called in my study of documentary generally the discourses of sobriety (Nichols 1991). As systems of discourse, science, economics, politics, foreign policy, education, religion, and welfare exercise instrumental power. They operate on the assumption that they can and should alter the world itself or our place within it, that they can effect action and entail consequences. Their discourse has the air of sobriety since it is seldom receptive to "make-believe" characters, events or worlds (unless these serve as pragmatically useful simulations of the "real" one).

Discourses of sobriety treat their relation to the real as non-problematic. Like Plato's Guardians their speakers return to the cave with a knowing sigh of disinterest in the shadow-play and story-telling distractions they now understand entirely and can explain to others. Through the discourses of sobriety knowledge/power exerts itself. Through them, things are made to happen. These are vehicles of domination and conscience, power and knowledge, pleasure and reason, desire and will (although the aura of science and sobriety—acute in U.S. anthropology—pushes the psychodynamics of domination, power, pleasure and desire squarely into the anthropological unconscious).

Between the "here" of anthropology and the "there" of another culture stands the border checkpoint where the passage of our bodies there and representations of them here is governed by the standards and principles of field work, and location filming. The separation of "here" and "there" is thus sharply demarcated. The predilection for "non-Western societies, particularly exotic cultures" (Balikci 1988: 33) heightens the sense of separation, of a passage to and fro, in which visible differences attest to both spatial and temporal separation. The act of travel and, consequently, arrival scenes play a central role here (Pratt 1986). In film such scenes may have a literal representation, as in *The Ax Fight* (Chagnon and Asch 1971) and *Before We Knew Nothing* (Kitchen 1988), or they may be diffused throughout the film in the observational stance that puts distance between another culture and the person behind the camera lens.

Also central to the impression of being there, while remaining separate from the reality that is represented are the indexical film image and synchronous location sound. These qualities of the realist image certify the authenticity of what is seen and heard as life-like even though they may represent lives conducted quite differently from our own. Voice-over commentary is another familiar form of binary support: fabricated here, it provides an applique for the sights and sounds from there, embellishing them. Sometimes a voice-over from there bumps against one from here, deferentially, as in *N!ai: Story of a !Kung Woman* (Marshall 1980). N!ai's voice-over, spoken by Letta Mbulu, is a vehicle for nostalgic reminiscence: "When [my father would] get up to go hunting . . . we'd be eating meat just like that." It is left to the anonymous male voice of anthropological authority, from here, to remind us of what Marshall's *The Hunters* (1956) chronicled and N!ai forgets: "It took four men five days to track the wounded giraffe."

Travel also underwrites the authority of ethnographic film with the powerful guarantee, "What you see is what there was. (I know; I was there.)" It may also guarantee that "What you see is what there would have been if I had not been there to film it. (I know; I was there and can attest to the representativeness of what you see.)" Being "on the scene" also allows anthropologists to identify the distorted representations of others, particularly when it is a case of footage they have shot being transformed into the dross of television documentary: "What you see is what there was, but it did not occur in this sequence, have this musical accompaniment, or bear these meanings. (I know, I was there and can identify the distortions.)"

Travel thereby underwrites authority by means of bodily presence although the body of the anthropologist/filmmaker usually disappears behind the optical vantage point where camera and filmmaker preside—a behind-the-scenes perspectival equivalent of the film frame's vanishing point. This disappearance, once valorized as part and parcel of observational respect for one's subjects but subsequently criticized as a masquerade of self-effacement that also effaces the limitations of one's own physicality in favor of omniscience and omnipotence (MacDougall 1981: 278), transforms first-hand, personal experience into third-person, disembodied knowledge.

As accounts of the personal, physical dimension of travel recede, invocations of the transpersonal, mythical dimension, distinctive to western culture, take on added prominence. Travel conjures associations with spiritual quests, voyages of self-discovery and tests of prowess, with the pilgrimage and the odyssey, as well as with the expansionist dreams of empire, discovery and conquest.[2] Movement and travel participate in the construction of an imaginary geography that maps the world required to support the sense of self for whom this world is staged (Biddock 1991; Bishop 1989; Said 1978). Travel, which began as something spiritual or economic, takes on the aura of something scientific and representational (Mukerjii 1983). An expanded moral framework, the discovery of cultural relativity, the heroics of salvage anthropology, the ritual of self-improvement, training in the civic responsibilities of neo-colonial power—travel supports them all.

Going there to get the story is one important part of the overall process; returning here is equally important. The act of representation always requires distance between the staging of a representation and its maker or *metteur en scène*, as well as between the world represented and its viewer. Questions of authority and authenticity arise from the effect of distance. This effect can be contested, subverted or displaced, as Brecht's theory of distanciation proposed. When left uncontested, this sense of distance—registered in the space between camera and event, in the observational stance from which it originates, in voice-over commentary, in the certifiable "ethnographicness" of sound and image (Heider, 1976), and in the construction of a factual story in accord with the canonic narrative form familiar in the west assures the viewer of the traveller's desire for a welcome return to the fold.

B.
Nichols

Talking Heads or Travel from the Waist Up

Our primary goal is the production of knowledge . . . (Ruby 1990: 16)

Only anthropology provides the cross-cultural framework that is sophisticated enough to deal with the range of variation that exists among human cultural systems. (Rollwagen 1988: 294)

The more crucial science and writing loom for anthropology, the more suspect ethnographic film becomes, especially when produced by "amateurs" (Ruby 1990: 15). Science is the institutional discourse of sobriety par excellence. Ethnographic films, like studies based on fieldwork, attempt to resolve an acute contradiction between impersonal, scientific knowledge and the personal experience on which it is based: "States of serious confusion, violent feelings or acts, censorships, important failures, changes of course, and excessive pleasures are excluded from the published account" (Clifford 1986: 13). Scientific knowledge travels from one mind to another, transported by bodies as cargo is by ships. Hence the disembodied quality of the voice of authority operating behind most ethnographic film. (The female voice-over commentary spoken by Mbulu in *N!ai* is clearly assigned to the physical person of N!ai as her restricted perception and opinion; the unidentified male voice-over that speaks on behalf of unrestricted ethnographic knowledge has no body; it projects itself from here to there as the voice of reason, personified only by the "grain" of the individual voice used to represent it.)

Disembodied knowledge causes problems of its own. It contrasts sharply with the storytelling traditions of other cultures where experiential, embodied knowledge is more highly prized. As Trinh puts it, "The words passed down from mouth to ear (one sexual part to another sexual part), womb to womb, body to body are the remembered ones. S/He whose belly cannot contain (also read 'retain') words, says a Malinke song, will succeed at nothing. The further they move away from the belly, the more liable they are to be corrupted. (Words that come from the MIND and are passed on directly 'from mind to mind' are, consequently, highly suspect . . .)" (1989: 136). The knowledge Trinh describes requires different stagings, different forms and styles of representation from those that have characterized ethnographic film.

The ethnographic message can serve as ethnographic mask, shrouding the body, and body knowledge (discussed below) from view. The mask of the depersonalized, disembodied investigator or filmmaker also allows the race and gender of the body to be relegated to the anthropological unconscious. Like a default value in cybernetics, reference to *the* body and *the* experience of the ethnographic fieldworker/filmmaker may mask the white male bodies of most anthropologists along with their distinctive ways of seeing and knowing. (Are the etic systems applied by the ethnographer as tools of the trade color and gender blind? If so, what consequences follow from such blindness?)

Feminism: The Body That Is Not One

> In my research I propose that ethnographic film and photographic images are a reflection of the gender stereotypes found in the filmmaker's (photographer's) dominant group, and thus reproduce the ethnographer's ideas and ideals about gender onto the visual representation of the cultural group being studied. (Kuehnast 1990: 24)

Feminism, as the articulation of issues that are inseparably linked to the physical body and its representation, to the personal and its political ramifications, has had noticeable trouble with ethnographic practice. Clifford laments the lack of a feminist contingent in the ranks of those who applied aspects of "textual theory" to ethnographic writing (1986: 20), without wondering if this "lack" might itself carry an implicit critique, and George Marcus identifies feminism (along with poststructuralism) as one of the major forces that has prompted a reevaluation of the nineteenth century realism supporting most ethnography only to drop it from the rest of his discussion of ethnographic writing and cinematic montage (Marcus 1990: 4).

Deborah Gordon specifies the dilemma posed by such gestures: "[Feminism] presents a face of similarity outward toward men who are its 'other.' Unlike experimental ethnography where the point is to establish a mutuality between self and other, feminism's relationship to its other is antagonistic" (1988: 17). On the other hand, films such as *Small Happiness: Women in a Chinese Village* (Hinton 1984), *The Women's Olamal* (Llewelyn-Davies 1985), *India Cabaret* (Nair 1986), and *Before We Knew Nothing* demonstrate that the apparently subordinate position occupied by women in a culture (something perhaps more "apparent" to men than women) need not be matched by a parallel subordination in representations of that culture. The possibility of a feminist ethnographic film aesthetic, however, has received no debate at all, to my knowledge.

Feminists recognize an acute predicament of either speaking "mind to mind," even in the dialogic play of modernist distanciation, or of speaking words from the belly that are meant to be of use-value to both those who utter them and those who hear them. Feminists may therefore have trouble with both realist and modernist camps, and with "textual theory" as a politically efficacious, rather than formally sophisticated, move. They may also make trouble for all these camps by posing the simple, yet "unscientific" question of what place does realism, modernism or textual theory lead one to occupy among the permeable, shifting, diverse subjectivities and ideological affinities operating at a specific historical moment?

The Master('s) Narrative

> We spent a hectic first day in Mina shooting as much footage of the Charriada as we could. (Olson 1988: 260)

> Actions filmed were, for the most part, spontaneous, candid, and one-time phenomena and not the result of any deliberately planned "staging." (Klima 1988: 228)

These epigraphs from *Anthropological Filmmaking: Anthropological Perspectives on the Production of Film and Video for General Public Audiences* (Rollwagon 1988) convey one of the central themes of the book: the disavowal of aesthetic intent. If aesthetic considerations should happen to slip in, despite the rough and tumble effort to catch-as-catch-can, safeguards must be taken. Participation in television productions based on anthropological footage generates tension largely because the anthropologist confronts a well-formulated television documentary aesthetic with only inchoate and semi-conscious aesthetic alternatives. Precepts based on content no longer carry their full weight. Precepts based on form circle back to a (discounted) content; they seldom address issues of audience and effect in any detail.

What is somewhat remarkable in this context is how often ethnographic films repeat similar cinematic qualities and narrative structures, without, apparently, knowing or acknowledging it. The canonic story form of an introduction to characters and setting, presentation of a disturbance or puzzle, a goal-oriented line of causally linked situations and events, followed by a resolution to the disturbance or solution to the puzzle that leaves the mind at rest recurs regularly in ethnography as well as fiction. Boiled down to a schematic template by Bordwell, this story format amounts to "setting plus characters—goal—attempts—outcome—resolution" (1985: 35). It has informed films from *Nanook of the North* to *The Hunters* and from *Tourou et Bitti* (Rouch 1971) to *Tong Tana* (Roed, et. al. 1990). The pervasiveness of this format in classic ethnography suggests it is not considered aesthetic at all but "natural," despite evidence to the contrary.[3]

Inherent in this preference for canonic story form is the idea of a "virtual performance," a performance, which, like a staged one, serves to represent significant themes but which is unscripted and unrehearsed. It is, instead, the performance of a lifetime: the condensation of a lifetime into representative moments. Filmmakers seek out those who "naturally" reveal or expose themselves, allowing their performance to engage a viewer's curiosity and empathy (while masking the filmmaker's own fascination or attraction—including the erotics of the gaze—behind the naturalness of discovering familiar (western, dramaturgical) codes of human expressivity among others. (MacDougall discusses this tendency in relation to his work among African pastoralists and Australian Aboriginals in "Complicities of Style," [1990].) Cinematic conventions of the close up and the long take, of the scene and the event, of continuity editing and synchronous sound reinforce virtual performances that fit the mold of what Brecht labelled "dramatic theater" (1964) in ethnographies from *Nanook* to *The Women's Olamal*.

What is most convenient about these conventions is that they not only serve to support the canonic form of narrative structure in western society, they also literally constitute an "imaginary geography." Like the imaginary geography constituted by the traveller, explorer and field worker, this map to an imaginary world reciprocally and recursively constitutes the self that produces it. This reassuring coherence may be one of the reasons why ethnographic film has not more readily adopted the conventions of modernism and cinematic montage championed by Marcus (1990). Modernist conventions upset the clean separation of here and there and the coherence afforded to the traveller who negotiates such spatial discontinuities by projecting onto other people and places systems of realist representation.

When rendered subservient to scientific knowledge, to the sobriety of discourses that distinguish themselves from fiction or "just stories," these realist conventions and narrative structures rupture the phenomenal, experiential bond of passing stories from one mouth to another, of a knowledge that is fully embodied (Ong 1982; Alter 1981; Trinh 1989). Trinh describes well the feminist and political dimension of what is at stake when stories become an explanatory template rather than an inseparable part of a life:

> Not only has the "civilized" mind classified many of the realities it *does not understand* in the categories of the untrue and the superstitious, it has also turned the story—as total event of a community, a people—into a *fatherly* lesson for children of a certain age. (1989: 124, italics hers)

> This is why we keep on doing violence to words: to tame and cook the wild-raw, to adopt the vertiginously infinite. Truth does not make sense; it exceeds meaning and exceeds measure. It exceeds all regimes of truth. (123)

A fascination with that which exceeds the grasp prepares the way for fetishism. Science can serve as talismanic fetish for the production of knowledge. Other cultures, caught in the thickness of ethnographic representation, as fetishized images of a pastoral Eden, offer a lost past, a reflection of the selves we might have been. To the extent that this process depends on an other scene, separated off, distant, available for representation, others will exist within the framework of an oscillatory ambivalence. The desire to know or possess, "to tame and cook," is constantly juxtaposed to the desire for the experience of strangeness itself, which will hold the Other at the distance of fetishistic contemplation. Ethnographic realism serves this ambivalence well. The arrival scene and the distance required by the act of representation confirm the sense of otherness, strangeness. The canonic narrative format, in either fictive or expository forms, produces a sense of similarity and the familiar.

Elsewhere I have discussed this ambivalence as part of a much larger set of parallelisms between the licit knowledge produced by classic ethnographic film and the illicit knowledge produced by classic heterosexual pornography (Needham, Hanson, Nichols, 1989). The parallels are quite extensive even though the institutional frames, discursive practices, and ostensible purposes seem sharply distinct. (Parallelisms include: 1) efforts to establish the authenticity of what we see via arrival tropes and scenes or via images of male ejaculation, aka "cum shots"; 2) emphasis on "whole acts" defined in ritualistic, empirical terms, 3) on the hierarchical effect of a voyeuristic gaze or a panoptic gaze [Foucault, 1980a], and 4) on a fetishization of phallic power or cephalic knowledge ["talking heads"].) In many ways the parallels recapitulate the mind/body split epitomized by a scientific production of knowledge. What Foucault called a *scientia sexualis* detaches itself from the body in order to understand, label, codify and cure the body and its sexuality (1980b). This detachment from that which becomes the object of study allows science, or ethnographic film, to disavow its attachment to the body. And yet, like the repressed, disavowal returns as fetish and ambivalence.

Ambivalence derives from the dependence on the other for a sense of identity that, in its imaginary coherence or autonomy, would deny the centrality of the other upon whom it is dependent. In pornography this ambivalence involves a paradoxical desire for a pleasure that is not one, is not fully available. Pornography sets out to please but not please entirely. It affords pleasure but not the pleasure that is (only) represented. The pleasure that is represented remains deferred, perhaps indefinitely, in favor of its (fetishistic) representation. The result is a gendered viewing subject caught up in a desire for this oscillatory pleasure per se. The completion of desire is deferred in favor of perpetuating a set of staged representations of desire (for more pornography).

In ethnographic film this ambivalence involves the paradoxical desire for a knowledge that is not one, that is not fully "ours" nor theirs. Rather than seeking to make strangeness known, we seek to *know* strangeness (the mythos of travel enters here). By being beheld at a distance strangeness eludes full comprehension but supports an imaginary coherence, what Said would call Orientalism, what we might more generally call the self that constitutes itself through an imaginary geography. Ethnography affords knowledge passed from mind to mind, but not the knowledge that is (only) represented, which is *their* knowledge, embodied knowledge located *there*, in other bodies. The result is a viewing subject caught up in a desire for this oscillation between the strange and the familiar. The satisfaction of the desire to know is deferred in favor of perpetuating this set of staged representations of knowledge (by means of more ethnographies).

Break on Through to the Other Side

These parallelisms might seem to deal a fatal blow to conventions of ethnographic film that bind its representational strategies so tightly to the culture of origin that misrecognition and misrepresentation are all but inevitable. I wish to suggest that what requires concerted effort is not the redemption of ethnographic film from its apparently fallen state, but heightened exploration and utilization of its material, experiential dimensions. Eliminating the perpetuation of ambivalence from the representation of experience, the body and the Other would be one important step forward. In her provocative book on hard-core film pornography, Linda Williams refuses to choose between the binary either-or of pro- and anti-pornography positions. She concludes by arguing that a feminist pornotopia—akin to an ethnotopia constructed by the Others who have been represented as source of the knowledge produced by anthropology—is preferable:

> An ideal of bisexuality drives the quest for the knowledge of the pleasure of the other: that one sex can journey to the unknown other and return, satiated with knowledge and pleasure, to the security of the "self." . . . Of course . . . there is no such thing as a discrete sexed identity who can journey from fixed self to fixed other . . . these identities themselves are constructed in fluid relations to fictional "others" who exist only in our relation to them . . . If the sexual other is ultimately unknowable, then all the more reason to desire this knowledge, especially now that what was once the "other" has begun to make the journey herself. (1989: 279)

Breaking through to the other side would mean making a similar journey, and helping others do so as well. The body—with its truth that exceeds all regimes of truth, its excess of physical specificity and historical situatedness—rather than being contained within (Western) story formats and ethnographic "attribute dimension grids" (Heider 1976) might provide the focus for speculation about experience and knowledge beyond the valley where our ethnographic shepherds have built their house of science. Just as a pornotopia requires not disavowal but a more intensive exploration of the sexual imagination to represent a dispersal of pleasures no longer focused on phallocentric tales, an ethnotopia would disperse experience and knowledge far beyond the binary, realist, canonic narratives of the classic ethnographer's tale. Rather than dismissing ethnographic film for failing to fulfill (generally unspecified) criteria of anthropological validation based on a conception of anthropology as science and professional discipline (Rollwagon 1988b; Ruby 1990) we might push forward, as Williams does, toward an ethnotopia that will not abolish experience, the body, and knowledge from the belly but affirm it.[4]

Nausea, Anomaly, Excess

> Viewers do not share the cultural context, and the background is not thus anchored in familiar assumptions, but begins to float in a sea of questions . . . (Jablonko 1988: 175–6)

> The message goes straight to the stomach . . . (Tambs-Lyche and Waage 1989: 32)

> Just because the world goes round is no reason for getting seasick. (Svevo 1923)

Sometimes bodily experience exceeds intellectual understanding. Cognitive processing and bodily experience produce contradictory responses that disorient the mind. Visceral reactions occur that are uncontained by the descriptive or explanatory grid utilized by a given film. To a large extent, such reactions appear as anomaly (they normally fall within the anthropological unconscious). My contention, however, is that such responses indicate a possible direction forward, toward an ethnotopia that does not arise from a discourse conveyed from mind to mind. Such an ethnotopia may provide a meeting ground for ethnographic film and those cross-cultural journeys that "others" have already begun.

Two fascinating accounts indicate just how visceral the cinematic experience of another culture can be. Tambs-Lyche and Waage report that fourteen and fifteen year old Norwegian schoolchildren, shown a series of ethnographic films that included nudity, violence and "strange scenes," were nonetheless overwhelmed by *The Nuer* (Harris and Breidenbach 1970) in particular (1989: 31–33). Several students fled the classroom; "some were found vomiting, one crying" (31). In describing their responses the students identified with the Nuer as "so much like us" but also found their actions "disgusting."

Though seemingly anomalous and theorized as an hysteria-like display of emotion at behavior that could not be assimilated within a cognitive frame (partly because the film did not provide a conventional one), this report has its echo in a study done by Martinez (1990). In this case a group of U.S. university students' responses to a series of ethnographic films were carefully monitored. Responses varied considerably and different qualities came to the fore with different films, but *The Nuer* again scored highest of all the films shown in terms of emotional response. Typical comments were: "I didn't like the film at all . . . I found it long and boring . . . I was in awe when I saw it . . . The droning of the cattle almost drove me crazy . . . The people were dirty" (1990: 41). These emotional responses which accompanied every ethnographic film to some degree, blocked more elaborated readings of the film, leaving the student feeling boredom and disgust, or awe. This pattern recalls Mulvey's comment that patterns of identification, or scopophilia, have their own aims which create the eroticized, imagized world needed to support the subject's image of him-or herself, aims which make "a mockery of empirical objectivity."

These visceral reactions float in a sea of questions, for viewers and ethnographers alike. Strong emotional reactions that block movement toward more generalized perspectives are not unique to *The Nuer* and its distinctively poetic, associative editing pattern. Such emotional disturbance is not limited to students: Balikci recounts how Representative Conlan of Arizona attacked *The Netsilik Eskimo Series* (Balikci 1967–68) as unfit for American schoolchildren because it undermined morality, patriotism, and American values by means of its lack of contextualizing commentary in the face of numerous scenes of "violence and death" (Balikci 1988: 42–43). Such disturbances are not limited to events in other cultures: Sobchack makes a compelling case for the extent to which the representation of death in any documentary is vividly different from its representation in a fiction film, a difference that prompts a qualitatively different form of response (1984). The disturbances are not limited simply to students and non-professionals: the

Reassemblage, Trinh T. Minh-ha.

extraordinarily diverse set of opinions occasioned by Robert Gardner's *Forest of Bliss* (1985) that appeared in the last issue of *SVA Newsletter* and the first issue of *SVA Review* (1990) also give evidence of emotional reactions of such unfathomed strength that more elaborate analysis is blocked.

These responses float in a sea of questions because they lack an interpretive frame within which they can be addressed. They represent a short-circuit. An aesthetic, visceral response translates into expressive excess, spillage from reactions unconnected to a self-reflective, consciousness-raising means of contextualizing and understanding them. Instead of comprehension, assimilation and interpretation these reactions surge past the mind in a guise that allows expression to what remains ultimately repressed within the unconscious. They are ego-defensive and boundary-protective rather than catalysts to relationality and exchange. This is not emotion as liberatory escape from Platonic hyper-rationality or sobriety, but emotion as the return of the repressed in forms that fail to lead to increased self-awareness or a heightened sense of permeable boundaries and partial subjectivities. Instead, "any scene is immediately either 'domesticated' by being naively explained as analogous to something in our culture, or it is dramatized and appears as a projection of unconscious or suppressed elements of our own culture" (Jablonko, 1988: 175).

Shifting Paradigms and Changing Times

How can we account for our bodily response to the sight of a film? This question exceeds the bounds of debate involving a new paradigm for ethnography based on a shift from a social science model to a cultural studies and textual theory model. This latter shift opposes: the transparency of discourses of sobriety to an emphasis on the content of the form—on rhetoric and style as producers more than bearers of meaning; the imaginary geography of the Orientalist to the heterogeneity of interpenetrating categories and worlds; the fullness of empirical knowledge to the partiality of experiential knowledge; disembodied, impersonal logic to a situated historical voice; a zero-degree style of institutionally regulated objectivity to the purposeful style of intersubjective communication and exchange; conventional story formats to experimental ones; self-sufficient, full narratives to self-reflexive, incomplete ones; realism to montage or collage, univocality to dialogism, and hierarchy to difference.

Such a paradigm shift recapitulates the last thirty years of debate in documentary and ethnographic filmmaking that began with the introduction of lightweight, synchronous recording equipment. It leaves many of the same problems unanswered: how can dialogism, polyvocality, heteroglossia and reflexivity avoid the fundamental rebuke of sustaining hierarchical relations and minimizing use-value to others when the questions, technologies and strategies are so heavily of "our" own devising?

Hardly insignificant, this paradigm shift does not yet, in and of itself, suffice to account for the nausea and excess ethnographic film may produce. What remains to be proposed, not as an alternative but an adjunct, is a reconceptualization of what visual anthropology itself might mean.

Reinterpreting the Visual

From the first moment [of *Forest of Bliss*] then we are confronted with a central principle of Hindu thought—the juxtaposition and interpenetration of oppositions (Creation: Destruction; Life: Death). (Chopra 1989: 2)

I rarely can figure out what the people are doing [in *Forest of Bliss*] and when I can, the significance of the action is lost to me. (Ruby 1989: 12)

. . . literary practice remains the missing link in the socio-communicative or subjective-transcendental fabric of the so-called human sciences. (Kristeva 1980: 98)

If the status of ethnographic film within anthropology signals a tension within the field as a whole in terms of epistemological theory and modes of representation, the status of Gardner's *Forest of Bliss*, and the films of Trinh T. Minh-ha, signal a tension within visual anthropology between social science canons of evaluation and cultural theory modes of interpretation (or "literary practice" in the Kristeva epigraph). So far there has been minimal dialogue between these two camps since anthropology and cultural theory, like communication studies and film studies, occupy very distinct sites within the U.S. academy: the former located more squarely within a social science tradition geared to the interpretation of data and the latter within a humanities tradition of hermeneutic interpretation. The adoption of reflexive, text-centered strategies in many cross-cultural forms of representation has yet to be matched by a comparable adoption of cultural theory in ethnographic film criticism.

A visual anthropology devoted to the interpretation of texts might raise from the anthropological unconscious questions regarding the viewer and viewer response. Repressed questions of the body, experience and sensory knowledge that figure forcefully into the rituals of fieldwork—even if they are largely suppressed from finished reports—might return, addressed to the viewer's bodily, affective experience of an ethnographic film. Interpreting the experience of the text and the forms of knowledge it makes possible is precisely what Chopra attempts in her close textual reading of *Forest of Bliss* (1989).

Going further, it is not interpretation but theories of interpretation, not one reading of a text vs. another but questioning historically conditioned and ideologically inflected mechanisms of textual representation that is at stake. Sarah Williams, in a response to a trio of commentaries on the work of Trinh T. Minh-ha, poses this more radical challenge by asking "Is it possible 'to know' difference differently?" (1991: 12). And doesn't such "knowing" require putting current practices, prevailing conventions governing the ethnographer's tale, what takes places behind the scenes of anthropological discourse into suspension? ". . . suspension is deferment, dispersion, cessation . . . To put into suspension is to support, to hang, to postpone, to interrupt" (1991: 9).

Reviewing the scope and application of cultural theory, literary theory, hermeneutics and interpretation is well beyond the scope of this essay. Clifford and Marcus have offered a useful prolegomenon for anthropology in their *Writing Culture* (1986) and Trinh T. Minh-ha has offered a symptomatic, distanciated reading of anthropological practice designed to put its underlying assumptions into critical suspension (1989). There also exists a tradition already represented, though often neglected, within sociology and anthropology that offers something of a bridge from paradigms lost to paradigms regained.

A Method in the Mist

> . . . it is crucial to realize that events take place not as representatives or examples of abstract categories ("marriage payments," "dispute settlement") but as contingent phenomena [which can be] far more important than the label which is attached [by analyst or actor] to the interaction. (Banks 1990: 32)

> Seeking to perforate meaning by forcing my entry or breaking it open to dissipate what is thought to be its secrets seems to me as crippled an act as verifying the sex of an unborn child by ripping open its mother's womb. It is typical of a mentality that proves incapable of touching the living thing without crushing its delicateness. (Trinh 1989: 48–49)

The method glimpsed in the mist shrouding current discussions of the scientific dimension of anthropology is phenomenology. The phenomenological tradition shares with ethnographic film a commitment to the appearance of things in their specificity. It takes considerable interest in the question of the body and how embodied action—performance—constitutes a sense of self in relation to others. Phenomenology addresses the issue of experience directly. It brings into focus the (largely absent) body of the filmmaker him- or herself as the organizing locus of knowledge. Phenomenology, and kindred approaches such as ethnomethodology or symbolic interactionism, offer a framework within which to displace the problematics of observation and the professional gaze with questions of interaction and participatory dynamics.[5]

Like a feminist ethnographic film aesthetic, a phenomenological aesthetic remains underdeveloped, and often overlooked as a possible point of departure. (It does figure, sometimes implicitly, in the largely informal discourse of ethnographic filmmakers attempting to articulate the problems and conflicts they experience in which bodily presence, emotional response, erotic engagement and ethical dilemmas inextricably confront one another.) It may be no coincidence that both David MacDougall and Alison Jablonko envision an experiential or perhaps gnosiological, repetitive, poetic form of filmic organization that would foster "haptic learning, learning by bodily identification" (Jablonko 1988: 182) or would replace subject centered and linear models with ones "employing repetition, associative editing and non-narrative structures" (MacDougall 1990: 9).[6]

Efforts such as these would move away from attempts to speak from mind to mind, in the discourse of scientific sobriety, and toward a politics and epistemology of experience spoken from body to body. Hierarchical structures designed for the extraction of knowledge (the interview, the informant, the case study) might yield to more fully personal, participatory encounter that makes an expansion or diffusion of the personal into the social/political inevitable. Rather than "perforate" the surface of things to extract concepts and categories, falsifiable rules and generalizations, ethnographic film might respond to the call for evocation rather than representation in order "to provoke an aesthetic integration that will have a therapeutic effect. It is, in a word, poetry" (Tyler 1986: 125). Its production and interpretation requires both a poetics, and a phenomenology, to accompany, if not displace, the "production of knowledge" and interpretation of data that prizes referential and explicit meanings—pertaining to another culture—over implicit and symptomatic meanings—pertaining to "our" own.

Beyond the Binary

Its sequences [*Appeal to Santiago*] contain superb visual ethnography, but when finally produced, these scenes are montaged primarily for artistic effect with no respect for spatial or temporal context . . . When the artistry becomes

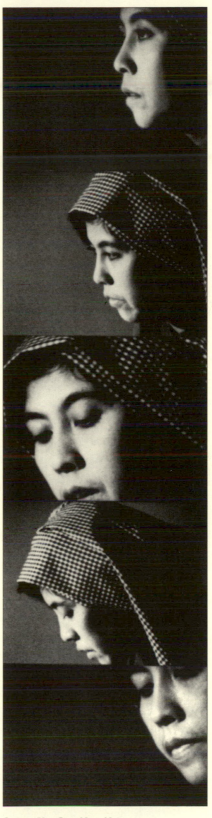

Surname Viet Given Name Nam,
Trinh T. Minh-ha.

an end in itself, then film on human behavior can become scientifically worthless. (Collier, 1988: 88–89)

[*The Nuer*] is one of the most visually beautiful films ever made . . . But the film is almost without ethnographic integrity. By this I mean that its principles are cinema aesthetic . . ." (Heider 1976: 35)

Thus, Nuer culture, or our experience of it, can be known through a formal strategy of "making strange" in order that overlooked qualities of the everyday can be rediscovered. *The Nuer* attempts to restore a sense of the poetic to the everyday world of another culture. (Nichols 1981: 252)

Cultural studies, phenomenology, and Tyler's particularly evocative description of a transformative ethnography conceived and practiced with social use-value foremost in mind, refutes the self/other opposition and its inevitable slide toward hierarchy in the service of the "production of knowledge." An interpretive method that centers on the form and texture of the text, and our experience of it, also holds the potential to bridge the divide between the practice of interpretation as the scientific derivation of data, facts or "ethnographicness"— with code words like "cinema aesthetic" to locate the author cleanly on one side of a self-constructed art/science divide—and interpretation as a hermeneutic act that locates the interpreter, viewer and text in the midst of both a formal and an ideological, aesthetic and social web of significance, stylistically inflected, rhetorically charged, affect-laden.

In short, bridging the gulf between interpretation as content analysis and interpretation as discourse analysis, between seeing *through* a film to the data beyond, and *seeing film* as cultural representation, may give visual anthropology a much needed reorientation toward questions of form and their inextricable relation to experience, affect, content, purpose and result. The emotional distress occasioned for some by seeing *The Nuer* can compel interpretive engagement and embodied awareness. Reworking the boundaries between the anthropological "discipline" and the anthropological unconscious can challenge the domesticating/ exoticizing tendencies of representation and the gaze. There is no reason why nausea should lead to protracted sickness.

To the Back of Beyond: Other Voices, Other Places

[As anthropologist/filmmakers] we will communicate from the subjects to the audience with the minimum distortion and with the maximum effort to tell the subject's story the way they would *if they could speak* to the audience *themselves*. (Olson 1988: 271, my italics)

To return the ethnographic gaze, both women and other non-hegemonic groups must begin to write and make visual images of the world according to their own viewpoint. (Kuehnast 1990: 25)

Clifford's map of consciousness with its sense of history and maturation from a state of belief in total knowledge to experimentation threatens to collapse under the weight of feminism and non-Western writings which make this division unstable. (Gordon 1988: 16)

But feminist ethnography . . . has not produced either unconventional forms of writing or a developed reflection on ethnographic textuality as such. (Clifford 1986: 21)

New paradigms and their application not only carry the possible taint of appearing as merely fashionable—celebrated with all the fanfare of millenarianism—they risk proposing a new balance of forces on the same, old, binary checkerboard. Dialogism, heteroglossia, reflexivity and experimentation with form can all be recuperated into new and improved ways for institutionalized ethnographers to vex each other more precisely by involving Others more thoroughly in the process. Giving Others a chance to speak (on terms not finally of their own choosing), is not a radical break with past convention. (And the thirty-odd years of debate on this topic, inaugurated by cinema-verité, has clearly not set the record straight, resolving issues and blazing trails written ethnographies need only follow.) Questions of how ethnography matters to Others, in what way it does more than refine a professional pursuit and project the imaginary geography peculiar to a modernist or postmodernist sensibility onto the world around it, remain unspecified, perhaps because, like women, Others have not participated in such debates as one among many, or, more precisely, as many among one—fracturing, reconfiguring, even dissolving that "one" into the many it too readily subsumes.[7]

New strategies for film structure and film interpretation, incorporating a poetics and phenomenology, will make a difference but perhaps not enough to know difference differently. To go beyond is to go outside. It is to discover other voices in other places that, as members of a diasporic or exiled community, frequently are neither here nor there in terms of fixed location, that bring the Third World inside the First, that have undertaken their own experimentations with form to give voice to subjectivities, perspectives and commitments that stem from other places and other experiences rather than to improve the existing ethnographic filmmaking tradition. These are voices from which we can learn.

Marilu Mallet's *Unfinished Diary* (1983) is a case in point. Refusing to tell the story of a people, a culture or a general situation, this personal, diaristic account of a Chilean exile's experiences in Montreal, in the midst of a crumbling marriage (to Australian-born Canadian documentarian Michael Rubbo), and with the burden of memories of a Chile that no longer is, *Unfinished Diary* demonstrates the death of those master narratives that have organized so many other stories in other times. Partial satisfactions, diverse affinities, overlapping but incongruent affiliations and imperfect utopias replace the ordered lives constructed according to the premises of Aristotelian logic, Christian salvation, Keynesian economics, or Marxist revolution. How can the gulf between a past there, in Chile, and a present here, in Montreal, be spanned without the logic of problem-solving, the theology of damnation and redemption, the dynamics of the marketplace or the dialectical materialism of revolution? How do we represent—that is, depict, speak for, and argue about what is no longer present under conditions such as these?

Mallet's answer is to speak from and about the self, with the sense of an ever widening web of implication that spins outward from this singular but incomplete nodal point, one among many that we see as the film unfolds. Like so many inhabitants of the great global village of political refugees, exiles, immigrants, and diasporic communities, Mallet is not "one of us" in terms of the classic, conventional image of the settled native informant as key to region and culture. She lives "inside" but perceives from "outside." Her split perspective leaves her acutely aware of the emotional resonance of minor moments such as when Rubbo matter-of-factly staples sheets of translucent plastic to all the windows as a heat-saving procedure. To her, the rationale is understandable but it does not eliminate the felt experience of encryptment that Rubbo's calm rationality only intensifies.

Unfinished Diary is the opposite of the travelogue or the conventional ethnography. Movement and travel no longer serve as a symbol for the expansion of one's moral framework, the realization of cultural relativity, the heroics of salvage anthropology, the rituals of self-improvement, or as training in the moral responsibilities that befall the custodians of a post-colonial order. Movement and travel no longer legitimate the subject's right to speak through/with disembodied discourses, master narratives and mythologies in which the corporeal "I" who speaks dissolves itself into the disembodied, depersonalized, institutionalized discourse of power and knowledge. This is the Cartesian, Griersonian, scientific legacy in documentary film that Mallet rejects.

For Mallet—as for others among the dispossessed and displaced for whom "de-territorialization" is not a concept but an experience—movement and travel become emblematic of dislocation, of social and cultural estrangement, of survival and self-preservation (what self is it that one preserves in the midst of dispersal and fragmentation?). Mallet explores and proposes strategies of resistance, of struggle and resolution (displayed vividly in the weave of Spanish, French and English speaking voices that situates characters within their own distinct, decentered locus of communication). Location stems from an embodied, corporeal discourse, and resistance from the material practice of communication and exchange.

Representing a politics of location—of living both here and there, of linguistic circles of affiliation, of work, family and friends—points toward the importance of testimonial literature and first-person filmmaking as an alternative tradition to master narratives and canonic stories. Testimonials are first person, oral more than literary, personal more than conceptual. Such works explore the personal as political at the level of textual self-representation as well as at the level of lived experience. Testimonial contrasts with the traditional essay or documentary where the authorial "I" speaks to and on behalf of a universalized collectivity. The "I" of testimonials *embodies* social affinities and collectivities. It is acutely aware of hegemonic discourse and social difference, historical conjuncture, material practice, and marginality. (Rigobert Menchu's *I, Rigoberta* [1984] and Cherie Moraga's *Loving in the War Years* [1983] are excellent examples of written testimonials that parallel many of the preoccupations of Mallet's *Unfinished Diary*.) Mallet's placement of herself within the film as a person whose authority derives from experience more than from theories, methods or institutional legitimacy, her displacement of the "history lesson" or "ethnographic message" from its privileged position of justification for her diaristic account, her refusal to make herself into the figure of the one-who-knows that most voice-over commentary in documentary evokes, all propose a radically distinct model of social representation.

Her scenes cannot be described as examples, models, or representative evidence in the service of an argument without betraying the very strategy she adopts. They are scenes not from *a* marriage but *her* marriage, not from *a* life but *her* life. Their significance within a wider web of implication resides in their particularity not their typicality, their phenomenological aura not their conceptual essence. To treat them as examples is to slide toward a Geertzian problematic where representation becomes the province of Us discussing Them in ways that no longer matter very much to Them.

These qualities of testimonial are taken up in different and suggestive ways in other works as well. *Films Are Dreams*, for example, traces a journey to Tibet by a political refugee, Lobsang Dakpa, and the ethnographic filmmaker herself, Sylvia Sensiper. News of the journey first comes to us through a staged television news report. The device aptly introduces the theme of mediating images, memories and discourses that the remainder of the video explores. Both Lobsang and Sensiper speak for themselves about what the journey means. In each case they envision a pre-existing Tibet: the Tibet of 1959 for Lobsang, the year his exile began, and the Tibet of *Lost Horizon* (Capra 1937) for Sensiper, the film that pre-figured the world she thought she might discover. By intercutting footage shot by Dakpa and Sensiper separately, clips from Capra's *Lost Horizon*, newsreel footage of China's annexation of Tibet and the Dali Lama's (and Dakpa Lobsang's) exile, and more formal interviews with Dakpa, the film explores the construction of the imaginary geographies that usually remains unacknowledged in ethnographic work. Characters, institutions and nations bring their pre-existing maps with them. Dissonance and conflicts arise. Contradictions reveal the premises and limitations, the dream-world quality to imaginary geographies which, at first, seem boundless. The tension between past and present is also rendered far more palpable than a salvage anthropology of disappearing customs can accommodate. There is no direct access to that imagined realm at the other end of memory; there are only memories and dreams that make more vivid the lineaments of the present from which past and future extend.

Another film that works against the grain of the ethnographer's tale is Diane Kitchen's *Before We Knew Nothing*. This film is close to a conventional ethnography in its description of living among the Ashinka Indians of the Amazon river basin, but Kitchen's stress on the physical experience of being there; her admission of being drawn to the tribe by early photographs of them as fierce warriors fending off the first waves of intruders earlier in the century (conveyed by cutting these photographs into the flow of present events, something like the intercut scenes from *Lost Horizon* in *Films Are Dreams*), her very limited use of synchronous sound, and her total reliance on a whispered voice-over for her own commentary construct a very vivid sense of distance and separation. Rather than being the space necessary for representation and fetishization of the other, this distance provides the space for critical reflection.

The whispered commentary in particular conveys a sense of intimacy and respect rather than confiding a secret or suggesting gossip. The whisper erases any sense of authoritativeness from the commentary. The grainy whisper localizes and personalizes the commentary and yet holds it apart from the visible scenes where its point of enunciation, Kitchen's body, is plainly in evidence. Now and then, like here and there, interpenetrate in the shadowy echoes of a voice that does not restore the past but identifies it as available to consciousness and the present but irreducible to these or any other essentializing formulations.

Other voices propose yet other directions. These works reconfigure strategies and assumptions that underlie the ethnographic film tradition from the outside, in relation to other concerns and priorities. Brenda Longfellow's *Our Marilyn* (1988), for example, is a poetic first-person meditation on the formation of female subjectivity in relation to the female body. The film positions the first-person, voice-off narrator between the body image of physical prowess represented by Canadian long distance swimmer Marilyn Bell and the image of physical allure represented by American film star Marilyn Monroe. The narrator, drawn to both images, confounds any sense of fixed position or transcendental coherence to individual identity. Her dilemma magnifies that of N!ai or

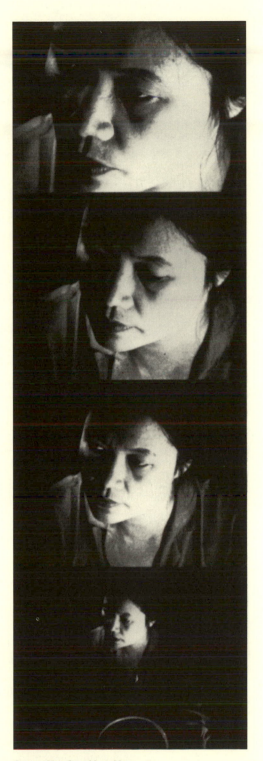

Surname Viet Given Name Nam,
Trinh T. Minh-ha.

the Masai women in *The Women's Olamal*. *Our Marilyn* adopts subjective means to give representation to a divided, reticulated, sedimented self. Realist tropes and canonical story structure no longer occupy center stage. Poetic impressions of marathon swimming, and extended passages representing duration itself, confound the notion of causal sequence and logical exposition. What would be treated in summary fashion, the hours and hours of arduous swimming required by Bell's attempt to traverse Lake Ontario, move to the fore. The film stresses prolongation, physical exertion, the experience of fatigue and hallucination with rhythmic, expressive patterns that seem reminiscent of how *The Nuer* conveys the poetic cadences and textures of everyday life among a pastoral people. Our sense of time and identification are transformed, momentarily. We enter into a different experiential realm, distinct from the representations others might apply to an experience they have only known vicariously. Representing the subjective interiority of this experience offers a distinct alternative to the erotics of a voyeuristic gaze and the construction of the self.

I'm British But (Chadha 1989) addresses similar questions of identity in relation to nationality and individual subjectivity. It presents a series of interviews with Pakistani-British who begin by describing themselves as Welsh or Scottish only gradually to speak more emphatically about their position between national identities—aware of their British present, conscious of their Pakistani heritage, and unwilling to choose within an either/or binary. Like Marilu Mallet, they, too, convey a both/and subjectivity that does not mistake transnationalism for privilege: the residue of racism and xenophobia is far too strong.

Another Canadian film, *Speak Body*, also sidesteps concepts and categories, in this case regarding the issue of abortion, in order to evoke the experience entailed. Using a collage of voices that deliver diary-like commentary about specific moments in the passage from the awareness of pregnancy to its termination, the film couples these voices to fragmentary images of different women's bodies. Placed in this emotionally charged and de-eroticized context, the images do not encourage voyeurism or fetishism, as much as identification with the body as the personal and physical site of an experience that reverberates outward across the tissue of our culture. *Speak Body* represents an instructive experiment in conveying whole bodies/whole acts without showing either the entire body or the culminating act. Like *Our Marilyn* and *I'm British But*, *Speak Body* reconceptualizes holism outside the confines of an empirical realism and places it more squarely within the domain of a phenomenological and cultural whole. It does so without attaching its representation of a whole act to preconceived political positions, cultural assumptions, or moral judgments.

Not only *Unfinished Diary*, *I'm British But* and *Our Marilyn* but also *Handsworth Songs*, *Des grands evenements et de gens ordinaires (Of Great Events and Ordinary People)* (Ruiz 1979), *Surname Viet Given Name Nam*, *Films Are Dreams* and *Who Killed Vincent Chin?* offer compelling representations of the interpenetration of cultures and sensibilities in a world of guest workers, refugees, exiles, diasporic movements and ethnic diversity. Some, like *Who Killed Vincent Chin?*, reckon the enormous price this diversity sometimes exacts when differences serve to justify racism and conflicts turn to violence. (It follows the prolonged and desultory quest for justice in the wake of the murder of Vincent Chin by an out-of-work Detroit autoworker who mistook him for Japanese.) *Who Killed Vincent Chin?* exposes the workings of institutional and habitual racism at the level of everyday life. (Compared to the virulent ideology of racism promulgated by groups like the Klu Klux Klan, the autoworker insists he had no racial motives whatsoever. His own blindness challenges the viewer to identify and understand dynamics unrecognized or misunderstood by the murderer himself.) Like *I'm British But*, *Who Killed Vincent Chin?* examines racial and cultural differences at home, not in exotic locales, and makes clear what is at stake for others when difference succumbs to objectifying stereotypes and racist phobias.

Another film outside the ethnographic tradition but instructive to it, *Surname Viet Given Name Nam*, hinges on subverting the construction of authenticity and the representation of others as "informants" by presenting scripted and rehearsed interviews with women in Vietnam that use Vietnamese women in the United States to play the parts of the women who remained behind after they left. Trinh's film, like her earlier *Reassemblage* (1982) and *Naked Spaces: Living Is Round* (1985), acts as a metacommentary on documentary form and ethnographic intent. Trinh stages the other culture (postwar Vietnam) as "there," only to reveal it to be "here" in ways that demonstrate continuing difficulty for women within the sex-gender system of both cultures; Trinh subverts standard assumptions about travel, fieldwork, and ethnographic authority and she presents translation and transcription as processes that distort or betray that which they represent. Rather than allowing sub-titles to give the impression of representational adequacy, Trinh sets up vivid discrepancies and counter-pointing between what is said and what is written. *Surname Viet Given Name Nam* not only brings Vietnam inside the United States, it embeds the experience of cultural difference within the film experience.

Dream, Memory, History, Representation

> We need a dream-world in order to discover the features of the real world we think we inhabit. (Sylvia Sensiper, quoting Paul Feyerabend, in *Films Are Dreams*)

Dreams rework everyday experience according to the distinct processes of the unconscious mind. They are a way of re-membering the past and addressing its lingering conflicts, traumas and contradictions. Memory often plays a similar role. Adjunct or alternative to third-person historical narratives, it is another way of discovering features of the real world we think we inhabit. And in many of these films, time, memory and the past are a recurring motif. As in Marshall's film *N!ai: The Story of a !Kung Woman*, *Before We Knew Nothing*, *Lorang's Way* (MacDougall 1980) and *Kenya Boran*, *Handsworth Song*, *Unfinished Diary*, *I'm British But* and *Passion of Rememberance* (Julien 1986) all address the question of how the past persists in the present or of how the present includes a partiality, a lack of fullness, resulting from the undertow of the past. (No longer a repository of "our" lost horizon of idyllic bliss or savage ancestry, the past takes on a living presence perceived and felt from the inside by those for whom it matters.) What has come before—often in another place, another country—confirms the self as multiple, split and layered, built up of sedimented acts and revised memories. The hearty individuality of a Nanook shatters against such forces but is none the worse for it. What is re-membered serves to constitute a body of knowledge and experience that inflects the politics of location and subjectivity. The Pakistani-British in *I'm British But*, who begin by calling themselves Welsh or Scottish, conclude by remembering the massacre of Jallianwala Bagh, the kind of memory that identifies a place apart.[8]

Handsworth Songs vivifies the memory of immigrant parents and the dreams they bore with them on the boats that plied the Atlantic through the use of a poetic voice of reminiscence describing their aspirations in a diaristic mode. Sometimes this commentary is juxtaposed with footage showing new arrivals disembarking at dockside, sometimes it accompanies the camera as it slowly tracks past poster-sized photographs of the wedding pictures of Afro-Carribean immigrants in an otherwise dark, open studio space. These passages abut others built from journalistic footage covering the riots in Handsworth. There is no attempt to reconcile the two forms of representation. The memories of past hopes provide a contextualizing aura of historical consciousness for the next generation of blacks, those who made the film. It is little wonder that their imagination sees, and is compelled to help others see, ignorance, racial blindspot and misrepresentation—in sum, incommensurate realities—where their parents saw new beginnings.

These films, a few of the many available for discussion, interpretation, and use, step beyond realist conventions, canonic story formats, modernist montage and disciplinary purity. These films *already* use cinematic montage in ways Marcus calls for in the future (1990) but are also perceived as outside the ethnographic tradition Marcus addresses. They are films with use-value for those of whom they speak; they come from women/natives/others; they reconfigure the imaginary geography of cross-cultural representation itself and place ethnographic film as one, marginalized voice among many. These films move beyond the challenge of developing a better way for ethnographers to vex one another with their precision, proposing instead bold and innovative directions for cross-cultural representation in which others are no longer objects of study—however sensitive to needless perforations that study might be—no longer even equals in the production of work that will enlist their efforts in the redemption of western anthropology. They are now themselves the founding voices—the pioneers, provocateurs and poets—of a discourse of their own making, made with full, sometimes painful awareness of what has come before and of the representational residue they may choose to adapt, ignore or redress.

Some works such as Trinh's *Reassemblage* and *Naked Spaces: Living Is Round*, or Sensiper's *Films Are Dreams* clearly address assumptions and conventions behind the scenes of visual anthropology, but most do not. If this larger body of work contributes to the formation of an ethnotopia, it displays a very different geography from the one imagined by most ethnography and a viable answer to the question of whether it is possible to know difference differently. These works draw much of their inspiration from elsewhere, from other traditions, other forms, other perspectives and emphases. If other voices, speaking from other places, do not turn to ethnographic film as a primary source of inspiration, this should be occasion for pause. It invites "us" to reflect on the current state of, and discourse about, an ethnographic film tradition that has sought to represent others when, "we" have been told, they could not represent themselves.

Notes

1.   This body of work is primarily feminist in emphasis. Representative works include: Mulvey (1985); Studlar (1988); De Lauretis (1984); Doane, Mellencamp, Williams, eds. (1984); Gaines and Herzog, eds. (1990), and Kuhn (1982).

2.   Marianna Torgovnick (1991) offers an extended account of the central, allegorical role played by the tale of Odysseus in western travel narratives ever since, including ethnographic ones.

3.   The Twelfth Annual Nordic Film Festival revolved around the question of whether ethnographers could construct their work in accord with the narrative traditions and conventions of the cultures they study. MacDougall had explored the extent to which western conventions such as the canonical story format inform not only the films but also the selection of cultures to be studied (1990). Trinh's book, *Woman, Native, Other* also discusses alternative story forms at length, especially in her final chapter, "Grandma's Story" (1989).

4.   Interestingly, those engaged in the creation of virtual realities (computer-based worlds that simulate our experience of this world) find that it is difficult for subjects to locate or orient themselves without some representative of themselves in virtual space. Programmers often design "default heads," visual representations of a human head, that will perceive and move through virtual reality in the same manner as the subject would if she or he were physically, as well as perceptually, "there." These guides or "tricksters" take cognizance of our inability to act if we cannot locate our own body in relation to the world around us. When limited to a head, such figures would seem to offer one more example of an imaginary geography where the mind/body split of western civilization prevails. The mind enters into a strange and exotic realm, attaching itself to the guidance of a default head, while the physical body, left at the threshold, splits the mind's consciousness between two different streams of contradictory sensory input, leading, quite possibly, to nausea. As one participant at a recent conference remarked, there is considerable need for "default bodies" that locate the entire self within a virtual reality. Our experience and accountability within a distinctly different perceptual world depends on taking full account of our bodies and our selves, not just our mind and its theories.

5.   I discuss the professional or clinical gaze as well as the interactive mode of documentary filmmaking more extensively in *Representing Reality* (1991).

6.   Discussions of the use-value of phenomenology to a feminist theory of gender suggest something of its relevance to ethnographic film interpretation. Butler (1990), for example, argues, after Merleau-Ponty, for a conception of gender in which the body is "a historical idea" that renders gender specific through

individual acts that are also socially indicative. These acts accumulate into a "legacy of sedimented acts" that constitute the self in a continuously open-ended yet stable fashion (1990: 274). Such acts, and their sedimentation over time, of course, are the very stuff of ethnographic film.

7.   Stephen Lansing reminds us that the model of ethnographic film discussed here, of work aimed at a larger public, is not the only pertinent model (1990). His discussion of the National Film Board of Canada Fogo Island films and other works structured for use-value for their subjects rather than for their informational or affective value to others is a salutary reminder that ethnographic film can have more than one definition or purpose.

The direct usefulness of films to those about whom they are made also raises, by extension, a variation on the question that has reverberated through the museum world for some time now: should film footage be repatriated to the cultures where they were shot? Significant differences obtain when what is taken away are sounds and images rather than artifacts but the use-value of these materials, perhaps rushes and discarded footage even more than finished films since they bear a weaker imprint of the ethnographer's tale, may well be considerable. The time when their repatriation becomes a serious question may well be approaching.

8.   Recurring through *I'm British But* is a pop tune sung in Punjabi by a Pakistani-British rock group standing on the roof top of a small neighborhood store. The lyrics, printed in intertitles to make the point more clear, are a vivid reminder of roots and the price of dislocation. One verse, referring to the massacre, goes:

Recall that it was these same foreigners
That took their rifles to us
Innocent, fair flourishing lives
How they stood and destroyed us
And every corner bears witness
At Jallianwala Bagh

(refrain)
And you, my friend, come to England
Leaving your Punjab.

References

Alter, Robert. 1981. *The Art of Biblical Narrative*. New York: Basic Books.

Balikci, Asen. 1988. "Anthropologists and Ethnographic Filmmaking." In *Anthropological Filmmaking*, ed. J. Rollwagon.

Banks, Marcus. 1990. "Experience and Reality in Ethnographic Film." In *Visual Sociology Review* 5, 2: 30–33.

Biddick, Kathleen. 1991. "Uncolonizing History in Cyberspace: Memory, Artificial Memory, Remembering." Unpublished ms. delivered at the Second International Conference on Cyberspace, UCSC, Santa Cruz, Ca., April 1991.

Bishop, Peter. 1989. *The Myth of Shangri-La*. Berkeley: University of California Press.

Bordwell, David. 1985. *Narration in the Fiction Film*. Madison: University of Wisconsin Press.

Brecht, Bertolt. 1964 (1957). "The Modern Theatre Is the Epic Theatre." In *Brecht on Brecht*, ed. John Willet. New York: Hill and Wang.

Butler, Judith. 1990. "Performative Acts and Gender Constitution: An Essay in Phenomenology and Feminist Theory." In *Performing Feminisms: Feminist Critical Theory and Theatre*, ed. Sue-Ellen Case. Baltimore: The John Hopkins University Press.

Chopra, Radikha. 1989. "Robert Gardner's Forest of Bliss." In *SVA Newsletter* (Spring): 2–3.

Clifford, James. 1986. "Introduction." In *Writing Culture*, 1–26.

Clifford, James and George E. Marcus, eds. 1986. *Writing Culture: The Poetics and Politics of Ethnography*. Berkeley: University of California Press.

Collier, John. 1988. "Visual Anthropology and the Future of Ethnographic Film." In *Anthropological Filmmaking*, ed. J. Rollwagon, 73–96.

De Lauretis, Teresa. 1984. *Alice Doesn't: Feminism, Semiotics, Cinema*. Bloomington: Indiana University Press.

Doane, Mary Ann, Patricia Mellencamp and Linda Williams, eds. 1984. *Re-Vision: Essays in Feminist Film Criticism*. Frederick, MD.: University Publications of America.

Feingold, Ken. 1988. "Notes on India Time: The First in a Series of Videotapes." *CVA Newsletter* (May): 16–22.

Foucault, Michel. 1980a. *Power/Knowledge*. Ed. Colin Gordon. New York: Pantheon-Random House.

———. 1980b. *The History of Sexuality*. Trans. Robert Hurley. New York: Vintage-Random House.

Gaines, Jane and Charlotte Herzog, eds. 1990. *Fabrications: Costume and the Female Body*. New York: Routledge.

Geertz, Clifford. 1973. "Thick Description: Toward An Interpretative Theory of Culture." In *The Interpretation of Cultures*. New York: Basic Books.

Gordon, Deborah. 1988. "Writing Culture, Writing Feminism: The Poetics and Politics of Experimental Ethnography." *Inscriptions* 3/4: 7–23.

Heider, Karl. 1976. *Ethnographic Film*. Austin: University of Texas Press.

Jablonko, Allison. 1988. "New Guinea in Italy: An Analysis of the Making of an Italian Television Series from Research Footage of the Maring People of Papua New Guinea." In *Anthropological Filmmaking*, ed. J. Rollwagon, 169–96.

Klima, George. 1988. "Filming As Teleological Process." In *Anthropological Filmmaking*, ed. J. Rollwagon, 223–36.

Kristeva, Julia. 1980. *Desire in Language*. Ed. L. S. Roudiez. New York: Columbia University Press.

Kuhn, Annette. 1982. *Women's Pictures: Feminism and Cinema*. London: Routledge.

Kuehnast, Kathleen. 1990. "Gender Representation in Visual Ethnographies: An Interpretivist Perspective." *CVA Review* (Spring): 21–29.

Lansing, Stephen. 1990. "The Decolonization of Ethnographic Film." *SVA Review* 6 (1): 13–15, 81.

MacDougall, David. 1981 (1975). "Beyond Observational Cinema." In *Movies and Methods II*, ed. Bill Nichols. Berkeley: University of California Press.

———. 1990. "Complicities of Style." Unpublished ms. presented at RAI International Festival of Ethnographic Film (24 September).

Marcus, George. 1990. "The Modernist Sensibility in Recent Ethnography: Writing and the Cinematic Metaphor of Montage." In *SVA Review* 6 (1): 2–12, 21, 44.

Martinez, Wilton. 1990. "Critical Studies and Visual Anthropology: Aberrant vs. Anticipated Readings of Ethnographic Film." *CVA Review* (Spring): 34–47.

Menchu, Rigoberta. 1984. *I . . . Rigoberta Menchu: An Indian Woman In Guatamala*. Trans. Ann Wright. London: Verso.

Metz, Christian. 1974. "On the Impression of Reality in the Cinema." In Christian Metz, *Film Language*, trans. Michael Taylor. New York: Oxford University Press.

Moraga, Cherrie. 1983. *Loving in the War Years*. Boston: South End Press.

Muckerjii, Chandra. 1983. *From Graven Images: Patters of Modern Materialism*. New York: Columbia University Press.

Mulvey, Laura. 1985 (1975). "Visual Pleasure and Narrative Cinema." In *Movies and Methods, II*, ed. Bill Nichols. Berkeley: University of California Press.

Needham, Catherine, Chris Hansen and Bill Nichols. 1989. "Skinflicks: Ethnography, Pornography and the Discourses of Power." *Discourse* 11 (2): 65–79.

Nichols, Bill. 1981. *Ideology and the Image*. Bloomington: Indiana University Press.

———. 1991. *Representing Reality: Issues and Concepts in Documentary*. Bloomington: Indiana University Press.

Olson, Jon L. 1988. "Filming the Fidencistas: The Making of We Believe in Nono Fidencio." In *Anthropological Filmmaking*, ed. J. Rollwagon, 259–72.

Ong, Walter J. 1981. *Orality and Literacy: The Technologizing of the Word*. London: Methuen.

Pratt, Mary Louise. 1986. "Fieldwork in Common Places." In *Writing Culture*, ed. Clifford and Marcus.

Rollwagen, Jack, ed. 1988. *Anthropological Filmmaking: Anthropological Perspectives on the Production of Film and Video for General Public Audiences*. New York: Harwood Publishers.

———. 1988. "The Role of Anthropological Theory in 'Ethnographic' Filmmaking." In *Anthropological Filmmaking*, ed. J. Rollwagon, 287–315.

Ruby, Jay. 1988 (1977). "The Image Mirrored: Reflexivity and the Documentary Film." In *New Challenges for Documentary, ed.* Alan Rosenthal. Berkeley: University of California Press.

———. 1989. "The Emperor and His Clothes." *SVA Newsletter* (Spring): 9–11.

———. 1990. "Eye-Witnessing Humanism: Ethnography and Film." *CVA Review* (Fall): 12–16.

Said, Edward. 1978. *Orientalism*. New York: Vintage-Random House.

Sartre, Jean-Paul. 1965 (1948). *Anti-Semite and Jew*. New York: Schocken Books.

Silverman, Kaja. 1988. *The Acoustic Mirror: The Female Voice in Psychoanalysis and Cinema*. Bloomington: Indiana University Press.

Sobchack, Vivian. 1984. "Inscribing Ethical Space: Ten Propositions on Death, Representation, and Documentary." *Quarterly Review of Film Studies* 9 (4): 283–300.

Studlar, Gaylyn. 1988. *In the Realm of Pleasure: Von Sternberg, Dietrich, and the Masochistic Aesthetic*. Urbana: University of Illinois Press.

Svevo, Italo. 1958 (1923). *The Confessions of Zeno*. New York: Vintage.

Tambs-Lyche, Harald and Kjellaug Waage. 1989. "Intimacy, Recognition and Nausea: Reflections on the

Perception of Ethnographic Film by Norwegian Youth." *CVA Review* (Fall): 31–33.

Torgovnick, Marianna. 1991. *Gone Primitive: Savage Intellects, Modern Lives.* Chicago: University of Chicago Press.

Trinh, T. Minh-ha. 1989. *Woman/Native/Other.* Bloomington: Indiana University Press.

Tyler, Steven. 1986. "Post-Modern Ethnography: From Document of the Occult to Occult Document." In *Writing Culture*, ed. Clifford and Marcus, 122–40.

Williams, Linda. 1989. *Hard Core: Power, Pleasure and the 'Frenzy of the Visible'.* Berkeley: University of California Press.

Williams, Sarah. 1991. "Suspending Anthropology's Inscription: Observing Trinh Minh-ha Observed." *Visual Anthropology Review* 6 (3): 7–14.

B.
Nichols

Filmography

The Ax Fight, Napoleon Chagnon and Timothy Asch, Venezuela/ United States, 30 min., 1971.

Before We Knew Nothing, Diane Kitchen, Peru/ United States, 62 min., 1988.

Bitter Melons, John Marshall, Kalahari desert/ United States, 30 min., 1971.

Dead Birds, Robert Gardner, New Guinea/ United States, 83 min., 1963.

Films Are Dreams, Sylvia Sensiper, Tibet/ United States, 30 min., 1989.

First Contact, Bob Connelly and Robin Anderson, New Guinea/ Australia, 54 min., 1984.

Forest of Bliss, Robert Gardner, India/ United States, 90 min., 1985.

Handsworth Songs, John Akomfrah, Black Audio Collective, Great Britain, 52 min., 1986.

The Hunters, John Marshall, Kalahari desert/ United States, 73 min., 1956.

I'm British But, Gurinda Chadha, Great Britain, 30 min., 1989.

India Cabaret, Mira Nair, India, 60 min., 1986.

Jaguar, Jean Rouch, Ghana/ France, 57 min., 1967.

Kenya Boran, David MacDougall and James Blue, Kenya/United States, 66min., 1974.

Last Grave at Dimbaza, Nana Mahamos, South Africa, 57 min., 1975.

Moi, un noir, Jean Rouch, Cote d'Ivoire/ France, 80 min., 1957.

N!ai: Story of a !Kung Woman, John Marshall, Namibia/ United States, 58 min., 1980.

Naked Spaces: Living Is Round, Trinh T. Minh-ha, West Africa/ United States, 135 min., 1985.

Nanook of the North, Robert Flaherty, Canada/ United States, 55 min., 1922.

The Netsilik Eskimo Series, Asen Balikci and Guy Mary-Rousseliere, Canada, 18 episodes, approx. 10 hours, 1967–68.

The Nuer, Hillary Harris and George Briedenbach, Sudan/United States, 75 min., 1970.

Of Great Events and Ordinary People, Raul Ruiz, France, 65 min., 1979.

Our Marilyn, Brenda Longfellow, Canada, 22 min., 1988.

Passion of Remembrance, Isaac Julien, Sankofa Film Collective, Great Britain, 82 min., 1986.

Reassemblage, Trinh T. Minh-ha, Senegal/ United States, 40 min., 1982.

79 Springtimes, Santiago Alvarez, Cuba, approx. 30 min., 1969.

Small Happiness: Women in a Chinese Village, Carmen Hinton, China/ United States, 60 min., 1984.

Speak Body, Kay Armatage, Canada, 20 min., 1979.

Surname Viet Given Name Nam, Trinh T. Minh-ha, United States, 108 min., 1989.

Tong Tana, Jan Roed, Fredrik von Krustenstjirra, Bjorn Cederberg, Krisian Petri, Sarawak-Malaysia/ Sweden, 88 min., 1990.

Tourou et Bitti, Jean Rouch, Niger/ France, 8 min., 1971.

Unfinished Diary, Marilu Mallet, Canada, 55 min., 1983.

Who Killed Vincent Chin? Christine Choy and Renee Tajima, United States, 87 min., 1988.

The Women's Olamal: The Organization of a Masai Fertility Ceremony, Melissa Llweleyn-Davies, Kenya/ Great Britain, 110 min., 1985.

Artaud, Rouch, and the Cinema of Cruelty

Paul Stoller

IMAGINE THE FOLLOWING SCENE. WE ARE SEATED IN THE FILM THEATER OF THE MUSÉE de l'Homme. It is 1954, and a select audience of African and European intellectuals has been assembled to see a film screening. Marcel Griaule is there as is Germaine Dieterlen, Paulin Vierya, Alioune Sar and Luc de Heusch. Jean Rouch, who is in the projection booth, beams onto the screen the initial frames of *Les Maîtres Fous*. Rouch begins to speak, but soon senses a rising tension in the theater. As the reel winds down, the uncompromising scenes of *Les Maîtres Fous* make people in the audience squirm in their seats. Rouch asks his select audience for their reaction to the film.

Marcel Griaule says that the film is a travesty; he tells Rouch to destroy it. In rare agreement with Griaule, Paulin Vierya also suggests that the film be destroyed. There is only one encouraging reaction to *Les Maîtres Fous*, that of Luc de Heusch.[1]

This reaction clearly wounded Jean Rouch. Should he destroy this film? In filming *Les Maîtres Fous* Rouch's intentions were far from racist; he wanted to demonstrate how Songhay people in the colonial Gold Coast possessed knowledge and practices "not yet known to us." Just as in one of his earlier films, *Les Magiciens de Wanzerbé* (1947), in which a sorcerer defies common sense expectations by vomiting and then swallowing a small metal chain of power, so in *Les Maîtres Fous*, Rouch wanted to document the unthinkable—that men and women possessed by the Hauka spirits, the spirits of French and British colonialism, can handle fire and dip their hands into boiling cauldrons of sauce without burning themselves. Always the provocateur, Rouch wanted to challenge his audiences to think new thoughts about Africa and Africans. Could these people of Africa possess knowledge "not yet known to us," a veritable challenge to racist European conceptions of Africa's place in the history of science?

P. Stoller

Perhaps Rouch's intent in *Les Maîtres Fous* was naive. The brutal images overpower the film's subtle philosophical themes. After other screenings to selected audiences in France, Rouch decided on a limited distribution—to art theaters and film festivals.

Rouch was troubled by such criticism, for his prior practices and commitments were clearly anti-racist, anti-colonialist, and anti-imperialist. Critics have suggested that the controversy surrounding *Les Maîtres Fous* compelled Rouch to make films, especially his films of "ethno-fiction," that more directly confronted European racism and colonialism. Such a view may well be correct, for after *Les Maîtres Fous* Rouch made a series of films that portrayed the political and cultural pernicious-ness of European ethnocentrism and colonialism in the 1950s. But Rouch's political films are not simply the result of his reaction

Les Maîtres Fous, Jean Rouch.

to stinging criticism; they also embody, in my view, a cinematic extension of Artaud's notion of the theater of cruelty. In a cinema of cruelty the filmmaker's goal is not to recount per se, but to present an array of unsettling images that seek to transform the audience psychologically and politically. In the remainder of this essay I first discuss the Artaudian theories of the cinema and theater and speculate about the contours of a cinema of cruelty. I then use those contours to analyze four of Rouch's more politically and philosophically conscious films (*Jaguar* [1953–66], *Moi, un Noir* [1957], *La Pyramide Humaine* [1959], and *Petit à Petit* [1969]). I conclude with a discussion of the contemporary philosophical and political importance of Rouch's cinema—of cruelty.

Artaud and the Cinema

Throughout his life Artaud (1896–1948) suffered from long bouts of incoherence—the result of schizophrenia and drug addictions. Despite these difficulties, Artaud broke into the theater as an actor in 1921. Between 1921 and 1924 he joined the experimental repertory company of Charles Dullin for whom he acted and designed sets and costumes. He also acted with Georges and Ludmilla Pitoefs who produced plays by Blok, Shaw, Pirondello, Capek, and Molnar. During this period, Artaud also began to write plays, essays, poems, manifestoes, and film scenarios. In 1925 he joined André Breton and other Surrealists contributing essays to the review, *The Surrealist Revolution*. Between 1926 and 1929, he, Roger Vitrac and Robert Aron founded the Theatre Alfred Jarry, which briefly became a center of the avant-garde stage in France. After three years of meticulous planning in the early 1930s, Artaud opened his short-lived Theatre of Cruelty. The failure of this experiment did not dampen Artaud's creative spirit, for Artaud traveled widely and continued to write plays, essays and manifestoes. In 1938 Artaud's influential book of essays, *The Theatre and its Double*, was published. Critics hailed it as an important work. This recognition, however, did not exorcise Artaud's existential demons. He spent much of the last part of his life in asylums and died in 1948 (Bermel 1977: 113–19).

Les Maîtres Fous, Jean Rouch.

Once in Paris Artaud was quickly drawn to the magic of the cinema, the subject of many of his early essays, especially during his tenure as director of the *Bureau de Recherches Surrealistes*. Like Robert Desnos, Artaud penned many film scenarios (only one was ever produced). He wrote scenarios not to sell his ideas to producers, but to explore his thoughts about the relationship between films and dreams (Kunezli 1987; Williams 1981). Like other Surrealists, Artaud found an affinity between dreams and the cinema, and his analyses of film, according to Linda Williams (1981), probed this relationship with great sensitivity. Unlike Robert Desnos who unproblematically accepted a link between the experience of dreams and film, Artaud focused upon how film signifies.

In his writings on film Artaud's great enemy is language, for it is language's arbitrary connection of things (referents) to sequences of sound that stifles the human imagination. "What Artaud wanted was a language that would not only *express*, but also—impossibly—be—the very flesh and blood of his thought" (Williams 1981: 20). Artaud saw film as a possible means of escaping the perils of linguistic signification. Williams goes on to suggest a link between Artaud's cinematic theories and Christian Metz's notion of the imaginary signifier.

> The notion of the immediacy of film, of its ability to bypass the usual coded channels of language through a visual short circuit that act "almost intuitively on the brain," is Artaud's attempt to rediscover what he terms the primitive arrangement of things . . . For the film image, unlike an accumulation of words on the page or an enactment of these words in a theater, cannot be pointed to as a thing that is actually *there*. In other words, the film (as Christian Metz has shown, but as the Surrealists had already intuited) is an *imaginary signifier* . . . Briefly, the term refers to the paradoxical fact that, although film is the most perceptual of all the arts and even though its signifier (the play of light and shadow on the screen representing objects of the real world) gives a powerful impression of reality, this impression is only an illusion. (1981: 21–22)

As Artaud recognized, human beings are lulled into accepting the reality of the images in dreams and films; they "misrecognize," following the terminology of Lacan and Williams, the illusion of the image. As a result the scenarios of Artaud and Desnos attempted to construct films that would deconstruct our fundamental relationship to the image. In this way, film could be a means of unveiling the fundamental structure of the unconscious thereby liberating it from the tyranny of language.[2]

Artaud and the Theater of Cruelty

By the time of the publication of André Breton's *Second Surrealist Manifesto* (1929), Artaud had become less enamored of the cinema and its revolutionary possibilities. "Movies in their turn, murdering us with second-hand reproductions which, filtered through machines, cannot unite with our sensibility, have maintained us for ten years in an ineffectual torpor, in which all of our faculties appear to be foundering" (Artaud 1958: 84).

Perhaps Artaud realized that the seductive qualities of the cinema can also create a kind of anesthetized state that promotes inactivity (see Buck-Morss, nd.). Artaud may have recognized that the cinema's immediacy was not immediate enough for his revolutionary program of social transformation.

In time Artaud turned more and more of his attentions to the theater, specifically to his Theater of Cruelty. Considering the impact that Artaud's writings have had on the theory and practice of theater in the Twentieth Century, it is ironic that his great dramatic experiment closed only two weeks after it opened in June of 1935. Like other aspects of Artaud's voluminous work, his writings on the Theater of Cruelty are fragments, jagged pieces of puzzle that never form a coherent whole.

Artaud's early experience in the Parisian theater disillusioned him. He reviled so-called masterpieces. "One of the reasons for the asphyxiating atmosphere in which we live without possible escape or remedy . . . is our respect for what has been written, formulated, or painted, what has been given form" (Artaud 1958: 74). In fact, Artaud felt that the literary staidness of the cerebral arts was socially unhealthy.

> Masterpieces of the past are good for the past: they are not good for us. We have the right to say what has been said and even what has not been said in a way that belongs to us, a way that is immediate and direct, corresponding to present modes of feeling, and understandable to everyone. (Ibid.: 74)

For Artaud, the Theater of Cruelty was the solution to social asphyxiation, for it constituted a space of transformation in which people could be reunited with their life forces, with the poetry that lies beyond the poetic text.[3] More specifically, the Theater of Cruelty

> . . . means a theater difficult and cruel for myself first of all. And on the level of performance, it is not the cruelty we can exercise upon each other by hacking at each other's bodies, carving up our personal anatomies . . . but the much more terrible and necessary cruelty which things can exercise against us. We are not free. And the sky can still fall on our heads. And the theater has been created to teach us that first of all. (Ibid.: 79)

In some respects Artaud yearned for the participatory theater of yore which foregrounded transformative spectacle. According to Artaud, that idea of theater had long been lost. He traced this loss to Shakespeare and Racine and the advent of psychological theater, which separates the audience from the immediacy of "violent" activity. The advent of the cinema compounded this loss.

It is clear from Artaud's comments about myth, spectacle and "theatrical violence" that his vision for the Theater of Cruelty was inspired by pre-theatrical rituals in which powerful symbols were employed for therapeutic ends. In his first manifesto on the Theater of Cruelty (1933), Artaud wrote:

> But by an altogether Oriental means of expression, this objective and concrete language of the theater can fascinate and ensnare the organs. It flows into the sensibility. Abandoning Occidental uses of speech, it turns words into incantation. It extends the voice. It utilizes the vibrations and qualities of voice. It wildly tramples rhythms underfoot. It pile-drives sounds. It seeks to exalt, to benumb, to charm, to arrest the sensibility. It liberates a new lyricism of gesture which, by its precipitation or its amplitude in the air, ends by surpassing the lyricism of words. It ultimately breaks away from the intellectual subjugation of language, by conveying the sense of a new and deeper intellectuality which hides itself beneath gestures and signs, raised to the dignity of particular exorcisms. (Ibid.: 91)

Although Artaud disassociated himself from the Surrealists in the late 1920s, the influence of Surrealism twists its way through his writing: the suspicion of logic, language and rationality; the use of the arts to liberate the power of human vitality from the repressed unconscious; the promotion of social revolution; the juxtaposition of "primitive" and "civilized" imagery to create transformative poetry (see Breton 1929; Lippard 1970; Balakian 1986; Clifford 1988; and Richman 1990).

Artaud's writings on the Theater of Cruelty also evoke spirit possession rituals. Albert Bermel, an Artaud critic, suggests that the rites associated with the Corybantes, an early Greek secret society, are quite similar to those proposed for the Theater of Cruelty. Through music and dance the Corybantes initiates were whipped into a frenzy, a crazed state that was

Jaguar, Jean Rouch.

expiated through purification rituals, "an experience not dissimilar in kind to the one Artaud seems to have had in mind" (Bermel 1977: 40).

Bermel is not the only scholar to suggest links between ritual and theater. Gilbert Rouget (1980) argues that classical Greek theater evolved from the Corybantes, which he calls a possession cult. Other French scholars have proposed links among possession, poetry and theater (Schaeffner 1965; Leiris 1958; Gibbal 1988). The Artaudian scenario outlined for the Theater of Cruelty also bears striking resemblance to many West African possession rituals, including those practiced by the Songhay in the Republic of Niger—the subjects of most of Jean Rouch's films.[4]

Rouch and the Cinema of Cruelty

It is clear that Artaud believed that the Theater of Cruelty could not be transferred from stage to screen. Although he was fascinated by the cinema in his earlier writings, his interests gradually gravitated toward the more ritualized framework of the theater. Given Artaud's dispositions, is a cinema of cruelty possible? Like the sets and costumes of Artaud's shortlived Theater of Cruelty, the images of the great Surrealist films wage war against culturally conditioned perception. Films like *Un chien andoulou* (1929) and *L'âge d'or* (1930) play with generally recognized patterns of perception; namely, the illusion that that which is patently unreal (the images of the cinema) is, in fact, real. Surrealist film, following the argument of Linda Williams (1981), exposes the illusion—some would say, delusion—of the perceptual processing of imaginary signifiers. Artaud's scenarios, in fact, dwell on themes that expose the "misrecognition" of the cinematic image. In this sense, Surrealist film meets some of the criteria of Artaud's Theater of Cruelty. But are these films transformative? Do they alter behavior? Do they purify the spirit? Do they release pent-up vitality?

Although the cinema can seduce us into a highly personalized but relatively inactive dreamlike states, its culturally coded images can at the same time trigger anger, shame, sexual excitement, revulsion, and horror. Artaud wanted to transform his audiences by tapping their unconscious through the visceral presence of sound and image, flesh and blood. He wanted to revert to what André Schaeffner (1965) called the "pre-theater," a ritualized arena of personal transformation, a project for a ritualized stage.

Although Jean Rouch has concentrated his artistic efforts exclusively on the cinema, his path shares much with that of Artaud. Like Artaud, he was very much influenced by Surrealism. In his various interviews, both published and broadcast, he often pays homage to the Surrealists. When Rouch witnessed his first possession ceremony among the Songhay of Niger in 1942, it evoked for him the writings of Breton and the poems of Eluard (Echard and Rouch 1988; Stoller 1992). Perhaps the vitality of Songhay possession rituals, a virtual pre-theater—compelled Rouch to make "cruel" films. In some of his films, especially those he refers to as "ethno-fiction," Rouch pursues an Artaudian path. Rouch always tells a story in his films, but the narratives in these films are secondary to his philosophical intent. In these films Rouch wants to transform his viewers. He wants to challenge their cultural assumptions. He wants the audience —still mostly European and North American—to confront its ethnocentrism, its repressed racism, its latent primitivism.

La Pyramide Humaine, Jean Rouch.

Anyone who has been assailed by the brutal images of *Les Maîtres Fous* has experienced Rouch's cinema—of Cruelty. In *Les Maîtres Fous*, "Rouch's path is correct not only because he doesn't ignore colonialism, but because leaving constantly his own environs and exhibiting nature through the massive effects she produces elsewhere, it at no time allows the spectator to remain indifferent, but compels him in some way if not to take a position, at least to change" (Bensmaia quoted in Predal 1982: 55). Rouch's *Les Maîtres Fous* evokes the meaning of decolonization: namely, that European decolonization must begin with individual decolonization—the decolonization of a person's thinking, the decolonization of a person's "self." Such an effect is clearly an element of a Cinema of Cruelty, a cinema that uses humor as well as unsettling juxtapositions to jolt the audience.

Jaguar

Jaguar is not an insufferably "cruel" film; rather, it is infused with what Italo Calvino once called the brilliance of "lightness." I like to call *Jaguar*, "*Tristes Tropiques*, African style"—with a very significant twist. Like *Tristes Tropiques* and other works in the picaresque tradition, *Jaguar* is a tale of adventure, a story of initiation to the wonders of other worlds and other peoples. The

La Pyramide Humaine, Jean Rouch.

protagonists, Damoré, un petit bandit, Lam, a Fulani shepherd, and Illo, a Niger River fisherman, learn a great deal from their adventures in the colonial Gold Coast. The difference between *Tristes Tropiques* and *Jaguar* is an important one. We expect Claude Lévi-Strauss to be enlightened by his voyage to Brazil. But do we expect the same for three young Nigeriens from Ayoru? Can Others embark on philosophical journeys of Enlightenment? In *Jaguar*, Rouch forces us to confront a wide array of colonialist assumptions: that in their "backwardness" all Africans are alike; that in their "backwardness" Africans have no sense of the wanderlust; that in their "backwardness" Africans do not extract wisdom from their journeys. With great humor, *Jaguar* shatters our expectations. Along their journey to the colonial Gold Coast, the Others (Damoré, Lam and Illo) confront their own Others: the Gurmantche who file their teeth into sharp points and drink millet beer; the Somba who eat dogs and shun clothing. At the Somba market Damoré says to Lam:

> "Mais, il sont complement nus, mon vieux."
> "Complètement," says Lam.

For Lam, Illo and Damoré such a corporeal display is unthinkable. They have encountered the "primitive's primitive," thus affirming Montaigne's affirmation that "each man calls barbarism whatever is not his own practice; for indeed, it seems we have no other test of truth and reason than the example and pattern of opinions and customs of the country we live in . . ." (1948: 152). Later in *Jaguar*, Damoré becomes very "jaguar," (with it),

Lam becomes a small time entrepreneur (*nyama izo*—the children of disorder), and Illo toils as a laborer in the port of Accra. At all junctures in the film, difference is underscored: distinctions are made between northerners and southerners, Christians and Muslims, traditionalists and moderns. In *Jaguar*, Africa is not a continent of sameness; it is rather a land of finite distinctions, a space for the politics of difference. Commenting critically on Kwame Nkruma and his cronies, Damoré says:

"Ils sont bien nourris, ceux-la." (These ones are well nourished.)

A political commentary of visionary proportions, for the leaders of newly independent Africa would become very well nourished, indeed—fed by the political systems they created.

And so in *Jaguar*, Africa emerges from the shadows of sameness and is cast into the swift cross-currents of political fragmentation. Rouch's protagonists, like Susan Sontag's Lévi-Strauss, are heros—adventurers in a heterogenous Africa who confront their own primitives as well as the stormy politics of their epoch. As such, these wise and articulate "Others" defy our expectations and make us ponder our own categories of sameness and difference, civilized and primitive. In this way, Rouch uses *Jaguar* to critically juxtapose Europe and Africa.

Petit à Petit, Jean Rouch.

Like the Artaudian wanderer, Rouch's "fictional" wanderers in *Jaguar* challenge the cultural assumptions of viewers, forcing them to confront the centuries-old legacy of European ethnocentrism and racism. *Jaguar* makes us laugh as it subverts the primitivist imagery of Africa. True to a cinema of cruelty, *Jaguar* compels viewers to decolonize their thinking, their "selves."

Moi, un Noir

To make *Jaguar*, Rouch employed his friends as actors. Although Damoré, Lam, and Illo acted well in the film, they had never been migrants. While he was editing *Jaguar*, Rouch asked Oumarou Ganda to attend a screening. Ganda, who *had* been a migrant in Abidjan, challenged Rouch to make a film about real migrants like himself. Rouch took up Ganda's challenge which resulted in *Moi, un Noir*, one of the first films, ethnographic or otherwise, that depicted the pathos of life in changing Africa. In the film, we follow Ganda and his compatriots as they work as dockers in Abidjan's port. We see how hard they work, how little they are paid, and how they are belittled as human beings. We see how work and life steal from them the last vestiges of their dignity. In this space of deprivation and demoralization, we are touched by Oumarou Ganda's fantasies. We are saddened by his disappointments. We are outraged by his suffering. We hear his sad voice. In this film one of the silent ones tells his sad tale. Oumarou Ganda's story enables us to see how the discourse of colonialism and racism disintegrates the human spirit. Are not the dreams of Oumarou Ganda the dreams of the oppressed—the hope against all hopes that someday . . . ?

Like *Jaguar, Moi, un Noir* is a film that obliterates the boundaries between fact and fiction, documentary and story, observation and participation, objectivity and subjectivity. Rouch calls *Moi, un noir* and *Jaguar* works of "ethno-fiction," works in which the "fiction" is based upon longterm ethnographic research. In this way, both *Jaguar* and *Moi, un Noir* are biting critiques of the staid academicism that pervades the university in Europe and North America. Imprisoned by eighteenth century intellectualist assumptions in a postcolonial epoch, the academy was and is ill-equipped to deal with the complexities of the changing world. These films, which are also indictments of European modernity, remind us that in a world in which expectations are continuously subverted, the sky, to paraphrase Artaud, can suddenly fall down on our heads. The intent of these films is clearly political; through the subversion of "received" categories, they challenge us to confront our own ugliness—an exercise in Artuadian "cruelty."

La Pyramide Humaine

Rouch's early critique of European modernity does not end with *Moi un Noir*. As Rouch is fond of saying, "one film gives birth to another." *Moi, un Noir* prompted Rouch to make another film set in Abidjan—*La Pyramide Humaine*. In this film, the title of which is taken

Petit à Petit, Jean Rouch.

Petit à Petit, Jean Rouch.

from one of Paul Eluard's Surrealist poems, Rouch explores the relations between French and African students at an Abidjan high school. Here viewers observe the divergent lives of impoverished African and affluent European students. Some of the African students hate the Europeans; some of the European students are unabashedly racist. The students argue about colonialism and racism. The debate intensifies when a new female student from Paris begins to date an African. This social act, which taps the fear of interracial sexuality, unleashes a torrent of emotion and prejudice on both sides. While *Moi, un Noir* focused upon the plight of African migratory workers, *La Pyramide Humaine* sets its sights on the sexuality of interracial relations in a colonial state—a volatile topic in 1959. Not surprisingly, the film was banned in most of Francophone Africa. And yet, even today, it speaks eloquently to issues of the repressed fear of interracial sex and of liberal duplicity and racism in Europe and North America.

   La Pyramide Humaine is also very conscious of its own construction. Rouch qua filmmaker appears in several sequences of the film, using his presence to carefully weave a subplot through the text. The main story involves the confrontation of two worlds, two sets of prejudices; it is about how confrontation can be transformative. The subplot recounts how the making of the film transformed the lives of the actors. The subplot, then, subverts the specious boundary between fact and fiction and shows how film constructs and transforms, how film is "cruel" in the Artaudian sense. Shot in color, this film is "cruel," indeed, for it impels viewers to acknowledge in black and white their culturally conditioned sexual fears and fantasies.

Petit à Petit

"One film gives birth to another." *Moi, un Noir* gave birth to *La Pyramide Humaine*, which gave birth to Rouch's most famous work, *Chronique d'un Été*, a film about Rouch's own "tribe," les Français. In 1960 how did the French deal with difference—with Jews, Arabs, and Africans? The film, which was politically provocative, is considered a landmark in the history of the cinema for two reasons: 1) it is among the first works filmed in synchronous sound; and 2) it launched the Nouvelle Vague in French cinema. In the 1960s Rouch continued to film in Africa. He completed *The Lion Hunters* in 1964, and began to film the magnificent Sigui ceremonies of the Dogon of Mali in 1967.[5] But he wanted to make yet another film in France and decided on Jaguar II, which he called *Petit à Petit*, after the corporation formed by Damoré, Lam and Illo in the original *Jaguar*.

The scenario of *Petit à Petit* focuses upon two entrepreneurs, Damoré and Lam, who want to build a luxury hotel in Niamey, Niger, which would cater exclusively to Europeans. But Damoré and Lam know nothing about Europeans. Like a good anthropologist, Damoré decides to travel to Paris to study the lifeways of the French tribe: to observe and measure them. How else would they know how to design the hotel's interiors? How else would they know how to order sofas and beds of the correct dimensions? And so Damoré flies to Paris, where he embarks on his study. But Lam becomes so worried about the impact of France on Damore's being, he decides to join his friend in Paris. With great humor, Rouch tells the story of Damoré and Lam's Parisian experience. As in *Jaguar*, Damoré and Lam turn the tables of our expectations. Europeans are usually the filmmakers, not the filmed. Europeans are usually the observers, not the observed.

Among the most memorable scenes occurs on the Place Trocadero, between La Musée de l'Homme and the Cinemathèque Française, a space filled with academic significance. It is winter and Damoré, posing as a doctoral student, approaches several French people armed with anthropometric calipers.

"Excuse me sir," he says to an elderly gentleman, "I am student from Africa working on my thesis at the university. Would you permit me to measure you?" With the gentleman's willing consent, Damoré measures his skull, his neck, his shoulders, his chest and waist. Damoré then approaches a young woman, and again makes his request. He measures her dimensions and then asks:

> "Excusez-moi, mademoiselle, mais est-ce que je pourrais voir vos dents?"
> The woman opens her mouth.
> "Ah oui. Tres bien. Merci, mademoiselle."

There is much, much more to this film, but I describe this scene to underscore Rouch's ongoing contempt of the academy's conservatism, its uneasiness with innovation and

Petit à Petit, Jean Rouch.

change. Throughout his films Rouch casts aspersions on what he calls "academic imperialism." Such a theme blazes a "cruel" trail for scholars who believe in the superiority of Reason.

And so, Rouch's films of ethno-fiction cut to the flesh and blood of European colonialist being. His films compel us to reflect upon our latent racism, our repressed sexuality, the taken-for-granted assumptions of our intellectual heritage. In so doing, Rouch's films expose the centrality of power relations to our dreams, thoughts and actions. Such exposure is a key ingredient to a cinema of cruelty.

The Poet's Path

During my research on Rouch's *oeuvre* I wondered why the philosophical aspects of his work—embodied in filmic images—are underappreciated in Europe and unknown in North America. Why is it that until recently contemporary critics in European and North America rarely, if ever, considered the pioneering work of Rouch? The answer, I think, is that most critics, philosophers and anthropologists are still part of the academy that Rouch so skillfully reproaches for its conservatism. Academics are still bound to reason, to words, to plain style. Scholars seek the discursive and eschew the figurative. Images are transformed into inscriptions that form a coherent discourse. Poetry and what Merleau-Ponty called "the indirect language" are out-of-academic bounds.

More than a generation ago Jean Rouch understood the transformative power of poetry. Many of his films are poetic in the sense recently invoked by Trinh T. Minh-ha (1992: 86)

> For the nature of poetry is to offer meaning in such a way that it can never end with what is said or shown, destabilizing thereby the speaking subject and exposing the fiction of all rationalization . . . So to avoid merely falling into this pervasive world of the stereotyped and the clichéd, filmmaking has all to gain when conceived as a performance that engages as well as questions (its own) language . . . However . . . poetic practice can be 'difficult' to a number of viewers, because in mainstream films and media our ability to play with meanings other than the literal ones that pervade our visual and aural environments is rarely solicited.

Literalness is the curse of the academy, and yet the strong poetic undercurrents of a few films and ethnographies somehow survive.

Because of their literalness, academics are often the last people to stumble upon innovation. Such is the case in anthropology—visual or otherwise. One of my philosopher friends admitted that professional philosophers are 50 years behind the times. For inspiration, he advised me, look to the arts. Indeed, for most of us the epistemology of plain style means that photography and film are, to use Jake Homiak's phrase, "images on the edge of the text" (1991). In Rouch's case, this means that his films are most often judged in terms of technological innovation rather than philosophical lyricism.

A generation before the "experimental moment" in anthropology, scores of filmmakers, artists and poets evoked many of the themes that define the condition of postmodernity: the pathos of social fragmentation, the recognition of the impact of expanding global economies, the cultural construction of racism, the legacy of academic imperialism, the quandaries of self-referentiality, the rewards of implicated participation, the acknowledgment of heteroglossia, the permeability of categorical boundaries (fact/fiction//objectivity/subjectivity). In one of his many interviews Rouch said:

> For me, as an ethnographer and filmmaker, there is almost no boundary between documentary film and films of fiction. The cinema, the art of the double, is already a transition from the real world to the imaginary world, and ethnography, the science of

thought systems of others, is a permanent crossing point from one conceptual universe to another; acrobatic gymnastics where losing one's footing is the least of the risks. (Rouch 1978)

Perhaps the way to the future of anthropology is to follow Rouch's "cruel" path and confront the sometimes inspiring, sometimes fearsome world of incertitude.

The sky is lower than we think. Who knows when it will crash down on our heads?

P. Stoller

Notes

1. This scenario is reproduced from Echard and Rouch (1988).

2. Williams's semiotic and psychoanalytic analysis of Surrealist film is an important contribution. Contrary to the uncritical analysis of the Surrealism and the cinema that preceded her work, Williams suggests that Surrealist films "are about the signifying processes of desire in the human subject." Her careful frame by frame analysis of *Un chien andalou* is revelatory and demonstrates how Surrealist filmmakers used formal cinematic devices to promote their revolutionary ends.

3. Tyler (1987) makes a similar point in his analysis of Paul Friedrich's poetry, some 50 years after the initial publication of Artaud's manifesto.

4. Influenced by Aristotle's writings on trance in *The Politics*, a group of French scholars consider possession as a kind of cultural theater (see Schaeffner 1965, Leiris 1958, and Rouget 1980). This hypothesis is a highly attractive one, but my own suspicion is that while spirit possession is doubtless a dramatic form, one cannot reduce such a complex phenomenon to "drama" or "theater" (See Stoller 1989). The great majority of Rouch's films are about Songhay possession ceremonies, a ritual that has fascinated him since 1942 when he witnessed his first ceremony in Gangell, Niger.

5. For a detailed analysis of Rouch's Sigui films and their relation to the Dogon origin myth, see Stoller 1992.

References

Artaud, Antonin. 1958. *The Theatre and Its Double*. Trans. Mary Caroline Richards. New York: Grove Press.
————. 1956. *Antonin Artaud: Oeuvres Completes*. Paris: Gallimard.
Balakian, Anna. 1986. *Surrealism*. Chicago: University of Chicago Press.
Bermel, Albert. 1977. *Artaud's Theatre of Cruelty*. New York: Taplinger Publishing Company.
Breton, André. 1929. *Manifestes du Surrealisme*. Paris: Kra.
Buck-Morss, Susan. n.d. "The Cinema Screen as Prosthesis of Perception: A Historical Account." A paper read at the Annual Meetings of the American Anthropological Association, Chicago, Illinois, November 17–21, 1991.
Clifford, James. 1988. *The Predicament of Culture*. Cambridge, Mass.: Harvard University Press.
Echard, Nicole and Jean Rouch. 1988. "Entretien avec Jean Rouch. À Voix Nu. Entretien d'hier à Aujourd'hui." Ten-hour discussion broadcast in July of 1988 on France Culture.
Gibbal, Jean-Marie. 1988. *Les Genies du Fleuve*. Paris: Presses de la Renaissance.
Homiak, John. 1991. "Images on the Edge of the Text." Forthcoming in *Wide Angle*.
Kuenzli, Rudolph, ed. 1987. *Dada and Surrealist Film*. New York: Willis, Locker and Owens.
Leiris, Michel. 1980. *La Possession et ses Aspects Theatraux Chez les Ethiopiens de Gondar*. Paris: Le Sycomore.
Lévi-Strauss, Claude. 1955. *Tristes Tropiques*. Paris: Plon.
Lippard, Lucy, ed. 1970. *Surrealists on Art*. Englewoods Cliffs, N.J.: Prentice Hall.
Montaigne, Michel de. 1948. *The Complete Essays of Montaigne*. Trans. Donald Frame. Palo Alto,CA: Stanford University Press.
Predal, Rene, ed. 1982. "Jean Rouch, un griot Gallois." Special issue of *CinemAction* 17. Paris: Harmattan.
Richman, Michelle. 1990. "Anthropology and Modernism in France: From Durkheim to the College de Sociologie." In *Modernist Anthropology*, ed. Mark Manganaro, 183–215. Princeton: Princeton University Press.
Rouget, Gilbert. 1980. *La Musique et la Trance*. Paris: Gallimard.
Schaeffner, André. 1965. "Rituel et Pre-Theatre." In *Histoire des Spectacles*, 21–54. Paris: Gallimard.
Stoller, Paul. 1989. *Fusion of the Worlds: An Ethnography of Possession Among the Songhay of Niger*. Chicago: University of Chicago Press.
————. 1992. *The Cinematic Griot: The Ethnography of Jean Rouch*. Chicago: University of Chicago Press.

Trinh, T. Minh-ha and Nancy Chen. 1992. "Speaking Nearby: A Conversation with Trinh T. Minh-ha." *Visual Anthropology Review* 8 (1): 82–91.

Tyler, Stephen. 1987. *The Unspeakable: Discourse, Dialogue, and Rhetoric in the Post-Modern World*. Madison: University of Wisconsin Press.

Filmography

Buñuel, Luis and Salvador Dalí. 1929. *Un chien andalou*. Paris.

Buñuel, Luis. 1931. *L'age d'or*. Paris.

Rouch, Jean. 1949. *Les Magiciens de Wanzerbe*. Paris: Comite des Films Ethnographiques (CFE).

———. 1955. *Les Maîtres Fous*. Paris: Films de la Pleiade.

———. 1957. *Moi, un Noir*. Paris: Films de la Pleiade.

———. 1959. *La Pyramide Humaine*. Paris: Films de la Pleiade.

———. 1960. *Chronique d'un Été*. Paris: Films de la Pleiade.

———. 1964. *The Lion Hunters*. Paris: Films de la Pleiade.

———. 1967. *Jaguar*. Paris: Films de la Pleiade.

———. 1969. *Petit à Petit*. Paris: Films de la Pleiade.

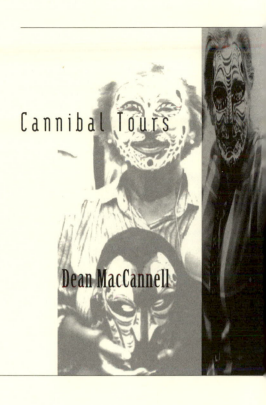

Cannibal Tours

Dean MacCannell

DENNIS O'ROURKE'S *CANNIBAL TOURS* IS THE LATEST OF HIS DOCUMENTARY FILMS ON Pacific peoples, following his *Yumi Yet* (1976), *Ileksen* (1978), *Yap . . . How Did They Know We'd Like TV?* (1980), *Shark Callers of Kontu* (1982), *Couldn't Be Fairer* (1984), and *Half Life* (1986). The narrative structure of the film is unremarkable. A group of Western Europeans and North Americans, by appearance somewhat wealthier than "average" international tourists, travel up the Sepik river in Papua New Guinea in an ultra-modern, air-conditioned luxury liner, and up tributaries in smaller motor launches, stopping at villages along the way to take photographs and buy native handicrafts. The travelogue is inter-cut with ethnographic still photographs and with "talking head" interviews of both tourists and New Guineans who try to answer questions about the reasons for tourism and its effects on the local peoples. The background soundtrack contains occasional shortwave messages from the wider world, a Mozart string quartet, and an Iatmul flute concerto. O'Rourke (1987) says of his own film:

> "Cannibal Tours" is two journeys. The first is that depicted—rich and bourgeois tourists on a luxury cruise up the mysterious Sepik River, in the jungles of Papua New Guinea . . . the packaged version of a "heart of darkness." The second journey (the real text of the film) is a metaphysical one. It is an attempt to discover the place of 'the Other' in the popular imagination. [Ellipsis in the original.]

The film makes it painfully evident—the choice of the Sepik region drives the point home with precision—that this primitive "Other" no longer exists. What remains of the primitive world are ex-primitives, recently acculturated peoples lost in the industrial world, and another kind of ex-primitive, still going under the label "primitive," a kind of performative "primitive."

This loss and transformation can be linked historically and conceptually to the shift from the *modern* to the *postmodern*. During the first slow phase of the globalization of culture, colonialism and industrialization, eventually tourism and modernization, modernity, the modern—during this phase the energy, drive and libido for the globalization of culture came from Western European and North European cultures. But today, the older centers of modernity are demanding a return on their investments, an implosive construction of primitivism (and every other "ism") in a postmodern pastiche that might be called "globality."

Postmodernity is itself a symptom of a need to suppress bad memories of Auschwitz, Hiroshima and the other genocides on which modernity was built. Of course it is not possible to repress the past without denying the future. Thus the central drive of postmodernity is to stop history in its tracks. One finds, even within critical reflections on the postmodern, a strange glee over the failed revolutionary potential of the western working class and all the various socialisms.

The opening scenes of *Cannibal Tours* neatly frame several postmodern figures. A voiceover taken from Radio Moscow world service announces a Paul Simon rock concert in Lenin Auditorium. But the film's postmodern figure *par excellence*, is a self-congratulating German tourist who comes as close as anyone in the film to being its central character. He compulsively records his travel experiences on film while speaking into a handheld tape recorder: "Now we see what remains of a house where cannibalism was practiced. Only the posts remain." His age is ambiguous. He might be old enough to have fought in World War II, a suspicion not allayed by his attire, which is designer re-issue of African campaign stuff. He explains to O'Rourke's camera, "Yes I have been to Lebanon, Iran, India, Thailand, Burma, China, Japan, the Philippines, Indonesia, the Pacific Islands, Australia two times, once to New Zealand, South Africa, Rhodesia, all of South America . . . I liked Chile. Next year, Middle America and Panama." He appears in the film as someone under a biblical curse to expiate the sins (or would it be the failures?) of National Socialism, and also to displace certain memories. He goes where the German army was not able to go, expressing a kind of laid back contentment when he encounters a fascist regime: "I liked Chile. Next year Middle America . . ." Only the United States is unmentioned in his recounting of his itineraries. He asks his Iatmul guide, "where have they killed the people. Right here. People were killed here? [He pats the stone for emphasis.] Now I need a photograph for the memory."

The Economics of Tourist/Recent Ex-primitive Interaction

The little reliably obtained ethnographic evidence we now have, tends to confirm a central theme of *Cannibal Tours*: that the relations between tourists and recent ex-primitives are framed in a somewhat forced, stereotypical commercial exploitation model characterized by bad faith and petty suspicion on both sides. Ex-primitives often express

Cannibal Tours, Dennis O'Rourke.

their belief that the only difference between themselves and North Americans or Europeans is money. The German in Cannibal Tours, responding to what was supposed to have been a high level question from the film-maker about commercial exchanges spoiling the New Guineans, "agrees" that "these people do not know the value of money," but the workmanship "often justifies" the prices they ask. In short, he thinks it is he, not the New Guineans, who is being exploited. He is doing them a favor by not paying the asking price— he simultaneously gives them a lesson in commercial realism and, by withholding his capital, he helps delay their entry into the modern world. He thinks their eventual modernization is inevitable, but they would benefit from a period of delay. The dominant view of white Europeans and North Americans expressed by recent ex-primitives is that they exhibit an unimaginable combination of qualities: specifically, they are rich tightwads, boorish, obsessed by consumerism, suffering from collectomania. The Sioux Indians call whiteman *wasicum* or "fat taker." This arrangement can devolve into hatred. Laureen Waukau, a Menonimee Indian told Stan Steiner:

> Just recently I realized that I hate whites. When the tourist buses come through and they come in here and stare at me, that's when I hate them. They call me "Injun." Like on television. It's a big joke to them. You a "drunken Injun," they say . . . I hate it.

And, of course, it should not go unremarked that *intention* in these exchanges does not alter the outcomes. The tourist who calls an Indian "Injun" means to insult, but the well-intended tourist on the same bus is no less insulting. Steiner describes an encounter between Waukau and a tourist:

> One lady gently touched the young girl's wrist. "Dear, are you a real Indian?" she asked. "I hope you don't mind my asking. But you look so American." (Both incidents are reported in D. Evans-Pritchard, 1989: 97.)

The commercialization of the touristic encounter extends to the point of commodification not merely of the handicrafts and the photographic image, but to the person of the ex-primitive. Southwest American Indians complain that tourists have attempted to pat up their hair and arrange their clothing before photographing them, and that they receive unwanted offers from tourists to buy the jewelry or the clothing they are actually wearing.

As degenerate as these exchanges might at first appear, there is no problem here, really, at least not from the standpoint of existing social conventions. All these behaviors are recognizably boorish, so the "problem" as represented is entirely correctable by available means: counseling ("don't use ethnic slurs"); education ("Indians were the original Americans"); etiquette ("don't be condescending in conversation," "don't violate another's person or privacy," "don't comment on how 'American' they appear"); etc. With a bit of decency and sound advice these "problems," including their New Guinea equivalents, would go away.

Or would they? I think not. Because I detect in all these reports on exchanges between tourists and others a certain mutual complicity, a co-production of a pseudo-conflict to obscure something deeper and more serious: namely, that the encounter between tourist and "other" is the scene of a shared utopian vision of profit without exploitation, logically the final goal of a kind of cannibal economics shared by ex-primitives and postmoderns alike. The desire for profit without exploitation runs so strong, like that for "true love," even intellectuals can trick themselves into finding it where it does not exist, where, in my view, it can never exist.

The touristic ideal of the "primitive" is that of a magical resource that can be used without actually possessing or diminishing it. Within tourism, the "primitive" occupies a position not unlike that of the libido or the death drive in psychoanalysis, or the simple-minded working class of National Socialism which was supposed to have derived an ultimate kind of fulfillment in its labor for the Fatherland. Or the physicist's dream of room temperature superconductivity and table top fusion. These are all post-capitalist moral fantasies based on a desire to deny the relationship between profit and exploitation. Let's pretend that we can get something for nothing. The fable is as follows: The return on the tour of headhunters and cannibals is to make the tourist a real hero of alterity. It is his coming into contact with and experience of the primitive which gives him his status. But this has not cost the primitives anything. Indeed, they too, may have gained from it. Taking someone's picture doesn't cost them anything, not in any Western commercial sense, yet the picture has value. The picture has no value for the primitive, yet the tourist pays for the right to take pictures. The "primitive" receives something for nothing, and benefits beyond this. Doesn't the fame of certain primitives, and even respect for them, actually increase when the tourist carries their pictures back to the west? It seems to be the most perfect realization so far of the capitalist economists' dream of *everyone* getting richer together.

Of course this is impossible. If a profit has been made, some bit of nature has been used up or some individuals have worked so that others might gain. It is easy enough to see how the advanced techniques of modern statecraft and stagecraft, recently merged into one, permit the destruction of nature and the alienation of work to be hidden from view. But how are they hidden from consciousness? The only way is by negative education, specifically the suppression of an understanding of exchange within exchange relations. In the relation between tourists and primitives, this pretense transforms the literally propertyless state of primitives into a property. Tourism has managed (and this is its special genius in the family of human institutions) to put a value on propertylessness itself. "Look, there are no fences around their fields. That's worth a picture!" "They work only for their own subsistence. That's worth reporting back to our overly commercial society at home!"

And for their part, the performative primitives, now ex-primitives, have devised a rhetoric surrounding money that perfectly complements the postmodern dream of profit without exploitation. They deny the economic importance of their economic exchanges. They will explain that they are exploited absolutely in their merely economic dealings with tourists, but also as far as they are concerned, at the level of symbolic values, these exchanges count for nothing. By the ex-primitives' own account, their economic dealings with tourists are spiritually vacuous and economically trivial, producing little more exchange than what is needed to buy trousers.[1] Their problem is not petty exploitation by tourists. Rather it is getting money and having it. The New Guineans in *Cannibal Tours* repeat to the point that it becomes a kind of litany, their position that money is simply "had" and "gotten," never *earned* and spent, and are quick to guard against the formation of any idea that the tourists, especially, earned their money. An old admitted ex-cannibal speaks to the camera about the tourists: "These are very wealthy people. They got their money, I know not where, perhaps their parents earned it and gave it to them, perhaps their governments give it to them." Clearly, he is thinking not in terms of earnings but capital. Sounding more like Donald Trump than a Western proletarian, the old warrior complains, "I have no way of persuading them to give me money." From an ethnological standpoint, this is not especially surprising coming from a people whose basic unit of money, their equivalent to the American dollar or the British pound, is the *tautau*, *nassa*, or *maij*, a string of shells, which at the time of first European contact, was estimated by Mrs. Hingston Quiggin (1949: 172 ff.) to be worth the value of between two and ten months of labor. There is a deeply ironic movement of the camera in the scene in *Cannibal Tours* in which a New Guinea woman complains with bitter eloquence that "white men got money . . . you have all the money." For an instant, the camera drops down to the blanket in front of her showing what she is selling: it is *maij*, strings of shell money. She knows herself to be positioned like the Western banker, trading in currencies under enormously unfavorable exchange conditions. The tourists think they are buying beads.

In sum, there is so much mutual complicity in the overall definition of the interaction between the postmodern tourist and the ex-primitive that the system comes close to producing the impossible economic ideal. The performing primitives claim to be exploited, but in so doing they take great care not to develop this claim to the point where their value as "primitive" attraction is diminished. In short, they must appear as almost noble savages, authentic except for a few changes forced on them by others: they sell beads, they do not trade in currencies. They gain sympathy from the tourist based on the conditions of their relationship to the tourist. And the entire arrangement almost works. O'Rourke asks a young man on camera how it feels to have his picture taken, and points out that as he (O'Rourke) takes his picture, one of "them," (a woman tourist) has also come up behind to take yet another picture. "One of them is looking at you now." The woman tourist gets her shot and awkwardly steps into O'Rourke's frame sidewise to give the young man some money for letting himself be photographed. O'Rourke comments dryly, "It's hard to make a dollar." We can feel sympathy, but only to the point of considering the working conditions of a steel worker in a foundry, an agricultural worker in the fields of California, or even a model in Manhattan who is also paid to have her picture taken, but under conditions of somewhat greater performative demand.

Performances

The conditions of the meeting of tourists and ex-primitives are such that one predictably finds hatred, sullen silence, freezing out. Deirdre Evans-Pritchard (1989: 98) reports that sometimes this sullenness is heartfelt and at other times it may be performed as a way of humoring the tourist. Southwest American Indian males hanging out in a public place and

D.
MacCannell

joking around with each other, for example, have been known to adopt a frozen, silent, withdrawn stance on the approach of tourists, then they break back into a joking mode as soon as the tourist is gone, their jocularity redoubled by their mutual understanding that the tourists accepted their "hostile Indian" act. This is only one of the ways that ex-primitives knowingly overdose tourists with unwanted pseudo-authenticity.[2]

The micro-sociology of the arrangement between tourists and ex-primitives reveals an interesting balancing mechanism. Even if the tourists bring greater wealth and worldly sophistication to the encounter, the ex-primitive brings more experience in dealing with tourists. Most tourists do not repeatedly return to a specific site; they go on to new experiences. But ex-primitives who have made a business of tourism deal with tourists on a daily basis and soon become expert on the full range of touristic appearances and behavior. I have personally been picked out of a crowded Mexican market by a vendor who called me over to look at his wares, "Ola, professor!" Jill Sweet (1989) reports on a Zuni Pueblo four-part typology of tourists labeled by them as: (1) New Yorker or East Coast type, (2) Texan type, (3) Hippie type, and (4) "Save-the-whale" type. In the Zuni typology as reported by Sweet, "Texas types" wear cowboy boots and drive Cadillacs. "Hippies" are represented as wearing tie-die T-shirts, attempting uninvited to join in the Indian's dances, and as incessantly asking questions about peyote and mescal, etc. All of these figures are beginning to appear in Indian dance routines, sometimes in the dances they do for tourists. The "save-the-whale" tourist dancer is played by an Indian wearing hiking boots, tan shorts, a T-shirt with a message, and a pair of binoculars carved out of a block of wood that he uses to study the Indians. The "East Coast" tourist is represented as a woman played by a male Indian wearing high heels, wig, dress, mink coat, dime store jewelry, clutch purse, and pillbox hat. As "she" awkwardly approaches the dance ground, she stops to coo and cluck over the small Indian children along the way. In their tourist routines, the Zuni represent all types of tourists as disappointed that they (the Zuni) do not fit the stereotype of plains Indians who hunt buffalo and live in tipis.

The more elaborated performances that occur in the relations between tourists and ex-primitives assume what are according to Jameson (1984) characteristically postmodern dramatic forms: parody, satire, lampooning, and burlesque. All these forms involve identification, imitation, emulation, impersonation, to make a point. No matter how negative this point might at first seem to be, even if it might hurt a bit, it is always ultimately positive, because it suggests that relations could be improved if we pay more attention to our effects on others. Parody builds solidarity in the group that stages it and potentially raises the consciousness of an audience that is the butt of it. But to accomplish this the parodist must take risks. Intercultural burlesque is necessarily structurally similar to efforts on the part of individuals from stigmatized minority groups to emulate the appearances and behaviors of representatives of the dominant culture. So any dramatically well-constructed parody that misses its mark, even slightly, becomes self-parody, just as postmodern architecture always risks losing its ironic referentiality and simply becoming tacky junk, not a parodic "comment" on tacky junk. It may well be insecurity in this regard that drives performers of tourist routines to cast their burlesque in such broad terms: to cause an Indian male to represent a tourist woman, etc. A Japanese-American student of mine recently remarked to me that some of her friends lighten their hair and wear blue contact lenses in order to look like Anglo-Americans. "But," she added perceptively, "they end up looking like Asian-Americans with dyed hair and blue contacts." Something like this seems to have happened toward the end of *Cannibal Tours* in a party scene where a heavy-set male tourist attempts to act savage for his fellow tourists. He has the necessary props. He is stripped to the waist. His face is painted (he would like to think, for war) by his New Guinea hosts. Only he can't act. His hackneyed way of making himself seem to be fierce for others is to strike a pose similar to that seen in pre-1950s publicity shots of professional boxers. It is so profoundly embarrassing that no one can even tell him that he is making an ass of himself. The new Guineans could not have done him better.

It is harrowing to suggest that these performances and aesthetic-economic exchanges may be the creative cutting edge of world culture in the making. But I think that we cannot rule out this possibility. In a very fine paper, James Boon (1984) has argued that parody and satire are at the base of every cultural formation. Responding to A. L. Becker's question concerning Javanese shadow theater ("'Where,' he ponders, 'in Western literary and dramatic traditions with their Aristotelian constraints' would we find 'Jay Gatsby, Godzilla, Agamemnon, John Wayne and Charlie Chaplin' appearing in the same plot?") Boon answers: "I suggest we find such concoctions *everywhere* in Western performance and literary genres except a narrow segment of bourgeois novels." Further suggesting that Becker has not even scratched the surface of the "riot of types" found linked together in cultural (as opposed to Cultural) performances Boon throws in Jesus Christ, the Easter Bunny, Mickey Mouse and Mohammed.

> The remainder is, to say the least, impressive: miracle plays, masques, *Trauerspiele*, follies, carnivals and the literary carnivalesque, everything picaresque, burlesque or vaudevillian, *Singespiele*, gests, romances, music drama, fairy tales, comic books, major holidays (Jesus cum Santa; Christ plus the Easter Bunny), Disney, T.V. commercials, the history of Hollywood productions, fantastic voyages, sci-fi, travel*liars'* tales, experimental theater, anthropology conferences . . . (1984: 157)

Boon's comment precisely affirms the logical procedures employed in the selection of figures for a wax museum: Jesus, Snow White, a Headhunter from New Guinea, John Wayne, Aristotle. Framed in this way, the absorption of the ex-primitive into the new cultural subject is theoretically unremarkable. It simply repeats the logic of the wax museum and "hyperreality," which is Eco's term for the valorization of absolute fakery as the only truth. Still, there is something O'Rourke has caught in the eyes of these New Guineans, perhaps a memory that they cannot share, that suggests there remains a difference not yet accounted for.

Let me summarize: Overlaying our common ancestors, primitive hunting and gathering peoples, we now have a history of colonial exploitation and military suppression, missionary efforts to transform religious beliefs and secular values, anthropological observations and descriptions, and now the touristic encounter. This complex system of overlays is all that is left of our common heritage and it has, itself, become the scene of an oddly staged encounter between people who think of themselves as being civilized or modernized and others who are said to be "primitive," but this can no longer be their proper designation. The term "primitive" is increasingly only a response to a mythic necessity to keep the idea of the primitive alive in the modern world and consciousness. And it will stay alive because there are several empires built on the necessity of the "primitive": included among these are anthropology's official versions of itself, an increasing segment of the tourist industry, the economic base of ex-primitives who continue to play the part of primitives-for-moderns, now documentary film-making, and soon enough music, art, drama, and literature. The rock star David Bowie takes several Indians from the Amazon basin, carrying spears and painted for "battle," with him on tour.

• • •

I am arguing that at the level of economic relations, aesthetic exchange (the collecting and marketing of artifacts, etc.), and the sociology of interaction, there is no real difference between moderns and those who act the part of primitives in the universal drama of modernity. Modern people have more money usually, but the ex-primitive is quick to accept the terms of modern economics. This may be a practical response to a system imposed from without, against which it would do no good to resist. But it could also be an adaptation based on rational self-interest. The word has already gone around that not everyone in the modernized areas of the world lives a life as seen on television, that many ex-primitives and most peasants are materially better off, and have more control over their own lives than the poorest of the poor in the modern world. Perhaps a case for difference could be made in the area of interactional competence. Ex-primitives are often more rhetorically and dramaturgically adept than moderns, excepting communications and media professionals. Still, up to this point, it would be tenuous and mainly incorrect to frame the interaction as "tourist/other" because what we really have is a collaborative construction of postmodernity by tourists and ex-primitives who represent not absolute difference but mere differentiations of an evolving new cultural subject. Probably, if James Boon's formulation is acceptable, the new cultural subject is no more or less of a pastiche than any other culture was before it got an official grip on itself.

The Psychoanalytic and the Mythic

Still, one cannot visit the former scene of the primitive without concluding that even within a fully postmodern framework, there is a real difference that might be marked "primitive," but it is not easy to describe. It does not deploy itself along axes which have already been worked out in advance by ethnography. These former head-hunters and cannibals in *Cannibal Tours* are attractive, have a lightly ironic attitude, and are clearsighted and pragmatic in their affairs. The tourists are most unattractive, emotional, self-interested, awkward and intrusive. It is difficult to imagine a group of real people (i.e., non-actors) simply caught in the eye of the camera appearing less attractive. This is not because of any obvious filmic trick. There is no narrator to tell the viewer how to think. Everyone on camera, the Iatmul people and tourists alike, is given ample opportunity for expression. The film is not technically unsympathetic to the tourists. The ostensible perspective is emotionless and empirical. The tourists do themselves in on camera. So the effect is really unsympathetic. The film often feels as if O'Rourke instructed his subjects to do an insensitive tourist routine, and they tried to oblige him even though they are not good actors.

That the tourists should come off second best to the Iatmul provides a clue to the difference, but to follow up on this clue requires yet another trip up the Sepik River. Here is the scene of much more than *Cannibal Tours*. It is, not by accident, also the place of perhaps the thickest historical and ethnographic encounter of "primitive" and "modern" on the face of the earth, suspended between perfect historical brackets marking the first 1886 exploration of Europeans in the Schleinitz expedition, and the 1986 filming of *Cannibal Tours*. During this 100 years the headhunters and cannibals of the Sepik region were visited by explorers, prospectors, missionaries, German colonists, labor contractors, anthropologists, government district police, Rockefeller the younger, and now, tourists. The anthropologists who have visited the Sepik include John Whiting, Reo Fortune, Gregory Bateson, and of course Margaret Mead.

The images that appear in *Cannibal Tours* are mainly tight shots that are geographically nonspecific. Dennis O'Rourke is careful to name the villages which hosted him in the credits at the end. But at any given point in the film, the viewer, especially one unfamiliar with the Sepik region, cannot know the precise location of the action. The only places mentioned by name on film are Kanganuman and Anguram villages and Tchamburi lake, where the stones used in the beheading ceremonies were found. An old warrior says "Here in Kanganuman we . . ." It is remarkably strange that these lapses into specificity should also have named Anguram and Kanganuman, Gregory Bateson's headquarters while assembling his observations for writing his ethnographic classic, *Naven*, and Tchamburi lake where Margaret Mead lived while making her observations for *Growing Up in New Guinea*. Kanganuman was also where Bateson hosted his friends and colleagues Margaret Mead and Reo Fortune, sharing his eight by twelve mosquito enclosure with them while they wrote up their field notes, the scene of an anthropological romance properly-so-called, where

Cannibal Tours, Dennis O'Rourke.

Margaret Mead changed husbands, or as she more delicately puts it, where she fell in love with Bateson, without really knowing it, while she was still married to Fortune.[3]

There is a gravitational pull, operating at a level beyond myth and psychoanalysis, between Western ethnography and these people of the Sepik who, I am arguing, only seem to put the anthropological doctrine of cultural relativism to its ultimate test. Consider *Naven*, the Iatmul ceremonial celebration of cultural accomplishments. Bateson tells his readers straight away that among the Iatmul, the greatest cultural achievement is "homicide":

> The first time a boy kills an enemy or a foreigner or some bought victim is made the
> occasion for the most complete *naven*, involving the greatest number of relatives and the
> greatest variety of ritual incidents. Later in his life when the achievement is repeated,
> there will still be some *naven* performance . . . but the majority of ritual incidents will
> probably be omitted. Next to actual homicide, the most honored acts are those which

help others to successful killing [. . . such as] the enticing of foreigners into the village so that others may kill them. (6)

Ritualized murder among the Iatmul is a reciprocal form embedded in intra-and inter-group social control mechanisms to the point that a victim's own people may arrange for a kill, for example by letting it be known to an enemy group that reprisals will be light if they select the "right" individual. But this should not be taken to mean that only delinquents and misfits are killed. The Iatmul people and their neighbors, it has often been noted, are remarkably free from status distinctions, and this certainly shows up in the range of victims, by no means limited to initiated males but inclusive of men, women, children, pigs and dogs. A more recent ethnographer, William Mitchell, who took his young children into the field with him describes a recent raid on his village:

> Entering the unprotected village, the Taute men shot and killed the first human they saw. It was a little boy. Returning victorious to their village, the Tautes beat their signal drums in triumph and danced through the night while the Kamnum women wailed the death of Wuruwe's small son. (Mitchell, 1978: 92)

And he captions a photograph of his children playing with Kanmun kids: "On the sandy plaza where little Tobtai was murdered, Ned and Elizabeth now played with their new friends." (131)

The anthropologists' fascination (the sheer number of Sepik ethnographies is a symptom), and the tourists', with ecstatic violence, taking heads, eating human brains, involves displaced anal-sadism which is a strong, albeit necessarily denied, component of Western culture and consciousness. A side benefit of Sepik ethnography is free psychoanalysis, and not cheap stuff either, but a one that finds its authentic substrate in the Western cogito and consciousness. For the Iatmul people of the Sepik and their neighbors, male homosexuality and anal sadism are not deep secrets accessible only by psychoanalytic methods. They are openly avowed, key features of the ritual and social order, open to ethnographic observation.

In *naven* celebrations, according to Bateson's account, the maternal uncle dresses in women's clothing and goes about the village in search of the nephew who has done his first murder, carved his first canoe, or other major cultural accomplishment. The uncle's purpose is supposed to be to offer himself to the nephew for homosexual intercourse. The nephew is painfully embarrassed by this and usually manages to absent himself from the ceremony, leaving the uncle to sprawl about in the sand in a burlesque agony of sexual desire, a show which delights everyone, especially the children. Sometimes the uncle's wife will put on mens' clothing and act the part of the nephew, pantomiming homosexual intercourse with her husband in the presence of the entire village. Very rarely is there actual physical contact between the *wau* (uncle) and the *laua* (nephew whose deed is being celebrated). A gesture, which Bateson calls a "sort of sexual salute," the possibility of which is at the heart of all *naven*, is called *mogul neggelak-ka* which literally means "grooving the anus." Bateson describes his only sighting as follows:

> This gesture of the *wau* I have only seen once. This was when a *wau* dashed out into the midst of a dance and performed the gesture upon his *laua* . . . The *wau* ran into the crowd, turned his back on the *laua* and rapidly lowered himself—almost fell—into a squatting position in such a way that as his legs bent under him his buttocks rubbed down the length of the *laua*'s leg. (13)

Fascination for these Sepik peoples and their highland neighbors, has always been a reflex of our own economic values and associated gender order. No matter whether we are for or against the homoeroticism of our own social order, in which everyone, not just women are supposed to adore the "great man," New Guinea provides a certain comfort. If we oppose the arbitrary segregation of the sexes in our society and gendered hierarchies, we can tell ourselves that at least we have not gone so far as the Iatmul. If we favor our own phallic order, we can use the New Guinea materials to support our claims that the separation of the sexes and hierarchical arrangements are "natural." If we are for or against our system of economic exploitation, we can take certain comfort from a people who actually eat the brains of their dead enemies. I have long suspected that this "either-orism" is the unwritten social contract that establishes the conditions for the widespread acceptance of the doctrine of "cultural relativism." The peoples and cultural practices which are handled "relativistically" must seem to support both sides of the deepest oppositions and ambivalencies of their observers. No ethnographic case accomplishes this at a level of intensity and detail that can compete with the New Guineans. In a celebrated remark, the father of modern phenomenology, Edmund Husserl states: "[J]ust as a man, and even the Papuan, represents a new stage in animality in contrast to the animals, so philosophical reason represents a new stage in humanity . . ." (Quoted in Derrida, 1978, 62, and in Ferry and Renault, 1988, 102).

D.
MacCannell

Another highland New Guinea case has become famous because they have universally enforced homosexuality for young boys until marriage, after which they are said to begin practicing normal heterosexual relations. We can read a brief account of these people in a recent *New York Times Magazine* article on homosexuality:

> Consider the Sambia of New Guinea, described by Gilbert Herdt in "Guardians of the Flutes." They belong to a group of cultures in which homosexual practices are actually *required* of boys for several years as rites of passage into adulthood. After adolescence, the young men abandon homosexual practices, marry women, father children and continue as heterosexuals for the rest of their lives. The lesson is threefold: first, a culture can make such a rule and get every person to conform; second, years of obligatory homosexuality apparently do not commit the average man to a lifetime of homoerotic desires. Third . . . (April 2, 1989: 60)

The normalizing tone of this account is remarkable in view of the subject. The "Sambia" (it is a pseudonymous case) practice referred to, but not specified in the *Times* article, is young-boy-to-adult-male fellatio. "Sambia" initiates are required to eat semen on a daily basis from about age seven through adolescence. The justification given for this practice is that male stature and strength, courage in war, and the ability eventually to be reproductively competent requires the ingestion of enormous quantities of semen. The more semen you eat, the bigger, stronger, more intelligent and more masculine you will become.[4] The "Sambia" point to the first growth of pubic and facial hair, and the first appearance of adult muscle contours as proof of the effectiveness of their initiation procedures. Herdt (1981: 3) comments:

> ritualized homosexuality becomes the center of their existence. Born from the deepest trauma of maternal separation and ritual threats, homosexual fellatio is dangerous and enticing, powerful and cruel. And from such experience is born a boy's sense of masculinity .
> . . . In short, Sambia boys undergo profound social conditioning through early, exciting homosexual experiences that continue for years. Yet they emerge as competent, exclusively heterosexual adults, not homosexuals. Contrary to Western belief, transitional homoeroticism is the royal road to Sambia manliness.

These statements can be read, indeed they must be read, as expressing what is meant by "manliness" and "competent heterosexuality" in current Anglo-European culture. We can discover, for example, that "competent heterosexuality" means only that men marry women and have children. Modernized cultures contain well-developed internal mechanisms that effectively resist the detailed specification of behavioral rules for adult heterosexual males. The

"Sambia," even in the context of marriage and "normal" heterosexual relations, consider the female sex to be so polluting, that if a man should utter the word for vagina, he must spit repeatedly lest he be poisoned by his own saliva that has come into contact with the word. At about the time the boys end their homoerotic career they are subjected to the ramming of a long cane down their throats to the point of forcing (they believe) out of their anus the last bits of filthy contaminated food, and also words, given to them in their youth by their mothers.[5] Let me suggest that the cessation of homosexual activities on the part of "Sambia" boys does not end in heterosexual relations, at least not from their perspective. It ends with the taking of heads. When they stop giving head and start taking heads ritually marks the transition when they join with the men as a man. In Herdt's accounting scheme, only the youthful fellators are engaged in homosexual activity, the adult male fellatees have "abandoned their homosexual practices" and are simply going about the business of their offices as competent adult male heterosexuals. They also get married and father children, and initiate the young boys. Still, attention to the ethnographic record reveals that heterosexual relations remain for them, frightening, dirty, and dangerous, the way that women steal their strength. Apparently also, according to Herdt's account, the kind of contamination and danger associated with hetero-sexual relations can be sexually exciting, working a powerful erotic attraction on certain adult males in the direction of what would be for them the exotic and the alien, i.e. sex with women.

Viewing *Cannibal Tours* in the context of Sepik ethnography one necessarily begins to wonder about what Freud gave us. It is not so much a question of psychoanalysis as mythology, a mythology of modernity which includes the primitive as a veil for our cannibal and other homoerotic desires. The primitive modality in the new cultural subject is already contained, or almost contained, in a touristic frame. Certainly O'Rourke's camera has assumed the point of view of the old paternal analyst, steady, listening, silent, pretending to be non-judgmental. Its gaze remains when the subject has run out of things to say. The tourists in O'Rourke's movie, after a pause, begin to say anything that comes into their minds; this is how O'Rourke finds the modern myth of the primitive in the touristic unconsciousness. When the camera is left running, the Italian girl blocks on decapitation and castration: "It was *symbolic*. For survival but also *symbolic*. It was *symbolic* when they cut off the heads of the white explorers. Not with malice, but a part of a *symbolic* tradition."

The ex-primitives, for their part, maintain much more rhetorical control. When the camera is left running, they often comment, "that is the end of my story," or "that's all I have to say," gladly telling about taking heads and eating brains, but stopping short of revealing the secret of *Naven*. But their rhetorical brilliance does not nevertheless permit them completely to escape the touristic, or postmodern frame around their consciousness. Within this frame, it is the ex-primitives who have internalized and who rigorously apply the doctrine of cultural relativism. They maintain that there is no difference between themselves and Europeans with the single exception that the Europeans have money and they don't. An old warrior relates his past making an ultimate statement of the principle of relativism. "We would cut off the heads, remove the skin and then eat. The Germans came, but white men are no different."

Language

All that remains is the question of language. Within the touristic frame, there is a characteristic deformation of language. This deformation might originally have resulted from noncompetency ("the breezy from high mountains which surrounding . . .") but now it has grammaticality and intentionality of its own. Deirdre Evans-Pritchard describes an interchange between an Indian artist, and a tourist who unfortunately mistakes him for someone with less than full competence in English:

> A lady was examining the balls on a squash blossom necklace. She turned to Clippy
> Crazyhorse and in the slow, over-emphasized fashion for someone who does not

understand English, she asked "Are these hollow?" Clippy promptly replied "Hello" and warmly shook her hand. Again the lady asked, "Are these hollow?" pronouncing the words even more theatrically this time. Clippy cheerily responded with another "Hello." This went on a few more times, by which time everyone around was laughing, until eventually the lady herself saw the joke. (Evans-Pritchard, 1989: 95–96)

D.
MacCannell

Jacques Lacan (1966: 113) once remarked, "beyond what we call the 'word' what the psychoanalytic experience discovers in the unconscious is the whole structure of language." I prefer to take this as a methodological, not theoretical, statement to mean that we can arrive at the unconscious without necessarily naming it as our destination if we are sufficiently attentive to language. Attention to the structure of tourist language suggests the possibility of building a case for real differences in primitive vs. modern modalities and to find a way out of the singularity of the postmodern touristic frame. Tourist language, pidgin English, or, in pidgin, "Tok Pisin," has reached its point of greatest perfection on the Sepik.

Tok Pisin, Tourist English, Tourist German, or, viewed from the other perspective, what some of my respondents call "Tarzan English," like all other languages are built out of transvaluing mechanisms. This is so they can draw upon their own internal resources for meaning, which is only another way of saying that they can function as languages. In the early stages of its development, the transvaluing exchange of tourist language may be between language and language, or even language and some extra-linguistic material. A woman tourist repeatedly asks a New Guinean to smile and gets no result. Finally, in frustration, she asks "can you smile like this?" and pushes up the corners of her own mouth with her fingers. Clippy Crazyhorse would have obliged her, saying in effect, "sure I can smile like that," by manually pushing up the corners of his own mouth.

The two master tropes on which all languages depend for internal self sufficiency are metaphor and metonymy. The transvaluing mechanism is blatant in *metaphor*: "my love is like a red, red rose." *Metonymy* depends on concrete association and a violation of the boundaries western science has erected around "cause and effect" relations. A metonymic transvaluation has occurred, for example, when we think something is poisonous because it tastes bitter. Metaphor contains much more potential power to transvalue across originally disconnected and separate matters. A "shining" example rests on a metonymic association of glittering, glistening, diaphanous, golden, perhaps crystalline exemplarity. But effectively to "make an example" of someone requires false identification with a victim, necessarily a metaphoric reach and suppression of one's own humanity.

Gregory Bateson provided a model that is potentially helpful here: the double-bind theory of schizophrenia (Bateson *et al.*, 1956). I would like to think that "the hand that strikes the blow can heal the wound"; that Bateson's later work on language and madness was also a product of his earlier New Guinea experience, at least in part. According to Bateson, well-formed language is so because its users have achieved a synthesis, balance and harmony between metaphoric and metonymic mechanisms of transvaluation, to the point that both are found in any given utterance. Deformed languages develop increasing specialization, dependence and separation of the two master tropes, eventually prizing one over the other as the only "proper" medium of exchange. The talk of schizophrenics is rigorously tropo-logical, that is, overly metaphoric, for example, as when a patient refuses to state anything directly, coding every message in elaborate allusions and allegories. Or it may be defensive in a metonymic direction, admitting no allusion, as when an unguarded remark like, "there were about a thousand people in the elevator" causes a schizophrenic to hallucinate a compact cube of gore.

This kind of imbalance is well-documented at the level of the "speaking subject." What I want to suggest here is that we begin to attend to something like the same phenomenon at the level of *language*. This move potentially leads to real analysis of Fredric Jameson's (1984) assertion that "postmodern society is schizophrenic" which is airy in the way he presented it, but also intuitively correct. Tourist language is deformed by an odd internal specialization and separation. There is a basis in the language that is used in tourist settings for designating a primitive modality deployed along the metonymic axis and a modern modality along the metaphoric. At least there is a strong statistical tendency in all the examples that I have collected for tourists to speak metaphorically and primitives to speak metonymically. If this is supported by further investigation, we would have a case of a discourse which is itself, in its totality, perfectly normal, built out of two complementary schizoid subvariants. This is a theoretical model for a structural mechanism for producing a normal speech community within which all discourse is schizophrenic, a postmodern speech community.

The raging metaphoricity of the language of the tourists marks virtually every one of their utterances. In rejecting a large mask, a woman in *Cannibal Tours* cannot bring herself to say "I think it's ugly." She cannot even say "it would not look good in my house." Instead, she says, "it would not go in a house *such as* mine, in Chicago." Each metaphoric move to disconnect and to separate (her husband might take note—at some level she evidently desires to exchange her own house for one like it in Chicago) builds up an absent authority, or standard, a power that controls every decision, a power that has no name except, perhaps, "Chicago." Another Papuan mask is said to be "like Modigliani." Even direct experience is assimilated only as metaphor: a couple walks briskly down a path, "This is *definitely* jungle." A German man gazes across the Sepik, "it reminds me of the Zambezie." This same man understands himself, only as metaphor, "for me *as tourist* it is very impressive."

The ex-primitives in *Cannibal Tours*, for their part, appear unable to get a metaphor past their lips in either direction. Their way of assimilating the German colonist was to eat his brains. It is noteworthy in this regard that Americans also eat their former enemies, the Germans, but only metaphorically, of course: as frankfurters, and hamburgers.[6] When the old ex-cannibal told O'Rourke's camera about the loss of his "sacred symbols" he was not speaking of traditional values, beliefs, ideals which are fading from thought. What he has in mind were some carved wooden objects that had been stolen from the spirit house and destroyed by the German missionaries or sent to European museums. New Guinea languages are possessive, imperative, even when command and presence is not called for. One of the most frequently occurring words in Tok Pisin is "bilong." The Tok Pisin name for a dildo-like penis sheath, an instrument that teleotypically stands for standing in, that is, for absence, is "skin bilong kok." The term itself takes the form of a miniature moral harangue about the importance of presence, association, connection: this is a dildo but don't forget, skin belong cock.

Metaphor always involves suppression: a veiling of the obvious through which the outlines of the obvious can be seen. The tourists' historical dependence on metaphor necessarily produces something like an unconscious. The cannibalism, violence, homoeroticism, of the primitives are openly avowed and principled. The New Guineans experience their myths as myths, while the tourists experience their myths as symptoms and hysteria. It should not go unnoticed that this is the exact opposite of the difference conventionally attributed to "primitive" vs. "modern." An old man tells the story of the reaction to the arrival of the first ships carrying German colonists. This is a fascinating moment in O'Rourke's film because the ex-primitive mobilizes a strong metaphor, "the tourists are like death," which he deftly proceeds to explicate, situate historically, and render concrete. In listening to this story, neatly packaged as it is with its own interpretation, we must not forget that death for an old Iatmul warrior is close and real. The tour boat as the death star would be a fitting end to a tragic narrative. He tells the camera with a smile that his grandparents ran down to the river to look at the ship, shouting "Our dead ancestors have arrived! Our dead have come back! They have gone someplace and gotten new faces and skin, and now they are back!" And he continues, the sly grin never leaving his face, "Now when we see the tourists, we say the dead have returned. That is what we say. We don't seriously believe they are our dead ancestors—but we say it." He might also believe it. It is possible to frame his point with some theoretical precision: that the Western tourists are indeed the embodiment of the spirit of dead cannibals.

One does not find among the tourists any similar lightness of sensibility, any detachment from what might be taken as their deepest insights. The woman in *Cannibal Tours* who is perhaps an "art historian" from New York explains that after the "disappearance" of Governor Rockefeller's son in New Guinea, "I became an exponent of primitive art." The word "art" as it escapes her lips inscribes itself heavily on the film. At this embarrassing moment, in searching for another place to look, the viewer's gaze may fall upon her eyebrows which seem to have been penciled onto her forehead with an almost brutal force. Again, there is the same contrast with the New Guinea face painting scenes where the touch is always light.

D. MacCannell

Here is the only difference between primitive and modern, as best as I can make it out from the materials at hand. The modern-day tourists are incapable of a conscious detachment from their values, a detachment that is the most evident feature of the New Guinean images and discourse. As the tourists cannibalize the primitive, they repress and deny the myth of modernity so it necessarily expresses itself always as an out-of-control force leading to a kind of violence that has no ritual outlet. An Italian family states, "We must enter their villages as the missionaries did. We must make them desire our values, our convictions, to teach them something, to do things for themselves, to teach them to desire our point of view, to make them want to wear our kind of clothes." The language of the Iatmul people is filled with concrete images of violence: "one of our spears went down the barrel of his gun . . . it wouldn't fire, so we captured him and took his head." The language of the tourists is filled with repressed violence: "we must make them want to wear our kind of clothes." The "art historian" never confronts her own denial and suppression of the "primitive" on the Sepik and in her own soul. Instead, she states somewhat shrilly as she buys artifacts, "I for one think it is too bad if they deviate [from their traditions] and work for tourism as such." The potential for evil and cruelty lurking unsaid in this statement is far greater than anything openly expressed by the old warriors.

Notes

The author wishes to thank Deirdre Evans-Prichard for calling O'Rourke's film to his attention.

1. Few accounts of cannibals neglect to remark that they need exchange to buy pants. Montaigne ends his essay "On Cannibals" with the words, "All this is not too bad. But wait. They don't wear trousers." (92) It should not come as any surprise that covering the penis is the first requirement for absorption in a new cultural arrangement in which hierarchy based on material wealth, with males at the top, is taken to be the "natural" order. Any re-appearance of the penis in this context would reveal the ludicrous basis for the rather vast claims made on behalf of males. Primitive men can afford to expose themselves because so long as they live in a primitive condition, they have nothing to lose: men and women, the young and the old, the rulers and the ruled all live in virtually the same material circumstances. But as soon as differences in material well-being become socially significant, the men begin to cover their "privates": the wealthier, the more covered. The young man in *Cannibal Tours* says simply that he needs money to buy the "things I like," and the woman says she needs it to send her children to school. But the powerful old men and the tourists always give the purchase of "trousers" as the reason these almost ex-primitives need money.

2. I reported on some others in D. MacCannell (1973).

3. Amply described by Mead (1972) and interpreted by James Boon (1985).

4. On the relationship between eating semen and such intelligence factors as ability to learn foreign languages, See Schieffelin, 1978.

5. See the references to ramming out "bad talk" in Herdt (1981: 224). "Bad talk" is the mother's nagging reprimands and insults that stultify and "block his growth."

6. Marshall Sahlins (1976: 166–79) has provided an alternate, more normative, "vegetarian," solution to the problem of the cannibalistic drive in contemporary culture. He refuses to use the term "frankfurter." For him, they are only "hot dogs."

References

Bateson, Gregory. 1958. *Naven*. 2nd ed. Stanford: Stanford University Press.

Bateson, Gregory, D. Jackson, J. Haley, and J. Weakland. 1976 (1956). "Toward a Theory of Schizophrenia."

In *Double Bind: The Foundations of the Communicational Approach to the Family*, Carlos E. Sluzki and Donald C. Ransom. New York: Gune and Stratten.

Boon, James A. 1984. "Folly, Bali and Anthropology, or Satire Across Cultures." In *Text, Play, and Story*, ed. E. Bruner. Washington, D.C.: Proceedings of the American Ethnological Society for 1983.

———. 1990. *Affinities and Extremes: Crisscrossing the Bittersweet Ethnology of East Indies History, Hindu-Balinese Culture, and Indo-European Allure*. Chicago: University of Chicago Press.

Derrida, Jacques. 1978. *Origin of Geometry*. Trans. John Leavey, Jr. Brighton: Harvester Press.

Evans-Prichard, Deirdre. 1989. "How 'They' See 'Us': Native American Images of Tourists." *Annals of Tourism Research* 16: 89–105.

Ferry, Luc and A. Renault. 1990. *Heidegger and Modernity*. Trans. Franklin Philip. Chicago: The University of Chicago Press.

Herdt, Gilbert. 1981. *Guardians of the Flute*. New York: McGraw Hill.

Jameson, Fredric. 1984. "Postmodernism, Or the Cultural Logic of Late Capitalism." *New Left Review* 146: 53–92.

Lacan, Jacques. 1966. "The Insistence of the Letter in the Unconscious." *Yale French Studies* 36/37: 112–47.

MacCannell, Dean. 1973. "Staged Authenticity: Arrangements of Social Space in Tourist Settings." *American Journal of Sociology* 79 (3): 589–603.

Mead, Margaret. 1930. *Growing Up in New Guinea*. New York: William Morrow.

———. 1972. *Blackberry Winter: My Earlier Years*. New York: William Morrow.

Mitchell, William E. 1978. *The Bamboo Fire: An Anthropologist in New Guinea*. New York: W.W. Norton.

Montaigne, Michel de. 1943. *Selected Essays*. Trans. Donald Frame. New York: Walter J. Black.

O'Rourke, Dennis. 1987. *Cannibal Tours*. Canberra: O'Rourke and Associates.

Quiggin, A. Hingston. 1949. *A Survey of Primitive Money: The Beginnings of Currency*. London: Methuen.

Sahlins, Marshall. 1976. *Culture and Practical Reason*. Chicago: University of Chicago Press.

Sweet, Jill. 1989. "Burlesquing 'The Other' in Pueblo Performance." *Annals of Tourism Research* 16: 62–75.

Schieffelin, Edward L. 1976. *The Sorrow of the Lonely and the Burning of the Dancers*. New York: St. Martin's.

Filmography

Cannibal Tours. 70 minutes. 35mm and 16mm. Color. 1987. Produced, Directed and Photographed by Dennis O'Rourke. Associate Producers: Laurence J. Henderson, Chris Owen. Sound Recordists: Tim Litchfield, Chris Owen. Film Editor: Tim Lichfield. Distributed by Direct Cinema, P.O. Box 69799, Los Angeles, CA 90069.

Trinh T. Minh-ha Observed
Anthropology and Others

Henrietta L. Moore

ONE OF THE MOST REMARKABLE THINGS ABOUT THE WORK OF TRINH MINH-HA IS THE continuity between her writing and her filmmaking. Her work is marked through by disruption, juxtaposition and dislocation. There is, therefore, much irony in the perception of continuity. Irony is in evident play in both the written and the cinematic texts, but irony is an unstable realm and much of the difficulty in interpreting Trinh Minh-ha's work arises from this instability. The difficulty of interpretation, or rather, the anxiety the activity produces, is compounded further by the clear recognition that her work eschews narrative and actively resists any attempt by the reader to impose narrative structure or closure. However, her work has a political project; it is engaged in a series of discursive practices with a clarity of purpose which accounts, in part, for the strong sense of continuity in the work. It is in reading the purpose of the work against the work itself that interesting tensions and ambiguities arise.

Deconstructing Ethnography

Trinh Minh-ha's *Reassemblage* (1982) and *Naked Spaces: Living is Round* (1985) are both films shot in West Africa. These films are not intended to be ethnographic in any conventional sense, they are concerned instead to challenge and undermine the ethnocentrism of Western anthropological studies of "other cultures" and to criticize the way those cultures are habitually perceived and represented in Western discourse. There are times when this critique is made explicit in the commentary in the film, as in the following excerpt from the sound track of *Reassemblage*.

The land of the Manding and Peul peoples

A film about what? my friends ask.
A film about Senegal, but what in Senegal?

I feel less and less the need to express myself
Is that something else I've lost?
Something else I've lost?

Filming in Africa means for many of us
Colorful images, naked breast women,
exotic dances and fearful rites.

The unusual.
First create needs, then, help
Ethnologists handle the camera the way they handle
words
Recuperated collected preserved
The Bamun the Bassari the Bobo
What are your people called again? an ethnologist
asks a fellow of his

In numerous tales

Diversification at all costs
Oral traditions thus gain the rank of written heritage.
Fireplace and woman's face
The pot is known as a universal symbol for the
Mother the Grand-Mother the Goddess

Nudity does not reveal
The hidden
It is its absence

A man attending a slide show on Africa turns to his
Wife and says with guilt in his voice; "I have seen some
pornography tonight"

Documentary because reality is organized into an
explanation of itself

Every single detail is to be recorded. The man on
the screen smiles at us while the necklace he wears,
the design of the cloth he puts on, the stool he sits
on are objectively commented upon

It has no eye it records

This extract contains a number of the themes which are important in Trinh Minh-ha's work. For example, it challenges the objectivist pretensions of a scientific, comparative anthropology. It criticizes the objectivist language of anthropological discourse which is laden with metaphors of collecting, specifying and recording. It undermines the realist pretensions of documentary and ethnographic film. It questions Western representations of Africa and of African women, and it comments on the self-serving nature of Western discourses on the Other and 'otherness.' These are all themes which are present in Trinh Minh-ha's work.

H. Moore

Reassemblage and *Naked Spaces* are both sensual films full of powerful and rich images that cut in upon each other. For the most part, these films refuse their role as bearers of messages, as fixed forms of representation, as structured narratives. This is consistently impressed upon the viewer through the use of jump-cuts, close-ups of parts of human bodies, changes in the mode and register of commentary, and the frequent repetition of key phrases. The overall impression is one of discontinuity, disruption and juxtaposition. Meaning is open-ended and unstable. The commentary and the images are often at odds with each other, they do not work together to produce a single comprehension. The conventional Western discourse on the Other is pushed aside and the result is a view of the Other which does not conform to expectations.

However, in spite of an initial impression of discontinuity and disruption, where images and commentary are in conflict, there is another level at which the constant repetition of certain images and phrases works to produce an all encompassing narrative structure which threatens to subvert the fragmentation and plurality which the film seeks to convey.

For example, *Naked Spaces* could be considered as a film about the poetics of space (Bachelard is mentioned in the credits). It covers the architecture, material culture and cosmology of villages in six West African countries (Mali, Senegal, Mauritania, Burkina Faso, Togo and Benin). The architecture of this region is famous for its splendor and symbolic complexity, and it is here shown off at its best. The camera takes up the theme that "living is round" and it focuses intently, lovingly and obsessively on curves and round shapes in the landscape: breasts, pots, rows of water jars, pot-bellied houses, round decorations, circles of light, openings and the bellies of children. The themes of fertility and female sexuality are obvious.

In her book, *Women, Native, Other*, and in interviews, Trinh Minh-ha has criticized the scientific, comparative project of anthropology, where the universalistic pretensions of the discourse create objectified Others. However, *Naked Spaces* often reads like comparative ethnography. It moves from one context to another, and each context is characterized by a distinctive architecture, which the unwary viewer is apparently encouraged to associate with the name of the group written on the screen. The lasting image is one of different cultures, and yet the repetition of certain images and phrases provides a form of linking narrative which suggests that these cultures share certain cosmological beliefs, architectural motifs, and ideas about gender relations. The result is a representation of Africa, where cultures are complete and are possessed of distinctive world views which guarantee their authenticity, as well as their difference from an unspecified, but equally monolithic, "West."

The irony of this is both disconcerting and painful. There were moments in both *Reassemblage* and *Naked Spaces* when I felt I was in the midst of an older anthropological discourse which many anthropologists would claim they have been striving to escape over the last twenty years: a discourse which stresses the wholeness of cultures, their distinctiveness and coherence of values, their authentic—that is, ahistorical—nature. A discourse which claims to be able to represent others, and through representing them to know them. Modern anthropology, by contrast, is much more concerned to set cultures in their historical context, to stress the constructed nature of social and cultural identities, to examine the conflicting and often contradictory nature of social values and self-understandings, to emphasize the historical specificities and power dimensions of representations of 'other cultures', and when representing other people and other people's lives, to underline their changing, processual and dynamic nature. There are, therefore, areas of overlap between modern anthropology's project and the project in which Trinh Minh-ha is engaged. Given this fact, the question is why did it seem so easy to interpret *Reassemblage* and *Naked Spaces* as partially, at least, representative of an anthropological and Western discourse of the Other from which they were specifically designed to distance themselves and of which they were intended to be rightfully and forcefully critical?

There are several kinds of possible answers to this question. One answer has to do with the hegemonic nature of a particular anthropological discourse on the Other and the way in which it has informed the representation of 'non-Western' societies, including those representations which are not intended to be anthropological *per se* (e.g., Hollywood adventure movies set in Africa). Trinh Minh-ha speaks explicitly about this problem, and in an interview on her filmmaking she says: "Often I would realize that I was shooting in conformity with anthropological preoccupations and expectations and have to stop in the midst of action" (Penley and Ross, 1986: 93). However, Trinh Minh-ha makes it clear that in the process of editing she made no attempt to cut such moments out of the film. In this way, she tries to avoid didacticism and to allow such moments to appear self-critical in the context of the film overall. This is a brave strategy, but given the hegemonic nature of this particular anthropological discourse, it does carry possible risks, because it seems likely that many viewers will gravitate towards those images and representations which appear familiar to them, and make their interpretations accordingly. Interpretations which then govern the way they interpret subsequent images in the film, even if such images could equally well be interpreted as critical of conventional representations of 'other cultures' or African women.

Trinh Minh-ha discusses a shot of a man carving wood in *Reassemblage* as an example of an image which is constructed in terms of a dominant anthropological discourse, in that it seems to be exactly the sort of image which is so familiar from hundreds of documentary and ethnographic films. She points out, however, that the difference between this image and its familiar counterpart is that it is specifically not part of some developing narrative or characterization of the Other. It is not intended to be explanatory, to be part of a single truth about another culture. As a result, no explanation or information is given about what the man is carving, or about any possible local meanings or interpretations (Penley and Ross, 1986: 95).

Trinh Minh-ha makes a similar sort of argument about the repetition of certain images and phrases. She sees this repetition as working against conventional narrative understandings, and far from seeing it as a substitute for narrative, she envisages it as a way of unsettling conventional images and representations, as specifically working against the unity of the dominant anthropological discourse.

> . . . repetition can serve many purposes. Those used in the spoken text, for example, (fragments of sentences) are never identical. It suffices to pull one word out of the repeated sentence to shift its meaning. As viewers, we often fix a meaning or metaphor by identifying or associating the image with the commentary that accompanies it. Repetitions of the same sentence in slightly different forms and in ever changing contexts help to unsettle such a fixity, and to perceive the plural, sliding relationship between ear and eye, image and word. In instances, where repetition functions as a substitute for lengthy scientific-humanistic explanations, it leaves room for the spectator to decide what to make out of the statement or sequence of images in its diversely repeated forms. (Penley and Ross, 1986: 92)

Repetition can indeed serve many purposes, because for the viewer it often seems to provide a substitute for an all-encompassing narrative, while for the filmmaker it is intended to work as a shifter, something which unsettles the fixity of meaning and moves it onward. There might be a number of reasons for these differences in interpretation. It could be that viewers are insufficiently attentive to changes in the relationship between visual and linguistic representations. More plausibly, it might be that viewers are used to a cinematic form with a strong narrative structure, and indeed to ethnographic films with a fixed didactic line, and that consequently they seek out narrative even where it does not exist. However, the problem could also have something to do with the question of context.

In spite of brief references in both *Reassemblage* and *Naked Spaces* to the negative political and economic effects of colonialism and, latterly, international aid, the societies and individuals represented in both films are actually presented out of context. This lack of contextualization works in a number of different dimensions. The first dimension is perhaps most evident in the treatment of space in *Naked Spaces*. This is a film which gives full attention to the creativity and social and cosmological complexity of West African architecture. An explicit homology is established between architecture or physical space and cosmological beliefs or people's "inner lives." This homology is reinforced technically through the use of shots through spaces (i.e., from the inside of the house, through a famed doorway or pool of light, to the outside) and through sequences of images which establish visual connections between different shapes and patterns in architectural forms, decorative motifs, items of material culture and parts of human bodies. These visual images are powerful and very beautiful, but they are not accompanied, as has

H. Moore

already been discussed, by any narrative or explanation which would fix them as objects within a closed set of meanings. Instead, they are accompanied by a commentary which has no discernable narrative form and which is juxtaposed to, and often in conflict with, the visual images. On one level, this has the effect, which the filmmaker desires, of providing a critical space and unsettling the fixity of meanings. However, on another level, it has the unintentional effect of transforming both the images and the commentary into assertions, bald statements of some kind. The commentary, in spite of its fragmentary nature, is particularly resistant to critical interpretation. Many of the sentences and phrases are actually derived from the writings of anthropologists, philosophers and poets (Griaule, Rattry, Heidegger, Diop, Shakespeare, Bachelard and Cixous are amongst those mentioned in the credits). Even statements which are not so derived often appear very

Trinh T. Minh-ha.

anthropological or philosophical in tone because they share with those disciplines precisely those comparativist, universalistic pretensions which Trinh Minh-ha rightly criticizes. To the viewer, it is not always clear that these statements should be read critically, and when certain phrases are repeated—albeit with slight variations or shifts in context—it is even harder to appreciate the necessity for a critical distance.

The second dimension in which there is a lack of contextualization is clearly related to the first. In many deconstructionist texts—whether written or otherwise—the striving for plurality and multivocality often leads to the kind of decontextualization I have just described; however, it can lead also to a situation where because no single interpretation or set of meanings are privileged over others, representations are just left to "speak for themselves."[1] The result is a form of empiricism, where unsorted images, both visual and linguistic, jostle each other. In this situation, it is often impossible, paradoxically, to do what we as viewers or readers are being encouraged to do and that is to deconstruct the constructed, ideological nature of such representations. For example, in *Naked Spaces*, it is quite impossible for a viewer to deconstruct—beyond the point of assuming that they are constructed—such statements as the following: "Rhythms are built into the way people relate to each other"; "she who wears the antelope headdress is said to portray the deceased's daughter"; "The house, like a woman, must have secret parts to inspire desire." These statements, which are repeated, are presented in the film as if they are of equal status, which in one way they are because there is no reason to privilege one over the others. However, if I had to make a decision, I would suggest that the first can be attributed to the filmmaker, the second to an anthropologist, and the third to an African villager (possibly in conversation with the filmmaker). But, while it is possible to argue that these statements ought to be treated equally, since there is no necessary reason to privilege anthropological over any other form of knowledge, when they are presented in the film without any indication of the context in which they were produced, it is absolutely impossible to critically deconstruct them. The only option is to take them or leave them. This cuts the viewer off from any understanding of the ideological formation of other people's understandings, whether those of the filmmaker, the African villagers participating in the film or the anthropologist. It also severs the viewer from any historical understanding of the construction of different ideologies and perspectives, and of how these change through time.

This last point leads us on to the third dimension in which a lack of contextualization is relevant. The failure to specify the ideological basis of certain interpretations and representations is most crucial with regard to the representation of the African societies and individuals in the film. The depiction of a variety of societies through their architecture, supported by a variety of statements about the relationship between inner and outer space, between the living and the dead and between women and men, has the unintended effect of creating a series of bounded cultures, each with their distinctive lifeways and beliefs. The repetition of certain images and phrases serves to emphasize continuities and similarities between the groups. This means that while there is a certain play on the similarities and differences between groups, what is completely absent are the differences and conflicts which exist within groups. For example, in spite of an expressed desire to avoid explanation and objectification, a relatively coherent set of meanings is attributed to the organization of domestic architecture, especially in the homology established between people's beliefs and the organization of space. This implies—quite accurately, of course—that people give meaning to the world around them, but it also implies that there are fixed cultural meanings and that all persons within the culture subscribe to those meanings. There is no discussion of the fact that certain groups in society may interpret space differently, that the meanings given to certain spaces can vary according to the activities carried out in them, or that those meanings might change over time (Moore, 1986). Once again, African societies seem to have authentic cultures ascribed to them, and this prevents the viewer from analyzing the ideological construction of certain architectural forms and of certain cultural statements. This is particularly crucial with regard to women. In the section of the film dealing with Birifor architecture much use is made of light and dark, and women are seen moving through dark spaces into light as they go about their daily activities. These shots are accompanied by commentary and two statements which follow each other within a relatively brief period of 2–3 minutes: "The house, like a woman, must have secret parts to inspire desire"; and "A man should not see all the dark corners of another's house." In so far as these statements are out of context and no information is given regarding the context of their production or use, there is no possibility of the viewer achieving any critical distance from them. Once again, the option is simply to take them or leave them. They float free from their context as straightforward assertions. It seems quite likely that these are ideological statements concerning gender relations, and that women and men, old and young might dispute the meaning and validity of such statements. They may well have as much and as little meaning as the statement "Gentlemen prefer blondes" would have in an American context.

If cultures are portrayed as coherent, unified and unchanging then there is the possibility that they appear also as passive, and this is the fourth dimension in which a lack of contextualization is important. Trinh Minh-ha is concerned to undermine and disrupt the conventions of the Western discourse on the Other, but in *Reassemblage* and *Naked Spaces* African societies are represented out of their historical context. This means that there is no possibility of representing the historical circumstances in which the Western discourse on the Other took shape and, as a result, there is no space to represent the active engagement of African with Western societies. An engagement within which Western discourse on the Other was produced and developed. In *Reassemblage* and *Naked Spaces* the Western discourse on the Other is presented by implication as the sole creation of the West; this deprives African societies of a significant part of their history and of their role in world history. In making this point, there is no necessity or intention to appropriate or subjugate all of African history to the history of contact. As Nicholas Thomas says: "There were always, and still are, a number of indigenous histories—but their discovery need not deny the other histories we share and interact through" (Thomas, 1990: 66). The important point here is the one of interaction. The pervasive and brutal nature of Western domination, both material and discursive, is not in doubt. However, that domination cannot be understood without a clear recognition of the way it was, and still is, subverted and resisted by African societies. There are points in both films when reference is made to resistance to colonialism, so resistance is not ignored, but it is not portrayed as an active moment in the historical production of a discourse on self and other, for African as well as for Western societies.

Women, Native, Other:
Identity, Difference and Authenticity

In her book *Women, Native, Other*, Trinh Minh-ha develops many of the themes with which she is concerned in her films, but she adds also new critical perspectives on writing, difference and subjectivity. On a first reading, one of the most striking things about her writing is its cinematic quality. It moves quickly from one point to another, changing perspective and tone. It is eloquent and vital, but she seems to strive for a staccato effect which recalls the techniques of disruption and dislocation used in her cinematic texts. The aim of the written text is to undermine forms of representation, to question the Western discourse on the Other and to unsettle meaning. However, the book is more sustained in its didactic line, more detailed in its treatment of issues and, as such, it overcomes many of the problems which seem apparent in the films. The book consists of four chapters, each with a number of still photographs from her films. The first chapter is about writing; the second is about anthropology; the third is concerned with difference and authenticity; and the fourth reflects on questions of history and identity. In fact, the subject matter of chapters is by no means discrete, and themes are built up and developed through the text.

Many of the anxieties and confusions which I experienced when watching and thinking about *Reassemblage* and *Naked Spaces* were dissipated by the book which directly addresses issues of marginal voices, displaced and fragmented identities, cultural hybridization and plurality, historical shifts in discourses, the mutuality of representation, and the question of authorship itself.

The Question of Anthropology

In Chapter Two, Trinh Minh-ha addresses the objectifying, comparativist discourse of anthropology, and the relationship of language to power.

> Like any common living thing, I fear and reprove classification and the death it entails, and I will not allow its clutches to look down on me . . . What I resent most, however, is not his inheritance of a power he so often disclaims, disengaging himself from a system he carries with him, but his ear, eye and pen, which record in his language while pretending to speak through mine, on my behalf. (48)

The power of naming, and the power of language is to subdue and subjugate. In order to try and subvert this power, Trinh Minh-ha uses the male pronoun throughout this chapter when referring to anthropologists, and uses stereotypical labels in the place of proper names when referring to specific anthropologists; for example, Malinowski becomes the "Great Master" and Lévi-Strauss becomes the "modern anthropologist." Trinh Minh-ha specifically distances herself from "academic" modes of argumentation and writing. She is concerned less to refute arguments using well-worn and compromised methods than to engage in a heterogeneity of free play in an attempt to unsettle meaning, to let "his" language speak against itself. She clearly recognizes the perils of this strategy and addresses it directly:

> Perhaps by persisting in this new play, I shall succeed in reproducing a few traits of the numbness of a tradition which he happily spreads about, often "without his being aware of it." Perhaps, also, I shall succeed in exposing some of the premises of oppression and hegemony I and you often accept into our discourse the very moment we apply ourselves to denouncing them. (49)

The strategy works to a certain extent, shifting anthropology's language against itself. However, in order for the strategy to work, anthropology, as practice and as discourse, has to become something monolithic, fixed, an entity of sorts. This is achieved in the text by focussing almost exclusively on the writings of Malinowski and Lévi-Strauss (Geertz, Diamond, Griaule and one or two others get brief references). The terms of the discourse on anthropology are thus firmly set by these two men. It is not appropriate here to argue about how representative they might be of anthropology as a whole. One would certainly have to acknowledge their formative influence on the discipline, but likewise it should be pointed out that many other anthropologists are in profound disagreement with them. The most notable problem here concerns the lack of reference to the writing of feminist and/or critical anthropologists.[2] It is in this work that one can see most clearly the shifts which have taken place in the discourse of anthropology in the last twenty-five years, and it is also here that one finds deconstructed and laid out for examination the ambiguous, conflicting and often contradictory elements which make up that complex and compromised discourse on the Other which is labeled anthropology. Feminist and critical anthropologists struggle to shift the ground of language and representation, and to dislocate the dominant Western discourse on the other. To write only in the male pronoun and to refer only to male anthropologists makes it hard to see the differences within the discourse of anthropology, and those differences are significant ones.

Trinh Minh-ha correctly identifies a discourse on the Other which classifies, dichotomizes and essentializes in its depiction of other people, and which performed, and continues to perform, a significant role in the exercise of colonial and post-colonial domination. This discourse should be actively resisted in all its manifestations, but it is incorrect to assume that the Western discourse on the Other is synonymous with anthropology or vice versa.[3] Anthropology is merely one of several Western discourses on the Other, or, more accurately, it represents one aspect of Western discourses on the Other.

Anthropology never had a monopoly of the Other and although it was frequently in alliance with parallel discourses on otherness, it was also, at times, in opposition to such discourses. The murky history of anthropology and colonialism has been written—the equally murky history of anthropology and neocolonialism is being written—but to assume that anthropology was the only discourse on which the regimes of domination and exploitation drew is misleading, not least because it seriously underestimates the real power of the Western discourse on the Other and fails to adequately locate its generative points of power. The contemporary discourse on otherness animates the geo-politics of the modern world, and this seems most apparent as the world waits to see what will happen in the Gulf. What part does anthropology play in the generation of this contemporary discourse? It is certainly far from blameless, and it is equally clear that this discourse profoundly influences the discourse and practice of modern anthropology, but it is not easy to answer such a question. Discourses on difference mimic each other, and it seems quite likely, for example, that the Civil Rights Movement is equally responsible, if not more so than anthropology, for the contemporary American discourse on otherness. This emphasizes the further point that if once we could talk of a Western discourse on the Other, we can do so no longer. North American and European societies are highly plural, diverse and differentiated. Muslim youth in the north of England support Iraq in the current crisis in the Gulf, and the British establishment talks characteristically and idiotically about ingratitude. In this battle of identities and allegiances, there are many discourses on otherness and their pervasive power is only revealed if we examine the ways in which they mock and mimic each other, but not if we assume that they are part of a single discourse.

The multiplicity of discourses on otherness raises the question of participation. In other words, there may be many discourses, but who decides which of these will be dominant, and who benefits from the elaboration of dominant discourses? It is the urgency of these questions which informs Trinh Minh-ha's critique of anthropology, but by treating anthropology as effectively synonymous with a single Western discourse on the Other she is in danger of over-emphasizing the role of the dominant at the expense of the sub-dominant. It is an obvious fact that in spite of the multiplicity of discourses on otherness, it has been possible to identify historically a hegemonic Western discourse on the Other which played a significant role in the process of the subjugation of colonial peoples. The terms of this discourse were largely set by the technologically and economically more powerful Western nations, and subjugated peoples were certainly not equal partners in the setting up of this discursive formation. However, to imply that the Western discourse on the Other was merely a tool for the purposes of colonial (and neocolonial) domination implies that this discourse was simply something imposed on the world by the West. In one sense, of course, this is true, but in another it is not. Western discourses on otherness are not, and were not, all powerful, nor were they, or are they, static. Western discourses on otherness are not just the products of an over-heated collective imagination, but were forged in the context of a set of mutual experiences; the experience first of mercantilism and slave trading, then of colonial rule, and lately of international aid and super power politics. The experiences of dominant and sub-dominant are clearly not the same, but they are interactive, and, to that degree, they are mutual.

African societies, like many others, resisted colonial domination, but they did not always do so through direct military or economic confrontation. They constructed their own discourses on otherness and they used them to engage with and deal with colonial rule, and these discourses continue to develop and evolve in the post-colonial context. In many instances, individuals and groups took up aspects of what seemed to be part of Western discourses on the Other and played it back at their oppressors at high speed, or in a different register or simply absolutely straight, and, in so doing, they turned the West's discourse against itself. This "deconstructive *bricolage*" played an important part in the rise of nationalist movements and the overthrow of colonial governments; it also materially shaped western discourses on otherness.

H.
Moore

Identity and Authenticity

In Chapter Three, Trinh Minh-ha takes up the theme of difference in relation to women as Other, and discusses the representation of difference and the way it is incorporated into a discourse about identity and roots. She shows how difference becomes distorted in political discourse into a spurious argument about origins and authenticity, so that policies of separate development in South Africa (and elsewhere) have been readily justified on the basis of an appeal to supposed cultural and ethnic histories and needs. She goes on to argue that the treatment of women of color and "Third World" women in feminist academia can be and should be subject to the same sort of critique because these women are consistently incorporated into discussions on the basis that questions of racism, ethnic identity, religion and Third World exploitation are "their" issues. "We did not come to hear a Third World member speak about the First (?) World, we came to listen to that voice of difference likely to bring us what we can't have." (88). This is the tyranny of specialness, and Trinh Minh-ha describes it as "planned authenticity." Difference is no longer to be erased, it is to be remembered, and through this process of remembering we will all remember not just that we are authentic, but that we are different. Difference as identity and authenticity is thus a discourse of racism and division.

The point that Trinh Minh-ha makes is that difference is socially constructed, and that what we need to do is to unpack those discourses which constantly seek to naturalize it, to make it a question of essentialisms, of authenticity. However, in interrogating the socially constructed nature of difference, she is drawn into the question of how to handle identity, of the politics and practice of working as a specifically situated individual, as a Third World woman. Is it possible to write as a woman, as a Third World woman, as a man? What difference does it make? She approaches these questions, in part, through a critique of the Western idea of identity as being connected to an all-knowing subject. She touches on the question of whether it would be or should be possible to dissolve the subject-object opposition. This is a question which has been addressed by feminist scholars for some time, but which has only really achieved intellectual respectability since it has been taken up by those who are self-identified as post-modernists. The main theme of her argument, however, is that difference is not to be understood as the difference between fixed entities, whether these are cultures or individual identities. We need to be alive to the differences within such entities; the differences within, rather than between all of us.

The usual response to arguments of this kind is that if we do away with fixed identities, if we release the notion of identity from its restricting association with essentialism then we undermine the possibilities for political practice. Trinh Minh-ha deals with this response by making the case for seeing the ethnic female subject as a site of multiple differences. These differences are produced in language and are experienced through engagement in the world, and it is on the basis of recognizing these differences and making them work against each other that we will be able to take political action. The proper understanding of differences is a shared responsibility, and it is time that this responsibility were equally shared.[4]

Notes

1.   This is a point which is made most clearly and elegantly by Bruce Kapferer in his review of postmodernist anthropology (1988).

2.   Trinh Minh-ha does make a brief reference to the writings of critical or post-modernist anthropologists in a footnote (157). She notes her agreement with some of the arguments made by James Clifford in his introduction to *Writing Culture* (1986).

3.   I have been strongly influenced in my argument here by Clifford's brilliant essay on Edward Said's book *Orientalism* (Clifford, 1988). Many of the points Clifford makes about Said could be made about Trinh Minh-ha's work.

4.   There are very obvious parallels between Trinh Minh-ha's work on this point and that of Teresa de Lauretis (1986; 1987).

References

Clifford, J. 1988. *The Predicament of Culture*. Cambridge: Harvard University Press.

Clifford J. and Marcus, G., eds. 1986. *Writing Culture*. Berkeley: University of California Press.

De Lauretis, T., ed. 1986. *Feminist Studies/Critical Studies*. London: Macmillan.

De Lauretis, T. 1987. *Technologies of Gender*. London: Macmillan.

Kapferer, B. 1988. "The Anthropologist as Hero: Three Exponents of Post-Modernist Anthropology." *Critique of Anthropology* 8 (2): 77–104.

Moore, H.L. 1986. *Space, Text and Gender: An Anthropological Study of the Marakwet of Kenya*. Cambridge: Cambridge University Press.

Penley, C. and Ross, A. 1986. "Interview with Trinh T. Minh-ha." *The New American Filmmakers Series* 32: 87–103.

Thomas, N. 1990. "Taking People Seriously: Cultural Autonomy and the Global System." *Critique of Anthropology* 9 (3): 59–69.

H.
Moore

Filmography

U.S. Distribution by: *Women Make Movies, Inc. 225 Lafayette. Suite 212. New York, NY 10012. (212) 925-0606.*

U.K. Distribution by: *Circles, 113 Roman Road, London E2 0HU. (071) 981-6826.*

Reassemblage. 1982. Color. 40 mins. Rental: (16mm) $90.00. Purchase: (16mm) $800.00.

Naked Spaces: Living is Round. 1985. Color. 135 mins. Rental: (VHS) $225.00. Purchase: (VHS) $495.00 (16mm) $1,600.00.

Surname Viet Given Name Nam. 1989. Color. 108 mins. Rental: (VHS) $225. Purchase: (VHS) $495.00 (16mm) $1,500.00.

Marketing Alterity

Rachel Moore

We have, throughout this volume, followed the convention of designating kinship terms
by their first letter (M for mother), except Z for sister to distinguish it from S for son.
>—Prefatory page
> to David Maybury-Lewis'
> *Dialectical Societies*

Facts can very seldom be caught without their clothes on,
and [...] they are hardly seductive.
>—*Brecht on Theatre*: 226

ETHNOGRAPHIC FILM IS CONTINUALLY SUBJECTED TO CRITIQUES THAT MEASURE HOW MUCH
of what is represented to us as them is really just us. We have opined that the use of narrative
form, of authoritarian voice-over, of presenting the part for the whole, obscures authentic
representation in the service of ethnographic explanation. Likewise, the authority of the
anthropologist to structure and interpret them for us in writing was suspect. Much like the
self-critique of current written anthropology, a need for showing us showing or reflexivity
surfaced, and was duly noted. Microphones and cameras are as awkwardly inserted into films
as they were once avoided. But for all the direct address and soft peddling question and
answer—the filmic acknowledgements that what you are seeing is a representation defined

by power relations—the imbalance of power between those behind and those in front of the camera as with that of its ever-allegorized twin, the gun, could never really be negotiated. It was time to hand the camera over.

Indigenous Video is one answer to the troubles that plague ethnographic authority. Presumably montage and image-based, language loses its linear tyranny in this visual media (Marcus 1990: 8). If, indeed, it is the camera that means power, it too is ceded. Moreover, such a mobile and accessible medium provides a venue for political organization and advancement to groups whose dispersion and lack of representation could mean their doom. Just when ethnographic authority seemed its most untenable, anthropologists have found solid ground again as conduits for the filmic, and, they hope, virtual redemption of physical reality by producing indigenous video and film. Notwithstanding the laudable claims to be made for the political and cultural redemption their production represents, questions remain about a formulation in which indigenous video inherits the theoretical burdens of representation—problems that are, after all, as Marcus Banks has noted (1990), ours, not theirs.

R.

Moore

The Kayapó Video Project, along with earlier films made for the Granada Television's *Disappearing World* series, and the reports that accompanied them suggest that their use of media has served the Kayapó well. The work done for and then by the Kayapó successfully negotiates not only between first and fourth world concerns but also between often antagonistic factions within the Gê language community. The Granada *Disappearing World* series' encounter with the Kayapó, for example, produced a situation in which the Kayapó turned their own filming into a stage for their effective protest against the building of a hydroelectric dam. Not only could they galvanize support for the cause through taped messages, Kayapó leaders were able to document their international and internal visits to delight as well to maintain credibility with those who stayed at home. One remarkable Kayapó film was created to steady internal tension between two chiefs and their respective followers. They have also made a great effort to document their own rituals on video, which serve as part home movie, part cultural archive.

Like the cinema of Lumière, video is useful to the Kayapó as empirical documentation of a world that is physically out of reach but whose influence has real consequences. For the colonial culture in which cinema developed, this represented yet one more instance of capturing not just the exotic and far-away but also the routine, like workers leaving a factory, men fishing, women caring for children. The image of the Indian with a camera which now adorns book jackets, film festival posters, and journal covers, charms us by reversing this metaphor of capture. But the charm of this reversal very much still rests on the primitiveness of the bare-chested Indian, who holds the state of the art camera confidently up to his painted face. The Indian's clever adaptation to this image-producing machine makes both the primitive and the machine all the more wondrous. In what follows I will investigate the confidence this image restores for us, confidence, first of all, as regards the authenticity of the Indian who holds the camera, and confidence, secondly, in the authority of the camera itself. My contention however, is that the primacy of "culture" on the one hand, and the optical, on the other, so easily ceded to such ventures as indigenous video, begs the questions posed by difference at every turn. Instead, I suggest that we take the encounter with radical difference that ethnography, that film, can produce seriously, seriously enough not only to change our own methods of representation, but seriously enough to shatter our own otherwise stable logic and routine customs, which very much include film form.

What follows here then is not about those Kayapó videos produced by Terence Turner, directed by Kinhiabieti, Payakan, Tamok Mokuka, edited by Vincent Carelli, Mokuka, Terence Turner, Antonio Cioccari, funded by the Centro de Trabalho Indigenista, and the Spencer Foundation, made in 1990–91 that I watched up at the Museum of the American Indian. Instead, it is about what the production of Indigenous Video means to the disciplines of Anthropology and Ethnographic Film. With no access to the language spoken in the films and outdated accounts of the rituals to which they correspond, any attempt to speak about them inevitably leads me back to my understanding of film language. Operating at such a remove from the process by which they shot and edited the tapes, let alone their social context, it is difficult to tell where conventions have been learned, created or broken, and how form, as Terence Turner argues, follows function, albeit in a structural mode (1991a). For example, the camera follows men's dynamic movement in the field of action and centers them in the frame when they are speaking. Women, by contrast, are more often filmed immobile, framed off center and close-up; when they are moving they are shot with a static camera, closer up than men thus weakening the dynamism of their movement (amongst other things). Are these conventions learned from television and anthropologists, or do they reflect the general state of affairs there as well? What appear to be endless processions of men singing and dancing, casting glances to make sure they are in step, relentlessly perform culture as a fixed ritual at the start of the tape of the men's naming ceremony. Although the taping finally loosens up, its pomp is more akin to the local Veteran's Day Parade than the danger, transformation, and celebration that otherwise fuel probably equally packaged representations of such meaningful actions. The questions that arise from such long distance scrutiny are rhetorical if not imperialistic, at best. Moreover, Indigenous Videos' status within Ethnographic Film and Anthropology is not primarily tied to their representational strategies, or even their content, but to the rock solid fact of their authenticity, a value hardly unnoticed by the Kayapó filmmakers who never miss a chance to film their brethren cameramen in action.

Indigenous Video's value in the academic field is not only its (for once) unquestionable ethnographic authority, that it bypasses the dangers of interpretation, but also that it lightens the moral load of representation. The three articles of the Fall 1991 *VAR* discussed below exemplify a greater trend to see Indigenous Video as the just telos of Ethnographic Film's otherwise beleaguered project:

> By challenging the traditional structure of ethnographic authority, indigenous forms of self-representation are transforming the historical power relationship between the Self and the Other in a way that permits a more equal re-encounter in which differences are *no longer inscribed in a hierarchical power structure*. In the end, this might indicate that the solution to what is emphatically our crisis of representation might not come from the Us within but may be forced upon us by the Other from without. (Feitosa: 49; my emphasis)

This argument assumes that Indigenous Videomakers are immune from "hierarchical power structures" and ignores the possibility that image-making itself carries its own hazards. Who gets the video camera and how they get it is here a simpler matter than the envy-ridden struggle for control of the image and its interpretation that characterize Euro-American film production. Without the barriers of power and finance, of structures of thought and representation which so scuttle our own other worldly ventures, Indigenous Video performs a theoretical feat for us by taking up the mechanical tools of representation.

The teleology of the filmmaker's attempt to faithfully represent another culture's plight is clearly mapped out by Jay Ruby (1991: 50–59). It begins with varying degrees of participation and input from them, passes through direct cinema and *cinéma vérité*, cooperative and collaborative productions, and leads finally to films by *The Other*. Although Ruby is not sanguine about the ability of indigenous video to redress the structural problems of mediating knowledge, authority, and the great power of media itself, his greatest worry is the cooptation of indigenous media. Again, the authenticity of the native's voice, rather than its representational characteristics, is the most pertinent feature of Indigenous Film in his argument:

> . . . some [documentarians] recognize that audiences need to understand that documentaries always speak about and never for a subject and that films never allow us to see the world through the eyes of the native, unless the native is behind the camera.

Ruby's piece comes the closest to recognizing, albeit in a footnote (1991: 64, n. 31), what Fred Myers so gently reminds us in his article on the MacDougalls' recent films. Anthropology is not about us or about them, it's about us and them: "The problem of all ethnography, as Evans-Pritchard long ago noted, is that of translation, an act of interpretation that necessarily involves a meaningful integration for the reader/viewer" (1988: 218). Myers argues that ethnography is really only ethnography when performing its toughest of tasks, the task of manifestly figuring between us and them: "Our writing involves the exploration of our own vision, our sense of problem, within the ethnographic material. This metaphorical exploration is a source of strength as well as weakness; it alone gives relevance and relationship to brute fact" (1988: 218). Myers makes the relationship between his theory of anthropology and the function of film form explicit in his discussion of participant reflexive ethnographic film (and here the qualifiers highlight the charged issue of representing others). Reflexive ethnographic film at its best admits both of its own authority and the clash between us and them, not as a sop to "*greater honesty*," but as the structuring element of the film's form (1988: 207). The structuring element of Indigenous Videos' academic attention is the brute fact that they are made by them. If one accepts Myers' definition of ethnography, Indigenous Video would present the chore of discovering how, in viewing tapes often not made for our reception, we then figure between us and them. It is therefore not surprising that laudatory claims for Indigenous Video rest on quite different assumptions in the New World's bastion of otherness, Amazonia.

Timothy Asch, whose film work was done under the auspices of a most pernicious positivism,[1] now tells us that "a goal of anthropology has been to understand and represent, as much as possible, the insider's point of view" (1991: 103). "The Story We Now Want to Hear Is Not Ours to Tell" again presents his facilitating Yanomami self-representation as a moral solution to ethnographic authority and verity. The Asch/Chagnon films, however, used formal tropes for disorientation and unfixing authorial positions to gain a rhetorical advantage for science and explanation. Awash in constant havoc, foaming noses, screaming and crying women, their films allowed no recognizable expression or meaning to be generated out of the people's actions themselves. Instead, these films operated with a shrewd realist framing of apparent chaos so that we learned from these films that science can, after all, fix, organize the chaos. What comes to us from the synch sound and apparently candid images of people is, always, strange and chaotic. The sound from the ethnographers by contrast, the narration, and their visual organizations—i.e. the kinship charts in *The Ax Fight*; its severely edited reenactment; the didactic prologue to *The Feast*; and the calmly whispered tutorial in *Magical Death*—is full of reason and explanation. Asch's grand leap now from privileging our voices to theirs—both projects which avoid Myers' notion of the ethnographer's task—is more theoretically consistent than the expeditious change of heart which might otherwise explain such an extreme reversal. Rather, it represents the flip side of the same positivist coin.

The shift from the filming and study of groups noted for their primitive customs to assisting their own production of images has become a phenomenon that has proven particularly amenable to solving Kayapó problems. The Kayapó's success at forging alliances with the First World on a range of issues now has its own popular trajectory. Contrary to the fast theoretical and moral fix Indigenous Video appears to represent from the comments of Feitosa, Ruby and Asch, the Kayapó Video Project evolved out of many years of media and anthropological contact. It does not represent the mere act of handing over the camera, but rather a result of the long term interdependence between anthropological and indigenous interests. It is to the profound ties between shifting anthropological and Kayapó interests that we must turn to understand the success of the Indigenous Video as academic theory and Kayapó political practice.

As early as Nimuendajú in 1937, anthropology faced the problem of reconstructing culture from old informants and earlier ethnographic sketches because indigenous culture was already in an advanced state of decay. Nimuendajú begins his chapter reconstructing Sere'nte society, a Gê speaking group like the Kayapó, with the following alarm:

> In the beginning of the twentieth century the Sere'nte became demoralized by Neo-brazilian contacts, and in 1937 I found the aboriginal culture in a state of collapse. Economically and socially ruined, hemmed in by Neobrazilian settlers, the people were on the verge of complete subjection to these influences. Once more the leap from prim-itive collectivism to individualism had failed: I know not a single Indian in even fairly satisfactory circumstances under the new règime. Hence a Sere'nte prefers loafing, begging, and stealing among Neobrazilians to providing for his needs. His native village has turned into a place of scarcity; tribal influence steadily wanes as the settlers' increas-es; miscegenation extends, altering the tribal character. Thus parents who are no longer pure Indians sometimes deviate from their traditional system of educating children without scolding and blows. (1942: 8)

The fact that the decay of traditional culture also means material poverty would be confirmed by Turner when he recalls his arrival at Gorotire (1991b). Such material and cultural change, largely accounted for by colonial contact also, obviously enough, threatens the anthropologist's access to primitive society. The degree to which one can freeze and describe traditional Kayapó culture was complicated not only by the vicissitudes of contact by colonists, missionaries, anthropologists and the like, but the lack of stability in "culture" itself. Still, both Nimuendajú and Turner manage to describe traditional culture, the former by active reconstruction in a then declining culture, the latter by discerning it from underneath modern trappings. Another possibility, which still preserves primitive autonomy, describes the instability which so troubled anthropologists as itself Kayapó tradition.

"Village Fission"

Colonial encroachment, a history of fighting other indigenous neighbors for lack of territorial limits, are causes that had traditionally explained "village fission" when Joan Bamberger looked instead to internal causes for such fission amongst the Kayapó in 1979. Bamberger looks over Kayapó history and finds the break up of villages and the diminution of their size to be due to social and political factors endemic in what she understands as Kayapó culture itself. This is true to such a degree that she finds the traditional village structure, based on a division between two men's houses merely a "stated ideal" for the Kayapó themselves since there have been no such villages reported since 1936 (1979: 133).

She devotes an article to the native accounts, which "document a long-standing pattern of factionalism and feuding among Kayapó males." Quickly rejecting the "Helen of Troy theory of war, so readily proffered by the Kayapó,"—that all the major divisions have come about by quarrels between men over the adulterous liaisons of their women—Bamberger maintains that the real reason for Kayapó divisiveness is a "function of their diffuse system of political authority" (1979: 133).

A number of points emerge from her carefully detailed account of the political and kinship systems. Authority, based on popularity, age, accomplishment, generosity, and not kinship, is continually contested, requiring constant reenforcement through hierarchical naming ceremonies and initiation rituals. In so far as these ceremonies constitute tradition, it is as much the site as it is the solution for conflict. Communal rituals themselves are often "catalysts for village disturbances" (1979: 141), so that when a group breaks off from a village, while they may feel impoverished for the lack of personnel to perform most of the great Kayapó ceremonies, the possibility of conflict which "inevitably arise during performance" (1979: 141) is reduced. The danger and tension that surround ritual in Bamberger's account disturb any notion of an easy regeneration of culture through ritual itself let alone visual representations thereof. Instead it presents conflict as an integral part of cultural regeneration.

The Emergence of Kayapó "Voice"

R.
Moore

Conflict, for Bamberger, has two possible resolutions. The most common had been the "exit option" wherein the exiled group eventually itself establishes a village, and reproduces the society along with its political system, which in turn seems overdetermined to produce at some time yet another rupture, and in this unsettling manner maintain and disseminate Kayapó culture. The problem, as Bamberger saw it in 1979, was that the previously relatively simple "exit option"—which she characterizes as a mark of political underdevelopment encouraged by the availability of new village sites—was no longer appropriate to their situation in a developing environment. She stresses the need for the Kayapó to develop the "voice" option. Expressing differences vocally, a rhetorical solution to conflict, substitutes for taking territory. What seems crucial to note from this 1979 assessment, albeit based on earlier fieldwork and other documentation, is that by exercising the "voice" option, the Kayapó are doing something new to them which accommodates the Brazilian state's need to contain the population. While Bamberger denigrates the "exit option" as "nonprogressive," and, adopting Albert O. Hirshman's terms, an "avoidance mechanism," it had nonetheless been the "tradition" (1979: 144). "Voice," far from being an extension of any tradition of Kayapó oratory, debate, and political conversation which now characterize the political sub-genre of Kayapó Video, was a direct consequence of, to use Hirshman's wording, "raising the cost of exit" and "increasing the rewards of voice" (1979: 144). The assumption here is that "voice" is in and of itself a good thing. The clear consequence of developing and exercising the "voice" option however, is forgetting that other option, that option which for us here and now in the academy, as for the Kayapó in the ever diminishing forests of Central Brazil, is unthinkable, to just get up and leave, taking your associates, and perhaps your family—for in Kayapó culture familial kinship is a much weaker force than political affiliation—with you, graduate students and all. The voice option was privileged not because it might prove efficacious, but because it fit into dominant (both Brazilian and Harvard) logic. The emergence of voice is thus part of the project of containment:

> The National Indian Foundation (FUNAI) has severely reduced opportunities for the Indians to continue their practice of exiting, while at the same time raising opportunities for voice, not from any grand concern for the preservation of indigenous communities as such, but from a more practical interest in promoting peaceful relations between Indians and Brazilian settlers in the Amazon region. (1979: 145)

The ascendence of indigenous media within Kayapó culture is a consequent development this voice "option." Bamberger ends her article with a figure that readers of *Time* and *Variety* would now recognize. Robni (Raoni), whom she had met ten years previously when he had just been appointed a tribal leader, has indeed become an accepted spokesman for his group capable of negotiating with Brazilian officials as opposed to the custom of "mannered harangues and exhortations [which] served to safeguard village traditions" (1979: 145). Robni, wrote Bamberger, "can be said to exemplify a new voice which has been activated from the outside. It appears that the Kayapó voice mechanism, once so rudimentary, needed only to receive the right impetus to discover itself" (1979: 145).

The Brazilian government, lacking any experience in the shifty and potentially volatile method of traditional Kayapó debate, and certainly not willing to have either party exercise the "exit" option, must be spoken to by someone with "voice." Voice itself here is thus a construction, predicated on that which it is believed will be listened to, or in some cases quite bluntly, who the Brazilians say they want to talk to (1979: 145).

From Authoritarian to Authentic Voices

Terence Turner's account of the emergence of Kayapó "voice," written with a set of new concerns in mind, would appear to bear out Bamberger's prediction in its final analysis of chief Ropni's[2] oratory (1988). But it differs in that it weaves Kayapó "voice" back into Kayapó tradition in the process of producing a general theory about the way in which myth and history intertwine.

To counter our mistaken belief that contact is their defining myth and not ours, Turner finds a congruity between the myths and histories of contact with Brazilians and with those that deal with other indigenous people. He takes care to both distinguish and then disrupt the conventions of myth and history showing the Kayapó capable of wittily "mythologizing" the past to suit present day reality. Turner provides plentiful examples of myths and historical tales from Johannes Wilbert's *The Folk Literature of the Gê Indians* and Lux Vidal's 1977 ethnography which support his final claim as regards the similar historical and mythic content of Ropni's oratory. Only two paragraphs, however, are given over to describing the way in which these tales function in everyday life, the way stories are told (1988: 198). Similarly, notwithstanding his precaution that we look at specific genres of representation before assuming them to be homogeneous, we are given no understanding of how the filmed "political oratory" relates to other forms of Kayapó political talk. Instead, they relate to his universal theory that myth and history are not mutually exclusive, self-contained categories. "Myth" and "history," sums Turner, "are thus deployed side by side in a dialogically sophisticated performance in which different modes and levels of consciousness are synthesized into an effective rhetorical unity" (1988: 211). Finally, the oratory is reminiscent of a form we know all too well: "This situation certainly has its counterparts in our society: witness the speeches of our current political leaders" (213). Turner concludes by noting the similarity between Kayapó political rhetoric and that of modern capitalism. The transformation to authoritative and at the same time authentic "voice" from the "harangues" as they are characterized by Bamberger's account, is also an adoption of good rhetoric, whose "sophisticated performance" can hardly fail to be "effective." The question here is not if the oratory serves Kayapó interests, but if, in so serving, their accomplishment also sustains our own belief in rhetorical authority whose shrewd performance on their part is discerned with such pleasure.

Whether learned, created, or reinvented, Kayapó political rhetoric before the camera reproduces the authoritarianism and chauvinism of our own. George Bush could not end a call to unity as Raoni did in *Peace Between Chiefs* by saying "and when I get home I'm going to fuck my wife," but what better way to characterize the situation in which power has been put to rights. The rhetoric of the family is a poor second to the warm kick of recognition this statement provokes. Nor could a politician here refer to the deleterious effects of the slit-eyed people as Raoni does, but merely the apparently innocuous 'fair trade agreement.' By relegating now odious positions safely to the primitive realm they can be enjoyed from a distance or alternatively, for their distance. Spectator "pleasure" here derives not from directly participating in the film's content, but from discerning the mimetic residue activated by the encounter between primitive and civilized. If contact is, indeed, our defining myth, Indigenous Video becomes one long performance of that myth in its first world reception.

Theory and Practice

Turner rethinks the integration of indigenous and Western practices when he charts the parallel change in his Anthropology and Kayapó society (1991b). He recalls his first arrival at Gorotire and with all the irony hind-sight allows describes a young couple "depressed, upset, and confused [. . .] by the Kayapó's failure to live up to our idea of what a Kayapó village should look like" (1991b: 289). The Kayapó had also the suffered severe material consequences of contact: "They had lost all but one hundred of their population to disease, further internal

schisms, and starvation resulting from administrative incompetence and neglect" (1991b: 287).
The Kayapó, in the middle of two competing interests, the SPI (The Brazilian Government's
"Service for the Protection of Indians") and the Missionaries, both of which were intent on
destroying Kayapó culture in the interests of keeping them both contained and dependent on
the government on the one hand, and Christian conversion on the other, had modified their
savage appearance in order to deal with the SPI and Missionaries. "By the time of our arrival in
1962," Turner disparages, "most men had removed their lip plugs, had their hair cut short
Brazilian style, and had taken to wearing shorts and occasionally T-shirts in the village,
although some still appeared in long hair, lip plugs, and penis sheaths" (1991b: 289). But then,
to the anthropologist's delight, the western trappings disappear and the couple find
themselves in the midst of a women's naming ceremony (1991b: 289). Kayapó culture was alive
and well beneath the veneer they had produced to accommodate colonial domination.

The anthropological interest for Turner back then seemed to "lie in discovering the
authentic Kayapó social and cultural system beneath the corrosive overlay of imposed
political, social and ideological forms constituting the situations of contact, and in analyzing
how this system might work, or might have worked, in its own terms" (1991b: 292). That
defining codicil, "in its own terms," much like the concept of indigenous "voice," is difficult
to locate. The terms Turner used to sum up his essay on "Kinship, Household and
Community Structure amongst the Kayapó" in 1979 suggest that Kayapó thought must
have had a strong, as yet undocumented influence on Talcott Parsons, not to mention Marx
and Lévi-Strauss:

> The analysis I have presented has been an experiment in the synthesis of structuralist,
> functionalist, and system theoretical notions with a dialectical point of view. The model
> developed in the preceding general paper has been put to the test of accounting for the
> normative and dynamic features of a particular Gê society, including the contradictions
> implicit in its structure and the short-run and long term forms of instability and
> structural change resulting from them. I suggest, on the basis of the success of the
> model in meeting this test, that it might profitably be applied, *mutatis mutandis*, to other
> societies of the same type. (1979: 214)

The discovery and rescue of real Kayapó culture from beneath the corrosive western overlay
not only proffered a parallel material gain for the Kayapó, but also provided anthropological
capital, if profitably applied. The authenticity of Kayapó ritual practice, kinship structures,
hunting forays, etc. maintained a valuable anthropological object of study, allowing us to
confirm or disprove theories, say, that it is the superstructure and not the base that is the
privileged term, or that dual societies exist, thus providing fuel for various understandings of
the creation of meaning, or whatever our problems may turn out to be.

More relevant to the rescue of *current* Anthropology, however, is that the assertion of
Kayapó culture was, by itself, also defiant, subversive. Back then, writes Turner, the Kayapó
had no "notion that their assemblage of received customs, ritual practices, social values, and
institutions constituted a 'culture' in the anthropological sense, nor any idea of the reflexive
role of that culture in the reproduction of their society and personal identities" (1991b: 301).
By participating in the creation of a consciousness which allows the Kayapó to see their own
culture's autonomous value, the anthropologist sees himself aligned with an inherently
radical project. The effect of contacts with anthropologists, "photographers, ethnozoologists,
ethnomusicologists, museum collectors, journalists, cinematographers," (1991b: 300) was "to
catalyze the development of an awareness on the part of the Kayapó of the potential political
value of 'culture' in their relations with the alien society by which they found themselves
surrounded" (1991b: 301). Kayapó realization of their own culture's political value as a
"culture" is a major reason, in Turner's opinion, for their material success such that the
Gorotire, continuing the particular example with whose poverty he began, now manage their

own affairs and profit from mahogany and gold concessions on their communal land (1991b: 302). The reification of culture turns out to mean the redemption of culture. This transformation from reification to redemption, while it might have remarkable consequences for a theory of realism, sidesteps what to my mind is still the unanswered central question. Why, we should ask, does "Culture" have such political and mythic value that it is not just the means, but the very grounds for "survival?"[3] This question is posed not only by the successful Kayapó, but also by the current clamoring of multitudinous historically disenfranchised peoples (perhaps more often, their academic or journalistic hangers-on) for traditions, histories, languages that will satisfy culture's daunting requirements.[4]

Daunting as these requirements may be, Turner's report is testimony to the thoroughness with which they are so quickly understood. The stakes, after all, are none other than survival. And while Turner sees anthropological attention (the category into which he places all studious or observant visitors) as the catalyst for self-awareness, film and video lend themselves to the project of defining and sustaining culture particularly well. Since Lumière, (Barnouw: 22–23), however, the filming of events has shaped and altered the events themselves. Power plays for the camera, as well as posturing for the image are almost endemic to visual media. It is hardly surprising that the filming and video-taping of Kayapó culture and politics have had effects on Kayapó culture and politics themselves. As Turner's reports on the Kayapó Video project indicate, the use and ownership of the video camera quickly became an integral part of political power in internal as well as external struggles (1991a: 71–74). The ascendence of video also corresponds to a kind of self-fashioning amongst the Kayapó as traditional Indians. The resurgence of Kayapó body and face painting, long hair, and bare chests so evident at Altamira in the Granada film reverses the westernizing trend Turner found in earlier self-fashionings amongst the Kayapó as evidenced by the photo he reproduces from his early fieldwork which shows the bare chested anthropologist next to a Kayapó Indian in a black shirt and pants wearing sun-glasses. Although these striking images of resistance as ceremonial culture, first made by foreign film crews and then authorized by the Kayapó themselves, may well be in the end what we want to see, the question of their "authenticity" in this charged and shifting environment is, as Turner pointed out on *Latinos en Accion*, moot. The more relevant issue for both anthropology and film theory, in so far as this conception of indigenous video relies so heavily on a theory of the visible as real, is the degree to which the real (and, hence, that which may be redeemed), in turn, becomes limited to that which can be represented in reified visual form.

From Reification to Redemption

The case for redemption through the film image is made by Siegfried Kracauer in his *Theory of Film: The Redemption of Physical Reality* (1960). Kracauer's early work paid radical homage to the fetish quality of a surface reality available exclusively in film which he felt gave the audience visual access to the magical machinations that informed their daily lives. The disembodied, multiple legs of the famous "Tiller Girls" produced the undulating, abstract pattern which served Kracauer in 1927 to describe reification's inverse potential power in the form of the "Mass Ornament." Not only does film give the spectator access to and experience of things otherwise out of reach in their fetish—and thus for Kracauer real—form, it gives visual representation to things and people from which we would otherwise turn away. By the time he produced his later work in exile, Kracauer was so thoroughly bound to the world of objects that the function of the film image was to redeem physical reality. The film screen functioned, as Athena's sword did for Perseus, to allow one to see what we could not bear to see in reality, so that one might incorporate that reality back into experience.

> The mirror reflections of horror are an end in themselves. As such they beckon the
> spectator to take them in and thus incorporate into his memory the real face of things

too dreadful to be beheld in reality. In experiencing the rows of calves' heads [in Franju's famous documentary film about the slaughterhouse in Paris] or the concentration camps, we redeem horror from its invisibility behind the veils of panic and imagination. (Kracauer, 1960: 305–306)

Given the primacy thus placed on the optical, the "redemption of physical reality" through visual representation, which provides the living "animistic solidarity with the dead," runs up against what Gertrude Koch defines as "intrinsic limits" when faced with experiences that have no corresponding physical form: "If 'seeing' is understood as 'experiencing,' then mass annihilation could only be experienced to the extent that it is possible to give it visual form. Only that which is concrete in nature, that which belongs to the world of physical things, can be visualized" (100). "Thus arises," as Koch puts it, "a horrifying hierarchy extending from the mountains of corpses of those whose bodies remained to be captured on film, to the people who literally went up in smoke, having left behind them no visual mnemonic trace that could serve their redemption" (104).

R.
Moore

Walter Benjamin in 1936 Europe remarked that "Any man today can lay claim to being filmed" (231). Such egalitarian access to visual representation is also now possible for Kayapó men today, given the presence of no less than two indigenous video projects, as well as numerous documentary and feature films, not to mention the miscellaneous footage such ventures inevitably produce. The project of redemption through the image would seem well on its way. Distances of space, differences in taboos in the case of indigenous societies, make the category of what belongs to the world of physical things more elastic and difficult than Koch's example implies. We look across boundaries of space at the living rather than across time at the dead. This project, however, so dependent on the fidelity of the image to reality, so tied to documentation, to the empiricism of being there, runs up against similar limits to those Koch points out by virtue of such boundless faith in the image. Such faith in the visible always raises, at the same time, the ghost of what remains invisible. This ghost can be said to haunt, and thus necessarily propel the project of producing indigenous video towards infinity. Hence the inevitable call for more images (and more grants to facilitate them) thinly veiled by Turner's rather naive musings:

> Will video become a political possession of communal chiefs, or remain a more open field of social praxis available to younger men and women? Will Kayapó video documentarians of their own culture be able to step beyond the traditional mounds of communal ceremony to focus on the less glamorous but no less significant activities and family relations of everyday life? Can the accumulation and circulation of a common stock of videos of their own culture become a genuine focus of intercommunal relations among the mutually autonomous and factious Kayapó villages? (1991a: 76)

The possibilities, indeed, the necessity for getting everything on tape in this empirically bound schema of capitalist accumulation where stock in images is running high, are endless . . . Meanwhile, if media exposure comes to mean cultural survival, if ethnographic film continues to maintain that what you see represents the significant rather than the selected, regardless of who has the camera, a less horrific, but still crude hierarchy emerges separating visible people and practices from those that defy visual representation.[5]

Faith in the value of film as documentary evidence, whether for legal, ethnographic, or moral courts, is, to my mind, a desperate faith. It is not easily dismissed. David Macdougall concludes his recent essay on memory by insisting on the physical nature of the filmic medium unavailable to verbal forms:

> Film images may be reinterpreted in a variety of new contexts but the unalterable record of appearance and place contained in them may ultimately prove to have a more

profound effect upon our "memory" of history than the interpretations we attach to them. (1992: 36)

The obstinate theory that film provides an "unalterable record," informs Turner as well, who reaches towards video recording as, as he puts it, a "concrete medium"(1991a: 70). Unfortunate as this description may be, it nonetheless points to the paradox of a form that is at once merely light and shadow, and at the same time one that uses real objects and real people for its gums and varnishes.

We all have before us now an example that pits the physical reality of the image against its interpretation in very blunt terms. The faith that police violence could be exposed, that finally we had it on tape was shattered by a classic cinema studies exercise which will doubtless in turn fuel scholars' pens for months to come. The filmed image's redemptive value for physical reality is paradoxical. That which constitutes the empirical value of the physical reality at the same time limits that value to the image itself. Belief in the filmic image as a document which can redeem an otherwise irrecuperable past or suppressed contemporary truth is desperately necessary. But the firm grip of the present on the past and the magnitude of the contemporary lies which obtain also make that belief necessarily desperate. It is in desperation that we turn to filmic proof of a reality recognized everyday by victims and victimizers alike. What hides the truth is not an absence of evidence, but lies and beliefs large enough to obscure it. The magnitude of such despair, held in the balance by eighty one seconds of videotape, is all too evident. The "physical nature" of film, its ability to serve the record, has its limits inscribed in its very form: the frame, the shot, the cut. The redemptive value of the filmic image is limited not only from without to that which has a physical form, but also from within the image. Trapped in the frame, its very "concrete" nature weighs hard on the image. It is at once set in whatever truth it is cast and set up by the form in which it is fixed.

This paradox is worth bearing in mind as more and more eggs get dropped in the positivist basket. On the one hand, it accounts for the image delirium of the Kayapó Project, desperately collecting more images. On the other hand, such accumulation suggests a neglect of the invisible. That is not to say, we need more and different "concrete" images, but rather to ask what our stake is in the primitive's image; what are we desperate for? We have no easy access to our own consciousness with regards to the now, and I suspect always "disappearing" Other.[6] Lacking the means to register, let alone reflect on the "shocks" that radical difference engenders which might lead us to question our own beliefs and practices, we choose yet another source of mastery and turn to the authentic voices and images made by that other whose relationship to our own consciousness otherwise remains a mystery. Turning the camera over, just at the point when our own methods and theories appear to be exhausted, not only defers their critique (and thus assures their recycling), but far more importantly, preempts the creativity, already up against enormous odds,[7] required to change them.

Ethnographic film can be both daring and honest enough to pursue and reveal its own stakes in cultural difference. It is severely hampered, however, when film's domain is limited to either a reproduction of physical reality or narrative conventions. Defined by Hollis Frampton as "anything that you can fit in the projector's sprockets" (Jenkins 1984: 27) avant-garde film significantly expands the notion of what film can be. James Clifford looked to ethnography's surrealist heritage to find a "situation in which ethnography is again something unfamiliar and surrealism not a bounded province of art and literature" (1981: 539). A similar appreciation for avant-garde film can't be confined to a particular period. Looking over the avant-garde's near century long and extremely diffuse heritage to learn some of the potential of the film form, however, produces an exhaustive compendium of relational problems for the spectator, rather than a well worn system of habitual devices. "Establishing shots," "reaction shots," for example—the traditional tools of the trade in ordering the filmic universe—are either dispensed with or parodied. René Clair's *Entr'acte*

(1924) debunks a host of conventions in just twenty-five minutes. Graphic matches turn a ballerina into a bearded man, matches on action have people running in chase the wrong way, panning the crowd yields spatial confusion rather than perspective. When the pursued man breaks through the screen at the film's end, even the frame, for a moment, is not sacrosanct. Ethnographic film, never fun and games, nonetheless has failed to interrogate its language with the excruciating rigor that characterized say, the "structural" avant-garde.[8] It is therefore largely from the filmmaker's side of the divide today that we get films which can speak unabashedly about difference. Self-consciousness about form feeds, rather than frustrates representational strategies in the work of Marlon Riggs, Yvonne Rainer, and Trinh T. Minh-ha, three well known avant-garde filmmakers whose work could not be placed in the context of Ethnographic Film without mutual strains and groans.

Ethnographic Film ignores the many avant-gardes film has produced in much the same way anthropology ignored the surrealist elements of ethnography:

> The surrealist elements of modern ethnography tend to go unacknowledged by a science that sees itself engaged in the reduction of incongruities rather than, simultaneously, in their production. But is not every ethnographer something of a surrealist, a reinventor and reshuffler of realities? Ethnography, the science of cultural jeopardy, presupposes a constant willingness to be surprised, to unmake interpretive syntheses, and to value—when it comes—the unclassified, unsought Other. (Clifford 1981: 564)

Films that produce incongruities and sustain a willingness to be surprised nonetheless continue to be made but continue to be exceptional. Just as ethnography shied away from the perils and pleasures of surrealism, turning in some cases towards abstract empiricism, ethnographic filmmaking now risks a similar loss by embracing the savage empiricism indigenous video cannot help but represent to the discipline.

The power that Indigenous Video can help regain for the dispossessed, as well as the creative potential this extends to alter film and video form is beyond question. The more credibly indigenous the medium, however, the more it solves their problems and not ours. To annex our academic/artistic discipline's redemption to that of indigenous peoples without allowing their work to prompt self-conscious and daring exploration of our politics of theory, our politics of style, furthers neither the projects of Ethnography nor Filmmaking. A redemption so effected belongs rather, along with a host of other image-bound enterprises, to the fundraiser's and to the patron's calling. Hence the brooding sermons of *Cultural Survival*'s David Maybury-Lewis as he introduces public television's *Millennium* series in a segment humbly called, "The Shock of the Other." This "melancholy meditation about 'trying to capture the wisdom of tribal peoples before it is all gone'" (Goodman: C13) comes from a man who, in 1979, was primarily preoccupied by the fear that we might mistake a sister for a son (see the epigraph above). That project of extracting, preserving and packaging culture to be negotiated as academic capital then, and moral capital now, was and is, well, beyond redemption.

Notes

I thank Catherine Benamou (Latinos en Accion) and Emelia Seubert (Museum of the American Indian) for their generosity in giving me invaluable access to visual material; Faye Ginsburg and Elizabeth Weatherford for that and their commitment to exposure and debate in both formal and informal contexts; Nicole Ridgeway, Lucien Taylor, and Ximena Vargas for providing the measured degrees of criticism, encouragement and tolerance needed to get things done.

1.   For a detailed discussion of the scientific drive behind the Asch/Chagnon project see Eliot Weinberger's "The Camera People," *Transition* 55: 40. It is also noteworthy that the project was partially funded by geneticists. Chagnon's initial study of the Yanomami was instigated by the Atomic Energy Commission who sought scientific access to an untouched, primitive society for comparative analysis.

2.   Bamberger and Turner give either two different names or spell the same name differently. The possibility that there are two leaders who qualify as subjects for a Marlon Brando film is daunting.

3.   And indeed, if Payakan (who, beginning as head of the Brazilian Bureau of Indian Affairs post at Gorotire became leader of the protest against the Hydroelectric Dam, was the visionary for the Kayapó Video Project) is to withstand the rape charges now leveled against him, it will be from behind the skirts of culture. Whether by diverting blame to the wife who is considered too primitive to be tried by law, blaming the white man's drink, the infusion of the white woman's/man's money which disturbed his place within his own culture, or an impulsive redress to the hateful practices of whites towards Kayapó women, Payakan's defenses find their best ground in the purity of Kayapó culture, compromised severely by his career as a mediator between the Kayapó, the Brazilian Government, International Business and various NGOs.

4.   Renato Rosaldo discusses the vicissitudes of "Culture" for both us and them in "Ideology, Place, and People without Culture." He contrasts his experience with people who half-joked "that they were people without culture" (1988: 7) in the Philippines to the ideology of culture within the academy as well as in the social and political sphere. For the academy, Rosaldo fabricates an "Imaginary Handbook for Young Anthropologists" which "could even advise members of theoretical schools about their preferred places. During my graduate school days in the 1960s, for example, we all knew that smart structural anthropologists could best find what they were looking for either in eastern Indonesia or among Brazil's Gê-speaking peoples whose dual organizations were strikingly visible in aerial photographs of their villages. Ethnoscientists, on the other hand, prospered most in the Philippines or in the highlands of Chiapas, Mexico, where people seemed to care about nothing so much as naming plants" (1988: 79). Rosaldo presents instead "border zones," so feared and repressed by Reagan and the media, "along with our supposedly transparent cultural selves, [. . .] as profoundly cultural as anything else" (1988: 87).

5.   While the category is as shifting as it is self-defining, Kayapó practices of violence towards women, gang rape, (See Joan Bamberger, 1974: 275, n. 5 and 277–78), the very danger embedded in ritual, and the always evasive "everyday life" are still on the agenda for Athena's polished shield. Perhaps, given the apparently cyclical nature of filmic and physical reality, since they don't lend themselves to the screen image, they will drop out of practice all together.

6.   As Turner points out, the Kayapó are not disappearing but rather growing in number and adapting to change on their own terms.

7.   These odds are also very practical. Filmmakers have marginal relationships to institutions, they live by the seat of their pants between occasional funding for their films. Anthropologists, by contrast, have steady incomes and institutional channels available to fund special projects. Their academic and fieldwork credentials can suffice in the social sciences to fund projects in visual anthropology which sees the visual as an obvious extension of science and not the new and different form, requiring likewise different talents, that it is.

8.   See, for instance: Ken Jacobs' *Tom Tom the Piper's Son*, (1969, 86 min); Kubelka's *Unsere Afrikareise*; Joyce Wieland's *Sailboat*; Hollis Frampton's *(nostalgia)*, Snow's *Wavelength*. Given the patience required for some to watch ethnographic film and video, asking visual anthropologists to screen such classics seems only fair.

References

Asch, Timothy. 1991. "The Story We Want to Hear is Not Ours to Tell." *VAR* 7 (2).
Bamberger, Joan. 1974. "The Myth of Matriarchy: Why Men Rule in Primitive Society." In *Women, Culture and Society*, ed. Rosaldo, M.A. and Lamphere, L. Palo Alto: Stanford University Press.
———. 1979. "Exit and Voice in Central Brazil." In *Dialectical Societies*, ed. David Maybury-Lewis. Cambridge: Harvard University Press.
Banks, Marcus. 1990. "The Seductive Veracity of Ethnographic Film." *VAR* 6 (1).
Barnouw, Erik. 1983. *Documentary, A History of the Non-Fiction Film*. Oxford: Oxford University Press.
Benjamin, Walter. 1969 (1936). "The Work of Art in the Age of Mechanical Reproduction." In *Illuminations*, trans. Harry Zohn. New York: Schocken.
Clifford, James. 1981. "On Ethnographic Surrealism." *Comparative Studies in Society and History* 23 (4).
Feitosa, Monica. 1991. "Guest Editorial—The Other's Visions: From the Ivory Tower to the Barricade." *VAR* 7 (2).
Goodman, Walter. 1992. "A Sermon on Capturing Tribal Peoples' Wisdom." *New York Times* (11 May): C13.
Jenkins, Bruce. 1984. *The Films of Hollis Frampton: A Critical Study*. Dissertation, Northwestern University.
Koch, Gertrude. 1991. "'Not yet accepted anywhere': Exile, Memory and Image in Kracauer's Conception of History." *New German Critique* 54.
Kracauer, Siegfried. 1960. *Theory of Film: The Redemption of Physical Reality*. New York: Oxford University Press.

—. 1975 (1927). "The Mass Ornament." Trans. Barbara Correll and Jack Zipes. *New German Critique* (5).

MacDougall, David. 1992. "Films of Memory." *VAR* 8 (1).

Marcus, George. 1990. "The Modernist Sensibility in Recent Ethnographic Writing and the Cinematic Metaphor of Montage." *VAR* 7 (1).

Myers, Fred R. 1988. "From Ethnography to Metaphor: Recent Films from David and Judith MacDougall." *Cultural Anthropology* 3 (2).

Nimuendajú, Curt. 1942. *The Serente*. Trans. Robert H. Lowie. Los Angeles: Frederick Webb Hodge Anniversary Publication Fund.

Rosaldo, Renato. 1988. "Ideology, Place and People without Culture." *Cultural Anthropology* 3 (1).

Ruby, Jay. 1991. "Speaking For, Speaking About, Speaking With, or Speaking Alongside." *VAR* 7 (2).

Turner, Terence. 1991a. "The Social Dynamics of Video Media in an Indigenous Society." *VAR* 7 (2).

—. 1991b. "Representing, Resisting, Rethinking." In *Colonial Situations*, ed. George Stocking.

—. 1988. "History, Myth and Social Consciousness among the Kayapó of Central Brazil." In *Rethinking History and Myth*, ed. Jonathan Hill. Urbana: University of Illinois Press.

—. 1979. "The Gê and Bororo of Central Brazil." In *Dialectical Societies*, ed. David Maybury-Lewis. Cambridge: Harvard University Press.

Weinberger, Eliot. 1992. "The Camera People." *Transition* 55.

two

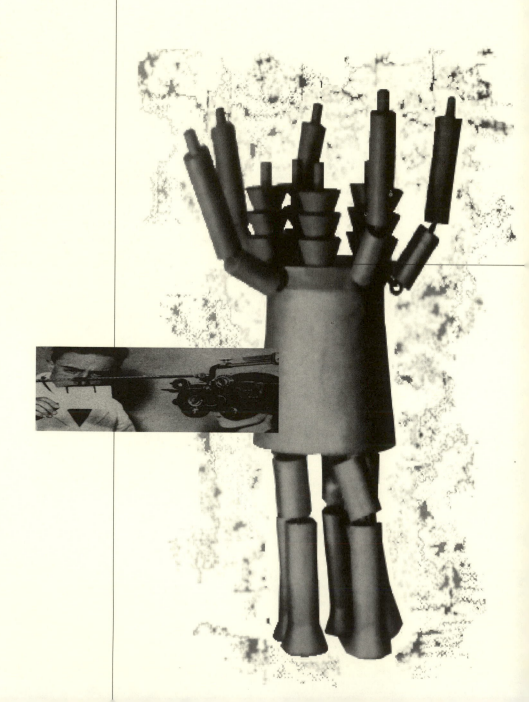

Surrealism, Vision, and Cultural Criticism

Between the Street and the Salon
The Dilemma of Surrealist Politics in the 1930s

Susan Rubin Suleiman

> How are we to imagine an existence oriented solely toward Boulevard
> Bonne-Nouvelle, in rooms by Le Corbusier and Oud?
>
> —Walter Benjamin, "Surrealism"

WHY SHOULD AN AMERICAN INTELLECTUAL TODAY (SPRING 1991) CARE ABOUT THE POLITICAL dilemmas of a European avant-garde movement more than half a century ago? I can think of at least two reasons. The war in the Persian Gulf, catching many of us by surprise, once again brought History with a capital H to the forefront of consciousness; and with that has come, for many, the renewed question of the political responsibility of artists and intellectuals in a time of historical crisis. But already in 1989, the Mapplethorpe affair and the Helms Amendment had produced the paradoxical result of politicizing certain artistic practices which, without the attention paid to them by the would-be censors, might well have faded into the general postmodern spectacle.

The second reason is linked to the ongoing theoretical debate about postmodernism and the possibilities of oppositional or critical art in the age of instant commodification and "spectacularization."[1] It seems obvious that any understanding of the avant-garde's political aspirations, let alone any attempt to revive similar aspirations, must include a historical examination of Surrealism, as both influence and example—example not in the edifying sense, but in that of a still relevant case. Such an examination might well take as its epigraph Michel Foucault's reflection, in the opening chapter of *Discipline and Punish*, on why he wants to write the history of the birth of the prison: "Simply because I am interested in the past? No, if one means by that writing a history of the past in terms of the present. Yes, if one means writing the history of the present."[2]

I. The Ground On Which to Stand.

In June 1936, there opened in London the first great international exhibition of Surrealist art. On that occasion, which coincided with the official founding of the British branch of the Surrealist movement, the leader of the French Surrealists, André Breton, gave a public lecture titled "Limites non-frontières du surréalisme," "Limits Not Frontiers of Surrealism."[3] The concern with a kind of geopolitics of Surrealism indicated by the title of this lecture/essay (it was published a few months later) is linked to a programmatic question that can also be formulated in topographical terms: What is the ground on which Surrealism stands, in 1936? Breton's clear spelling out of the "fundamental propositions" to which all Surrealists necessarily subscribed ("I would like you to believe that no effort has been spared from the very beginning to discourage those who could not subscribe to a fundamental and indivisible scheme of propositions which I shall now briefly restate" [152]) have made some commentators refer to this text as a "third manifesto of Surrealism."[4]

According to Breton, the two fundamental propositions of the collective Surrealist project in 1936 were the same as they had always been: first, "adhesion to the theory of dialectical materialism," with all of its accompanying theses, including the necessity of social revolution and class struggle; second, adhesion to the idea (for which Breton quotes the authority of Marx and Engels) that the "economic factor is not the *only* determining factor in history"—in other words, that work on the level of superstructures is also necessary and effective. This second proposition allows Breton to affirm the importance of Surrealist discoveries and innovations in what he calls the "highways of great mental adventure"—highways which, for him, necessarily traverse the domain of poetry and art, without being restricted to that domain. Surrealism, as he and other members of the group have been repeating for more than ten years, is not merely an aesthetic style, it is "a new consciousness of life" (152).

One path that leads to the new consciousness sought by the Surrealists (here again, the topographical metaphor is Breton's) is the path of objective chance, "le hasard objectif," that curious phenomenon of sudden, illuminating, soul-shattering coincidences in individual life, whose manifestations Breton had been exploring in his life and writings ever since the early 1920s. Another path is what Breton calls objective humor, a kind of gallows humor that he would later call "humour noir." The link between these "two poles between which surrealism will be able to produce its most far-reaching sparks" (again, Breton's spatial metaphor) is that of *automatism*, which Breton does not bother to define other than to say that it alone provides a chance of "resolving, outside the economic plane, all the antinomies which, since they existed before our present social regime was formed, are not likely to disappear with it" (155). Echoing, and even exaggerating, the affirmations of the *Second Surrealist Manifesto* (1930), Breton once again claims as the ultimate ambition of Surrealism to resolve seemingly irreconcilable contradictions: "of reality and dream, of reason and madness, of objectivity and subjectivity, of perception and representation, of past and future, of the collective sense and individual love; even of life and death" (155).

Surrealism, in short, is the superstructural equivalent of the class struggle, whose ultimate aim is to abolish social and economic contradictions. That is why Breton can consider Surrealist activity in the realm of poetry and art as the genuine artistic counterpart of social revolution; and why he can combat, as a Surrealist, the aesthetic doctrine which by 1936 had become the official doctrine in Soviet Russia and in Western communist parties—the doctrine of socialist realism, which (in Breton's words) "attempts to impose on the artist the exclusive duty of describing proletarian misery and the struggle for liberation in which the proletariat is engaged." The trouble with socialist realism—aside from the fact that it seeks to regiment what should be the totally free activity of the individual artistic imagination—is that it deals only with clearly declared intentions and surface representations. As such, says Breton, "this new doctrine flagrantly contradicts marxist teaching"—for as Engels himself wrote in a letter in 1888, "'The more the [political] opinions of the author remain hidden, the better it is for the work of art'" (155).

S.
Suleiman

Surrealism, which pursues the unexpected discoveries of dreams and of automatic writing, thus turns out to be more in keeping with Marxist teaching than socialist realism. And as if that bit of dialectical provocation were not enough, Breton now rephrases the whole argument in Freudian terms (thus seeking to resolve, perhaps, what in the 1930s was felt by many to be an insurmountable contradiction between Freud and Marx): "We expressly oppose the view that it is possible to create a work of art or even, properly considered, any useful work by expressing only the *manifest content* of an age. On the contrary, surrealism proposes to express its *latent content*" (155). Socialist realism, by that criterion, is neither art nor useful; Surrealism is both.

Having declared that Surrealism proposes to express, in its works and *as* its work, the latent content of an age, Breton goes on to an extremely interesting analysis of the English Gothic novel, which he claims accomplished a similar work in the late eighteenth century, another time of general European crisis. Besides pointing out this historical parallel, Breton identifies the Gothic novel as a precursor of the Surrealist preoccupation with dreams and with a kind of automatic writing. He quotes a letter by Horace Walpole ("the initiator of the genre") in which Walpole explains that the origin of *The Castle of Otranto* was a curious dream, which impelled him to sit down and start to write "without knowing in the least what I intended to say or relate" (157). But even more interesting, from my present point of view, is the attention Breton pays to the preferred site of the Gothic novel—the castle. "Are there places predestined for the accomplishment of the particular form of mental transmission [*médiumnité*] that manifests itself in such a case?" he asks. "Yes, there must exist observatories of the inner sky. I mean, naturally, observatories already existing in the outer world. This we may describe, from the surrealist point of view, as the *castle problem*" (157–58).

The "castle problem," for Breton, does not concern the specific trappings of the Gothic castle, but rather its extraordinary power as a collective myth. This power to engage the imagination is, he explains, at the source of the continuing appeal of the Gothic genre—but the Surrealist challenge is not to rewrite the Gothic; it is to find *another* place, as powerful in its mythical effect and psychic affect as the castle. "Human psychism in its most universal aspect found in the Gothic castle and its accessories a point of fixation so precise that it would be essential to discover the equivalent of such a place for our period. (*Everything leads us to believe that it is not a factory*)" (158, my emphasis).

Breton's parenthetical dismissal of the factory as mythic site must be read, I contend, as highly overdetermined and symptomatic. The most obvious way to read the parenthetical remark is as one more barb against socialist realism and its prescriptions about the representation of workers. Wrong again, says Breton ironically—a factory will never produce the powerful affect of the Gothic castle. This meaning becomes interestingly complicated, however, if one takes into account the introduction Breton provided for his London lecture in its published version, which appeared eight months later. Looking back at June 1936 from the vantage point of February 1937, what does Breton see? "The International Surrealist Exhibition opened and was enjoying its success at the very moment when the French workers, employing for the first time tactics quite unpremeditated on their part, were forcibly *occupying the factories* and, as a direct result of the simultaneous adoption of this attitude, were everywhere triumphant in their principal demands" (151, my emphasis). Breton is referring here to the famous "June days," the workers' strikes during the first month of the Popular Front government, which led to major labor reforms in France, including the institution of the still sacred four weeks' paid vacation. The triumph of the workers and the success of the Surrealist Exhibition thus become linked in the opening paragraph of the essay; and the link between them is not only one of temporal simultaneity, it is also one of metaphorical equivalence.

The paragraph begins, in effect, by speaking about the international influence of Surrealism, which "has grown with ever increasing rapidity during recent years." But although success is often the prelude to inaction and "stupor," this will not be the case with

Fig. 1. Plate 8 in *Nadja*. "No: not even the extremely handsome, extremely useless Porte Saint-Denis . . . "

Surrealism: "If we talk here of the highest point [of Surrealism's influence], it is only because we wish to make clear those curves whose intersection produces this point with its peculiar significance and to help to *situate* it in relation to the coordinates of time and place. This intention should be enough to silence any suggestion that we are marking time, and to make us advance without hindrance, unhampered by our own laurels" (150–51, Breton's emphasis). Besides initiating the series of spatial metaphors that dominate the essay, this passage affirms that Surrealism has lost none of its dynamism and forward movement. The strategic importance of this affirmation becomes especially clear if one recalls that by 1936 it had become a journalistic commonplace to declare Surrealism "dead" as an avant-garde movement, or at the very least exhausted; and that a number of major figures had defected from the Surrealist group during the preceding years in order to join the Communist Party, the party of the working class.[5] After this affirmation comes the sentence about the triumph of the French workers, which is followed by a very long sentence that makes two major points: first, the workers' occupation of the factories was so spontaneous and sudden that "none of the existing political parties can properly claim the responsibility" (read: the Communist Party must not be given credit for this triumph). Second, the workers' action "spread [so] widely and swiftly," its forward movement was so strong, that it definitively "gave the lie to those who, since the war, have never tired of denying the militancy of the French proletariat." Indeed, this action suggests nothing less than that (Breton quotes Trotsky here) "the French revolution has begun" (151).

S. Suleiman

Breton claims, then, in the opening paragraph, that both the French proletariat, which occupied the factories, and the largely French Surrealist movement, which was spreading all over the world, had proved their power and influence in June 1936, independently of party control. And yet, he will state between parentheses toward the end of his essay that the factory is not the mythologically charged place in which Surrealism might seek the powerful equivalent of the Gothic castle. Does he suggest what that place might be, if not the factory? No. All that Surrealism can do, he states after dismissing the factory, is to "register the displacement, from the period of the Gothic novel to our time, of the highest emotional charge from the miraculous *apparition* to the shattering [*bouleversante*] *coincidence*, and to ask that we let ourselves be guided toward the unknown by this latest flash, brighter than any other at the present time, isolating it whenever possible from the trivial facts of life" (158, Breton's emphasis).

The fact that Breton here refuses—or is unable—to name the place most favorable to the "shattering coincidence," but insists that it be isolated from the trivial facts of life, cannot but surprise any reader of *Nadja* or of the two prose works that followed it, *Les Vases communicants* (*The Communicating Vessels*) and *L'Amour fou* (*Mad Love*). (Earlier in the essay, Breton cited all three works in a note about his own explorations of objective chance). In *Nadja*, to stick to that example, it is quite clear that the "predestined place" for the experience of the shattering coincidence is both nameable and part of the trivial facts of life: it is the street, and indeed not just any street but the streets of a particular area of Paris. "Meanwhile, you can be sure of meeting me in Paris, of not spending more than three days without seeing me pass, toward the end of the afternoon, along the Boulevard Bonne-Nouvelle between the *Matin* printing office and the Boulevard de Strasbourg. I don't know why it should be precisely here that my feet take me, here that I almost invariably go without specific purpose, without anything to induce me but this obscure clue: namely that it (?) will happen here."[6]

This area, roughly a triangle whose three points are the Opéra, the Porte St. Denis and the Gare du Nord, was in the 1920s (and still is, to a large extent) an extremely busy and heterogeneous place. One could find there the main newspaper offices, the bookstore of the Communist Party paper *L'Humanité*, the covered commercial passages celebrated by Aragon in *Le Paysan de Paris*, the Grévin wax museum celebrated by Breton in *Nadja*, and a number of theaters, including the sublimely tawdry Théâtre Moderne, destroyed by the late 1920s (Walter Benjamin declared himself "inconsolable not to have known" it[7]), and the equally tawdry Théâtre des deux Masques where Breton saw the horror play *Les Détraquées*, whose star Blanche Derval became for him a precursor of Nadja. It was a neighborhood whose streets were filled by office workers, salesclerks, skilled laborers, "better class" prostitutes, tourists, and of course *flâneurs* of every kind. It was the neighborhood where Breton met Nadja, one day in 1927 "after stopping a few minutes at the stall of the *Humanité* bookstore and buying Trotsky's latest work" (63). Finally, as Benjamin noted in his 1929 essay on Surrealism, this neighborhood was the neighborhood of popular uprisings, such as the Sacco and Vanzetti riots of 1927 on the Boulevard Bonne-Nouvelle, which Breton mentions at the end of *Nadja*. Noting that unfortunately he was not in Paris at the time and therefore missed participating in the riots, Breton nevertheless cites them as a moment when the Boulevard (living up to its promise of "good news," Benjamin glosses) seemed to fulfill his expectations by becoming a "strategic point of disorder," of "love or revolution" (*Nadja*, 153).

The street as the place for the ultimate Surrealist experience, that of love or revolution—but in the best of circumstances, of love *and* revolution—is so anchored in the imagination of early Surrealism (and in the imagination of critics influenced by Benjamin's writings on both Surrealism and the city of Paris) that one can only wonder at the way in which Breton manages to avoid speaking about the street in his reflections on the "predestined place" that would correspond to the displacement of the Gothic "apparition" by the Surrealist "coincidence." This wonder increases all the more if one returns again to the beginning of the "Limits" essay. There, after noting that the opening of the 1936 London exhibition coincided with the triumph of the French workers in June and heralded a new "French revolution," Breton notes, more somberly, that the closing of the exhibition coincided with Franco's counter-revolutionary offensive against the "young Spanish Republic." (Actually, the exhibition closed on July 4 and the Spanish Civil War began on July 18—but it was close enough.) "If at the time I am writing there is no doubt that the French revolution has just begun, it is certain that the Spanish revolution is reaching its peak" (151). In Spain, too, Breton has hopes for the triumph of the workers, who have been called to the defense of the Republic as an armed militia. He then turns once again to France, noting that "it is only a revolutionary minority in France which demands the formation of such a militia in the teeth of opposition from the Popular Front government . . . which puts off as long as possible the moment for the resolution of social crisis in the only place where it can be resolved—*in the street*" (152, Breton's emphasis).

Breton does not identify the "revolutionary minority in France" that demanded the arming of workers, but we can be sure that it was not the Communist Party, which had given up its hard-line class-war rhetoric of the 1920s and was engaged in 1936 in the parliamentary politics of the Popular Front. The demand for

Fig. 2. Plate 17 in *Nadja*. "The Humanité Bookstore."

arming the workers seems more likely to have been formulated by the theorists of *Contre-Attaque*, the ultra-Left group led by Georges Bataille and other former members of a dissident Marxist group associated with Boris Souvarine; the Surrealists also participated in *Contre-Attaque*, during its short existence between 1935 and 1936.[8] The call for a "descent of the masses into the street" *against* the politicians of the Popular Front government was Bataille's, and for a while it was evidently shared by Breton and the Surrealists. The Surrealists soon realized, however (as, indeed, did Bataille himself), that this call had fascist overtones; they left the *Contre-Attaque* movement, which was disbanded as a result.[9] It would seem, therefore, that the evocation, by Breton, of the "resolution of social crisis . . . *in the street*" was more a rhetorical flourish than the expression of a political program (a program which, given its possible fascist associations and its lack of support by the organized Left, would in any case have been a highly problematic one for a leftist movement.) This conclusion is reinforced by the fact that "Limites non-frontières du surréalisme" was published in the *Nouvelle Revue Française*, an eminent, Parisian bourgeois literary journal that was anything but political and anything but revolutionary— and that had been strongly critical of Surrealism's "excesses," including its revolutionary politics and its provocatively anti-literary stance, from the very beginning of the movement.[10]

S. Suleiman

I suggest that the parenthetical dismissal of the factory and the disappearance of the street at the end of Breton's essay, combined with the publication of the essay in the *Nouvelle Revue Française* (it's true that the alternative place of publication open to Breton, the review *Minotaure*, would have made no difference, for despite being dominated by Surrealist work *Minotaure* was a luxurious, apolitical art magazine destined for a wealthy public), must be read as symptoms of a displacement that had occurred in and of Surrealism itself, and that Breton was the last person to have wanted to acknowledge. This displacement is what I am calling, in metaphorical shorthand, the gradual, reluctant, perhaps totally unwilling but nevertheless indubitable movement of Surrealism during the 1930s from the street to the *salon*.

II. Slipping.

In this metaphorical shorthand, the street stands not only for the early Surrealist program of "love and revolution"—or, in the slightly different terms employed by Breton as late as 1935 in a famous speech, for the union of Rimbaud's watchword "Change life" with Marx's injunction "Transform the world."[11] It also stands for what was again a hope of early Surrealism—the hope that Surrealist experimentation in the domain of art and poetry, and the Surrealist revaluation of the literary tradition (celebrating Sade, Rimbaud, Lautréamont and other marginalized or ill-understood writers) could become known and available to a large public, in particular the public of workers. To discuss this hope about experimentation and the public in detail would require a whole separate essay. I will simply mention here the Surrealists' ongoing feud, throughout the late 1920s and early 1930s, with those Communist theorists (represented in France by Henri Barbusse) who advocated a "proletarian literature" that would either be written by actual workers, or else be written for workers in an easily readable, traditional style like that of the popular realist novel. This, of course, was anathema to the Surrealists, who had been railing against realist fiction, with its banality and small-mindedness (as they saw it) ever since the First Surrealist Manifesto. Even at the height of their allegiance to the Communist Party, during the years of the journal they placed "at the service of the Revolution" (*Le Surréalisme au service de la Révolution*, *SASDLR* for short, 1930–1933), they refused to endorse any idea of "proletarian literature" that would betray their own conceptions of artistic practice.[12]

Breton, in an article published in one of the last issues of *SASDLR*, suggested that before the proletariat was asked to produce literary works (*L'Humanité* had just organized a contest of "proletarian literature"), it should be properly educated, for one of the bourgeoisie's biggest sins was precisely to "paralyze the intellectual development of the working class, in order to assure its passivity."[13] Breton volunteered to work on a "Marxist Manual of General

Literature," and proposed a series of more advanced lectures on literature to be given at the Université Ouvrière, the workers' university run by the Party. Naturally, none of this was put into practice, and indeed Breton's call to educate the workers so that they could appreciate modern (Surrealist) art could very well be used by hostile critics to castigate the Surrealists' "elitism." When, at the 1934 Writers' Congress in Moscow, the Soviet Union changed aesthetic doctrines and abandoned the idea of proletarian literature, it was only to adopt the equally non-Surrealist doctrine of socialist realism.

So much for a quick approximation of what I mean when I say that Surrealism's first and most lasting aspiration was to "be in the street." The question is: What historical and political circumstances moved Surrealism, willy-nilly, into the *salon*? In trying to answer that question, we will do well to recall that the reasons for asking it are not merely historical.

What does the *salon* stand for in my metaphorical equation? On the one hand, obviously, it stands for the bourgeois public—and not just any bourgeois public, but the educated, wealthy, "adventurous" *grand bourgeois* public (which overlapped with some segments of the aristocracy) who were the patrons and consumers of modern art between the wars. Breton's first (indeed, only) paid job, in the early 1920s, was as an artistic and literary adviser to the art collector and *couturier* Jacques Doucet, who added considerably to his impressive collection of modern art and literature during those years: among his purchases was Picasso's *Demoiselles d'Avignon*, upon Breton's advice. Breton stopped working for Doucet at the end of 1924, shortly after the publication of the first Surrealist Manifesto, and just about never accepted any salaried work after that. (He supported himself, quite minimally, by buying and selling modern art, much of it the art of his friends, and ran a gallery for a while around 1937. He made almost nothing on his writings during those years, even though his work was published by the prestigious publishing house Gallimard.)[14]

My mentioning Breton's relation to Doucet is not intended to cast doubt on his or the Surrealists' good faith when they declared their war against the bourgeoisie, but merely to suggest one of the dilemmas that Surrealism faced from the beginning: insofar as it required financial support, the most likely place where it would find it was not in the street, but in the *salons* of certain "enlightened" bourgeois—who nevertheless remained bourgeois. This dilemma did not escape the Surrealists who lived it. André Thirion, who in 1930 was an active member both of the Surrealist group and of the French Communist Party, recounts in his memoirs an episode from that year which shows just how complicated this lived experience was.

In October 1930, Thirion attended a special showing of the newly made film by Buñuel and Dali, *L'âge d'or*, at the Studio 28, a small art cinema in Montmartre. A few weeks later, when the film opened to the public in late November, it caused a veritable scandal, as it had been fully intended to do. The final sequence—which shows the hero of Sade's *120 Days of Sodom* emerging from his castle after unspeakable orgies, costumed and made up to look like Jesus Christ—was merely the culmination of a series of insults hurled at Church, Family, Country, all the "sacred values" that Surrealism despised. To make sure that everyone understood the revolutionary intention of the film, the Surrealists published a forty-eight-page brochure that included the scenario, thirty of the more provocative stills from the film, and short essays by Breton, René Crevel, Paul Eluard and André Thirion, each one devoted to a particular aspect of the film's subversive intent. (Several stills from *L'âge d'or* were also reproduced in the first issue of *SASDLR*—cf. Figs. 4 and 5). The brochure further included a list of works by Arp, Dali, Ernst, Miro, Man Ray and Yves Tanguy, which were exhibited in the entrance hall of the movie theater.

This was, in short, a major collective provocation—and it worked. A few days after the film's opening, on 3 December, the movie theater was invaded by a "commando" of right-wing demonstrators representing the Ligue des Patriotes and the Ligue Anti-Juive (one wonders what all this had to do with Jews, but evidently the anti-Jewish league saw it as a good opportunity—possibly the owner of the Studio 28 was Jewish, for one of the Algerian newspapers reporting the event referred to it as a "Judeo-Bolshevik movie house").[15]

The commando, shouting "We'll see if there remain any Christians in France!" and "Death to the Jews!" threw purple ink at the screen, then launched a stink bomb and attacked the spectators with billy clubs to try and force them to leave. The commando then proceeded to the exhibition hall and tore the place up, including all the paintings hanging there. This incident was widely reported in the press, and became a minor *cause célèbre* for about a week. Nine days after the attack, the government (incited by, among other papers, the liberal bourgeois daily *Le Figaro*) halted the showing of the film—and *L'âge d'or*, generally recognized as the masterpiece of Surrealist cinema, was never again shown in a commercial theater in France until 1981, when the newly elected Socialist government lifted the ban. (It was often shown at the Cinémathèque in the intervening half-century).

If one wanted to argue for a successful "street effect" by Surrealism, the *L'âge d'or* scandal would certainly be one good example.[16] But as Thirion recounts in his memoirs, the special showing in October that he attended with Breton and other Surrealists was followed by a sumptuous reception at the home of the Viscount and Viscountess de Noailles, who had financed the making of the film. "My intolerance was so total at

Fig. 3. Plate 26 in *Nadja*. "The Sphinx-Hôtel, Boulevard Magenta."

the time," writes Thirion, "that the role played by rich and titled people in the making of a revolutionary work disturbed me. I saw it as a flaw. Yet, in thinking about it a bit, I would have had to admit that without the Noailles there would have been no *L'âge d'or*."[17] Conquering his hesitation, Thirion went to the reception—but as he walked up the grand staircase, past the liveried footmen stationed there, his anger rose again; entering the reception room where a buffet was being served, he started breaking glasses, throwing bottles at the mirrors, and hurling insults at all present. He thus brought into the *salon* not only the street tactics of the "patriots" who would invade the movie theater a few weeks later, but also repeated the action of one of the chief sequences of *L'âge d'or*, where the hero, in search of his beloved, creates a

Fig. 4. "Parfois le dimanche . . . ," *L'âge d'or*, Luis Buñuel.

scandal at a fancy reception. Both in the film and in real life, the effects produced were momentary: In the film, the hosts are outraged and throw the hero out (he manages to sneak back); in real life, not even that was accomplished. "Charles de Noailles remained impassible," and his wife "had the elegance not to notice anything" (284). Somehow, one cannot help but see an allegory here.

The dilemma presented by the *salon* was not only social and financial, however. It was also a question of aesthetics, and in that sense the further French meaning of *salon*, that of a large collective art exhibition, also comes into play. The fact is that the public who was most willing to take Surrealism seriously as an artistic practice was precisely the public of the *salon*, in both senses of the word. But the price they exacted for their interest was the reduction (or, in their mind, the elevation) of Surrealism to the status of a "style," rather than a recognition of it as a revolutionary program or way of life. Aragon, in what was to be his last contribution to a Surrealist journal before he left the movement, analyzed the dilemma thus posed in the most lucid terms. In his 1931 essay, "Le Surréalisme et le devenir révolutionnaire" (published in *SASDLR*), he spoke of a new form of censorship, even more pernicious than the nineteenth century method of arresting writers and seizing their works. The new method was "more elegant": it consisted in muzzling the Surrealists by publishing their works in ever more restricted luxury editions. "In 1930 and 1931, we have arrived at this paradoxical result: that our thought has been considered as a luxury item *precisely* because of its revolutionary character. Bourgeois society refuses to allow it except in more and more limited editions."

What's even worse, he continued, is that certain self-styled revolutionaries hypocritically accept "the legend according to which we are writers *for* society snobs, whereas the truth is that if we are confined (by means of financial coercion) to this public which we have never considered with anything but scorn, this confinement is itself a perfected form of repression."[18]

In Aragon's analysis, the responsibility for Surrealism's lack of contact with a mass public lay entirely at the door of the bourgeois publishers who refused to make their work widely available, fearing its revolutionary content. But things were not quite so simple. The Communist Party, which had not only *L'Humanité* with its huge circulation but a number of other publications at its disposal, was generally hostile and uncomprehending toward Surrealist work, even at the height of its supposed collaboration with the Surrealists. It strongly disapproved of Surrealism's emphasis on eroticism and the exploration of erotic fantasies, for example. When Dali published a frankly masturbatory fantasy (entitled "Rêverie") in the issue of *SASDLR* immediately following the one with Aragon's article, Aragon and several other Surrealists who were assiduous members of the Party were strongly taken to task by the editors of *L'Humanité*.[19] The Revolution was far too serious a thing to be confused with Surrealist notions of "rêvolution."[20] When, a few months after publishing "Le Surréalisme et le devenir révolutionnaire," Aragon left the Surrealists and became the "official" Party writer, he totally changed his mode of writing, embarking on a series of realist novels under the rubric "the real world," "le monde réel" (not "surréel"). In return, he gained steady employment and praise in various Party publications, and thousands of readers.

In early 1935, by which time *SASDLR* and the hope it had represented (that there might be a real place for Surrealism, without compromises, in the ranks of the Communist Party) were dead, Breton summed up the aesthetic dilemma (he used the word "dilemma") in a highly succinct way. Innovative artists and writers, he wrote, find themselves in a position where "either they must give up interpreting and expressing the world in the ways that each of them finds the secret of in himself and himself alone—it is his very chance of enduring that is at stake—or they must give up collaborating on the practical plan of action for changing this world . . . It has become a commonplace . . . to point out that leftist political circles appreciate in art only time-honored, or even outworn, forms . . . whereas rightist circles are peculiarly friendly in this respect . . . What to do? Avant-garde art, caught between this total lack of comprehension [by the left] and this completely relative, self-seeking comprehension [by the right] cannot in my opinion long put up with this compromise."[21]

According to Maurice Nadeau, it is around this time, "the moment when Breton classifies himself, whether willingly or not, in the category of the *artists*, that we must date the failure of the surrealist movement."[22] In a more recent analysis, Peter Bürger has argued that the tendency to regard art as independent of political exigencies (a tendency he calls "modernist," identifying it with the "autonomy of art" theory inherited from Kant) was there in Surrealism from the very beginning, in tension with the opposing tendency (which Bürger calls "avant-gardist") to integrate art and life. The "modernist" tendency simply became more pronounced in Breton's writings, according to Bürger, after 1935.[23] But things may be more complicated, in historical context, than either Nadeau's or Bürger's argument suggests. For it is not the case that Breton classified himself and the Surrealists exclusively in the category of "artists," even after their break with the Communist Party; nor is it the case that he gave up what Bürger calls the "avant-gardist" position after 1935 in favor of a "modernist" one emphasizing the autonomy of art. Rather, he continued *trying* to satisfy both the demands of individual artistic freedom and the demands of what he considered "Marxist teaching," notably the necessity of social revolution. If he failed in this attempt—and Nadeau and Bürger are undoubtedly right in their assessment that he failed—it was certainly not for lack of trying.

After the 1936 London exhibition, the newly formed English Surrealist group published a collective declaration that Breton also signed, which stated that negative reactions to the exhibition had come from two quarters: from the "Marxists and Communists," who "refuse to accept the existence of the world of the unconscious" and who therefore cannot "appreciate our strictly dialectical and materialist synthesis of inner and outer world as the basis of general theory"; and from the "smart Society critics," for whom "Surrealism is merely another 'ism'. They conceive it as a new style of painting or theory of art . . . Surrealism comprehends all human activity, and as a total attitude to human life is beyond the habitual petty scale of their thought. They know nothing of either Freud or Marx."[24]

In London 1936, then, the Surrealists considered themselves misunderstood by both the Marxist street and the bourgeois *salon*, and they took pride in that fact. Their own program was to know something about both Freud and Marx, to pursue both the path of dreams and the road to revolution—a program that, in theory at least, can hardly be identified with the "autonomy of art" theory advanced by certain modernists or by Kant. In practice, however, and despite its program, Surrealism found itself increasingly pushed (or pulled) out of the *political* street into the *artistic salon*. The second International Surrealist Exhibition, held in Paris in January 1938, drew many visitors, but apparently offended none. *Le Figaro*, which had called for the closing down of *L'âge d'or* seven years before, now advised its readers to go see the show: Surrealism, it wrote, "defies the years, financial crises and political crises," and "takes us far away from the realities of the day."[25] This was not exactly what the Surrealists had in mind when they proclaimed, in the first issues of *La Révolution Surréaliste* and of *SASDLR*, that they wanted to "do away with reality."

The 1938 exhibition was accompanied by no collective (or, for that matter, individual) programmatic declaration; rather, there appeared in the guise of a catalogue the first "dictionary of Surrealism," put together by Breton and Eluard.[26] Although, as Henri Béhar suggests, it could to some extent be considered a parodic antidictionary, the *Dictionnaire abrégé du surréalisme* also functioned as a genuine reference work: it provided historical information about the movement, listing even those artists and writers who were no longer members, like Aragon, Artaud, or Desnos; and like all good dictionaries, it gave basic definitions of terms (some of them derisive, but most of them serious), supported by plenty of quotations and illustrations. This was not a manifesto; it looked more like a monument. Marx and Lenin figured among the entries, as did "dialectic." There was a long entry for "rêve," but none for "révolution."[27]

Can one see here a recognition, however implicit, on Breton's part that Surrealism's double program ("dream *and* revolution") was no longer viable? Yes and no. Yes, because by January 1938 it had become even clearer than before that any revolutionary politics that tried to exist outside the confines of the Communist Party in Western Europe during those years was doomed to fail.[28] This lesson was driven home not only by the savage feuding between Stalinists and anarchists and Trotskyists in Spain (the Stalinists won—and some of their adversaries on the left claimed that they helped defeat the very Republic they ostensibly supported), but also by the general silence among leftists (Trotskyists excepted) concerning the Moscow trials of August 1936 and January 1937. Breton, in the name of the Surrealists and of "true Marxism," spoke out against the trials in forceful and courageous terms, just as he had spoken out against Stalinist policies at the Writers' Congress for the Defense of Culture in Paris in 1935. But few people on the left listened to these criticisms—and as hardly needs to be said, Breton was not speaking to those on the right, or even to those in the center.[29]

The reasons why the left was so reluctant to criticize Stalinist Russia in the late 1930's have often been rehearsed by historians. Besides the continuing aura of the Communist state, which many on the left were unwilling to see stripped away (this might be called the sentimental reason) there was the influence of the *realpolitik* argument: Stalin appeared to many as a necessary ally, indeed the only bulwark, against Hitler. To criticize him was therefore seen as playing into the hands of a far more evil and dangerous enemy. The Surrealists, with their insistence that revolutionary principles were more important than *realpolitik*, could appear to many as downright naive, and blamable. Of course, when it turned out that Stalin's own *realpolitik* included an alliance with Hitler, that particular argument collapsed and it was those who had trusted in it (including some notable Communists, like Paul Nizan) who could feel naive, or betrayed. Still, reading today some of the Surrealist declarations of 1938 and 1939, one understands why the position that Surrealism staked out as its own was—in that place, in that time—impossible. They railed against what they called the "pseudo-democratic powers," crying "Neither your war nor your peace!" They railed against French nationalism, imperialism, the exploitation of workers and their certain sacrifice in yet another senseless capitalist war. Meanwhile, Hitler was building the concentration camps and preparing to swallow Europe whole.[30]

At the same time, I would suggest that there is something admirable (as well as consistent with Surrealist principles, for better or worse) about this refusal to bow to reality. The document that Breton composed, with Leon Trotsky, in Mexico a few months after the 1938 Surrealist Exhibition in Paris, "Pour un art révolutionnaire indépendant" ("Manifesto for an Independent Revolutionary Art"), is a case in point—and it replies with a resounding "No"

Fig. 5. "J'ai blasphémé peut-être . . . ," *L'âge d'or*, Luis Buñuel.

to the question about whether Breton admitted the defeat of the Surrealist double program. This document, unique in its collaboration between an artist and a world-historical political figure, was indeed the last of the great Surrealist manifestoes: it affirmed that "true art" must be both absolutely free and committed to social revolution; that it could be aspired to by all, not just by isolated geniuses; that to call for an independent art was not the same as to call for a "pure" or disinterested art (so much for the "autonomy of art" argument); that to criticize the Soviet Union was not to criticize communism, but its worst enemy; and that to be against both Hitler and Stalin did not mean one had to approve of the bourgeois democracies. Finally, the manifesto called for the union of all "revolutionary writers and artists" on a "common ground," to be staked out by a newly formed association, the International Federation of Independent Revolutionary Art.[31]

It was a statement of principles and a call to action, inspiring on both counts. Unfortunately (but after the preceding pages, the news can hardly surprise us), very few writers and artists came to the rendez-vous.[32] A little over a year after the publication of the "Manifesto for an Independent Revolutionary Art," Hitler and Stalin marched into Poland. That was common ground all right, but not the one the manifesto had called for.[33]

Notes

1. I have tried to summarize the major issues of the debate in the concluding chapter of my book, *Subversive Intent: Gender, Politics, and the Avant-Garde* (Cambridge, Mass.: Harvard University Press, 1990).

2. Michel Foucault, *Discipline and Punish: The Birth of the Prison*, trans. Alan Sheridan (New York: Vintage Books, 1979), 31.

3. First published in the *Nouvelle Revue Française* 281 (February 1937): 200–15. I shall be quoting from the English translation by David Gascoyne, often modified by me: "Limits Not Frontiers of Surrealism," in A. Breton, *What Is Surrealism?*, ed. Franklin Rosemont (New York: Monad Press/Pathfinder Press, 1978). All page references will be to this edition and will be given parenthetically in the text.

4. Yves Bridel, *Miroirs du Surréalisme: Essai sur la réception du Surréalisme en France et en Suisse française (1916–1939)* (Lausanne: L'Âge d'Homme, 1988), 62.

5. On the journalistic view of Surrealism, see Elyette Guiol-Benassaya, *La Presse face au Surréalisme, 1925–1938* (Paris: Editions du CNRS, 1982), and Bridel, *Miroirs du Surréalisme*; Maurice Nadeau, in his *History of Surrealism*, considers 1935 as the watershed year, after which the avant-garde aspirations of the movement foundered (Nadeau, *The History of Surrealism* [Cambridge, Mass: Harvard University Press, 1989], chapter 17). The most highly publicized defection from Surrealism to the Communist Party was that of Louis Aragon, in 1932; René Crevel, who committed suicide in 1935, was also claimed by the Communists after his death; the next big defection, that of the poet Paul Eluard, would come in 1938.

6. A. Breton, *Nadja*, trans. Richard Howard (New York: Grove Press, 1960), 32. Subsequent page references will be given parenthetically in the text.

7. W. Benjamin, "Surrealism: The Last Snapshot of the European Intelligentsia," in *Reflections* (New York: Harcourt, Brace Jovanovich, 1978), 183.

8. For the texts of the tracts published by Contre-Attaque, as well as detailed background and commentary, see *Tracts Surréalistes et Déclarations Collectives*, Vol. I (1922–1939), ed. José Pierre (Paris: Le Terrain Vague, 1980), 281–301 and 498–506. For a brief narrative account emphasizing Bataille's role, see Michel Surya, *Georges Bataille: La Mort à l'oeuvre* (Paris: Editions Garamont-Frédéric Birr, 1987), 223–31. See also my "Bataille in the Street," in *Georges Bataille: Writing the Sacred*, ed. Carolyn Gill (Routledge, 1994).

9. Bataille's position was most fully stated in his essays "Front Populaire dans la rue" and "Vers la révolution réelle," published in the single issue of *Les Cahiers de CONTRE-ATTAQUE*, May 1936 and reprinted in his *Oeuvres Complètes*, I (Paris: Gallimard, 1970), 402–28. The Surrealists broke with the group in March 1936, after the publication of a tract written by Bataille but carrying all of their names, which could be interpreted as sympathetic to Hitler. (See "Travailleurs, vous êtes trahis" and "La Rupture avec 'Contre-Attaque'," in *Tracts Surréalistes* I, 299–301).

10. For a brief history of the NRF's reactions to Surrealism during the 1920s and 1930s, see Bridel, *Miroirs du Surréalisme*, 27–80.

11. A. Breton, "Speech to the Congress of Writers," in *Manifestoes of Surrealism*, trans. Richard Seaver and Helen R. Lane (Ann Arbor: University of Michigan Press, 1972), 241.

12. André Thirion, a member of the Surrealist group at the time, reports in his memoirs that Breton was extremely concerned about attracting a mass public for *SASDLR*. During a meeting with Eluard, Aragon, and Tristan Tzara in October 1931, Breton affirmed that he was even willing to "change a text" in order to have it read by certain readers. He also claimed, however, that his own difficult style was not incompatible with his desire to "write for the masses." (See Thirion, *Révolutionnaires sans révolution* [Paris: Laffont, 1972], 323–24). In fact, *SASDLR* never sold more than a few hundred copies.

13. "A Propos du concours de littérature prolétarienne organisé par L'Humanité," *SASDLR* 5 (1933); reprinted in Breton, *Point du jour* (Paris: Gallimard, 1970), 113. Unless otherwise indicated, translations from the French are my own.

14. The biographical information in this paragraph comes from Henri Béhar's detailed and carefully researched biography, *André Breton: le grand indésirable* (Paris: Calmann-Lévy, 1990). Although Béhar, a recognized expert in the field, cites his numerous sources in a Bibliography, his book suffers from the decision to omit all footnotes or other specific forms of documentation.

15. Article from *Le Petit Oranais*, quoted in *Tracts Surréalistes* I, 449. José Pierre's commentary on the *L'âge d'or* affair is wonderfully detailed and informative (see *Tracts*, 435–41, 445–50) and is the basis for my own account here.

16. Public scandal as a form of provocation and protest was a favored activity by Surrealists (and before them by the Dadaists) during the early 1920s. The one closest to the *L'âge d'or* scandal in its political effect was the "St. Pol Roux banquet" of July 1925, which ended in a street fight and aroused a great deal of indignation in the bourgeois press. For details, see Guiol-Benassaya, *La Presse face au Surréalisme*.

17. Thirion, *Révolutionnaires sans révolution*, 283. Other page references will be given parenthetically in the text. Charles and Marie-Laure de Noailles, well known as patrons of modern art, were famous for their extravagant masked balls and other fêtes throughout the 1920s. Before financing *L'âge d'or*, they had commissioned, among other projects, Man Ray's film, *Mystères du Château de dés*, shot in their country château in 1929. (See Neil Baldwin, *Man Ray, American Artist* [New York: Clarkson N. Potter, 1988], 150–52).

18. Aragon, "Le Surréalisme et le devenir révolutionnaire," *SASDLR* 3 (1931): 3.

19. Thirion, *Révolutionnaires sans révolution*, 337.

20. For reflections on this wonderful portmanteau word ("rêve" and "révolution," dream and revolution), see Jean-Luc Steinmetz, "L'Homme aux ânes: surréalisme, politique et psychanalyse dans les années trente," in Anne Roche and Christian Tarting, ed., *Des Années trente: groupes et ruptures* (Paris: Editions du CNRS, 1985), 274.

21. Breton, "Political Position of Today's Art," in *Manifestoes of Surrealism*, 214–15. This essay, published as part of a book, *Position politique du Surréalisme*, in 1935, was delivered as a speech in Prague in April of that year.

22. Nadeau, *The History of Surrealism*, 202.

23. Peter Bürger, "Surréalisme et engagement," *Avant-garde*, (1987): 84–94.

24. *International Surrealist Bulletin*, 4 (September 1936): 16, 17.

25. Quoted in Guiol-Benassaya, *La Presse face au Surréalisme*, 142.

26. See Béhar, *André Breton*, 306.

27. *Dictionnaire abrégé du Surréalisme* (Paris: Galerie des Beaux-Arts, 1938). One area in which the dictionary appears to be sorely lacking, looked at with today's eyes, is in the listing of names of women artists, even though several women artists (Eileen Agar, Leonora Carrington, Meret Oppenheim, Toyen, Remedios Varo) were represented in the 1938 exhibition and some of their works were reproduced in the dictionary. Lacking an alphabetical entry, the women artists become less visible. The only women's names to receive alphabetical entries are a few who figure as "muses," even if—like Jacqueline Lamba, Breton's wife—they were artists in their own right. The "muses" are listed under their first name only, again leading to a kind of invisibility. All of this is probably an accurate reflection of the ambiguous position of women in the Surrealist group at the time: welcomed as companions and even recognized as artists, but not quite seen as full-fledged members of the movement.

28. One of the most acute analyses of the trend toward party orthodoxy, on both the right and the left, was written in 1936 by the liberal humanist philosopher (Albert Camus' teacher), Jean Grenier. In his essay "L'Âge des orthodoxies," *Nouvelle Revue Française* (April 1936), Grenier notes the "nobility" of Breton's position, but also adopts a condescending tone toward it: "[Breton] proclaims the rights of the intellect and sides for the ideal Revolution, against actual revolutionaries. But that is quite useless: the age of heresies is over . . . we are now in the age of orthodoxies . . . To be a revolutionary, today, against Stalin, is like being a monarchist against Maurras and Catholic against Pius X. These are very noble attitudes, but they are admissible only for young people. Maturity . . . hungers for achievements. What is urgent is not to proclaim a faith, but to join a party" (482). Grenier himself was against orthodoxies and party lines, and was writing from the somewhat ironic point of view of a bourgeois humanist—a position Breton continued to attack, even while refusing orthodoxy and party lines. As Grenier saw, this left him open to the charge of "idealism" or "immaturity." Sartre, in his famous attack on the Surrealists' political aspirations in *Qu'est-ce que la littérature?* (1948), would repeat the same charge; in the postwar period, when Communism was a dominant force among intellectuals in France, this charge made Surrealist political ideas ("revolutionary but anti-Communist") virtually devoid of influence.

29. For a brief account of left-wing reactions to the Moscow trials in France (which makes no mention, however, of Breton or the Surrealists), see David Caute, *Communism and the French Intellectuals, 1914–1960* (New York: Macmillan, 1964), 127–36.

30. "Ni de votre Guerre ni de votre Paix!" was the title of a tract published in September 1938, in response to the Munich agreements. José Pierre notes that although the tract is "altogether rigorous from the point of view of revolutionary ethics, it still manifests a strange blindness" in not recognizing the threat posed by Hitler. (*Tracts Surréalistes* I, 525).

31. See Breton, *What Is Surrealism?*, 183–87; in French, in *Tracts Surréalistes* I, 335–39. Although in 1938 the published text was signed by Breton and Diego Rivera, the actual authors of this manifesto were Breton and Trotsky; subsequent publications (including the one in *Tracts Surréalistes*) carry Breton's and Trotsky's names as authors.

32. Among those who did join the Federation was the star of *L'âge d'or*, Gaston Modot; others included Jean Giono, André Masson, Victor Serge, Jef Last, and Herbert Read. Aside from Read, many of the British Surrealists were hesitant, precisely over the question of what "attitude to adopt toward the USSR." (See "Lettre à nos amis de Londres," an attempt to convince the British to join, in *Tracts Surréalistes* I, 340–43). In retrospect, the Federation, like certain pacifist movements at the time, can be seen to have played into the hands of those who followed a politics of appeasement with regard to Hitler. This was obviously not Breton's intent.

33. I wish to thank Guy Ducornet and Lucien Taylor for their careful readings of this essay and their useful suggestions.

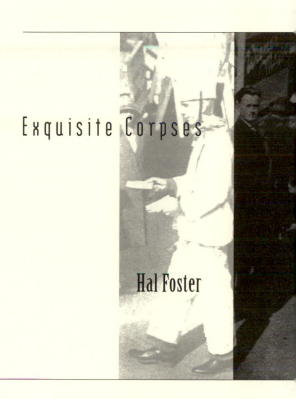

Exquisite Corpses

Hal Foster

Industry as it objectively exists is an open book of the human faculties,
and a human psychology which can be sensuously apprehended.
—Karl Marx,
Economic and Philosophical Manuscripts
(1844)

IT IS NO SECRET THAT SURREALISM CONCERNS TRAUMA.[1] THE USUAL DEFINITION OF THE
Surrealist image as a coupling of different elements in space can be read in terms of a working
over of different memories and/or fantasies in time, a working over of trauma. Here, however,
I want briefly, even telegraphically, to suggest that Surrealism also concerns shock—in
particular that it contains a reflection on the machine and the commodity no less important
than that of any other modernism. Of course, Surrealism hardly engages the processes of
mechanization and commodification as directly as does Constructivism, for example, or even
Dada. Yet whereas Constructivism does not really question the social ramifications of the

mechanical order which it embraces, Dada does not fully address the psychic effects of the commodified order which it mocks. Surrealism does both—in a way crucial to any dialectical understanding not only of various machinic modernisms (such as the Bauhaus) but also of various fascist modernisms.

I want to concentrate on the Surrealist relation to the mechanical-commodified through two figures in particular: the automaton and the mannequin. The Surrealists were fascinated by such figures because they evoke an uncanny doubling of the body. But not just any uncanny doubling: they evoke its estranging as machine and commodity under capitalism. Historically, of course, the machine and the commodity were often seen as demonic, disruptive as they were of traditional social practices. But both forms are uncanny in other ways too, for both suggest a confusion between the animate and the inanimate, between life and death—a confusion which the Surrealists sought to exploit.

In his famous remarks on commodity fetishism Marx argues that producers and products trade semblances: social relations take on "the fantastic form of a relation between things," and commodities assume the active agency of people (1977: 165). In effect, the commodity becomes our uncanny double, evermore vital as we are evermore inert. A similar inversion occurs in the technical history of the machine. In the premodern instance the machine is thought to mimic the organic movements of the body; in the modern instance, however, the machine becomes the model, and the body is disciplined to its mechanistic specifications. Like the commodity, the machine is uncanny because it assumes our human vitality and because we take on its deathly facticity. Both forms draw out human labor and will, animation and autonomy, and return them in alien guises; both are other yet not-other, strange yet familiar. The Surrealists seize upon this uncanny aspect of mechanization and commodification, on the irrational residue of rationalization. Insistent on the somatic disruptions of the unconscious ("convulsive beauty" is nothing less than hysterical beauty), they resist this double reification even as they explore its psycho-physical effects, and again they do so, at least in part, through automaton and mannequin figures.

This exploration, these figures, are not without typological precedents. Two familiar ciphers of the mechanical-commodified are the ragpicker and the prostitute. These Baudelairean ciphers, decoded by Benjamin in the milieu of Surrealism, are still active in its imaginary. But by the time of Surrealism it is no longer only a question of representation— of ambiguous identification with industrial detritus as figured in the ragpicker, or of ambivalent empathy with commodity status as figured in the prostitute. This rapport now also concerns an actual reification and fragmentation of the body, a condition addressed in Surrealism not only in its critical deployment of automaton and mannequin figures, but also in its political rejection of mass production and consumption—in the recoding of the commodity in Surrealist objects, in the recovery of the outmoded in Surrealist images, in the refusal of work in Surrealist *dérives*, in the *détournement* of the mechanical in Surrealist automatism (consider the Surrealist game of the exquisite corpse, whereby different parts of a drawing or text are produced by different hands, as a perverse assembly-line).

The becoming machine and/or commodity of the body is not often figured in Surrealism simply or as such. A becoming animal is much more common in its image-repertoire, and such grotesques primarily address a redefining of the human in terms of sexual drives and unconscious conflicts. Yet this psychological redefinition cannot be separated from the sociological transformations. And in fact in Surrealism the two are often expressed in terms of each other: the unconscious as an autonomous machine, the sexual as a mechanistic act, the commodification of sexuality as the sexualization of the commodity, the difference between male and female projected as the difference between the human and the machinic, an ambivalence concerning women as an ambivalence regarding the mechanical-commodified, and so on. These conflations are enacted in another familiar type, the bachelor machine, as figured most famously by Roussel and Duchamp. But here again by the time of Surrealism it is no longer only a question of representation: in some sense the Surrealists *become* bachelor machines. Long before Warhol, Ernst took the machine as a persona (as in "Dadamax, the self-constructed small machine"), just as his fellow Cologne Dadaist Alfred Gruenwald identified with the commodity (with the pseudonym "Baargeld" or cash). Like the Surrealists, they assumed the trauma of these social forms in order to delineate the psycho-physical effects attendant upon them—more, to deploy these effects against the very social order which produced them.[2]

In the early years after World War I this traumatic becoming machine and/or commodity of the body is focused in the figure of the mutilated and/or shocked soldier. Then, in the mid-1920s, with the spread of Taylorist and Fordist disciplines of the industrial body, the worker becomes the epitome of these processes. Finally, with the fascism of the 1930s, a new figure, the worker-soldier, the armored body become weapon-machine, emerges to overdetermine the other two. Together these figures form the dialectical object of attack of the mechanistic grotesques that Surrealism developed, after Dada, to contest the modern cult of the

Mascarade publicitaire

Photo A. Dubreuil
Le mannequin-élégant dans les rues de Paris   Hommes-sandwich à la foire de Leipzig

Fig. 1. "Le mannequin-élégant dans les rues de Paris"/"Hommes-sandwich à la foire de Leipzig."

machine—a cult variously promulgated not only in technophilic movements such as Futurism, Constructivism, Purism and the middle Bauhaus, but also in the everyday ideologies of the Fordist state, whether capitalist, communist, or fascist.

Although these types are not always distinct, I want to concentrate on the second one, the worker as machine, as elaborated in the Surrealist milieu. To do so I will lean heavily on images rather eccentric to the canon: several suites of photographs of automatons, mannequins and the like printed in *Variétés*, a modish Belgian review published under the influence of Surrealism from May 1928 to April 1930. This is Surrealism at a remove, headed towards fashion; yet if some of its complexities are lost, some of its concerns are clarified. The photographs are by artists and nonartists alike; not every image is pertinent, but the editorial complexes as a whole are. (Incidentally, these photo-complexes are fairly typical of Surrealist journals; they comprise an important practice of juxtaposition seldom ackowledged as such, in which Surrealism appears precisely as the transformative *colle* of the collage.)

In the early 1929 issues of *Variétés* a proposition about fetishism emerges, one implicit in both Marxian and Freudian accounts: that we moderns are also fetishists; more, that our machine and commodity fetishes irrationalize us, even reritualize us. For example, in "Surrealism in 1929," a special issue of *Variétés* edited by Breton and Aragon, one finds under the rubric "Fétiches" a female automaton juxtaposed with a Northwest Coast Indian figure. In another 1929 series (March 15) this fetishism of the body as machine is developed in terms of the body as commodity. Here two photographs, one of "a mannequin-man of fashion in the Paris streets," another of two "sandwichmen at the Leipzig fair," are juxtaposed with two

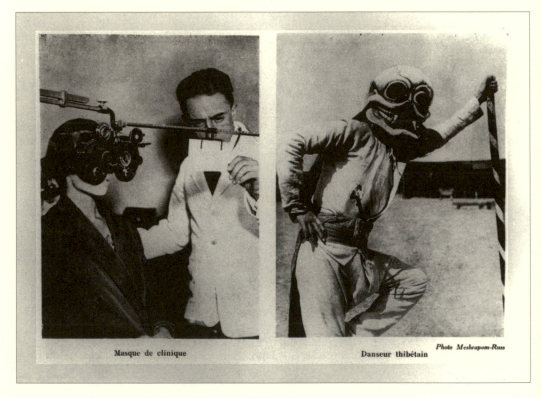

Masque de clinique   Danseur thibétain   *Photo Meshrapom-Russ*

Fig. 2. "Masque de clinique"/"Danseur thibétain."

photographs of masks, one from the old Belgian Congo (used by priests who perform circumcisions), another apparently from a classical tragedy (Fig. 1). The primary initiations in high-capitalist society, the spread suggests, also involve sacrifical rites, those of the commodity: to become a social being is to accede to its condition, literally to assume its character. A later 1929 photo-essay (October 15) makes a similar point in relation to the machine, specifically medical apparatuses and technological protheses. In one representative spread a modern woman behind an optometrical device is paired with a Tibetan dancer in a horrific ceremonial mask (Fig. 2).

The captions of these photographs often stress the term "masquerade," which suggests that these identities are in some sense performed. However, that the disciplines of commodity and machine are not voluntary is underscored by several images. In one image the face of a modern woman is usurped by a collaged advertisement, then paired with a prettified doll (Fig. 3). In another image the heads of two people have become photographic apparatuses (Fig. 4). In the first image the commodity is no longer simply supported by the female body; it is inscribed on her very face, once the sign of individual subjectivity. In the second image the machine is no longer only a technical prosthesis; it becomes an organ substitute— modern vision as photographic gun. Just as the first image is hardly a proto-Pop embrace of the modern commodity world, so the second is scarcely a Bauhausian celebration of a technogical New Vision, much less a proto-fascist exaltation of the body become weapon. In these images the uncanny underside of the commodity and the machine is again exposed, and the world-views that might celebrate them are ridiculed.

Only in two photo-essays in *Variétés* (January 15, 1930) is modernist art specifically related to machine and commodity forms, and in both essays the determinant ur-figure is taken to

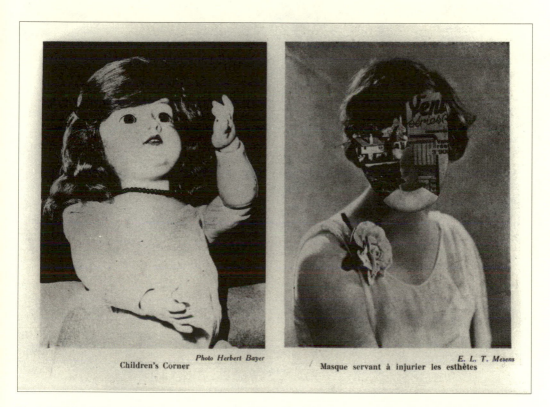

Photo Herbert Bayer   *E. L. T. Mesens*
Children's Corner   **Masque servant à injurier les esthètes**

Fig. 3. "Children's Corner"/"Masque servant à injurier les ethétes."

be the mechanical-commodified body. The principal complex of the first essay includes three modernist works: an abstracted puppet by Man Ray, a primitivist *Child* by Brancusi, and a marionette *Soldiers* by Sophie Taeuber-Arp (Figs. 5a and 5b). All three images are referred to a fourth: "a steel automaton that performs human movements on command" (the letters on its chestplate, R.U.R., allude to the Karel Capek play, *R.U.R. (Rossum's Universal Robots)*, that popularized the term "robot" in the 1920s). Here the paradigm of the modernist figure is the worker become machine; the usual art-historical references—to tribal, folk or childhood objects—are displaced.

The second photo-essay addresses not only this modernist ur-form of the machinic worker but also the very relationship of different modernisms to the machine. Titled "Aboutissements [effects] de la mécanique," it begins with three photographs of human-machinic

Fig. 4. "Voir ou entendre."

hybrids: two figures in gas masks, a third masked by an optometrical device (fig. 6). The caption, "the protection of men," is mordantly ironic: technology here does not extend bodily limbs and senses; it constricts and deforms them (somewhere between Kafka and Cronenberg, these people have become mechanical insects). This effect of the machinic nuances the constellation of four images that follow: a photograph of Fernand Léger on the laboratory set of the L'Herbier film *The Inhuman* (1923), the stage apparatus designed by Lyubov' Popova for the Meierkhol'd production of *The Magnanimous Cuckold* (1922), and the painting *Factory of My Thoughts* (1920) by Suzanne Duchamp, all of which are referred to a photograph of several dirigibles captioned "Trafic" (Figs. 7a and 7b). The three art images triangulate the machinic aspect of modernism; that is, they suggest a partial map of cultural responses to technological modernity at this time. This modernity is represented by the dirigibles, the very emblem of new forms of mobility, visuality, spatiality—of new freedoms of the body. Yet, announced by the mechanical insects, this image is hardly celebratory; and indeed those freedoms are only apparent, grounded as they are in a capitalistic, militaristic base: the *trafic* of products, weapons, people, soldiers.

I want to linger on this constellation of images for a moment in order to ask what map of machinic modernisms is sketched here. The Suzanne Duchamp image deploys a machinist idiom; its very title, *Usine de mes pensées*, suggests a mechanization of artistic craft as well as of (un)conscious thought. However, this is done to mock traditional representation and

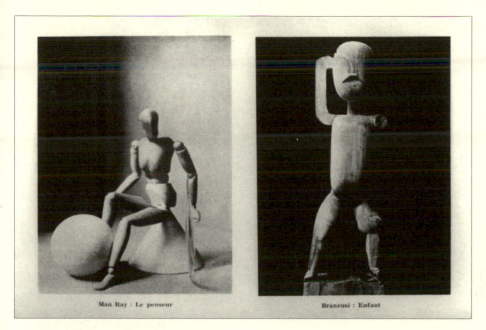

Fig. 5a. "Man Ray: Le Pensur"/"Brancusi: Enfant."

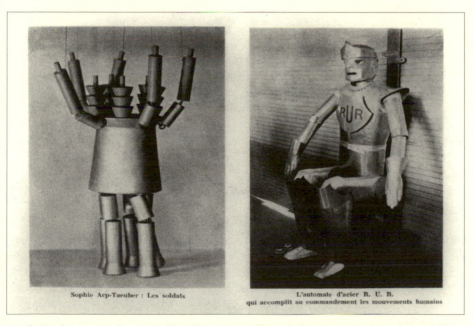

Fig. 5b. "Sophie Arp-Tæuber: Les Soldats"/"L'automate d'acier R.U.R. qui accomplit au commande-ment les mouvements humains."

Fig. 6. "La protection des hommes."

modernist expressivity rather than to embrace industrial production as such. In this regard the Duchamp is dialectically opposed to the Popova. Hardly parodic, this Constructivist stage set is an affirmative sketch of industrial communism to come, which the Meierkhol'dian actors who perform on the apparatus are to evoke with biomechanical gestures (Meierkhol'd based these gestures on Taylorist time-motion studies of labor). The Léger position differs from both the Duchamp and the Popova; neither a parody nor a subsumption of art vis-à-vis industry, Léger proposes a populist aesthetic based on the capitalist object. In so many words he celebrates the machine and the commodity, specialization and shock, as he seeks to "renew the man-spectacle mechanically" (1973: 36).

The Léger position is the other to the Surrealist position, the absent fourth term in this grouping. For if Dada and Constructivism form one dialectical pair (especially regarding the critique of the institution of art), the dysfunctional devices of Surrealism and the machinic models of Léger, Le Corbusier and the middle Bauhaus comprise another such pair. Whereas Léger and company insist on the rational beauty of the "manufactured object", Surrealism stresses the uncanny repressed of this modern rationality: desire and fantasy. Under its gaze the dirigibles here may become so many fantastic fish or innocuous bombs, pneumatic penises or inflated breasts—part objects of desire rather than mass paradigms of objectivity. "[I]n every [utilitarian] object," Roger Caillois writes around this time, "[there is] an irrational residue," and it is precisely this residue that the Surrealist gaze seizes upon.[3] It does so in order to save the modern object from strict functionality, total objectivity, to restore its fantasy, its subjectivity—or at least to make sure that the body, its traces, are not entirely effaced. Obviously this cannot be done completely or cleanly, as the young Marx had dreamed.

Cinéma:
Le peintre Fernand Léger dans le décor du film « L'Inhumaine »

Russphoto

Théâtre:
Décor pour « Le Cocu Magnifique » de Fernand Crommelynck
au Théâtre Meierhold, à Moscou

Fig. 7a. "Cinéma"/"Théâtre."

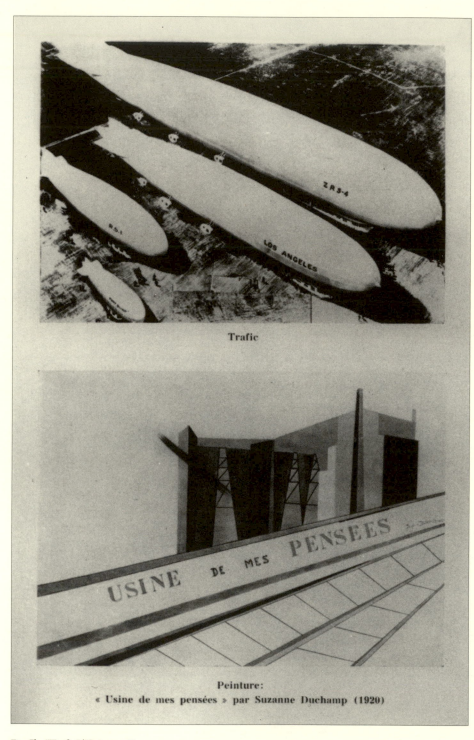

Trafic

Peinture:
« Usine de mes pensées » par Suzanne Duchamp (1920)

Fig. 7b. "Trafic"/"Peinture."

And Adorno, unlike Benjamin no friend of Surrealism, grasped the raggedness of this redemption precisely: "Surrealism," he wrote, "recaptures what functionality denies to man; the distortions demonstrate what the taboo did to the desired" (1954: 224).

All this might be dismissed as another form of romantic anticapitalism. But that is too easy: the Surrealists, after all, are not Expressionists. They do not reject the becoming machine and/or commodity of the body in reactive nostalgia; they resist it with dialectical wit. Significant in this regard is another photo-text on the automaton and the mannequin published by Benjamin Péret in a 1933 issue of *Minotaure* under the title "Au paradis des fantômes." The first spread includes several automatons (including *The Young Writer* by Jacquet-Droz) from its greatest era, the late eighteenth century (Fig 8). This was the epoch of the mechanistic model of man as presented primarily by La Mettrie and figured principally by the automaton, especially as constructed by the premier automaton-maker of the Enlightenment, Jacques Vaucanson. For Péret, however, this figure of materialist rationality has become an irrational "phantom", and in the second spread he relates this irrational phantom to modern rationalization by reference to a robot (Fig. 9). Here, it is implied, the Enlightenment automaton is the historical prototype not only of the modern worker but also of the modern consumer—the mannequin man in tuxedo, the casual woman in the café, the touristic figure on safari.

However elliptically posed here, this historical connection between Enlightenment automaton and capitalist worker is quite close. Indeed, they intersect in the figure of Vaucanson, who also developed the first industrial plant rationalized in plan and power. In a sense, then, the automaton or machine-as-man is a historical figure that announces the industrial laborer or man-as-machine. *L'Homme Machine*: this was in fact the title of the 1748 La Mettrie text that attempted to define the human in terms of mechanical laws. Though set against the metaphysical claims of the *ancien régime*, this mechanistic model was one beginning, according to Foucault, of the discipline of "docility," of the analyzable body joined to the manipulable body, as produced by modern institutions of all sorts (factories, prison, schools, etc.). This relation between Enlightenment man and docile body, between automaton and worker, was not lost on nineteenth-century theorists, whether celebrated as an ideal of productive efficiency (as it was by Andrew Ure) or denounced as a figure of capitalist subjection (as it was by Marx). But it is only, I would argue, in the historical period of Surrealism—when automatons were outmoded but automation had become structural to production and emergent in consumption—that the full effects of the industrial process were thought.

In 1922, at the very rise of Surrealism, Lukács wrote that the law of capitalist production, the fragmentation of subject and object, was now extended "to cover every manifestation of life in society" (1971: 91–92). And in 1939, at the effective end of Surrealism, Benjamin argued that this fragmented rhythm of repetitive shock and reaction to shock had become the perceptual norm in the capitalist city, that once complex acts of all kinds were now mechanically automatic. (Here again Surrealist automatism must be placed in apposition to these other routines.) Finally, not much later Sigfried Giedion wrote that such mechanization had "impinged upon the very center of the human psyche, through all the senses," and that Surrealism alone "has given us keys to the psychic unrest" produced in the event (1948: 42). My suggestion here falls in this line of analysis: that the Surrealists figured the uncanny aspects of reification and fragmentation in order to make these processes reflexively perverse, critically absurd, that they deployed the "mere sources of error" to which subjectivity is reduced in capitalist production against the supposed objectivity, the second nature, of its social order. Finally, this may be where the political in Surrealism lies: less in its stormy party affiliations and isolated anarchistic gestures than in its uncanny ability to oppose to modern rationalization its other face.

H.
Foster

SINGE MUSICIEN HABILLÉ EN MARQUIS ET COIFFÉ D'UN BONNET
ROUGE A COCARDE TRICOLORE. JOUE LA MARSEILLAISE ET LA
CARMAGNOLE. FIN DU XVIIIᵉ SIÈCLE (COLLECTION CORTI).

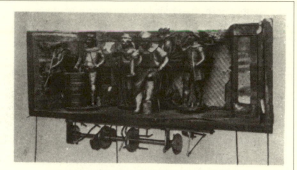

GROUPE D'AUTOMATES : AU CENTRE, UN CORDONNIER ASSIS SUR UN ESCABEAU
TIRE LE FIL DE SA COUTURE. IL BAISSE LA TÊTE ET OUVRE LA BOUCHE. A SA DROITE,
INCLINANT LE CHEF UN PHYSICIEN SOULÈVE LE COUVERCLE D'UN TONNEAU D'OÙ
ÉMERGE UNE TÊTE DE NÈGRE. A GAUCHE, UNE FIGURINE — PROBABLEMENT UN
BERGER — PORTE SUR SON DOS UNE HOTTE DE LAQUELLE SORT PAR INSTANTS UNE
PETITE CHÈVRE. AU SECOND PLAN, UNE FEMME AUX CHEVEUX DÉFAITS, COIFFÉE D'UN
CASQUE, PORTE UNE SORTE DE CORBEILLE DONT, DE SA MAIN DROITE, ELLE SOULÈVE
LE COUVERCLE, FAISANT APPARAITRE UN OISEAU. PUIS, LE CASQUE SE RABATTANT
SUR SON VISAGE, ELLE PRÉSENTE UNE FIGURE MASCULINE. DANS LE FOND, LES
BRANCHES D'UN PALMIER LAISSENT VOIR LORSQU'ELLES S'ENTROUVRENT UN
COUPLE ENLACÉ CACHÉ DANS L'ARBRE.

FEMME POUSSANT UNE BROUETTE SUR LAQUELLE
EST ASSIS UN HOMME (MUSÉE DE CLUNY).

MÉCANISME DES YEUX
DE L'« ÉCRIVAIN » DE
JAQUET-DROZ.

MÉCANISME DE L' « ÉCRIVAIN »
DE JAQUET-DROZ.

Nous devons à l'obligeance de M. Édouard Gélis, auteur, avec
M. Alfred Chapuis, du remarquable ouvrage : « Le Monde des
Automates » (Paris, 1928), la plupart des illustrations de cet article.

Fig. 8. Cluster of 5.

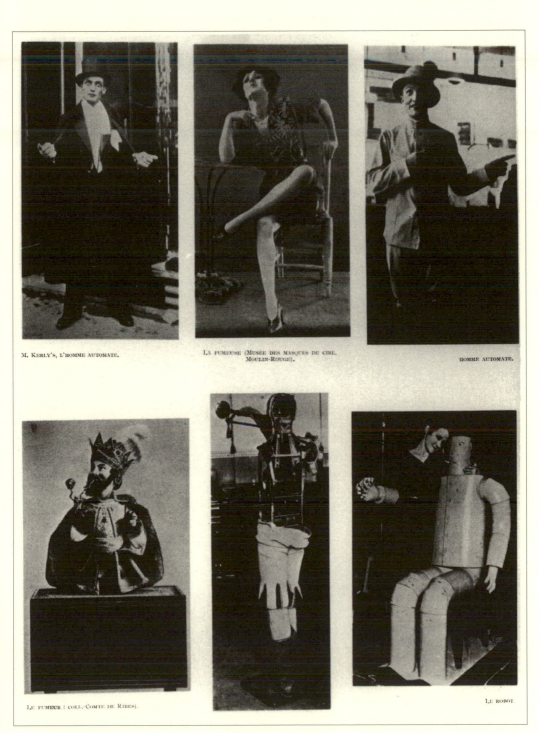

M. KERLY'S, L'HOMME AUTOMATE.

LA FUMEUSE (MUSÉE DES MASQUES DE CIRE,
MOULIN-ROUGE).

HOMME AUTOMATE.

LE FUMEUR (COLL. COMTE DE RIBES).

LE ROBOT.

Fig. 9. Cluster of 6.

Notes

1.   This paper was presented as a talk at a symposium on Surrealism held at UC Berkeley in October 1990 and then at a panel concerning questions of "high" and "low" culture held at the Dia Art Center in New York in November 1990. It appears here essentially as it was delivered then. For an extended discussion of Surrealism in these terms see my *Compulsive Beauty* (1993).

2.   For an extended account of this cultural politic of "kynical irony," see Peter Sloterdijk (1987).

3.   The Surrealists detected this modern dialectic of reason and unreason in the everyday object, "the irrational knowledge" of which they examined collectively in texts, inquiries and exhibitions.

References

Adorno, Theodor W. 1967 (1954). "Looking Back on Surrealism." In *The Idea of the Modern in Literature and the Arts*, ed. Irving Howe. New York: Horizon.

Benjamin, Walter. 1969. "On Some Motifs in Baudelaire." In *Illuminations*, trans. Harry Zohn. New York: Schocken Books.

Foster, Hal. 1993. *Compulsive Beauty*. Cambridge, Mass: M.I.T. Press.

Foucault, Michel. 1977. *Discipline and Punish*. Trans. Alan Sheridan. New York: Pantheon.

Giedion, Sigfried. 1948. *Mechanization Takes Command*. New York: W. W. Norton.

Léger, Fernand. 1973. *Functions of Painting*. Ed. Edward Fry. New York: Viking.

Lukacs, Georg. 1971. *History and Class Consciousness*. Trans. Rodney Livingstone. Cambridge, Mass: M.I.T. Press.

Marx, Karl. 1977. *Capital* Vol. 1. Trans. Ben Fowkes. New York: Vintage Books.

Sloterdijk, Peter. 1987. *The Critique of Cynical Reason*. Trans. Michael Eldred. Minneapolis: University of Minnesota Press.

The Disenchantment of the Eye
Surrealism and the
Crisis of Ocularcentrism

Martin Jay

"It is time to abandon the world of the civilized and its light."
—Georges Bataille[1]

"I have discarded clarity as worthless. Working in darkness,
I have discovered lightning."
—André Breton[2]

IF, AS IT IS OFTEN CLAIMED, THE FIRST WORLD WAR CHALLENGED AND IN CERTAIN CASES toppled the traditional hierarchies of European life, the domination of sight, long accounted the "noblest of the senses," was by no means impervious to its impact.[3] The interrogation of sight's hegemonic role in Western culture begun by certain prewar philosophers like Nietzsche and Bergson and artists like Mallarmé and Cézanne was given an intense, often violent inflection by the war, which also helped disseminate an appreciation of its implications. The ancient scopic régime, which might be called Cartesian perspectivalism,[4] lost what was left of its leading role, and the very premises of ocularcentrism themselves were soon being called into question. In certain cases, the crisis of visual primacy expressed itself in direct terms; in others, it produced compensatory vindications of an alternative scopic order to replace the one that seemed lost. These effects were perhaps nowhere as evident as in interwar France, where many intellectuals from a wide variety of different camps experienced a palpable loss of confidence in the eye, or at a very minimum, in many of its time-honored functions. Even in the case of those who sought to reenchant the world, and thus renew the alleged innocence of the eye, an unexpectedly critical attitude towards visual experience ultimately developed. Even, that is, the Surrealists, who are often accounted among the most starry-eyed exponents of visionary redemption, came to question the possibility or even the desirability of that goal. In what follows, I hope to demonstrate the reasons for so counter-intuitive a claim, and in so doing, situate Surrealism in the context of the much larger anti-ocularcentric discourse whose outlines I have probed elsewhere.[5]

•   •   •

To generalize about the effects on visual experience and the discursive reflection on that experience stimulated by the first world war is very hazardous. Recent commentators such as Paul Fussell, Eric J. Leed, Stephen Kern, Kenneth Silver and Sidra Stich have made, however, a suggestive start.[6] The Western front's interminable trench warfare, they point out, created a bewildering landscape of indistinguishable, shadowy shapes, illuminated by lightning flashes of blinding intensity, and then obscured by phantasmagoric, often gas-induced haze. The effect was even more visually disorienting than those produced by such nineteenth-century technical innovations as the railroad, the camera or the cinema. When all that the soldier could see was the sky above and the mud below, the traditional reliance on visual evidence for survival could no longer be easily maintained. The invention of camouflage and the disappearance of differences in uniform between men and officers added to the experience of war as at once a frightening reality and a not so grand illusion. According to Leed, "the invisibility of the enemy, and the retirement of troops underground, destroyed any notion that war was a spectacle of contending humanity . . . The invisibility of the enemy put a premium upon auditory signals and seemed to make the war experience peculiarly subjective and intangible."[7]

One reaction was a compensatory exaltation of the aerial perspective of the flyer, able to rise above the confusion of the earth-bound—and often earth-bespattered—combatants. Nadar's balloonist became St. Exupéry's aviator, heroically embodying the ancient myth of Icarian freedom.[8] From the air, the labyrinth of trenches could seem like a patterned carpet. Perhaps this was the perspective which earned Gertrude Stein's appellation "the cubist war."[9] Cubism, which was in fact on the wane in Paris, grew increasingly popular among artists with experience at the front.[10] But whereas from the perspective of the ground, it expressed the decomposition of spatial order, from that of the air, it suggested a landscape with unexpected intelligibility. Within the internal history of Cubism itself, the shift may have been reflected in the transition from its analytical to synthetic phases.

Another escape was provided by focussing on the one thing that remained visible from the trenches, at least when the gas or smoke was not interfering: the boundless sky, whose dreamy beauty could be ironically juxtaposed to the brutal reality of earthly combat. Such a sky could also become the locus for a projected, split vision in which the victim could somewhere become the distanced observer of his own fate. "The sky," Leed writes, "is charged with intense significance: It *must* be the residence of the observer watching himself struggle through the nightmare of the war, for only then will the eye survive the dismemberment of the body."[11]

Still another reaction, manifest in the avant-garde visual arts themselves, was the willed return to visual lucidity and clarity, which Silver has shown accompanied a new nationalist-inflected classicism in the arts as a whole. The new mood in Paris was evident in the waning popularity of Cubism, the reevaluation of Cézanne in non-Bergsonian terms, the revival of interest in Seurat's serene canvases, and the newly sober preoccupations of artists like

Delaunay, Picasso and Gris. It culminated in the uncompromising Purism of Ozenfant and Le Corbusier in the late teens.[12] Postwar reconstruction would require, they reasoned, the restoration of a unified scopic regime, which would be compatible with the disciplined collectivist society they saw emerging from the ashes of the conflagration. Here the precarious "recall to order" of the 1920s found one of its origins, as certain modernists sought to contain the more explosive and disintegrative implications of their predecessors' work.

But despite such compensatory myths and exercises in nostalgic purification, the actual impoverishment of normal visual experience also produced more directly disturbing effects. For, to cite Leed again, "the deterioration of the visual field experienced by many in trench warfare removed those visual markers that allow an observer to direct his attention to what comes first and what later . . . The constriction of vision eliminated most of those signs that allow individuals to collectively order their experience in terms of problems to be solved in some kind of rational sequence . . . Naturally, this chaotic world was judged entirely on the basis of the individual's own perspective, a perspective that mobilized deeply layered anxieties, animistic images, and surprising and unbidden associations."[13] "The cubist war" could thus also mean the practical collapse of that transcendental notion of a shared perspective that had been theoretically undermined by Nietzsche. And with it could come the return of all of the demons seemingly repressed by the "civilizing process," which was grounded to a significant extent in the domination of the dispassionate gaze.

Perhaps no figure during the subsequent decades expressed both the trauma and the ecstasy of that liberation as powerfully as did Georges Bataille. Certainly none tied it as explicitly to the dethronement of the eye as did he. Bataille's own wartime experiences have, however, rarely been given their due in the now voluminous literature on him, and one can indeed only conjecture about their direct impact. Perhaps, as his friend Pierre Andler contended, they left him with a visceral pacifism that undermined his willingness to endorse violent means even against fascism.[14] Yet on a deeper level, the war seems to have exercised a certain positive fascination. For it is striking that many of Bataille's obsessive themes would betray an affinity for the experiences of degradation, pollution, violence and communal bonding that were characteristic of life in the trenches. Perhaps none of those themes was as dramatically intertwined with the war's impact as that of the eye.

According to his own testimony (which not all commentators have accepted with equal trust), Bataille, born in 1897, fled the invading German army in 1914, was called up in January, 1916, fell seriously ill and was discharged a year later.[15] Although there is little to indicate he had any combat experience, it is significant that two decades later, on the eve of another war, he could exult in the risking of life in battle as a joyous release from petty, selfish concerns.[16] "Conflict is life," he insisted. "Man's value depends upon his aggressive strength. A living man regards death as the fulfillment of life; he does not see it as a misfortune."[17]

In seeking to evoke the mystical experience of "joy before death," Bataille turned to typical images from the first world war of the all-encompassing sky and blinding light. His sky, however, participated in the general destruction, rather than served as an escape from it: "I imagine the earth turning vertiginously in the sky, I imagine the sky itself slipping, turning and lost. The sun, comparable to alcohol, turning and bursting breathlessly. The depth of the sky like an orgy of frozen light, lost."[18] "I MYSELF AM WAR," he proclaimed, and added, "there are explosives everywhere that will soon blind me. I laugh when I think that my eyes persist in demanding objects that do not destroy them."[19]

Bataille's deeply charged summoning of blindness had another likely source, which has been remarked by virtually all of his commentators: his blind and paralyzed father, who died insane in November, 1916. Here too, however, the experience of the war seems to have played a role. For Bataille and his mother had abandoned the father to his fate when the Germans invaded Rheims in August, 1914. The son returned two years later to find only the sealed coffin of his dead father, with whom he at least partly came to identify.[20] "Today," he would write in 1943, "I know I am 'blind,' immeasurable, I am man 'abandoned' on the globe like my father at N. No one on earth or in heaven cared about my father's dying terror. Still, I believe he faced up to it as always. What a 'horrible pride,' at moments, in Dad's blind smile."[21]

Before Bataille came to identify with his father, however, he seems to have felt closer to his mother instead. The first essay he published, in 1920, was a lyrical reflection on the cathedral of Notre-Dame de Rheims, which had been destroyed during the German invasion.[22] According to Denis Hollier,[23] the cathedral functioned for Bataille as a visual metaphor of maternity, a regressive symbol of continuity and repose. Significantly, it was also linked to images of illumination. "Joan of Arc's vision," the young Bataille wrote, "still so thrilling to myself four years later, is the light I offer up to your desires, the vision of Notre-Dame de Rheims bathed in sunlight."[24] Shortly thereafter, for reasons that remain murky, Bataille repudiated this maternal identification, and with it his celebration of visions of clarity. "All of Bataille's writings would be aimed at the destruction of this cathedral," Hollier concludes; "to reduce it to silence he would write against this text."[25] In fact, he would write "against architecture" of any kind, because it represented visual order and legible space, covering over tomb-like the subterranean disorder it abhorred.

Whatever the personal sources of Bataille's subsequent lucubrations, at once tormented and triumphant, on death, violence, eroticism, religious transgression[26] and blindness, the results would slowly find an appreciative audience able to understand their implications for the traditional privileging of vision. The first attempt he made to reach that audience came in 1926 with the composition of a short book written under the pseudonym Troppman and called *W.C.* "Of violent opposition to any form of dignity,"[27] it was never finished, its fragments burned by the author. Significantly, it contained a drawing of an eye, the eye of the scaffold, which he called in tribute to Nietzsche "the Eternal Return." "Solitary, solar, bristling with lashes," he would later recall, "it gazed from the lunette of a guillotine."[28] This lunette, he confided, was mixed up in his mind with that of the toilet seat on which his blind father sat to void his bowels. A symbol of terrorist surveillance, it thus also stood for the liberating blindness through which the expended waste Bataille was to celebrate as *dépense* could explosively pass.

A year later, a slim volume published under the pseudonym Lord Auch appeared in a private edition of 134 copies, accompanied by eight lithographs drawn by Bataille's friend André Masson. It was called *Histoire de l'Oeil* (*Story of the Eye*) and was so transgressively pornographic that it never appeared under Bataille's name during his lifetime.[29] After his death and then with its republication in 1967, however, it became a widely discussed classic, eliciting commentaries by Roland Barthes, Michel Foucault, Susan Sontag and a host of scholarly interpreters.[30] There can, in fact, be few works of this genre since Sade that have generated so much earnest exegesis.

Story of the Eye is a pivotal text for our own story of the eye's interrogation for a variety of reasons. Whatever else it may be, the eye in this story is, to borrow Brian Fitch's phrase, *l'oeil qui ne voit pas*.[31] Bataille finishes his tale with the enucleated eye of a garroted priest inserted in the anus and then vagina of the heroine, as the narrator realizes that he finds himself "facing something I imagine I had been waiting for in the same way that a guillotine waits for the neck to slice. I even felt as if my eyes were bulging from my head, erectile with horror . . ."[32] Enucleation, is in fact, a central theme of the story, which reproduces an actual episode Bataille witnessed in 1922: the ripping out of the matador Granero's eye by a bull's horn in Seville. Until he saw the famous scene of the slit eyeball in the Surrealist masterpiece *Un chien andalou* by Dali and Buñuel in 1928, about which he wrote enthusiastically in the pages of *Documents*,[33] he had no more vivid image to express his obsessive fascination with the violent termination of vision. For the enucleated eye was a parodic version of the separation of sight from the body characteristic of the Cartesian perspectivalist tradition. No longer able to see, it was then thrown back into the body via the anal or vaginal cavities, thus mocking in advance Merleau-Ponty's benign reembodiment of the eye in the "flesh of the world."

Photo by Man Ray.

In more subtle ways, as well, the novel challenges the primacy of sight. As Barthes pointed out in an essay that in any other context could innocently be called seminal, Bataille's narrative can be read not merely as a sado-masochistic erotic revery, but also as a linguistic adventure. That is, the tale is motivated less by the increasingly bizarre couplings of its ostensible protagonists than by the metaphoric transformations of the objects on which they fetishistically focus. The most notable series is that linked to the eye itself, which is enchained with images of eggs, testicles and the sun. A second train is composed of the liquids associated with them (tears, egg yolks, sperm) and others like urine, blood and milk. According to Barthes, none of these terms is given any privilege, none has any foundational priority: "it is the very equivalence of ocular and genital which is original, not one of its terms: the paradigm *begins* nowhere . . . everything is given on the surface and without hierarchy, the metaphor is displayed in its entirety; circular and explicit, it refers to no secret."[34] Thus, the time-honored function of the penetrating gaze, able to pierce appearances to "see" the essences beneath, is explicitly rejected.

Bataille furthermore links the two metaphoric chains to each other in metonymic ways, so that signifiers from one, (e.g., eggs) are coupled with signifiers from others (e.g., urination). The result, Barthes concludes, are typically Surrealist images produced through radically decontextualized juxtapositions (e.g., suns that cry, castrated or pissing eyes, eggs that are sucked like breasts). Thus, what is transgressed is not merely normal sexual behavior, but also the rules of conventional language. Because in French, words like *couille* are near anagrams of *cul* and *oeil*, the effect of linguistic promiscuity is as strong as that of its more obvious sexual counterpart.

Barthes's structuralist reading, with its strongly textualist rather than experiential bias, may have its flaws,[35] but it points to one important implication of the novel: that whether understood literally or metaphorically, the eye is toppled from its privileged place in the sensual hierarchy to be linked instead with objects and functions more normally associated with "baser" human behavior. This is, indeed, the most ignoble eye imaginable.

To understand fully the depths of that ignobility, we have to recall the speculative claim Freud was advancing at virtually the same time in *Civilization and its Discontents*.[36] Human civilization, Freud conjectured, only began when hominids raised themselves off the ground, stopped sniffing the nether regions of their fellows and elevated sight to a position of superiority. With that elevation went a concomitant repression of sexual and aggressive drives, and the radical separation of "higher" spiritual and mental faculties from the "lower" functions of the body.

Bataille was himself in analysis with Dr. Adrien Borel when he wrote *Story of the Eye*. He later contended that "by August 1927, it put an end to the series of dreary mishaps and failures in which he had been floundering, but not the state of intellectual intensity, which still persists."[37] Nor would his fascination with Freudian ideas end, as he continued to draw on them throughout his life. Although there is no evidence that he knew of Freud's specific conjectures about the connections between elevated vision and repression—indeed, the chronology of their respective publications suggests otherwise, even if it is possible that Freud's ideas were in circulation among analysts before coming into print—*Story of the Eye* can be read as a tacit plea for the reversal of this most fateful of human developments. Bataille's later defense of what he called a "general" as opposed to "restricted" economy, one based on *dépense* (waste or expenditure), loss, transgression and excess, rather than production, exchange, conservation and instrumental rationality, was closely tied to this critique of the primacy of vision.[38] The only light cast by the potlatch ceremonies he found so fascinating was produced by the flames consuming the wealth destroyed. So too Bataille's critique of absolute knowledge, most notably that sought by Hegel, in favor of a "non-knowledge" or "un-knowing," which always defeats the ability to think it clearly and distinctly, drew on the same impulse.[39] If, as Robert Sasso puts it, Bataille wanted to go "*du savoir au non-savoir*,"[40] he certainly understood the importance of *voir* for *savoir*. It could be undermined only through the explosive sound of laughter or the blurred vision produced by tears.[41]

No less subversive of traditional ocularcentrism was Bataille's unprecedented transfiguration of the familiar metaphor of the sun. In a short piece entitled "The Solar Anus," written in 1927 and published, with drawings by Masson, four years later, he identified himself with the sun, but one of violent aggression rather than benign illumination, a "filthy parody of the torrid and blinding sun."[42] It was a sun that loves the night and seeks to copulate with it: "I want to have my throat slashed," Bataille wrote, "while violating the girl to whom I will have been able to say: you are the night."[43] Such a sun could thus be conflated with an anus, the darkest of possible holes.

In another brief essay, written in 1930, Bataille invoked the "rotten sun" as an antidote to the elevated sun of the dominant Western tradition.[44] The latter was based on the prudent refusal to stare directly into it, the former with the self-destructive willingness to do so. The Platonic tradition of rational heliocentrism could thus be subverted by a mythic alternative, which he identified with the Mithraic cult of the sun: "If we describe the notion of the sun in the mind of one whose weak eyes compel him to emasculate it, that sun must be said to have the poetic meaning of mathematical serenity and spiritual elevation. If on the other hand one obstinately focuses on it, a certain madness is implied, and the notion changes meaning because it is no longer production that appears in light, but refuse or combustion, adequately expressed by the horror emanating from a brilliant arc lamp. In practice the scrutinized sun can be identified with mental ejaculation, foam on the lips, and an epileptic crisis. In the same way that the preceding sun (the one not looked at) is perfectly beautiful, the one that is scrutinized can be considered horribly ugly."[45] The two ways of conceiving the sun are represented in the myth of Icarus, who seeks the sun of elevated beauty, but is destroyed by the vengeful sun of combustion.

Bataille furthermore linked the ability to stare at the "rotten sun" with artistic creativity. This essay was itself written as a brief tribute to Picasso, whose decomposition of forms challenged the search in academic painting for elevated beauty. Later, in a celebration of Blake, Bataille would write of *The Tyger*, "never have eyes as wide open as these stared at the sun of cruelty."[46] But it was perhaps in two essays of 1930 and 1937 on Van Gogh that he made the connections between looking at the sun, self-destruction and aesthetic creativity most explicit.[47]

Drawing on a case study of an auto-mutilator called Gaston F, written up by Dr. Borel and two collaborators, he pondered the implications of the painter's own auto-mutilation.[48] The patient had torn off one of his fingers after staring at the sun, symbolically instantiating the psychoanalytic link between blindness and castration. For Bataille, Van Gogh's sun paintings and his severed ear enacted a similar sacrificial mutilation: "The eagle-god who is confused with the sun by the ancients, the eagle who alone among all beings can contemplate while staring 'at the sun in all its glory,' the Icarian being who goes to seek the fire of the heavens is, however, nothing other than an automutilator, a Vincent Van Gogh, a Gaston F."[49] Such a sacrifice, according to the logic of Bataille's general economy, was an act of de-individuating freedom, an expression of ecstatic and "sovereign" heterogeneity. At the moment Van Gogh introduced the sun into his work, "all of his painting finally became *radiation, explosion, flame,* and himself, lost in ecstasy before a source of *radiant* life, *exploding, inflamed*."[50]

If the sun could thus be split into an elevating, ennobling, rational source of light, not to be looked at directly, and an aggressive, dismembering, sacrificial source of destruction, joyously blinding those who dare to stare at it unflinchingly, so too the eye itself could have several conflicting meanings for Bataille. In a 1929 essay for *Documents*, simply entitled "Eye," he explored examples of the fears and anxieties engendered by the experience of ocular surveillance.[51] Citing such instances of the "eye of conscience" as Grandville's lithograph "First Dream: Crime and Expiation," Hugo's poem "La Conscience," and the illustrated weekly "The Eye of the Police," he emphasized the sadistic implications of being the object of the punishing gaze. The slitting of the eye in *Un chien andalou*, "this extraordinary film,"[52] showed, he claimed, how the eye could be related to cutting, both as its victim and as its perpetrator. But such violence, Bataille concluded, was not without its positive implications: "If Buñuel himself, after filming of the slit-open eye, remained sick for a week . . . how then can one not see to what extent horror becomes fascinating, and how it alone is brutal enough to break everything that stifles?"[53] For Bataille, submission to the aggressive power of the "cutting" gaze, like that to the blinding power of the sun, could be a source of liberating subversion.

In two other essays written around 1930, Bataille turned to another concept, that of the "pineal eye," which had played a central a role in Descartes's philosophy.[54] Strictly speaking, Descartes had known it only as a gland, not a vestigial eye, which was understood only by nineteenth-century science. But significantly, he had accorded it a pivotal role in the transformation of the visual experience of the two physical eyes into the unified and coherent sight of the mind or soul. The pineal gland was thus the very seat of rational intellection. In contrast, Bataille concocted a phantasmatic anthropology which pitted the pineal gland against both the two eyes of everyday sight and the rational vision of the mind's eye.

Interestingly, he did so by subtly reversing the axes of verticality and horizontality posited by Freud as connected, respectively with civilization and bestiality. Normal sight, he claimed, was a vestige of man's originally horizontal, animal status. But it was a burden rather than a

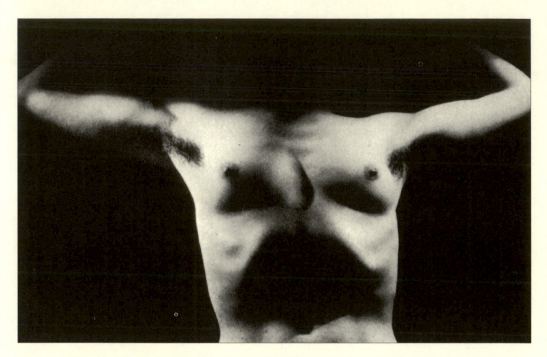

Photo by Man Ray, published in *Minotaure* in 1935, and referred to in footnote 64.

blessing: "the horizontal axis of vision, to which the human structure has remained strictly subjected, in the course of man's wrenching rejection of animal nature, is the expression of a misery all the more oppressive in that it is apparently confused with serenity."[55]

In contrast, the pineal eye yearns to burst out from its confinement and blind itself by staring at the sun, that destroying sun ignored by rational heliocentrism: "the eye, at the summit of the skull, opening on the incandescent sun in order to contemplate it in sinister solitude, is not a product of the understanding, but is instead an immediate existence; it opens and blinds itself like a conflagration, or like a fever that eats the being, or more exactly, the head."[56] This version of verticality is not, *pace* Freud, an escape from man's "lower" functions, but is intimately linked with them. Its volcanic eruptions are "discharges as violent and as indecent as those that make the anal protuberances of some apes so horrible to see;" its bursting through the skull is like an erection, "which would have vibrated, making me let out atrocious screams, the screams of a magnificent but stinking ejaculation."[57]

The sun that it seeks to reach through these explosions is at once a solar anus and a fecal or bronze eye. Here the distantiating function of normal sight and the elevating tradition of rational heliocentrism are undone, as eye, sun and anus are all indiscriminately mingled in a general economy of ecstatic heterogeneity. Here blindness and castration are less to be feared than welcomed as the means to liberate the mundane self from its enslavement in a restricted economy based on the fastidious discriminations of servile sight.

Bataille's radical devaluation of conventional visual experience and its metaphorical appropriation continued to be manifest throughout his career. Thus, for example, during his most Marxist phase, around 1930, he defended a version of "base" materialism very different from the conventional philosophical kind, linking it to the Gnostic principle of darkness which was opposed to the Hellenic worship of clarity and light.[58] Like Bergson, although without acknowledging the similarity, he rejected a materialism based on a visual image of matter in favor of one derived from the bodily experience of materiality. Likewise, he repudiated the classical—and, we might add, high modernist—fetish of form, which was so dependent on visual distance. Instead, he privileged the *"informe,"* that formlessness apparent in phlegm and putrefaction.[59] As Rosalind Krauss has shown, the same sentiment generated the fascination shown by Bataille and other contributors to *Documents* for primitive art.[60] Unlike most modernists who saw in primitive artifacts models of universal, abstract form, the group around Bataille appreciated instead their links with sacrificial rituals of mutilation and waste.

Later in the 1930s, Bataille adopted the image of the headless, "acephalic" man as the central symbol for the community he and his friends Michel Leiris and Roger Caillois wanted to create around the Collège de Sociologie.[61] *Acéphale*, their journal, published four issues between 1936 and 1939.[62] Here the explosion of the pineal eye was understood to have taken with it the head, that symbol of reason and spirituality based on the hegemony of the eyes. The gruesome work of the guillotine was also invoked as still haunting the Place de la Concorde. Today, that square was dominated, Bataille wrote, by "eight armored and acephalic figures" with helmets "as empty as they were on the day the executioner decapitated the king before them."[63] Even the bull's head affixed to another symbol beloved by Bataille's circle, the minotaur, was gone.[64]

The sacred community he wanted to resurrect would only come when "man has escaped from his head just as the condemned man has escaped from prison . . . He reunites in the same eruption Birth and Death. He is not a man. He is not a god either. He is not me but he is more than me: his stomach is the labyrinth in which he has lost himself, loses me with him, and in which I discover myself as him, in other words as a monster."[65] Rather than seeking a way out of the labyrinth through aerial flight, that compensatory myth sustaining so many veterans of the trenches on the western front, Bataille urged instead a joyous entanglement in its coils.[66] The labyrinth, as Hollier has noted, served as the antidote to the pyramid, that architectural symbol of solidity and substance, which was homologous to the optical cone.[67]

Even after the second world war, when the ambiguous political implications of Bataille's interwar fantasies had a certain sobering effect on him, he continued to criticize the ocularcentric traditions of our culture in a variety of ways. Taking issue with Sartre's defense of pellucid prose as the clear passage of ideas from one subjectivity to another, he contended that true communication at the deepest level demands obscurity. "Communication, in my sense," he wrote in *Literature and Evil*, "is never stronger than when communication, in the weak sense, the sense of profane language or, as Sartre says, of prose which makes us and the others appear penetrable, fails and becomes the equivalent of darkness."[68] Like Maurice Blanchot, with whom he became friends in 1940, Bataille came to see literature, prose no less than poetry, as the privileged locus of obscure communication, the guilty repository of sovereign and transgressive Evil.

There were visual manifestations of the same phenomenon as well, for Bataille was deeply taken with the possibility of what one commentator has called an anti-idealist "iconography of the heterogeneous."[69] Fascinated by the primitive cave paintings discovered at Lascaux,[70] Bataille invidiously contrasted the visual tradition that emerged when men left the cave and sought to paint in the clarity of sunlight with one in which darkness and obscurity still reigned supreme. And even his book of 1955 on Manet, in many ways a conventional appreciation of modernist opticality, contained, as Rosalind Krauss has noted, a short paean to Goya, whose art of excess and violence provided a counter-model comparable to those he had celebrated in Van Gogh and Picasso during the interwar years.[71] In short, when Bataille was discovered in the 1960s by a generation of post-structuralist thinkers eager to follow his philosophical, literary and anthropological lead, his critique of vision was also readily available as a vital inspiration to their own ruthless interrogation of the eye.

• • •

Bataille's obsessive visual concerns may well have had a personal source, as his own reminiscences of his blind father imply. But the frequency of themes in his work that can be traced to the wartime experiences of so many others of his generation suggest that they were by no means uniquely his own. The group of artists and writers who came to be called Surrealists were themselves deeply disturbed by those experiences. As their first historian Maurice Nadeau observed, "Breton, Éluard, Aragon, Péret, Soupault were profoundly affected by the war. They had fought in it by obligation and under constraint. They emerged from it disgusted; henceforth they wanted nothing in common with a civilization that had lost its justification, and their radical nihilism extended not only to art but to all its manifestations."[72] Was ocularcentrism one of the manifestations they chose to reject? If, as Sidra Stich has argued, the traumas of the war were reproduced in the "anxious visions" of Surrealist art, did they lead as well to an anxiety about vision itself? And if so, were the mainstream Surrealists as violently hostile to the hegemony of the eye as Bataille?

To answer these questions is no simple task, as the Surrealists were a large and heterogeneous group of artists with countless internal quarrels and many reversals of opinion over the long duration of the movement (which has not entirely given up the ghost even today). Despite all the best efforts of their "pope" André Breton, to keep order, they remained an unruly and obstreperous assemblage of individuals radically unwilling to submit to discipline for very long. However much the Surrealists wanted to suppress the traditional idea of the artistic genius and work collectively, the narcissism of small differences often interfered. Moreover, the many visual artists associated with them—painters, photographers, cinematographers and those who invented their own media of expression—developed clearly disparate and individual styles; no one can confuse an Ernst with a Dali or a Miró with a Magritte. And although there is no shortage of verbal statements of their intentions in manifestoes, memoirs, interviews and exhibition catalogues, the visual results cannot be assumed to correspond with or merely exemplify their avowed purposes. Thus, to pretend to have located a monolithic Surrealist attitude towards the visual would indeed be foolish.

Still, what allows us (and allowed them) to call Surrealism a relatively coherent phenomenon suggests that at least some recurrent patterns can be discerned, which with due caution can be called typical. One way to approach them would be to focus for a moment on the quarrel between Bataille and Breton, which involved, *inter alia*, a difference of opinion about vision.[73] As Bataille would remember it, contact began around 1925, was almost immediately followed by a falling out which came to a head in 1929, then was succeeded by a rapprochement in 1935 with their joint membership in a political group called *Counterattack*.[74]

Part of the tension was caused by Breton's suspicion that Bataille wanted to challenge his leadership and set up a rival group, which became a self-fulfilling prophecy when he did become the figure around whom disaffected Surrealists like Caillois, Leiris, Masson, Desnos, Vitrac and Limbour could rally. Another part was due to Breton's personal distaste for Bataille's perverse pornographic and excremental obsessions,[75] as well as for the hypocritical contradiction he saw between Bataille's advocacy of violence and his professional career as a librarian at the Bibliothèque Nationale. But issues of substance were also involved, which bear on their different attitudes towards vision.

Breton's rejection of Bataille was made public in the *Second Manifesto of Surrealism* of 1930, where he defended himself against what he called Bataille's "absurd campaign against . . . 'the sordid quests for every integrity'."[76] Bataille, he claimed, was interested only in the vilest and most corrupt things, was indifferent to anything useful, and had returned to an old anti-dialectical notion of materialism, which was simply the reverse of idealism. Moreover, his wholesale repudiation of the homogenizing powers of rationality produced a performative contradiction, in so far as he had to engage in communicative rationality to express it (a charge that would be repeated against Bataille many years later by Jürgen Habermas[77]):

"M. Bataille's misfortune is to reason: admittedly, he reasons like someone who 'has a fly on his nose,' which allies him more closely with the dead than the living, but *he does reason*. He is trying, with the help of the tiny mechanism in him which is not completely out of order, to share his obsessions: this very fact proves that he cannot claim, no matter what he may say, to be opposed to any system, *like an unthinking brute*. What is paradoxical and embarrassing about M. Bataille's case is that his phobia about the 'idea,' as soon as he attempts to communicate it, can only take an ideological turn."[78]

Bataille's response came in two pieces written around 1930, although not immediately published: "The Use Value of D.A.F. Sade (An Open Letter to My Current Comrades)" and "The 'Old Mole' and the Prefix *Sur* in the Words *Surhomme* [Superman] and Surrealist."[79] The former, which was one salvo in an ongoing war over the correct reading of Sade involving many other combatants,[80] contains little directly bearing on the issue of vision.[81] The latter, however, drew on and expanded Bataille's earlier ruminations on the contrast between ennobling vision and baser forms of knowledge (or non-knowledge). Here the metaphor he introduces pitted the eagle against the "old mole," the latter derived, of course, from Marx's celebrated image of the Revolution in *The Eighteenth Brumaire*.

The eagle, Bataille points out, is more glamorous and virile a symbol than the mole. With its hooked beak, it has "formed an alliance with the sun, which castrates all that enters into conflict with it (Icarus, Prometheus, the Mithraic bull.)"[82] As such, it might be expected that Bataille would interpret the eagle as an ambivalent figure, like the sun, at times Platonic and at times "rotten," with whom it allies itself. But because of the polemical intent of the essay, it is only its unattractive implications that he chose to stress: "politically the eagle is identified with imperialism, that is, with the unconstrained development of individual authoritarian power, triumphant over all obstacles. And metaphysically the eagle is identified with the *idea*, when, young and aggressive, it has not yet reached a state of pure abstraction."[83] Breton's desire to ride the eagle on a revolutionary flight would thus be disastrous: "revolutionary idealism tends to make of the revolution an eagle above eagles, a *supereagle* striking down authoritarian imperialism, an idea as radiant as an adolescent eloquently seizing power for the benefit of utopian enlightenment. The detour naturally leads to the failure of the revolution and, with the help of military fascism, the satisfaction of the elevated need for idealism."[84] Even Nietzsche, Bataille concedes, fell prey to the same temptation with his concept of the Superman, despite his understanding of the base roots of the "highest" ideas.

Instead, the Revolution must look to the bowels of the earth, where the blind mole burrows. Its materialism must reject any Icarian strategy of idealizing that base world. "The passage from Hegelian philosophy to materialism (as from utopian or Icarian socialism to scientific socialism)," he insisted, "makes explicit the necessary character of such a rupture."[85] Although Bataille's own engagement with Hegel would grow more complex after his attendance at Alexander Kojève's famous lectures in the mid-1930s, his disdain for the Surrealist appropriation of the Hegelian themes of transcendence and sublation would remain constant. The identification of the eagle with Hegel, which is especially compelling in French because both words sound alike, would also have a long future in the anti-visual discourse Bataille helped disseminate; it would reappear in spectacular fashion in Derrida's *Glas* in 1974.

How justified, we must ask, was Bataille's characterization of Surrealism as an Icarian movement that sought out heterogeneous, transgressive material only to transfigure it in an idealist direction? How bewitched were its adherents by a positive notion of visual sublimity? Or did even the Surrealist search for new visual experience, for what may well be called visionary redemption, paradoxically contribute to the crisis of ocularcentrism?

•   •   •

The tenacious hold of ocularcentrism over Western culture was abetted by the oscillation among models of speculation, observation and revelation. When one or another faltered, a third could be invoked as the foundation of a still visually privileged order of knowledge.

In the case of Surrealism, it is readily apparent that speculative reason, bathing in the light of clear and distinct ideas mirrored in the mind's eye, and mimetic observation, trusting in the reflected light of objects apparent to the two physiological eyes, were both explicitly scorned. It is no less evident that the third tradition, that of visionary illumination, was elevated in their place to a position of honor.

Once the more nihilistic and destructive impulses of Dadaism, out of which Surrealism emerged in the early 1920s, were overcome (or at least so it seemed), the movement sought to realize the avant-garde's optimistic project of transforming daily existence by infusing it with the redemptive power of art. Although often employing the provocative verbal violence we've seen in Bataille,[86] the Surrealists were never as willing to celebrate waste, expenditure and destruction as ends in themselves. Combining, as Breton famously put it, Rimbaud's injunction to "change life" with Marx's call to "transform the world,"[87] they hoped to revolutionize more than just aesthetic fashions.

This ambition not only led them into a series of tragi-comic alliances with Communist and Trotskyist parties,[88] but also permitted them to adopt the self-image, as old as the earliest prophetic religions and as recent as Rimbaud's "*Lettres du voyant*," of the seer. One of Breton's first manifestoes, written in 1925, was in fact called "A Letter to Seers" and in 1934, he would still insist that "'I say that we must be *seers*, make ourselves seers': for us it has only been a question of discovering the means to apply this watchword of Rimbaud's."[89] As Blaise Cendrars put it in 1931, "let us open this third eye of Vision; let us surnaturalize."[90] Max Ernst would add in 1936, "Blind swimmer, I have made myself a seer. *I have seen.*"[91] Indeed, as late as 1943, Benjamin Péret would embrace Novalis' dictum "the man who really thinks is the seer."[92]

The Surrealist adoption of the visionary model was evident both in their verbal and their plastic creations. Indeed, virtually from its inception, Surrealism would be fascinated by the interaction of the eye and the text.[93] Mallarmé's *Un Coup de dés* was one of their most admired poems. Apollinaire's *Calligrames* were no less revered. Indeed, Apollinaire, who had coined the term Surrealism for his 1917 drama, *Mamelles de Tirésias*, was instrumental in redirecting French poetry away from its Symbolist stress on musicality.[94] "Until the beginning of the twentieth century," the editors of *Surréalisme* wrote in 1924, "the *ear* had decided the quality of poetry: rhythm, sonority, cadence, alliteration, rhyme; everything for the ear. For the last twenty years, the *eye* has been taking its revenge. It is the century of the film."[95] Breton's personal distaste for music has been widely acknowledged,[96] and indeed, there was little, if any explicitly Surrealist musical composition. Surrealism, as Breton put it in *Mad Love*, sought instead to recover the virginal sight, the *jamais vu*, that would be the uncanny complement of the *déjà vu.*[97]

This visionary project would involve following two trails already blazed by Rimbaud: self-conscious sensual derangement and the suppression of the mundane, rational ego. Breton explicitly contended in 1925 that "to aid the systematic derangement of all the senses, a derangement recommended by Rimbaud and continuously made the order of the day by the Surrealists, it is my opinion that we must not hesitate to *bewilder sensation*."[98] The Surrealist painter Paul Nougé added that the production of radically new experiences in the viewer could only be brought about by creating forbidden images, "bewildering objects."[99]

The suppression of the rational self was to be sought through the celebrated and controversial technique of automatic writing, which allowed free association to produce arresting images unobtainable by conscious creative effort.[100] Chance, which Mallarmé had realized could never be abolished by the throw of the dice, was thus preferable to deliberate manipulation.[101] Other techniques included the game that became known as "exquisite corpse,"[102] which involved the stringing together of arbitrarily chosen phrases by different poets unaware of what preceded or followed, and Raymond Roussel's method of writing a novel by beginning with one sentence and ending with its homophonic, but semantically distinct double. Although the precise proportion of chance to contrivance in all of these techniques continues to spur debate, the results were often strikingly unexpected images, unlike virtually any in previous Western literature.

The nature of Surrealist images, verbal and pictorial, has been the subject of extensive critical reflection, only a few of whose conclusions can be advanced here.[103] As in the case of Bergson, "image" was a counter-term to "concept," the latter being identified with the stifling logic of the rationalism Surrealism generally denigrated.[104] Also reminiscent of Bergson, when he used the term honorifically, was the Surrealists' refusal to identify "image" with a mental representation of an external object, a thing in the world, a mimetic sensation. It referred instead to the revelation of an internal state, a psychological truth hidden to conscious deliberation, what Mary Ann Caws has called an "inscape" rather than an "outlook."[105]

M. Jay

The often-cited classic example of the quintessential Surrealist image was Lautréamont's "chance meeting of an umbrella and a sewing machine on a dissecting table" from his *Chants de Maldoror*. What made it so arresting for Breton and his collaborators was the effect produced by the juxtaposition of two incongruous and seemingly unrelated objects in a space utterly unlike their normal context (although they may well have also liked its scarcely veiled sexual connotation). As Breton put it, images of this kind were "incandescent flashes linking two elements of reality belonging to categories that are so far removed from each other that reason would fail to connect them and that require a momentary suspension of the critical attitude in order for them to be brought together."[106] The relationship between the two objects is not, strictly speaking, metaphorical because the principle of paradigmatic similarity does not work to create a unified symbol. Nor do such images signify through metonymic linkages along a syntagmatic chain, as is the case with realist prose. Instead, their ineffable effect is produced by their very resistance to such traditional modes of signification. Their power, when they succeed, is produced by their evocation of that uncanny "convulsive beauty" Breton would call "the marvelous." They are, he claimed, "endowed with a persuasive strength rigorously proportional to the violence of the initial shock they produced. Thus it is that close up, they are destined to take on the character of things *revealed*."[107]

Because of the Surrealists' fascination with psychoanalysis and F.W.H. Myers's "gothic psychology" of the subliminal,[108] what was revealed was often understood as a direct manifestation of unconscious desire.[109] Reversing Augustine's anxiety about the "lust of the eyes," they reveled in the fact that, as Breton put it, "as far as the eye can see, it recreates desire."[110] More precisely, the Surrealist image sought to duplicate the mysterious workings of dreams, which allowed desire to be expressed, without conscious intervention, in plastic and verbal form. Rejecting Bergson's metaphysical belief in *durée* as the locus of human volition, the Surrealists claimed that the onrush of oneiric images evinced a kind of causality of desire, which overwhelmed the conscious will. Although the Surrealists contrived mechanisms that could be manipulated to produce "the marvelous," once it came, conscious volition was left far behind. Breton may have denied the resemblance to a spiritualist who is merely a vessel for external voices,[111] but the Surrealist poet nonetheless succumbed to powerful forces beyond his or her conscious control. Citing Baudelaire on the effects of drugs, Breton claimed, "it is true of Surrealist images as it is of opium images that man does not evoke them; rather they 'come to him spontaneously, despotically. He cannot chase them away, for the will is powerless now and no longer controls the faculties'."[112] This process corresponded to what in life Breton called the law of "objective chance," in which serendipitous meetings—like that he describes with Nadja in *Mad Love*—produce the "marvelous."

Surrealism began by stressing poetic language as the medium through which its images could best be expressed, but soon its emphasis shifted to include the visual arts as well. Breton himself noted that automatic writing could induce visual hallucinations.[113] The unconscious could also be visually manifest in hysterical symptoms, which Breton and Aragon, sounding more like Charcot than Freud, celebrated in 1928 as "the greatest poetic discovery of the later nineteenth century."[114] Was it also possible to achieve convulsive beauty by more conventional visual means, such as painting? Could one make visible—*donner à voir*, in Eluard's phrase,[115]— the lightning flash of profane illuminations? Not all Surrealists were immediately convinced. In the third issue of *La Révolution surréaliste*, Pierre Naville, fearing that it would become just another art journal and betray its revolutionary mission, claimed that "everyone knows that there is no *surrealist painting.*"[116] Even when Naville's objections were brushed aside, Breton could still call painting a "lamentable expedient" and confess his boredom in art museums in the essays that became *Surrealism and Painting.*[117]

But the title essay of that book did appear in 1928, thus ratifying what was already clear in practice: Surrealism was as much a visual as verbal phenomenon. In a few years, Breton could proclaim that "at the present time there is no fundamental difference between the ambitions of a poem by Paul Eluard or Benjamin Péret and the ambitions of a canvas by Max Ernst, Miró, or Tanguy."[118] Breton himself even tried his hand at fashioning collages and what he called "poem-objects," integrating ready-mades and poetry. He and his collaborators sat for or composed innumerable portraits, individual and group, which presented their images to the world.[119]

What in part allowed the visual in through the side door, as Nadeau has remarked, was the trick of defining what the Surrealists championed as being "beyond painting"[120] or "painting defied."[121] And indeed, like Duchamp, whose "anti-retinal" work they so much admired, Surrealism sought to challenge many of the received truths about the creation of visual beauty. Even their self-portraits problematized the narcissistic premises of the genre, relentlessly displacing, as Martine Antle has put it, "the 'who I am' toward the 'whom I haunt,' the visible toward the invisible, the 'figural' toward the 'spectral' elements."[122]

If the Surrealists radically defied visual conventions, they did so, at least initially, in the hope of restoring the Edenic purity of the "innocent eye," an ideal which had been defended by the Romantics, if not earlier.[123] By violently disturbing the corrupted, habitual vision of everyday life, the visionary wonder of childhood, so they believed, might be recaptured. "The eye," Breton began *Surrealism and Painting* by announcing, "exists in its primitive state."[124] Unlike the music he generally denigrated, painting could therefore provide spiritual illuminations: "auditive images, in fact, are inferior to visual images not only in clearness but also in strictness, and with all due respect to a few melomaniacs [passionate lovers of music], they hardly seem intended to strengthen in any way the idea of human greatness. So may night continue to fall upon the orchestra, and may I, who am still searching for something in this world, may I be left with open or closed eyes, in broad daylight, to my silent contemplation."[125]

How did painting (or going "beyond" it) provide the occasion for stimulating the eye to regain its innocence? Revitalizing a metaphor seemingly discredited by modernist abstraction, Breton admitted "it is impossible for me to consider a picture as anything but a window, in which my first interest is to know what it *looks out on,* or, in other words, whether, from where I am, there is a 'beautiful view,' for there is nothing I love so much as that which stretches away before me and *out of sight.* Within the frame of an *unnamed figure, land- or seascape,* I can enjoy an enormous spectacle."[126] But rather than revealing an external world situated in Cartesian perspectivalist space, the window opened "out" on the psychic world within: "the plastic work of art, in order to respond to the undisputed necessity of thoroughly revising all real values, will refer to a *purely interior model* or cease to exist."[127]

Windows, as Susan Harris Smith has recently shown,[128] were, in fact, an abiding preoccupation of the Surrealists, and by pausing with their complicated meaning, we can begin to understand the implicit tensions in their visionary celebration of the innocent eye. The epiphanous experience Breton himself underwent before hitting on automatic writing as the royal road to the unconscious was produced by an image that suddenly came to him, "a phrase . . . *which was knocking at the window,*" of a man being cut in two by a window.[129] Many Surrealist painters would later play on the theme of the window as a transitional or liminal plane between reality and imagination, foreground and background, external and internal worlds. Often deploying it to suggest yearning for the beyond, they also used the window as an aperture through which a face could look into the shadowy room of the unconscious.

More unsettling, however, were the uses to which Surrealists like Magritte could put windows. In a number of his works, such as *La Condition Humaine I* (1933), *The Domain of Arnheim* (1949) or *Euclidean Walks* (1955), he used them to create visual paradoxes or puns, incommensurable spatial orders which were disjunctively combined to challenge the viewer's faith in his eyes.[130] At times, the Surrealists could also play on the theme of the shattered window, literally embodied in Duchamp's *Large Glass*, or the opaque window, as in his *Fresh Widow* (1920), thus problematizing the notion of the transparency of visual experience, even when it pretended to be that of the seer.

These last uses alert us to some of the ways in which Surrealist painting could defy the high modernist ethic of pure opticality. Even as they self-consciously sought to renew vision, the Surrealists were calling into question many of the assumptions underlying that very project. They did so in part by rehabilitating subject matter and resisting the lures of nonrepresentational abstraction, based on the dream of complete visual presence and self-sufficient form. The rehabilitation of subject matter did not, of course, mean restoring naive mimesis, but rather wrenching objects out of their original contexts and allowing them to follow the uncanny logic of the Surrealist image. Representation was resurrected only to call it into question, thus exposing the arbitrary nature of the visual sign. As Magritte put it in "Words and Images" in *La Révolution surréaliste* in 1929, "everything points to the fact that scarcely any relationship exists between the object and that which represents it."[131] In relation to the conventions of realist art, Surrealist painting thus could seem to be, following the title of one of Magritte's most famous works, "the betrayal of images."

In fact, titles themselves played a key role in this effort. Often chosen with the goal of disrupting or contesting the apparent meaning of the image, titles could also be introduced directly into the picture, as in Miró's *Un Oiseau poursuit une abeille et la baisse* (1941).[132] Or words could be introduced into the painting calling its apparent visual meaning into question, the most famous example being Magritte's *"ceçi n'est pas une pipe"* under the image of a pipe painted in 1928.[133] As in the case of Duchamp, the discursive was thus allowed to undermine the self-sufficiency of the figural in radical ways. "Painting the impossible," as Magritte liked to call it, meant giving "precedence to poetry over painting."[134] As Breton recognized, Magritte "put the visual image on trial, stressing its weakness and demonstrating the subordinate character of figures of speech and thought."[135] The eye should not only be in the text, the Surrealists seem to be saying; the text must also be in the eye.[136]

In a very different register, Surrealist experiments in producing arresting visual effects by techniques such as collage, frottage, decalcomania, fumage, coulage and *étréticissements*,[137] also challenged the integrity of optical experience. Their tactility invoked the hegemony of touch over vision, which Diderot had defended during the Enlightenment.[138] Ernst, who was the pioneer in developing certain of these methods, saw them as the visual equivalent of automatic writing, and Breton compared them to a graphic version of the "exquisite corpse" game.[139] One Surrealist painter, the Rumanian-born Victor Brauner, took them to an extreme by drawing with his eyes entirely closed. Such techniques problematized the adequacy, self-sufficiency and, in Brauner's case, even the necessity of perception in general, and of vision in particular. As Rosalind Krauss has argued, collage provided a kind of metalanguage about the visual, which makes explicit the differential play of presence and absence, presentation and representation, that high modernism sought to efface. "Collage," she argues,

> operates in direct opposition to modernism's search for perceptual plenitude and unimpeachable self-presence. Modernism's goal is to objectify the formal constituents of a given medium, making these, beginning with the very ground that is the origin of their existence, the objects of vision. Collage problematizes that goal, by setting up discourse in place of presence, a discourse founded on a buried origin, a discourse fueled by that absence.[140]

Other techniques like frottage and fumage generated whatever meaning they did by a combination of indexical signification, produced by the physical residue of their material source, and the pattern "discovered" in them by their viewers. As such they were related to another medium to which the Surrealists turned for help in their search for "the marvelous": photography.[141] For despite its more iconical character, its signification by resemblance, the index-ical quality of the photograph was often explicitly foregrounded by its Surrealist practitioners.

The importance of this medium for the Surrealist project has only recently come, as it were, into focus. It has, to be sure, often been noted, that the movement's first journal, *La Révolution surréaliste*, lacking the typographic fireworks of its Dadaist predecessors, would have seemed like an austere scientific journal, if not for the presence of photographs by Man Ray, as well as sketches by other Surrealist artists.[142] It has also been remarked that many other Surrealist texts, such as Breton's *Les Vases communicants* (1932), *Mad Love* (1937), and *Nadja* (1938), had accompanying photos by Jean-André Boiffard, Brassaï, and Man Ray. And the Surrealists' discovery of Eugéne Atget, then virtually unknown, has also not gone unnoticed.[143]

But in general, the putative mimetic or iconic imperative of the medium—acknowledged by Breton himself when he credited photography with undermining realist painting[144]—seemed to make it an unlikely tool for Surrealist purposes. Thus, Simon Watney articulated a widespread assumption, when he claimed that "photography proved by and large to be resistant to the surrealist imagination, and Man Ray's photographs have far more to do with a Modernist aesthetic derived from Cubist painting than with Surrealism . . . In the majority. of cases the long-term influence of Surrealism meant little more than the creation of the extended sense of the picturesque."[145] Even when the links between Surrealist photography and the politically motivated defamiliarization effects sought by other modernist artists such as the Russian Futurists are acknowledged, its ultimate impact has seemed limited. For as a tool of radical social enlightenment, it had little direct success.

In the different context of our narrative of the interrogation of vision, however, the Surrealists' experiments with the medium can be deemed of greater importance. As Rosalind Krauss has suggestively demonstrated,[146] Surrealist photography presented a dual challenge to the high modernist attempt to wrest a new visual order from the wreckage of Cartesian perspectivalism. First, it introduced into the photographic image a kind of temporal deferral or "spacing,"[147] which might be called internalized montage. Second, it often drew on the explicitly anti-visual implications of Bataille's work, rather than on the search for an "innocent eye" in Breton.

Despite the extraordinary heterogeneity of Surrealist photographic practice, ranging from Boiffard's close-ups of big toes to Man Ray's solarizations, Krauss finds a common theme in all of them. Implicitly introducing the principle of Dadaist photomontage into a seemingly intact and undoctored image, they undercut the temporal instantaneity of the traditional snapshot: "without exception the surrealist photographers infiltrated the body of this print, this single page, with spacing . . . more important than anything else is the strategy of doubling. For it is doubling that produces the formal rhythm of spacing—the two-step that banishes the unitary condition of the moment, that creates *within* the moment an experience of fission. For it is doubling that elicits the notion that to an original has been added its copy."[148] A famous example of the technique was Man Ray's portrait of *La Marquise Casati* of 1922, which seems to have two or maybe three sets of eyes superimposed on each other.

The importance of spacing is that it destroys the fateful linkage of vision with pure synchronous presence and introduces the interruption of discursivity, or in the Derridean terminology Krauss adopts, *écriture*. The photograph is particularly adept at instantiating the deferral and doubling of writing because of its dual status as indexical and iconic sign, signifying both by the physical trace left by light waves and by the resemblance its image bore to the object off which those waves bounced:

> Surreality *is*, we could say, nature convulsed into a kind of writing. The special access that photography has to this experience is its privileged connection to the real. The manipulations then available to photography—what we have been calling doubling and

spacing—appear to document these convulsions. The photographs are not *interpretations* of reality, decoding it, as in Heartfield's photomontages. They are presentations of that reality as configured, or coded, or written.[149]

Conventional notions of Surrealist imagery as wholly independent of external reality and based solely on the imagination were thus explicitly called into question by the mixed quality of photography. Rather than allowing the "innocent eye" of the seer to look inward into his unconscious to "see" images of the marvelous, Surrealist photographs were often as much creations of the darkroom as windows on reality, internal or external. They thus showed, even more than its painting, the composite quality of internal and external objects as well as the imbrication of the figural and the discursive, and thus the impure status of vision itself.

Even more disruptive of the assumption that Surrealism merely celebrated visionary optics is Krauss's demonstration that Bataille rather than Breton may best be seen as the inspiration for much of its photography. Noting that a number of visual artists excommunicated by Breton, such as Masson, Desnos, and Boissard, gravitated into Bataille's orbit around the journal *Documents*, she remarks that even before their break with mainstream Surrealism, they—and others like Man Ray—were already exponents of Bataille's notion of *informe*, the anti-idealizing distortion of the body's integral form. Bataille's influence was also apparent in the photographs in *Minotaure*, launched in 1933, with their degrading transformations of the human body into animal-like images and their confusion of organs, such as mouths and anuses. Such photographers as Boiffard, Bellmer, and Raoul Ubac subjected the body to a series of violent visual assaults reminiscent of *Story of the Eye*, producing images "of bodies dizzily yielding to the force of gravity; of bodies in the grip of a distorting perspective; of bodies decapitated by the projection of shadow; of bodies eaten away by either heat or light."[150] Their often fetishistic, sexually charged displacements of familiar human forms were accompanied by an uncanny denaturalization of the spatial order in which they were situated. The results exemplified the nonreciprocal chiasmic intertwining of the eye and the gaze, each the apex of a different visual cone, that Lacan was beginning to explore at the same time and in the same milieu.[151]

As a result, Surrealist photography proved a scandal for what can be called the dominant tradition of "straight photography," with its assumed spectator still the unified subject of the Cartesian perspectivalist tradition. "That subject," Krauss concludes, "armed with a vision that plunges deep into reality and, through the agency of the photograph, given the illusion of mastery over it, seems to find unbearable a photography that effaces categories and in their place erects the fetish, the *informe*, the uncanny."[152] Thus Surrealist photography, long in the shadow of its other visual practices, must be seen as one of the movement's most consequential contributions to the twentieth century's crisis of ocularcentrism.

Can the same be said of another realm of Surrealist optical experimentation, the cinema?[153] Eschewing the skepticism that can be seen in Bergson, the Surrealists avidly embraced the new medium. One of its earliest French champions had, in fact, been Apollinaire, who introduced cinematic effects into such poems as "Zone" and even tried his hand at writing a film script. As early as 1917, Soupault had written "cinematographic poems," based on montage-like transitions and the sudden transfiguration of objects; he too composed films scripts. Jacques Vaché, the absurdist whose life (and self-inflicted death) so inspired the Surrealists, was also spellbound by film. The year Breton spent with Vaché in Nantes in 1916 turned him as well into a passionate convert, who with his friends would hop from movie house to movie house seeing snatches of as many films as they could. Robert Desnos, who was the Surrealists' most serious film critic, spoke for many of them when he gushed, "for us and only for us had the Lumière brothers invented the cinema. There we were at home. That darkness was the darkness of our rooms before going to sleep. Perhaps the screen could match our dreams."[154]

The 1920s in France were especially congenial to experimental cinema, partly because the widespread ciné-club movement allowed the easy distribution of non-commercial films.[155] Dada artists like Francis Picabia and René Clair exploited the new medium's capacity for trick photography in such works as *Entr'acte*, which owed more to the visual prestidigitation of Georges Méliès than to the realism of the Lumière brothers. Others drew on film's completely non-mimetic, mechanical potential, often producing non-narrative, illogical effects, like those developed in Duchamp's "Anemic Cinema." Man Ray's first film, *Le retour à la raison* of 1921, for example, included animated rayographs. But the Dadaists soon came to distrust the cinema's spectacle-like closeness to the nineteenth-century ideal of synaesthesia and the *Gesamtkunstwerk*, which rendered the audience overly passive.[156]

The Surrealists, on the other hand, admired precisely that result. They restored narrative, character and optical realism, but imbued them with the oneiric effects they sought elsewhere through poetic and plastic means. As early as 1911, the critic Jules Romains had noted a link between films and dreams in his discussion of the cinema audience: "the group dream now begins. They sleep; their eyes no longer see. They are no longer conscious of their bodies. Instead there are only passing images, a gliding and rustling of dreams."[157] Not surprisingly, the affinity between Surrealism and the film would be quickly recognized. Perhaps its classic statement came in a widely cited essay by Jean Goudal, not himself a member of the movement, in 1925.[158] The cinema, he contended, promotes conscious hallucinations in which the ego is suppressed; "our body itself undergoes a sort of temporary depersonalization which robs it of the sense of its own existence. We are nothing more than two eyes riveted to ten meters of white screen."[159] Cinema, he claimed, also brilliantly realizes the Surrealist project of generating meaning without recourse to the logical entailments of conventional language. It could even more vividly produce profane illuminations through visual juxtapositions than the verbal images in Surrealist poems.

How successful were the Surrealists in producing films of their own to realize this promise? Much of their talent was, in fact, spent in devising scenarios rather than shooting actual films, that is, in verbal rather than visual endeavors. Often published as *ciné-romans* in film journals, their scripts tried to transgress the stabilizing, conventionalizing function of the typical *"film racontés"* available on the mass market.[160] As a result, some of them are of considerable interest, for example certain of Antonin Artaud's, which play with the theme of high-altitude flight so popular in the aftermath of World War I.[161]

But the inability to transform most of them, for financial as well as aesthetic reasons, into actual films soon took its toll. The invention of talkies made production costs prohibitive for esoteric experiments without a mass audience. By the early 1930s, the Surrealists' infatuation with the cinema had begun to cool down. Breton himself had done little beyond his expression of youthful exuberance to sponsor their production. It was one thing to enjoy watching films, but quite another to make them. Few Surrealists became as explicitly bitter as the frustrated Artaud, who proclaimed in a 1933 essay called "The Premature Senility of the Film," "The world of the cinema is a dead world, illusory and truncated . . . we must not expect of the cinema to restore to us the Myths of the man and the life of today."[162] But most would come to share the later lament of Benjamin Péret: "Never had a means of expression witnessed as much hope as the cinema . . . And yet never has one observed such disproportion between the immensity of possibilities and the derisory results."[163]

Although the number of its successes was small, Surrealism did produce two universally acclaimed masterpieces before its interest waned: *Un chien andalou* (1929) and *L'âge d'or* (1930). Both were by the Spanish artists Luis Buñuel and Salvador Dali, who in this period were very much part of the Parisian avant-garde community. An enormous amount of critical attention has been devoted to both of these works, discussing everything from the relative role of the two collaborators to the shift in the political implications from one film to the other.[164] Rather than rehearse all of its conclusions, I want to probe the meaning of only one of these films' central episodes, which has special significance for the Surrealist contribution to the crisis of ocularcentrism: the celebrated slitting of the eye in *Un chien andalou*.

The film consists of a series of loosely linked, rebus-like scenes, which powerfully evoke the Surrealists' fascination for the world of dreams. According to Buñuel, "the plot is the

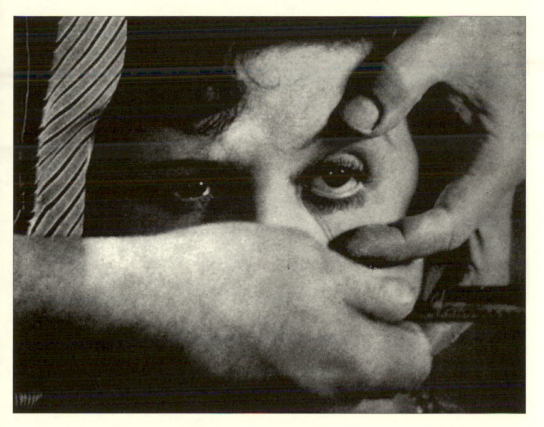

Un chien andalou, Luis Buñuel and Salvador Dali.

result of a CONSCIOUS *psychic automatism* and, to that extent, it does not attempt to recount a dream, although it profits by a mechanism analogous to that of dreams."[165] Bataille, one of the work's most enthusiastic supporters, described its power as follows: "Several very explicit facts appear in successive order, without logical connection it is true, but penetrating so far into horror that the spectators are caught up as directly as they are in adventure films. Caught up and even precisely caught by the throat, and without artifice; do these spectators know, in fact, where they—the authors of this film, or people like them—will stop?"[166]

Another source of *Un chien andalou*'s fascination was its defiance of attempts to interpret it, even as it insistently solicited such attempts. Buñuel claimed that "NOTHING in the film SYMBOLIZES ANYTHING,"[167] but admitted that psychoanalysis might help to make sense of it. Its most widely interpreted episode occurred at the beginning, in what is sometimes called the film's prologue. Introduced by the caption, "once upon a time . . ." invoking mythic temporality, a cloud slices across the moon, to be followed by the slow, deliberate and unresisted slashing of a woman's eyeball with a razor. According to Bataille, Buñuel told him that it had been devised by Dali, "to whom it was directly suggested by the real vision of a narrow and long cloud cutting across the lunar surface."[168] Years later, Buñuel would say he had dreamed it himself.[169] Whatever its provenance, it was realized with stunning efficacy, as the dead cow's eye substituted for the woman's by the magic of montage burst apart with devastatingly gruesome horror. Buñuel, who actually held the razor, was reported (rather gleefully) by Bataille to have been sick for a week afterwards.

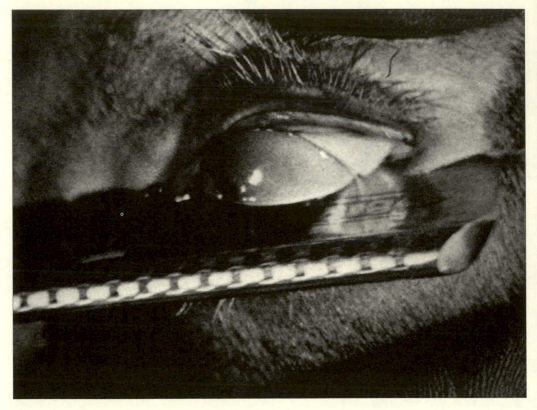

Un chien andalou, Luis Buñuel and Salvador Dali.

Variously interpreted, *inter alia*, as a simulacrum of sexual cruelty against women, a symbol of male castration anxiety, the conception of an infant, an indication of homosexual ambivalence, and an extended linguistic pun,[170] the act's literal dimension has sometimes been overlooked.[171] That is, the violent mutilation of the eye, that theme so obsessively enacted in Bataille's pornographic fiction, is here paradoxically given to the sight of those with the courage not to avert their eyes from what appears on the screen. There is little visual pleasure, to put it mildly, in the result, which defies reduction to that seductive lure of the cinema critics like Christian Metz would later so vehemently denounce.

The eye was, in fact, a central Surrealist image, and indeed can be discerned in much twentieth-century visual art.[172] Anticipated by Odilon Redon's haunting images of single eyes as balloons, flowers or Cyclops staring towards heaven, artists like de Chirico, Ernst, Dali, Man Ray and Magritte developed a rich ocular iconography. In most cases, the eyes (or often the single eye) were enucleated, blinded, mutilated or transfigured, as in *Story of the Eye*, into other shapes like eggs, whose liquid could easily be spilled. Ernst's *Two Ambiguous Figures* (1919), with its transparent heads fitted with opaque goggles, Man Ray's *Object of Destruction* (original version, 1923), with its eye cut from a photograph of a lover and mounted on a metronome, Dali's *The Lugubrious Game* (1929), with its chilling mixture of images of castration and enucleation, Giacometti's *Suspended Ball* (1930–31) with its globe erotically/sadistically split by a crescent wedge,[173] all typify the violent denigration of the visual that culminated in Buñuel's slashing razor.

Here the third eye of the seer is deprived of its spiritualizing, elevating function and compelled to reveal its affinity with sadistic and erotic impulses instead. The Icarian flights of Breton's seer end in the bowels of Bataille's labyrinth.[174] Indeed, if Jeanne Siegel's conjecture is right, the explicit link between the third eye and transgressive sexuality argued by the psychoanalyst Rudolf Reitler in 1913, may have directly influenced Max Ernst and through him other Surrealists.[175] Whatever the source, there can be little doubt that the eye seemed to many Surrealist artists less an object to be revered, less the organ of pure and noble vision, than a target of mutilation and scorn, or a vehicle of its own violence. It is largely on the basis of an analysis of Surrealist eye imagery that the art historian Gerald Eager could generalize about all twentieth-century painting, whose eyes

> are not moist or movable, they are not alive and do not suggest the power to look back and see. When the viewer looks at them, they do not have the power to look back and see. So the individual or divine spark of contact does not exist in the missing or mutilated eye. In place of contact there is rejection; instead of sight, there is complete blindness.[176]

Although this analysis of the implications of Surrealist painting, photography and cinema might well be construed as demonstrating the triumph of Bataille over Breton, it should be noted in conclusion that the latter also came to evince doubts about the privileging of the visual. In "The Automatic Message" of 1933, he admitted that "verbal inspiration is infinitely richer in visual meaning, infinitely more resistant to the eye, than visual images properly so called."[177] Such a belief, he then confessed, "is the source of my unceasing protest against the presumed 'visionary' power of the poet. No, Lautréamont and Rimbaud did not *see* what they described; they were never confronted by it *a priori*. That is, they never described anything. They threw themselves into the dark recesses of being; they heard indistinctly . . ."[178] It is thus no surprise to find Breton, like Bataille, availing himself of the metaphor of the labyrinth, as the enfolded, convoluted, unilluminated space where the Surrealist confronts the unconscious.[179]

Whether or not Breton's protest against the "visionary" model of poetic creation was quite as unceasing as he claimed—as we've seen, he approvingly cited Rimbaud's *Lettre d'un voyant* again in his 1935 "Surrealist Situation of the Object"—he clearly revealed his priorities, when he insisted that "I believe as fully today as I did ten years ago—I believe blindly . . . blindly with a blindness that covers all visible things—in the triumph *auditorily* of what is unverifiable visually."[180] Thus, when the painters ultimately failed Breton by remaining dogged egotists rather than submitting themselves to the discipline of collective work—even the much admired Ernst was excommunicated for accepting the Grand Prix at the Venice Biennale in 1953—he could fall back on his original distrust of the "lamentable expedient" that was the direct visual expression of the marvelous.[181]

In short, with the provocative slitting of the cow/woman's eye in *Un chien andalou*, we have come a long way indeed from the serene dissection of the *oeil de boeuf* in Descartes' *Dioptrique*. Surrealism, whether understood in Breton's terms or Bataille's, I hope it is now sufficiently clear, must be accounted a central episode in the progressive denigration of the noblest of the senses, whose full ramifications would only come, as it were, into view in our own day.[182]

Notes

1. Georges Bataille, "The Sacred Company," in *Visions of Excess: Selected Writings, 1927–1939*, ed. Allan Stoekl, trans. Allan Stoekl et al. (Minneapolis, 1985), 179.

2. André Breton, written in collaboration with Jean Shuster, "Art Poétique," (1959); in Breton, *What is Surrealism?: Selected Writings*, ed. Franklin Rosemont (London, 1969), 299.

3. According to Paul Virilio, "1914 was not only the physical deportation of millions of men to the fields of battle, it was also, with the apocalypse of the deregulation of perception, a diaspora of another kind, the moment of panic in which the American and European masses no longer believed their eyes . . . " *La Machine de la Vision* (Paris, 1988), 38.

4. For a discussion of its implications, see Martin Jay, "Scopic Regimes of Modernity," in Hal Foster, ed., *Vision and Visuality* (Port Townsend, Washington, 1988).

5. See, for example, Martin Jay, "In the Empire of the Gaze: Foucault and the Denigration of Vision in Twentieth-Century French Thought," in *Foucault: A Critical Reader,* ed. David Couzens Hoy (Oxford, 1986).

6. Paul Fussell, *The Great War and Modern Memory* (London, 1975); Eric J. Leed, *No Man's Land: Combat and Identity in World War I* (Cambridge, 1979); Stephen Kern, *The Culture of Time and Space: 1880–1918* (Cambridge, Mass., 1983); Kenneth E. Silver, *Esprit de Corps: The Art of the Parisian Avant-Garde and the First World War, 1914–1925* (Princeton, 1989); Sidra Stich, *Anxious Visions: Surrealist Art* (New York, 1990).

7. Leed, *No Man's Land,* 19.

8. St. Exupéry himself, as Leed notes, was too young to have flown in the war, but his writings of the 1920s drew on many actual accounts of aerial combat. The Icarian parallel, of course, holds as well for the outcome that many flyers suffered. Some 50,000 airmen died by the end of the war. See J. M. Winter, *The Experience of War* (London, 1988), 108.

9. Gertrude Stein, *Picasso* (New York, 1959), 11. The precise formulation "cubist war" is actually a paraphrase of this passage by Kern, *The Culture of Time and Space 1880–1918,* 288. Ernest Hemingway made a similar observation. See his remarks in "A Paris to Strasbourg Flight," in *By-Line Ernest Hemingway* (New York, 1968), 38. Other modernist movements also appropriated the visual experience of the war for their own purposes. Constructivists like El Lissitzky and Suprematists like Kasimir Malevich were fascinated by the implications of aerial photographs. As late as 1939, Italian Futurists like Tullio Crali were painting vertiginous scenes of pilots diving over geometrically rendered urban landscapes.

10. Silver, *Esprit de Corps,* 79.

11. Leed, *No Man's Land,* 137.

12. Kenneth E. Silver, "Purism: Straightening Up After the Great War," *Artforum* (March, 1977). "Instead of indeterminacy, simultaneity, the mutability of time and space, the Purists will substitute something stable and durable. In place of Cubist complexity Jeanneret [Le Corbusier's original name] and Ozenfant will provide images with a freshly starched spiritual and moral rectitude, showing the certainty and direction of 'the great collective current'." (57).

13. Leed, *No Man's Land,* 130–31.

14. Andler's personal recollections are discussed in Rita Bischof, *Souveränität und Subversion: Georges Batailles Theorie der Moderne* (Munich, 1984), 292.

15. Georges Bataille, "Autobiographical Note," *October* 36 (Spring, 1986), 107.

16. Georges Bataille, "The Threat of War," *October* 36 (Spring, 1986), originally written in 1936; and "The Practice of Joy Before Death," in *Visions of Excess,* originally written in 1939. In notes written in 1941, however, Bataille contended that his personal relation to war was always that of an outsider, who had never experienced ecstatic release at the front. "In war what is arresting for me," he wrote, "is a means of agonized contemplation. For me that is still connected to a nostalgia for ecstatic states, yet this nostalgia today seems dubious and lugubrious to me: It never had, I must say, any active value. I never fought in any of the wars in which I might have been involved." Cited in Denis Hollier, ed., *The College of Sociology* (1937–1939), trans. Betsy Wing (Minneapolis, 1988), 139.

17. Bataille, "The Threat of War," 28.

18. Bataille, "The Practice of Joy Before Death," 238.

19. *Ibid.,* 239.

20. According to Rita Bischof, Bataille's disgust with the war was also directed against the paternal order which spawned it, an order represented by his own father. Thus the pseudonym used in his first published work was in part a repudiation of his patronym. His strong identification with certain maternal values, those of the "earth" as opposed to those of the heavens, may reveal the force of this choice. See Bischoff, *Souveränität und Subversion,* 293. Although Bataille was certainly no friend of paternal authority in its traditional guises, when it came to his father's blindness, it is hard not to discern an ultimate identification with him as well.

21. Bataille, "W.C. Preface to Story of the Eye," appended to *Story of the Eye,* trans. Joachim Neugroschel (New York, 1982), 123.

22. Lost until after his death, it is reprinted in Denis Hollier, *Against Architecture: The Writings of Georges Bataille,* trans. Betsy Wing (Cambridge, Mass., 1989), 15–19.

23. *Ibid.,* 19.

24. *Ibid.,* 16.

25. *Ibid.*, p. 15.

26. In 1917, he thought of becoming a monk and in 1920, went to stay with a Benedictine order on the Isle of Wight, only to lose his faith "because his Catholicism has caused a woman he has loved to shed tears." (*Autobiographical Note*, 107).

27. *Ibid.*, 108.

28. Bataille, "W.C. Preface to *Story of the Eye*," 120.

29. There were two other, changed editions published when he was alive, in 1940 and 1943, both in Paris, although giving Burgos and Seville as places of publication. In the *Oeuvres* published by Gallimard in 1967, five years after his death, the 1928 and the later editions appear as separate texts. The English translation is made from the 1928 edition. In 1943, Bataille explained the provenance of his pseudonym: "Lord Auch [pronounced *osh*] refers to a habit of a friend of mine; when vexed, instead of saying 'aux chiottes!' [to the shithouse], he would shorten it to 'aux ch'." *Lord* is English for God (in the Scriptures): Lord Auch is God relieving himself." (W.C. Preface to *Story of the Eye*, 120).

30. Roland Barthes, "The Metaphor of the Eye," in *Critical Essays* (Evanston, 1972), first publication in 1963; Michel Foucault, "A Preface to Transgression," in *Language, Counter-Memory, Practice: Selected Essays and Interviews*, ed. Donald F. Bouchard, trans. Donald F. Bouchard and Sherry Simon (Ithaca, N.Y., 1977); Susan Sontag, "The Pornographic Imagination," in *Styles of Radial Will* (New York, 1981); among the more scholarly commentaries, see Michele H. Richman, *Reading Georges Bataille: Beyond the Gift* (Baltimore, 1982), chapter 3; Brian T. Fitch, *Monde à l'envers/ texte réversible: la fiction de Georges Bataille* (Paris, 1982), chapters 4 and 5; Peter B. Kussel, "From the Anus to the Mouth to the Eye," *Semiotext(e)* II, 2 (1976), 105–19; Paul Foss, "Eyes, Fetishism, and the Gaze," *Art & Text* XX (February–April, 1986), 24–41; Susan Rubin Suleiman, "Pornography, Transgression and the Avant-Garde: Bataille's *Story of the Eye*," in Nancy K. Miller, ed., *The Poetics of Gender* (New York, 1986).

31. Fitch, *Monde à l'envers*, chapter IV.

32. Bataille, *Story of the Eye*, 103.

33. See his 1929 essay "The Eye," reprinted in *Visions of Excess*, 17–19.

34. Barthes, "The Metaphor of the Eye," 242.

35. For critiques, see the work cited above by Suleiman, Kussel, and Fitch. Suleiman contends that its blindspot is the importance of the view of the body, in particular the female body, in the story, which she connects to Bataille's castration anxiety produced by looking at his mother's genitals. Kussel claims that Barthes underplays the real fear of blindness in Bataille, which is underlined by the autobiographical information about his father he provides in his later prefaces. Fitch, however, argues that it is less a case of an object than a word, "*l'oeil*," that is at issue; he claims Barthes is too interested in objects in fictions, rather than words in texts.

36. Sigmund Freud, *Civilization and its Discontents*, trans. James Strachey (New York, 1961), 46–47.

37. Bataille, "Autobiographical Note," 108.

38. For a short presentation of these concepts, see "The Notion of Expenditure" in *Visions of Excess*. For a good summary of their roots in Bataille's reading of anthropology, especially that of Marcel Mauss, see Richman, *Reading Georges Bataille*. The distinction between the two economies has had a widespread impact in post-structuralist thought. See, for example, Jacques Derrida's influential essay "From Restricted to General Economy: A Hegelianism without Reserve," in *Writing and Difference*, trans. with intro., Alan Bass (Chicago, 1978).

39. See, for example, his remarks on Hegel's search for transparency in "*L'expérience intérieure*," in his *Oeuvres complètes*, vol. V (Paris, 1973), 141; and his three essays on "Un-knowing" in *October* 36 (Spring, 1986).

40. Robert Sasso, *Georges Bataille: Le Système du Non-Savoir* (Paris, 1978), chapter IV.

41. Bataille, "Un-Knowing: Laughter and Tears," *October* 36 (Spring, 1986), 89–102.

42. Bataille, "The Solar Anus," in *Visions of Excess*, 9.

43. *Ibid.*

44. Bataille, "Rotten Sun," *Visions of Excess*.

45. *Ibid.*, 57.

46. Bataille, *Literature and Evil*, trans. Alastair Hamilton (New York, 1973), 73.

47. Bataille, "Sacrificial Mutilation and the Severed Ear of Vincent Van Gogh," in *Visions of Excess*; "Van Gogh as Prometheus," *October* 36 (Spring, 1986).

48. H. Claude, A. Borel and G. Robin, "Une automutilation révélatrice d'un état shizomaniaque," *Annales médico-psychologiques* I (1924), 331–39. Bataille notes that Borel told him of this case after he first thought to link Van Gogh's automutilation and his solar obsessions.

49. Bataille, "Sacrificial Mutilation," 70.

50. Bataille, "Van Gogh as Prometheus," 59.

51. Bataille, "Eye" in *Visions of Excess*.

52. *Ibid.*, 19.

53. *Ibid.*

54. Bataille, "The Jesuve," and "The Pineal Eye," both in *Visions of Excess*; for a comparison of his usage with that of Descartes, see David Farrell Krell, "Paradoxes of the Pineal: From Descartes to Bataille," in *Contemporary French Philosophy*, ed. A. Phillips Griffiths (Cambridge, 1987).

55. Bataille, "The Pineal Eye," 83.

56. Ibid., 82.

57. Bataille, "The Jesuve," 77.

58. Bataille, "Base Materialism and Gnosticism," *Visions of Excess*, 47.

59. Bataille, "Formless," in *Visions of Excess*.

60. Rosalind E. Krauss, *The Originality of the Avant-Garde and Other Modernist Myths* (Cambridge, Mass. 1985), 67f.

61. For a history of the group, see Hollier, ed., *The College of Sociology*.

62. For its program, see *October* 36 (Spring, 1986), 79; and the essay "The Sacred Conspiracy" in *Visions of Excess*. The latter is accompanied by a picture by Masson of an acephalic man, holding a sword in one hand, a flaming sacred heart in the other, his labyrinthine bowels open to view and a skull in the place of his genitals.

63. Bataille, "The Obelisk," *Visions of Excess*.

64. *Minotaure* was a journal to which Bataille's friends often contributed in the 1920s and 1930s. The marvelous photograph by Man Ray published in volume 7 (1935) of a torso with its head in shadows transformed into a bull's head suggests that even this symbol could somehow be acephalic. The prevalence of the image during this period is shown by its frequent adoption by Picasso after 1937.

65. Bataille, "The Sacred Conspiracy," 181.

66. The labyrinth, in fact, was a frequent image used by other modernist writers from Joyce to Borges. Guy Davenport goes so far as to call it "a life-symbol of our century." See his *The Geography of the Imagination* (San Francisco, 1981), 51. Its coils evoke those of the ear from whose power Icarus tried to escape by privileging the eye. Many years later, Jacques Derrida would spell out the connection. See *The Ear of the Other: Otobiography, Transference, Translation*, ed. Christie McDonald, trans. Peggy Kamuf and Avital Ronell (Lincoln, Nebraska, 1985), 11. Still another evocation of the image appeared in the work of Luce Irigaray, who speculated that its etymology may have been the same as that for "lips," *labra*, whose self-touching was emblematic of women's sexuality. See her essay "The Gesture in Psychoanalysis," in *Between Feminism and Psychoanalysis*, ed. Teresa Brennan (London, 1989), 135. It should also be noted that even earlier it was a favorite symbol of Nietzsche, who wrote "we are especially curious to explore the labyrinth, we try to make acquaintance with Mr. Minotaur, about whom they tell such terrible things . . . you wish to save us with the aid of this thread? And we—we pray earnestly, lose this thread!" *Werke*, ed. Kröner, 2nd ed., 20 vols. (Leipzig, 1901–1913, 1926), vol. XVI, 439–40. Ariadne was one of Nietzsche's heroines as well, and seems to have been identified with Cosima Wagner. For a general account of the labyrinth in world literature, see Gustav René Hocke, *Die Welt als Labyrinth* (Reinbeck, 1957).

67. Hollier, *Against Architecture*, 72.

68. Bataille, *Literature and Evil*, 170.

69. Bischoff, *Souveränität und Subversion*, chapter 1, which provides a thorough survey of Bataille's visual preoccupations. Hollier also remarks on Bataille's interest in painting as "the defacement of the human figure," which he contrasts with Bataille's distaste for architecture. "The space of painting," he writes, "is space where someone who has torn his eyes like Oedipus feels his way, blinded. Thus it is not to the eye but to the missing-eye that painting corresponds . . . automutilation needs to be thought of as a pictorial act, even *the* pictorial act, par excellence. For painting is nothing if it does not attack the architecture of the human body." (79–80).

70. Bataille, *Lascaux ou la naissance de l'art* (Paris, 1955).

71. Bataille, *Manet*, trans. Austryn Wainhouse and James Emmons (Geneva, 1955); Rosalind Krauss, "Antivision," *October* 36 (Spring, 1986), 152. Jean Starobinski's use of Goya in *1789: The Emblems of Reason*, trans. Barbara Bray (Charlottesville, Va., 1982) was similar.

72. Maurice Nadeau, *The History of Surrealism*, trans. Richard Howard, intro. Roger Shattuck (London, 1987), 45.

73. For a general overview of the dispute, see Richman, *Reading Georges Bataille*, 49f.

74. Bataille, "Autobiographical Note," *October* 36 (Spring, 1986), 108–109.

75. Salvador Dali noted the limits of Breton's tolerance for the scatological and perverse phenomena that so obsessed Bataille: "Blood was acceptable. Even a little excrement. But not excrement alone. I could portray sexual organs, but not anally oriented optical illusions. The arsehole was frowned upon! Lesbians were welcomed, but not homosexuals." *Journal d'un génie* (Paris, 1964), 23.

76. André Breton, *Manifestoes of Surrealism*, trans. Richard Seaver and Helen R. Lane (Ann Arbor, Michigan, 1972), 180.

77. Jürgen Habermas, *The Philosophical Discourse of Modernity: Twelve Lectures*, trans. Frederick Lawrence (Cambridge, Mass., 1987), 235–36. A similar complaint was made earlier by Raymond Queneau in 1939, who contended that "there is no antipathy between reason and that which exceeds it, whereas antireason only cures myopia with enucleation and headaches with the guillotine." Cited in Hollier, ed., *The College of Sociology*, 161.

78. Breton, *Manifestoes of Surrealism*, 184. The irony of this charge is that Breton was normally anxious to transcend the confinements of the very logical consistency that he here invoked against Bataille.

79. Both are translated in Bataille, *Visions of Excess*.

80. Along with Lautréamont and Rimbaud, Sade was the great example of the *poète maudit* so beloved by Surrealism. See the issues of *Le Surréalism au service de la revolution* from October, 1930 on. The great Sade scholar of the era was Maurice Heine, with whom Bataille was close friends. He asked him to verify the story he had told in an earlier essay, whose veracity Breton had attacked, concerning Sade's dipping rose petals in liquid manure. Heine could not. The battle over Sade's legacy continued after the war; see Pierre Klossowski, *Sade, Mon Prochain* (Paris, 1947), and the chapter on Sade in Bataille's *Literature and Evil*. For a good account of the stakes in the controversy, see Carolyn Dean, "Sadology," in Denis Hollier, ed., *History of French Literature* (Cambridge, Mass., 1989).

81. It does include, however, a kind of answer to Breton's charge of performative contradiction: "*As soon as the effort at rational comprehension ends in contradiction, the practice of intellectual scatology requires the excretion of unassimilable elements*, which is another way of stating vulgarly that a burst of laughter is the only imaginable and definitely terminal result—and not the means—of philosophical speculation." (99).

82. Bataille, "The 'Old Mole' and the Prefix Sur," 34.

83. *Ibid.*

84. *Ibid.*

85. *Ibid.*, p.43.

86. See for example, their diatribes against the corpse of Anatole France in 1924, collected in Nadeau, 233f. What suggests an important difference between them and Bataille, however, is their respective attitudes towards war. As we have seen, he glorified the experience of sacrifice, whereas they were almost all pacifists.

87. Breton, "Speech to the Congress of Writers" (1935), in *Manifestoes of Surrealism*, 241.

88. For an account of their political affiliations, see Helena Lewis, *The Politics of Surrealism* (New York, 1988).

89. Breton, "Surrealist Situation of the Object," *Manifestoes of Surrealism*, 274.

90. Blaise Cendrars, *Aujourd'hui* (Paris,1931), 31.

91. Max Ernst, *Au-delà de la peinture* (Paris, 1936), excerpted in Patrick Waldberg, *Surrealism* (New York, 1971), 98.

92. Benjamin Péret, "A Word from Péret," in *Death to the Pigs and Other Writings*, trans. Rachel Stella et al. (Lincoln, Nebraska, 1988), 197.

93. For an exploration of this theme, see Mary Ann Caws, *The Eye in the Text: Essays on Perception, Mannerist to Modern* (Princeton, 1981).

94. For an analysis of the visual dimensions of Apollinaire's poetry, see Timothy Mathews, *Reading Apollinaire: Theories of Poetic Language* (Manchester, 1987), esp. chapter 2.

95. "Manifeste du surréalisme," *Surréalisme* 1 (October, 1924), 1. This was the only issue of a journal edited by Ivan Goll, who ultimately had little to do with the group around Breton. The manifesto was followed by a short piece on the cinema, which extolled the virtues of its French versions over its American or German.

96. René Held, for example, speaks of Breton's "aversion towards music." See his *L'Oeil du psychanalyste: Surréalisme et surréalité* (Paris, 1973), 164. After World War II, however, Breton and the Surrealists came to appreciate American jazz, in part because of its Black roots. See his "Silence is Golden" (1946), in André Breton, *What is Surrealism?*

97. Breton, *Mad Love*, trans. Mary Ann Caws (Lincoln, 1987), 90. *Jamais vu* was used by Breton as early as his appreciation of Francis Picabia in the early 1920s. See *What is Surrealism?*, 14.

98. Breton, "The Surrealist Situation of the Object," 263.

99. Paul Nougé, *Histoire de ne pas rire* (Brussels, 1956), 239.

100. The origins of automatic writing have been variously attributed to the "mental automatism" examined by the French psychiatrist Pierre Janet, the nineteenth-century debates over sleep-walking and hysteria, and the literary experiments of the German writer Ludwig Börne, whom Freud later acknowledged as one of the forerunners of free association.

101. Man Ray produced a film in the late 1920s entitled *Le Mystère du Château de Dés*, which explicitly drew on Mallarmé's poem. See the discussion in Steven Kovács, *From Enchantment to Rage: The Story of Surrealist Cinema* (London, 1980), 143.

102. The term comes from a phrase in the first game they played: "the exquisite corpse will drink new wine." Americans who grew up in the 1950s will remember the introduction of a related game called "Madlibs," which involved the insertion of arbitrarily chosen words in blanks in a narrative. The results were often hilarious, but rarely approached what Walter Benjamin had called the "profane illuminations" of Surrealism.

103. For a helpful account, see J.H. Matthews, *The Imagery of Surrealism* (Syracuse, 1977).

104. The qualifier has to be added, for, as we noted in examining Breton's critique of Bataille, Surrealism could employ rational arguments when it needed them.

105. Caws, *The Eye in the Text*, chapter 6.

106. Breton, "On Surrealism in its Living Works" (1953), in *Manifestoes of Surrealism*, 302.

107. Breton, *Mad Love*, 88.

108. Breton, "The Automatic Message," *What is Surrealism?*, 100. Myers, an English psychologist of the paranormal, wrote *The Human Personality and its Survival of Bodily Death* (London, 1903). For an account of its importance for Breton, see Jennifer Munday, "Surrealism and Painting: Describing the Imaginary," *Art History* 10, 4 (December, 1987), 501.

109. The belief that language could somehow serve as the transparent medium for the revelation of desire was at odds with the often hermetically obscure nature of Surrealist poetry and prose. In fact, because of their sensitivity to the arbitrary, non-representational quality of language, they have sometimes been praised for understanding what more systematic linguists like Saussure and his followers were discovering at roughly the same time. Not surprisingly, the two intellectual currents could later mingle in thinkers like Lacan.

110. Breton, *Mad Love*, 15.

111. Breton, "The Automatic Message" (1933), in *What is Surrealism? Selected Writings*, ed. Franklin Rosemont (London, 1978), 105, where he writes, "contrary to what spiritualism proposes—that is, the dissociation of the subject's psychological personality—surrealism proposes nothing less than the unification of that personality."

112. Breton, "Manifesto of Surrealism," 36.

113. Breton, "The Automatic Message," 108.

114. Editorial entitled "The Fiftieth Anniversary of Hysteria," *La Révolution surréaliste* 11 (1928), in *What is Surrealism?*, 320. The original was accompanied by six plates from Albert Londe's *Iconographie photographique de la Salpêtrière*. Other Surrealists would also draw on the iconography of hysteria, for example Dali in his *Phénomène de l'ecstase,* in *Minotaure* (December, 1933).

115. Paul Eluard, *Donner à voir* (Paris, 1939).

116. Pierre Naville, "Beaux-Arts," *La Révolution surréaliste* I, 3 (April, 1925), 27. The quarrel over painting was part of a larger political dispute, which ultimately led to a break with Naville in 1929.

117. Breton, *Surrealism and Painting*, trans. Simon Watson Taylor (London, 1972), 3. It is often pointed out that rather than referring to Surrealist painting, Breton still uneasily linked them together as two distinct categories.

118. Breton, "Surrealist Situation of the Object," 260.

119. See Martine Antle, "Breton, Portrait and Anti-Portrait: From the Figural to the Spectral," *Dada/Surrealism* 17 (1988), 46–58.

120. Nadeau, *The History of Surrealism*, 110. *Beyond Painting*, was in fact, the title of a book by Max Ernst, trans. Dorothea Tanning (New York, 1948). He had used it as early as the announcement of one of his exhibitions in 1920.

121. Aragon, *La peinture au défi* (Paris, 1926).

122. Antle, "Breton, Portrait and Anti-Portrait," p. 48.

123. For a discussion of its history and revival among twentieth-century photographers, including the Surrealists, see Simon Watney, "Making Strange: The Shattered Mirror," in Victor Burgin, ed., *Thinking Photography* (London, 1982). The idea of the "oeil sauvage" included the connotation of savagery, as well as innocence. The Surrealist eye was never very remote from the cruel potential in vision, perhaps most explicitly thematized in the work of Artaud and Bataille.

124. Breton, *Surrealism and Painting*, 1. The phrase *l'état sauvage* was a reference an earlier description of the visionary Rimbaud by Paul Claudel. See the discussion in Mundy, "Surrealism and Painting," 498. Later, in an interview in 1946, Breton would continue to defend the Surrealist interest in non-European art by claiming "the European artist in the twentieth century can ward off the drying up of the sources of inspiration swept away by rationalism and utilitarianism only by resuming so-called primitive vision, which synthesizes sensory perception and mental representation." "Interview with Jean Duché," in Breton, *What is Surrealism?*, 263.

125. *Ibid.*, 1–2.

126. *Ibid.*, 2–3.

127. *Ibid.*, 4.

128. Susan Harris Smith, "The Surrealists' Windows," *Dada/Surrealism* 13 (1984), 48–69. Windows were also a favored metaphor of French poets much admired by the Surrealists, such as Baudelaire and Apollinaire. For a discussion of the former's use, see Sima Godfrey, "Baudelaire's Windows," *L'Esprit Créateur* XXII, 4 (Winter, 1982), 83–100. For an extensive analysis of Apollinaire's "Les Fenêtres" of 1913, which was written in connection with Robert Delaunay's Cubist canvases on the same theme, see Mathews, *Reading Apollinaire*, 132f.

129. Breton, "Manifesto of Surrealism," 21. Italics in original.

130. Describing *The Human Condition*, Magritte wrote: "I placed in front of a window, seen from inside a room, a painting representing exactly that part of the landscape which was hidden from view by the painting. Therefore, the tree represented the real tree situated behind it, outside the room. It existed for the spectator, as it were, simultaneously in his mind, as both inside the room in the painting, and outside in the real landscape. Which is how we see the world: we see it as being outside ourselves even though it is only a mental representation of it that we experience inside ourselves." Cited in Suzi Gablik, *Magritte* (London, 1970), 184. Lacan was to invoke Magritte's windows in his discussion of phantasy in his 1962 Seminaire. See David Macey, *Lacan in Contexts* (London, 1988), 45.

131. Magritte, "Les Mots et les images," *La Révolution surréaliste* 12 (December 15, 1929), 32. Magritte's close relations with the Paris Surrealists lasted only for three years, from 1927 to 1930, and he ultimately came to regret his connection. But his work was always admired by Breton.

132. For a discussion of the function of titles in Surrealism, see Laurie Edson, "Confronting the Signs: Words, Images and the Reader-Spectator," *Dada/Surrealism* 13 (1984), 83–93.

133. On the incorporation of words into images, see John Welchman, "After the Wagnerian Bouillabaisse: Critical Theory and the Dada and Surrealist Word-Image," in Judi Freeman, ed., *The Dada and Surrealist Word-Image* (Cambridge, Mass., 1990) and Georges Roque, "Magritte's Words and Images," *Visible Language* XXIII, 2/3 (Spring, Summer, 1989). For an earlier reflection on this theme, see Michel Butor, *Les mots dans la peinture* (Geneva, 1969).

134. Magritte in a letter to James Thrall Soby, May, 1965, cited in Matthews, *The Imagery of Surrealism*, 34. Apparently, it was the sight of de Chirico's *The Song of Love*, with its surgeon's rubber glove combined with an antique statue, that led to his decision to paint the impossible. See the discussion in Gablik, *Magritte*, 25.

135. Breton, "Genesis and Perspective of Surrealism in the Plastic Arts," in *What is Surrealism?*, 226.

136. For these reasons, it is hard to accept Mundy's contention that Surrealist painting is essentially an affair of transparent internal perception in which "the image must simply be seen." ("Surrealism and Painting," 499.)

137. Collage involved the chance juxtaposition and reassembling of different found objects on a canvas, without the goal of creating *trompe l'oeil* effects as in Cubist *papier collé*. Frottage meant rubbings of textures such as the grain of wood or the veins of leaves. Decalcomania meant spreading color on a sheet of paper, placing another sheet on top of it, then separating them to reveal a chance pattern. Fumage functions with the traces of smoke. Coulages were paint drippings on a canvas, anticipating the technique of Jackson Pollock. *Étrécissements*, developed in the 1960s by Marcel Mariën, are commercial photographs with parts of the original cut off (the word comes from *rétrécissements* with the first letter snipped off).

138. Breton explicitly praised Diderot's inspiration of "the possibility of a purely tactile art which would aim at apprehending the object by primitive means and reject all that might be tyrannical and decadent in the realm of *sight*." "Genesis and Perspective of Surrealism in the Plastic Arts" (1942), in *What is Surrealism?*, 220.

Here the connection was made with Futurism, but it would work as well with certain Surrealist practices too.

139. Ernst, "*Au-delà de la peinture*", in Waldberg, *Surrealism*, 98; Breton, *Le Cadavre Exquis: Son Exaltation*, in *Ibid.*, 95.

140. Krauss, *The Originality of the Avant-Garde*, 38.

141. For a wide selection of Surrealist photographs with excellent annotations, see Edouard Jaguer, *Les mystères de la chambre noire: le surréalisme et la photographie* (Paris, 1982).

142. Pierre Naville, who with Bernard Péret, was the initial editor, deliberately sought to emulate a scientific journal, thus conceding nothing to "the pleasure of the eyes" (Nadeau, *The History of Surrealism*, 98).

143. Walter Benjamin, "A Short History of Photography," *Screen* 3 (Spring, 1972), 20; and Watney, "Making Strange: The Shattered Mirror," 171. Four of his works were reprinted in *La Révolution surréaliste* in 1926. In the 1930's, Man Ray's assistant Berenice Abbot brought Atget's work to the United States and helped stimulate Surrealist photography in America. In a different light, however, Atget can also be seen as a forerunner of the *neue Sachlichkeit* sensibility of the German New Vision of the 1920s. However he is understood, Atget's work represented a kind of voyeuristic capturing of urban life, often in danger of disappearing, that fit well with the Surrealists' fascination with wandering through the modern city.

144. Breton, "Max Ernst," in *What is Surrealism?*, 7; and "The Surrealist Situation of the Object," in *Manifestoes of Surrealism*, 272. Breton, to be sure, did appreciate the non-mimetic potential of the medium as well, as shown by his enthusiasm for Man Ray's rayographs. He also saw its resemblance to automatic writing, which he calls "the true photography of thought" in the piece on Ernst.

145. Watney, "Making Strange: The Shattered Mirror," 170–71. These claims are part of a larger argument that challenges the political sufficiency of estrangement and defamiliarization as a means to expose social contradictions. He contends that different contexts of reception have to be taken into account as well, because certain contexts more easily absorb shocks than others. The history of Surrealism's refunctioning for advertising purposes bears out his warning.

146. Krauss, "The Photographic Conditions of Surrealism," in *The Originality of the Avant-Garde and Other Modernist Myths*; "Corpus Delicti," *October* 33 (Summer, 1985), 31–72; with Jane Livingston, *L'Amour Fou: Surrealism and Photography* (New York, 1985).

147. The term is Derrida's and it suggests an interplay of absence and presence, the sequential temporality lurking in even the most apparently static spatiality, that defeats "the metaphysics of presence."

148. Krauss, "The Photographic Conditions of Surrealism," 109. The recent montage photographs of David Hockney, in which sections of an original image are dissected and then resynthesized, would seem to take the technique of spacing to an extreme.

149. *Ibid.*, 113.

150. Krauss, "Corpus Delicti," 44. The gender dimension of this attack on the body, most obvious in Bellmer's dismembered dolls, has been the subject of considerable controversy. Krauss has argued against its importance, but other commentators are not convinced. See, for example, Steve Edwards, "Gizmo Surrealism," *Art History* 10, 4 (December, 1987), 511f. His critique is situated in a larger defense of the value of Breton over Bataille because of their respective political implications. See also Hal Foster, "L'Amour Faux," *Art in America* 74, 1 (January, 1986).

151. To be precise, the chiasmic intertwining she evokes was really only spelled out in Lacan's later work, *The Four Fundamental Concepts of Psychoanalysis*, but in the 1930s, his theory of the mirror stage was already developed and available to the group around Bataille. In fact, *Minotaure* published an essay in 1938 by Pierre Mabille, entitled "Miroirs," which discussed it.

152. *Ibid.*, 72.

153. The literature on the Surrealist cinema is now very extensive. Among the most helpful treatments are J.H. Matthews, *Surrealism and Film* (Ann Arbor, Mich., 1971); Steven Kovács, *From Enchantment to Rage: The Story of Surrealist Cinema* (Rutherford, N.J., 1980); Linda William, *Figures of Desire: A Theory and Analysis of Surrealist Film* (Urbana, Ill., 1981); and the special issue of *Dada/Surrealism* 15 (1986), which has a full bibliography. For Surrealist writings on film, see Paul Hammond, ed., *The Shadow and its Shadow: Surrealist Writings on Cinema* (London, 1978).

154. Robert Desnos, *Cinéma*, ed. André Tchernia (Paris, 1966), 154; cited in Kovács, 15.

155. For histories of French cinema, see Richard Abel, *French Cinema: The First Wave, 1915–1929* (Princeton, 1984), Roy Armes, *French Cinema* (New York, 1985), and Alan Williams, *The Republic of Images* (Harvard University Press, 1992).

156. For an account of their disillusionment, see Thomas Elsaesser, "Dada/Cinema?," in *Dada/Surrealism* 15 (1986), 13–27.

157. Jules Romains, "La Foule au cinématographe," *Puissances de Paris* (Paris, 1911), 120.

158. Jean Goudal, "Surréalisme et cinéma," *Revue Hebdomadaire* 34, 8 (February 21, 1925), 343–57, in English in Hammond, ed. , *The Shadow and its Shadow*.

159. *Ibid.*, 308.

160. For an account, see Richard Abel, "Exploring the Discursive Field of the Surrealist Scenario Text," *Dada/Surrealism* 15 (1986), 58–71.

161. Kovács, *From Enchantment to Rage*, 170. In a note on p.180, he posits a connection between films and flight, which draws on Freud's speculations about their common links to sexuality, but he neglects the specific postwar context in which the aviator's vision was glorified.

162. Antonin Artaud, "La vieillesse précose du cinéma," *Les cahiers jaunes* 4 (1933), in *Oeuvres complètes* (Paris, 1970), 104 and 107; for an account of his disillusionment, see Kovács, *From Enchantment to Rage*, chapter 5 and Sandy Flitterman-Lewis, "The Image and the Spark: Dulac and Artaud Reviewed," *Dada/Surrealism* 15 (1986), 110–27. The latter focuses on his disastrous collaboration with Germaine Dulac in the making of *The Seashell and the Clergyman* in 1927.

163. Benjamin Péret, cited in Kovács, *From Enchantment to Rage*, 250.

164. For an extensive selection, see the entries under Buñuel and Dali in Rudolf Kuenzli's bibliography of works on Dada and Surrealist film in *Dada/Surrealism* 15 (1986).

165. Luis Buñuel, "Notes on the Making of *Un chien andalou*," in Frank Stauffacher, ed., *Art in Cinema* (New York, 1968), 29.

166. Bataille, "Eye," *Visions of Excess*, 19.

167. Buñuel, "Notes on the Making of *Un chien andalou*," 30.

168. Bataille, "The 'Lugubrious Game'," *Visions of Excess*, 29.

169. Carlos Fuentes, "The Discreet Charm of Luis Buñuel," *New York Times Magazine* (11 March, 1973), 87, cited in Kovács, *From Enchantment to Rage*, 191.

170. Buñuel himself seems to have been satisfied with none of these interpretations. See his remarks to François Truffaut in "Rencontre avec Luis Buñuel," *Arts* (25 July, 1955), 5; cited in Kovács, *From Enchantment to Rage*, 245.

171. One recent exception is Mary Ann Caws, "Eye and Film: Buñuel's Act," in *The Art of Interference: Stressed Readings in Verbal and Visual Texts* (Princeton, 1989).

172. For discussions, see Jeanne Siegel, "The Image of the Eye in Surrealist Art and its Psychoanalytic Sources, Part One: The Mythic Eye," *Arts Magazine* 56, 6 (1982), 102–106 and "Part II: Magritte," 56, 7 (1982), 116–19; and Gerald Eager, "The Missing and Mutilated Eye in Contemporary Art," *The Journal of Aesthetics and Art Criticism* XX, 1 (Fall, 1961), 49–59.

173. For an analysis of this sculpture, which links it to *Story of the Eye* and *Un chien andalou*, see Krauss, *The Originality of the Avant-Garde*, 58.

174. For a reading of *L'âge d'or* that also interprets it in terms of Bataille's worldview, see Allen Weiss, "Between the Sign of the Scorpion: *L'âge d'or*," *Dada/Surrealism* 15 (1986), 159–75.

175. Siegel, "The Image of the Eye in Surrealist Art," 106. Reitler's essay was "On Eye Symbolism," *Internationale Zeitschrift für Ärztliche Psychoanalyse* I (1913).

176. Eager, "The Missing or Mutilated Eye in Contemporary Art," 59.

177. Breton, "The Automatic Message," 107.

178. *Ibid.*

179. For a discussion of the various uses of the metaphor in Breton, see John Zuern, "The Communicating Labyrinth: Breton's 'La Maison d'Yves'," *Dada/Surrealism* 17 (1988). He notes that Breton identified himself more with Theseus than the Minotaur, but adds, "the surrealist Theseus, the revolutionary, does not free the world from tyranny by entering the labyrinth and destroying the beast, but by taking the entire world into the labyrinth with him, where, confounded with the liberated unconscious, the world is transformed . . ." (118).

180. *Ibid.*

181. For Breton's disillusionment with painters, see "Against the Liquidators" (1964), in *What is Surrealism?*

182. I spell these out further in my *Downcast Eyes: The Denigration of Vision in 20th-Century French Thought*, (Berkeley: University of California Press, 1993).

M.
Jay

three

Modernity's Mediations

The Scopic

and the Haptic

Physiognomic Aspects
of Visual Worlds

Michael Taussig

> Nature creates similarities. One need only think of mimicry. The
> highest capacity for producing similarities, however, is man's. His gift of seeing
> resemblances is nothing other than a rudiment of the powerful compulsion in
> former times to become and behave like something else. Perhaps there is none of his
> higher functions in which his mimetic faculty does not play a decisive role.
>
> — Walter Benjamin, first paragraph
> of "On the Mimetic Faculty." (1934)

PLEASE NOTE THE PITCH MADE FOR THE IMPORTANCE OF THE "MIMETIC FACULTY" IN all of our "higher functions." For this four-page essay of Benjamin's is by no means an esoteric aside. All the fundamentals are herein composed; from his theories of language of persons *and* of things, to his startling ideas concerning history, art in the age of mechanical reproduction and, of course, that infinitely beguiling aspiration, the profane illumination achieved by the dialectical image dislocating chains of concordance with the one hand, reconstellating in accord with a mimetic snap, on the other.

His fascination with mimesis flows from the confluence of three considerations: alterity, primitivism, and the resurgence of mimesis with modernity. Without hesitation Benjamin affirms that the mimetic faculty is the rudiment of a former compulsion of persons to "become and behave like something else." The ability to mime, and mime well, in other words, is the capacity to Other. Second, this discovery of the importance of the mimetic is itself testimony to an enduring theme of Benjamin's, the surfacing of "the primitive" within modernity as a direct result of modernity, especially of its everyday-life rhythms of montage and shock alongside the revelation of the optical unconscious made possible by mimetic machinery like the camera and the movies. By definition this notion of a resurfacing of the mimetic rests on the assumption that "once upon a time" mankind was mimetically adept, and in this regard Benjamin refers specifically to mimicry in dance, cosmologies of microcosm and macrocosm, and divination by means of correspondences revealed by the entrails of animals and constellations of stars. Much more could be said of the extensive role of mimesis in the ritual life of ancient and "primitive" societies. Third, Benjamin's notion regarding the importance of the mimetic faculty in modernity is fully congruent with his orienting sensibility towards the (Euro-American) culture of modernity as a sudden rejuxtaposition of the very old with the very new. This is not an appeal to historical continuity. Instead it is modernity that provides the cause, context, means, and needs, for the resurgence—not the continuity—of the mimetic faculty. Discerning the largely unacknowledged influence of children on Benjamin's theories of vision, Susan Buck-Morss makes this abundantly clear with her suggestion that mass culture in our times both stimulates and is predicated upon mimetic modes of perception in which spontaneity, animation of objects, and a language of the body combining thought with action, sensuousness with intellection, is paramount. She seizes on Benjamin's observations of the corporeal knowledge of the optical unconscious opened up by the camera and the movies in which, on account of capacities such as enlargement and slow motion, film provides, she says, "a new schooling for our mimetic powers."[1]

The Eye as Organ of Tactility: The Optical Unconscious

> Every day the urge grows stronger to get hold of an object
> at very close range by way of its likeness, its reproduction.
>
> — Benjamin, "The Work of Art in the
> Age of Mechanical Reproduction."

To get hold of something by means of its likeness. Here is what is crucial in the resurgence of the mimetic faculty, namely the two-layered notion of mimesis that is involved—on the one hand a copying or imitation and, on the other, a palpable, sensuous, connection between the very body of the perceiver and the perceived (which ties in with the way Frazer develops what he takes to be the two great classes of sympathetic magic in *The Golden Bough*, the magic of *contact,* on the one hand, and that of *imitation,* on the other). Elementary physics and physiology might instruct that these two features of copy and contact and are steps in the same process, that a ray of light, for example, moves from the rising sun into the human eye where it makes *contact* with the retinal rods and cones to form, via the circuits of the central nervous system, a (culturally attuned) *copy* of the rising sun. On this line of reasoning contact and copy merge with each other to become virtually identical, different moments of the one process of sensing; seeing something or hearing something is to be in contact with that something.

Nevertheless the *distinction* between copy and contact is no less fundamental, and the nature of their interrelationship remains obscure and fertile ground for wild imagining— once one is jerked out of the complacencies of common sense-habits. Witness the bizarre theory of membranes briefly noted by Frazer in his discussion of the epistemology of sympathetic magic, a theory traced to Greek philosophy no less than to the famous Realist, the novelist Honoré de Balzac, with his explanation of photographs as the result of membranes lifting off the original and being transported through the air to be captured by the lens and photographic plate![2] And who can say we now understand any better? To ponder mimesis is to become sooner or later caught, like the police and the modern State with their fingerprinting devices, in sticky webs of copy *and* contact, image *and* bodily involvement of the perceiver in the image, a complexity we too easily elide as non-mysterious with our facile use of terms such as identification, representation, expression, and so forth—terms which simultaneously depend upon and erase all that is powerful and obscure in the network of associations conjured by the notion of the mimetic.

Karl Marx deftly deployed the conundrum of copy and contact with his use of the analogy of light rays and the retina in his discussion of commodity fetishism.[3] For him such fetishization resulted from the curious effect of the market on human life and imagination, displacing contact between people onto that between commodities, thereby intensifying to the point of spectrality the commodity as an autonomous entity with a will of its own. "The relation of producers to the sum total of their own labor," wrote Marx, "is presented to them as a social relation, existing not between themselves, but between the products of their labor." It is this state of affairs that makes the commodity a mysterious thing "simply because in it the social character of men's labor appears to them as an objective character stamped upon the product of that labor." What is here decisive is the displacement of the "social character of men's labor" into the commodity where it is obliterated from awareness by appearing as an objective character of the commodity itself. The swallowing up of contact we might say, by its copy, is what ensures the animation of the latter, its power to straddle us.

Marx's optical analogy went like this. When we see something, we see that something as its own self-suspended self out there, not the passage of its diaphanous membranes or impulsions as light waves or howsoever you want to conceptualize "contact" through the air and into the eye where the copy now burns physiognomically, physioelectrically, onto the retina, and as physical impulse darts along neuroptical fibers to be further registered as copy. All this contact of perceiver with perceived is obliterated into the shimmering copy of the thing perceived, aloof unto itself. So with the commodity, mused Marx, a spectral entity out there, lording it over mere mortals who, in fact, singly and collectively in intricate divisions of market orchestrated interpersonal labor-contact and sensuous interaction with the object-world bring aforesaid commodity into being. We need to note also that as the commodity passes through and is held by the exchange-value arc of the market circuit where general equivalence rules the roost, where all particularity and sensuosity is meat-grindered into abstract identity and the homogeneous substance of quantifiable money-value, the commodity conceals in its innermost being not only the mysteries of the socially constructed nature of value and price, but also all its particulate sensuosity—and it is this subtle interaction of sensuous perceptibility and imperceptibility that accounts for the fetish quality, the animism and spiritual glow of commodities, so adroitly channeled by advertising (not to mention the avant-garde) since the late nineteenth century.

As I interpret it (and I must stress the idiosyncratic nature of my reading), not the least arresting aspect of Benjamin's analysis of modern mimetic machines, particularly with regards to the mimetic powers striven for in the advertising image, is his view that it is precisely the property of such machinery to play with and even restore this erased sense of contact-sensuous particularity animating the fetish. This restorative play transforms what he called "aura" (which I here identify with the fetish of commodities) to create a quite different, secular, sense of the marvelous. This capacity of mimetic machines to pump out contact-sensuosity encased within the spectrality of a commoditized world is nothing less than the discovery of an optical unconscious, opening up new possibilities for exploring reality and providing means for changing culture and society along with those possibilities. Now the work of art blends with scientific work so as to defetishize yet take advantage of marketed reality and thereby achieve "profane illumination," the single most important shock, the single most effective step, in opening up "the long-sought image sphere" to the bodily impact of "the dialectical image." An instance of such an illumination in which contact is crucial is in his essay on Surrealism. Here Benjamin finds revolutionary potential in the way that laughter can open up the body, both individual and collective, to the image sphere. What he assumes as operant here is that images, as worked through the surreal, engage not so much with mind as with the embodied mind where "political materialism and physical nature share the inner man, the psyche, the individual." Body and image have to *interpenetrate* so that revolutionary tension becomes bodily innervation. Surely this is sympathetic magic in a modernist, Marxist revolutionary key? Surely the theory of profane illumination is geared precisely to the flashing moment of mimetic connection, no less embodied than it is mindful, no less individual than it is social?

The Third Meaning

Benjamin's theses on mimesis are part of a larger argument about the history of representation and what he chose to call "the aura" of works of art and cult objects prior to the invention of mimetic machines such as the camera. These machines, to state the matter simplistically, would create a new sensorium involving a new subject-object relation and therefore a new person. In abolishing the aura of cult objects and artworks, these machines would replace mystique by some sort of object-implicated enterprise, like surgery, for instance, penetrating the body of reality no less than that of the viewer. All this is summed up in his notion of the camera as the machine opening up the *optical unconscious*, yet before one concludes that this is ebullient Enlightenment faith in a secular world of technological reason, that the clear-sighted eye of the camera will replace the optical illusions of ideology, we can see on further examination that Benjamin's concept of the optical unconscious is anything but a straightforward displacement of "magic" in favor of "science"—and this in my opinion is precisely because of the two-layered character of mimesis as both (1) copying, and (2) the visceral quality of the percept uniting viewer with the viewed, the two-layered character so aptly captured in Benjamin's phrase, *physiognomic aspects of visual worlds*. Noting that the depiction of minute details of structure as in cellular tissue is more native to the camera than the auratic landscape of the soulful portrait of the painter, he goes on to observe in a passage that deserves careful attention that

> at the same time photography reveals in this material the physiognomic aspects of visual worlds which dwell in the smallest things, meaningful yet covert enough to find a hiding place in waking dreams, but which, enlarged and capable of formulation, make the difference between technology and magic visible as a thoroughly historical variable.[4]

But where do we really end up? With technology or magic—or with something else altogether where science and art coalesce to create a defetishizing/reenchanting modernist magical technology of embodied knowing? For it is a fact that Benjamin stresses again and again that this physiognomy stirring in waking dreams brought to the light of day by the new mimetic techniques bespeaks a newly revealed truth about objects as much as it does about persons into whom it floods as tactile knowing. "It hit the spectator like a bullet, it happened to him, thus acquiring a tactile quality," Benjamin pointed out with respect to the effect of Dada artworks which he thus considered as promoting a demand for film, "the distracting element of which is also primarily tactile."[5] The unremitting emphasis of the analysis here is not only on shocklike rhythms, but on the unstoppable merging of the object of perception with the body of the perceiver and not just with the mind's eye. "I can no longer think what I want to think. My thoughts have been replaced by moving images," complains one of Benjamin's sources.[6] By holding still the frame where previously the eye was disposed to skid, by focusing down into, by enlargement, by slowing down the motion of reality, scientific knowledge is obtained through mimetic reproduction in many ways. We see and comprehend hidden details of familiar objects. We become aware of patterns and necessities which had hitherto invisibly ruled our lives. But what is the nature of the tactile seeing and comprehension here involved?

Automatic Pilot

M.
Taussig

Habit offers a profound example of tactile knowing and is very much on Benjamin's mind because only at the depth of habit is radical change effected, where unconscious strata of culture are built into social routines as bodily disposition. The revolutionary task—using the term with all the urgency of the time Benjamin was writing, and now, once again, as I write in the late twentieth century—the revolutionary task could thus be considered as one in which "habit" has to catch up with itself. The automatic pilot functioning while asleep has to be woken to its own automaticity, and thus go traveling in a new way with a new physiognomy—bursting its "prison-world asunder by the dynamite of a tenth of a second."

Benjamin asks us to consider architecture as an example of habituated physiognomic knowing. How do we get to know the rooms and hallways of a building? What sort of knowing is this? Is it primarily visual? What sort of vision? Surely not an abstract blueprint of the sort the architect drew? Maybe more like a mobile Cubist constellation of angles and planes running together in time where touch and three-dimensioned space make the eyeball an extension of the moving, sensate body? Which is to say there is an indefinable tactility of vision operating here too, and despite the fact that the eye is important to its channeling, this tactility may well be a good deal more important to our knowing spatial configuration in both its physical and social aspects than is vision in some non-tactile meaning of the term. Of course what happens here is that the very concept of "knowing" something becomes displaced by a "relating to." And what is troublesome and exciting is that not only are we stimulated into rethinking what "vision" means as this very term decomposes before our eyes, but we are also forced to ask ourselves why vision is so privileged, ideologically, and other sensory modalities are, in Euro-American cultures at least, so linguistically impoverished yet actually so crucial to human being and social life. I am thinking here not only of tactility and tactile knowing, and what I take to be the great underground of knowledges locked therein, as conveyed in the mysterious jargon of words like "proprioception," but also, in an age of world historically unprecedented State and paramilitary torture, of the virtual wordlessness of pain too—a point recently made clear and important for us by Elaine Scarry.[7]

Benjamin wants to stress a barely conscious mode of apperception and a type of "physiological knowledge" built from habit. The claim is grand. "For the tasks which face the human apparatus of perception at the turning point of history cannot be solved," he writes, "by optical means, that is, by contemplation, alone. They are mastered gradually by habit, under the guidance of tactile appropriation."[8]

So far, of course, history has not taken the turn Benjamin thought that mimetic machines might encourage it to take. The irony that this failure is due in good part to the very power of mimetic machinery to control the future by unleashing imageric power on a scale previously only dreamed of, would not have been lost on him had he lived longer. But, as he was ready to note, we live constantly in the shadow of history's incompleteness, in the aftertaste of the sound bite's rolling echo.

"I Fall and I Fly At One With The Bodies Falling"

"It almost makes you seasick," comments the Lt.-Colonel in the U.S. Air Force as, with quiet pride two days into the Persian Gulf war in 1991, he queasily displays for U.S. television news a prolonged video shot taken by one of his precision bombs seeking its target, gliding in a soft wavy motion through the Iraqi sky. "Cinema isn't I see, it's I fly." Thus Paul Virilio in his *War and Cinema* paraphrases New York video artist Nam June Paik, assuming this free-falling image of sensuous filmic participation into his argument about the role of the camera and the type of visualization it opens up for massive destruction as in war.[9] In the same work Virilio cites a Russian pioneer of cinema, Dziga Vertov:

> I am the camera's eye. I am the machine which shows you the world as I alone see it. Starting from today, I am forever free of human immobility. I am in perpetual movement. I approach and draw away from things—I crawl under them—I climb on them—I am on the head of a galloping horse—I burst at full speed into a crowd—I run before running soldiers—I throw myself down on my back—I rise up with aeroplanes—I fall and I fly at one with the bodies falling or rising through the air.[10]

Or, to take a recent commentary on a Hollywood film, Vincent Canby's *New York Times* review of David Lynch's *Wild at Heart* "is all a matter of disorienting scale, of emphases that are out of kilter. The same object can as easily be the surface of the moon, seen in a long shot, or a shriveled, pockmarked basketball photographed in close-up." A shot of a traffic light held too long is no longer a traffic light. When a match is struck behind the credits, "the screen erupts with the roar of a blast furnace. The flames are of a heat and an intensity to melt a Cadillac Seville." And in an inspired act he draws the parallel of a trip in a fun house ghost train: "Nightmares are made real. Without moving one seems to plummet through pitch darkness."

From pioneers of Soviet avant-garde to the capitalist ghost train so it goes, tactility all the way:

> —Tatlin, 1913: "The eye should be put under the control of touch."
> —Hollywood, 1989: Burning Cadillacs erupting from screens, *Wild at Heart*.
> —Duchamp: "I want to abolish the supremacy of the retinal principle in art."
> —A Lieutenant Colonel of the U.S. Air Force at war having his tummy churned as his mechanical eye smartly dances death through the sky, linking so many tons of explosive with a programmed target on the ground.

And, of course, we must add that consummate theoretician and sometime (when he was allowed) maker of films, Sergei Eisenstein, contemporary of Vertov and Tatlin (and surely a profound influence on Benjamin), who time and again in word and image expressed those principles at the heart of Benjamin's fascination with the mimetic faculty—namely alterity, primitivism, and the resurgence of mimesis with mechanical reproduction. Especially pertinent was the way Eisenstein came to understand within and as a result of those principles the interdependence of montage with physiognomic aspects of visual worlds.

Taking his cue from the Kabuki theater of pre-modern Japan, Eisenstein complicated the theory of montage in filmmaking with his notion of the "visual overtone," first established with his making of *The Old and the New* in 1928. "The extraordinary physiological quality in the affect of *The Old and the New*," he explained, is due to such an overtone, a "filmic fourth dimension" amounting to a "physiological sensation." He concluded,

> For the musical overtone (a throb) it is not strictly fitting to say: "I hear."
> Nor for the visual overtone: "I see."
> For both, a new uniform formula must enter our vocabulary: "I feel."[11]

And it was precisely the venerably aged techniques of Kabuki theater that provided specific ideas no less than stimulus for the modernist theory and film practice of montage itself. Eisenstein understood Kabuki acting, for instance, as "organic to film," and in this regard emphasized its "cut acting" with sudden jumps from one depiction to another. There was also unprecedented slowing down of movement "beyond any point we have ever seen," and "disintegrated" acting as with the depiction of a dying woman, the role being performed in pieces detached from one another, acting with the right arm only, acting with the leg only, acting with the head and neck only (compare with break-dancing by African-Americans in the streets and subways of New York City). Each member of the death agony played a solo performance, "a breaking up of shots," as Eisenstein gleefully put it, working at a faster and faster rhythm.[12] Thus was the yoke of naturalism lifted for this early theoretician of mimetic machinery.

"The Genuine Advertisement Hurtles Things At Us With the Tempo of a Good Film"

I have concentrated on film in my exploration of the rebirth of the mimetic faculty. But what about that other great explosion of the visual image since the late nineteenth century, namely advertising? Does it not also provide the everyday schooling for the mimetic faculty? Even more so?

In his essay, "Transparencies on Film," Adorno makes the muted criticism that Benjamin's theory of film did not elaborate on how deeply some of the categories he postulated "are imbricated with the commodity character which his theory opposes."[13] Yet is it not the case that it is precisely in the commodity, more specifically in the fetish of the commodity, that Benjamin sees the surreal and revolutionary possibilities provided by the culture of capitalism for its own undoing, its own transcendence? Far from opposing the commodity, Benjamin seeks to embrace it so as to take advantage of its phantasmogoric potential. Take as an example his 1928 montage-piece, "This Space For Rent," concerning what he declared to be "today, the most real, the mercantile gaze into the heart of things, is the advertisement."

It abolishes the space where contemplation moved and all but hits us between the eyes with things as a car, growing to gigantic proportions, careens at us out of a film screen.

Lusting to exploit the optical unconscious to the full, advertising here expands, unhinges, and fixes reality which, enlarged and racy, hitting us between the eyes, implodes to engulf the shimmer of the perceiving self. Corporeal understanding: you don't so much see as be hit. "The genuine advertisement hurtles things at us with the tempo of a good film." Montage. Bits of image suffice, such as the shiny leather surface of the saddle pommel and lariat of Marlboro Man filling the billboard suspended above the traffic and prostitutes hustling on the West Side Highway—in a strange rhythm, as Benjamin puts it, of "insistent, jerky, nearness," the monteur's rhythm bartering desired desires internal to the phantom-object world of the commodity itself. And as with the fantasy-modeling of much shamanic ritual, as for instance with the Cuna shaman's figurines and the Emberá *gringo* boat, there is a cathartic, even curative, function in this copy-and-contact visual tactility of the advertisement such that

"matter-of-factness" is finally dispatched, and in the face of the huge images across the walls of houses, where toothpaste and cosmetics lie handy for giants, sentimentality is restored to health and liberated in American style, just as people whom nothing moves or touches any longer are taught to cry again by films.

Frightening in the mimetic power of its own critical language, what could be a more convincing statement of the notion that films—and beyond films, advertisements—reschool the mimetic faculty than this observation that "people *whom nothing moves* or touches any longer are *taught to cry again* by films"? And how mobile, how complicated, the interconnected dimensions of copy and contact turn out to be with this dispatching of matter-of-factness! The copy that is as much a construction as a copy, and the sentient contact that is another mode of seeing, the gaze grasping where the touch falters. Not just a question of changing the size and fragmenting the copy, but at the same time contact with it through an ether of jerky, insisting, nearness that, gathering force, hits us between (not in) the eyes. The question of being moved, *again*. The question of being *touched*, again. Rebirth of mimesis. Short-circuit. Copy fusing with contact. Fire in asphalt. For the person in the street, says Benjamin, it is money that arouses sentience. It is money that liberates these healthy American sentiments and brings the person into perceived contact with things. Hence, the gnomic parting shot to "This Space For Rent":

> What, in the end, makes advertisements so superior to criticism? Not what the moving red neon says—but the fiery pool reflecting it in the asphalt.

The Surgeon's Hand: Epistemic Transgression

Here we do well to recall Benjamin likening the process of opening the optical unconscious to the surgeon's hand entering the body and cautiously feeling its way around the organs. For there is, as Georges Bataille would insist, great violence and humor here as a tumultuous materialism is ushered into modernity's epistemological fold. The taboo is transgressed, the body is entered, the organs palpated. Yet we are told, as a result of Bataille's intellectual labors on taboo and transgression, that it is the function of the taboo to hold back violence, and that without this restraint provided by the unreason of the taboo, the reason of science would be impossible.[14] Thus insofar as the new form of vision, of tactile knowing, is like the surgeon's hand cutting into and entering the body of reality to palpate the palpitating masses enclosed therein, insofar as it comes to share in those turbulent internal rhythms of surging intermittencies and peristaltic unwindings— rhythms inimical to harmonious dialectical flip-flops or allegories of knowing as graceful journeys along an untransgressed body of reality, moving from the nether regions below to the head above—then this tactile knowing of embodied knowledge is also the dangerous knowledge compounded of horror and desire dammed up by the taboo. Thus if science depends on taboos to still the ubiquitous violence of reality—this is the function of the whiteness of the white coats, the laboratory, the scientifically prepared and processed sociological questionnaire, and so forth—if science requires a sacred violence to hold back another violence, then the new science opened up by the optical unconscious is a science to end science because it itself is based first and foremost on transgression—as the metaphor of the mimetically machined eye as the surgeon's hand so well illuminates. Confined within the purity of its theater of operation, science can proceed calmly despite the violence of its procedure. But . . . in the *theater of profane and everyday operations*, which is where, thanks to the ubiquity of mimetic machinery, the optical unconscious now roves and scavenges, no such whiteness cloaks with calm the medley of desire and horror that the penetrating hand, levering the gap between taboo and transgression, espies—and feels. And "every day the urge grows stronger to get hold of an object at very close range by way of its likeness, its reproduction."

This is why the scientific quotient of the eyeful opened up by the revelations of the optical unconscious is also an artistic and hallucinatory eye, a roller-coastering of the senses dissolving both science and art into a new mode of truth-seeking and reality-testing—as when Benjamin, in noting the achievement of film to extend our scientific comprehension of reality also notes in the same breath that film "burst our prison world asunder by the dynamite of a tenth of a second, so that now, in the midst of its far-flung ruins and debris, we calmly and adventurously go traveling."[15] And it is here, in this transgressed yet strangely calm new space of debris, that a new violence of perception is born of mimetically capacious machinery.

Notes

1. Susan Buck-Morss, *The Dialectics of Seeing: Walter Benjamin and the Arcades Project.* (Cambridge, Mass.: MIT Press, 1989), 267.

2. Yrjo Hirn, *Origins of Art* (London,1900; New York: Benjamin Bloom, Reissued 1971), 293.

3. Karl Marx, *Capital: A Critique of Political Economy*, Vol. 1 (New York: International Publishers, 1967), 72.

4. Benjamin, "A Short History of Photography," in *One-Way Street and Other Writings*, trans. and ed. E. Jephcott and K. Shorter (London: New Left Books), 243–44.

5. Benjamin, "The Work of Art in the Age of Mechanical Reproduction," in *Illuminations*, ed. Hannah Arendt, trans. Harry Zohn, (New York: Schocken), 238.

6. Georges Duhamel, *Scenes de la vie future*, (Paris, 1930), cited in Benjamin, "The Work of Art in the Age of Mechanical Reproduction," 238.

7. Elaine Scarry, *The Body in Pain: The Making and Unmaking of the World* (New York: Oxford University Press, 1985).

8. Benjamin, "The Work of Art in the Age of Mechanical Reproduction," 240.

9. Paul Virilio, *War and Cinema: The Logistics of Perception*, trans. Patrick Camiller (London: Verso, 1989), 11.

10. Virilio, 20.

11. Sergei Eisenstein, "The Filmic Fourth Dimension," in *Film Form: Essays in Film Theory*, ed. and trans. Jay Leyda (New York: Harcourt, Brace, Jovanovitch, 1949), 71.

12. Eisenstein, "The Cinematographic Principle and the Ideogram," in *Film Form: Essays in Film Theory,* 42.

13. T. W. Adorno, "Transparencies on Film," *New German Critique* 24–25 (Fall–Winter, 1981): 199–205, 202.

14. Georges Bataille, *Erotism, Death, and Sensuality* (San Francisco: City Lights, 1986), 37–38.

15. Benjamin, "The Work of Art in the Age of Mechanical Reproduction," 236.

The Memory of the Senses
Historical Perception, Commensal Exchange, and Modernity

C. Nadia Seremetakis

THIS IS A PAPER IN FIVE ACTS—SALIVA, THE JOURNEY, TRAFFIC, DUST, AND REFLEXIVE Commensality—that explore the senses and material culture as exchange, memories, ethnographic description, and as a conceptual problematic of fieldwork and modernity. The montage of these impinging fragments concurs with my proposal that the numbing and erasure of sensory realities are crucial moments in socio-cultural transformation. These moments can only be glimpsed at obliquely and at the margins, for their visibility requires an immersion into interrupted sensory memory and displaced emotions. Thus the use of montage here is not simply an aesthetic or arbitrary choice. Sensory and experiential fragmentation is the form in which this sensory history has been stored and this dictates the form of its reconstruction. For I believe that there can be no reflexivity unless one passes through an historical reenactment of perceptual difference.

Montage also reflects the transactional dimensions of my research in rural and urban Greece on sensory experience, memory and material history which combines traditional fieldwork inquiry with the biographical experience of my generation; a generation that straddles the admixture of rural and urban economies and cultures that has taken place since the postwar period. In fusing the ethnographic and the biographical I focus on everyday language use, and the symbolic and affective dimensions of material culture which serve as passageways into those experiential fragments, deferred emotions and lost objects that were not part of the public culture of Greek modernization, yet were integral to the tangible force of its historical passage. The mixture of fieldwork inquiry, biography and narrative styles here also refracts the ready-made montage that organizes that hybrid figure called the "native anthropologist"; a figure that is the very embodiment of the syncretism of incomplete modernization.

Saliva

The grandma dressed in black, sitting at home or at the edge of the fields, feeds the baby.[1] The baby in the cradle or on her lap is wrapped tightly in strips of cloth. She takes a piece of crustless bread, the inside of the bread known as *psíha*, crumbles it with her fingers and puts a few crumbs in her toothless mouth. The rotating tongue moistens the bread with saliva till it becomes a paste, "clay." She molds the bread till its texture signals that it is ready for the child. She takes the bread from her mouth and places it in its toothless mouth.[2] The baby swallows it as she swallows her saliva flavored by the bread. Her fingers reach for more bread and the act is repeated. On other occasions she dips the crumbs first in olive oil before molding them with her saliva. She talks and chants to the baby, calling to it: "my eyes," "my heart," "my soul," "my bread loafs" (*frajolítses mou*—when referring to the pudgy white legs), "my crown." She continues till the baby sleeps, as they wait for the child's mother to return from the fields.[3]

Different names pertain to this process of feeding a child in various parts of Greece. In the Southern Peloponnese, for instance, this child has been "raised" with *masoulíthres* or *ladhopsíhala* (the former derives from the verb *masáo*, to chew; the latter from the nouns *ládhi*, olive oil, and *psíhala*, bread crumbs). They are described as claylike substances (*pilós*) resembling that prepared by the birds to feed their little ones in the nest. The process of raising a child is known as "resurrecting a child" (*anasténo pedhí*). This child will often be described as having been "resurrected with *masoulíthres* by his grandma" (*anastíthike me masoulíthres* or *i yiayiá tou to anástise*). The notion of resurrection is connected to the movement from down to up, from death to life, from sleeping to awakening, and from the raw to the baked (cooked). A woman raises a child as she raises dough into bread. Working the bread with the tongue and the saliva, the grandma changes it to dough which is then used to raise the child. Raising here is akin to baking. Children are also "baked in the ocean." There the "salt and sun bake the child (*to psínoun*)" transforming a pale body into a "crusty skin." Baking gives form: color, shape, texture. Enculturation here is a sensory process and tied to the acquiring of form. It draws its imagery (color, shape, texture) from the body and food processing. There is no rigid dichotomy between enculturating and natural processes that transform the body. Northerners, for instance, or dull persons are often characterized as "raw" or "dough" or "inedible" precisely because they are not properly enculturated (raised) in Greek ways. Baking results in an upward movement: coffee is "baked" until it rises to form a top (*kaimáki*)—the top implies sedimentation, texture in taste. Bread and desserts are baked to rise and/or till they form a crust. When they are not raised, they are not "ready" and thus considered "raw"; as Greeks say, "pale like dead." The stiff, raw and dead can be raised to life, can be baked. The raw food is termed *omó*—which is also a metaphor for the uncultivated person.

Baking involves the alternation between raising (the up) and sleeping (the down). The act of baking and cooking in general, is always a trial. The cook "has to be fully alert" because cooking is a sudden awakening of substance and the senses. It is often said after a dish has finished cooking "let it sleep now, let it rest." The cook also rests at this point; most of the time she does not eat the food she prepares for others, for she is "filled with the smells."

The child is resurrected because the passage from the womb is a passage out of the dark and from a state of sleep. Babies are wrapped in cloth, and the dough is covered with blankets and towels to rise. The mouth of the grandma (softening the bread) is an oven, as is the womb (see also duBois 1988). The grandma feeding the baby with her mouth is resurrecting it by awakening its body point by point, by calling and naming points[4] (*semía*) of the body: "my eyes," "my heart," "my soul," or "my olive,"[5] referring to a birth mark. These are inferential codes for a complex act that engages other parts and points of the body not explicitly named. The entire act of feeding the child and naming the points of the body is an awakening of the senses. The act of talking to the child engages hearing. Naming the eyes awakens vision, the transference of substance from mouth to mouth animates taste and tactility.

The act of calling and naming is also an act of exchange. The substance transferred from the mouth of the grandma to the mouth of the child is her saliva, her taste or flavor, that becomes its own taste. It is food baked within her, with parts of her, her substance which is then transferred. This act can be contrasted to the feeding of the child with baby food from a jar bought in the store. By naming the child's gaze "my eyes," the grandma exchanges body parts and establishes vision as a social and sensory reciprocity. She calls the child "my heart" for the emotions in this awakening are as sensual as the senses are emotive. This act of sharing and naming parts and senses constructs one heart for two bodies, as one food was baked with saliva for two mouths, as one soul is raised for two persons, as one pair of eyes is imprinted on two bodies. The grandma gives her parts to see them inscribed on the child over time. *This is what she receives back from the child: the memory of herself in parts.*

The points of the body once awakened are not merely marks on the surface but are an active capacity. Awakening these points as sensate is opening the body to semiosis. The senses, the "points" (*semía*) of the body, are the sites where matter is subjected to signification. Semiosis here is inseparable from interpersonal exchange. The child is not only exposed to substance but to *shared substance*. The grandma's molding of the bread crumbs with saliva is a transcription of the self onto matter which is then transferred into the body of the child. This is the materialization of the person and the personification of matter.[6] The transcription of self onto substance and then into the child's body is inseparable from the transmission of emotions as a fuel of this exchange—which is why this is understood as "one heart for two bodies." Or as the sayings go," we are one breath," "we are one home," we grew up "with one food, one water."

The act of exchange is registered on the senses that seal it as a social relation. In turn, the senses are synchronized and crossed with each other and with *the Other*, so that senses and subjects can witness and be witnessed. "Listen to see" is the colloquial Greek phrase to demand attention in conversation, or "I can(not) hear it"[7] in reference to tasting a food flavor. The memory of one sense is stored in another: that of tactility in sound, of hearing in taste, of sight in sound. Sensory memory is a form of storage. Storage is always the embodiment and conservation of experiences, persons and matter in vessels of alterity. The awakening of the senses is awakening the capacity for memory, of tangible memory; to be awake is to remember, and one remembers through the senses, via substance. Cooking food in grandma's mouth with saliva imprints memory on the substance internalized by the child. Memory is stored in substances that are shared, just as substances are stored in social memory which is sensory.

Grandma feeding the child is also resurrecting it from death as a kind of generational sleep. She feeds the child that is often named after herself, her husband or one of her dead children. Personal names are passed down in families through alternate generations. This naming system endows the exchange of food, body parts and senses with a historical inflection—which is why it is all the more important for the senses and memory to witness and to record (historicize) the acts of exchange.[8] In this context, the food is not only cooked by saliva but also by emotions and memory. In turn, social memory is baked (raised) and thus reproduced by awakening the child. The dead can be raised through cooking, eating, awakening and exchanging, which all require memory. Ceremonial eating follows all death rituals.

The storage of memory in the senses, which awakens both, is based, like any other form of storage, on deferred consumption. Women in this culture distribute before they consume. Cooking is always for others. Cooking defers the immediacy of consumption. This is epitomized by the grandma who molds the food in her mouth and instead of swallowing it, places it in the mouth of the baby. A common Greek expression is "she was taking the food out of her mouth to feed him" referring literally to how one was raised and metaphorically to how two people relate; another expression of exchange is "you eat and I am filled." The deferment of consumption is affective because one always cooks for significant others. To

defer and to store is to place into alterity, the self registering substance and emotions in the other. Storage by both donor and recipient encodes the material world. If matter was to be subjected to immediate consumption, there would be no senses, no semiosis, and no memory. The senses defer the material world by changing substance into memory.

The return to the senses (experiential or theoretical), therefore, can never be a return to realism; to the thing-in-itself, or to the literal. In realism, matter is never deferred, but supposedly subjected to total consumption. When the child returns to the senses, this passage will always be mediated by memory, and memory is concerned with, and assembled from, sensory and experiential fragments. This assemblage will always be an act of imagination—thus opposed to the reductions of realism.[9]

The Journey

The child now living in the city returns to visit the grandma in the country. The trip to the village to visit grandma was by train. It meant camping out on a long journey. This entailed elaborate preparations, such as the packing of functional items for surviving the trip and numerous gifts for friends and relatives. Every station was identified with specific foods, their particular tastes and smells—one station with *souvláki*, another with rice pudding, pistachios, *pastéli*, dried figs. The child traveled through substances to reach grandma; a journey that sharpened the senses and prepared the child for diving into the village. The child arrived to the smell of the ocean, the trees, lemon, orange, olive, the sound of the donkey's bray, and the omnipresent, loud, loud music of the cicadas: sensory gates that signified entry into a separate space. The child greets the grandma who has been surveying the road like a gatepost, and passes into her world through the smells and texture of her dress. Shoes are removed as the child enters the main door and the pebbled floor leaves an indelible mark on the insteps. Its feet soon move from the hard pebbled floor to the soft mud of the gardens soothing its insole; an ingestion of the wet and the dry through the insole. Tactility extends beyond the hands.

There is also a tactility of smells. Each smell generates its own textures and surfaces. No smell is encountered alone. There are combinations of smells that make up a unified presence, the grandma's house: the garden aroma combined with the animal dung; the oregano bunch hanging over the sheep skin containing the year's cheese; the blankets stored in the cabinet which combine rough wool with the humidity of the ocean; the oven exuding the smell of baking bread and the residue of the ashes; the fresh bread in the open covered with white cotton towels. Nothing is sealed for the sake of preserving. To do so would mean to silence the smells preventing them from being "heard." As one moves from place to place in the house and gardens, these smells come in waves.

The senses in this place are moving constantly, they are not stationary. They blend, combine and recombine, shifting positions and transforming contexts. The fig is on the tree in the field one day, and next morning hundreds of figs are gathered and placed on bamboo mats on the beach, by the ocean to sundry. They look like pebbles and their strong sour taste blends with the smell of the sea. Then comes the olive season or the noodle making. For smells have seasons and each season smells. There is no watermelon in the winter, for instance, as in America. For taste has seasons too, and each season tastes. Each season also has its colors, as well as its sounds: cicadas, winds, ocean, earth.

Traffic

The grandma sits on a wooden stool, her legs comfortably spread apart with her skirt around them forming an armchair. Her face dark, her hair tied in a bun, her hands freckled and rough. The child slips into her lap. It is time for fairy tales. Slipping into her lap is slipping into a surround of different smells and textures, sediments of her work in the fields, the kitchen, with the animals. Through the anxieties of the parents, the child has learned that the grandma is the person who places it in contact with things dangerous and improper. She is the one who has a different relation to water, its qualities and economy, and thus to washing. She is the one who introduces "dirt."

She cracks a walnut. She "cleans" the inside, the "bread" (*psíha*), by pealing off the thin membrane that covers it. She splits the inside into pieces and reveals the parts of a new cosmos. She is a woman in the middle of chickens, dogs, cats, rabbits, goats, wells, mountains, oceans. These become the material emblems of her fairy tales, and the countryside the allegory of her stories. The landscape exhibits the fragments and ruins of her tales; its topography becomes a narrative sequence in itself. Her stories, inscribing the ocean, will come in waves. Yet, these tales are not the mere combination of her physical world. Outside invisible forces crack the surface and pop up to disorder and repatch that reality. Pirates and brigands raiding the ocean, monsters in the mountains, bad and good fairies fighting, snakes laying in ambush for passersby, ghosts talking, guiding and misguiding you. In one instance a child will be born by popping out from the woman's calf. The parts of the body, like the parts of the world, are mobilized; parts that were stationary and insignificant. These parts now recombined begin to signify. This is a repatching of the human body and of the "body" of the world.

This recombination and mobilization of the "body" through the fairy tale is staged on the grandma's own body in the way she performs and tells her story. Through breathing, vocal tones and gestures, her body enacts all the forces, characters and movements of the story. As the grandma and child eat the walnut, the fairy tale and its telling become the saliva on the "bread" of the present, bringing the past into the child's mouth.

Next morning the ocean will no longer be the ocean, a flat surface for play. It will also be a surface cracked by the raiding pirates. In this cosmos, the unexpected, the incongruous will appear suddenly from the casual and the everyday through their interruption and transformation. Sitting between her legs, the child is split between two worlds like the tree in her fairy tales that grows in between two rocks which make its abode; a split home formed by a stereoscopic vision ignited by the fairy tales in which the past and the present, the phantasmagoric and the everyday are juxtaposed on the material landscape and the senses.

When the fairy tale is remembered through play in the city, the child's new stereoscopic vision infiltrates the urban space, the city apartment, the parlor and the bedroom, creating an alternative geography. Within the apartment, the child will uncover obscure spaces, corners, closets that will become separate and imaginary and within which the fairy tales will be reenacted. These can be "old rooms" or unfinished rooms and alcoves which contain discarded objects of all sorts, colors and shapes. They become artifacts, actors of the fairy tale landscape. On the street old buildings, abandoned buildings, or buildings under construction will be transformed into "open" spaces for the transcription of the fairy tale surround.

Through her fairy tale (*paramythi*), the grandma brings the past into the present as a transformative and interruptive force. This very action defines the efficacy of the fairy tale as post-mythic—something related to myth but beyond it, a narrative that extracts and liberates, disassembles and reassembles the substance and fragments of myth in order to create passageways between times and spaces. Just as she chops up the landscape of the countryside rearranging its parts in order to convey her tales, the infiltration of the child's present by these narratives chops into pieces its world picture, undermining surface coherence with foreign elements. The fairy tale as narrative, performance and persona is post-mythic to the extent that it challenges and decenters contemporary myths that divorce and segregate the past from the present; myths that respectively depict the past and the present as separate homogeneities. The grandma's narration hooks things, shifting them from one space and time to another. This narrative redistribution interrupts the present as a closed continuum because it inserts and works with objects and experiences that are qualified by their spatial and temporal strangeness. Thus she becomes a colporteur [10] similar to the journeyman, the carnival performer, the sailor, who are comfortable moving between the city and the country and who bring with them glittering trinkets and other exotica; everyday objects from different sites and epochs. Colporteurs tell stories of the exotic and the different with artifacts as well as with language. Their stories, their small goods are bits and pieces of alterity that bring with them semantic possibility in miniature.

A characteristic figure of colportage, in urban and rural Greece has been the *pramateftís* or *yirológos* (*práma* means thing, event—deriving from the verb *pramatévo,* which means I handle, trade, deal with, or put together; *yíro* means (a)round, and *lógos* discourse). Both terms concern the circulation of things, words, signs, and sounds, as inseparable elements of trafficking, understood as a symbolic, performative and economic practice—a way of telling stories with objects and a way of circulating other cultures and their objects through stories. Colporteurs have also been repairmen of all sorts, fruit and vegetable vendors, fishmongers who traveled with donkeys and later motorcycle trucks, the newspaper man, and earlier the gypsy with his little monkey that danced to the tunes of the *défi* (a drum) and caricatured known personalities. On special days in the cities, this traffic was joined by the *ghaitanáki,* a carnival figure of a donkey formed by two men under a frame covered with multicolored strips of paper and dancing to the beat of a drum played by a third man. All these figures, along with the sailor and the returned emigrant, created a traffic of exotica, an alternative economy that transcended urban/rural spatial and temporal boundaries within a periphery. Many of them were also envoys of an invisible market network that connected this periphery with the markets of other peripheries in distant parts of the world, all of which bypassed and/or exploited dominant economies.

This traffic was a choreographed timekeeping mechanism. Hours, days and seasons were measured in alternating performances, each accompanied by its own sounds, smells, textures and visual spectacle. Colporteurs were figures stepping on and off the road as if it were a public stage, and in the eyes of the child they were akin to the fairy tale as the entry of the "fantastic" into the everyday.

There was traffic at night as well. When all movement stopped, the drunkard would appear. Staggering and stuttering, he passed next to low windows scaring everybody, especially the children. The drunkard of the urban neighborhoods, singing and grumbling against the world, interrupting the silence of the night was feared though tolerated. Nobody would call the police. He was the scarecrow people would play with but not expel.

The ingredients of colportage, the scattered contents of the unpacked myth that is disseminated through fairy tales and exotic traffic ornamented the everyday character of the child's present, lending it new auras. Colportage has nothing to do with completed appearances and geometric closures; rather, in ornamenting the everyday with the sensibility of the different it cuts up the edifice of the routine and prosaic, it forms fragments and animates broken up pieces of multiple realities in transit. This is the migration of sensory forms via material artifacts, and the memory they leave behind. The traffic of exotic matter here is both literal and symbolic, actual and remembered; the transport (*metaphorá*) of artifacts and narratives from one historical or cultural site to another is their metaphorization. Therefore colportage and its engagement with what can be shifted and altered is neither nostalgic nor realist.

In colportage, moments of the past and the different are glued onto the experience of the present. This is both montage and the fermentation of nonsynchronicity in the present. Colportage is not the transfer of parts and meanings into predetermined functions nor is it mechanical substitution.[11] With her saliva and stories, the grandma glues past generational and collective history onto present biographical experience. This dynamic traces how the imaginary and mythic postures of one generation are received within the childhood experience of another. The colportage of the grandma and its witnessing by the child does not fashion a noncontradictory totality. The grandma and child collaborate in the sensory and narrative refiguration of the rural landscape; a refiguration that also functions as a meta-commentary on the urban landscape because it recharges the marginalized and the ephemeral within the urban with exotic[12] meanings. This transcoding is all the more poignant because within modernity and between the rural and the city landscapes, the worlds of memory are rapidly replaced. Through the underground passageways between grandma and grandchild, through saliva and fairy tale, through evocations of persons, dead and/or supernatural, and through shared food, an alternative world of memory is set up against the structure of repression and displacement called modernity.

•   •   •

Once upon a time my son
a good king ruled over a faraway land

I remember to this day grandma starting
this way, her mind sailing in different times,
tenderly talking to me of this and that
witchcraft, love and great killings
Of good young kings who
conquered castles, killed the witches
and defeated monsters

And when the sweet sleep targeted my mind
my thought returned to the world of the fairy tales

Bad times took away from my dreams,
along with my joy, grandma's stories
They often come back from the old times
—God if it were only true—
like a gust of wind, those fairy tales

Don't cry my little girl for you open
wounds on my chest,
the two of us will make the world
a fairy tale.

> — *Grandma's Fairy Tales*, Cretan *mandinádha*
> composed and sung by the Cretan group
> *Hainidhes*, popular among Greek youth.

Dust

When the grandma comes from the village to visit her children in the urban center, she has to be patched up to appear publicly in the metropole. This is a montaging that only the grandchild can read. For occasions like a family wedding or baptism, grandma is taken to the hairdresser to get her hair fixed, given a hat with a veil, a matching suit or dress, special shoes that constrain her feet, a small purse otherwise useless to her, with some money and a handkerchief placed in it so it won't be empty. She is dressed and staged in this manner to make

an appearance, for she is the hidden element of her children's past. In the city she is the exposure of the inside to the outside, the rural to the urban. It is at this moment that the grandchild catches the present fabricating the past. The child is between two loving worlds and split into two, as if in between two mirrors never able to capture its full image in any one of them.

For the grandma this dressing up and ornamentation is inappropriate to her life cycle where one only dresses this way for death. She can sense that she is modernized as an element of a no longer pertinent reality which is now named "the past." For the grandchild, however, the dressing of the grandma transforms her into a redecorated artifact. The extraction of the grandma from her rural context and her transformation becomes in the child's perception analogous to its own coercive extraction from imaginary places and play and its insertion into an adult world. Dressing up the grandma forms a dialectical image in which two failed utopian expectations or sensibilities converge within the same form: that of the rural and that of the urban. In this simultaneous investiture and divestiture of the grandma, the child witnesses the repression of the rural, its historical vulnerability and at the same time the inability of modernity to fully transform the grandma. There is one such "grandma" in every other Greek household.

In comparison with the sensory layers and residues with which grandma is dressed in the village, she is now covered with "dead" objects. In this masquerade, she becomes the negated past, a fossilized display in the urban museum: the living room, the parlor. The deadening of the rural "past" and its framing in the parlor-museum transforms the sensory alterity of the grandma into dust. Dust is the perceptual waste material formed by the historical-cultural repression of sensory experience and memory. It is also the form that residual culture takes once it is compartmentalized as the archaic and sundered from any contemporary pertinence and presence.

Throughout the Mediterranean, the undusted house is a "dead" house, very much like the rural house "devoured" by overgrown weeds or abandoned by emigration (Seremetakis 1991). Dust offends the senses. It is the loss of the home to otherness: the temporal effacement of its semantic "surface," and its historical sedimentation. There is a relation between the accumulation of dust and the displacement of memory. The dust covered surface is alien to that sensory sedimentation that characterizes the grandma's house as a storage site of sensory memory where no odor or tactility is sealed—where not even the soil, the dirt with its smell and texture, can be left to become "dust," i.e., agriculturally dormant.

In Greek exhumation practices women mourners, after bringing the bones up from below the earth and back into their perceptual field, dust, wash, and sun dry the bones. This eliminates any foreign particle on the bone and restores the legibility of the artifact which is to be used as divination text. Without dusting they cannot "see" the bone in the divinatory sense nor touch it in the emotional sense. To make sensory contact with the bone without cleaning it, is to touch only the "dust." It is as if the bone, artifact of the remembered dead, has its own senses always in communication with the mourner's memory which can be blocked by the dust. Yet the dust is not devoid of signification. The dust on the bones and their cleaning encapsulates a material allegory of the temporal chasm that separates the living from the dead. This is the distance that is crossed by exhumation, an act of ritual purification that is understood as a sensory restoration and awakening of both the mourner and the bones which places them in communication. This awakening through the senses is divination (Seremetakis 1991).

In modernity dust forms around the culturally hollow space of the old that has been emptied of all indigenous meaning but which leaves its traces behind. Antiquarian, "tribal" and "folk" exotica inserted into the parlor space and then defined, encysted, encased and isolated as dust, emerge as fossilized displays, as a collector's artifact—a direct antithesis of the

sensory mobility of living colportage. The past collected and encased is the past devoid of semantic possibilities because its meaning has been completed, exhausted, totalized and consumed; that is, turned to historical dust. Historical and cultural difference introduced into the parlor settles in as surface without depth, devoid of the record of exchanges that produced it; thus devoid of emotions, memory and the senses.

In the late nineteenth and early twentieth centuries, the process of collecting, staging and displaying exotica archaicized the past and domesticated cultural otherness. This interiorization was mediated by a circuit of spaces of containment, typified by the urban parlor, a space which communicated with the museum and the academic study. The logic of the museum was inscribed into the parlor, and the museum itself was inhabited and enjoyed as an enlarged public living room. The parlor-museum encapsulates western modernity's petrifaction and consumption of ethnological and historical difference. In parlor sites, items of older periods and other cultures which had their particular aromatic, tactile, and auditory realities were desensualized and permitted a purely visual existence. In this process, vision itself was desensualized and subsequently metaphorized as and reduced to a transparent double of the mind unmediated by any material, spatial and temporal interference (Corbin 1986; Foucault 1979; Fabian 1983). The taming of difference through sensory neutralization, fabricated a false historical continuity between past and present through the cover of dust. The history of fieldwork, the anthropology of the senses and the archaeology of dust are linked to the extent that spatial devices like the parlor and the museum mediated the modern perceptual experience of culture-bound sensory alterity. The encounter with the ethnographic other was filtered by the spatial containment and sensory repression of the parlor exhibit.

In the first decades of the twentieth century, fieldwork and ethnography were informed by the impulse to exit from spaces of epistemological, textual and artifactual containment, such as the academic study and the ethnological museum—sites that were cultural variants of the parlor. Recent criticism emanating from within the discipline and from post-colonial sites inadvertently disclose the spatial and sensory continuity between parlor site and field site

(see Fabian 1983; Asad 1975). Fieldwork depended on spatial instruments such as the political geography of colonial pacification and tribalization. These spatializing grids were reinforced by parlor-like sensory orientations and homogenizing representational strategies that privileged vision-centered consumption of ethnographic experience, the reductive mapping of cultural traits, and the narrative genre of a static ethnographic present (Clifford 1988; Fabian 1983). This flattening of cross-cultural sensory experience into visual diagrams and atemporal spatial metaphors exported the parlor to the field site and transformed the latter into an open-air museum.

Reflexive Commensality

Between grandma and grandchild sensory acculturation and the materialization of historical consciousness occurred through the sharing of food, saliva and body parts. Another expression of this type of reciprocity is encountered in Maniat mourning ceremonies (Seremetakis 1990, 1991) where the lament circulates from mouth to mouth among singers as a shared substance. This sharing imparts a material density to the antiphonic exchanges of mourners from which oral history emerges. In Greek exhumation practices, the sensory presence of the dusted bones of the dead reawakens the memory of past commensal exchanges with the dead. Ignited by the collective memories invested in the bone as emotive artifact, the exhumers create a commensal ritual grounded on material substances, present and absent (past).

Commensality here is not just the social organization of food and drink consumption and the rules that enforce social institutions at the level of consumption. Nor can it be reduced to the food-related senses of taste and odor. *Commensality can be defined as the exchange of sensory memories and emotions, and of substances and objects incarnating remembrance and feeling.* Historical consciousness and other forms of social knowledge are created and then replicated in time and space through commensal ethics and exchange. Here each sense witnesses and records the commensal history of the others. In this type of exchange, history, knowledge, feeling and the senses become embedded in the material culture and its components: specific artifacts, places and performances. In processes of historical transformation and/or cross-cultural encounter, divergent sensory structures and commensalities can come into conflict with each other, and some are socially repressed, erased or exiled into privatized recollection and marginal experience. These dynamics indicate profound transformations in a society's relation to material culture and to systems of knowledge bound up with the material.

The history of the senses in modernity (see Corbin 1986; Vigarello 1988; Gay 1984; Crary 1991) can be understood as the progressive effacement of commensality; that is of a reflexive cultural institution that produced and reproduced social knowledge and collective memory through the circulation of material forms as templates of shared emotion and experience. In modernity, commensality is not absent but is rendered banal, functional or literal and increasingly reserved for the diversions of private life.[13] Yet commensality leads an underground existence as a repressed infrastructure of social knowledge (see also Marcus 1991).[14] In current ethnographic discourse commensality either has the status of fieldwork anecdote, or it is reified as a discrete object of inquiry internal to the culture of the Other. This is a curious pattern in a discipline that frequently worries over its own commodification of ethnographic knowledge, and which associates its progress with the recent expansion of surfaces of knowledge-consumption resulting from the multiplication of subdisciplines and specializations.

How can inquiry into the commensal practices of other cultures be undertaken when researchers do not consider nor generate accounts of the historical formation-repression of commensal ethics and sensory reciprocities within their own culture and particular discipline?[15] Is there a commensal structure for the social production of knowledge in anthropology? Does this structure communicate with the organization of the senses and material culture in modernity? If so, how does this affect the ethnographer's perception of the commensalities of cultural others?

The
Memory
of the
Senses

• • •

The relation between dust and what it covers is not a relation of appearance and essence. It is a relation of historical sedimentation. *Dust is not deposited only on the object but also on the eye.* Sensory numbing constructs not only the perceived but also the perceiving subject and the media of perception; each of these are reflexive components of an historical process. Thus dust can be a subject of historical analysis just as much as the senses, objects and experiences that dust interrupts and blurs.

When the anthropologist first enters the field site the sensory organization of modernity, the perceptual history and commensal structure of the discipline direct her/him to first see dust. Without long-term fieldwork and sensory archeology the anthropologist may never come to know that this dust is a surface residue of the researcher's own acculturation that obscures depth: other sensory surfaces that embody alternative materialities, commensalities and histories. Without a reflexive anthropology of the senses, fieldwork, short-[16] or long-term, remains trapped in the literal, captive of realist conventions that are themselves unacknowledged historically determined perceptual and commensal patterns. This is well understood by those who inhabit the memory of other sensory and material reciprocities. How can they take anthropologists seriously if the latter go with the dust?

• • •

"When I die, I am going to leave this gold tooth for you."
"But Grandmother, how are you going to pull it out once you
are cold and gone?" . . . "You'll pull it out."
Empty the table, and over the emptiness, dust. Over the dust the habitual
searching of your bony fingers. Is it a candle, or a tooth? Whenever I see that glow
in the dark I'll know it's you coming home to visit.

— Excerpt from Stratis Haviaras' novel
When the Tree Sings.

Notes

This paper was presented in the panel "The Anthropology of the Senses and European Modernity" organized and chaired by the author (sponsored by the Society for the Anthropology of Europe) at the 90th Annual Meetings of the American Anthropological Association, Chicago, 1991. It was also presented to the faculty of the department of anthropology at the University of Chicago in the spring of 1992. I wish to thank all anonymous reviewers for their comments, and most of all the editor of V.A.R., for his sensitive reading of this paper and for his decision to publish it without revisions. Thanks to Paul Stoller for his constructive remarks as a discussant at the AAA panel at which this paper was first given. This paper would not have been possible without my fierce dialogues with Allen Feldman.

**N.
Seremelakis**

1. Given the incomplete and uneven character of capitalist penetration and modernization in Greece and the accelerated rural to urban migration, which still allows for reverse seasonal migration (back to the country), the structure of the Greek family particularly from the perspective of a generational profile, can span rural and urban economies and cultures (for a fuller discussion see Seremetakis 1991). Therefore in Greece as in other cultures that have undergone similar uneven transformations, e.g., Latin America, the grandmother has been a central and ubiquitous figure in the popular imagination, literature and cinema, representing the anomalous persistence of the past in a present that has not superseded it.

2. Mutual toothlessness points to the twinship of grandma and child as liminal figures in this social context. Greek folksayings and humor on the mimetic relations between old age and infancy are common; they concern the lack of teeth and the inability to consume "adult," that is, hard food. The elderly frequently comment with irony on this resemblance. For instance, the perceived similarity between the physical, mental and social aspects of the life-cycle stages of old-age and infancy, informs the organization and intensity of mourning rituals in Inner Mani (see Seremetakis 1991). Also, in Inner Mani there are strong semiotic parallels between the imagery of birthing and dying (*ibid.*). The association sparked by toothlessness does not imply the infantilization of the elderly. In Greek rural culture, the infant, like the grandma, participates in a liminality with divinatory and cosmological implications. With the intensification of modernity and the internalization of Western notions of the life cycle and human development both the infant and grandma, particularly in the urban milieu, undergo a reciprocal infantilization as helpless entities.

3. The use of the present tense here does not imply the narrative strategy of the ethnographic present, but simply replicates the style of storytelling in Greek culture. If we accept that anthropology is another form of storytelling, we must allow for indigenous forms of narration to infiltrate the ethnographic narrative.

4. See Seremetakis (1991) for a discussion of the "points" of the body as liminal orifices where exchanges between the outside and inside take place.

5. For a fuller description of olive cultivation as well as the emotional and symbolic connotations of olives and the olive tree see Seremetakis 1991.

6. See Weiner (1976) and Strathern (1988) for analogous descriptions of the personification of matter in Melanesian contexts. However, their accounts do not explicitly focus on the link between emotions and historicization (witnessing) which is central to the understanding of exchange both in Greece and in other cultures.

7. Expressions such as "I hear the garlic" are used throughout Greece and most commonly in Crete and the Peloponnese. Dictionary definitions of the verb *akoúo* (I hear) associate it with the auditory, including literal hearing, but also receptive learning and obeying an order; the latter indicating that hearing is never passive but tied to the notion of agency. It is also tied to witnessing as in the phrase "I hear in the name of" (my name is). At issue in this article is the metaphorization of hearing in other senses such as taste and vision. This metonymic displacement violates any segmentation of the senses as discrete perceptual organs. One reviewer of this article suggested that it be translated as a generic term for perception ("encoded sensation"). This gloss loses the inflection of metaphorical transfer from one sense to another. *Akoúo* is not a generic phrase that takes on the character of a particular sense in changing situations. To maintain this is to assume a division of the senses. To translate it as generic perception is also to maintain a Cartesian distinction between language and material experience which reduces the polysemy of sensory crossing to rhetorical word-play.

8. The naming of body parts and sensory capacities throws new light on Greek personal naming and exchange. Earlier discussions of Greek naming practices in anthropology viewed naming as the mechanical reflex of kinship rules, inheritance requirements and collective religious identity (see for instance Bialor 1967; Kenna 1976). Personal naming was understood as upholding homeostatic, atemporal or cyclical institutions; it was also primarily viewed as an ideational-linguistic practice. Alternate generational naming is supposed to assimilate the individual to the kin collective of persons who share names

and eventually depersonalize those whose names are transferred to later generations. This style of naming replicates collective institutions by suppressing the passing of finite time (see for example Herzfeld 1982). Herzfeld added a performative element to this model by suggesting that Greek naming constructs social identity through the instrumental manipulation of rules and norms; the ultimate concern was what one "gains" from the conferral. Here, naming was associated with the rhetorical side of performance and value manipulation.

Baptismal naming has also been linked to the symbolic "resurrection" of the person whose name is transferred. But here the vernacular use of the term "resurrection" has been restricted to the theological sense of the term as an event and final outcome which preserves individual identity against death. In contrast, this paper shows that "resurrection," "raising" and "baking" are neither isolatable nor terminal events, but speak to ongoing and accumulated reciprocities, and to long term caring for the other. This is the storage and personification of the self in the other over time which cultivates, matures and individualizes the recipient through the poetic intensification of sensory memory. Personification *must* be distinguished from any dichotomy of the individual and the collective that informs all discussions of Greek naming (see for example Stewart 1988.) Personification is the transcription of the self into alterity, *not* the recycling of identity onto a blank mimetic slate. It does not aim at producing repetitive sameness, it is instead, a thoroughly historical and historicizing process that recuperates the difference between the young and the old, the living and the dead, the past and the present. This historical sensibility, with its focus on the shifting of emotions, identity, substance and memory from one form or vessel to another, also carries with it an aesthetic sensibility for variety and multiplicity. Personification through sensory and personal naming does not lead to depersonalization but rather to the cultivation of the distinct through transformative exchange, which preserves nothing that is not first altered by being exchanged.

Thus to limit naming practices to mentalist-linguistic and instrumental formulas, is to cover with dust the sensorial, materially dense, performed *poesis* (making and imagining) of naming. Through reciprocities of naming and other modes of exchange the self is, via the senses, dispersed and transcribed in parts onto diversity and history. These issues have been discussed in length in *The Last Word* (Seremetakis 1991).

9.   The critique of descriptive realism here does not necessarily mean to say that there is no reality outside the text, but rather points to the possibility of alternative modes of describing and depicting the Real which retroactively locate realism as a cultural construct with its own historical and social specificity.

10.   Colporteurs or colporteurs are hawkers and peddlers (originally of books, pamphlets and religious tracts). For a literary analysis of colportage, colporteurs, and their relation to spontaneous cultural montage see Bloch (1989). He associates it with " . . . the yearning for a constellation in the world, made out of esoteric and weird things, the yearning for the curious as objective quality." (Bloch 1991: 181)

11.   These characteristics distinguish colportage as defined here and by Ernst Bloch (1988), from Lévi-Strauss' famous notion of *bricolage* which emphasizes the ordered placement of a serendipity of materials within a stabilized structure which then endows these elements with a classificatory order. Colportage contests discrete systems of classification.

12.   Recently it has become fashionable in anthropology to criticize any tendency to exoticize as ethnocentric and romantic. However such criticism has been deployed in such a reductionist manner as to efface indigenous fascinations with the exotic and local "romanticisms" in diverse societies which may have little to do with nineteenth-century European predilections and their contemporary holdovers.

13.   This correlates with the privatization of what is actually social memory, which is consequently removed from collective historical consciousness.

14.   Marcus' discussion of "corridor talk" indexes a repressed commensality in academia since it engages unofficial practices for consuming and exchanging disciplinary knowledge.

15.   See Stoller (1989), for an analogous critique of fieldwork and protocols of representation in anthropology.

16.   The growing legitimacy of short term fieldwork within anthropology merely exacerbates this situation.

References

Asad, Talal, ed. 1975. *Anthropology and the Colonial Encounter*. Atlantic Highlands: Humanities Press.
Bialor, Perry. 1967. "What's In a Name? Aspects of the Social Organization of a Greek Farming Community Related to Naming Customs." In *Essays in Balkan Ethnology*, ed. W.G. Lockwood, Kroeber Anthropological Society Special Publication 1: 95–108.

Bloch, Ernst. 1989. "Better Castles in the Sky at the Country Fair and Circus, in Fairy Tales and Colportage (1959)." In *The Utopian Function of Art and Literature: Selected Essays*, trans. J. Zipes and F. Mecklenburg, Cambridge: MIT Press.

————1991. *Heritage of Our Times*. Trans. Stephen and Neville Plaice. Berkeley, Los Angeles: University of California Press.

Buck-Morss, Susan. 1989. *The Dialectics of Seeing: Walter Benjamin and the Arcades Project*. Cambridge, Mass.: MIT Press.

Corbin, Alain. 1986. *The Foul and the Fragrant: Odor and the French Social Imagination*. New York: Berg Publishers.

Clifford, James. 1988. *The Predicament of Culture: Twentieth-Century Ethnography, Literature and Art*. Cambridge, Mass.: Harvard University Press.

Crary, Jonathan. 1991. *Techniques of the Observer: On Vision and Modernity in the Nineteenth Century*. Cambridge, Mass.: MIT Press.

duBois, Page. 1988. *Sowing the Body: Psychoanalysis and Ancient Representations of Women*. Chicago: University of Chicago Press.

Fabian, Johannes. 1983. *Time and the Other: How Anthropology Makes Its Object*. New York: Columbia University Press.

Feldman, Allen. "On Cultural Anesthesia: From Desert Storm to Rodney King." *American Ethnologist* (forthcoming).

Foucault, Michel. 1979. *Discipline and Punish: The Birth of the Prison*. London: Perigrin Books.

Gay, Peter. 1984. *The Education of the Senses*. Oxford: Oxford University Press.

Harvey, David. 1989. *The Condition of Postmodernity: An Inquiry into the Origins of Cultural Change*. Oxford: Blackwell.

Haviaras, Stratis. 1979. *When the Tree Sings*. New York: Simon and Schuster.

Herzfeld, Michael. 1982. "When Exceptions Define the Rules: Greek Baptismal Names and the Negotiation of Identity." *Journal of Anthropological Research* XXXVIII: 288–302.

Kenna, Margaret. 1976. "Houses, Fields and Graves: Property Rites and Ritual Obligation on a Greek Island." *Ethnology*, vol. XV: 21–34.

Marcus, George. 1991. "A Broad(er)side to the Canon." *Cultural Anthropology* 6 (3): 385–405.

Seremetakis, C. Nadia. 1984. "The Eye of the Other." *Journal of Modern Hellenism* 1 (1): 63-67.

————.1990. "The Ethics of Antiphony: The Social Construction of Pain, Gender and Power in the Southern Peloponnese." *Ethos* 18 (4): 481–511.

————.1991. *The Last Word: Women, Death, and Divination in Inner Mani*. Chicago: University of Chicago Press.

————, ed. 1993. *Ritual, Power and the Body: Historical Perspectives on the Representation of Greek Women*. New York: Pella Publishing Co.-Greek Studies.

Stewart, Charles. 1988. "The Role of Personal Names on Naxos, Greece." *Journal of the Anthropological Society of Oxford* XIX (2) no. 2: 151–59.

Stoller, Paul. 1989. *The Taste of Ethnographic Things: The Senses in Anthropology*. Phila: University of Pennsylvania Press.

Strathern, Marilyn. 1988. *The Gender of the Gift: Problems with Women and Problems with Society in Melanesia*. Berkeley: University of California Press.

Vigarello, G. 1988. *Concepts of Cleanliness: Changing Attitudes in France since the Middle Ages*. Cambridge: Cambridge University Press.

Weiner, Annette. 1976. *Women of Value, Men of Renown: New Perspectives in Trobriand Exchange*. Austin: University of Texas Press.

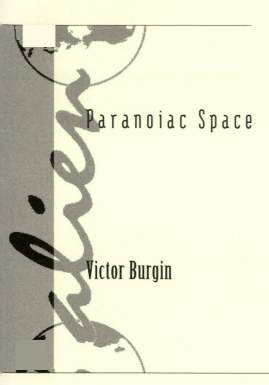

Paranoiac Space

Victor Burgin

At the beginning of his essay "reflections on exile" edward said tells anecdotes about friends, mainly writers, which testify to their pain in being separated from their home-land and their mother-tongue. He is quick to acknowledge that exile is suffered not only by a comparatively small number of writers and artists, but that it has "torn millions of people from the nourishment of tradition, family and geography." He speaks of the "hopelessly large numbers, the compounded misery of 'undocumented' people suddenly lost, without a tellable history." Here, he says, we must "leave the modest refuge provided by subjectivity and resort instead to the abstractions of mass politics."[1] But this early interruption to his text, this irruption of a public voice, soon gives way to the privacy of another anecdote about a friend. The clash of private and public voices in Said's essay represents the difficulty of placing the exile. Said's anecdotes show the experience of exile as lived in irreducibly subjective isolation; at the same time, he observes, the exile exists only in relation to nationalism, the "assertion of belonging in and to a place, a people, a heritage."[2] But here Said asks, "What is there worth saving and holding on to between the extremes of exile on the one hand, and the often bloody-minded affirmations of nationalism on the other? . . . Are they simply two conflicting varieties of paranoia?"[3] Said does not answer this question, but to ask it suggests that between the anecdotal expression of "personal feelings" and the abstractions of political discourse we must interpellate the discursive space of that "other locality" of which Freud spoke; that place, as Lacan put it, "between perception and consciousness." The term "paranoia" has of course passed from psychoanalysis into everyday use, but the "ordinary language" sense of the word generates little of interest in answer to Said's question. In everyday use, "paranoia" means "a feeling of persecution unjustified in reality." In so far as the exile has, in Said's own words, been "torn . . . from the nourishment of tradition, family and geography" then the feeling of persecution is surely justified. As for nationalism, it depends on the case, but there are instances where such a feeling would be equally justified. For example, the discourses of both Israeli and Palestinian nationalisms express feelings of persecution, for which both may legitimately argue a basis in reality. Some might judge one of these realities to be now past, while the other remains present. But at this point we encounter precisely the necessity of understanding the term "paranoia" in its psychoanalytic setting. There is no "past reality" in the *psychical reality* which is the object of psychoanalysis. Freud puts it simply: "there is no time in the unconscious": the past event, whether actual or fictional, produces real effects in the present.[4] Said recognizes this when he defines exile as a "condition of terminal loss," which also acknowledges that the space of exile is a psychical space as much as it physical. Before considering this space in its unconscious dimensions however we should first fix its coordinates in the space of instrumental reason.

The opposition "exile"/"nation" rests on a logic of exclusion/inclusion. According to this logic "exile" is not the only term which may appear opposite "nation." Said, for example, distinguishes between "exiles," "refugees," "expatriates" and "émigrés." The origin of exile, he observes, is in the ancient practice of banishment, which stigmatizes the exile as rejected. Refugees, he finds, are a by-product of the modern state, political innocents united in bewilderment. Expatriates share the condition of the exile in all respects but one: having chosen to leave their homeland they are therefore free to return. The status of the émigré, Said says, is "ambiguous": the émigré may once have been an exile but, like the european settler in Africa, Asia or Australia, may have constructed a new national identity away from national origins. As one category of displaced subject tumbles on the heels of another in Said's text the term "exile," no longer connoting fixity, comes to indicate a contingent resting place in a world in which today's exile may be yesterday's tourist. The subject positions Said mentions are in differing relations to their homeland, but in the same relation to their host country: they are all "foreigners." One of Julia Kristeva's more recent books, *Étrangers à nous-mêmes*, is a book about the foreigner. She writes: "To live with the other, with the foreigner, confronts us with the possibility . . . of *being an other*. It is not simply a matter—humanistically —of our aptitude for accepting the other; but of *being in his or her place*, which amounts to thinking of oneself and making oneself other than oneself. Rimbaud's "I is an other" was not only the avowal of the psychotic phantom which haunts poetry. The word announced exile, the possibility or the necessity of being foreign (*être étranger*) and of living in the foreigner's country (*vivre à l'étranger*), thus prefiguring the art of living in a modern era, the cosmopolitanism of the excoriated (*écorchés*)."[5] Kristeva here makes a mirror of the foreigner: to encounter the other in one's own space is to confront one's own alterity to that other's space. The phrase by Rimbaud she invokes, "I is an other," moreover perfectly describes the alienated identification which the infant makes in the "mirror stage," as described by Lacan. In further presenting Rimbaud's phrase as haunted by psychosis, as announcing exile and as "prefiguring the art of living in a modern era," Kristeva echoes Said's assimilation of exile to paranoia, makes this the common condition of us all, and associates the condition with a changed global space.

It is now a familiar observation that our subjective sense of the spatial relations ordering our world has undergone a historical mutation. The unprecedented speed of the locomotives and aeroplanes of modernity had the effect on the popular imaginary of causing geographical space to shrink; extensive contact with other cultures nevertheless still entailed actual bodily displacement and was available to comparatively few. The space engendered by the communication technologies of postmodernity however, as Paul Virilio puts it, ". . . is not a geographical space, but a space of time."[6] Historical events no longer simply "take place" in their immediate locality, but may be broadcast at the speed of light to simultaneously appear in a myriad other places. Jean Baudrillard has described the consequent tendency of historical reality to "disappear behind the mediating hyperreality" of the "simulacrum." In the classical mimetic theories of representation which dominated Western thought before modernism the image was a mirror of reality—not of any contingent reality but an ordered reality, the anticipation of a perfected reality. Today that mirror has shattered. Its fragments, perpetually in motion, reflect nothing reassuring. The psychoanalytic concept of the mirror stage, which I have already mentioned and to which I shall return, has alerted us to the importance of our relation to the image in the formation of a coherent identity out of pre-oedipal fragmentation and disorganization. From a Western world in which images were once limited in number, circumscribed in meaning and contemplated at length, we have today arrived at a society inundated with images consumed "on the fly"—from glossy magazines, from photomats, video rental stores, broadcast and cable TV, communication satellites and increasingly realistic computer simulations. Flipping and "zapping" through avalanches of books and journals, TV channels and CD-ROM, we are in turn bombarded by pictures not only of hopelessly unattainable images of idealized identities, but also images of past and present suffering, images of destruction, of bodies quite literally in pieces. We are ourselves "torn" in the process, not only emotionally and morally but in the fragmentary structure of the act of looking itself. In an image saturated environment which increasingly resembles the interior space of subjective fantasy turned inside out, the very subject-object distinction begins to break down, and the subject comes apart in the space of its own making. As Terry Eagleton has written, the postmodern subject is one "whose body has been scattered to the winds, as so many bits and pieces of reified technique, appetite, mechanical operation or reflex of desire." Such fragmentation, decentering and loss of subject-object boundaries, is characteristic of paranoia.

The term "paranoia" is derived from the Greek words for "changed reason" (*para, nous*) and originated in the Hippocratic school in the fifth-century B.C. when the word was used to denote all manifestations of severe mental disorganization. There then intervened that period of Western history in which religious explanations of such mental states prevailed: for example, in the idea of demonic possession. The word "paranoia" returned to the medical literature in 1863 when the German psychiatrist Karl Ludwig Kahlbaum used it to speak of persecutory and megalomaniac delusions. Said may very well have had this picture in mind—persecution and megalomania—when he spoke of exile and nationalism as "two conflicting varieties of paranoia." By the end of the nineteenth century then the term "paranoia" was used in a restricted sense; the function of denoting the more general field of severe mental illness having passed to the word "psychosis."[7] In his introduction to a recent collection of "Essential Papers on Psychosis" the editor remarks that although psychotic states have come to be "roughly grouped into two major categories, the affective psychoses and the schizophrenias," nevertheless their "ætiology and pathogenesis remain unknown." He remarks, for example, that the term "schizophrenia" has come to be used as if it signified a singular "disease" whereas in fact, "all that the term represents is a description of a cluster of symptoms which have no clear prognosis or definitional implications by themselves."[8] The psychoses are defined and classified therefore only according to the symptomalogical pictures they present, to their "phenomenology." Patients who present symptoms which lie in the area of overlap between extant nosological categories have traditionally been termed "borderline cases." The clinically psychotic person, in everyday language, is "raving mad"; in extreme cases of paranoia the paranoiac is clearly and completely out of touch with reality. Psychoanalysis however recognizes only differences of degree between normal and abnormal psychology. Unconscious processes are the same in all of us, and we all experience psychotic states when we dream. Just as the neurotic who enters analysis may be only a step away from the neurotic who would never think of such a thing, at the other end of the spectrum the borderline case in analysis may be only a step away from institutionalization. In a recent paper the American psychoanalyst John Frosch has proposed that the comparatively vague term "borderline" be replaced by the expression "psychotic character." Frosh derives his diagnostic category from the presence of "ill-defined psychotic-like features" in patients who are "not clinically psychotic." The idea acknowledges the often intermittent and short-lived nature of psychotic episodes in otherwise normal, or normally neurotic, people. In looking at the paranoid process in more detail then we should bear in mind that to whatever extreme it may appear to take the subject, it is never far from "normal" psychology.

V.
Burgin

Freud's first substantial discussion of paranoia is in his long paper of 1911, "Psycho-analytic notes on an autobiographical account of a case of paranoia (Dementia Paranoides)." The case is that of the German jurist Daniel Paul Schreber, who had the delusion that he had been chosen by God to restore the world to a lost state of bliss, and that in order to do this it was necessary that he be transformed into a woman in order that God might inseminate him. Schreber also believed that his doctor was conspiring against him to commit "soul-murder."[9] In an 1895 communication to Fliess, Freud had proposed that paranoia is one of the "neuroses of defense" and that its mechanism is projection. In letters to Ferenczi and Jung written thirteen years later (1908) Freud further hypothesized that the root of paranoia is in repressed passive homosexuality, a finding that both of his correspondents confirmed from their own case studies.[10] Freud finds that paranoia is to be defined in the *form* of the defense against the admission of homosexual desire. He writes: "It is a remarkable fact that the familiar principal forms of paranoia can all be represented as contradictions of the single proposition: 'I (a man) love him (a man),' and indeed that they exhaust all the possible ways in which such contradictions could be formulated."[11] The "principal forms of paranoia" of which Freud speaks are: delusions of *persecution*; *erotomania*; *delusional jealousy*; and *megalomania*. All are derived from the different ways in which the proposition "*I love him*" may be denied. In the case of persecutory paranoia it is the verb which is contradicted; that is to say the proposition "I love him" is denied in the form "I *hate* him." However, Freud writes: "the mechanism of symptom-formation in paranoia requires that internal perceptions—feelings—shall be replaced by external perceptions. Consequently the proposition 'I hate him' becomes transformed by *projection* into another one: '*He hates* (persecutes) *me*, which will justify me in hating him.' And thus the impelling unconscious feeling makes its appearance as though it were the consequence of an external perception."[12] In the case of erotomania, it is the object of the sentence which is contradicted: "I love him" becomes "I love *her*"; this in turn, through projection, becomes "*She* loves me," and "she" in return is loved with a vengeance. Delusional jealousy contradicts the subject: "I love him" becomes "*She* loves him." Here, Freud comments, "distortion by means of projection is necessarily absent . . . since, with the change of the subject who loves, the whole process is in any case thrown outside the self."[13] Finally, in megalomania, the basic proposition is denied in its entirety and becomes, "I do not love anyone"; but, "since, after all, one's libido must go somewhere, this proposition seems to be the psychological equivalent of the proposition: 'I love only myself.'"[14]

After Freud the next substantive contribution to the psychoanalytic description of psychosis came from the work of Melanie Klein. It is often observed that much as Freud discovered the child in the adult, so Klein found the infant in the child. Klein's primary innovation, apart from her therapeutic technique, was her description of the infant's internal "object" world.[15] We are familiar with such expressions as "a lump in the throat," or, "butterflies in the stomach"; we are also accustomed to hear that hunger "gnaws" at the stomach, or fear "grips" the heart. In these examples from ordinary language, bodily sensations are identified with actual entities, endowed with an agency of their own, either benevolent or malevolent. As adults we employ such metaphors without abandoning our knowledge of actual physiology. The infant however has no such knowledge, its primitive understanding of its own bodily feelings is its only reality. What we call "milk" the infant may experience, after feeding, as a benevolent object which emanates bliss. This object is destined to fade. Hunger will take its place—a malevolent agency, bringing destruction of the "good object," and pain. What Klein calls the "object," then, is the fantasmatic representation of the phenomenological form of the infant's earliest bodily experience, experience centered upon orality. In his book *The First Year of Life*, René Spitz emphasizes the primacy of the oral phase in human development, he writes, ". . . all perception begins in the oral cavity, which serves as the primeval bridge from inner reception to external perception."[16] Jean Laplanche observes that in these earliest months of life, "There is a sort of coalescence of the breast and the erogenous zone . . . the breast inhabits the lips or the buccal cavity." In Klein's description, this primitive oral world splits in the experience of loss of the breast. The "breast" here does not correspond to the anatomical organ but is the name given to that constellation of visual, tactile, kinæsthetic, auditory and olfactory memory-traces which serve as the psychical representatives of the experience of somatic satisfaction. From the physiological ingestion of the milk, then, we pass to the psychological incorporation of an "object." More specifically, as Laplanche emphasizes: "we pass from 'ingest' not to 'incorporate' but to the couple 'incorporate/be-incorporated' [for] . . . in this movement of metaphorization of the aim, the subject . . . loses its place: is it on the side this time of that which eats, or the side of that which is eaten?"[17] Devouring, being devoured: the violent poles of infantile experience often represented in the fantasies and play of small children, and in adult horror films. In her paper of 1935, "A Contribution to the Genesis of Manic-Depressive States," Klein writes: "quite little children pass through anxiety situations (and react to them with defense mechanisms), the content of which is comparable to that of the psychoses of adults."[18] In 1946, in "Notes on Some Schizoid Mechanisms," Klein named this stage of infantile development, belonging to the earliest months of life, the "paranoid-schizoid position." Klein's use of the term "position," as Juliet Mitchell notes, "facilitates the making of a connection between adult psychosis and infant development—a 'position' is an always available state, not something one passes through."[19]

Klein's work forms the essential backdrop to Lacan's paper on the "mirror stage." The concept is well-known to those familiar with critical theory. The mirror is not essential, any source of a simulacrum will do but the infant at the mirror makes the most engaging picture. Somewhere between the age of six and eighteen months it gets the idea that the image is of itself. It is as if the infant (*infans*, without speech), has found the means to acknowledge, "Yes, that's me, over there," and, says Lacan, it "jubilates" in its own reflection. Catherine Clément gives the most succinct definition of the mirror stage: "the moment when one becomes oneself because one is no longer the same as one's mother."[20] The imago of a unitary ego, Freud's "body-ego," has coalesced out of the primitive flux of the "body in pieces" in which, as Clément puts it, "[The infant's] body does not exist. It is a mere pile of parts. A piece of the mother's breast, a bit of skin, a fragment of shoulder, a part of a lip. It has no body of its own. At this early stage the child is a fragmented body, a violent body."[21] The mirror stage unifies these warring organic cantons and encloses them within a frontier: the psycho-corporeal equivalent of the nation state. The bounded identity assumed in the mirror stage however is an *identification*, an alienation in the image of the other: "that's me, *over there*." Moreover the infant's self-image is a self-idealization; as Lacan writes, it, "anticipates on the mental plane the conquest of the functional unity of [its] own body, which, at that stage, is still incomplete on the plane of voluntary motility."[22] In his paper of 1948, "Aggressivity in Psychoanalysis," Lacan speaks therefore of the "primary identification that structures the subject as a rival with himself."[23] Lacan's concept of the mirror stage was extensively informed by his early studies of adult psychotics. Lacan trained as a psychiatrist; his thesis, written while he was a resident in a psychiatric clinic and published in 1932, is titled "On Paranoid Psychosis in Relation to the Personality." The subject of the thesis is a woman Lacan refers to as "Aimée," who had attempted to stab a celebrated Parisian actress. Aimée's ambition was to be a famous writer; for Aimée the actress she attacked represented herself in the ideal form to which she aspired. Aimée had never quite drawn the line between herself and her mother, whom she never ceased to idealize. After the mother's death, Aimée displaced her feelings towards her onto a series of substitute female figures. The actress, the last in line of these, finally received the aggression which Aimée had never allowed herself to feel towards her ego-ideal, that composite figure in which her narcissism fused with her identification with her mother. More accurately: she had felt hostility but had refused to symbolize it. Refused access to the word, the aggression returned in the deed, in what psychoanalysis calls "acting out." In his thesis Lacan wrote: "In the form of her victim Aimée struck the exteriorization of her ideal, as the perpetrator of a crime of jealous passion strikes the unique object of her hatred and her love."[24] In the year following the publication of his thesis Lacan contributed an essay to the Surrealist journal *Minotaure* called "Motifs of the Paranoid Crime (The Crime of the Papin Sisters)."[25] Léa and Christine Papin were domestic servants who for six years, in the words of the Surrealists Paul Eluard and Benjamin Péret, ". . . endured, with the most perfect submission, commands, demands, insults," until the day they, "literally massacred their employers, tearing out their eyes and crushing their heads."[26] Léa and Christine Papin were twins who had never really come to distinguish themselves from each other. The only other inhabitants of the house in which they lived were the mother and daughter couple they served as maids. As Catherine Clément comments, "Christine had been so close to Léa that she could only project her hatred along with Léa onto another female couple. Aimée, on the other hand, would take some time to work out the amorous hatred that she secretly bore toward her alter ego, and the forms taken by the fantasies derived from this hatred became increasingly remote from their original object."[27]

Aimée was inseparable from her mother. Christine and Léa Papin were similarly inseparable. Clément reports that one of the women to whom Aimée subsequently became attached had the opinion that Aimée was "masculine." Christine said she was certain that in another life she was intended to be Léa's husband. We will recall that Freud found the cause of paranoia in repressed homosexuality. According to his own findings however all heterosexuals necessarily harbor a repressed homosexual component of their sexuality—but not all of them become paranoid as a result. There is another problem in Freud's account. He says that the characteristic mechanism of paranoia is projection, but the case of Schreber leads him to explicitly question his previous ideas about the functioning of this mechanism. He writes: "It was incorrect to say that the perception which was suppressed internally is projected outward; the truth is rather, as we now see, that what was abolished internally returns from without."[28] As Lacan is later to express it, in his own terms, "what has been foreclosed from the Symbolic reappears in the Real." The concept of foreclosure represents Lacan's summary of Freud's attempts to describe a defense mechanism specific to psychosis. The foreclosed element has never gained access to the discourse of the subject; it can therefore be neither repressed nor projected. When the foreclosed element "returns" it returns not to the symbolic but to the real, in the form of a delusion or hallucination. Freud found paranoiacs to be "people who have not freed themselves completely from the stage of narcissism." In Lacan's account the paranoiac is fixated at the the narcissistic mirror stage, the pre-oedipal stage of the ego-ideal. This fixation will entail the foreclosure of sexual difference. Freud's use of the term "homosexuality" presupposes a subject who has knowledge of sexual difference and is therefore certain of his or her sexual identity. In the paranoid episode, however, the subject regresses to a stage where there is no such certainty. The apparently homosexual object choice in paranoia therefore is an epiphenomenon of the auto-erotism of this stage. In 1953 Schreber's translators, Ida Macalpine and Richard Hunter, published a paper in which they explicitly rejected the idea that the repression of homosexuality is at the origin of paranoia.[29] Lacan writes of Macalpine, "Her critique of the cliché . . . is masterly . . . Homosexuality, supposedly a determinant of paranoiac psychosis, is really a symptom articulated in its process."[30]

Paranoiacs do not clearly differentiate themselves from other people and things. Their speech does not coincide with their identity, they speak as if they were an other, or simply an object in a world of objects. They have lost the illusory but necessary sense of transcendence which would allow them to position themselves at the center of their own space. In her essay, "Space, Time and Bodies," Elizabeth Grosz writes: "It is our positioning within space, both as the point of perspectival access to space, but also as an object for others in space, that gives the subject any coherent identity." The matrix of space is the body. Grosz continues: "The subject's relation to its own body provides it with basic spatial concepts and terms by which it can reflect on its own position. Form and size, direction, centeredness (centricity), location, dimension and orientation are derived from the perceptual relation the subject has to and in space."[31] Subjectivity "takes place" in corporeal space. "The ego," says Freud, is, "a mental projection of the surface of the body." The psychical representations of the body and the space it inhabits first form under the anarchic hegemony of the drives. The unitary body does not yet exist, there is only the borderless space of the body in fragments described by Klein. If we want a picture of this space, Lacan suggests: "We must turn to the works of Hieronymous Bosch for an atlas of all the aggressive images that torment mankind."[32] In the mirror stage the child anticipates its future coherence in an act of identification. However, as Edith Jacobson expresses it, such early identifications are founded on: "fusions of self and object images which disregard the realistic differences between the self and the object. They will find expression in illusory fantasies of the child that he is part of the object or can become the object by pretending to be or behaving as if he were it. Temporary and reversible in small children, such ideas in psychotics may turn into fixated, delusional convictions."[33] In psychosis boundaries fail, frontiers are breached. In psychotic space an external object—a whole, a part, or an attribute of a person or thing—may be experienced as if it had invaded the subject. In his *Memoirs Of My Nervous Illness*, Schreber writes: "From the first beginnings of my contact with God . . . hardly a single limb or organ in my body escaped being temporarily damaged by miracles . . . my lungs were for a long time the object of violent and very threatening attacks . . . the *gullet* and the *intestines* . . . were torn or vanished repeatedly."[34] The sense of being invaded may be projected onto some larger screen than that of the psychotic's own body; the threat may be seen as directed against some greater body with which the psychotic identifies: for example, the "body-politic" of nation, or race. Psychosis, moreover, may be infectious. Speaking of the trial of the Papin sisters, Lacan remarks: "One has heard in the course of the debates the astonishing affirmation that it was impossible that two beings should both be struck, together, by the same madness . . . This is a completely false affirmation. Joint deliriums (*les délires à deux*) are amongst the most ancient of known forms of psychosis."[35] In the age of the intimate address of the national imago to its counterpart before a television screen, the *folie à deux* may take on national proportions.

The same logic which generates the opposition "exile"/"nation" across national frontiers, may oppose one racial group to another within national borders. History has familiarized us with the insidious movement in which "nation" is confused with "race." Institutionalized racism may ensure that racial minorities live in a condition of internal exile within the nation of which they are citizens—an exile which, if it is not legal, cannot be named. Roland Barthes once defined the bourgeoisie as "the social class which does not want to be named." He wrote, "Politically, the hemorrhage of the name 'bourgeois' is effected through the idea of *nation* . . . today the bourgeoisie merges into the nation."[36] By refusing to be named the bourgeois class represents itself and its interests as a universal norm, from which anything else is a deviation. In the West the Caucasian race has in effect "ex-nominated" itself in the word "White."

Whether or not there is any scientific justification for Blumenbach's term "Caucasian" it does at least have the advantage of simply naming one racial category amongst others. "White" however has the strange property of directing our attention to color while in the very same movement it ex-nominates itself *as* a color. For evidence of this we need look no further than to the expression "people of color," for we know very well that this means "not White." We know equally well that the color white is the higher power to which all colors of the spectrum are subsumed when equally combined: white is the sum totality of light, while black is the total absence of light. In this way elementary optical physics is recruited to the psychotic metaphysics of racism, in which White is "all" to Black's "nothing"—as in the attitude of those white colonialists Hélène Cixous speaks of, who live in a country they have stolen "as if the eyes of their souls had been put out."[37] To speak of the color of skin is to speak of a body. "People of color" are embodied people. To have no color is to have no body. The body denied here however is a very particular body, it is the abject body: the body that defecates, vomits and bleeds; the entropic body that dies. In Kristeva's account, infantile abjection of the maternal body is the irreducible imperative which impels any subject whatsoever towards its necessary identity. Abjection, establishing the first line of demarcation, is the zero degree of identity; as inevitable as it is beyond reason, it cannot be explained. The paranoid racist subject, seeking to take its place on the "clean and proper" side of abjection, has refused to symbolize the abject within itself. It has foreclosed its abject body only to have this body return to it in the form of the "dirty Jew," the "dirty Italian" . . . and "people of color"—or as an American colleague once said to me about the English, "They're a people who think their shit doesn't smell."

I have noted the tendency for "nation" to be confused with "race." Nazism is the most horrific example, but there are many others. At the end of the First World War, the armies of each of the Allied Nations marched in a Victory Parade in the Champs Elysées. The Harlem Hellfighters were a battalion of Black American soldiers. Highly decorated, they served longer than any other American unit and were the first Allied unit to reach the Rhine. They were not allowed to march in the Victory Parade.[38] Clearly it was felt that there would be something wrong with the picture of America that this would present. In *The Four Fundamental Concepts of Psycho-Analysis*, Jacques Lacan tells an anecdote about a day when he, "a young intellectual," was out in a small boat with "a few people from a family of fishermen." As they were waiting for the moment to pull in the nets, one of the fishermen pointed out to Lacan something floating toward them on the waves. It was a sardine can, glittering in the sun. "You see that can?," said the fisherman, "Well, it doesn't see you!" The fisherman found the incident highly amusing, Lacan "less so." Searching for the reason for his discomfort, it occurred to Lacan that "in a sense" the can *was* looking at him, and that from the can's point of view—that is to say, from the position represented by the reflected point of light—Lacan "looked like nothing on earth . . . rather out of place in the picture."[39] A young bourgeois among workers, we might say, "his face didn't fit." On an afternoon in November of 1988, Karen Wood, a White woman from Binghamton, New York, was killed by a rifle bullet as she stood in the backyard of her new home in Bangor, Maine. The man who shot her was a local hunter, who said he believed he had seen a deer. According to an article in *The New York Times*[40] the man was obviously criminally negligent, in clear contravention of Maine laws governing hunting, and liable in Maine law to prosecution for manslaughter. However, he was not prosecuted. The *Bangor Daily News*, referring to the shooting as "a double-tragedy," reflected overwhelming local sympathy for the man. The newspaper criticized the victim for wearing white gloves in her garden, as these may have made the man think he saw a white-tailed deer. Another local journalist wrote that if Karen Wood "had been wearing one piece of blaze-orange clothing, she'd be alive today." The consensus expressed in readers' letters to local newspapers was that "out-of-staters ought to learn a thing or two about Maine's traditional way of life." On a night in August of 1989, Yusuf K. Hawkins, a Black teen-ager, was shot to death by White teen-agers as he was on his way to look at a second-hand car in the

Bensonhurst section of Brooklyn. Hawkins was from a mainly Black neighborhood of the East New York section of Brooklyn; Bensonhurst is predominantly White. *New York Times* journalists noted that many Bensonhurst residents expressed sympathy for the killers, reporting a White teen-age girl on the scene as telling them, "The black people don't belong here. This is our neighborhood."[41] A racist decision by the military; an unkind joke; a tragic accident; a vicious murder. Certainly, it makes no sense in common sense to juxtapose these incidents. Nevertheless each incident may be seen as exemplifying the more or less aggressive defense of a space perceived as violated by an invader. Common sense, reason, is not at issue. What a situation may be in reality is quite simply disregarded by unconscious processes. Speaking of Aimée, Clément remarked, "the forms taken by the fantasies derived from [her] hatred became increasingly remote from their original object." Psychical space may have much the same relation to real space that the dream has. In another *New York Times* story I read of two communities in the town of Malverne, New York: one mostly Black, the other mainly White. The Times reporter writes, "The two are divided by Ocean Avenue, and residents on both sides refer to the other as "over the ocean."[42] In this example, and in the extreme case, the clinically paranoid person would quite simply *see* an ocean, in a less marked paranoid attitude the subject would behave exactly *as if* there were an ocean—with all the absolute territorial imperatives, all the patriotic moral fervor attached to the defense of the motherland, that this could invoke.

Moral fervor is frequently a characteristic of racism, and the morality is generally sexual. There has been no more strident call to White racist arms than that of the "defense" of White women. The mobilizing fantasy image of this particular racist discourse is that of the sexual penetration of a body. The image seems to be one of invasion, the fantasy seems to be paranoid. We should however distinguish between two forms of the perceived threat: rape and seduction. One is invasive, the other is not. Even in the former case the structure seems neurotic rather than psychotic, seems more likely to involve repression rather than foreclosure. The White male racist who fantasizes a White woman's rape by a Black man might be seen as defending himself against his own aggressive sexual impulses. He represses the fantasy in which he himself is a rapist; the emotional investment in the unconscious fantasy forces it back into consciousness but now in an acceptable disguise: the rapist is identified as Black, absolving the subject of the fantasy of any culpability in the imaginary crime. Moreover the violence of the fantasy, as it may now lay claim to moral justification, can be unleashed in its full force ("projection" here may take on a deadly physical materiality). The racist's fear that the White woman may be seduced by the Black man however suggests delusional jealousy—a paranoid, rather than neurotic, symptom. It is the inverted form of his fear that the woman will actively seduce the man. Which in turn is derived from the White's jealous envy of the Black, an unconscious envy untouched by statistics on unemployment or death rates. As a small child at school, in the late 1940s in the industrial North of England, I was told that there were three types of people in the world: those who lived in very cold climates, those who lived in very hot climates, and those like ourselves who lived in temperate climates. The people in cold climates had to work so hard just to stay alive that they never had time to create things, as a consequence they had no civilization. Those who lived in hot climates on the other hand were so well provided for by nature that they never had to work at all, they ate the fruits which fell into their laps and enjoyed their leisure. Needless to say, they had no civilization either. People in temperate climates however, people like us, had to work hard to feed themselves, but not so hard that they never had time to work at other things. That was why people like us had created civilization. I distinctly remember the envy I felt towards the people of the hot climates. It was a guilty feeling, as I knew I was supposed to feel proud to be a temperate and civilized person. Today I see that my teacher had communicated his own unconscious envy and guilt to me; it cannot have been much fun being a school teacher in a working-class neighborhood of a bomb-ruined steel town in austere post-war Britain. The Garden of Eden my teacher created for the people of the hot climates, the people "over the ocean," was a Garden of Earthly Delights: a paradise where pleasure came as easily as the fruit on the trees, and one never lost one's appetite. Jealous envy is an unavoidable component of our relation to the other, the one who is different, who knows something we do not, who experiences things we shall never know. There is always something we want, and it is easy to believe that the other has it. In Spike Lee's film, *Do The Right Thing*, Mookie, the Black employee of "Sal's Famous Pizzeria," has the following exchange with Pino, Sal's White racist son:

> Mookie: Who's your favorite basketball player?
> Pino: Magic Johnson
> Mookie: And not Larry Bird? Who's your favorite movie star?
> Pino: Eddie Murphy
> Mookie: Last question: Who's your favorite rock star?
> *Pino doesn't answer.*
> Mookie: Barry Manilow?
> *Pino's brother Vito supplies the answer.*
> Vito: It's Prince. He's a Prince freak
> Mookie: Sounds funny to me. As much as you say nigger this and nigger that, all your favorite people are "niggers"
> Pino: Its different. Magic, Eddie, Prince are not niggers, I mean, are not Black. I mean they're Black but not really Black. They're more than Black. It's different.
> Mookie: Pino, I think secretly that you wish you were Black. That's what I think.[43]

Mookie has spotted Pino's envy. The exchange might have taken place in an analysis, albeit Mookie's technique would probably be judged overly interventionist. But if Pino has now accepted his admiration of Black achievements why is it that his racism remains intact? As already noted, from infancy onwards the formation of an identity takes place through a series of identifications with others, alienated "ego-ideal" models "to which the subject attempts to conform."[44] The mirror stage shows us the primacy of the visual image in this process. Our media-saturated environment provides an almost limitless choice of images which may serve to represent the "ego-ideal." Just as Aimée identified with a series of women celebrities, Pino identifies with a chain of literally spectacular Black men—"magic" and "princely" men who would not be found sweeping the sidewalk in front of a pizzeria (one of the unheroic tasks assigned to Pino by his father). As passive spectator to his Black heroes' media-amplified activity Pino has adopted a "feminine" attitude. In order to fully assimilate his self-image to the model of his ego-ideals, and to regain the aggressively "masculine" identity required of a young man of his class and ethnic background, he must foreclose their difference from him, of which Blackness is the privileged signifier. Blackness, foreclosed in the symbolic, returns in the real as the defining attribute of his persecutory bad object, the "nigger." Pino's racism then, far from being expunged by his love for Black entertainers will only intensify, for his hostility draws its strength from his jealous admiration.[45]

This is not to "psychoanalyze" Pino; that would be preposterous. By definition, a psychoanalysis entails a proper clinical setting in which an adequately experienced analyst gains access to a wide range of detailed materials over a long period of time. This is rather an instrumental use of psychoanalytic theory. I began with a now familiar situation in which someone writing in the area of critical theory of culture—"cultural studies"—uses psychoanalytic terminology in a text from which psychoanalytic theory is, in any substantive sense, absent. The recourse to such terms is nevertheless meaningful. In Said's text I saw the use of the term "paranoia" as marking the place of a caesura between personal anecdote and political discourse. Taking Said at his word I have begun to look at nationalism, at racism, *as if* they might indeed be paranoid structures. Psychoanalytic theory here functions as a heuristic device, a means to reinscribe a *space between* positions which have become frozen in opposition.[46] There are good reasons why debates over nationalism and racism are emotive, consequently they often generate more heat than light. We cannot afford to dispense with any source of illumination by which we may examine the images—real and fantasmatic—across which we construct our conflict-ridden identities. The conflict which flares into violence in Spike Lee's film is precisely over images, identities. On the walls of Sal's Famous Pizzeria are photographs of Italian-American celebrities. Buggin' Out wants to see some Black faces on this wall of fame. Sal defends his own sovereign space. In this territorial dispute however neither party may claim original rights. When the sons of émigré Italians confront the descendants of abducted Africans in Sal's Pizzeria they do so in a Black and Hispanic district with a Dutch name, which was stolen from Native Americans. Most of us know the melancholy tension of separation from our origins. Said defines exile as a "condition of terminal loss." Kristeva chooses a more painful image to express this loss: she sees exile as the "cosmopolitanism of the excoriated." Excoriation, the loss of one's skin: violent image of the destruction of that first and last barrier between the ego and paranoiac space.

Notes

This paper was originally presented in the context of the conference Displacements, Migrations, Identities, *held at the Center for Cultural Studies, University of California, Santa Cruz, Spring, 1990.*

1.   Edward Said, "Reflections on Exile," *Granta*, 161.

2.   *Ibid.*, 162.

3.   *Ibid.*, 162.

4.   Indeed, in what Freud termed the "compulsion to repeat" the subject repeats what it does not remember precisely in order to avoid bringing it to consciousness.

5.   Julia Kristeva, *Etrangers à nous-mêmes* (Fayard, 1988), 25.

6.   See Paul Virilio, *L'Espace Critique* (Paris: Christian Bourgois, 1984).

7.   The word "psychosis" was introduced into medical psychology by Feuchtersleben in 1845. See Ida Macalpine and Richard Hunter, introduction (1955) to Daniel Paul Schreber, *Memoirs Of My Nervous Illness* (Harvard, 1988), 24–25.

8.   Peter Buckley, ed., *Essential Papers on Psychosis* (New York University, 1988).

9.   William G. Niederland reports that, "the expression 'soul murder' is used by Strindberg, whose essay 'Själamord' (Soul Murder), originally published in France in 1887, also appeared later in the Swedish and German literature." It is possible that Schreber was familiar with Strindberg's essay. See William G. Niederland, *The Schreber Case* (New York Times Books, 1974), 28, n. 2.

10.   In his essay on Schreber of 1911, Freud writes: "we are . . . driven by experience to attribute to homosexual wishful phantasies an intimate . . . relation to this particular form of disease. Distrusting my own experience on the subject, I have during the last few years joined with my friends C. G. Jung of Zurich and Sándor Ferenczi of Budapest in investigating upon this single point a number of cases of paranoid disorder which have come under observation. The patients whose histories provided material for this enquiry included both men and women, and varied in race, occupation, and social standing. Yet we were astonished to find that in all of these cases a defense against a homosexual wish was clearly recognizable at the very center of the conflict which underlay the disease."

11.   Sigmund Freud, "Psycho-analytic notes on an autobiographical account of a case of paranoia (Dementia Paranoides)" (1911), in *The Standard Edition of the Complete Psychological Works of Sigmund Freud*, Vol. XII (London: Hogarth, 1955), 74, 63.

12.   *Ibid.*, 63.

13.   *Ibid.*, 64.

14.   *Ibid.*, 65.

15.   See Jean Laplanche and Jean-Bertrand Pontalis, "Fantasy and the Origins of Sexuality," in Victor Burgin, James Donald and Cora Kaplan, eds., *Formations of Fantasy* (Methuen, 1986).

16.   René A. Spitz, *The First Year of Life* (New York: IUP, 1965), 62.

17.   Jean Laplanche, *La sublimation*, (Paris: Presses Universitaire de France, 1980), 62.

18.   Juliet Mitchell, *The Selected Melanie Klein* (Free Press, 1987), 116–17.

19.   *Ibid.*, 116.

20. Catherine Clément, *The Lives and Legends of Jacques Lacan* (Columbia, 1983), 76.

21. *Ibid.*, 90.

22. Jacques Lacan, "Aggressivity in Psychoanalysis," in *Ecrits: A Selection* (Norton, 1977), 18.

23. *Ibid.*, 22.

24. Quoted in Elisabeth Roudinesco, *Histoire de la psychanalyse en France*. 2, (Seuil, 1986), 128–9.

25. Jacques Lacan, "Motifs du Crime Paranoïaque (Le Crime des Soeurs Papin)," *Minotaure* 3, (15 Décembre 1933). [Lacan's first presentation of the idea of the mirror stage was in 1936.]

26. *Le Surréalisme au Service de la Révolution* 5. (1933), 28.

27. Catherine Clément, *The Lives and Legends of Jacques Lacan* (Columbia, 1983), 74.

28 Sigmund Freud, "Psycho-analytic notes on an autobiographical account of a case of paranoia (Dementia Paranoides)" (1911), in *The Standard Edition of the Complete Psychological Works of Sigmund Freud*, Vol. XII (London: Hogarth, 1955), 74, 71.

29. In their 1955 introduction to the English translation of Schreber's *Memoirs Of My Nervous Illness*, Macalpine and Hunter write, "We showed that projection of unconscious homosexuality, though playing a part in the symptomatology, could not account for the illness . . . ætiologically. [Schreber] . . . showed what we have come to regard as the two pathognomonic features of schizophrenia: doubt and uncertainty in sex identity . . . If such confusion about sex identity is termed homosexuality then of course schizophrenic 'homosexuality' is of a different order [from that] implied in Freud's use of the term. This last presupposes certainty in one's sex identity which Schreber had so obviously lost from the beginning of his illness."

30. Jacques Lacan, "On a question preliminary to any possible treatment of psychosis," in *Ecrits: A Selection* (Norton, 1977), 190.

31. Elizabeth Grosz, "Space, Time and Bodies," in *On The Beach* (Sydney: 13 April 1988).

32. Jacques Lacan, "Aggressivity in Psychoanalysis," in *Ecrits: A Selection* (Norton, 1977), 11.

33. Edith Jacobson, *The Self and the Object World* (International Universities Press, 1964), 47.

34. Daniel Paul Schreber, *Memoirs Of My Nervous Illness* (Harvard, 1988), 131–34.

35. Jacques Lacan, "Motifs du Crime Paranoïaque (Le Crime des Soeurs Papin)," *Minotaure* 3, (15 décembre 1933), 27.

36. Roland Barthes, "Myth Today," in *Mythologies* (Hill and Wang), 138.

37. Hélène Cixous, "Sorties," in *The Newly Born Woman* (University of Minnesota, 1986), 70. I offer the following as a depressingly typical example of the ordinary racism inscribed in everyday connotations of the black/white opposition: "black usually indicates death, misfortune or evil, or simply opposition to white's yielding and acceptance and purity." James Stockton, *Designer's Guide to Color* (San Francisco: Chronicle, 1984).

38. See Phyllis Rose, *Black Cleopatra: Josephine Baker in Her Time* (Doubleday, 1989), 67.

39. Jacques Lacan, *The Four Fundamental Concepts of Psycho-Analysis* (Hogarth, 1977), 95–96.

40. *New York Times Magazine* (Sunday, 10 September 1989).

41. *New York Times*, (Friday, 29 August 1989).

42. *New York Times*, (Tuesday, 19 December).

43. See Spike Lee, "Do The Right Thing" (script), in Spike Lee with Lisa Jones, *Do The Right Thing* (Simon & Schuster, 1989), 184–85.

44. Laplanche and Pontalis, *The Language of Psycho-Analysis* (Hogarth, 1973), 144.

45. We may recall that Schreber similarly "split" his object: turning his doctor both into a God, in order that he might adopt a feminine attitude towards him without conflict, and also into a hated "soul murderer," so that he might be protected from acknowledging the homosexual nature of his own feelings.

46. I have appropriated (or misappropriated) the idea of "reinscription" in the space of the "caesura" from Homi Bhabha. ["Postcolonial authority and postmodern guilt," unpublished paper, 1990.]

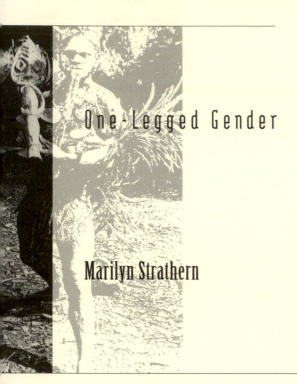

One-Legged Gender

Marilyn Strathern

Among the several contributions to the Hansons' recent book on art and identity in Oceania (1990), three have prompted the present exercise. One is Schwimmer's reminder that Lévi-Strauss referred to art as miniaturization; the second is the Hansons' brief reference to Maori figures which, posted at door lintels, appear to recompose body features into new forms; and the third an essay by Smidt on "one-legged" figures from the Middle Ramu (Kominimung) area of Papua New Guinea. This last is a rather odd but nonetheless evident presentation of bodily form—he records the spontaneous gesture of a man who turned himself into a one-legged figure to show Smidt what it all meant.

Among the challenges that Papua New Guinean and other Melanesian cultures present to visual interpretation, people's play on form has also prompted the present exercise. Smidt's

Papua New Guinean demonstrator dressed up the part with considerable flamboyance, stuffing the end of an elongated apron into his mouth and jabbing at an unseen novice with the one-legged figure in his hands. This was a display. A tension that runs through Melanesian display is the tension between what is concealed and what is revealed. The invitation to "see" is an invitation to witness the appearance of a specific form, and to have in that sense elicited it. The individual witness is inevitably placed by the performer, then, into the position of seeing only what is revealed. It is as though the witness "sees" one side of the performer. Indeed, in the tales people in the Papua New Guinea Highlands sometimes tell, one-sided creatures, with back but no front, or with one eye rather than two, occasionally flit across human vision.

Among the many refinements of analytical pleasure that inspire the present wave of anthropological interest in aesthetics, we should not forget that vision is embodied. In that case, in what kinds of bodies are the eyes set? I ask the question as a commentary on modernist assumptions that run through the best efforts to avoid the traps of representationalism and constructionism.

It is no good simply putting the endless sophistication of knowing displacement in the place of authoritative modeling nor, indeed, complaining about the disembodiment of knowledge while imagining that all that is at issue is greater reflexivity. Nichols (1991: 34) refers to the body blindness which afflicts depersonalized film narration. It is an insistence on embodiment that marks certain feminist quests. Sometimes, though, the discourse on the embodiment of vision seems to share with rather than obviate earlier representationalist obsession with uncovering facts about the world. Embodiment is brought from under the text—a hidden influence is made explicit, and analysis invites us to see what we did not see before. So such appeals to vision often serve as metaphors for greater awareness. What in that case does the anthropologist do in the face of deliberate provocations to vision? The question would be particularly acute when s/he in being shown something is also being forced to see with one eye only—insofar as vision itself is, in the context of Melanesian display, rendered one-eyed.[1]

I focus on the effects of particular kinds of displays, such as accompanying initiation practices or ceremonial exchange, though I suspect the point could hold more generally across Melanesian social life. Display always selects out of multiple possibilities the one made evident, and one only ever sees what is displayed. What is hidden is deliberately hidden, yet the secret may also be trivial: with the other eye one would simply see the other side. That fact about vision is only ever made evident through embodiment. As a consequence, there is nothing in this visual play to be "uncovered" about embodiment, since the body is the medium—and deliberately incomplete.

So what is this one-sided body that is imagined as the only kind of body that can be seen because it is the body that elicits vision? It is a personified body: a person only sees such a form as the outcome of relationships with others. It is also a gendered body: a man or woman only sees it as male or female.

One-Legged

One postulate of feminist critique is that it is a mistake to imagine we know what a body is when we see one. Much effort has gone into denaturing the received "body" of Euro-American discourse, and what is thus brought to view is the trivialization or the aggrandizement of sexual identity (the effort is how to get "between" gender obsession and gender blindness). But in denaturing the gender of he body perhaps we ought also to denature body composition. I mean the arrangement of torso, limbs, and organs. However labile contemporary analytic strategies appear to be in seeing or not seeing gender, their conclusions may already be compromised by modernist and Euro-American naturalizations that locate a principal source of sexual difference in one part of the body. Sexual symbols tend to be interpreted as phallic or vulvic/uterine before they are interpreted as anything else. The problem is not that Euro-Americans cannot imagine almost any part of the body as genitalized, but that it tends to be only the genitals that migrate in their imagination. Melanesians present gender through refigurations of which genitalia are only a part—limbs, organs and insides, including the eye, may all migrate. That figuration can as much be created between persons as made manifest in one.

It was sheer inspiration on Smidt's (1990) part to call the Kominimung figures "one-legged." However, I suspect that it was for naturalistic and compositional reasons: these carved wooden figures with a head and torso from which extends a single limb/organ could be stood upright as though this extension were its (single) leg. In any case, the carver whose activities Smidt followed seems to have supported his inference, dividing the carving into head, torso and leg.

Fig. 1. An informal demonstration of how one-legged figures are used to prod initiates on the back.

But, then, as Forge (1966) observed of the Abelam men's house, it is alright to infer that the ridge pole of a house is being treated as though it were a phallus, but what is a phallus? We might ask what a leg is.

In another context, Forge comments on the fact that "art" is supposed to have an effect. "One of the main functions of the [Abelam] initiation system with its repetitive exposure of initiates to quantities of art is, I would suggest, to teach the young men to see the art, not so that he may consciously interpret it but so that he is directly affected by it" (1970: 290). The enthusiastic Kominimung who showed Smidt what the "one-legged" figures meant was showing him what they could *do*. These wooden figures kicked. At one point in the course of male initiation, novices are rounded up and prodded with them. Smidt has an illustrative photograph (Fig. 1) of a man in ordinary dress jabbing such a figure—"leg" extended—at the back of a pretend novice. The figure held by one strikes the other. On the following page is the photograph (Fig. 2) of the enthusiast who dressed up, his own two legs firmly planted wide apart. Among other decorations, on his chest is a string bag with female breasts; nipples are also painted on the wooden figure. In this guise, the performer makes visible a powerful *tambaran* (ancestral spirit) as does the wooden figure itself. The figure is held in alignment with the man's head and chest, projecting downward and out. Indeed, the photograph draws attention to the way that the gesture is, so to speak, repeated in the long, narrow apron that forms a loop between the legs and is drawn up into the man's mouth. Visually, however, there is no direction to this wrapping—it could as well be coming from the mouth as entering it. In the same way, the figure that is held by a body also finds its mark on a body: the novice presents his back (novices may be beaten on the back or chest, but archetypically the back) to be kicked. So the figure in effect points in either direction, from the body that projects it and from the body that invites it.

Elsewhere in the same volume, the Hansons (1990) draw on an analysis offered by Jackson (1972) to make a point about the otherwise awkward composition of Maori lintel carvings over house doorways. What is disjoined is then conjoined in a new juxtaposition of elements. The body is thereby reassembled in the same way as the person entering and coming from the house is redefined by his or her actions. Such decomposition and recomposition "may be taken to represent the individual's dual roles in society—as a tribal, public figure and as a domestic, private figure" (1990: 192). In the Maori case, the body is recreated within the confined space of the structure of the door.[2] If the Melanesian example from Kominimung is also the recreation of a body, there is no such architectural confinement. Yet the one-legged figure, protruding from the head/chest or jabbed at the back, is not extended into space either. Rather, it is specifically aimed at another. *More than one person is required for this recomposition.* I infer that the composition is of relationships, and that the relationships contain and create an internal difference: initiator and novice are differentiated by the kicking act.

If novice and initiator are to naturalistic eyes evidently two persons, I want to suggest that the duo exists also within the one. The man who holds up the one-leg parallel to his body is paired with it, in the sense that both present *tambaran* to the novice. Yet while Euro-Americans would have little trouble in considering the man

Fig. 2. An initiation dancer with a one-legged figure.

and his wooden figure as a pair of sorts, they might less easily see that the wooden figure itself, with its own head and torso and the organ that extends from it, is also a set of relationships. But in fact any singular figure is already a composite. The man who grips his penis-covering between his teeth conveys that. Like the ancestral monsters that elsewhere in Papua New Guinea may appear alternately as swallowing and as regurgitating (initiates), persons cannot act—on themselves or on others—without instantiating the difference between them.

If the differentiation of persons here follows the Melanesian aesthetic of gender, then are these not single-sex but androgynous figures? (The performers, as Smidt remarks (1990: 34), show both male and female elements in their dress.) Indeed, there is a sense in which all objects are androgynous (cf. Mackenzie 1991) insofar as their personification requires that they are composed.[3] I suspect that Kominimung novices and initiators are gendered by the *actions* that one does to another, just as the penis-swallower/child-regurgitator recapitulates the gendering of any extensive activity.

It is thoroughly consonant with what is known from other parts of Papua New Guinea to suggest that extensive activity itself may be imagined in terms of receiving sexual attention or giving birth—including relations between partners in gift exchange who may stand momentarily male and female to each other. I say "extensive" insofar as one body takes in/brings forth another body. Together, the bodies form a single androgynous figure; insofar as the capacity to form such a figure is also present in the singular body, that body is inevitably androgynous as well. It does not matter how many people you see: each is a composition of persons.

But you do not see the composition. That is, as a witness you do not see both genders at the same time; you only ever "see" one, because that is what being made to see means. Let me explain the observation.

Look at the novice. The novice may eventually equate himself with the man holding the one-leg, for he is being made into the kind of man who can do exactly that to novices. At the end of the initiation sequence where the former initiate has been transformed into a marriageable person, he now appears decorated "in the same fashion as the one-legged figures and the *tambaran* performers" (Smidt 1990: 31). But at the moment of impact, the novice-initiate is in one position only. He sees, that is, "feels" the jab, is receptive to it, and can only be receptive. He is the "other side" of what one-leg can do. The recipient who feels one-leg, in feeling it gives it "back" to the man who is jabbing it at him. The novice is in this sense a spectator. He responds to what he is shown.

The Kominimung who dressed up to display to Smidt what a man holding a one-leg looks like might imagine he was putting the spectator into a recipient position, as though the camera could respond. Now in being on one side, the spectator can only ever see the "other" one side that is being presented: s/he does not see her or himself, for s/he is coerced (like the novice) into having the sight (a view) of someone else. What the spectators see is an androgynous figure in a single-sex form. Smidt infers that the one-legged figures connote male fertility. This is the male side: the men create a male version of a figure composed of both male and female elements.

So what you see in this photograph is an all-male version of a figure that in its composition is androgynous. But you are not meant to see the composition, for it is *out of* composite relations that the singular form-to-be-seen comes. And since it is the spectator who elicits the appearance of the singular form, the spectator is part of the composition that is not available to sight.

So what is a leg? Perhaps the leg in the one-legged Kominimung figures is an extended body. It is both organ and product, we might say, just like the shells that circulate in exchange in the Papua New Guinea Highlands. And the extension that is both body and organ product may be perceived as belonging to and coming from a body that is either male or female. For to be in an extended state means that in being detached from one body the organ/ product is taken into another. Unextended, it remains part of an androgynous composition that cannot itself be felt or seen. With its potential extension in mind, people may say it is still "hidden."

Gender

The accompanying photograph (Fig. 3) was taken in 1964 in Hagen, in the Papua New Guinea Highlands. There is hardly a woman in sight, though several were present. However, the products of women are evident: the children (including the little girl at the far end of the

Fig. 3.

line who glances in the photographer's direction), the Goldlip pearl shells laid out in front of the men's house, many of which will have come to the men via their connections through women, and the empty pig stakes to which women's pigs will be attached. If children and pigs are acknowledged extensions of women, so too are the men themselves. Every one of them is a mother's son, and on some occasion in their lives will have acknowledged the fact in gifts to matrilateral kin.

None of this was in the photographer's mind. She was too preoccupied with the sequence of events. (The shells were still being laid out, and she had turned back from the main bustle of activity to view the line that already existed.) It was the first public *moka* (ceremonial exchange) she had witnessed. Subsequently she would be aware of the fact that shells circulate exclusively among men and never come into the care of women except only in the most notional way; she would know that the men's house at the head of the ceremonial ground is an all-male preserve; that although the men have not decorated elaborately for this occasion they sport the long bamboo tallies (*omak*) which indicate their successes at earlier exchanges, and that the discussion and calculating going on would be about the kind of politics with which men are preoccupied (the occasion was a compensation payment between the clans of two tribes [from Kawelka to Roklaka, see A. Strathern 1971: 124]). But in any event, the photographer probably took it for granted that she was seeing an all-male affair. Retrospectively, the fact that women hardly appeared in the photograph indicated a kind of truth, for women were effectively excluded from active roles in shell exchange.

This particular event was a relatively small version of what is played out on a much larger scale at displays that demand formal decoration. On such occasions, the appropriation of public space by men, and when pigs are involved, of women's products, may be made evident by women's participation as "producers." But they have produced the objects, so to speak, not the performance: that is men's creation.

Yet suppose I choose to see this as a moment in miniature, what is being miniaturized? I suggest it is not the scale of the performance. Schwimmer (1990: 11) cites Lévi-Strauss' observation about art; as a reduction from nature (and thus a miniature), art implies abstraction. He adds that people who decorate as spirits thereby miniaturize the spirits, for they abstract from the idea of spirit certain qualities or features which can be made visible. Let me suggest what the Hagen performance here miniaturizes.

In my understanding of Melanesian practices, a performance is always a reduction: a single act created out of composite relationships. It appears gendered, as the display of single-sex qualities detached from androgynous ones. In this case, for all the appearance of masculinity, one is looking at a male side of male version of an androgynous composition. I do not mean that women are implicitly present, although they are; I mean that the whole event is a recomposition of relationships. Indeed, that recomposition involves two kinds of reductions rendered visible by the gender of persons and their extensions.

Recomposition is made possible, first, by the division of the men into donors and recipients: what the men recipients see are other men in the guise of donors. This is the side that the performers present. Dual possibilities are reduced to one. The same (donor) men are recipients on other occasions and indeed may well be giving to those from whom they previously received. So too are the shells reduced: they are laid out in one line, streaming from the mouth[4] of the men's house at the head of the ceremonial ground. The event shows time to be recursive: what flowed before "into" the house now flows "out" again. But the event also momentarily detotalizes the flow (cf. Weiner 1991) into one of its two directions, that is, towards these recipients.

Second, multiple possibilities are reduced to one. The clan is sustained by more than its relationship with the recipients, and the particular shells are not those the recipients might have given but others gained through other relationships. Yet the diverse relations that formed the composite, and androgynous, figure of relationships "out of which" the shells have come *cannot be seen*. They are in the background: other events, other exchanges other partners. The shells instantiate the recomposition: drawn together from many relationships, they are now presented in a single line, as the "one" gift that will make the recipients "see" and "feel." (When pigs are handed over, a donor will kick the stake as he marks out the gifts).

The extended line is thus a reduced figure of the clan body. We might put it that the recomposition of the body is effected through reduction by making the body appear as its own extension: it is as though the extension were also the body. Thus the body is presented through an extension which is also only a part of itself. Certainly the donor clans appear in an extended form through the way their shells are being brought "outside," and what the male shells are seen to do is extend a male "men's house." Potentially detachable, any part of the body may then become the subject of differentiation from other parts. Either house or shell could be imagined as male or female in relation to the other. Thus the shells with their red ochre surround can be thought of as little embryos in the womb, carried by the handles women once netted (cf. Clark 1991). In that case, the long line of shells extending from the house decomposes the male clan into its procreative (male and/or female) body and its countless "children."

M. Strathern

To all appearances, the procreative body and organ/product is replicated in several forms. The photograph (Fig. 3) shows that on this occasion, while the shells extend (from) the house where they were once notionally hid, they also stream out from another shell, the single one standing at the head of the line as though it were the source of them all. Each individual shell in turn is positioned on its board with its opening downwards, out of which (barely visible on the photograph) extends a short bamboo "tally" like the tallies men wear; this is where the carrying handles to bear the shells away are attached. These replications suggest a series of figures: the house door and the line of gifts that come forth/go in; the head shell and the shells that come forth; the mounted shell and the tally that come forth with the handle so that the whole thing can be lifted up and away. Yet this is not a series contained in any simple way by diminishing scale. Look at the man close to the photographer. He is another figure, similar to all or any of these.

This man is looking intently: what is looking at the pearl shells is a figure with an enlarged head from whose neck falls a line of bamboo sticks, the *omak* tally which records previous shell transformations and hangs down over his apron. On ceremonial occasions, large aprons are elongated to conceal the displayer's two legs behind one single sweeping cover.

Whether the man is a donor or recipient, or one of the visitors whose interest in the destiny of the shells is more indirect, in looking at the shell he is looking at a transformed version of himself. Conventionally speaking, however, it is the recipients of the gifts who are marked as "the spectators." The donors are on display to these receptive partners, these witnesses who will later take the donated shells (and pigs) into their own men's houses. Hence the recipients look not at mirror images of themselves, but at the *other side of* themselves: the extended body (the line of shells) of the donors. What is replicated in each figure is the capacity to bring that extension forth. If each shell is such a figure, so too is the spectator in the photograph; but while his *omak* tally and apron falling from the enlarged head is like the tally and handle of the rounded shell itself, his extension is not contained in what the observer would see as his individual figure. He is a person who moves in/through relations with others. In the same way as the shells have been brought forth and will be borne away, his body extension lies first in his presence and second in his seeing. True for all spectators, this extension is condensed, abstracted and miniaturized for the recipients of gifts as the explicit object of the donors' endeavors. It is the recipients who are bound to receive the gifts.

The donors have composed the shells on their own ceremonial ground, in front of one of their men's house. The recipients have come out of their houses in distant territories and have come to the open ground—elicited forth by the promise of shells. In being present, and in gazing at the shells, the recipients extend their own men's house body: what they "see" is what they have brought forth from the bodies of other men. If one were to make explicit for Hagen what other Highlanders abstract in terms of gender, the feminized recipients masculinize themselves by eliciting the gifts and detaching them from the donors. If this were so, what would be miniaturized in that spectacle becomes the procreative possibility of gender difference.

•   •   •

These are speculations. Yet suppose, as Wagner (1991) suggested, Melanesian sociality implies that persons are fractally realized.[5] That is, insofar as persons are imagined as entities with relations integral to them, they cannot be thought of in terms of whole numbers, whether as entire units or as parts of a whole. Persons act as though they have a fractal dimensionality: however much they are divided or multiplied, persons and relations remain in proportion to each other, always keep their scale. Indeed, persons can only exist so divided or multiplied (by relations). It is as though their relationships were also themselves. There is no reason, of course, why the fractal person so conceived should be visible to the anthropologist. Yet if it were, what might it look like?

The anthropologist would be looking for a figure that keeps its complexity through all the scales of diminution and enlargement (cf. Wagner 1991: 172). What keeps its (complex) form in these Hagen performances is the reducibility of the body: every appearance manifests its reduction from a dual or multiple composition to the single side it inevitably presents to the world. For the extended body contains the elements of its reduction, as we might say that in separating into its constituents a relationship is made visible. What is made up of multiple relations decomposes into the entity that seeks relations with others.

Reducibility is thus the *capacity* to be effective, that is, to procreate, to bring forth a product that is also the body itself, to realize "a" relationship. If the capacity lies in the future, it also lies in the past. So the fractal person appears in the *effectiveness* of those relations integral to it, and thus always as an instantiation of itself. Now if persons can turn complete relations into relations requiring completion, one way to be completed is to be seen by others. That means, first, that the person is only ever "seen" as a (partible) extension of itself. It means, second, that it is only ever "seen" from one side, for the other side of the (one) person is the (other person of the) elicitor who evokes and completes the relation. And it means, third, that everything one "sees" oneself is one's own other side. In this world, persons eye the effects of their extensions.

It is not a place that the photographer inhabits. She belongs to a world where it is thought possible to see without having an effect. She also belongs to a world that understands likeness as copy or image as representation, that inspects photographs and endlessly compares graphics.[6] Indeed, she would not have looked again at this particular photograph if she had not been so intrigued by the computer graphics of fractal geometry. Yet drawing replications out of the photograph, seeing the same form in every form, making visual connections between entities that are all part of a single image, is far removed from the procreative activity which in Hagen must rest on its effects. There, effectiveness is gendered: it lies in the way persons draw one form out of another. Each form is divided from the other in the process, as recipients are divided from donors. Two persons but one figure: the body of one of them is also the body of the other.

We might imagine this as the figure of a body whose organs are distributed between persons (much as Euro-Americans think of "society," their own miniaturization of sociality, when they imagine it as so many roles distributed between individuals). For to be effective is to witness the impact—through seeing, say, or kicking—of one's own body on another. But in this mode of Melanesian imagining, the body that is seen or kicked is already only "half" the figure; the eliciting organs are located in the other half. So it would be a one-eye that "sees" one-leg.

Notes

Some of the theoretical work on which this paper is based can be found in The Gender of the Gift *(1988) and in* Partial Connections *(1991). I thank Sarah Williams and Lucien Taylor for allowing me to present this in such an experimental manner. I am grateful to Dirk Smidt, as well as Alan and Louise Hanson, for permission to reproduce the photographs (Figs. 1 and 2), and for Nigel

Rapport's comments. A version was presented to the workshop "Material Culture, Anthropology of Art," convened by José-António Fernandes-Diaz and Cesare Poppi at the 2nd EASA conference, Prague 1992, and comments made there have been most useful.

1. And in people's commentary on themselves. Biersack (1991: 260; also 1990: 78–9) observes that the Paiela people of the Papuan New Guinea Highlands contrast themselves with the all-seeing, all-knowing sun in the phrase: "We are one-eyed: the sun is two-eyed." The sun includes everyone in his vision, and is himself thereby without body (cf. 1981: 260). The interest of the point will be evident in the argument that follows.

2. Though the form that the recomposed body takes (a double-sided or "split" figure) is found in a variety of contexts, not only doorways, and may also be freestanding.

3. The performer who holds one-leg may be referred to as a "child" in relation to male and female guardians of the *tambaran* who accompany the performer; a fourth actor is the *tambaran's* "friend." On the androgyny of children see, for example, M. Strathern (1992).

4. Melpa *keta*, "mouth," "door," "opening."

5. The context is Wagner's reflection on the kind of individual/society antinomy anthropologists have conventionally brought to the analysis of Big Men regimes in the Highlands of Papua New Guinea, prompted by Maurice Godelier's counter-figure of the Baruya Great Man. The idea of individuals somehow aggregated into society contains an implicit mathematics which Wagner here uncovers through another mathematic metaphor (fractals as conceptualized in chaos theory).

6. On modernity's commitment to mimesis, see Taussig 1992. Per contra, Don Kulick and Margaret Willson ("Rambo's Wife Saves The Day: Subjecting the Gaze and Subverting the Narrative in a New Guinean Swamp," manuscript) describe how Gapun villagers seeing films try to make the films "work" for (have an effect on) them.

References

Biersack, Aletta. 1990. "Histories in the Making: Paiela and Historical Anthropology." *History and Anthropology* 5: 63–85.

———1991. "Prisoners of Time: Millenarian Praxis in a Melanesian Valley." In *Clio in Oceania: Towards a Historical Anthropology*. Washington: Smithsonian Institution Press.

Clark, Jeffrey. 1991. "Pearlshell Symbolism in Highlands Papua New Guinea, with particular reference to the Wire people of the Southern Highlands Province." *Oceania* 61: 309–39.

Forge, Anthony. 1966. "Art and Empowerment in the Sepik." *Proceedings of the Royal Anthropological Institute, 1965*, 25–31.

———1970. "Learning to see in New Guinea." In *Socialization: The Approach from Social Anthropology*, ed. A. Mayer. London: Tavistock Public.

Hanson, Allan and Louise Hanson. 1990. "The Eye of the Beholder: A Short History of the Study of Maori Art." In *Art and Identity in Oceania*, ed. A. and L. Hanson. Honolulu: University of Hawaii Press.

Jackon, Michael. 1972. "Aspects of Symbolism and Composition in Maori Art." *Bijdragen tot de Taal-, Land- en Volkenkunde* 128: 33–80.

Mackenzie, Maureen. 1991. *Androgynous Objects: String Bags and Gander in Central New Guinea*. Chur: Harwood Academic Publishers.

Nichols, Bill. 1991. "The Ethnographer's Tale." *Visual Anthropology Review* 7: 31–47.

Smidt, Dirk. 1990. "Kominimung One-Legged Figures: Creative Process and Symbolic Function." In *Art and Identity in Oceania*, ed. A. and L. Hanson. Honolulu: University of Hawaii Press.

Schwimmer, Eric. 1990. "The Anthropology of the Ritual Arts." In *Art and Identity in Oceania*, ed. A. and L. Hanson. Honolulu: University of Hawaii Press.

Strathern, Andrew. 1971. *The Rope of Moka. Big Men and Ceremonial Exchange in Mount Hagen*. Cambridge: Cambridge University Press.

Strathern, Marilyn. 1992. "The Mother's Brother's Child." In *Shooting the Sun: Ritual and Meaning in the West Sepik*, ed. B. Juillerat. Washington: Smithsonian Institution Press.

Taussig, Michael. 1992. "Physiognomic Aspects of Visual Worlds." *Visual Anthropology Review* 8: 15–28.

Wagner, Roy. 1991. "The Fractal Person." In *Big Men and Great Men: The Personifications of Power*, ed. M. Godelier and M. Strathern. Cambridge: Cambridge University Press.

Weiner, James F. 1991. *The Empty Place: Poetry, Space, and Being Among the Foi of Papua New Guinea*. Bloomington: Indiana University Press.

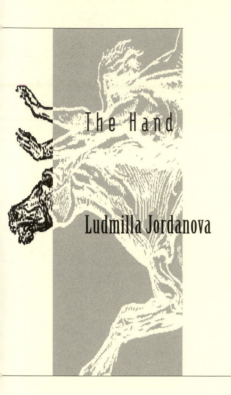

The Hand

Ludmilla Jordanova

Many scholars have explored the kinships between history and anthropology; for historians of science and medicine the affinity between these two disciplines is of a quite specific kind. It hinges on a shared concern with the relationships between what is natural and what is conventional. Cultural anthropology proved enormously enabling to those historians who sought to demystify and undermine the claims at the heart of the natural sciences. Two closely related claims were subjected to critique: first that science gave a true picture of the world, and second that the possession of natural knowledge conferred social authority and privilege upon experts. By contrast, the "new" history of science suggested that natural knowledge, like other kinds of power, was made, and hence the challenge was to show precisely how this was achieved, and, once achieved, sustained. No anthropologist was more influential in the quest to demonstrate the conventional in the putatively natural than Mary Douglas. Here I shall put her enormously influential collection of readings *Rules and Meanings* to heuristic use in a discussion of *The Hand*, a nineteenth-century treatise by the anatomist and artist Charles Bell (1774–1842)[1]

L. Jordanova

Bell was intensely concerned with physiological theory, with visual representation, and with effecting a marriage between science and religion. At first sight he is a classic instance of a thinker who constructed "nature" in order to do other political and social jobs with it. While this is not an inaccurate representation of his life and work, it fails to do justice to the complexity of his enterprise. *The Hand* is a work of extraordinary interest. Illustrated by the author himself, it ranges widely through the animal kingdom and in terms of its subject matter, which includes art history, theories of perspective, taxonomy, animal behavior, and comparative anatomy. Bell was well aware that in taking the hand as his subject he was dealing with one of the most commonly used symbols in human history, with one of the most emotive parts of the body and with one of the most challenging areas for scientific explanation. Bell did indeed insist that the specialness of the hand was in nature; but this nature was created by God, and then explicated, insofar as this was possible, by science. As a natural theologian, Bell was interested in how God's hand was visible in the natural world, and how seeing design made nature comprehensible to mankind. "The hand" was thus shorthand for an unusually dense cluster of ideas, images and beliefs.

In *Rules and Meanings*, Mary Douglas included a section on "Physical Nature Assigned to Classes and Held to them by Rules." Given her belief that reality is socially constructed, it is easy to see why she is interested in the ways classificatory systems carry both meanings and rules, and why she asserted that everyday knowledge and scientific knowledge are closer together than is often supposed. "Physical nature" embraces animals and plants, human behavior and bodily characteristics, including body parts. Douglas selected for inclusion a part of Herz's book on the hand, first published in 1909, in which he argued that the distinction between right- and left-handedness concerned the sacred and profane. He saw this as a widespread distinction, which could *not* be explained in terms of "nature." He did not deny that there were physical differences between the two sides of the body, he only denied that such differences explained the consistency with which diverse cultures affirm the priority of the right hand. Herz's interest in the hand derived from the fact that it stood for a general and abstract principle—the sacred and profane must be kept separate and their relationship strictly controlled for the sake of (a sense of) order. Hands literally embody this principle.

The cultures that Herz mentions have much in common with Western ones, in which for centuries the hand has also embodied abstract social principles. Along with the face, it has long been understood as the main instrument of expression. Conventionalized gestures involving the hands have been central to visual traditions as they have to practices that carry an exceptionally heavy symbolic load—worship, king-making, marriage, making agreements, eating and formal greetings. Europeans also "read" the hand as part of a whole constellation of divinatory practices. And, they have used the word "hand" metonymically, most importantly, to speak of those who depend upon their physical labor. Doing justice to the scientific and medical analysis of the hand may, however, require a different kind of approach. Douglas' emphasis was on the way in which societies derive prescriptions from apparently natural categories. In the treatment of the hand that I am concerned with here, Bell's Bridgewater Treatise of 1833, social rules do not flow directly from constructed nature. Rather, a naturalistic analysis of the hand becomes the occasion for meditation, and for drawing together a number of threads—theological, zoological, medical, aesthetic and epistemological. To be sure some of the same themes come up, but formally speaking the functions of the argument are different, since in Bell the hand is used to gather together insights, beliefs and feelings, not as an element in a system, which *directly* yields *rules*. For anthropologists such as Douglas the passage from natural symbol to social prescription is obvious, unproblematic. For those who wish to understand figures such as Charles Bell, it may be more useful to think about how the hand held meanings, not how it generated rules.

It is noteworthy that Bell, who can be characterized as a holistic thinker, took a single body part—a fragment—as his theme. Yet the notion of fragmentation does not seem helpful here. Hands are important anthropologically precisely because they are so bound up with everything else, they are so thoroughly conventionalized as instruments and indexes, that they cannot be understood as fragments. One dictionary defines fragment as a "part broken off, detached piece; isolated or incomplete part, reminder of lost or destroyed whole . . ."[2] The conclusion is inescapable that fragmentation evokes violence, damage, a sense of loss. Clearly there are *medical* traditions where specific parts are treated as fragments, but this is not the case with the hand; its capacity to be an index (as in the case of rheumatoid arthritis) and a symbol is striking.[3] The hand is a convenient and emotionally powerful exemplification.

But what, precisely, does it exemplify? Here it is necessary to be historically specific, despite the persistence of evocative images over many centuries, for which Dürer's drawing of hands in prayer stands as the classic instance. For the hand to have the exemplifying role I just sketched in, it has to generate specific meanings in an immediate context. Let us take, therefore, the situation at the end of the eighteenth century. Three areas—natural theology, comparative anatomy, the study of the senses—are of special concern, for in all of them the hand could be assigned a special role, which will help to explain the nature of Bell's meditation.

Natural theologians saw the design of God everywhere in the living world.[4] Bodies were perfectly adapted to carry out the tasks they had been assigned; this was simultaneously an aesthetic vision, which celebrated the beauty of perfect design, and a functional one, which admired the perfect fit between purpose and instrument. And, the more complex or elaborate the tasks, the greater the sense of wonder and awe, so that the human body, and its unique capabilities, stood at the summit of the created world. The capacity of the human hands to be dextrous, sensitive, expressive and versatile fitted neatly into this framework. It is important to recognize, however, that natural theology posed a formidable intellectual challenge, above all to medicine. Given its guiding beliefs, there was much to explain, and to resist. A mechanistic view of adaptation and of physiology had to be refuted. Pathological examples involving appalling suffering and pain had to be dealt with in a manner that was consistent with divine beneficence. The nature of human consciousness had to be accounted for so that concepts such as soul and will could form part of scientific explanations alongside the most sophisticated anatomical and physiological insights.

Clearly, adaptation was a central concept in the developing science of comparative anatomy, which paid most attention to skeletal structures across a variety of animal forms, just as it was in natural theology. In comparative anatomy it was necessary to explain both the differences and the similarities that were observed across the animal kingdom in this, a pre-Darwinian worldview. The resulting strategies were highly diverse, but at quite a simple level, comparative anatomy encouraged people to compare limbs of many different kinds with respect to their forms and functions; it sanctioned several forms of empiricism, one of which involved the description and recording of bone structures, often in visual form. "Hands" (we should note the anthropomorphism of the term) are easy to observe in action, and so links between structure and behavior could be elaborated without difficulty. Since comparative anatomy encouraged the construction of graded series of forms, the human hand could be put at the head of a series of limbs, thereby affirming its difference and superiority, while saving a sense of kinship with other vertebrates (this was, more or less, Bell's approach). According to Bell: "To comprehend the perfection of the structure even of any single organ of an animal body, we must take it comparatively, that we may see how the same system is adapted to an infinite variety of conditions" (Bell 1837: 2). It was also possible to compare human hands with one another, as Lavater did in four plates of *La Physiognomie* (Lavater 1845; and Tytler 1982).

Discussions on the nature of the senses were conducted with intense interest in a century during which sensualist epistemology occupied a prominent place. Philosophers, medical practitioners, educationalists and natural philosophers all debated the matter. Analyses of the senses generally concentrated on human beings, not least because only there was it possible to observe phenomena and link them up with experiences. It was precisely because the senses shaped experience and behavior, and generated knowledge, that eighteenth-century intellectual traditions found them endlessly fascinating. One result was an interest in the distinct contributions the five senses made, which could be conveniently studied using unusual medical cases and information about those who did not have the use of one or more of their senses. For a variety of reasons, the blind, the deaf and the dumb were of particular interest; they became the recipients of an Enlightenment reformist zeal that was based upon careful observation and experimentation. In the last two cases, sign language, where the hands "speak," came into prominence, but this was largely an extension of existing traditions that studied and interpreted manual expressiveness (including in the theater). Where the hand really came into its own was in discussions of the sense of *touch*. This sensory capacity was most elaborated in the hand and above all in the fingers. The fact that this part was under voluntary control suggested that touch was an active sense. By the late eighteenth century, then, the hand was available as an important test case, body part and exemplification of claims made by dominant medical, scientific, and philosophical traditions.

L.
Jordanova

It was in this intellectual environment that the Scottish anatomist, surgeon and artist Charles Bell grew up. Born in 1774, he was reared on the medicine and philosophy of the late Enlightenment, and grew to prominence as a devout man, an able surgeon, a skilled draughtsman and an innovative physiologist in the London of the 1820s and '30s. In 1830 he was invited to compose a Bridgewater Treatise on the hand, a topic specifically mentioned in the will that funded this series of publications. They were to illustrate "the Power, Wisdom, and Goodness of God, as manifested in the Creation," "by all reasonable arguments." Bell, intensely conscious of his status and reputation, was clearly pleased with the invitation, which came with the approval of the scientific and church establishments stamped upon it. He saw the project as one that required the elegant exposition of ideas he was already master of— it was not an occasion for new research, but for bringing together his prolonged reflections on the design and perfection of one part of the body. The treatise appeared in 1833, with illustrations by himself, by which time he was also preparing for publication an edition of Paley's enormously popular *Natural Theology* jointly with Lord Brougham (1836). By 1837, *The Hand, its Mechanism and Vital Endowments as Evincing Design* was in its fourth edition.

In a letter to his brother of August 1830, he set out his reactions to the prestigious invitation:

> Behold with what I point! [he then drew a hand on a shield]—This hand, how exquisite in form and motion. But first turn over—use it and learn to admire!
> I have a letter this morning from the President of the Royal Society, who, with the counsel and approbation of the Archbishop of Canterbury have proposed to me to write on the *Human Hand* . . . I think I know now what to engrave on my seal—a hand. I shall introduce it on all occasions, sometimes doubled . . . as implying the pugnacious nature of the man—sometimes smooth and open, as ready to receive—sometimes pointing, as from the master. In short, I shall make use of this hand until they acknowledge me a handy fellow! (Bell 1870: 314).

This, to my mind uncharacteristically playful, statement by Bell is revealing. It indicates the ready range of associations that the hand provoked among educated people of the time, including the sense of wonder that is so marked a feature of Bell's response to the human body. His letter also reveals that the hand had an immediate *personal* significance for him.

At this point I would like to consider the illustrations to Bell's *The Hand*. Many of them are all of a piece with the unexpected manner in which he approached his assignment. Much of the book concerns vertebrates rather than human beings, and hence many of the pictures show animal skeletons both whole and in part; a relatively small number depict human bones, while several are vignettes of animals and people in little scenes. I find particularly striking the inclusion of two images; one of a bear with a fish it has just caught, the other of a monkey apparently eating out of a bowl. They are inescapably anthropomorphic, while by contrast, the text relentlessly asserts that, despite their morphological kinship with vertebrates, human beings are unique and, it is made clear, to think otherwise is profoundly *impious*. Although the inclusion also of a bear on display in a zoo might suggest that Bell was critical of making animals humanoid, the other bear and the monkey are so deftly and warmly presented that this seems unlikely. Equally curious is the inclusion of a satyr bouncing a child on his knee! We know that Bell thought the project should not be taken too earnestly (he made this clear in a letter to his brother on 3rd September 1831, Bell 1870), but the text is evidently a serious essay on medicine and natural theology. Yet this kind of "play" should not be lightly dismissed, even if it cannot easily be explained, and I mention it to suggest the possibility that Bell's treatise is working at more levels than at first sight appears. And it is worth noting that Bell included *no* pictures at all of living human hands, with flesh upon them, despite his eloquence on the subject, and his August 1830 letter. The final vignette of the book is of a centaur with a little cupid on his back holding an arrow!

Perhaps Bell's reluctance to provide a lifelike image of the human hand was connected with a refusal to see it as a fragment. If the treatise has any message it is that webs of relationships exist between parts of the body and between human beings and God. Expounding upon the anatomy and physiology of the hand enabled him to make the point powerfully. This organ of touch and expression is perfectly constructed for human needs, hence it fits in with the rest of the body and with the material circumstances within which the body has to function—this was a standard view in comparative anatomy.

Bell's principal claim to scientific fame was through his work on the nervous system, and specifically his discovery of the distinction between sensory and motor nerves. He engaged in a particularly bad-tempered priority dispute with the French physiologist François Magendie (1783–1855), which on one level was about who should have the credit for this discovery, but on another was about the different ideological agendas of British and French medicine as these were constructed by interested parties. Bell used every available opportunity in *The Hand* to refer to his own achievements and to press his claims for priority over Magendie, who is not, however, mentioned by name. The specific nature of the innervation of the hand enabled him to point to its unique sensory properties, while stressing its role as part of a larger system. In fact there were two larger systems involved. First, the nervous system as a whole, so that the hand, or rather its sensory capacities, were one element of this larger system. Second, the hand was part of an adaptive system that enabled human beings to function effectively in their environment: "our body . . . [is] created in accordance with the conditions of the globe, and [is a] systematic part of a great whole" (Bell 1937: 8). In this way the hand was one small part in the total providential picture.

A quite specific medical view underpinned this sense of connectedness. Bell argued that nerves had different functions; there is no scale of fineness or coarseness that accounted for the diversity of nervous response—which is to be explained in terms of functional differentiation. In other words, it was not a question of the physical attributes of nerves, such as size, but of function: some nerves respond to visual stimuli, others to tactile ones and so on. It was just this division of nervous labor that enabled the human body to display elaborate capacities and to function effectively in its surroundings. But this model of the nervous system immediately generated a potential problem; for if the claims about functional specificity were true then it might be possible eventually to explain everything mechanically, in terms of structures—the nervous system would then appear to be "self-starting," and the way was open to materialism. Bell dealt with this threat by denying that function could, ultimately, be rooted in structure; thus it was not the hand itself, or indeed any other organic

"The Comparative Anatomy of the Hand," in Sir Charles Bell, *The Hand, Its Mechanisms and Vital Endowments as Convincing Design*, p. 58, Chapter III. London: William Pickering, 1834. 3rd ed.

structure, that accounted for the sophisticated capacities with which it was associated (e.g., Bell 1837: 227). Although the superiority of "man" was indeed lodged in the hand—"in the sense of touch, seated in the hand, man claims the superiority" (Bell 1837: 185)—the hand was not the *cause* of this effect; rather, it was itself the effect of human wisdom, implanted by God. Thus explanations of the human body had to go beyond the body itself, to an order of being that could never be fully transparent to the human mind, nor be imaged. Materialism was resisted by locating active forces in the universe outside the order of nature; forces ("propensities," as he puts it) are needed "to put . . . into operation" wonderful instruments such as the hand (Bell 1837: 254). Appropriately enough, the appendix on the classification of animals presents man at the top alone in an order named "Bimana."

Bell's taxonomy conveniently brings us back to Mary Douglas' *Rules and Meanings*, where she insists on the cosmological significance of classificatory systems. We noted earlier Herz's ideas on handedness as expressions of the sacred/profane distinction, and his claim that the common separation of left and right *had to be* conventional. Bell too addressed these questions, and his assertions on the matter are revealing: "there is an universal consent, among all nations, to give preference to the right hand over the left. This *cannot* be a conventional agreement: it must have a natural source" (Bell 1837: 151)! He argued that the whole left side of the body was weaker than the right, and that this had adaptive value. He supported this claim by pointing to the difficulties left-handers experience in the world "opening the parlor door, or opening a pen knife" (154). We, now, immediately sense a difficulty in treating man-made objects, such as doors and knives, as entities to which the human frame is adapted, that is, in giving explanatory priority to artifacts when, supposedly, "nature" is being explicated.

In the twentieth century we are accustomed to seeing the interpretation of social differences as natural ones in terms of a usually conservative strategy that presents inequalities as natural differences and then finds them to be resistant to manipulation. The resulting images of the body we construe as static legitimations; historians and anthropologists refuse to take them at face value, seeing them as active constructions that use languages of nature as the idiom though which cultural, that is conventional, distinctions (clean/unclean, sacred/profane, white/black, and so on) are expressed. This approach presupposes the existence of societies where the natural has a certain kind of prestige.

At one level this kind of analysis can be applied to Bell. His fusion of medicine and natural theology certainly legitimated a particular sense of order: "man" was the top animal, religion was integral to science, and social-cum-political organization should reflect these facts. The language he developed for talking about the body, like the pictures he drew, helped to elaborate sets of body images that gave eloquent expression to his worldview. Yet to see this *simply* as legitimation would be unhelpful. Legitimation implies not only clearly articulated interests, both material and ideological, but a smooth passage between legitimating concepts and legitimated hierarchies. It was indeed exciting for critics to be able to unmask the naturalized categories of science and medicine, in order that they stand forth as mere conventions—and hence in the minds of liberal scholars, as capable of being changed. These strategies used, often quite naively, the natural/conventional polarity and cognate dichotomies without recognizing the need for their deconstruction, without taking on the complex mediations between natural knowledge and social life, and without appreciating the profound conflicts that have surrounded the dualisms in question. In fact, anthropological perspectives continue to have something to offer historians of science and medicine, which will help them appreciate the insufficiency of unmasking on its own. More specifically, the anthropological recognition that the *spiritual* life of cultures is important in its own right will help the practice of history. It will do so by showing that interests and legitimations exist within a larger framework that pertains to notions of what is sacred.

Bell did *not* in fact accord prestige to the natural order itself; ultimately God's creative design explains observed phenomena. Indeed "explain" must be used loosely here, since human beings cannot understand divine actions in the way they can comprehend skeletal structures, for example. For Bell, art was important precisely because it could, without conscious scientific or medical theorizing, display the eloquence of the hand. It did so indeed through "the ingenuity of the hand" of the artist; Bell thereby endowed the artist with special, quasi-divine status (258). Hence he considered that the privileged "expert" was as much the artist as it was the scientist, and that the privileged domain was the mind of God rather than the natural world. I began by suggesting that Bell's was in some sense a contemplative work. The combination of anatomy, physiology, natural theology and art enabled him to express a sense of the sacred in the human body through detailed biomedical researches. In doing so he explored the interplay between his own constructions of the divine, the natural and the conventional. His vehicle was a powerful natural symbol, which bore an unusually complex relationship to visualization. Bell was an artist, anatomist and surgeon whose manual dexterity was central to his being; he was also a theorist of vision; he studied how gestures were expressive; he believed that God was only known through the sophistication of human sight. It is precisely because the hand—a foundational metaphor of action—enabled him to work at so many different levels that scholarly responses cannot rest with simply unmasking his naturalizations. They must probe his historically specific sense of the hand as sacred.

Notes

An earlier version of this paper was presented to "Imaging the Body: Art and Science in Modern Culture," University of Chicago, April 1992.

1.   The recent secondary literature on Bell is surprisingly sparse. Most helpful are the following books, which place Bell's concerns in a broader historical context: Coleman (1972); Desmond (1989); Moore (1989).

2.   *Oxford Illustrated Dictionary* (1975), 30.

3.   It would be possible to read William Hunter's famous obstetric atlas in terms of fragmentation—see my essay on this in Bynum & Porter (1985). The point about rheumatoid arthritis was made to me by David Cantor (Institute for the History of Medicine, Johns Hopkins University), who is currently research-ing the imagery of that disease.

4.   The outstanding treatment of natural theology is Brooke (1991). See also Moore (1989).

L.
Jordanova

References

Bell, Charles. 1837. *The Hand*. London, 4th ed.

————. 1870. *Letters of Sir Charles Bell*. London.

Brooke, John Hedley. 1991. *Science and Religion: Some Historical Perspectives*. Cambridge: Cambridge University Press.

Bynum, W.F. and Roy Porter, eds. 1985. *William Hunter and the Eighteenth-Century Medical World*. Cambridge: Cambridge University Press.

Coleman, William. 1972. *Biology in the Nineteenth Century: Problems of Form, Function, and Transformation*. New York: John Wiley.

Desmond, Adrian. 1989. *The Politics of Evolution: Morphology, Medicine, and Reform in Radical London*. Chicago: University of Chicago Press.

Douglas, Mary, ed. 1973. *Rules and Meanings*. Harmondsworth: Penguin.

Lavater, J.C. 1979 (1845). *La Physiognomonie*. Reprinted Paris Lausanne.

1975. *Oxford Illustrated Dictionary*. Oxford: Oxford University Press.

Moore, J.R., ed. 1989. *History, Humanity and Evolution*. Cambridge: Cambridge University Press.

Tytler, Graeme. 1982. *Physiognomy in the European Novel: Faces & Fortunes*. Princeton: Princeton University Press.

Films of Memory

David MacDougall

The Mind's Eye

FILMS HAVE A DISCONCERTING RESEMBLANCE TO MEMORY. THEY REGISTER IMAGES WITH LENS and emulsion in a process better understood but often no less astonishing than the physiological processes of eye and brain. Sometimes film seems even more astonishing than memory, an intimation of memory perfected. Two of the journalists present at the Lumière brothers' "Salon Indien" screening of 1895 wrote that motion pictures bestowed a kind of immortality upon their subjects (Jeanne 1965: 10–12). But for many of the first viewers of films, what struck the imagination even more forcefully than the images of living people (who were regarded in the same light as performers) was the participation of the inanimate world in recording its own traces—the evocative minutiae of experience which the mind could only roughly register. It was such ephemeral images as the steam from a locomotive, the brick dust from a demolished wall, and the shimmering of leaves that seemed the real miracles of filmic representation (Sadoul 1962: 24; Vaughan 1981: 126–27).

And yet memory offers film its ultimate problem: how to represent the mind's landscape, whose images and sequential logic are always hidden from view. In the nineteenth century C.S. Sherrington described a sixth sense which he called "proprioception," that consciousness of our own body which confirms our physical identity (Sacks 1984: 46; 1985: 42). We might well consider memory our seventh sense, that record of an antecedent existence upon which our intellectual identity precariously rests.

D.
MacDougall

Memory is often apparently incoherent, and a strange mixture of the sensory and the verbal. It offers us the past in flashes and fragments, and in what seems a hodge-podge of mental "media." We seem to glimpse images, hear sounds, use unspoken words and reexperience such physical sensations as pressure and movement. It is in this multidimensionality that memory perhaps finds its closest counterpart in the varied and intersecting representational systems of film. But given this complexity, and equally the aura of insubstantiality and dreaming which frequently surrounds memory, we may ask whether in trying to represent memory in film we do something significantly different from other kinds of visual and textual representation. We create signs for things seen only in the mind's eye. Are these nevertheless signs like any other?

The Translation of Memory

Films which focus on memory do not of course record memory itself, but its referents, its secondary representations (in speech, for example) and its correlatives. In films, objects survive from the past, people reminisce, and certain objects evoke or resemble those of memory. We end by filming something far removed from memory as it is experienced, but instead a mixture of dubious testimony, flawed evidence and invention. Films of memory could thus be said to represent only the external signs of remembering.

How then are these signs to be read? For the filmmaker, how audiences read them is largely a matter of trial and guesswork, since the minds of viewers are as closed to direct inspection as those of the people filmed. Nor do films, once made, communicate an unequivocal message. They produce different readings in different viewers, and as time passes are open to continual rereading. If memory itself is selective and ideological, films of memory redouble this and add further codes of cultural convention.

Physical objects might be thought to be least subject to such vagaries, providing films with a kind of independent baseline for memory. This indeed is the rationale of many museums. But objects which survive from the past are not the same objects that they were in the past, and they can thus stand for the memory of themselves only obliquely. Unlike an object seen in a photograph, which bears a parallel relation to other objects around it in a specific past context, the patina of age on an old object tends to exaggerate its status as a sign. This sign is often confused with authenticity. But the least authentic thing about museum reconstructions of the past is that the authentic objects displayed in them are too old. At the time represented, many of them would have been new. Thus, whether displayed in museums or filmed in the recent past, the actual objects of memory are unreliable as expressions of memory. They can only be touchstones for its retrieval or construction.

Despite this, many films equate memory with surviving objects, including photographic images of the past. With the original sources of memory forever beyond reach, filmmakers are tempted to use the surviving photographic record *as if this were memory itself*. Thus documentary films and television programs persistently link interviews with photographs and newsreels, which are presented quite illegitimately as the memories of the speakers.

Such images nevertheless play an important part in our own memories, influencing how we think about the past. They take their place in our culture as physical artifacts, not mere media "messages." Many public figures whom we see on television are as substantial to us as the images of people we see in daily life. And as Frank Tillman has argued (1987), exposure to photographic images has altered the way recent generations imagine the world. We have always been able to think visually, but until photography we were unable to think photographically. As for most recent historical events, we remember not the events themselves (we were not present at them) but the films and photographs we have seen of them. But these may create a commonality of experience more powerful and consistent as social memory than the experiences of many of the actual participants. As Edmund Carpenter has commented, modern media, and particularly television, extend the images of our dream world (1976: 58).

These public images can serve society at large in the way that family photographs serve smaller communities—as emblems of significant events and transitions, constructing a concept of the past but also providing ways of overcoming it. They may assist in what Yannick Geffroy (using Freud's term *Trauerarbeit*) describes as the "work of mourning" the lost past (1990: 396ff). They do so through repetition and reduction, for representation usually entails both of these. Television news (like its predecessor, the newsreel) rings changes on an essentially unchanging catalogue of disasters, political meetings, sports events, and wars, and it is this limited set of themes, with minor variations, which reassures us that the world goes on as before. But the process is not without emotional cost: like all mourning, viewing the recent past, particularly its horrors, includes a measure of guilty relief at our own survival.

In films of memory, however, there is a frequent collapsing of memory and its sources. The distinction between photographic records and photography's place in people's minds is rarely made. Thus, among the variety of signs that films employ for the objects of memory, photographs and archival footage tend to be used the least critically and most misleadingly.

The Signs of Memory

Films of memory draw upon a distinctive repertoire of signs. Perhaps most common, and what might be termed *signs of survival*, are images of objects which have a physical link with the remembered past. These memorabilia serve half as symbols of experiences, half as physical proof that they occurred, and like Kane's "Rosebud" they often turn up amidst a clutter of other, less familiar objects. They are "astonishing" and precious not so much for their visual resemblance to remembered objects as for the fact that they are perceived, like Proust's handful of dried lime blossoms, as the "very same" objects.

These objects are remnants of a larger whole, sometimes declaring their connection to it only by the damage they have sustained: a tree whose broken branches tell of a storm, or a bullet-riddled helmet, or the wrinkles on the face of a person being interviewed. Old photographs and films belong to this group of signs not only as historical objects which bear the marks of handling, foxing and projection, but also (though more loosely) through the direct indexical link which their imagery—their photochemical "marking"—bears to past events.

If objects do not survive to be filmed, films of memory often resort to *signs of replacement*— similar objects and sounds and, at the farthest extent, reconstructions and reenactments, such as those of docudramas. If pressed lime blossoms are unavailable, new lime blossoms will do. In this way, a train rumbling through a modern railway yard becomes a 1940s train to London or Auschwitz. Journeys and the retracing of steps are especially favored by films of memory because revisiting places—like viewing photographs—produces emotions of both retrieval and loss.

At one remove from replacements in kind are replacements in form: what we might call *signs of resemblance*. These offer a looser, iconic link with their objects, filling in the missing pattern of the past by analogy—not, as it were, by striking the missing note, but by supplying its harmonic. They make possible major shifts of magnitude: a day's work or a short trip can now speak of a life's journey. This principle can be seen in Roman Kroiter's films *Paul Tomkowicz: Street-Railway Switch Man* (1953) and *Stravinsky* (1965), which "frame" life histories in a man's last day's work and an Atlantic crossing, and Renata and Hannes Lintrop's *Cogito, Ergo Sum* (1989), in which an elderly Estonian's daily physical struggle becomes a metaphor for his long resistance to Soviet rule. Resemblance, on any of several metaphorical and metonymic levels, allows a broad range of associative imagery to be brought into play. A cut to an eagle or seagull, for example, is rarely simply an evocative touch. In films, birds singled out for attention seem inevitably to carry an extra burden of aspiration, loneliness, hope or despair.

Among signs of resemblance, music is the analogue *par excellence* for emotion, and not surprisingly films of memory are choked with it. In these films music serves doubly for emotions imputed to the subject and meant to be aroused in the viewer. In addition, music is used by films of memory for its historical associations. Because musical styles "date" and are culturally specific they make ideal aural icons. A piece of music can almost always be found to fit a particular historical and social milieu. In the past, ethnographic films seemed invariably to use gratuitous (although culturally accurate) indigenous music for this single validating purpose. In mainstream documentary films, accordions, charleston orchestras and honky-tonk pianos become the equivalent clichéd accompaniments for archival footage of villages, nightclubs and working-class neighborhoods.

The conventions of film music persist despite their naivete and the obviousness with which they are used to manipulate audiences. Even in Ken Burns' recent and carefully wrought American television series, *The Civil War* (1990), period music is marshaled throughout as though better to authenticate photographs and quotations from the period. Although the music in the series has been defended as adding textual complexity, it has also been criticized for conditioning the audience to view history with a simplistic melancholia (Henderson 1991). By contrast, the British series, *The Great Depression* (1981), sometimes uses only the sound of a projector over compilations of archival footage. This device may be equally artificial, since even silent films were originally accompanied by music, but at least it has the merit of drawing attention to the contingent physical qualities of the film materials rather than cloaking them in an aura of fateful grandeur.

Although music is generally employed to "double" a specific historical setting, it can sometimes be cast against type, as Humphrey Jennings demonstrated in *Listen to Britain* (1942), when he juxtaposed Dame Myra Hess playing Mozart at a wartime London concert with the effects of Hitler's bombing. A more common alternative is to seek out music which is culturally and historically as neutral as possible, representing (it is hoped) nothing so much as pure emotion. Music may function in this fashion if it is new or has lost its original connotations through re-use. Electronic music is often chosen because it is cheap and anonymous, while Andean flutes and pan pipes have been used so typically to evoke memory that they are now part of an international style, stripped of other cultural meanings.

The Sense of Absence

The signs we have considered so far are those most often found in conventional films of historical reminiscence. They bolster the illusion of a recoverable past. They have coalesced to produce a cinematic subgenre whose ritual ingredients are aging faces (usually of interviewees), fetish-objects from the past, old photographs, archival footage and music. This formula is used with equal impartiality in everything from brief television items to twelve-part series and documentary features. It is a subgenre which purports to tell us our "true," unwritten history through the testimony of both ordinary people and famous eyewitnesses. It has a tendency to be elegiac, as though remembering were in itself a virtue. The age of a speaker is an important index of authority: The increasing reverence with which historical events are viewed as they recede into the past is transferred to those who remember them. Few films of this genre ask children what they remember about last week or last year, and few admit that the old may be forgetful or devious. Indeed, reminiscence is seen as a burgeoning richness which, if only it could be gathered up quickly enough, could tell us everything worth knowing about the past. Although such an approach acknowledges that memory is cultural, it tends to surround its own interviewees with a spurious neutrality (Nichols 1983).

A few films of memory employ one further class of signs, which we may call *signs of absence*. These provide a way of confronting the problems of forgetting and willful distortion, as well as the larger abyss between experience and memory. Although films of memory often claim legitimacy as a way of salvaging first-person experience, they rarely address slippage in the memories of their informants. At the very least, signs of absence place memory in the context of forgetting, and define the past by its irreducible distance from the present.

Signs of absence often make ironic use of objects and testimony, positioning the audience uncomfortably by asking them to make judgments and comparisons, to search for and interject meanings. Here the sign for a lost object becomes not its surrogate but what has displaced it. These signs define memory by its true opposite, an embodied absence. An empty factory thus represents a fully operating one. A market square teems not with peasants and bullocks but with youths on motorbikes. In another variation, first-person testimony is challenged (and reversed) by its positioning in a film—Nixon's air of ingenuousness, for example, in *The Trials of Alger Hiss*. Or it may be offset by the internal evidence of a shot (what Walter Benjamin called "dialectical" images), as in the presence of an overseer with interviewed workers in Amos Gitai's film *Ananas*, or signs of duress in televised statements by hostages and prisoners of war.

Some films go further still. Beyond the carefully counterpoised "now" and "then" of Resnais' *Nuit et Brouillard* (1955) or the verbal and visual evidence of Erwin Leiser's *Mein Kampf* (1960), Claude Lantzmann's *Shoah* (1985) not only asks us to query first-person testimony but to look at empty roads and fields where atrocities took place and search them for what happened there. We look in vain for the signified in the sign. In this constant reiteration of absence we are brought to the threshold of one kind of knowledge about history. In the failure of the sign we acknowledge a history beyond representation.

The Representations of the Mind

If memory forms an aspect of thought, it is possible to regard films of memory as efforts to approximate the processes by which the mind represents experience to itself. These films harness the memories of the film subjects, the filmmakers and, more indirectly, the film viewers. In a discussion of photographic imagery, Victor Burgin (1982: 194–8) has referred to M.J. Horowitz's classification of thought into "image," "lexical" and "enactive" categories (1970: 69–82). Horowitz based his tripartite structure on Jerome S. Bruner's "three systems for processing information and constructing inner models of the external world"—what Bruner called the "iconic," "symbolic" and "enactive" (1964). Both systems resemble, whether directly or indirectly, the sign classifications developed by C. S. Peirce and Roman Jakobson, and seem elaborations on them. Although these modalities of mental representation are usually intermingled in actual thought, they correspond very well to the strategies by which films render memory in images, words and physical behavior. Indeed, we may not fully understand how films use these elements, and how they ultimately affect us, until we have a better understanding of the processes of mind.

By "image" Horowitz means not only visual imagery, but the ability to recall sensory experience generally. It is possible to remember a specific smell or sound, or even "hear" in silence an entire Mozart symphony. Thus, although in films we are limited to sounds and visual images (forays into odorama and smellavision notwithstanding), Horowitz's concept of "image" is best understood as *sensory thought*.

The visual imagery of the mind appears to be both more complex and less systematic than the visual imagery of cinema. We might compare two of its operations to those of the voluntary and involuntary muscles of the body. Some images come to us unbidden, the material of dreams and daydreams. They are specific and sharply defined: a face, perhaps never consciously noted before, has the living detail of a face actually seen, or viewed on a movie screen. But images recalled through conscious effort are more often indistinct and elusive. It is a common experience to find the faces of loved ones the most difficult to recall. The more actively one pursues them the more effectively they sidestep the mind's gaze, as though long familiarity had rendered their object too complex and heterogeneous for a single image to suffice. Films condense such multidimensional thinking into concrete imagery, stripping the representation of memory of much of its breadth and ambiguity.

D. MacDougall

The counterpart of Horowitz's "lexical" thought is amply represented in films, although usually in a more studied form (such as commentary) than in the scribbled demotic of daily experience. Actual thought more typically consists of broken fragments of language and a sense of meanings hovering between the verbal and preverbal. Among the few films which attempt to duplicate this is Clément Perron's *Day After Day* (1962), which departs from conventional film writing to give us muttered pieces of nursery rhymes and sudden announcements ("The departure has been delayed indefinitely") as the accompaniment to monotonous piecework in a paper mill. There is also something rather like it in the headlong rush of notions and placenames in Auden's poetry for the film *Night Mail* (1936).

In representing sensory and lexical thought, films might be thought to have encompassed the essential elements of memory, for images, sounds and words tend to dominate our conceptions of our own consciousness. This assumption appears to be endorsed by many current social and political documentaries, which reduce these two categories to a simple format of archival footage (the sensory) and interviews (the lexical). It seems taken for granted that this not only represents memory adequately but also, quintessentially, history.

However, Horowitz's third mode of thought, the "enactive," is neither image nor word, but gesture—experience recalled, one might say, in the muscles. We imagine an action through the feel of it—for example, the sense of moving a hand in a familiar motion, such as stirring coffee. One might call this the kinesthetic dimension of thought, familiar to ourselves but only observable in others when it is translated into actual physical movement, just as lexical thought is only observable when translated into speech. That the images of words on a page are translated into an enactive version of sound production is perhaps well demonstrated by Edmund Carpenter's observation that throat surgery patients are forbidden to read because "there is a natural tendency for a reader to evoke absent sounds, and the throat muscles work silently as the reader scans the page" (1980: 74).

Enactive memory finds its primary filmic counterpart in images of physical behavior, especially behavior of an habitual kind. Of the three categories, the enactive is perhaps the mode of memory closest to the indexical sign, for its form is that of an imprint or direct extension of previous experience. It is evident in certain gestures—when, for example, artisans are at work and the memory of their craft seems to reside "in their hands." Such gestures can express not only the memory of an habitual activity but an attitude towards it, as when a cook breaks eggs with a flourish that combines both pride and expertise.

Enactive memory may take precedence over visual or lexical memory. In a French television report a man descends a stairway in a building in which he was imprisoned in total darkness for over a month. Although he can tell us in words the exact number of steps (there are thirty-one) and we can see the steps ourselves, it is in fact the movement of his feet which tells us most convincingly that he knows when he has reached the bottom.

We may postulate that of all the modalities of thought, the enactive is most closely associated with emotion: that, for example, the memory of shame or triumph is largely an enactive, physiological response, although linked to a visual memory of the situation in which it arose. The dynamics of film editing may constitute, after the portrayal of "habitual" gesture, a second level on which films reproduce the qualities of enactive thought, although precisely how this operates deserves further investigation. Eisenstein characterized the effects of montage as "psycho-physiological" phenomena, and described how in the film *The General Line* (or *Old and New*, 1929) a series of increasingly short shots of farmers mowing with scythes caused members of the audience to rock from side to side (1929: 80). At their junctions, film shots produce kinesthetic responses in the viewer; and much film editing may represent a translation of movement and gesture from enactive thought into a succession of juxtaposed images. Editing also creates imaginary geographies—cinematic landscapes of the mind in which we as spectators walk and take our bearings. It is one of the objectives of films of memory to create such spaces, as analogues of the spatial dimensions of memory. Other aspects of enactive memory may be represented in films through the synesthetic effects of movement, light, color and texture.

Horowitz's three modes of mental representation can thus help us to identify correspondences between the processes of memory and filmic representation. To these should perhaps be added a fourth category—that of *narrative* thought. More than simply a property of the other modes, narrative has, it seems to me, good reason to be considered a further primary constituent of thought. Time, which provides the continuum on which memory is registered, here underpins the arrangement of the sensory, lexical and enactive into sequences. Narrative governs the disposal of objects and actions in time, without which most memory, and even language, would be impossible. Although a certain part of thought is apparently incoherent (even if, perhaps, the product of a deeper logic) there is little we can think of without assigning it a narrative history or potential. We think within a set of narrative paradigms in which objects have origins and futures, and in which even simple actions are constructed out of a succession of lesser ones. This hierarchy of mental structures is reflected in the syntagmatic structures of many popular cultural products, from folktales to films.

Film & Thought

It is often asserted that the conditions of film-viewing induce a dreamlike state in which the self is stripped of its defenses. Films seem like dreams because we watch them helplessly, deprived of our volition. However, another explanation for this effect may be that films create a synthesis of varied modes of representation which closely mimic the modes of mental representation. Although films are visual, they are also aural, verbal, narrative and enactive. They slide through different cognitive registers in a way that we find strikingly familiar, so that even people who have never seen films before quickly find them comprehensible, despite culturally-specific codes of narration and editing. One may speculate that although experiments in artificial intelligence are widely based on linguistic and mathematical models, film may well offer a more convincing simulation of mind and memory than either of them.

The connections between cognition and film underlie many of the conventions of the cinema (as in the "psychological" editing of Fritz Lang or Alfred Hitchcock) but without, it seems, often being explicitly acknowledged as such. The reluctance to identify narrativity closely with actual processes of thought produces an ambiguity in the point of view of many films, as though films could somehow *think themselves* without reference to an identifiable consciousness. Films of memory, particularly documentaries, often seem uneasy about their own narrativity. Fiction films seem less troubled. Some, like Resnais' *Hiroshima mon amour* (1959) and Fellini's *8 ½* (1963), clearly seek to reproduce certain processes of thought through visual imagery and interior monologue. Others do so more obliquely, through strategies of identification with third-person characters, who recite or reenact their memories, as in *Citizen Kane* (1941) or—extraordinarily, since the narrator is supposed to be dead—*Sunset Boulevard* (1950).

Nonfiction films of memory more often seek to stand outside the narratives provided by their human subjects. Instead, they situate these stories in a structure which at times relies on them for narrative impetus but otherwise seeks to create its own narrative about an historical period or political issue. There is a general presumption of interest on the part of the audience, but precisely why they should be interested (or why the filmmakers are) is often never made clear.

There is a certain amount of journalist hubris in such a position. Frequently the presence of testimony itself is taken as its own sufficient justification. This approach dominates film portraits of famous people, such as *Portrait of Nehru* (1965), in which an interview was virtually forced upon Nehru, and John Else's study of Robert Oppenheimer, *The Day After Trinity* (1980), in which the film's authority and that of its subject seem curiously undifferentiated. Memory is *used*, but the fundamental link between constructing the past through reminiscence and constructing the audience's present experience through film is never made. We may thus conclude that many films of memory are uncertain about their own discursive status: in making the assumption that their subjects' reminiscences are worth knowing they somehow dispose of having to define, or speak from, their own particular interests. There is thus a certain emptiness at the heart of such authorship, a fundamental lack of conviction. It may well be that the common tendency to adopt a celebratory stance towards memory is a symptom, and a masking, of that uncertainty.

Processes of thought and memory are generally approached more directly in autobiographical documentaries, which constitute a rapidly growing subgenre of filmmaking. From the early work of Jonas Mekas and Stan Brakhage to later films such as Chris Marker's *Sans Soleil* (1982), these films show a concern for the workings of memory and the problem of how film can represent it. However self-absorbed and self-serving they may be, they are explicit about their uses of the past. Reminiscence is rarely treated as omniscient or transparent, and when photographs are used, as in such films as Corinne Cantrell's *In This Life's Body* (1984) and Antti Peippo's *Sijainen* (1989), they are presented as fragmentary documents, to be interrogated and filled with meaning.

These filmmakers are often dubious about the translation of memory, just as anthropologists have become more cautious about the possibility of cultural translation. They confront in the most personal way the "crime" of representation, the gap between signs and their objects. Most makers of films of memory confront the same problem, but often (it appears) in a different spirit. If they regret the sparseness of detail or the inarticulateness of filmed first-person testimony, their response is not to indicate the significance of this gap but to try to improve upon it. The unattainable richness trapped inside their subjects' memories is supplanted by the addition of much illustrative material. The viewer is drawn into a collusion in which the varied signs of memory are brought into play. These are not the abstract and regenerative symbols of literature, but images from the physical world. In fiction films (Robert Bresson's, for example) such representation is sometimes saved from the literalness of its images by a kind of minimalism, an exclusion of the too-explicit. In documentary the closest equivalent of this is perhaps the use of the single, mute object saved from childhood, or the perfectly enigmatic photograph, like that which Anitti Peippo shows us of his apparently happy family in *Sijainen*. But at this point we must ask whether films of memory are really engaged in representing memory at all. They may instead have moved outside the more verifiable significations of other documentary film texts and into a domain of evocation. Here film could be said to leave representation behind and to confront the viewer once again with the primary stimuli of physical experience.

Film, Ritual & Social Memory

Social memory in small communities is a matter of consensus, a version of the past accepted by various groups for reasons of convenience and solidarity. The particularities of social life prevent any one person from sharing precisely the same perspective or experience as others. Social memory is thus "social" in an active sense: negotiated, provisional, and indicative of relationships. But increasingly, access to common experiences and sources of information in modern society tends to create a monolexical culture, condensing useful fictions like social memory into realities. When momentous events occur it is quite common the next day for people hardly to speak of them, for by then they are already public icons and "news" to no one. This instantaneous production of social memory creates public perceptions which are widespread and seemingly unassailable, but also, because of their very rigidity, brittle and subject to sudden reversals. As the Iraq-Iran and Iraq-Kuwait wars show, the victims of today easily become the villains of tomorrow.

The images of film and television combine the durability of artifacts with the force of oral tradition. They are concrete reports from the physical world. In a preliterate society these reports are conveyed by art, ritual and word of mouth (all ephemeral) and become a constantly revised "tradition." With the advent of writing, printing, photography, and electronics they become fixed, even petrified points of reference. As Walter Benjamin (1936) observed, they also take on more explicitly political functions. Yet as film and television endlessly recapitulate past events they also regain some of the functions of ritual. Certain images of the past keep recurring and, like famous still photographs (the napalmed Vietnamese girl; the Andean flute-player in *The Family of Man*) lose their historicity (their status as photography) and become cultural symbols.

Marc Piault has noted that the controllers of ritual use it to inculcate an orthodox "tradition" which reinforces their own power, but in the process of constructing such a tradition ritual simultaneously makes possible its transformation by creating a stage for the confrontation of conflicting interests (1989). One might suppose that "fixed" media representations, which share with ritual the power of authority and repetition without offering such a stage, might avoid such a challenge. Indeed this seems to be widely assumed by their "controllers." From early in this century governments have seen film and other mechanically reproduced images as a safe means of inculcating patriotism and historical orthodoxy. In 1917 General Ludendorff wrote to the Imperial Ministry of War praising the superiority of photography and film as "a means of information and persuasion," an action which eventually led to the founding of the giant UFA studio (Furhammar & Isaksson 1971: 111–12). And in his well-known statement of 1922, Lenin told his Education Commissar, Lunacharsky, "Of all the arts, for us the cinema is the most important" (Leyda 1960: 161).

This trust in photographic iconography is in some measure confirmed by the way in which modern conceptions of the October Revolution are still defined and contained by Eisenstein's images of it. It is quite common for compilation documentaries dealing with the period to mix indiscriminately newsreel footage with scenes from the film *October* (1927). Such uses of fictional footage have occurred often, perhaps most notably in the American wartime film series, *Why We Fight*. The logical extension of using film to construct history is to tailor history to its filmic representation, as was done in 1934 in Nuremberg for Leni Riefenstahl's *Triumph of the Will* (1936), perhaps the world's first great "media event" and the outgrowth of such propaganda exercises as the manipulation of the Reichstag fire and the mythologizing of the story of the Hitler Youth hero, Herbert Norkus (notably, through the film *Hitlerjunge Quex* [1933]). But in doing so the creators of an orthodoxy also created a tool for its destruction. Here film images, despite their apparent permanency and consecrated meaning, have proven as open to challenge as earlier forms of ritualized persuasion.

In 1942, after viewing *Triumph of the Will*, Frank Capra (soon to be the producer of the *Why We Fight* series) decided to "use the enemy's own films to expose their enslaving ends" (1971: 332). He realized that by altering the context in which the footage appeared its meaning could be reversed. He thus began exploiting the "stage" which the original producers had created. Since then scenes from Riefenstahl's film have been endlessly repeated, but they have in effect become part of a transfigured view of German history, imbued with quite different ritual significance.

Thus, like ritual, the focal narratives of history provide a medium for political contestation and change. Social memory, although it may be powerfully shaped by film and television, is clearly as vulnerable to revision as the traditions of earlier times. In a description which interestingly parallels Piault's, Edward Bruner and Phyllis Gorfain (1984: 56) assert that such narratives "and similar cultural texts . . . are frequently national stories and rarely remain monologic. They do serve to integrate society, encapsulate ideology, and create social order; indeed, the story may become a metaphor for the state, and poetic means may be used for political purposes. But because these narratives are replete with ambiguity and paradox, an inherent versatility in interpretation arises that allows for conflicting readings and dissident, challenging voices."

Yet a residue of a clearly *physical* nature remains in film images which is not available in verbal narratives, and its importance should not be underestimated. Film images may be reinterpreted in a variety of new contexts, but the unalterable record of appearance and place contained in them may ultimately prove to have a more profound effect upon our "memory" of history than the interpretations we attach to them.

**D.
MacDougall**

Note

This paper is an expanded version of introductory comments made at the final discussion of the 5th "Regards sur les Sociétés Européenes" Seminar devoted to "Memory," held in Budapest, July 8–15, 1990. A related version of this article appears in French as "Films de mémoire" in Journal des Anthropologues *(Special Visual Anthropology issue 47/48, Spring 1992).*

References

Benjamin, Walter. 1936. "The Work of Art in the Age of Mechanical Reproduction." In *Illuminations*. Reprint. New York: Harcourt Brace Jovanovich, 1964.

Bruner, Edward M. and Phyllis Gorfain. 1984. "Dialogic Narration and the Paradoxes of Masada." In *Text, Play and Story: The Construction and Reconstruction of Self and Society*, ed. Edward M. Bruner. Washington: 1983 Proceedings of The American Ethnological Society, 56–79.

Bruner, Jerome S. 1964. "The Course of Cognitive Growth." *American Psychologist* 19: 1–15.

Burgin, Victor. 1982. "Photography, Phantasy, Function." In *Thinking Photography*, ed. Victor Burgin. London: Macmillan Education.

Capra, Frank. 1971. *The Name Above the Title*. Reprint. New York: Vintage Books, 1985.

Carpenter, Edmund. 1976. *Oh, What a Blow That Phantom Gave Me!* St Albans: Paladin.

———. 1980. "If Wittgenstein Had Been an Eskimo." *Natural History* 89 (2): 72–76.

Eisenstein, Sergei. 1957 (1929). "Methods of Montage." Reprint in *Film Form*. New York: Meridian Books.

Furhammar, Leif and Folke Isaksson. 1971. *Politics and Film*. London: Studio Vista.

Geffroy, Yannick. 1990. "Family Photographs: a Visual Heritage." *Visual Anthropology* 3 (4): 367–409.

Henderson, Brian. 1991. "The Civil War: Did It Not Seem Real?" *Film Quarterly* 44 (3): 2–14.

Horowitz, Mardi Jon. 1970. *Image Formation and Cognition*. New York: Appleton-Century-Crofts.

Jeanne, René. 1965. *Cinéma 1900*. Paris: Flammarion.

Leyda, Jay. 1960. *Kino*. London: George Allen & Unwin.

Nichols, Bill. 1983. "The Voice of Documentary." *Film Quarterly* 36 (3): 17–30.

Piault, Marc. 1989. "Ritual: a Way Out of Eternity." Paper presented at "Film and Representations of Culture" conference, Humanities Research Centre, Australian National University, Canberra, September 28, 1989.

Sacks, Oliver. 1984. *A Leg to Stand On*. London: Gerald Duckworth.

———. 1985. "The Disembodied Lady" In *The Man Who Mistook His Wife for a Hat*. London: Picador.

Sadoul, Georges. 1962. *Histoire du cinéma*. Paris: Flammarion.

Tillman, Frank. 1987. "The Photographic Image and the Transformation of Thought." *East-West Film Journal* 1 (2): 91–110.

Vaughan, Dai. 1981. "Let There Be Lumière." *Sight and Sound* 50 (2): 126–27.

Manufacturing Vision
Kino-Eye, The Man with a Movie Camera, and the Perceptual Reconstruction of Social Identity

David Tomas

Our eyes, spinning like propellers,
take off into the future
on the wings of hypothesis.

— Dziga Vertov [1]

THIS COMPELLING METAPHOR ENCAPSULATES THE PIONEERING MODERNIST SPIRIT OF ONE OF the twentieth century's most radical experiments in creating a working interface between social revolution and cinematic practice. The experiment was developed by the Russian filmmaker Dziga Vertov in the 1920s during the "golden age" of the Russian Revolution, one of the most fertile periods of cultural upheaval since the Industrial Revolution. Because of its documentary orientation, political engagement, and commitment to formal experimentation, Vertov's work has been a seminal influence on the *cinéma vérité* movement as well as avant-garde experimental film; it has had a decisive influence on filmmakers of the caliber of Jean-Luc Godard and Chris Marker; and has been the subject of numerous commentaries and analyses.[2] However, there has been no attempt to examine his work and, in particular, his classic 1929 silent film *The Man with a Movie Camera* from an "anthropological" point of view, that is, as the social symbolic product of a particular culture. This is surprising since his work has dual ethnographic value: as a documentary product of the making of a new society as well as the product of a new way of looking (cinema) and seeing (montage editing). Moreover, to approach Vertov's ideas and films from an anthropological point of view leads to a surprising observation, since the principal exemplar of this new way of looking and seeing—*The Man with a Movie Camera*—appears to have been cast in the form of an age-old panhuman ritual: a rite of passage.

If Vertov's films differ fundamentally from those of his great rival Sergei Eisenstein, it is precisely in their initial focus on the everyday world of Soviet Russia and in their attempt to critically engage this world in cinematic terms, that is in terms of a technology of representation which was the complex product of the kind of social environment they were examining. The importance of Vertov's films and writings is, however, not only to be measured in terms of their dual ethnographic value as products of a period of unparalleled revolutionary change or potential sources of information on the social construction of vision. Their ethnographic singularity and richness also resides in the fact that they represent a conscious, indeed reflexive, attempt to socially engineer vision in order that it could function in pace with social and political change.

While it can be argued that Vertov's cinematic practice provides an important object-lesson in the design of *social* imaging systems on the basis of existing hardware inasmuch as it directly and successfully links cinematic observation to social organization and the production of new cultural/perceptual spaces, and while it can be argued that this object-lesson is enhanced by a cinematic practice which was specifically designed to function in a period of rapid change, one must also situate such object-lessons in a broader political context. In Vertov's case, this context would prove overwhelming, since his work was eventually marginalized in the name of another social agenda. He was, of course, not the first or last casualty in a game of *Realpolitik*. Later politically engaged filmmakers would also find themselves in a similar position.[3] Nevertheless, Vertov's unusual model of collective observation and cinematic manufacture remain, to this day, one of the few coordinated attempts to design a "social technology of observation"[4] that could account for an expanding media culture while retaining a tactical political and social "situational reflexivity."[5]

In the following pages, I will present a case for considering film and photography as rites of passage. I will extend this discussion to *The Man with a Movie Camera*, detail the novel "social technology of observation" that served as its foundation and, finally, note their relationships to the production of new social identities. During the course of this discussion, I will have occasion to comment on some possibilities and questions raised by this approach to Vertov's cinematic theory and practice.

Photographic and Cinematic Rites of Passage

Rites of passage have traditionally been understood to be limited to the symbolic mediation of socially problematic and ambiguous biological processes such as birth, puberty, and death. They have also been identified as mediating major seasonal or cosmic transitions or, alternatively, conventional passages between important social stages, for instance, marriage.[6] These rituals have notably excluded technological and industrial processes in general and, in particular, those processes used in engendering and sustaining Western traditions of pictorial representation. However, there are two reasons why one should begin to consider these latter technologies as ritual systems and processes of social/symbolic transformation. First, photography and film are powerful systems of optical, mechanical, and chemical transformation, more accurately *transubstantiation*, that serve as well-defined spatiotemporal passages between the worlds of everyday human existence and parallel worlds of pictorial representations having very particular (i.e., coded) photochemical compositions and cognitive organizations. The efficiency of these mass-produced systems which are, in turn, able to mass-produce visual images and the ubiquity of their use in the modern world suggests that they might represent important portals between distinctive collective social states or stages. Second, these systems are, in fact, structured according to three clearly demarcated or differentiated stages of production that replicate, in important ways, the governing tripartite structure and corresponding symbolic logic of a classic rite of passage.

D.
Tomas

Thus, the first stage, or rite of separation, of an ideal form of photographic or cinematic rite of passage consists of the optical/mechanical procedures and photochemical reactions involved in physically "taking" photographs and films. The product of this stage (a latent image) is then chemically processed to produce a negative, which corresponds to the second or liminal stage of a photographic or cinematic rite of passage. The negative is an exemplary liminal artifact, a strange and uncanny social object in which light and dark, the binary components of many ocularcentric systems of social/symbolic classification, the most prominent of which is day/night, are reversed while a subject/image retains its given morphological characteristics. The negative is also rather unusual and unique in that its transparency provides the means for almost infinite reproduction. The third stage of an ideal photographic or cinematic rite of passage, which corresponds to a rite of incorporation in a classic rite of passage, comprises the optical, mechanical, and chemical procedures used for processing and printing a positive image. These procedures ensure an orderly transformation or passage from the liminal stage to a final "positive" social condition *represented* by a final photographic or cinematic print.

However, cinematic prints are part of a larger social system or technology of representation since they are designed to be viewed in the context of special environments called *cinemas*. These environments bear a striking resemblance to traditional liminal sites in their curious exclusionary spatial and social properties. Cinemas are dark, enclosed environments in which a group of people view physically nonexistent realities projected onto a two-dimensional surface by way of a beam of light. These realities, whose cultural contents are as diverse as their social and political inflections, range from depictions of the monstrous to the mundane. But in all cases they tell us something about the ways in which we live and behave, or the ways in which others live and behave. In other words, as in the case of a traditional liminal stage, they provide us with special insights into what it means to be human and social beings. The liminality of cinemas is further accentuated by a symbolic exchange between the "living" and "dead"—the former virtually presented on screen as moving, talking, interacting figures, while the latter are reproduced in the order and rigidity (almost a form of social rigor mortis) of an audience enveloped in a mausoleatory darkness.

A ritual approach to photographic and cinematic technologies, and the image cultures they generate, is therefore in order not only because such compelling similarities between traditional rites of passage and contemporary modes of image production warrant further investigation, but also because this approach would allow one to begin to address the social and cultural dimensions of the *technological* systems that produce photographs and films. In particular, such an approach would allow one to explore these extraordinary products of a Western industrial imagination from the view points of the overall functions of their systems of manufacture in order to answer such traditional "anthropological" questions as, what kind of social and symbolic transformations are they designed to deal with? How do they achieve these ends? For whom and in terms of whom do they operate?

One can also conceive of a whole series of other questions in connection with the so-called objective technological transparency of film and photography. What does it mean to take photographs and/or films of other cultures? What world(s) are these other peoples really entering when we film them or when they film themselves according to a ritual of technology that articulates Western technological and aesthetic values? While this is not the place to address such issues, Vertov's work on Kino-Eye should sensitize us to the politics—both symbolic and mimetic—implicated in film production and its culture of vision, while reminding us, once again, of the range of human expression that is possible when we begin to challenge inherited ways of looking at and seeing ourselves and others in the name of other visions, other realities.

Vertov's Kino-Eye project is especially significant in this regard, because it provides a unique, relatively well-documented attempt to perceptually reconstruct human vision by redefining its social/technological foundations and political orientation. In contrast to other types of film organization, Kino-Eye was dedicated to exploring, in an almost comparative ethnographic fashion, Soviet society at a given point in time. This attempt was, moreover, radical enough to have effectively challenged cinema practice as then understood, and its challenge continues to resonate to this day.

Preamble to a Kinomatic Rite of Passage: A Note on Vertov's Politics of Representation

Vertov's revolutionary film practice was founded on a "non-acted" or documentary model of film production. He argued that an inherent weakness of fictional films was their tendency to separate, too easily, the realms of work and leisure according to a governing opposition between methods of analysis (science) and practices of interpretation (art). In contrast, his factually based "non-acted" film practice was predicated on a synthesis of art and science, interpretation and analysis. This synthesis was carefully crafted, under the auspices of a logic of montage editing, to produce a revolutionary poetics powerful enough to induce a critical social consciousness in film audiences. Its power resided in its ability to redefine the parameters of binocular vision and thus challenge and transform an audience's habitual modes of perception according to cinematic knowledge (that is, knowledge of and knowledge by way of cinema). When considered in the context of the dominant models for early twentieth century film production, this poetics was nothing less than a carefully honed weapon with which to attack the literary and theatrical tendencies which Vertov considered to be destructive counterrevolutionary forces in a young Soviet film culture. Its main objective was to undermine their modes of social production and system of coding which, in the lattercase, amounted to an assault on their technological transparency, narrative linearity, and illusionism, the combination of which resulted, in Vertov's opinion, in the spectator's unconscious intoxication.[7]

This poetics was the product of three innovations. First, Vertov shifted the emphasis in film production's social logic from product to process of manufacture. He hoped, by doing so, to draw attention to film as mode of production as opposed to film as mode of entertainment. Second, he argued that it was necessary to recast the notion of process itself in a "non-acted" or documentary mold. Film production would thus be displaced from the studio to the street—propelled, in other words, into an industrialized culture and thus forced to take account of its new forms of manufacture, social organization, cultural expressions, and volatile post-Euclidean perceptual spaces. Moreover, as *The Man with a Movie Camera* illustrated, this shift allowed for the cinematic ingestion of a wide range of social protagonists, including "cameramen" and editors, as film characters and subjects. Third, Vertov developed a common basis of social/cinematic organization that would link these innovations directly to the most fundamental unit of film production/reproduction: The creation of difference between two frames of a film a) at the level of production in the passage of a filmstrip through a movie camera's film gate (the elementary procedure for recording movement) and b) at the level of reproduction in the passage of a film-strip through a projector gate (the elementary procedure for reproducing movement). The sum total of these innovations embodied, in Vertov's estimation, the spirit as well as the political and social aspirations of the October Revolution.

Man with a Movie Camera is the most radical statement of Vertov's Kino-Eye method, from the points of view of both its observational *and* documentary strategies. It is, moreover, a prototypical cinematic product of a society in transition and a cinematographer who was attempting to come to terms with this transition. At the level of manufacture, it links the activities of a "cameraman" to those of the editor and finally the audience, and grounds these activities in a wider industrial culture. As a visual artifact, it also represents a perceptual process of manufacture, its product a new social vision. The "conveyor belt" for these processes is provided by a formal and thematic itinerary which visually interweaves the human activities that define a society in the making with the socio-technological activities that generate and survey its new mode and domain of vision: a social/cinematic space. Together they (re)constitute themselves in the process of reconstituting a factually grounded day in the fictional life of a Soviet city. The film thus articulates two parallel interconnected rites of passage, the one that embodied and sustained its production as cinematic object, the other that articulates a particular "dioptric" solution to the problem of generating an alternative camera-based socialist culture of vision, a problem posed and solved in terms of an architectonics of collective observation.

D.
Tomas

The Man with a Movie Camera: A Kinomatic Rite of Passage

The Man with a Movie Camera (Chelovek s Kinoapparatom) is a six-reel, approximately 95-minute film released in 1929 under the auspices of the Ukrainian Film and Photography Administration (VUFKU). As credited on the film, Vertov was the "author-supervisor of the experiment," Elizaveta Svilova, his wife, the editor or montage assistant, and his brother, Mikhail Kaufman, the chief cameraman. Vertov considered the film to be a major statement of the "Kinoks" principles of nonfiction filmmaking, the first part of a projected two-part study of the language of the cinema, which would oppose a purely cinematic world—a world as seen and reproduced by Vertov's new mode of social/cinematic observation/manufacture, christened "Kino-Eye"—to the world as seen by the imperfect human eye.[8]

At once a brilliant exposition of film production's place in an industrialized society, a masterly display of the formal and rhetorical codes of cinematic representation, and a complex polythematic montage of everyday social activities in Soviet Russia, The Man with a Movie Camera is Vertov's most direct visual statement of Kino-Eye method[9]—not only "a practical result" but also, and most importantly, "a theoretical manifestation on the screen."[10] Finally, in keeping with its artifactual status as manufactured object, it was also considered a "film-thing" or "film-object."

Recently, the film has been described by Annette Michelson as a "meta-cinematic celebration of filmmaking as a mode of production and . . . a mode of epistemological inquiry" in which a "'world of naked truth' is, in fact, the space upon which epistemological inquiry and the cinematic consciousness converge in dialectical mimesis."[11] This space, whose specific social topography remains undefined in this cogent description of the film's status qua revolutionary film, is, perhaps, best defined by way of a new social/industrial matrix for cinematic communication: a hierarchic division of observational labor that functions as a technology or process for manufacturing cinematic vision. It is this social technology, a fusion of Vertov's Kino-Eye collective with the cinematic apparatus, which articulates the complex thematic armature consisting of a day in the life of the composite Soviet city depicted in The Man with a Movie Camera; and it is this technology that finally provides the visual means for staging a perceptually induced revolutionary transformation in the consciousnesses of both producers and spectator/audience.

However, it does so in a curious manner, for such an avowedly revolutionary visual experience, since the film appears to replicate in its overall organization the tripartite form and symbolic structure of a traditional rite of passage. Although there is no evidence to suggest that Vertov was aware of the cultural status and "anthropological" significance of this type of ritual, he was certainly aware of the existence of similar rituals in his culture,[12] and he did depict socially sensitive events widely subject to rites-of-passage mediation—events such as birth, marriage and death—albeit under the aegis of a new revolutionary social and cultural agenda and cinematic medium of representation.

As a cinematic rite of passage, the first section of the film reflexively introduces the spectator/audience to its own context of observation: the cinema. The sequence is introduced by the following warning: "Attention viewers: This film represents in itself an experiment in the cinematic communication of visible events; without the aid of intertitles (a film without intertitles); without the aid of a scenario (a film without a script); without the aid of theatre (a film without sets, actors, etc.); this experimental work was made with the intention of creating a truly international ultimate language of cinema on the basis of its total separation from the language of theatre and literature." This warning shatters any expectations about seeing a conventional fictional film while simultaneously sensitizing the audience to the rather unusual "story" that immediately begins to unfold before their eyes.

This "story" is introduced by a survey of the mechanics of cinema reproduction. Although it is presented under the sign of production, in this case a giant movie camera which serves as the platform for the appearance (introduction) of the cameraman and his camera (the film is always clear as to the priority of this distinction), representation is considered, in this separation sequence, from the point of view of the cinema as opposed to the movie camera: interior of cinema with its empty seats, projector and projectionist, film, chandeliers, seats (animated this time), audience, orchestra, and conductor. The audience is thus immediately presented as divided in terms of representation (an audience on the screen) and self-representation (the audience is depicted as preparing to watch a film). This ensures a common identification between "audiences" while introducing the idea that the film's "story" might have nothing to do with "the old 'artistic' [i.e., narrative] models" of literature or the theater that were based, as Vertov saw it, on "a literary skeleton plus film-illustrations."[13] In fact, the possibility that the old models, whose narrative unfurling was ultimately determined by a script's point of view, might be operating in this case, is almost immediately negated by the perceptual conjoining of audiences about to watch a "common" but highly unusual film in which they already have a collaborative role in ensuring its social articulation.

If the film goes on to produce a cinematic dislocation of the audiences's atomistic or individual powers of vision, powers previously governed by a "process of identification and participation,"[14] it nevertheless does so under a contradictory sign: the dialectic of identification and alienation first introduced in a separation sequence. The result is the inauguration of a "crisis of belief," as Michelson has succinctly described it, which will be consummated by the "exposure of the terms and dynamics of cinematic illusionism."[15]

The liminal phase of this kinomatic rite of passage, introduced by the numeral "1," is governed by a "dominant" dioptric symbol, the Camera/Eye, which is periodically foregrounded during the course of the film either in the form of a camera lens or a superimposition of camera lens and human eye.[16] The film articulates its socialist "vision," in this phase, according to a series of thematic vignettes of, amongst others, paradigmatic rites of passage subjects (birth, marriage, death), a series of social themes (work and leisure), and political issues (the constrast between socialist behavior and residues of bourgeois behavior); and it does so according to a pure film semio-logic based on the unique spatiotemporal possibilities offered by motion picture technology *when used outside of the studio and within the context of the "real."* It is, therefore, the Camera/Eye's ability to witness the full range of social life that is celebrated in this liminal phase.

The audience is then reintroduced, through a cinematic rite of perceptual reincorporation or aggregation, to the conditions of cinema representation: with "itself" *qua* audience; with the special context in which the film is being presented; and thus to its status as representation and self-representation. But the situation is somewhat different this time, because the audience is also introduced to an anthropomorphized movie camera who, in performing in front of the audience and in taking its bow, seems to be claiming a central role in the staging of this cinematic "event"—a claim apparently confirmed by the ensuing recapitulation of major themes, punctuated by copious references to the mechanics of cinema and cinematic representation highlighted by a constant montage of audience, screen, cameraman, and editor. This montage ensures that film and audience cross over into each other's domains and are incorporated in a spectacular perceptual *mise en abyme* in which the audience becomes spectator to an audience watching a film which turns out to be *The Man with a Movie Camera*, a connection that had not been made during the opening separation sequence. The film ends with the Camera/Eye staring at the audience, its diaphragm closing into pure light then darkness.

In sum, therefore, *The Man with a Movie Camera* is structured in the form of a rite of passage which connects and mediates two social stages of vision: a pre-revolutionary reality, whose dominant model Vertov isolated and defined in terms of the natural or unconscious acceptance of an unproblematized illusionism, and a post-revolutionary cubo-futurist model that took form as a dynamic, dialectical, "non-acted" cinematic culture predicated on a new logic of perception or method of constructing a film: *montage*.

The transformation between the two social stages was clearly mediated by an optically induced crisis of mimetic belief accompanied by a visual celebration of the transformative social powers of Kino-Eye—powers generated by "its own dimensions of time and space" and presented as if completely severed from "the weakness of the human eye."[17] The transformation was presented, moreover, through the medium of a new form of intelligence, in the words of an earlier 1923 manifesto, "the kinok-pilot [Mikhail Kaufman amongst others], who not only controls the camera's movements, but entrusts himself to it during experiments in space."[18] Vertov had anticipated the results of such a transformative union in this manifesto when he argued that as a "result of this concerted action of the liberated and perfected camera and the strategic brain of man directing, observing, and gauging—the presentation of even the most ordinary things will take on an exceptionally fresh and interesting aspect"—a comment that suggests a familiarity with Viktor Shklovsky's theory of defamiliarization or *ostranenie*.[19]

A cinematic version of Shklovskian defamiliarization was produced, in the case of *The Man with a Movie Camera*, by an array of visual strategies of perceptual distanciation which included references to the film screen as representational surface; the disruption of action sequences through the use of techniques of animation; the use of different film speeds to produce arrested, slow, and accelerated motion that call into question the notion of normal film speed and thus the pace of conventional cinematic vision; the disruption of filmic illusion by distinguishing between "illusion experienced" and "illusion revealed" or film and film screen as distinct surfaces of representation; the use of techniques of distortion and abstraction as means of drawing attention to the constructed nature of the image; and finally a consistent attempt to place cinematic understanding, according to these means of perceptual distantiation, on an intellectual as opposed to an emotive footing.[20]

The sum total of these strategies was a cinematically manufactured crisis of habitual ocular perception (that is belief based on the experience of eyesight conditioned by an inherited social and cultural environment whose demise was most prominently symbolized in the film by the optical implosion of the Bolshoi Theatre Building) and the aesthetic pleasure that was based on this habitual perception. This ocular crisis functioned as the motive force for a simultaneous thematic transformation in a given audience's patterns of social identity. As in some classic rites of passage,[21] the audience was introduced to the social and cultural mechanics of their (Socialist) way of life and its normative and ethical frameworks. Thus, in keeping with the "social" functions of liminal activities where a culture is decomposed along the lines of its dominant symbols and recomposed in new and unusual ways, this new pattern of existence was deployed in a new post-Euclidean cinematic space and based on a cinematic process of socialization whose thematic context was provided by new systems of communication, transportation, manufacture, and the patterns of work, including Kino-Eye work, and leisure they engendered.

However, Vertov's ambitions extended well beyond ocularcentric transformations in archaic social/cinematic practices. He was ultimately interested in inaugurating a revolutionary transformation in the total human sensorium. With this aim, we pass beyond the immediate experience of *The Man with a Movie Camera* in order to reconsider in detail the function of the kinoks and Kino-Eye in Vertov's model of film production.

On the Rationalization of Observation and its Linkage to Spectatorial Consciousness: Vertov on "the Work of the Kino-Eye"

Vertov's strategies of film production were deployed in relation to an inherited scopic regime: Cartesian perspectivalism.[22] He proposed to challenge this regime on its own terms, that is, through the use of a recently invented (1895) technology of observation/reproduction that embodied that regime in its optical system: the film camera. Thus, he argued:

> We . . . take as the point of departure the use of the camera as a kino-eye, more perfect than the human eye, for the exploration of the chaos of visual phenomena that fills space.
>
> The kino-eye lives and moves in time and space; it gathers and records impressions in a manner wholly different from that of the human eye. The position of our bodies while observing or our perception of a certain number of features of a visual phenomenon in a given instant are by no means obligatory limitations for the camera which, since it is perfected, perceives more and better . . .
>
> Until now, we have violated the movie camera and forced it to copy the work of our eye. And the better the copy, the better the shooting was thought to be. Starting today we are liberating the camera and making it work in the opposite direction—away from copying.[23]

However, it was not just the film camera's superior powers of observation that converted cinema into a tool of perceptual liberation. Transformation was the product of a complex mode of observation that was itself structured according to a new perceptual logic—montage—derived from a politically reconditioned cubo-futurist aesthetic. While Vertov's artistic generation was first to intuitively understand the role of powerful modern technologies and industries in mediating contemporary urban existence, the Russian constructivist artists were the first to seek to systematically articulate this understanding in terms of a political agenda that went beyond intellectual critique to embrace total social revolution.

The Man with a Movie Camera is an exemplary experiential product of this understanding, because it clearly proposes, in the overt linkage of its material, formal, and thematic organizational levels according to an acausal logic of representation (montage), that the technology *and* social organization of cinema directly "mediates," in the words of Judith Mayne, "perception and production";[24] indeed, that it can also mediate social existence. Thus, what Vertov described as "the *organization of the visible world*" (emphasis in the original)[25] was, in keeping with this understanding, considered to be a *complete* system and process of social manufacture: ultimately a collective *work of editing* that ranged from initial thematic research and primary observation "in the field" to a final product to be perceptually experienced in a cinema. As Vertov pointed out at the time:

> The Kinoks distinguish among:
> 1. *Editing during observation*—orienting the unaided eye at any place, any time.
> 2. *Editing after observation*—mentally organizing what has been seen, according to characteristic features.
> 3. *Editing during filming*—orienting the aided eye of the movie camera in the place inspected in Step 1. Adjusting for the somewhat changed conditions of filming.
> 4. *Editing after filming*—roughly organizing the footage according to characteristic features. Looking for the montage fragments that are lacking.

5. *Gauging by sight* (*hunting for montage fragments*)—instantaneous orienting in any visual environment so as to capture the essential link shots. Exceptional attentiveness. A military rule: gauging by sight, speed, attack.

6. *The final editing*—revealing minor, concealed themes together with the major ones. Reorganizing all the footage into the best sequence. Bringing out the core of the film-object. Coordinating similar elements, and finally, numerically calculating the montage groupings.[26]

It is clear from this passage that Kino-Eye was ideally composed of a hierarchic division of labor that functioned as a *technology of observation*—a kind of collective imaging system that had the capability to simultaneously observe a multitude of different social spaces. Moreover, this technology was also a *process of manufacture* socially defined in terms of editing stages and aesthetically defined in terms of montage stages. Thus, a clear practical logic linked social labor from the individual Kinok-observers to Kinok-cameramen, Kinok-constructors [designers], Kinok-editors (women and men), Kinok laboratory assistants[27] to the final cinematic experience (its decisive stage of manufacture and observation—a new visual consciousness in an audience).

The concept of Kino-Eye film production was therefore not only predicated on light-weight and mobile camera technology, a concern with a "culture of materials"—"the materiality of the [film] object and . . . its architectonics",[28] it was articulated in terms of a powerful social technology of observation/manufacture that ranged from the beginning to the end of production. Although one would imagine that, ideally, there were no privileged points of view or observers in this collective mode of observation/manufacture, its hierarchic organization implied, in keeping with Vertov's military model, coordination by a "leader" who ensured observational coherence according to an overall thematic goal.[29]

Traces of this technology of observation and process of manufacture are clearly visible in *The Man with a Movie Camera*. The film's thematic flow is governed by a cameraman (Kaufman) who is seen pursuing 'themes' and an editor (Svilova) who is seen classifying and working thematic components into a final product. Collective authority tends therefore to be foregrounded in terms of these activities as opposed to an individually defined directorial authority. The foregrounding of collective authority is also evident insofar as the division of editorial labor is dominated by an observational logic whose presence in the film is more than symbolized by the Camera/Eye.

In Kino-Eye terms, a kinematic rite of passage would involve the Camera/Eye, and its operator(s) (the Kinoks-cameraman), and an audience in a continuous vertically extended intersystem of manufactured perceptual transformation whose axis was precisely the Camera/Eye. As "masters of vision, the organizers of visible life, armed with the omnipresent Kino-Eye,"[30] the Kinoks would—after having gone through a process of resocialization marked by a shift of observational context from studio to the street—be in a position to be continually educated by "life": "that whirlpool of colliding visible phenomena, where everything is real."[31] In other words, far from being independent of the "real," as in the case of personnel involved in filming fictional films, camera/persons would become at once visible and invisible, submissive and sensitive to "life's" socio-political vicissitudes and cultural contradictions. It was this process of reeducation, grounded as it was in the reality of the everyday and subtly orchestrated by a system of observation, which ensured that Kino-Eye's collective consciousness and, by extension, the audience's collective consciousness would no longer fall prey to "the director's megaphone"[32] which stood, in Vertov's mind, as the symbol for all that was antithetical to a liberated and pure language of the cinema, and a liberated, critical, Soviet consciousness.

If Vertov's concept of Kino-Eye is clearly reflected in *The Man with a Movie Camera's* perceptual/thematic integration, his espousal of the title "author-supervisor" is a further, if oblique, acknowledgement of its collective authority. Thus, if, as Michelson suggests, *The Man with a Movie Camera* is a film that marks "a threshold in the development of consciousness" whereby the "cameraman" was transformed "through the systematic subversion of the certitudes of illusion . . . from a Magician into an Epistemologist,"[33] it is perhaps more accurate to suggest that the Kino-Eye model of cinematic production ensured that the cameraman, editor, and audience were collectively accorded a new epistemological identity in its name, the result of a coming of collective age by way of an uncompromising cinematic rite of passage.

Beyond Poetic Documentary: Orchestrating Vision
According to a Post-Ocularcentric Culture of Representation

Vertov considered himself a "film poet" who "wrote" "on film" and who produced "poetic documentary film."[34] Poetry, for Vertov, was cinematic truth rooted in the invisible. In other words, poetic documentary film was the product of strategic "comparisons" of social behavior which aimed "to decipher reality" by way of a particular social technology of observation/manufacture that worked on pieces of film "from the beginning to the end of production."[35] This process was governed, as we have seen, by a dialectical form of thought ("most easily translated by montage"[36]) which allowed for the exploitation of the inherent difference between two adjacent film frames—a difference defined, in the final analysis, in terms of *intervals*—but nevertheless experienced at all the levels of observation/manufacture.[37] As Vertov pointed out at the time,

> To find the most convenient itinerary for the eyes of the spectator in the midst of all these mutual reactions, of these mutual attractions, of these mutual repulsions of images among themselves, to reduce this whole multiplicity of intervals (of movements from one image to the other) to a simple spectacular equation: to a spectacular formula expressing in the best possible manner the essential theme of the cine-thing, such is the most difficult and important task of the author of montage.[38]

If montage functioned as the dialectical semio-logic articulating Kino-Eye's social technology of observation/manufacture and its tripartite ritual structure, Vertov's theory of intervals was its thematic complement inasmuch as it made perceptual sense of the visual connections that articulated particular thematic vignettes. From the point at which documents were to be related to a chosen theme ("montage evaluation"), through the stage of "montage synthesis" of the human eye ("montage of personal observation or of reports by the information-gatherers and scouts of the film") involving the "plan of shots"—the "result of the selection and classification of the observations of the 'human eye'" conceived in relation to the "peculiarities of the 'machine-eye' of Kino-Eye"—to the period of "general montage" when the visual equation is worked out, one can understand the *production of truth* to pivot on the interval, "upon a movement between the pieces." This is minimally expressed in the difference between two successive frames; "upon the proportions of these pieces between themselves, upon the transitions from one visual impulse to the one following it";[39] and upon the reflexivity generated at the thematic level by means of the "meaning ties" or formal linkages established by the visual rhythm created by orchestrating the intervals.[40]

The interval would thus serve to link montage technique directly to the mechanical and photochemical foundations of the film process: to the photochemical creation of difference in the movement of two frames through the film gate of a camera, and the reproduction of that difference in the movement of a film through a projector gate. A theory of the interval would, in other words, ensure a linkage and engagement between the evolving thematic geography of the film and a spectator's maturing consciousness by way of a specific perceptual itinerary plotted, as in the case of the *The Man with a Movie Camera*, under the aegis of the Camera/Eye.

In the process of reconstructing meaning, the audience, as both subjects and objects articulated in the context of a Kinomatic rite of passage, would no longer find themselves excluded from the process of observation/manufacture that constructed this cinematic experience. At the beginning of *The Man with a Movie Camera's* rite-of-incorporation sequence, the audience is introduced to the "real" author of the film: an anthropomorphic Camera/Eye. Thus, in the course of the film, consciousness has been gradually redefined from a human to a panhuman consciousness: its final form—an animated camera and tripod symbolizing the "birth" of a new type of collective consciousness whose "representation" or identity pattern is not the dense factually based thematic interpretation Kino-Eye had forged in relation to a contemporary Soviet reality in this film, but rather Kino-Eye's simple and refined observational logic, a logic that managed to articulate, as never before, a newly evolving social space in terms of a previously unmapped cinematic space. Had this blueprint for a kinomatic rite of passage found social sanction with post-revolutionary authorities, Vertov's dream of an open-ended socialist vision might have found broader collective expression. Instead, Vertov's film was ignored—its revolutionary impulse to be subsequently legitimated within the context of an avant-garde aesthetic tradition, the product of the kind of capitalist system that Vertov had attempted to systematically undermine through Kino-Eye's theoretical and practical work.

Kino-Eye's Logical Excess: Vertov on the Total Collectivization of the Human Sensorium

In retrospect, it is evident that the Kinoks were not, in fact, considered to be individual persons but rather basic elements in observational modules composed of two integrated components (film camera and Kinok intelligence) that together comprised a minimal social unit in a technology of observation whose collective cinematic intelligence was compounded through physical and emotional bonding into a perfect bio-cinematic consciousness. In terms of our current understanding of this linking of machine and human organism, these elements combined to form a prototype *cyborg* consciousness: a kinomatically integrated "brain" and consciously reflexive observational technology. It was this consciousness—whose dominant symbol was the Camera/Eye—which operated on the audience during the course of *The Man with a Movie Camera*.

However, Vertov proposed that the Kino-Eye mode of organizing observation/ manufacture also be extended *horizontally* in order to link together other technologies of the human senses with the aim of transforming human thought itself:

> The theoretical and practical work of the *Kinoks-radioks* . . . have run ahead of their technical possibilities and for a long time have been awaiting a technical basis the advent of which will be late, in relation to Kino-Eye; they await the Sound-Cine and Television.
>
> Recent technical acquisitions in this area lend powerful arms to the partisans and workers of *documentary sound cinegraphy* in their struggle for a revolution in the cinema, for the abolition of play, for an October of Kino-Eye.
>
> From the montage of visual facts recorded on film (Kino-Eye) we pass to the montage of visual and acoustic facts transmitted by radio (Radio-Eye).
>
> We shall go from there to the simultaneous montage of visual-acoustic-tactile-olfactory facts, etc.
>
> We shall then reach the stage where we will surprise and record *human thoughts*, and, finally, we shall reach to the greatest experiments of direct organization of thoughts (and consequently of actions) of all mankind.
>
> Such are the technical perspectives of Kino-Eye, born of the October Revolution.[41]

This passage, from a lecture delivered in the same year *The Man with a Movie Camera* was released, indicated the principal stage leading to a highly rationalized cultural politics of representation. As Kino-Eye's composite sense-organ became increasingly collectivized in relation to the other senses, and its powers were increasingly dissipated through sensorial integration, there would be a progressive erosion of its undisputed ability to claim a scopic sovereignty over the social spaces of an evolving Soviet culture. In hindsight, it is now possible to suggest that this democratization of the senses would ultimately lead to a kind of expanded sensorial intersystem—in other words, a comprehensive post-ocularcentric culture.

The model Vertov outlined in this 1929 lecture was, of course, directly patterned on Kino-Eye's organizational model for observational diffusion. However, at this final stage in Vertov's blueprint for a socialist reconstruction of the human sensorium, it was no longer a question of coordinating and structuring individual observers so as to form a flexible, multi-faceted, technology of observation/manufacture. There was now the suggestion of a new series of sensory possibilities, a new range of perceptual transformations rooted in new patterns of identity emerging from a range of "intelligent" sensorially integrated human/machine interfaces. It is not surprising, therefore, that totally global human thought would represent Kino-Eye's final threshold of revolutionary transformation, since transformations in habitual modes of thought and consciousness had already been prefigured in the structure and activities of its most "primitive," compact, and mobile observational unit: the Kinok "cameraman."

"Kino-Eye is learning" was Vertov's reply to a question by the poet Vladimir Mayakovsky concerning its progress in 1934.[42] That assertion best sums up Vertov's attitude to his project: Kino-Eye learns, which means that the Kinoks and the audience are collectively introduced to new identities which would ideally continue to be generated along a continuum of technologies of representation until the October Revolution would consummate itself in a spectacular sensorial excess.

Conclusion

There are a number of lessons to be extracted from Vertov's revolutionary but abortive experiment. First, there is the curious phenomenon of an ultramodern visual experience—
The Man with a Movie Camera's—being structured in terms of a panhuman ritual. Could this represent a profound intuition concerning the human capacity to negotiate radical change, or does it illustrate the limits of Vertov's vision? There is, of course, no clear answer to this question, other than to suggest that this mode of negotiating major social transitions deserves further investigation in the context of other technologies of representation. Of particular interest in this connection, and at this point in time, are powerful new imaging systems such as virtual reality which have the capacity to interface directly with the human sensorium and ultimately incorporate it, in one form or another, into a global information network.[43] While investigations in this direction do not preclude the investigation of other ways of negotiating change, just what form they might take is beyond this paper's speculative range.

Second, there is the question of Vertov's kinomatic practice and its relevance to contemporary cinematic practice. It is evident that Vertov still has much to teach us about the relationship of theory and practice, the politics of representation, vision, and its connections to social change, and the necessity of exploring different organizational models for technologies of observation (notwithstanding his utopian call for a global sensibility which, in hindsight, rings ominously in the late-twentieth century ear). One might, however, correctly point out that filmmakers such as Godard and Jean-Pierre Gorin have already attempted without much success to build on Vertov's legacy. While the failure of these attempts demonstrates, in no uncertain terms, the powerful political constraints under which all artists and political activists operate at any one point in time, they also make it very clear that without these kinds of challenges and continual attempts at redirecting social expectations and restructuring cultural experience, we are, at this point, in the late-twentieth century, in grave danger of succumbing to a kind of blind technological amnesia. It is therefore worth bearing in mind Vertov's arguments and demonstrations concerning the social foundations of imaging systems, since they sensitize us to the fundamental importance of developing a flexible and mobile politics of technology that is able to keep pace with economic, political, social, and cultural change. *The Man with a Movie Camera* is exemplary in this connection, for it clearly presents its particular vision as a product of a theoretical and practical conjunction of a given imaging system (the movie camera) and a social technology of observation/manufacture. In other words, it is a model technology that not only creates and controls space it is *in itself* an organization of space, an inner space of critical social consciousness.

Third, there is Vertov's suggestion that technologies of representation be considered relationally—socio-logically—within a given mediascape. And that they be defined in terms of a complex intersystem of technologies of observation and related image cultures whose impact on the human sensorium can be measured according to alterations in its sense ratios. Walter Benjamin and a number of contemporary theorists, notably Marshall McLuhan and Paul Virilio, have made similar observations. Benjamin, for example, noted the impact of media on the relationship between the human senses as did McLuhan almost thirty years later.[44] Recently Virilio has devoted considerable energy to describing the logistics of military perception and its penetration throughout our social fabric.[45] Clearly, Vertov's work on Kino-Eye predates the work of these theorists, and goes beyond them in the sense of *actively* seeking to articulate new perceptual relationships through Kino-Eye, to the extent of embracing new sensory possibilities which might exist beyond the limitations of specific technologies as in the case of his espousal of a military model for Kino-Eye (whatever apprehensions or criticisms one might have, in retrospect, of his choice of metaphor) or his radical call for a collectivization of the human sensorium.

There is, however, another direction in Vertov's work which might provide a more fruitful contribution to contemporary debates on media: his suggestion that a critical poetics is only possible at the cultural intersection of observational technologies which manufacture the "real" (clearly in Vertov's estimation, a floating signifier of the historical artifact "representation"), and that it can only take form through an active and critical engagement with the comparative differences generated by fundamental contradictions inhering in particular cultural formations. For Vertov, it was this conjunction which gave political sense to social consciousness and identity. Thus, it is perhaps this aspect of Vertov's legacy which will prove to be the most enduring, since it motivates and gives conscious form to an open and situationally reflexive poetics.

While production has given way to consumption as a cultural dominant and new technologies such as virtual reality threaten to redefine our sensorial landscape and, indeed, the very basis of our identities as human beings, Vertov's practice remains, to this day, a useful touchstone in the search for ways to foster new modes of looking, new ways of seeing ourselves and others.

Notes

An earlier version of this paper was presented at the "Film as Ethnography" conference, University of Manchester in September 1990.

1.   Dziga Vertov, "We: Variant of a Manifesto," in Annette Michelson, ed., *Kino-Eye: The Writings of Dziga Vertov*, trans. Kevin O'Brien (London and Sydney: Pluto Press, 1984), 9.

2.   On the avant-garde see Peter Wollen, "The Two Avant-Gardes," *Studio International* vol. 190, no. 978 (1975): 171–75. For a discussion of Vertov's influence on Godard see Kent E. Carroll, "Film and Revolution: Interview with the Dziga-Vertov Group," in Royal S. Brown, ed., *Focus on Godard* (Englewood Cliffs: Prentice Hall, 1972), 50–64. For a discussion of the social and political background to Vertov's work and its relationship to postrevolutionary Russian culture see Annette Michelson, Introduction, *Kino-Eye*, op. cit., xv–lxi and Stephen Crofts and Olivia Rose, "An Essay Towards *Man with a Movie Camera*," *Screen* vol. 18, no. 1 (1977): 9–58. An extensive formal analysis of *The Man with a Movie Camera* can be found in Vlada Petric,

Constructivism in Film: The Man with the Movie Camera, A Cinematic Analysis (Cambridge: Cambridge University Press, 1987).

3.   See, for example, Godard's comments in Kent E. Carroll, "Film and Revolution: Interview with the Dziga-Vertov Group," *ibid.*

4.   My use of the phrase "social technologies of observation" is derived, in part, from Teresa de Lauretis's influential definition of gender as a social technology. Thus, according to de Lauretis, gender can be considered "both as representation and as self-representation . . . the product of various social technologies, such as cinema, and of institutionalized discourses, epistemologies, and critical practices, as well as practices of daily life." *Technologies of Gender: Essays on Theory, Film, and Fiction* (Bloomington and Indianapolis: Indiana University Press, 1987), 2.

5.   I have borrowed the term "situational reflexivity" from *Femamatic* (L. Hissey, A. Hearn, L. McLarty), "Alice Does or Situational Reflexivity: Toward a Theory of Active Female Spectators" (unpublished manuscript, 1990) because it encapsulates the radical spirit, if not the gendered letter, of Vertov's Modernist cinematic practice. In Femamatic's words (11–12): "The term 'situational' refers to the immediate social context of subjects . . . those intersecting elements of . . . subjectivities: race, class, gender, sexual preference, age, etc. It also incorporates the specific context of viewing and the particular text in question. The situation is both materially and discursively constituted. In short, situation involves our momentary sense of 'self' and the representation of that 'self' to us through discourse. The situation is never static: its status is always changing and temporally defined . . . The notion of reflexivity adds to the immediacy and temporality of situation a reflective dimension which permits the apprehension of common experiences of oppression. This, in turn, points not only to the possibility, but to the very necessity, of making normative claims."

6.   For classic discussions of rites of passage, see Arnold Van Gennep, *The Rites of Passage,* trans. M. B. Vizedom and G. L. Caffee (Chicago: University of Chicago Press, 1960); and Victor Turner, "Betwixt and Between: The Liminal Period in Rites de Passage," in V. Turner, *The Forest of Symbols: Aspects of Ndembu Ritual* (Ithaca and London, Cornell University Press, 1977), 93–111. For an analysis of the photographic process as rite of passage see David Tomas, "Toward an Anthropology of Sight: Ritual Performance and the Photographic Process," *Semiotica,* vol. 68, nos. 3/4 (1988): 245–70.

7.   Vertov, "Kino-Eye," in *Kino-Eye,* op. cit., 63:

Musical, theatrical, and film-theatrical representations act, above all, on the viewer's or listener's subconscious, completely circumventing his protesting consciousness.

8.   cf. Vertov, "From Kino-Eye to Radio-Eye," *Kino-Eye,* op. cit., 87:

Kino-eye = kino-seeing (I see through the camera) + Kino-writing (I write on film with the camera) + kino-organization (I edit).

The kino-eye method is the scientifically experimental method of exploring the visible world—
  a. based on the systematic recording on film of facts from life;
  b. based on the systematic organization of the documentary material recorded on film.

Thus, kino-eye is not only the name of a group of film workers. Not only the name of a film . . . And not merely some so-called artistic trend (left or right). Kino-eye is an ever-growing movement for influence through facts as opposed to influence through fiction, no matter how strong the imprint of fiction.

9.   For a description of the film's rhetorically based cinematic language see Annette Michelson, "'The Man with the Movie Camera': From Magician to Epistemologist," *Artforum* vol. 10., no. 7 (1972): 66–67, 69.

10.   Vertov, "The Man with a Movie Camera," in *Kino-Eye,* op. cit., 83.

11.   Annette Michelson, "The Kinetic Icon in the Work of Mourning: Prolegomena to the Analysis of a Textual System," *October* 52 (1990), 19; Michelson, op. cit., 63 n. 7.

12.   Michelson, op. cit., n. 10.

13.   Vertov, "Kinoks: A Revolution," in *Kino-Eye,* op. cit., 13, 12.

14.   Michelson op. cit., 69, n. 7.

15.   *Ibid.*

16.   For a discussion of dominant symbols see Victor Turner, "Symbols in Ndembu Ritual," op. cit., 30–32, n. 11.

17.   Vertov, "Kinoks: A Revolution," in *Kino-Eye,* op. cit., 16. In Vertov's words (19):

The mechanical eye, the camera, rejecting the human eye as crib sheet, gropes its way through the chaos of visual events, letting itself be drawn or repelled by movement, probing, as it goes, the path of its own movement. It experiments, distending time, dissecting movement, or, in contrary fashion, absorbing time within itself, swallowing years, thus schematizing processes of long duration inaccessible to the normal eye.

18. *Ibid.*, 19

19. *Ibid.* For the standard discussion of *ostranenie* or defamiliarization see Victor Shklovsky, "Art as Technique," in *Russian Formalist Criticism: Four Essays*, trans. Lee T. Lemon and Marion J. Reis (Lincoln: University of Nebraska Press, 1965), 3–24.

20. Michelson, op. cit., 69–70 n.7.

21. cf. Turner, op. cit., 99–110 n. 11.

22. Martin Jay, "Scopic Regimes of Modernity," in Hal Foster, ed., *Vision and Visuality* (Seattle: Bay Press, 1988), 5.

23. Vertov, "Kinoks: A Revolution," in *Kino-Eye*, op. cit., 14–16.

24. Judith Mayne, "Kino-Truth and Kino-Praxis: Vertov's Man with a Movie Camera," *Cine-Tracts* vol. 1, no. 2 (1977): 88.

25. Vertov, "Kino-Eye," in *Kino-Eye*, op. cit., 72.

26. *Ibid.*

27. *Ibid.*, 75.

28. Michelson, op. cit., n. 7, 65.

29. Vertov, "Kino-Eye," in *Kino-Eye*, op. cit., 69. There is a parallel to be explored here between Vertov's project and the militarization of perception as described by Paul Virilio in *War and Cinema: The Logistics of Perception,* trans. Patrick Camiller (London: Verso, 1989). However, this is the subject of another paper.

30. Vertov, "Kinoks: A Revolution," in *Kino-Eye,* op. cit., 20.

31. *Ibid.*, "Notebooks, Diaries," 167.

32. *Ibid.*

33. Michelson, op. cit., 72 n. 7.

34. Vertov, "Notebooks, Diaries," in *Kino-Eye* op. cit., 199, 183.

35. Vertov, "Notebooks, Diaries," in *Kino-Eye*, op. cit., 197 and "Kinoks-Revolution," op. cit., 90, 103 n. 34,

36. Luda Schnitzer, Jean Schnitzer, and Marcel Martin, eds., *Cinema in Revolution* (London: Secker & Warburg, 1973), 85.

37. Vertov, "Kinoks-Revolution," op. cit., 104 n. 34:

The school of Kino-Eye requires that the cine-thing be built upon 'intervals,' that is, upon a movement between the pieces, the frames; upon the proportions of these pieces between themselves, upon the transitions from one visual impulse to the one following it.

38. *Ibid.*, 104–105.

39. *Ibid.*, 103, 104.

40. cf. Vertov, "From Kino-Eye to Radio-Eye," in *Kino-Eye*, op. cit., 90–91: The "movement between shots"—the transitions from one visual stimulus or "visual 'interval'" were negotiated by way of a "sum of various correlations," amongst which were:

  1. the correlation of planes (close-up, long shot, etc.);
  2. the correlation of foreshortenings;
  3. the correlation of movements within the frame;
  4. the correlation of light and shadow;
  5. the correlation of recording speeds.

Vertov goes on to note: "Besides the movement between shots (the 'interval'), one takes into account the visual relation between adjacent shots and of each individual shot to all others engaged in the 'montage battle' that is beginning" in order "to find amid all these mutual reactions, these mutual attractions and repulsions of shots, the most expedient 'itinerary' for the eye of the viewer, to reduce this multitude of 'intervals' . . . to a simple visual equation . . . expressing the basic theme of the film-object."

41. Dziga Vertov, "'Kinoks-Revolution,' Selections," in Harry M. Geduld, ed., *Film Makers on Film Making* (Bloomington and London: Indiana University Press, 1967), 101–102.

42. Vertov, "Notebooks, Diaries," in *Kino-Eye*, op. cit., 180.

43. See, for example, my "Old Rituals for New Space: *Rites de Passage* and William Gibson's Cultural Model of Cyberspace," in Michael Benedikt, ed., *Cyberspace: First Steps* (Cambridge Mass.: M.I.T. Press, 1991), 31–47.

44. Walter Benjamin, "The Work of Art in the Age of Mechanical Reproduction," in Hannah Arendt, ed., *Illuminations* (New York: Schocken Books, 1976), 222; Marshall McLuhan, *Understanding Media: The Extensions of Man* (New York: A Mentor Book, 1964), 61.

45. Virilio, *op. cit.*, n. 29.

Post-Bourgeois Tattoo
Reflections on Skin Writing in
Late Capitalist Societies

Marc Blanchard

THIS PAPER DOES THREE THINGS. IT DESCRIBES THE NATURE OF TATTOOING FROM A HISTORICAL and cross-cultural perspective. It argues that in the West tattooing has moved from the margins of society to the core of the middle class and it examines some of the politics and the economics of tattooing. Finally, the paper links the sociocultural and economic aspects of tattooing with its symbolic and communicative functions. Throughout the paper, the question is raised of the relevance of a tattooing practice and aesthetic to the postmodern or postbourgeois anthropological and humanistic perspective.[1]

Tattooing, like writing, is a socially significant practice. Unlike writing, however, it is absolutely context-specific. There is no tattooing on stone, paper or sheepskin. Tattooing may be writing of sorts, but precisely because it involves mutilation of the human body, it is also linked to religious practices and psychosexual tendencies. Although we recognize since Freud the libidinal energy invested in writing and the instruments of writing, tattooing, because it always involves a degree of pain, and certainly always a fear of pain, signifies the particular pain of having a message written or painted on and sent by one's own body. But because tattooing, by being of the body, also raises the question of the support it receives from the body or, to borrow a Heideggerian term, of the equipmentality of this body, tattooing's own field of inscription must be distinguished from that of other forms of body sculpture, from corset wearing to plastic surgery, without forgetting scarification and piercing of ear or nose and the numerous practices of self-mutilation à la Van Gogh. Practices of customizing the body must be seen not only in the context of the social conventions they underwrite, but also in the broader context where ethnography poses the question of boundaries between systems of meaning, and at a deeper level still, that of the processes of inclusion and exclusion which shape all cultures. Not only does tattooing, like other forms of body art, impose a distinction between marked and unmarked subjects, it also forces upon the viewer the perception of a special relation between image and support or frame. Not only does the tattoo's message establish normative differences (the image of the tattooed male as "tough guy" or that of the gang member displaying the symbol which certifies him a member of the group), but this message is itself carried in the context of an equivalence or an opposition between the body frame or support and the image itself. There are cases of tattooing so extensive, for instance, that distinguishing the limits between the body and the image becomes impossible. A tattoo can become a trompe l'oeil, as is clear from the image of the Breton warrior composed in the sixteenth century for a series of French *Cosmographies* (Fig. 1).

Tattooing is different from body sculpting—from, for instance, the footbinding of imperial Chinese women. The point of tattooing, as everyone knows, is to insert designs beneath the skin. And while scarification and piercing may also originally have had to do with asserting the bearer's status as well as masculine rites of passage (the subject is supposed to remain stoic and to bear without flinching the ritual procedures of cutting and insertion), tattooing had and may still have magical and religious purposes. It is part of a system of exoskeletal defenses: it can serve as a charm protecting the tattooee or giving him or her special benefits in the immediate environment as well as the afterlife. Thus in Borneo, spirits of certain women were assigned tasks after death based on the amount and the kind of tattoos they had received during their life (Hambly 1974 [1925]: 204–205; Vlahos 1979: 182–96 [quoted in Sanders 1989:11]). Tattoo, which works by insertion, must also be contrasted with the ephemeral painting decoration of the sort that Lévi-Strauss incautiously describes in *Tristes Tropiques* as merely the saving remnant of a complex technique of (permanent) tattooing that has grown extinct.[2]

Historically then, tattooing has four functions: a ritual function, as when an adolescent, usually male, goes through a rite of passage; an apotropaic or protective function (in this case the link between tattoo and taboo is clear, as the person with the sacred mark is sacred); an identificatory function, whereby the individual asserts his participation in a group, a sect or a gang; and finally, a decorative function. While I am making distinctions between separate functions, they are in fact related. Thus, the apotropaic or protective function is clearly related to the identificatory function, as was the case for the involuntarily tattooed numbers of the concentration camp inmates. Another example, that of eighteenth-century Japan, shows how the decorative and the identificatory function mesh. In mid-eighteenth-century Japan, a Chinese novel, the *Suikoden,* became so popular that many people, including the most famous outlaws of the time were inspired by the story to wear tattoos relating to characters or episodes of the story (Richie and Buruma 1980: 11–33; McCallum 1988). Incidentally, the reason there may be fewer tattoos inspired by Doonesbury, Pogo or Peanuts, is that those cartoons are not, strictly speaking, narrative stories but cartoons in which identification with the anecdotal hero could not be sustained enough to warrant the tattooing. However,

Fig. 1. Original drawing by John White, engraved by de Bry, Virginia c. 1589.

returning to the various functions of tattooing, the point is that no one has ever received a tattoo for one reason only and it is part of the power of tattooing that it fulfills more than one function at once in a complex signifying system.[3]

Historically, the point must also be made that the growth and epiphany of tattooing in our Western culture dates from the West's early modern travels and discoveries, and the beginning of the European colonial cycle in what is today the Third World. Tattooing was known in Antiquity and practiced only a little during the Middle Ages. But it is only after the Conquest of Africa, America, and Polynesia that tattoos and tattooing became recognized in Europe. Yet the reference to colonization is more than a historical marker. Indeed, there seems to be a link between the reception of tattooing in Europe and the ideology of colonization. Not only because Western man does *not* customarily tattoo his body, but precisely because tattoos are the mark of the colonized other: the difference between the colonizer and the colonized is in the texture of the skin. The former's skin is white and transparent. The latter's is made opaque by the designs in it.

The term *tatu* was brought back by Captain Cook from Polynesia, where it was used with political, military and/or religious connotations.[4] Chiefs and priests wore the most beautiful tattoos. In other words, tattooing consecrated the upper echelons of society, where it served both an aesthetic and protective function (the tattooee is protected by the intricate design [Kaeppler 1988]) as well as a geopolitical function (the tattooee's body reaffirms in a kind of physiography the integrity of the cultural anatomy and the political terrain [Steiner 1990]). The tattooing rage caught Europe by fire, but was subsequently limited to the lower classes, especially those, sailors, soldiers, and merchants, who could travel. Soon, however, heavily tattooed individuals exhibited themselves all over Europe, and members of the aristocracy had their body tattooed as well. In the United States it was during the Civil War that tattooing became the fashion among soldiers, especially sailors. By and large, however, the European and American middle classes were not interested in tattooing. I may be accused of muddling the field a bit with such varied geographic and cultural references, but tattooing and especially the acculturation of tattooing in the West has a complex history which can only be understood at the intersection of disciplines, viz., anthropology, sociology and psychoanalysis. It may be argued that reading tattoos from a Western point of view erases one fundamental cultural difference between non-Western and Western tattooing. But to the extent that in non-Western societies the body is not merely a support for the tattoo aesthetic but is an integral part of the message being communicated in a context where body and design are harmonized into one system of communication, an interdisciplinary inquiry into the phylogeny and the cultural translation of tattooing aims at being more than a comparative study of tattoo inscriptions. It will show that tattooing can be interpreted neither as total "native" communication system in an anthropology nostalgic for origins nor as postmodern aesthetic form in an ethnography unaware of its own wish to avoid origination. For tattooing always asks of its practitioners and its beholders the question of what kind of specialized writing it is. Indeed, tattooing is not only properly a sign which denotes social distinction on the body or part of the body. It is also a sign of a sign: in addition to specifying differences of status and class, it has generally been variously interpreted in the West as illustrating the many facets of the social bond between individual and society, the self and the Other.[5] And because of the postmodern interest in forms of writing, authority, violence, and representations of the body, tattooing can also be seen as an appropriate context in which to examine the issues of indelible writing, body gendering and the observer's gaze, among others.

A man named O'Reilly on the East Coast was alone responsible in the 1890s for spreading the vogue of the Japanese tattoo, not only because he invited Japanese practitioners to New York, but also because he was the first to sell sheets of tattoo designs by mail all over the country and thus was instrumental in homogenizing the production of tattoos across the country. Very soon after it was imported from Japan, tattooing became the rage in the United States, but again, only in certain quarters. It was considered taboo by a large segment of the press and the middle class developed a certain paranoia vis-à-vis individuals with indelible ink on their body. These exclusionary attitudes prevail until today, so that tattooing is considered either deviant or marginal or as the German would put it, *alternativ*, without much attention being paid to the role that tattooing plays in the consumer culture.[6] And yet the consideration of tattooing as a deviant practice seems to replicate to some degree the excluding and differing which surrounds tattoos in primitive cultures. There, although tattoos cannot properly be said to be deviant because they are often a mark of distinction to which non-tattooed individuals aspire, they remain essential to social stratification (puberty) and symbolic interaction. Those who are tattooed are set apart from the rest, they bear the mark of otherness and are often sacred. Wearing tattoos, they are both revered *and* feared precisely because of their otherness, and this is where the connection can be made between a gang member who acquires a tattoo because of a desire to instill fear and a South Sea chief who acquires *moko* (Maori tattooing) because of a latent birth/death symbolism in the concept of *moko*.[7]

M.
Blanchard

Today, in modern society, tattooing is seen as dispensing a product by unskilled practitioners, a product whose hygiene is dubious. In addition, tattoo shops are located in slums or peripheral areas and tattooing is perceived as bringing back the whiff of those neighborhoods (Steward 1990: 19–36). But there has been a tattoo renaissance since the 1960s, despite the fact that tattooing is still banned in many states of the Union (Rubin 1988). It is not uncommon now to see middle-class people having a part of their body tattooed, often the part that will be seen only by their loved ones. As tattooing has become more emotionally and socially upscale, it is also clear that the art critical world has taken notice of this change. And the vogue of discussions on the body has, no doubt, contributed to some degree to the reintegration of tattooing into the artistic canon. This acceptance must also be linked with the taste for replication and transformation of primitive styles. For instance, the primitive and Japanese traditions have had an impact on the patterns and designs of tattoos. We have thus examples of Japanese-inspired wave or plant motifs as well as neo-tribal designs, which closely follow body contours. On the other hand, it is also true that tattooing is now seeing a renewal of anthropological interest, as the decorating and magic practices of primitive people are considered not only part of a traditional body aesthetic but also as symbolic of the fundamental exclusions and polarities on which culture as a whole is constructed.

In the rest of this paper, I would like to reflect on the sociocultural shapes of modern tattooing. Tattooing belongs in systems of cultural commercial productions. Instead of being highly centralized, it is essentially diffused throughout the community and highly competitive. Tattooing tends to be individual, not centrally organized. In that sense it remains a form of art close to craft. However, because tattooing has been up to now part of a marginal economy, it has been limited by a market in which the demand is determined by a group whose tastes are defined by emulation. Most people want to have the tattoos their friends have. It is only recently that tattoo artists have attempted to develop tattoo patterns which are very much unlike those of the typical tattoo consumer. This is perhaps a consequence of the fact that there is a clientele for tattoos of a higher socioeconomic background, which can indulge its different tastes. The economic aspect is not unimportant. Tattooing is not simply a question of taste, but a question of the artistic empowerment of the subject. As tattoos are being favored by higher income groups, they gain cultural legitimacy with the middle class, following in this the pattern of other forms of art such as jazz, film, even graffiti, which were originally enjoyed by low status groups and are now part of an enlightened aesthetic canon. It can even be said that the acceptance of tattoo is part of the general glamorization of "trash" in popular culture and especially in the entertainment world (Madonna and Cher are good examples).[8] However, tattooing continues to remain different. For instance, the difference between tattoo and graffiti remains that tattooing is writing on the body while graffiti is writing on equipment and the environment.[9] Also graffiti attains the status of art object when it is taken out of this environment, whereas tattoos remain on the body forever. Just as removing tattoos is almost impossible without skin grafting, considering tattooing in the abstract, much as one would speculate on the hermeneutics of writing, is pointless. Because a person's skin is as close as you will ever get to his or her private self, because skin is in fact what ultimately guarantees a person's physical integrity, a skin tattoo, while usually inscribed by a third party, the tattooist, is more than any other art product taken to reflect and to affect a person's presentation of his or her self in everyday life. A tattoo, while social, is of the person: a signature on one's skin.

Having said this, let me return to the economic aspect of tattooing. First, tattooing is the scene of an economic exchange and of the first division of labor: that between artist producer and consumer who in effect consumes his or her own body, if only because it would be difficult for someone to tattoo himself or herself—which is another reason why tattooing must be distinguished from other body decorations and paintings. There are self-portraits, but I doubt if there are self-tattoos, if only because one cannot suffer the pain of the tattooing process *and* execute the process at the same time. In economic terms, tattooing implies a process where individuals set up shop to offer what is basically body decoration and other individuals contract to have that service performed on their body. In this sense the tattooist is probably not different from the cosmetician or the hairdresser. But there is today at least a marked gendered difference. While hairdressers and cosmeticians attend mostly to women, today tattooists, for the most part, attend mostly to men.[10] Second, the tattooist in most cases operates only once on his subjects' body, while the hairdresser and the cosmetician build up a support of steady regular customers. Third, because for most people tattooing occurs only once, and their body is the site of a permanent imprint, it can be said that there is something in tattooing which escapes the flow of commodification. Because the body is there always, the image, the writ of tattoo is not as reproducible, and even if the design for the tattooed image can indeed be mass produced, as has been possible since O'Reilly, it is the individual body which bears this image, thus making the replication of the tattoo contingent upon its siting on the body of a specific subject. Tattooing, its practitioners and its clients, thus remain artisanal.

Furthermore, to the degree that prospective clients have an important say in shaping the production capabilities of the tattoo cottage industry by requesting custom designs which the tattooist then must execute, the decision to acquire a tattoo remains an individual decision, however much this decision might be the result of peer pressure. This fact effectively limits the possibility that the relation between producer (the tattooist) and consumer (tattooee) could be entirely subject to the laws of the market. On this point, at least for now and waiting for tattooing chains on the model of beauty parlor chains, the modern tattooed body remains a precapitalist body.[11] Conversely, however, the tattooed symbol often becomes fetishized, because the psychosexual context of tattooing is one where the inscription of a permanent symbol on the body has the effect of presenting the symbol as more desirable precisely because it is indelibly part of the body. It apportions that part of the body on which it is drawn as the dual object of desire, something like the Lacanian or Kleinian partial object which is central, yet resistive to total possession. The body can be bled, carved, and inscribed, and yet it lives on after the inscription: reassuringly the same and yet different (Kafka 1969; Walsh 1988: 181). By being inscribed on the surface of the body, the tattoo suggests a fragmentation of the body as material object supporting the fantasy as well as entirely appropriated by it. The picture of the self-loving penis is very much an illustration of this curious narcissism in reverse where the subjective body is divested so as to make possible the immediate reinvestment on its surface of the pictured object in the tattoo (Fig. 2).

In any case, tattooing is moving away from being a disvalued craft to being redefined as a new art form seeking legitimation. This process of legitimation entails not only a return to tradition but an attempt to present tattoo as producing original designs, and not simply replicating exemplars of limited economic value. It entails as well the presentation of tattooing specimens in museums and archives and making films where tattooing where tattooing is a central theme, like *Tattoo* with the actor Bruce Dern or novels like *The Illustrated*

Fig. 2.

Man by Ray Bradbury, which was subsequently made into a film. In this legitimation process, however, photographic reproduction has played an essential role. In fact, Marcia Tucker (1981) insists that the growing vogue of tattoo as a basic art form is actually a by-product of the development of photography: people could look at pictures of tattoo without being confronted by the physicality of the body beneath the tattoo.

However, the photographic reproduction of tattoo is less interesting for its aesthetic than for its sociocultural aspects, as the exact replication of tattoo flaunts images of deviant practices into the eye of the beholder. Tattooing suggests deviance through an unorthodox or sacred mode of inscription, and on the other hand, it controls this deviance by making the pain of inscribing and the inscription itself part of an operation by which the tattooed subject is both excluded from the community of those without tattoo and identified in the process of that exclusion. In Auschwitz, prisoners were tattooed because they were Jewish. This was the end of an ongoing process of exclusion: first the yellow star and then the tattoo on the lower arm.[12] Indeed, while tattooing prisoners and slaves is related to a world wide practice of branding social captives as commodities, Jewish men were the only ones among the inmates who could have been identified by the fact that they had been circumcised (checking individual foreskins was an all too common practice of Gestapo agents and affiliates during interrogation of male suspects throughout Europe during World War II, the express purpose being to check for the trace of Jewish mutilation and decide who might have been lying about his racial status).[13]

In all this, the line between deviance and control is a very thin one. To the extent that male circumcision has now become generalized in the United States among Gentile males, the sacred motive for it has been displaced by a scientific one. Circumcision has received the broad support of the medical profession on hygienic grounds. However, there has been a recent shift in medical opinion: circumcision is no longer deemed necessary and many physicians are now recommending against it being routinely performed.[14] Conversely, tattoos, which not so long ago were perceived to be the mark of social misfits, have now gained acceptance into the middle classes. These examples show how in the world of tattooing, a problematic of deviance and control hinging on rites of exclusion is subject to mutation and reversal. While Jewish circumcision was grotesquely mimicked by the lower arm tattoo of Auschwitz, the art tattoo of the once social misfit finds its way into the middle classes.

How then should we read tattoos? To be sure, they have been and continue to be the mark of deviance. Tattooed persons use tattoos, supposedly, as a way to protect their ego. In prisons, old-fashioned psychiatric studies used to suggest that persons with tattoos (it was estimated in the nineteenth century that one-third of prisoners had tattoos [Lombroso 1902]) either had a pathological need for attention or had a propensity to crime. A more acceptable theory suggests that prisoners and the clinically insane tattoo themselves because they have a need for identity which their being incarcerated has only exacerbated (Goffman 1961: 14–21; Mosher 1967). But this interpretation applies essentially to men, since a certain research claims that women are more interested in the aesthetic value of tattoos than men and see tattooing as a device to control the viewer's gaze.[15] By tattooing their bodies and establishing their membership in a subculture group, prisoners who seek tattoos protect their identity from repressive authority.[16] In all cases, both that of the prisoner and the clinically insane, much is made of the tattooing procedure and equipment, to suggest in any case the importance of the sexual symbolism associated with it. Not only is the needle suggestive of penetration but it has been argued that tattoo artists are for the majority gay males who use their art to remain close to the male body, which they can handle and touch in the process of executing their designs (Sanders [1989: 191])—although the argument might also be made, as in the film with Dern, that the psychosexual charge can work both for homosexuals and heterosexuals. However, because in the tattooing process the body is essentially the object of the gaze in a context where the tattooed subject looks for identification and separation, tattooing in effect capitalizes on the specular effects of this gaze in what remains a masculine ideology regulating what may be seen and what may not be seen. Indeed body decoration and modification is strictly regulated in the West. For instance, limited body piercing is accepted. Women wear earrings, but until recently—that is, roughly until the emergence of street gangs—men wouldn't, unless they wanted to give a hint of "antisocial" behavior, to look like pirates or to send the message that they were gay.

In any case, tattooing's exclusion is always part of a process of the definition of the Self. Goffman (1963: 131–139) has insisted that displaying the tattoo not only has an affiliative effect, it is also linked to public accessibility, as the tattoo becomes a coveted form of visual communication. More often than not, persons wishing to be tattooed report having been influenced by a friend or having considered it for a long time. Often the decision to get tattooed and the choice of a particular tattoo underscore the significance of a highly significant symbolic choice. Thus a case story has it that a woman's desire for acquiring a tattoo originated in her mate's disapproval of her wish to wear a tattoo: being tattooed meant reclaiming her body from her husband. Then there is the story of the man who wanted the picture of a bee, because he was allergic to bees, and thought that no one would give him any problems on the street, if he himself carried the symbol of the killer bee (Sanders 1989: 46–47). Together, these trivial examples help us revisit the taboo aspects of apotropaic tattooing. It may not be for nothing that both tattoo and taboo are anthropological imports from the South Seas, and there may be a correlation between the two. Tattoos and taboos both speak to interdicted possession and gazing but, especially in the West, to the desire repressed by the interdiction and the uses, cultural, social, even economic, to which this interdiction can be put.[17] Not only is that which is not allowed desired, but the acquiring of the desired, the trafficking with the desired threatens or is fantasized to threaten, in all cases where wearing a tattoo is restricted, negative consequences. In the South Seas, only certain individuals could wear tattoos. In the West, the tattooed individual, by challenging a bourgeois exclusionary tradition, sets himself or herself as taboo: he or she sets himself or herself apart from a broad consensus on accepted cultural symbols in the society. In effect, by transgressing the norm of a transparent skin, the tattooee grapples with everyone else's epidermic anxiety and concern for skin integrity, and beyond that, he or she ends up questioning the rigidity of the social, cultural and economic order. The tattooing design implies that it is the body itself, and not a neutral object in space, which supports the ritual scene of representation.

M.
Blanchard

This scene is essentially apocalyptic. Tattoo is about revealing, being revealed and gazing upon the revealing. The tattooed subject focuses the public gaze on his or her body or part of the body while also delighting himself or herself as both exhibitionist and voyeur of his or her own spectacle, in a ritual of intense specularity. One could say that to wear a tattoo is to see and be seen by controlling the gaze, as the delight in revealing the tattoo is made more exquisite by the dreadful memory of a painful inscription: pleasure in the hint of pain. Tattoos remind us of stigmata. They are the objects of desire and they involve pain and the recognition of distinction and/or exclusion in all cultures.[18] Perhaps to seek the tattoo is the modern equivalent of seeking the stigma in our lay theology: a postmodern sainthood.

I have made a great deal in this paper of the radical difference of the tattoo. Let me, however, suggest in a paradoxical return to writing, that if tattoo is the saving remnant of the theological stigma, it haunts us as well for being the trace, the *arche* of the book: that which writers give their life and mind for without ever being able to write it: in another words, the impossible book, something like Mallarmé's or Blanchot's *Coming Book*. In a daydreaming moment, the French writer and anthropologist Michel Leiris (1981: 13) expresses the wish for tattooing his entire body with the text he has in his mind. He concludes, rather nostalgically, that he must have resorted to writing books after he realized that his dream of inscribing each and every part of his body with the conceptions of his mind could not be executed and instead of gazing and deciphering his own body, he would have to fill the blank pages of a book: his own. Let me suggest, then, that there is a way in which tattooing fulfills the writer's original ambition: to say it all and have it all at all times, instead of entrusting it, as Montaigne does, to the whims of fortune (Frame 1965: 764). One might even take the suggestion further, and state that the theories of the Book at the end of the nineteenth century, and I am thinking particularly of Mallarmé, and his legacy to Blanchot, Lévinas and Derrida, echo in a nostalgic way the Golden Age, or would it be Utopia, in which all there was to know about oneself and the world anyone in this world could carry written all over his or her own body without fear of ever losing it.

However, in this world where books are indeed different from tattoos, what kind of message is communicated by tattoo? The first is that writing is violent and that it hurts. In his description of the tribes in *Tristes Tropiques*, Lévi-Strauss (1974: 294–304) makes much of the fact that the origins of writing are associated with the beginnings of political violence and the push toward empire and domination. Derrida's (1975: 97–140) critique of this idealist conception is well known. There has always been violence and the justification for this violence begins with the idea that writing is the successor to voice and its civilized substitute and enforcer, when in fact this succession just confirms in the subordination of writing to speaking, the very authority that oppresses in the first place. And certainly there is violence in tattooing, as there is in the first form of writing. But the violence is physical: in the act of drawing letters on bare flesh, unlike the carving of wax tablets or sheepskins with a stylus or the inscribing of the first sheets of paper with a quill; and finally, in the needles and the electric machines with which the skin is decorated.

And it is that message which is communicated first. The recent resurgence of tattooing, even though the process may have been made less painful by enhanced technology (the degree of pain being largely dependent on the fineness of the needle), continues to speak to this violence. In the "Fifteen-Dollar Eagle," Sylvia Plath (1977), describing a tattoo shop, details a tattoo motif with Christ on Calvary: "If you've got a back to spare, there is Christ on the cross, a thief at either end and angels overhead to right and left holding up a scroll with 'Mt Calvary' on it in old English script, close as yellow can get to gold." The reference is obvious. The tattooee is identified as he or she that has suffered in order to be beautiful. This postmodern suffering has the significance of ritual thresholds in primitive societies—with the difference that in our time the tattooing imperative is now internalized and that in most cases, it is the individual who approaches the tattooist in a highly stylized, self-appointed rite of passage; and as in every rite of passage, the sacred situation or trial suggests a pattern of symbols that reveals the system of socially approved proper relations between individuals and groups.[19] Adapting Leach's (1954) theories, we can say that tattooing, as properly individual ritual, is especially rich because it pits the tattooee in an asymmetrical relation of dominance or subservience to the non-tattooed group. In this context, acquiring a tattoo in the West today can be seen as as a singular invocation of the power vested in primitive, nonliterate rituals which postmodern societies no longer authenticate. However, to the extent that tattooing represents the marking of a permanent territory of representation in postmodern societies now universally captive to transient images, a resurgence of tattooing also testifies to an ironic embrace of a proto-, an arch-writing, a durable *écriture* synonymous, less with the domestication of the savage mind than, pace Goody, with the harnessing of its power.[20] It is not a matter of simple scarification or of piercing an ear so that an earring can dangle. It is a matter of turning on the body's display function for ever. No longer is the body simply adorned. No longer is its surface a base for paints. It has itself become part of a permanent representation whose transparency it blocks. The first travelers to the New World were shocked by the primitives' complete nakedness and yet this nakedness was of another sort. The natives were not simply unclothed, their naked body was covered, "written" with decorations. And because many of those decorations were properly tattoos, the bodies were forever different, incomprehensible and irreconcilable: both naked and clothed in nakedness, so to speak (Cowan 1910: 189–90; Kaeppler 1988). Montaigne (Frame 1965: 159), following Jean de Léry, ironized on his cannibals: "All that is not too bad—but what's the use? They don't wear breeches."

The second message is that tattoos are meant to have a certain power different from that attached to painting, drawing or writing. Because tattoos can be deceptively simple, the explanation for the present vogue of tattooing is essentially the *belief* in tattoo. Better than writing or painting, tattooing, because of the specificity of its inserting modes, speaks to possession and the gaze authorizing it. In effect, the body absorbs the picture and projects it as a part of itself. The illusion is that there is no longer any distance between the image and its support: there is a belief that the image is forever.

The third message is that tattooing, working itself back from the margins of society into the reaches of middle-class suburbia, is one of the prime examples of the role of the body and a certain form of body art in negotiating the acceptability of deviant forms of representation in the whole gamut of social bonds available today. Unlike fashion, which covers the body, tattooing is basically about showing the body naked as the fundamental repository for a type of representation which mediates the other through a secondary narcissism. The tattooed subject displays his or her own body as the site of a mirror stage in which the body physically demonstrates its capacity to be seen directly as the site for presentation of the partial object which charms it and others, and for whose displaying it has, much as for a stigma, paid with its own blood.

Notes

1.   In the context of a partial economic view of the tattoo renaissance in late capitalist societies, I am using the term "postbourgeois" to deflect the thrust of a crude comparison between "bourgeois" and "tribal" societies such as is often presented in either Marxist or Structuralist anthropologies (see Sahlins 1976).

2. "Formerly, the designs were either tattooed or painted, but only painting now survives" (Lévi-Strauss 1974: 187).

3. This complexity is part of the richness and the secondary forming power of the tattooing semiosis, as is evidenced by the following quote:

> An indelible imprint, like a tattoo, is like a barrio imprimateur, locking a person in for what the group seemingly considers life. Members wear their tattoos with pride and gain a certain amount of status and adulation from barrio onlookers, especially siblings and younger individuals who look up to them. Often one's level of gang identity can be gauged by the amount and type of tattoo. Some might only place a small dot or a cross on their hand, between the thumb and forefinger, while others, especially the committed *veteranos*, might cover large parts of the body with a very elaborate art form. (Many of the latter have a practical reason for this, as tattoos help hide injection "marks" when they are "using.") (Vigil 1988: 115).

4. Cook himself is said to have introduced the word into the English language. The original morpheme was "ta," a Polynesian word connoting "striking" or "beating" (the OED notes that "tattoo" had been used since 1644 to denote the beating of drums). Scutt and Gotch (1974: 30) speculate that the word is onomatopoeic in origin, "representing the 'tat-tat' made by the tattooing tool." They argue further for a multiple origin of "tattooing" and suggest as well a Javanese derivation ("tau" = "scar"). It remains, in any case, that Captain Cook was the one to return from the South Pacific with a tattooed individual, Omai, who was exhibited throughout England.

5. The last avatar in this scouting for the original social bond takes the literal form of a theoretical projection of constructions of self-identity on the surface of the physical body touching and being touched. The idea is to suggest that the concept of person rests on a homology between inner self and outer corporeal envelope. Both function as interface in a psychoanalytical perspective redefining such "equipmental" concepts as "limit," "boundary," as well as simple "form" and "content" (Anzieu 1985).

6. Modern Western tattooing can be considered until recently as a "socially disvalued phenomenon" but sociology and anthropology have tended, with some exceptions (Adler and Adler 1983: 1987), to stay away from the analysis of consumption of marginal social services.

7. *Moko* also means "lizard" (Williams 1971: 207) and lizards were feared by the Maoris "and linked with both the dreaded mythical dragonlike *taniwha* and the very real *tuatara* (*Sphenodon punctatus*). The *tuatara* and the lizard shed their skins. In other words, their natural actions enact a metaphor, whereby they continually cycle from life to death to life, and so on, dropping one mask, one might say, in order to assume another" (Gathercole 1988).

8. It is also true that the incorporation of "trash" elements into middle class culture speaks more broadly to the overall relationship between deviance and social change. Material, especially sex-oriented material, which in previous decades had been considered deviant has now become relatively acceptable. Sociologists (Winick 1984) have been slow in analyzing what constitutes acceptability. In the main, however, Kunzle's (1982) thesis that the more provocative and controversial fashions, e.g., tight lacing which would leave erotic striations on the skin, have historically been adopted by "nomadic" elements in society, those willing to resist oppression and desirous to move upwards, can be applied to tattooing, with the restriction that tattooing is *not* ephemeral like fashion and therefore testifies to a basic need for permanent, irreversible inscription.

9. The difference between tattoo and graffiti should be modulated, however. There is a way to look at gang graffiti in particular as "public tattoos." Gang graffiti is a way not only for individual artists to show off their artistry but also for a gang to assert territorial dominance, as gang members put up their graffiti in areas contested by rival gangs (Vigil 1988: 115). However, the general effect of carving or painting on stone is different from that of skin inscriptions for one essential reason. Graffiti can be seen without the artist being there. A tattoo cannot be seen without the tattooee revealing or exposing his tattoo.

10. In primitive societies this may not have always been the case. An early traveler to East Africa notes that women, not men, were tattooed (Parkins 1853). Herman Melville (1958: 84) noted in *Typee* the elaborate tattoos that only Polynesian women were allowed to wear. From the late nineteenth century on, higher society women started flouting social and religious interdicts against tattooing. Lower class women were exhibited in circuses and fairs by the hundreds (Scutt 1974: 155).

11. This may change soon, however, as the commercialization of tattoo expands. A recent newspaper article comments on the downside of this commercialization, with "scratchers" (incompetent or amateur tattooists) giving the craft of tattoo a bad name. While the comment may be funny, it also underscores the degree to which tattooing, like any other art form in the late capitalist world, is subject to reappropriation.

Indeed, the skin is the last (indelible) frontier in a world where all differences are doomed to erasure, but what good is a difference so poorly etched that it no longer appears to make any difference at all? (*Village Voice* 1991). As far as the prospect of tattoo parlor chains is concerned, the idea is not in the future but in the past: "In 1927 Harry Lawson of Los Angeles worked out an elaborate organization to build up a chain of tattoo beauty parlors covering the whole of the U.S.A., involving plastic surgeons and beauticians as well as tattooists. Unfortunately the negotiations dragged on for too long and the idea collapsed with the Depression" (Scutt and Gotch 1974: 149).

12.   One might argue that the purpose of the Nazi tattoo, which brands and excludes under the Aryan rule, ends up parodying in a grotesque way the mutilation that Jewish males undergo by having their foreskin removed shortly after birth under the Semitic rule. Besides being a cleanliness measure, as is made clear by *Leviticus* 12:3, circumcision can also be seen as the tattoo of lack, the mutilation which God's brand requires, as is also made clear in another context in *Samuel* 18:25, where Saul tries to entrap David by offering him his daughter if he is willing to go out and bring back from battle a hundred foreskins from the Philistines (David brings back two hundred and becomes Saul's son-in-law).

13.   Two additional remarks on the subject of circumcision. First, Jewish men were not the only prisoners tattooed in Auschwitz. However, as Jews, they often wore additional symbols before or after the tattooed number signifying their racial origin. Second, while Auschwitz was the only concentration camp which tattooed inmates, it is worth noting that the tattooing was initiated in 1941, when the decision was made to engage in the "Final Solution." Outside markings, such as the yellow star on clothing, were no longer enough to keep track of the body count, as prisoners began dying by the thousands. Only tattoos on the body made the ultimate identification possible (Zielinska 1985: 54–55; Glicksman 1989: 924–85).

14.   The literature on male and female circumcision is extensive and beyond my purview. It should be noted, however, the female circumcision, a longstanding practice thought to enhance female orgasmic response, is, like male circumcision, the subject of contemporary medical debate (Wallerstein 1980: 187–90). With respect to tattooing, the whole controversy about circumcision suggests a history of practices and procedures where the search for symbolic, not real, efficacy, drives those practices and procedures. When symbolic factors reemerge, i.e., in the case of tattooing, when the belief in the symbolic efficacy of bodily inscription grows, the social, cultural and economic aspect of the practices are enhanced, and in this case, we witness the growth of the tattooing industry.

15.   Research (Sanders 1989: 48–49) shows that women are more interested in the aesthetic value of the tattoo. While this theory should be taken with a grain of salt, since it confirms an already established masculine model of the gaze, where the woman is the sole object of the gaze, the emphasis on controlling the viewer's gaze suggests an interesting feminist subversion of this model.

16.   A repressive authority which has also been known to use tattooing for its own purposes. It is reported that eighteenth century Japanese police forces had developed a tattoo system that could immediately reference the criminal's status and his violations (Richie and Buruma 1980: 12–13).

17.   Marshall Sahlins (1985: 142–43) has shown how sacred prescriptions intended for religious purposes were in the end counterpoised to the general welfare of the Hawaiian people. Just as secular practices, i.e., trading with Western merchants, were declared taboo, we can make the analogy that tattoos, originally the singular mark of symbolic difference, are now traded on a market of values.

18.   "The tattoo was not only an artistic achievement: it also demonstrated that its recipient could bear pain. On one island, the word to describe a person who was completely covered with tattoos is *ne'one'o*, based on a word meaning either "to cry for a long time" or "honorific." One observer in the Marquesas noted that whenever people discussed the tattoo-design, they emphasized the pain with which it was acquired" (Ebin 1979: 88–89; quoted in Sanders 1989, 182).

19.   Govenar (1988) actually reports having seen a prison tattoo which is reminiscent of the fictitious tattoo envisioned by Plath. "It is bordered on the top by the inscription, *Nuestra Familia* (Our Family) and on the bottom by an angel with flowing wings supporting the foundation of a prison cell. The central part of the tattoo is a man behind bars, shown from the waist up; the prison bars are piercing his hands, and Christ's head is in agony on his chest. For Honrada [the tattooee], this tattoo is a way of identifying with the suffering of Christ: 'In prison, I could understand better what Christ must have gone through as a victim and prisoner. The tattoo represented the quest for freedom that everyone in the joint must feel—Nuestra Familia.'"

20.   Indeed, in the last chapter of *The Domestication of the Savage Mind* (1977: 146–62), Goody opens up his argument to a more flexible understanding of the "domesticating" process, where it might look as though writing's ultimate advantage is no longer that it harks back to its own dichotomous origins (lists and tables

vs. nonliterate and more poetic forms of cognition) but rather, that it can in effect also record the very conditions, historical (or to put it *à la mode*, posthistorical), sociological and psychobiological, of its production: its inscription.

References

Adler, Patricia and Peter Adler. 1983. "Relationships between Dealers. The Social Organization of Illicit Drug Transactions." *Sociology and Social Research* 67: 260–78.

––––––. 1987. "The Past and Future of Ethnography." *Journal of Contemporary Ethnography* 16 (April): 4–24.

Anzieu, Didier. 1985. *Le Moi-Peau.* Paris: Dunod.

Cowan, James. 1910. *The Maoris of New Zealand.* London: Whitcombe and Tombe.

Derrida, Jacques. 1974 (1967). *Of Grammatology.* Trans. G.C. Spivak. Baltimore: Johns Hopkins University Press.

Ebin, Victoria. 1979. *The Body Decorated.* London: Thames and Hudson.

Frame, Donald M. 1965. *The Complete Essays of Montaigne.* Trans. Donald M. Frame (III:9). Stanford: Stanford University Press.

Gathercole, Peter. 1988. "Contexts of Maori Moko." In *Marks of Civilization: Artistic Transformations of the Human Body*, ed. Arnold Rubin, 171–77. Los Angeles: Museum of Cultural History.

Glicksman, W. 1989. "Social Stratification in the Concentration Camps." In *The Nazi Holocaust,* ed. Michael R. Marrus (Part VI [The Victims of the Holocaust], Vol. 2: 924–85). Wesport: Meckler.

Goffman, Erving. 1961. *Asylums.* Garden City: Doubleday.

––––––. 1963. *Behavior in Public Places.* New York: Free Press.

Goody, Jack. 1977. *The Domestication of the Savage Mind.* Cambridge, England: Cambridge University Press.

Govenar, Alan. 1988. "The Variable Context of Chicano Tattooing." In *Marks of Civilization: Artistic Transformations of the Human Body*, ed. Arnold Rubin, 209–18. Los Angeles: Museum of Cultural History.

Hambly, W.D. 1974 (1925). *The History of Tattooing and its Significance.* Detroit: Gale Research.

Kafka, J.S. 1969. "The Body as Transitional Object: A Psychoanalytical Study of a Self-mutilating Patient." *British Journal of Medical Psychology* 42: 207–11.

Kaeppler, Adrienne. 1988. "Hawaiian Tattoo: A Conjunction of Genealogy and Aesthetics." In *Marks of Civilization: Artistic Transformations of the Human Body*, ed. Arnold Rubin. Los Angeles: Museum of Cultural History.

Kunzle, David. 1982. *Fashion and Fetishism: A Social History of the Corset, Tight Lacing and Other Forms of Body-Sculpture in the West.* Totowa: Rowman and Littlefield.

Leach, Edmund. 1954. *Political Systems of Highland Burma: a Study of Kachin Social Structure*, preface by R. Firth. London: G. Bell.

Leiris, Michel. 1981. *Le ruban au cou d'Olympia.* Paris: Gallimard.

Lévi-Strauss, Claude. 1974 (1955). *Tristes Tropiques.* Trans. J. & D. Weigthman. New York: Atheneum.

Lombroso, Paola. 1902. *I Segni rivelatori della personalitá.* Torino: Fratelli Boca.

McCallum, Donald. 1988. "Historical and Cultural Dimensions of the Tattoo in Japan." In *Marks of Civilization: Artistic Transformations of the Human Body*, ed. Arnold Rubin, 109–34. Los Angeles: Museum of Cultural History.

McDonnell, Evelyn. 1991. "Physical Graffiti." Photographs by Brigitta Lund. *Village Voice* 36, 30 (23 July): 39.

Melville, Herman. 1958 (1846). *Typee.* London: J.M. Dent.

Mosher, Donald, Wayne Oliver and Jeffry Dolgan. 1967. "Body Image in Tattooed Prisoners." *Journal of Clinical Psychology* 23: 31–32.

Parkyns, M. 1853. *Life in Abyssinia.* London: J. Murray.

Plath, Sylvia. 1977. "The Fifteen-Dollar Eagle." In *Johnny Panic and the Bible of Dreams.* London: Faber and Faber.

Richie, Donald and Ian Buruma. 1980. *The Japanese Tattoo.* New York: Weatherhill.

Rubin, Arnold. 1988. "The Tattoo Renaissance." In *Marks of Civilization: Artistic Transformations of the Human Body*, ed. Arnold Rubin, 233–63. Los Angeles: Museum of Cultural History.

Sahlins, Marshall. 1976. *Culture and Practical Reason.* Chicago: University of Chicago Press.

Sahlins, Marshall. 1985. *Islands of History.* Chicago: University of Chicago Press.

Sanders, Clinton R. 1989. *Customizing the Body: the Art and Culture of Tattooing.* Philadelphia: Temple University Press.

Scutt, Ronald and Christopher Gotch. 1974. *Skin Deep: the Mystery of Tattooing.* London: Peter Davies.

Steiner, Christopher B. 1990. "Body Personal and Body Politic: Adornment and Leadership in a Cross-cultural Perspective." *Anthropos* 85: 43, 431–45.

Steward, Samuel M. 1990. *Bad Body and Tough Tattoos: a Social History of the Tattoo with Gangs, Sailors, and Street-Corner Punks, 1950–1965*. New York: Harrington Park Press.

Tucker, Marcia. 1981. "Tattoo: The State of the Art." *Artforum* (May): 42–47.

Vigil, James Diego. 1988. *Barrio Gangs: Street Life and Identity in Southern California*. Austin: University of Texas Press.

Vlahos, Olivia. 1979. *Body: the Ultimate Symbol*. New York: Lippincot.

Walsh, Barent W. and Paul M. Rosen. 1988. *Self-Mutilation: Theory, Research and Treatment*. New York: Guilford Press.

Williams, Herbert. 1971. *A Dictionary of the Maori Language* (6th ed.). Wellington: A.R. Shearer.

Winick, Charles. 1984. "From Deviant to Normative: Changes in the Social Acceptability of Sexually Explicit Material." In *Deviant Behavior: a Text-Reader in the Sociology of Deviance*, ed. Delos H. Kelly. New York: Saint-Martin's Press.

Zelinska, W. 1985. *Auschwitz: Nazi Extermination Camp*. Warsaw: Interpress Publishers.

Family Matters
Postfeminist Constructions of a Contested Site

Elizabeth G. Traube

I‍T WAS A RECEPTION THEORIST'S DREAM. WHEN DAN QUAYLE ATTACKED AN EPISODE OF *Murphy Brown*, a television series which he later conceded he had never watched, he confirmed the autonomy of the reception process from the media text. Moreover, Quayle's outrage over the show's glorification of unwed motherhood seemed to suggest that the utopian had prevailed over the ideological, a view of mass culture most often encountered in reception studies. For in a sitcom that a frustrated feminist of the second wave might have seen as one more foray in a campaign to redomesticate independent women, Quayle found an attempted subversion of patriarchal order consistent with and partly responsible for the upheaval in Los Angeles over the Rodney King verdict.

Quayle's attack derives from a long tradition of conservative cultural criticism which links the development of the modern mass media of communication—including the press, radio and television, the cinema, and the music industry—to a moral breakdown in society. While left-wing criticism of the media came to fasten on a threat from "above," defining social stabilization as the ideological project of the "culture industry," the danger discerned by the right is the eruption of social anarchy from "below," under the influence of cultural forces. Conservative intellectuals, Tony Bennett (1982: 35) notes, have typically "responded to the *political* problem of social disorder by redefining it as a *cultural* problem," or specifically, as a *mass*-cultural problem. Culture produced in commodity form by the few for the many has been repeatedly condemned by the right as corrupt and corrupting, a desecration of a unifying high culture by the low tastes of the masses, or alternatively, a manipulative assault on the consciousness of atomized masses, calculated to arouse and unleash their baser impulses.

Since the mid-1970s, New Right intellectuals and politicians have fine-tuned a conspiratorial version of the mass culture critique in which a "New Class" or "liberal elite" are identified as the real holders of social power. Borrowing the language if not the conceptual framework of recent developments in class theory, neoconservatives define the "New Class" as a loose alliance of government bureaucrats and assorted cultural producers who together control the State, the educational system, and the mass media, and who have launched a concerted attack on traditional American values from those bases.[1] Among the New Class's most insidious instruments of subversion are affirmative action programs, social welfare programs, assorted left-liberal educational initiatives, and the cultural commodities produced and distributed by the entertainment industry.

What links these disparate phenomena in New Right imagination is an underlying narrative of the patriarchal family under siege. Affirmative action contributes to the perceived crisis in multiple ways. By supporting the career ambitions of women, it lures them away from their domestic role and erodes the authority of male breadwinners, while it unmans minority men by enabling them to succeed without the traditionally "masculine" virtues of industry and self-reliance. Even more corrosive is the "dependency" fostered by the welfare system, to which conservatives attribute the notorious "breakdown of the family" among the minority poor. The black welfare queen at the bottom of the class ladder is the counterpart of the selfish career woman whom affirmative action and feminism have helped ascend to the top. Producing babies for profit, exchanging the disciplinary influence of masculine authority in the home for the largesse of an overly indulgent "liberal" welfare state, the poor black unwed mother melds with the professional woman in the New Right imaginary, a condensed figure of subversive female desire.[2]

Contra David Letterman, Quayle had not confounded a television fiction with reality.[3] Rather, he had mapped the same fiction onto both a mass-cultural representation of unwed motherhood and the growth of female-headed households in the inner cities. Within the terms of neoconservative discourse, a sitcom which celebrates an upscale life without father and the welfare system which undermines "family values" among the minority poor are both the artifacts of New Class liberals, the domestic enemy of New Right imagination, whom Quayle went on to attack as the enemy of domesticity. In a series of speeches to his core supporters Quayle lashed out at what he called "the cultural elite," an assortment of mental workers, ensconced "in newsrooms, sitcom studios and faculty lounges across America" (Rosenthal 1992a: A-1), who use their control of cultural institutions to infect us all with their lax moral values.

Feminism epitomizes moral laxity for neoconservatives, who view it as a collective expression of female selfishness and irresponsibility. Quayle's complaint about *Murphy Brown*, that "(b)earing babies irresponsibly is, simply, wrong" (Wines 1992: B-16), was a condensed allusion to welfare mothers and to the feminist values which have supposedly eroded elite family ties.[4] What he had neglected to consider, however, is the transformation that "feminism" has undergone in media representations. As Elspeth Probyn (1990) observes, the

New Women who populate late-1980s and 1990s mass culture are uniformly preoccupied with domesticity. If they have not already "chosen" to return home, like the "neotraditionalist" homemakers at the centers of *Parenthood* and *Thirtysomething*, they are either nervously listening to the ticking of their biological clocks or busy combining motherhood with career, whether effortlessly, like Claire Huxtable, Maggie Seaver, and other Super Moms, or with trepidation, like single mothers Molly Dodd and Murphy Brown. Not having paused to adjust his antifeminist rhetoric to this "postfeminist" turn in mass culture, Quayle found his routine condemnation of unwed childbearing being re-presented as hostility to a woman's choice of motherhood, and it was suggested (by *Murphy Brown* creator Diane English, among others) that such a sentiment logically presupposed support for abortion.

This charge left Quayle understandably disconcerted.[5] New Right "pro-family" ideology defines abortion and single motherhood as two sides of the same coin, alternative ways of enabling women to reject the discipline of marriage, and counters such assertions of female autonomy with the reassertion of traditional patriarchal authority. In its present postfeminist construction, however, unwed motherhood is an elusive target for antifeminist rhetoric, for it condenses the female autonomy which conservative antifeminists seek to curtail with the nurturing family values which they claim to defend.[6]

Postfeminist trends in media representations of women have also been attacked by feminist critics, as manifestations of what Susan Faludi (1991) calls a "backlash" against the women's movement. For Faludi, postfeminism is a soft-peddled, mass-mediated version of New Right antifeminism with a broader but fundamentally similar appeal.[7] Yet, as the *Murphy Brown* incident demonstrated, postfeminist fictions can give offense to feminists (Pollitt 1992) and antifeminists alike, and this capacity, to my mind, is not insignificant. It gives support, I will argue, to Judith Stacey's (1990) model of "postfeminism" as a mixed and contradictory gender consciousness which informs an ambiguous gender politics. In Stacey's ethnographic research on the postindustrial remaking of the family system, postfeminists are women and men who distance themselves from feminist identity and politics but have nevertheless absorbed many feminist assumptions into their strategies for family life.

Extended to media representations, this model suggests that postfeminist images of female domesticity are not adequately understood as antifeminist regressions. Rather, the family in media representations as in lived experience is a contested terrain, a site where desires for more egalitarian family and gender systems intermingle with pervasive anxieties over change. How mass-mediated fantasies of female autonomy in the domestic sphere intersect with ideologies of race and class is the subject of this paper. I focus on postfeminist media images of white single motherhood in which, I argue, imaginary identifications with women of subordinated racial groups and social classes are used to reconfigure middle-class femininity. The immediate roots of these fantasies lie in the 1950s when images of white and black single motherhood were split apart.

Rebel With Child

The dramatic postwar increases in fertility and marriage rates and in the number of households conforming to the male breadwinner-female homemaker ideal were soon revealed to be a temporary reversal of longterm trends. Even at the height of the 1950s, the ideology which glorified women's return to full-time domesticity did not completely regulate their lives. Gaps between the refurbished domestic ideal and social practice emerged within the postwar period itself, in the growing numbers of married women who quietly returned to work to help finance rising consumption needs (May 1988: 167; Marsh 1990: 186–87).

Nor was work the only sphere in which postwar women contested the cult of domesticity. The period that saw a spectacular rush of young people into marriage and parenthood also saw an increase in the official number of illegitimate births among white as well as black women. How the dominant culture responded to this perceived violation of its norms is the subject of *Wake Up Little Susie*, Rickie Solinger's (1992) compelling study of single pregnancy before Roe v. Wade. The response, Solinger shows, was differentiated on racial lines. Although both white and black unwed mothers were constructed as threats to the postwar "family ethic," different meanings were assigned to their pregnancies and justified their differential treatment.

Unwed black mothers continued to be constructed in biological and sociological terms, as "wanton breeders" or "breeders for profit," products of unrestrained sexual drives and degraded social environments. Upon their unruly wombs conservative politicians laid the blame for population increase, rising welfare costs, and urban poverty.[8] By contrast, Solinger argues at length (1992: 86–186), white single pregnancy was psychologized over the therapeutic fifties. Where traditional religious authorities had seen irreversibly fallen women, psychiatric professionals and social workers recast the white unwed mother as a treatable neurotic. Her pregnancy, according to the new paradigm, was unconsciously motivated, the symptom of inner conflicts which were found in case after case to revolve around problems in feminine sex-role identification. These, in turn, were traced to the failure of a girl's parents to provide appropriate models of sex-role identity.

Developmental psychology in this period was dominated by a neo-Freudian model of socialization in which children internalized their proper sex roles through identification with the same-sex parent (Ehrenreich and English 1978: 241–251; Pleck 1987: 92–95).[9] Applied to the pregnancies of single white girls, the sex-role model produced a variety of particular explanations along the same general lines. A girl who became pregnant, psychiatric professionals argued, was one who felt unappreciated by a weak or distant father and had failed to identify with a domineering or negligent mother. As a result, her femininity was insecure, and this caused her to become pregnant, an unconscious attempt either to get back at or reach out to the parents who had disappointed her. Her cure, as Solinger (1992: 127–47) describes it, entailed accepting and internalizing the blame for her condition. Through treatment she was expected: to confront and renounce her hostile, unfeminine wishes; to accept her inability to raise a child alone; and to relinquish the child for adoption by a normative couple, demonstrating through her sacrifice her future vocation for motherhood.

The psychological model of single pregnancy had a complex ideological effect. By removing the "biological stain" of illegitimacy from the babies of white unwed mothers, psychological explanation rendered the babies adoptable in a period of rising demand; at the same time, it worked to secure the unwed mother's complicity in the adoption mandate by representing any desire to keep her child as a prolongation of the pathology that had supposedly made her pregnant (Solinger 1992: 152–54).[10] In submitting to expert authority and giving up their children, Solinger argues more generally (1992: 16–17), unwed mothers enabled childless couples to realize the postwar family norm; they also reinforced the dominant norm indirectly, by validating the postwar redefinition of motherhood as a status that could not be achieved without a man, outside of a legally sanctioned, properly constructed, two-parent, male-headed family.

The psychological stereotype of white single pregnancy was one strategy in what Elaine May (1988) calls the postwar "ethos of containment," which defined the family as the uniquely safe site for all expressions of female desire. In terms of the history of domestic ideology, containment codified a shift in the dominant construction of femininity. Whereas the older Victorian ideal of true womanhood had represented women as essentially asexual, maternal beings, containment produced female sexuality as a dangerous but potentially productive force.[11] Women in the new model were entitled to sexual fulfillment so long as they accepted dependence on male breadwinners and used sex to enhance their marriages. Conversely, the model invested single women in general with the negatively valued sexuality once reserved in bourgeois consciousness for women of subordinated classes (Stansell 1987) and racial groups (Carby 1987). Moreover, *any* assertion of independence on the part of middle-class women, such as choosing career over marriage, became even more heavily freighted with the imagined threat of dangerous female sexuality.[12]

Events over the next decades would conspire to intensify the sense of threat among defenders of the traditional domestic ideal. For the fifties' family soon proved inadequate to its assigned task of containing desire. By 1960, marriage and birth rates began to fall once more, renewing the longterm trend, and as the baby boom ended, the divorce rate resumed what proved to be its giddy, largely uninterrupted climb (Levitan & Belous 1981). The heightened instability of marriage encouraged women to reject full-time domesticity for participation in the paid labor force at the same time as it reflected such decisions.[13] Over the next decades, the domestic ideal became increasingly remote from lived experience, as economic and cultural forces together pushed and pulled women of all classes out of the home and into the paid labor force (Gerson 1985; Stacey 1990).

Liberal feminism of the second wave took hold among white, college-educated, professional-managerial-class women, those best positioned to experience career commitment as fulfilling. Among these women, improved access to education and employment worked together with feminist aspirations to shape a new consciousness which also found expression, Rosalind Petchesky (1983: 142–48) suggests, in rising rates of abortion and out-of-wedlock births. Terminating an unwanted pregnancy and becoming a single mother offered alternative ways to contest the dominant cultural narrative of marriage as the defining event in their lives; for those with expectations of economic independence, both acts could express and reinforce a new sense of autonomy.

Dominant representations of single motherhood in the larger culture continued to be differentiated along racial lines. Over the 1960s black single pregnancies were subsumed under the metaphor of the "population bomb," for which they were supposedly the trigger, further hardening the already harsh attitudes toward black single motherhood (Solinger 1992: 206).[14] White single mothers, by contrast, became a subset of a larger group, the youthful, middle-class baby boomers who rejected their parents' ethos of sexual containment and made up the vanguard of the "sexual revolution."[15]

The white, unwed, middle-class pregnant girl lost her marginality through this shift. If premarital sex were now the rule among her peers, a widely accepted feature of the dating system, then premarital pregnancy was a misfortune that could befall any young woman and not, or not necessarily, a neurotic symptom. As the psychiatric construction of white single pregnancy lost its hold, the adoption mandate also came apart, not least of all because single mothers were increasingly likely to resist it. A decline in the number of women applying to adoption agencies indicated just such a development, and new studies began to represent this trend in relatively positive terms. By the mid-1960s, according to Solinger (1992: 224–28), it was generally accepted among the experts that a white unwed mother who elected to keep her child could be pursuing a rational plan.

Kinder Women in A Meaner Season

Dominant images of single motherhood in the 1990s continue to be polarized on racial lines. At one pole of the prevailing representational system, poor black single mothers remain under the sign of the irrational, constructed as "excessive" reproducers whose fertility must somehow be restricted. At the other pole, single motherhood appears as the rational "choice" of elite white career women who have revised an earlier life plan. Both images recur with different inflections across a range of political positions, embedded in a variety of discourses that center on the family.

Black single motherhood is pathologized in the dominant discourses on social welfare which have made the elimination of "welfare dependency" rather than of female poverty into the overriding concern (Abramovitz 1988: 367; Fraser 1989: 144–45). Within this definition of the situation, the problem is to explain why poor minority women supposedly perpetuate a cycle of dependency by repeatedly bearing children out-of-wedlock.[16] While conservatives attack the welfare system itself for creating an "underclass" deficient in "traditional values," liberals point to structural causes of urban poverty and to such putative psycho-cultural consequences as a low sense of "self-efficacy" among the chronically jobless urban poor (Wilson 1987, 1991).[17]

Pregnancy among inner-city minority teenagers is belatedly psychologized in this latter perspective, which corresponds to what Nancy Fraser (1989: 155) calls the "*therapeutic* moment" of the operation of the social-welfare system as a "juridical-administrative-therapeutic-state apparatus." Counseling sessions, the application of the therapeutic model, construct the poor, unmarried, pregnant minority teenager in terms formerly reserved for white girls. Her pregnancy now appears as an individual, psychological problem, a (doomed) attempt to overcome her inner lack of self-worth. As the feminine counterpart to the criminal activities of restless ghetto youth, teenage sexuality comes to represent the sexuality of all black women as a pathological activity in which the state may justifiably intervene.[18]

Proposed solutions to the so-called welfare crisis share an underlying assumption: that black women need to be drawn *out* of their state-supported, female-headed, "defective families" and *into* the paid work force, where they can become responsible, self-sufficient, productive individuals.[19] Various means to this end are now in circulation, such as the "New Covenant" set forth at the Democratic convention which combines automatic limits on welfare grants with training for jobs that are somehow to materialize. Conservative rhetoric continues to appeal to widely held fears about the breadwinner family by blaming unwed welfare mothers for its breakdown among the urban minority poor. Despite sporadic railing against "deadbeat dads," however (who tend to be represented as white and middle class), the punitive strategies favored by conservatives (stricter eligibility requirements, forced work requirements, and cuts in benefits to eliminate the "incentive" to bear illegitimate children) are not designed to strengthen masculine authority within poor minority families. Instead, it is the "public patriarch" who is asked to reassert himself and drive welfare mothers back to work (Abramovitz 1988: 355–58).

I will not undertake the economic analysis required to connect these trends to the postindustrial economy and the demands of capital for cheap labor. Rather, I want to consider the ideological system which generates symmetric narratives about the relative places of motherhood and work in women's lives. Even as the welfare debates converge on the beneficial effects of labor discipline on single black mothers, stories about white women have been circulating in the mass media which follow a reverse course. Since the mid-1980s, the increasingly common wisdom conveyed in fictional and nonfictional representations is that middle-class white women must either leave the work force or modify their commitment to it in order to recover their true womanhood.

Fictional constructions of women in different media have been working toward a similar effect, which is to reposition women in the home. In the movies, the independent heroines of the late 1970s and early 1980s were displaced by frustrated career women and self-sacrificing mothers, women who returned to or simply belonged to the sphere their feminist sisters had rejected.[20] On television, the few single, childless professional women who survived were made to appear increasingly neurotic. Workplace sitcoms are symptomatic of the wider trend. In the 1970s MTM enterprises produced the "family of co-workers," a variation on the nuclear family sitcom which, Jane Feuer (1984: 58–59) has suggested, offered a utopian alternative to bourgeois domesticity. Progressive aspects of the genre were particularly evident in its representation of women, for whom the generic requirement to preserve the unity of the work family precluded any withdrawal into the home. By the end of the 1980s, however, the female members of workplace families were no longer content with the substitution and they became fixated on motherhood, with a husband (temporarily, on *Night Court*) or without one (*Cheers, Designing Women, Murphy Brown*).

According to Susan Faludi (1991), such cinematic and televisual images are part of a wider campaign waged over the last decade to construct feminism as the enemy of women. By demonizing independent women while celebrating motherhood as women's primary role, the mass media, Faludi argues, have sought to substitute a regressive postfeminist disposition for the more hopeful and combative spirit which the women's movement expressed and reinforced. Postfeminism, in this view, is fundamentally a mass-cultural phenomenon with potentially negative effects on the consciousness of female audiences.[21] It consists of a set of ideological representations created by media professionals and deployed in a campaign against gender equality to which women are peculiarly susceptible.

By contrast, Judith Stacey (1987; 1990) has consistently and cogently used the concept of "postfeminism" to demarcate a symptomatically mixed-gender consciousness emergent among different social classes and also objectified in media texts. In a critique of media texts aimed at middle-class women, Deborah Rosenfelt and Stacey (1990: 549) define postfeminism as "an emerging culture and ideology that simultaneously incorporates, revises, and depoliticizes many of the fundamental issues advanced by second-wave feminism." As the definition suggests, Rosenfelt and Stacey see important distinctions between the ideologies and constituencies of postfeminism and those of antifeminism, "distinctions," they add, "that make it worthwhile [for feminism] to grapple with rather than simply dismiss the literature and issues of the former."

They proceed to reinterpret selected postfeminist texts which to many feminists exemplify antifeminist backlash: the June 2, 1986 *Newsweek* cover story, "Too Late for Prince Charming," about the grim marital prospects for educated women over thirty as documented by Yale and Harvard researchers; Sylvia Hewlett's *A Lesser Life: The Myth of Women's Liberation in America*, which accuses feminism of devaluing motherhood and privileging a "male model" of career success; and *The Good Mother*, a novel by Sue Miller about a divorced mother's unsuccessful struggle to integrate her erotic and maternal feelings.

Rosenfelt and Stacey recognize troubling antifeminist tendencies in each of these texts, noting how female autonomy is repeatedly made to appear responsible for difficulties faced by contemporary women. But the difficulties, they continue, are not manufactured by media texts, as some feminist critics have implied. The loneliness of single working women (*Newsweek*), the obstacles to combining motherhood and work (Hewlett), the vulnerability of single mothers (Miller), these are real and painful dimensions of women's lived experience in a society in which progress toward gender equality remains uneven and incomplete. Nor can the texts be dismissed as antifeminist, Rosenfelt and Stacey argue, for even as they retreat from feminist responses to social discontents into a more conservative profamily vision, they also incorporate selected features of the feminism they reject. Such textual incoherence, according to Rosenfelt and Stacey (1990: 564), is cause for "modest optimism" about the future. What the "potentially fruitful inconsistencies of postfeminist culture" indicate, they argue, is not an antifeminist closure but the contradictory consciousness of women and men in a period when family and gender arrangements are multiple, insecure, and pervasively contested. With this consciousness, they conclude, a third wave of feminism can and must engage.

In the following sections I treat postfeminist media representations as a locus of contradictions, a site where diffuse fears about the passing of the breadwinner nuclear family and nostalgia for the stability and security of an imagined home coexist in tension with longings for new, more egalitarian forms of family life. This mixed character sets postfeminism apart from New Right "pro-family" ideology, which appeals primarily to the socially conditioned fears, falsely promising to restore an order that is over by blaming feminism and the welfare state, rather than the postindustrial economy, for its collapse. But neither does postfeminism express the oppositional consciousness promoted on the left, where the struggle to redefine what constitutes a family is collectively waged by feminists, gay and lesbian activists, and welfare rights groups seeking both social legitimation and economic support for diverse, nontraditional households. Postfeminism resonates, however, with less dramatic, everyday forms of struggle which are carried on by women and men in all social classes, in different circumstances and with unequal resources, who find themselves obliged to invent new ways of being a family.

Rather than replicating conservative antifeminism in another key, as the backlash theory would have it, mass-mediated postfeminism recognizes and reworks selected elements from the opposed discourses on the family that are competing in the larger culture. It appeals to the mixed fears and desires of diverse, socially situated audiences, proffering multiple, contradictory possibilities of meaning. Contemporary media representations of white single motherhood exemplify the intricacies of the postfeminist interpretive situation.

The Maternal Rebel as Natural Woman: *Murphy Brown*

Over the course of the 1991–92 television season, the *Murphy Brown* series revolved around the single pregnancy of the lead character, a successful television journalist. As the season unfolded, Murphy Brown's body was made visible to viewers as a specifically female body, and an increasingly grotesque and demanding female body, to which Murphy was ritualistically required to submit herself in episode after episode. These insistent visual and narrative affirmations of what Denise Riley (1988) calls the "sexed body" culminated with the image of Murphy in the season finale, singing Aretha Franklin's "A Natural Woman" to her newborn babe in arms. To borrow a phrase from Dick Hebdige (1979: 45), "a phantom history of race relations" was embodied in that moment.

Appropriated and incorporated into middle-class youth culture, African-American music had provided a symbol through which single white middle-class women in the 1960s and 1970s identified with the represented sexual autonomy of black women. *Murphy Brown* had long since given this identification a new twist by converting the Motown music that opens every episode into a signifier of its elite white heroine's professional autonomy.[22] Sexuality was constructed in the show as an indulgence which Murphy had largely given up, along with alcohol and other "excesses" of the 1970s, and throughout the series viewers were made to understand that her primary fulfillment now came through work. This unilateral commitment was understood to have been costly. Murphy was supposed to have recently returned from the Betty Ford Clinic in the series opener, and many episodes drew attention to her loneliness. Nevertheless, the career achievement for which she had sacrificed her personal life was consistently represented as exhilarating.

Pregnancy initiated a change in the traits attributed to Murphy's character, or more precisely, the plotting of the pregnancy episodes confirmed what viewers had always been encouraged to believe, that Murphy's harsh, antimaternal, and, as Andrea Press (1991: 41) notes, stereotypically feminist personality masked the "natural woman" hidden within. In this context her postpartum performance of her favorite soul song decisively redefined professional autonomy in terms of lack, as an attempted denial of true womanhood which was shown to be rooted in the distinctive difference of the maternal body.

From the perspective of an egalitarian feminism that seeks to reduce the socially constructed difference between the sexes, the treatment of Murphy's motherhood negotiates a partial, disturbing return to the ideology of women as essentially maternal beings. If women cannot be fulfilled solely through motherhood in the show's postfeminist vision, neither can they fully realize themselves without it, and that caveat has an antifeminist force. At the same time, however, the show also transposed a feminist ideal of the independent woman to the domestic realm, where Murphy, assisted by her family of primarily male coworkers, will mother more or less autonomously in the coming season.[23] Only the struggles waged by "maternal rebels" over the past decades, and the dramatic shifts they produced in dominant constructions of white single motherhood and in women's experience of that status, allowed the *Murphy Brown* show's feminist critics to take the rights of single mothers largely for granted and not to see a feminist victory in their fictive reassertion.

Dan Quayle knew better. The intrepid ideologue of the New Right protested the show with good reason, for even as it absorbs elements of the traditional ideology of motherhood, it simultaneously contests the conservative definition of the family and envisions an alternative to full-time, mother-intensive child raising. What is more, Quayle had brought a hidden connection into the light. Dipping into the New Right politics of the imaginary, he condensed the independent white professional woman with the poor black welfare mother, and he reminded us that these figures have also been covertly conjoined in centrist symbolism of self-realization.

Black people, along with the white working class, were the largely absent presence in the middle-class "sexual revolution." As young white middle-class women and men asserted a more openly eroticized identity, claiming the right to direct their sex lives as they saw fit, they identified their new freedom with the idealized sexualities of subordinated classes and racial minorities.[24] Whether positively or negatively valued, white stereotypes of black promiscuity continued to be oppressive for black women and men. But expressed through cultural commodities such as music and dress, the imaginary affiliation with dominated social groups provided the youthful "sexual rebels" of the white middle class with a language of resistance to bourgeois respectability.

As the baby-boom generation aged, those career-oriented white middle-class women who also wanted children found themselves obliged to become "maternal rebels" to some degree. A minority who, whether through circumstances or sexual preference, had never built a stable relationship with a man chose to have children outside of marriage, sometimes with the aid of new technologies of reproduction. Many more became single parents through divorce, to which the additional strains of two-career marriages have no doubt contributed. But another group of work-committed wives became mothers on the understanding that they and their husbands would more or less equally share parenting responsibilities (see Gerson 1985; Hertz 1986; Ehrensaft 1987). Contesting the traditional ideology of motherhood as a full-time and exclusively female vocation, women and men in two-career families who "mother" together are attempting to redistribute parental responsibilities along egalitarian lines.

What seems to be emerging with these and other experiments is a new identification in which the family practices rather than the represented sexuality of subordinate groups become a symbolic resource for reconfiguring white middle-class identities. From a historical perspective, black women, together with white working-class women, have been what Judith Stacey (1990: 252) calls "the genuine postmodern family pioneers." Although full-time motherhood was constructed (against resistance) as a hegemonic ideal, it was only belatedly and temporarily attained in the postwar years by privileged sections of the white working class.[25] It has rarely been a possibility for black women, who for generations were denied the right to legal marriage and who have a long history of combining paid work with domestic responsibilities (Jones 1985).

Single motherhood, moreover, has a particularly respected place within African-American culture. While representations of the strong father as the solution to the "crisis" of the black family are not without appeal in black communities, they have not gone uncontested by black feminists and political leaders.[26] Against nostalgia for male-headed families, a black feminist literary tradition which dates back to the nineteenth century uses the absence of the black father as what Hazel Carby (1986: 315) calls a "utopian space" to imagine a range of egalitarian, nonpatriarchal unions between black men and black women.

What I am suggesting is that shadow traces of African-American family practices are inscribed in postfeminist visions of the family. In converting the utopian family of coworkers into a female-headed household sustained by a network of fictive kin, *Murphy Brown* unconsciously recognizes and disguises the long, quiet struggle of black women to construct alternatives to the dominant white middle-class family system. With that system now under attack from within the white middle class, other social groups who have contested it under different conditions and for other purposes take on heightened symbolic value. But inasmuch as *Murphy Brown* gives only displaced recognition to the struggles of black women, it remains complicit with the pervasive splitting of praise and condemnation on racial lines. By indiscriminately condemning white and black single mothers, Quayle challenged us to defend all maternal rebels, who fight their battles with the unequal means at their disposal.

Reforming Women: *Little Man Tate*

Given the historical connection between family life and the formation of middle-class identity, it is not surprising that when the family is in flux, the ideological boundaries between classes may become blurred. It was in the name of "the family" that middle-class men and women advanced their claim to status in the mid-nineteenth century and launched what Christine Stansell (1987: 65) has unmasked as a "class intervention" into urban working-class neighborhoods. There they encountered what Stansell calls a "city of women:" collectivities of laboring women who were unable to depend on men for support in the unstable industrial economy and became household heads themselves, supporting one another in times of distress; and independent, assertive, pleasure-seeking working girls who drew on new forms of commercial leisure to construct a vivid, prideful style of their own. In these alternative forms of working-class womanhood and family life, middle-class reformers saw only deviations from the "true" female nature which, they believed, was incarnated in their own genteel family practices. By the 1850s, Stansell concludes (1987: 219), a campaign was underway "to transform the character of working-class womanhood into one resembling more closely the female identity that the cult of domesticity celebrated." Mediated by a particular, class-based conception of gender, a moral reform movement that targeted the households of laboring women became linked to the wider efforts of the bourgeoisie to suppress an oppositional working-class culture.

Ironically, from the perspective of class history, a recent postfeminist fantasy assigns to its working-class heroine the true womanhood in which her middle-class rival is deficient. *Little Man Tate* was a modestly successful, female-oriented 1991 movie about a gifted child and the two women in his life. The directorial debut of Jodie Foster, who also stars as the boy's single working-class mother, the movie opened to generally courteous but unenthusiastic reviews and, with little support from its financially troubled distributor (Orion Pictures), it might have been expected to quickly disappear. Yet it lingered on the top 50 chart for eighteen weeks (six of them among the top 10), grossing a respectable $25 million.[27] The movie provides identification figures for working-class and professional women, and my anecdotal evidence suggests that it appeals across class lines.[28] For this analysis, it is an exemplary postfeminist text, symptomatic of the contradictory pressures negotiated in mainstream representations of gender and family.

Generically, *Little Man Tate* draws on variant forms of the "woman's film" (see Gledhill, ed. 1987), as female-oriented Hollywood melodramas are known. Its heroine, Dede Tate, is the sacrificing mother of maternal melodrama who effaces herself for the good of her child, but transposed to what resembles the plot of a romantic melodrama in which an estranged couple is reunited after a separation. As is common in both varieties of the woman's film, the narrative facilitates identification with multiple viewpoints, allowing female spectators to sympathize to some degree with Dede's rival for her son's affection.[29] Against this generic tendency to shift point of view, much of the story is told from the perspective of the central male protagonist, whose intimate relationship to his adoring mother is announced when "I Get a Kick Out of You" plays over the opening credits. Fred Tate is indeed the little man in his mother's life, a controlling figure in many ways. He keeps the household accounts, knows when Dede's period is due, and fully absorbs her maternal and erotic energies.[30]

Seven-year-old Fred is also given partial control over the narrative discourse. His voice-over frames the movie and exemplifies his omniscient knowledge, which he thinks may encompass his own birth. Whether or not Fred can actually remember being born, the movie has him miraculously narrate that event in his voice-over to the opening scene, Dede in the delivery room, joyfully greeting her newborn child. The boy's miraculous nature is reaffirmed in the next scene when he performs what proves to be the first of many prodigious feats of knowledge and becomes the object of his mother's reverential gaze.

In keeping with the theme of Fred's uncanny powers is the movie's treatment of his fatherless condition. While Dede horses around with him, displaying the playfully erotic physicality which the movie associates with her working-class background, he explains in a voice-over that he is son to no (mortal) man:

> People are always asking who my Dad is. Dede says I don't have a Dad. She says I'm an immaculate conception. That's a pretty heavy responsibility for a little kid.

It is also, at the very least, a rather extreme case of "father absence." Nor is the movie quite so blasé as Dede about the implications for Fred's masculinity. His first appearance at age seven finds him on hands and knees in a school yard, isolated and a bit forlorn. He is putting the finishing touches on a chalk mural of a mother and child, all the while wishing, his voice-over tells us, to be one of the boys roughhousing across the yard under the leadership of a particularly macho little kid whom Fred will try in vain to emulate as the story unfolds.

Dede is entirely devoted to Fred, like the Madonna in his mural. She hovers over the boy, seeking to attend to his physical, mental, and social needs, a caring, giving maternal presence whose every move is for her son. He is, she tells him just before their parting, "exactly what I want to be," the admired and idealized object in which her own self is submerged. It is her difference from him, however, that drives the plot along its halting oedipal trajectory.

In contrast to the unhappily married heroine of *Stella Dallas* (1937; recently recreated as a single mother in *Stella*, the 1990 Bette Midler remake), Dede never seeks to be "something else besides a mother." Where Stella tried, unsuccessfully, to keep her directly erotic, pleasure-seeking impulses separate from her maternal ones, in Dede the two appear successfully fused. Maternal concern predominates in her scenes with Fred, though always erotically tinged, but when she comes to pick him up at school in her slinky blue cocktail waitress dress, we briefly see her through his classmates' eyes as a desirable, seductive, excessively feminine presence. It is not just that she represents "body" in the conventional coding of "working-classness," but a specifically female body, a female *as* body, the source of sensuality, desire, feeling, and also of a powerful pull toward fusion which her "little man" must resist if he is to achieve autonomous, masculine selfhood.

Or so it seems, at first, as the movie launches Fred on the oedipal path of separation from the mother. In place of the absent father, his way into the larger world is a wealthy and accomplished female mental-health worker, a cultural intellectual who belongs to the upper echelons of the professional sector of the professional-managerial class. Jane Grierson (played by Diane Wiest) is a child psychologist of considerable means, both material and mental. She has her own institute for gifted children (of whom she was one), as well as a "ranch" in Virginia (apparently an inheritance from her physician parents) and a townhouse in Cincinnati. She wants Fred to spend time with her in all three places so that she can observe him and help him to develop his prodigious intellectual powers.

This entails taking him away from what Jane will prove unable to provide, the constrictive but supportive confines of a home. The movie contrasts the sleek, ultra-modern interiors of Jane's upscale world of the mind to the working-class streets, where Fred watches other boys play from his window, and to the shabby but snug nest which breadwinner-homemaker Dede struggles to maintain (she has to sell the piano when money is short but she paints one for him on the wall), a haven where mother and son dance together to jazz music, all bathed in a warm, golden light. From this last image the movie cuts to a blue-lit scene in the Grierson Institute and our first glimpse of Jane, who is viewing slides of gifted children while her male associate recites their respective qualifications. When he quotes from a poem by a girl who represents the housewife as a "pathetic phlegm hound with no sense of self-worth," Jane cannot contain her pleasure.

The visual contrast opposes the humanizing influence of maternal nurturance to education, which is equated with abstract control. Jane will often appear as in this scene, as the feminist agent of a bureaucratic system of surveillance, her Institute a plush panopticon where the child geniuses are the objects of the observational gaze. In the movie's vision of the educational process, the children's knowledge is rapidly converted into cultural capital with a high market value in the corporate world, while the children themselves, removed from their families, lose their humanity and become apprentice functionaries in the modern apparatus of power. At a convention for gifted children, for example, a boy prosecuting Goldilocks in a mock trial explains that compassion for the homeless is irrelevant to an issue of private property, echoing in a legal discourse the same contempt for the role of nurturer which won Jane's approval at the slide show.

But superimposed on the movie's pop-Foucaultian critique of the educational apparatus is a humanist model of education as an instrument of emancipation rather than of control. Jane, in this view, is truly a kindred spirit who understands Fred's longing for enlightenment and offers him access to a higher plane. Yet she also offers him what the movie represents as her own overly regulated and repressive domestic regime. When she insists to Dede that the boy is "starving for stimulation and challenge and for order in his life," she collapses the two views of education, and they remain entangled in the represented events.

It could be argued that the movie's inability or refusal to separate control from liberation evokes the structurally ambivalent, historically contradictory relationship of middle-class professionals to the working class (Ehrenreich and Ehrenreich 1979). Whether intelligence is irrevocably in the service of capital and class control or whether it can be enlisted in emancipatory projects remains uncertain in the movie, which stresses the first possibility but also hints at the second. At the margins of the plot, a disciplinary bureaucratic rationality is critically evaluated from the perspective of an expanded welfare state dedicated to satisfying basic human needs. This critique, however, is carried on in fragmentary and allusive form, condensed into peripheral moments such as when Fred abruptly switches off a television talk show on which a William Buckley stand-in is denouncing "welfare dependency." What is central to the story is the private sphere, where caring for dependents is not a public responsibility but a personal capacity, and one which is unequally distributed along class lines. To overcome class antagonism in this representation entails reforming the professional woman.

Fred leaves the television on at a later point, when the same conservative talk-show host is promoting a bestseller entitled *Family of One: Today's Career Woman*, and the title introduces the ensuing scene. Deflecting Jane's concern over Dede's apparent unwillingness to let him pursue his education, Fred forces Jane to confront her own neglected childhood in a two-career family and her loneliness as a childless single career woman. As events unfold, both Fred and the movie become more and more intent on exposing Jane's insufficiently maternal nature. When she burns a meatloaf for Fred's dinner or anxiously follows him on his way to school, the movie invites female viewers to feel condescending approval for her inept attempts at mothering, but it harshly condemns her for her selfish absorption in her own work, her one-sided attention to Fred's intellectual life, and her utter inability to respond to his emotional needs.

The movie's antifeminist tendency is most pronounced in its compulsion to construct the female intellectual as a failed woman. Having set up a polarity between Dede, as the devotee of the female cult of self-sacrifice, and Jane, as the implicitly feminist proponent of self-realization for men and women alike, the plot comes to the defense of the first woman, while requiring the second to undergo a protracted and increasingly punitive process of reeducation in the art of self-denial. At the same time, as if to underline Jane's stifled but essentially maternal nature, the narrative also calls into question her ability to provide Fred with a way into the world, that is, to perform the paternal function in oedipal socialization.

Fathers are conspicuously absent in this movie, and the occasional allusions to their presence are less than flattering. In the background, the conservative talk-show host would seem to represent stern patriarchal authority, as does the educational apparatus in its disciplinary function, while one of Fred's fellow geniuses speaks bitterly of his own ignorant and abusive father. What is missing is any participatory paternal figure of identification, and Fred is preoccupied with this lack. Like Mikey in *Look Who's Talking* (Traube 1992: 156–67), he spends much of the movie in search of a masculine role model, but without Mikey's success. His schoolyard idol is intellectually too far below him, while Damon, the other genius, is too close.

For a fleeting moment, he appears to have found the ideal balance in an amiable college student (played by Harry Connick Jr.), a breezy, fun-loving youth who instructs him in jazz piano and pool. But no sooner has Fred attached himself to Eddie then he is disappointed. When he arrives unannounced to find Eddie in bed with a woman, the young man makes clear that he is not going to let the boy intrude upon his sexual pleasure. Eddie's assertion of himself as a sexual subject marks him in this movie's view as unsuited for parenthood, a point which is driven home by his refusal to be continuously available. "I'm not your baby-sitter," explains Eddie, not unkindly, "I can't take that kind of responsibility."

Nor is he expected to. Eddie might have said that he is not the boy's mother, for it is only women in this movie who are expected to find their fulfillment in caring for others and are held accountable if they fail. While Eddie's rejection plunges Fred into a depression, Jane's inattentiveness compounds it and triggers an emotional crisis which only Dede can resolve. Fred flees from Jane and returns home, where he is reunited with Dede who promises to take care of everyone: "You, me, even Jane." As she speaks, a chastised Jane appears briefly in the doorway, and then retreats, unobserved.

In the next and final scene, however, Dede's promise has been magically fulfilled. It is Fred's eighth birthday party, and he is surrounded by friends, a joyous contrast to the previous year's party, which no one attended.[31] Moreover, the two women in his life have been reconciled. For Dede, this means accepting the role of the Institute in his development, but it is Jane who has been dramatically reformed, her domestic reeducation evident in the huge, homemade cake that she proudly presents. The intellectual has become a woman, and the reforged bonds of womanhood provide the basis for a class reconciliation.

As critic David Ansen noted (1991: 65), the happy ending is "frankly baffling" and tenuously related to the represented events. Such disregard for narrative coherence, however, is a characteristic feature of romantic melodrama, motivated, Steve Neale and Frank Krutnik (1990) suggest, by the genre's utopian avoidance of real-world restrictions that bear upon women in terms of marriage and family. In melodramas, they argue, the romance is conventionally opposed to marriage and genital sexuality, both of which would represent the subjugation of the heroine's desire to that of a man and to patriarchy. Hence a common tendency in the genre is for the union to fail, thereby deferring any resolution to the heroine's wish. Alternatively, Neale and Krutnik observe (1990: 136), when the union is achieved: "it tends to be marked as 'impossible, incredible, or fantasy' . . . What both tendencies suggest, then, is that these melodramas involve a triumph of fantasy over the conventional restrictions which are involved in 'realist' narrative closure, where desire is in some way *fixed*."

In fact, Fred concedes in his voice-over that the festive scene we are witnessing is his remembered and hence possibly wishful version of the past, which would seem to be an invitation for viewers to take the resolution as a fantasy. Here it seems to me that the utopian possibilities of this "maternal romance" lie in the disjunction between the plot and its fantastic resolution. For the plot, as I have suggested, initially appears to be governed by an oedipal logic in which to become an autonomous individual the boy hero would have to reject the nurturing mother of dependency for her symbolic opposite, a liberating father of separation. In these terms, adapted from Jessica Benjamin's (1988) critique of the gender-differentiated process of oedipal socialization, the movie starts out on the oedipal trajectory only abruptly to reverse it. At least in fantasy, home becomes the site where the principles of nurturance and freedom commingle, both of them represented, albeit in different proportions, by women.

With respect to gender and parental roles, events up to the resolution convey a mixed message. On the one hand, Jane, biologically female, appears to have failed in the culturally masculine role of liberator and way into the world, the implication being that she has been denying her essentially maternal nature. On the other hand, by sending the boy back home to Dede, Jane's failure as a liberator partially undoes the oedipal polarities which construct repudiation of the mother as the condition of masculine development. Moreover, when Jane reappears with her cake in the final scene, she is still the director of the Institute and so a representative of the culturally masculine sphere of intellectual activity. As the movie studiously refuses to provide Fred with any biologically male father figure, we may assume that Jane, as intellectual, and Dede, as breadwinner, together perform the paternal function of modeling independence and achievement, at the same time as they also provide maternal nurturance and emotional support.

As the product of this unusual shared parenting arrangement, Fred himself represents an increasingly secure balance of capacities that are traditionally polarized. Identified from the outset as a genius whose abilities range from art and music to math and physics, attributed a profound sense of attunement with nature and quasi-divine pity for the weak and helpless to accompany his awesome powers of abstraction, he embodies the wish for transcension of a gender system in which feminine and masculine, feeling and intellect, emotionality and rationality, compassion and instrumental reason, nurturance and freedom are constructed as antagonistic opposites.

It needs emphasis, however, that although both of the women occupy culturally feminine and masculine spaces, neither of them approaches Fred's level of gender indeterminacy. To identify with the women in this maternal romance is to assume a postfeminist viewpoint, with its characteristic blend of utopian longings for new gender and family arrangements and pessimism about the possibilities for change. I have argued that an essentializing tendency is pronounced in the movie's chastisement of Jane, which defines domestic womanhood as a universal standard against which all women must be measured. Moreover, the conflation of maternal with romantic melodrama constructs female sexuality on neo-Victorian lines, reversing such uneven progress as women have made under patriarchy in achieving recognition as sexual subjects. Women do enjoy a desire of their own within the nonpatriarchal space provided for them in the movie, but that desire is strictly sublimated into maternal affection for a dependent and seems to preclude directly (hetero)sexual love between adults.

I would not deny that Dede and Jane could be interpreted as a lesbian couple, an "over-reading" (Young: 1990) of their relationship which would give the movie's nontraditional family a radical slant. Indeed, if rumors concerning Foster are to be believed, it is quite possible that a lesbian subtext was at some level intended by the director and seems likely to contribute to the pleasure which lesbian viewers, among others, may negotiate from the movie.[32] Nevertheless, even interpreted on such lines, the movie does not affirm a female sexuality detached from maternal instinct. Woman's desire, whether heterosexual or nonheterosexual, appears as something fixed by nature, an essentially nurturing and pacific expression of a sexed, maternal body, rather than something socially constructed, fluid, and transformable.

In line with this underlying tendency to essentialize gender and sexual identities is the movie's tacit pessimism concerning men's ability to change. Fred, after all, is portrayed as a miraculous being. While he may represent the movie's ideal, its overall verdict on boys is that they will, alas, be boys, leaving the task of caring for dependents in the strong hands of women. Here again, I would stress the mixed character of the movie's family vision. In its nonpatriarchal household there is both a utopian assertion of female autonomy and a retreat from the struggle to restructure the domestic relations between women and men on egalitarian lines.

A similar pessimism about the "public patriarch" is implicit in the movie's confinement to the private sphere. This brings me to the final point I want to make, which has to do with how postfeminist fantasies of domesticity may reflect and reinforce a retreat from political engagement. The problem with celebrations of home and family is not only that they tend to essentialize gender identities, but also that they may contribute to a reluctance to imagine relationships of mutual commitment at levels other than the individual household unit. Whether two- or single-parent, male- or female-headed, breadwinner or two-career, hetero- or nonheterosexual, nuclear or extended, the family is all too easily constructed and experienced as the exclusive locus of nurturing activities, a privileged alternative to other modes of providing for human needs. Over the course of the Reagan-Bush era, the right used the rhetoric of family with considerable success to attack social welfare programs and to limit the provision of public goods and services. Softened by invocations of "family values," its authoritarian image of the state has threatened to eclipse the very idea of caring as a public responsibility that corresponds to a socially held right to receive basic necessities.

Little Man Tate, I have suggested, offers resistance to the conservative assault on social welfare, but of a limited and symptomatically passive sort. When mean-spirited voices drone on in the background, denigrating the needs of others in the name of private property and self-reliance, the movie asks us not to listen to them. It invites us to detach ourselves from the selfish children at the convention and follow Fred out of the hall, to turn off the television set, as he does, cutting short the conservative litany about the benefits of labor discipline. But what the movie fails to offer is any counter-vision of a generous, nurturing father and a social-service-oriented state. Its response to a situation in the public sphere which it seems clearly to regret is to withdraw into a private sphere presided over by women, whom nature alone suffices to unite.

Nature, however, will no more unite women with one another than it need divide them from men. What could bring together women differentiated by class or racial identity is the struggle to create a society in which caring is defined as both a public and a private concern and is equally shared between women and men. Inasmuch as postfeminist mass culture systematically fails to imagine that struggle, it retreats from the feminist program which it partially incorporates and pursues.

Notes

An earlier draft of this paper was presented to the CSST Faculty Seminar at The University of Michigan; I am particularly grateful to Nick Dirks, Nancy Lutkehaus, and Sherry Ortner for their comments and encouragement. Thanks to my colleagues Karen Bock, Sue Hirsch, and Dick Ohmann for their critical insights. Lastly, this paper would never have been written were it not for Len Tennenhouse and Nancy Armstrong, who hosted a collective viewing of the Murphy Brown *birth episode.*

1.   The right's "New Class" is an ideologically defined segment of the class to which the critics themselves belong. The larger formation has been variously designated and theorized on the left as a New Class of intellectuals (Gouldner 1979), a professional-managerial class of salaried mental workers (Ehrenreich & Ehrenreich 1979), a service class of bureaucrats (Abercrombie and Urry 1983), a credential or skill-based class of semi-autonomous employees (Wright 1985), a new middle class of knowledge workers (Frow n.d.). Although different groups are included and excluded in these models, most theorists agree that the boundaries separating the new middle class from those above and below it are not sharply drawn, and the class itself is understood to be internally differentiated. John Frow argues that being weakly formed is a crucial attribute of the New Class and reflects the mechanisms of its formation, which have to do with claims to knowledge as opposed to ownership of the means of production or direct exploitation.

2.   On the state as the substitute for the male breadwinner, see Mimi Abramovitz (1988: 313–14). Barbara Ehrenreich (1987: 180) notes the parallel which New Right critics draw between feminism and social welfare. On the condensation of the welfare queen with the upwardly mobile female professional, see Wahneema Lubiano (1992) and Nancy Fraser (1992).

3.   Letterman's contribution to the postmortem: "I'm going to say this only once, Mr. Quayle. Murphy Brown is a fictional character."

4.   Katha Pollitt (1992: 88) takes Quayle to be positing a causal connection whereby watching *Murphy Brown* would encourage inner-city women to bear fatherless babies. But the speech alluded, it seems to me, to the paradigmatic association of career women with welfare mothers, which presupposes the subversive activity of the New Class. Pollitt was also puzzled by Quayle's inclusion of TV writers in the cultural elite ("I thought they were the crowd pleasing lowbrows, and *intellectuals* were the cultural elite"), but within the terms of New Right ideology there was no inconsistency here. What is interesting about the neoconservative construction of the New Class (and overlaps with the theories cited in Note 1) is precisely that it encompasses such differentially credentialed knowledge workers as media professionals and the traditional intelligentsia.

5.   "That's the first time I've heard that," he said when a political analyst for a San Francisco television station brought the abortion connection to his attention: "It's far-fetched" (Rosenthal 1992b: 34).

6.   As the summer of 1992 unfolded, antiabortion rhetoric proved equally recalcitrant. Faced with the question of how they would respond should a pregnant daughter or granddaughter consider an abortion, both Quayle and Bush exchanged the image of the stern patriarchal disciplinarian for that of the supportive, caring father who would respect his child's decision, thereby backing themselves (perhaps intentionally) into what many took to be a pro-choice position. Marilyn Quayle was left to hold the line, promising that should her daughter become pregnant, "she would carry the child to term."

7.   Here, for instance, is Faludi (1991: 77) on the press: "Journalism replaced the 'pro-family' diatribes of fundamentalist preachers with sympathetic and even progressive-sounding rhetoric. It cosmeticized the scowling face of antifeminism while blackening the feminist eye. In the process, it popularized the backlash beyond the New Right's wildest dreams."

8.   Aid to Dependent Children, the basic program of the welfare state which provided limited financial support to unmarried mothers raising children, was established in 1935. By the postwar years a majority of ADC recipients were black women who were rendered increasingly visible to the public through the mediation of the welfare state's disciplinary gaze. Living without a husband but dependent on the state, these women appeared to violate both the family ethic and the work ethic (Solinger 1992: 52). Abramovitz (1988: 351) also links a perception of black welfare mothers as dual transgressors to the mobilization of antiwelfare sentiment. Similar stereotypes, Nancy Fraser (1989: 152) observes, influence how service professionals view their black female clients and have helped to justify the heavy component of surveillance which characterizes the "feminine" sector of the social welfare system.

9.   The model placed particular emphasis on the "instrumental" role of the father, who was supposed to guide both boys and girls into their respective masculine and feminine identities. Sons appeared to be especially at risk in the "father absent" suburban home, and child-care experts called on Dad to assert his manly presence on their behalf; an added benefit, said the experts, was that Dad's displays of appreciation would encourage daughters to develop their feminine selves.

Such calls were not unique to the 1950s. According to Margaret Marsh (1990), the fusion of the suburban and the domestic ideals at the turn of the century was accompanied by increasing emphasis on the husband's family obligations. Male advice writers in that period encouraged suburban middle-class men to exchange their all-male social networks for greater intimacy with their wives and children. The model of domestic masculinity which developed from such instructions contributed to the evolving ideal of companionate marriage. It also shaped a new, increasingly influential definition of the father's role as that of a "caring older companion rather than a stern patriarch" (Marsh 1990: 80).

The ideal of the participatory father has contradictory implications. While it is a necessary condition for an egalitarian sharing of domestic labor that would reduce gender polarity, it may also be realized as the transposition of separate spheres to domestic space, and such a division became the postwar family ideal (Segal 1990: 6). The united family, Lynn Spigel (1992: 36–72) observes, was divided on gendered lines, creating new signifiers of masculinity out of selective domestic responsibilities. Yet the "manliness" of the man around the house seemed to require continual reaffirmation, and in the fifties version of paternal participation "concern for masculinity . . . was expressed in terms that condemned women" (Solinger 1992: 21). At the underside of the experts' crusade against "father absence" lurked the symmetric threat of "mother presence," or more precisely, the presence in the home of discontented (hence "maladjusted") wife-mothers whose overprotective or rejecting behaviors could subvert their children's sexual development.

The assumption which underlies the sex-role model, more fully theorized in object relations psychoanalysis, is that boys, unlike girls, must repudiate their primary identification with the mother by identifying with the oedipal father. Within this conception of masculinity, "excessive" mothering compounded by "father absence" (or the relative unavailability of a weak, passive father) creates severe obstacles to masculine development. A feminist approach within object relations psychoanalysis (Chodorow 1978; Benjamin 1988) sees exclusive female mothering and father absence as problematic for boys and girls alike. The solution envisioned in this approach is an alternative to gender-differentiated parenting and a masculinity that would no longer be based on the repudiation of femininity.

10. As Solinger observes (1992: 40), the adoption plan which liberal service professionals designed and implemented in the 1950s has become a strategy of antiabortion activists. Had Quayle been quicker on the uptake and had he wished to embroil himself further in the debate over a fictional character's pregnancy, he could have suggested that Murphy Brown give her baby up for adoption after carrying it to term.

11. On the subordination of sexuality to nurturance in the Victorian construction of the Ideal Mother, see Smith-Rosenberg (1985). Ehrenreich and English (1978: 242–45) discuss the misogynistic slant which sexologists and child care experts gave to the sexualization of marriage by prescribing it as the remedy for overprotective mothering. As Elaine May (1988: 106–109) also argues, a homology between female sexuality and nuclear energy underlay such prescriptions: both were forces that would prove destructive unless they were tamed by men.

12. Increasing suspicion of independent women was manifested in postwar cinematic images of women. By the late 1940s, the relatively positive portrayals of single working women which both the Depression and wartime cinemas had made available all but disappeared. Emancipated heroines were converted into the dangerous *femmes fatales* of *film noir* or into neurotics in need of therapeutic intervention. Alternatively, feminine independence was absorbed by the spunky wives and mothers of liberal family movies. On representations of women in the late forties and fifties cinema see Susan Hartmann (1982), May (1988), and Peter Biskind (1983).

13. On the one hand, high divorce rates made women reluctant to depend on potentially unreliable male breadwinners, many of whom were becoming involved in what Barbara Ehrenreich (1983) has called the "male revolt" against the provider role. On the other hand, the feminist critique of domesticity (Friedan 1963) helped many women to leave unhappy marriages, especially those with access to the expanded employment opportunities. Economic opportunities, however, were unequally distributed along class lines, and women's differential experiences in the workplace, Judith Stacey (1990: 12–16) argues, would affect their perspectives on the family system that was passing. As Kathleen Gerson (1985) has also found, women whose earning power and mobility is strictly limited are more disposed toward a nostalgic view of the breadwinner family as a receding haven.

14. The population control movement clashed with religious defenders of traditional sexual morality over how best to halt what both sides viewed as the "excessive" reproduction of poor minority women (Petchesky 1983: 120–22; Solinger 1992: 211–13). This debate over means was never fully resolved, and consequently, Petchesky argues (1983: 120–30), the U.S. never developed a coherent policy. While support from the population control establishment contributed to the legalization of contraception and abortion, government policy shifted back toward sexual control in the late 1970s, under pressure from the religious right. The Hyde Amendment was passed in 1977 to curb "promiscuous sex" among the minority poor.

15. The repositioning of unwed mothers as sexual revolutionaries, Solinger notes (1992: 217–18), reflected a shift in the dominant models of behavior. As sociological displaced psychological explanation, sexual nonconformity became a social rather than an individual pathology to its critics, something to be blamed on the disintegrating values of a "permissive" society rather than on the maladaptive behavior of individual families.

16. The concept of "welfare dependency" presupposes the stereotype it reinforces of black unwed welfare mothers as promiscuous reproducers. In fact, as a recent New York Times series on welfare points out, almost three-fourths of the families on welfare have two children or less, according to the American Public Welfare Association, and long-term use is more the exception than the rule (Toner 1992b: A-16). Although the Times series repeatedly refuted the distorted perception of the welfare mother as a long-term, chronic user whose "dependence" on the system leads her to bear baby after baby, one entire article in the six-part series (Dugger 1992) was devoted to women who more or less fit that stereotype.

17. I have adapted this critique of Wilson's explanation from Gregory (n.d.), who argues that despite Wilson's emphasis on the role of structural processes in creating urban poverty, his appeal to psycho-cultural factors to account for the effects of poverty reinforces existing stereotypes of minority groups and obscures the role of power relations both in producing poverty and mediating its effects.

18. See Gilroy (1987: 104–105) for similar British constructions of black teenagers.

19. The phrase "defective families" is from Nancy Fraser's (1988: 150) critique of the dominant discourses on welfare.

20. In a *New York Times* article that called attention to the trend, film critic Caryn James (1989) cited *Baby Boom* and *Crossing Delancey*, in which professional women trade unfulfilling careers for marriage and motherhood, along with *Beaches* and *Stella* (the 1990 remake of *Stella Dallas*), which extol the joys of maternal sacrifice.

21. Andrea Press (1991: 49) also stresses the role of the mass media in "constructing and shaping postfeminist ideology," but her more sophisticated, reception-based model of media effects on consciousness explores how women's responses to television vary along lines of class and generation. Unfortunately, for my purposes, the reception analysis seems loosely connected to the text-based critique of postfeminist television. This makes it difficult to assess the critique, which to my mind overstates the regressive features of mass-mediated postfeminism. Press's textual analysis relies on a reflectionist model that takes realism as the criterion for assessing a text's progressive content. So, for example, while *Roseanne* is praised for reflecting the exploitation of women in the workplace, its idealized portrayal of working-class family life is criticized for ignoring such phenomena as the wife's double burden. Press argues, as I understand her, that the "retreat from all criticism of the family" (1991: 43) identifies the show's ideology as postfeminist. But leaving aside whether this is an adequate definition of postfeminism or an accurate account of the referential code in *Roseanne* (double burden issues were central to the series premiere, albeit resolved in comic fashion), the reflectionist model precludes attention to the internal dynamics of television fictions. For another perspective on *Roseanne*, see Kathleen Rowe (1990), who treats the central character as an instantiation of the "unruly woman," the antithesis of the self-sacrificing wife-mother of domestic ideology.

22. I am grateful to my colleague Indira Karamcheti who first called my attention to the disarticulation and rearticulation of African-American culture in *Murphy Brown*.

23. It came as no surprise to *Murphy Brown* viewers that Elden, the bohemian working-class housepainter, became the co-mother in the course of the 1992 fall season. Although intermittently associated with a rigid, undomesticated, stereotypically working-class masculinity, Elden also represented the artist as natural man, enemy of bourgeois conventions (including conventional breadwinner masculinity). Consistent with the analysis presented here is the historical connection between the "beat culture" evoked through Elden and African American street cultures.

24. On the imaginary relation of middle-class youth to the white working class, and in particular the projection of unrestrained sexuality onto the working class, see Barbara Ehrenreich 1989: 93–96 and Sherry Ortner 1991: 175–79.

25. In many ethnic working-class families during the early stages of capitalist development daughters were more likely to work outside the home than mothers (Lamphere 1987). The wife-mother, however, might contribute to the household economy by taking in boarders or industrial homework.

26. Michelle Wallace (1978) explicitly rejected the model, popularized by Daniel Patrick Moynihan, of "matriarchy" as responsible for the "breakdown" of the black family. Jesse Jackson also defended the integrity of female-headed black households in his critical response to Quayle's *Murphy Brown* speech. On the other hand, the movie *Boyz 'N the Hood* popularized conservative nostalgia for the strong father by constructing the male-headed family as necessary to black empowerment and community control.

27. In its first weeks of release *Little Man Tate* showed at only 327 screens. Over the next few weeks, its release was widened to slightly over 1,000 screens, after which it gradually contracted again. To gross $25 million with such a limited release, the movie had to have excellent word of mouth.

28. In my experience, it was frequently and heatedly discussed among college students and professors, while it was also warmly received in the nail salon where I sometimes conduct highly informal reception work.

29. On this feature of female-oriented genres, see Tania Modleski (1982: 85–109) and Linda Williams (1987: 314–20).

30. I thank the members of the Michigan CSST seminar who pointed out that child viewers may derive

pleasure from the antiauthoritarian fantasy of subordinating adults to their desires. Yet I would not overemphasize the liberatory aspects of such a fantasy, especially as the adults whom Fred controls in the movie are uniformly female. The image of the all-giving nurturer continues to bear unequally upon women and men, making it difficult for women to assert their independent subjectivity, and, Jessica Benjamin (1988: 213–14) observes, for children to work through their aggressive responses to any such assertions. In Benjamin's model, mother and child collude in the fantasy that he is the center of her life, a fantasy which denies her existence as an independent subject.

E.
Traube

31. The first birthday party scene alludes to the equivalent scenes in *Stella Dallas* and *Stella*, suggesting that Foster intended her movie to evoke the famous maternal melodrama. It bears mention that what spoils the birthday party in the *Stella* movies is the heroine's unrestrained and playful sexuality, which offends the stuffy parents of her daughter's friends, whereas Dede is insufficiently attentive to Fred's needs, failing to appreciate his estrangement from ordinary kids.

32. Perhaps a more plausible reading would take Dede and her friend and coworker Gina as lesbian companions. It would be interesting to compare *Little Man Tate* with another, even more popular movie marketed to women in 1991–2, the sleeper hit *Fried Green Tomatoes*, adapted from Fannie Flagg's novel about a Depression-era lesbian relationship.

References

Abercrombie, Nicholas, and John Urry. 1983. Capital, Labour and the Middle Classes. London: Allen and Unwin.

Abramovitz, Mimi. 1988. *Regulating the Lives of Women: Social Welfare Policy from Colonial Times to the Present*. Boston: South End Press.

Ansen, David. 1991. "Jodie Foster Lurches About." *Newsweek* (21 October): 65.

Benjamin, Jessica. 1988. *The Bonds of Love: Psychoanalysis, Feminism, and the Problem of Domination*. New York: Pantheon Books.

Bennet, Tony. 1982. "Theories of the Media, Theories of Society." In *Culture, Society and the Media*, ed. M. Gurevitch et. al, 30–55. London: Methuen.

Biskind, Peter. 1983. *Seeing Is Believing: How Hollywood Taught Us to Stop Worrying and Love the Fifties*. New York: Pantheon Books.

Block, Fred, Richard Howard, Barbara Ehrenreich, and Frances Fox. 1987. *The Mean Season: The Attack on the Welfare State*. New York: Pantheon Books

Carby, Hazel. 1986. "On the Threshold of Woman's Era: Lynching, Empire, and Sexuality in Black Feminist Theory." In *"Race," Writing, and Difference*, ed. H. L. Gates, Jr., 301–16. Chicago: The University of Chicago Press.

———1987. *Reconstructing Womanhood: The Emergence of the Afro-American Woman Novelist*. New York: Oxford University Press.

Chodorow, Nancy. 1978. *The Reproduction of Motherhood: Psychoanalysis and the Sociology of Gender*. Berkeley: University of California Press.

Dugger, Celia W. 1992. "In Newark, Single Mothers on the Edge of Survival." *New York Times* (6 July): A1, B6.

Ehrenreich, Barbara. 1983. *The Hearts of Men: American Dreams and the Flight from Commitment*. Garden City, N.Y.: Anchor Press/ Doubleday.

———1989. *Fear of Falling: The Inner Life of the Middle Class*. New York: Pantheon Books.

Ehrenreich, Barbara, and John Ehrenreich. 1979. "The Professional-Managerial Class." In *Between Labor and Capital*, ed. P. Walker, 5–45. Boston: South End Press.

Ehrenreich, Barbara, and Deirdre English. 1979. *For Her Own Good: 150 Years of the Experts' Advice to Women*. New York: Anchor Books.

Ehrensaft, Diane. 1987. *Parenting Together: Men and Women Sharing the Care of Their Children*. New York: Free Press.

Faludi, Susan. 1991. *Backlash: The Undeclared War Against American Women*. New York: Crown Publishers, Inc.

Feuer, Jane. 1984. "The MTM Style." In *MTM 'Quality Television,'* ed. J. Feuer, P. Kerr, and T. Vahimagi, 32–60. London: BFI Publishing.

———1986. "Narrative Form in American Network Television," in *High Theory/Low Culture: Analysing Popular Television and Film*, ed. C. MacCabe, 101–14. New York: St. Martin's Press.

Fraser, Nancy. 1989. *Unruly Practices: Power, Discourse and Gender in Contemporary Social Theory*. Minneapolis: University of Minnesota Press.

———1992. "Sex, Lies, and the Public Sphere: Some Reflections on the Confirmation of Clarence Thomas." *Critical Inquiry* 18: 595–612.

Friedan, Betty. 1963. *The Feminine Mystique*. New York: W. W. Norton.

Frow, John. n.d. "Knowledge and Class." Unpublished manuscript.

Gerson, Kathleen. 1985. *Hard Choices: How Women Decide About Work, Career, and Motherhood*. Berkeley: University of California Press.

Gilroy, Paul. 1991. *"There Ain't No Black in the Union Jack": The Cultural Politics of Race and Nation*. Chicago: The University of Chicago Press.

Gledhill, Christine, ed. 1987. *Home Is Where the Heart Is: Studies in Melodrama and the Woman's Film*. London: British Film Institute.

Gouldner, Alvin. 1979. *The Future of Intellectuals and the Rise of the New Class: A Frame of Reference, Theses, Conjectures, Arguments, and an Historical Perspective on the Role of Intellectuals and Intelligentsia in the International Class Contest of the Modern Era*. New York: Oxford University Press.

Gregory, Steven. n.d. "Power, Discourse and the Construction of the 'Ghetto Underclass.'" Unpublished manuscript.

Hebdige, Dick. 1979. *Subculture: The Meaning of Style*. London & New York: Methuen.

Hertz, Rosanna. 1986. *More Equal than Others: Women and Men in Dual-Career Marriages*. Berkeley: University of California Press.

James, Caryn. 1989. "Are Feminist Heroines an Endangered Species?" *New York Times* (10 July): 15, 20.

Jones, Jacqueline. 1985. *Labor of Love, Labor of Sorrow: Black Women, Work, and the Family from Slavery to the Present*. New York: Basic Books.

Hartmann, Susan. 1982. *The Home Front and Beyond: American Women in the 1940s*. Boston: Twayne Publishers.

Lamphere, Louise. 1987. *From Working Daughters to Working Mothers: Immigrant Women in a New England Industrial Community*. Ithaca: Cornell University Press.

Levitan, Sar A., and Richard S. Belous. 1981. *What's Happening to the American Family?* Baltimore: Johns Hopkins University Press.

Lubiano, Wahneema. 1992. "Black Ladies, Welfare Queens, and State Minstrels: Ideological War by Narrative Means." In *Race-ing Justice, En-gendering Power: Essays on Anita Hill, Clarence Thomas, and the Construction of Social Reality*, ed. Toni Morrison, 323–63. New York: Pantheon Books.

Marsh, Margaret. 1990. *Suburban Lives*. New Brunswick: Rutgers University Press.

May, Elaine Tyler. 1988. *Homeward Bound: American Families in the Cold War Era*. New York: Basic Books.

Modleski, Tania. 1984. *Loving with a Vengeance: Mass-produced Fantasies for Women*. New York: Methuen.

Neale, Steven, and Frank Krutnik. 1990. *Popular Film and Television Comedy*. London: Routledge.

Ortner, Sherry. 1991. "Reading America: Preliminary Notes on Class and Culture." In *Recapturing Anthropology: Working in the Present*, ed. Richard G. Fox, 163–89. Santa Fe: School of American Research Press.

Petcheskey, Rosalind. 1983. *Abortion and Women's Choice: The State, Sexuality, and Reproductive Freedom*. New York & London: Longman.

Pleck, Joseph. 1987. "American Fathering in Historical Perspective." In *Changing Men: New Directions in Research on Men and Masculinity*, ed. M. S. Kimmel, 83–97. Newbury Park: Sage Publications.

Pollitt, Katha. 1992. "Dan, Murph and Me: Why I Hate 'Family Values' (Let Me Count the Ways)." *The Nation* (20/27 July): 88–94.

Press, Andrea. 1991. *Women Watching Television: Gender, Class, and Generation in the American Television Experience*. Philadelphia: University of Pennsylvania Press.

Probyn, Elspeth. 1990. "New Traditionalism and Post-Feminism: TV Does the Home." *Screen* 31 (2): 147–59.

Riley, Denise. 1988. *"Am I That Name?": Feminism and the Category of 'Women' in History*. Minneapolis: University of Minnesota Press.

Rosenfelt, Deborah, and Judith Stacey. 1990. "Second Thought on the Second Wave." In *Women, Class, and the Feminist Imagination: A Socialist-Feminist Reader*, ed. K. V. Hansen and I. J. Philipson, 549–67. Philadelphia: Temple University Press.

Rosenthal, Andrew. 1992a. "Quayle Attacks a 'Cultural Elite' in Speech Invoking Moral Values." *New York Times* (10 June): A1.

———1992b. "Quayle's Moment." *New York Times Magazine* (5 July): 10–13, 30, 33–34.

Rowe, Kathleen K. 1990. "Roseanne: Unruly Woman as Domestic Goddess." *Screen* 31 (4): 408–19.

Segal, Lynne. 1990. *Slow Motion: Changing Masculinities, Changing Men*. New Brunswick: Rutgers University Press.

Smith-Rosenberg, Caroll. 1985. *Disorderly Conduct: Visions of Gender in Victorian America*. New York: Oxford University Press.

Solinger, Rickie. 1992. *Wake Up, Little Susie: Single Pregnancy and Race Before Roe V. Wade*. New York & London: Routledge.

Spigel, Lynn. 1992. *Make Room for TV: Television and the Family Ideal in Postwar America*. Chicago: The University of Chicago Press.

Stacey, Judith. 1987. "'Sexism by a Subtler Name?' Postindustrial Conditions and Postfeminist Consciousness in the Silicon Valley." *Socialist Review* 17 (6): 7–28.

———1990. *Brave New Families: Stories of Domestic Upheaval in Late Twentieth Century America*. New York: Basic Books.

Stansell, Christine. 1987. *City of Women: Sex and Class in New York, 1789–1860*. Urbana & Chicago: University of Illinois Press.

Toner, Robin. 1992. "Quayle, at Anti-Abortion Meeting, Presses 'Cultural Elite' Attack." *New York Times* (12 July).

Traube, Elizabeth. 1992. *Dreaming Identities: Class, Gender, and Generation in 1980s Hollywood Movies*. Boulder: Westview Press.

Wallace, Michele. 1979. *Black Macho and the Myth of the Superwoman*. London: John Calder.

Williams, Linda. 1987. "'Something Else Besides a Mother': *Stella Dallas* and the Maternal Melodrama." In *Home is Where the Heart Is*, ed. Gledhill, 299–325.

Wilson, William Julius. 1987. *The Truly Disadvantaged*. Chicago: The University of Chicago Press.

———1991a. "Studying Inner-City Social Dislocations: The Challenge of Public-Agenda Research." *American Sociological Review* 56: 1–14.

Wright, Erik Olin. 1985. *Classes*. London: Verso.

Young, Alison. 1990. *Femininity in Dissent*. New York: Routledge.

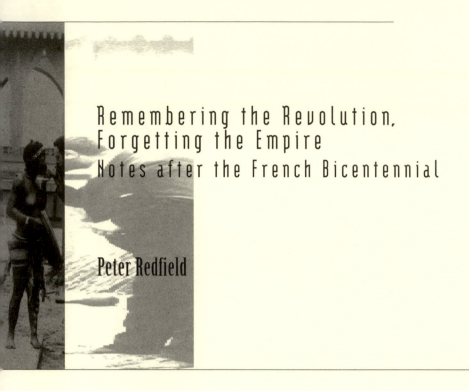

Remembering the Revolution, Forgetting the Empire
Notes after the French Bicentennial

Peter Redfield

TRAGEDY OR FARCE, SOME THINGS DO RETURN MORE THAN ONCE. THE FRENCH REVOLUTION has echoed many times, both on the street and across the printed page. It stands out as one of the most historicized events in Western history, with ample interpretations for every paving stone and proclamation. The summer of 1989 marked its bicentennial, and yet another interpretive overlay, the elaborate theater of official celebration and protest. Between opera at the Bastille and a flood of commemorative issues of stamps, T-shirts and journals left and right, the passions of the First Republic became the pageantry of the Fifth. The moment was fleeting; at the distance of several years the French commemoration lies buried beneath dramatic world events, and superseded by another historical anniversary, that of the arrival of Columbus to the New World. Yet in its brief glow the Bicentennial describes a remarkable attempt at spectacle, a modern ritual of national origin in a nation state claiming authority to Enlightenment, and the wellsprings of modernity. By way of introduction, let us open to a page seeking to provide a capsule summary of the French fireworks.

"*Les Jours de Gloire*," announces the headline in *Newsweek*, "France celebrates its bicentennial with the world's first postmodern patriotic festival." The article below lies offset against images of a black woman draped in the *tricolore*, an enormous burst of fireworks over the Arc de Triomphe, and, high in the corner, a grim clump of white men riding stiffly in military review. "We are all children of the Revolution now," it informs us, "—creatures of Liberty and survivors of the Terror, a perpetual bourgeoisie living off our wits" (Adler and Dickey 1989: 20–23). What surprises is both the strength of the claims ("postmodern . . . perpetual bourgeoisie"), and the manner in which they fall on the page—the touch of satire, poetry amid corporate journalism. This ironic tone continues through in offering a fuller description of events:

> Having turned the sacred commemoration of the Bastille over to an advertising man, Parisians were treated to a spectacle in the style of irrelevance that Americans pioneered . . . A new slogan taking shape in the streets: Liberty, Frivolity, Irony. . . A morning military parade with jet fighters streaming tri-color smoke was followed by a mile long parade in the evening dubbed "The Festival of the Planet's Tribes." This was a peculiar theme for a celebration of the French revolution, which in fact asserted the universality of mankind over parochial customs and loyalties. On the other hand, what does "universality" have in the way of spectacle to compare with zebra-striped horses and the Funky Chicken, with a phalanx of Chinese students towing a huge red Chinese drum in memory of Tiananmen Square and a platoon of Russian troops goose-stepping through ersatz snow to the beat of African drums? (Adler and Dickey 1989: 20–21)

It would be easy to glance briefly at this section and the accompanying photographs of the moonwalking Florida A & M marching band, the axe-carrying Foreign Legionnaires, the staring woman with a hoop dress bearing a child with the Palestinian flag, glance briefly and move on. Easy, yes, for this is *Newsweek*, not an academic journal, not even the French press, and yet—here, condensed through the distance of translation, linguistic and cultural, molded as a short and digestible piece, opened in irony and closed with light humor, here we find a discussion of postmodern society, human nature and difference.

In this essay I wish to pursue twin issues highlighted in the article, that of the possible "postmodern" status of this particular patriotic festival, and that of the modified relations of difference and universality in its reworking of the Revolutionary heritage. In question will be elements of time (change, continuity, and measurement) and elements of place (the political geographies of nation and world), together with those narratives which evoke time and place in larger constructions of historically similar and different identities (the traditional, the modern, the postmodern).[1] As historical anchors I propose two visual events: the Bicentennial, as replayed between personal notes, memories and published reports, and the most related antecedent, the Centennial World's Fair of 1889, especially as depicted in its own commemoration a century later.[2] At issue in each case will be the place of images of difference in the representation of revolution, nation and empire, alongside claims of universal meaning in the construction of a public France. The goal will be to better position the moment of the French Bicentennial with respect to anthropological categories of political ritual, while in turn positioning those categories over on the far side of modern identity.

> For the revolutionaries of 1789, there is no doubt: the message they express is addressed
> to the entire planet.
>
> —François Mitterand[3]

As a first step let us construct a social and historical frame around *Newsweek*'s account of the
Festival of the Planet's Tribes. At home in Paris, Bicentennial plans were laid, only to be unlaid
and relaid amid political squabbles, for years before *the* year. In September, 1981, the newly
elected Socialist administration announced that France would seek to hold a universal
exposition in honor of 1989, both commemorating the Revolutionary bicentennial and looking
forward at the possibilities of progress in the coming third millennium.[4] These grand designs
lasted less than two years before falling to political and economic realities, a reluctant Paris and
its conservative mayor, Jacques Chirac. Though denied an exposition, François Mitterand's
government nevertheless ploughed ahead with other monumental efforts, and despite
opposition and political turmoil during the period of *cohabitation*,[5] the central city would
eventually see some major reworking of its landscape. A controversial pyramid entrance for the
Louvre, former palace and totem museum; a gleaming science museum at La Villette, amid
traditional northeastern working-class neighborhoods; an intricate Arab World Institute near
the Seine, its panels combining Arabic patterns and complex technology; an enormous boxlike
arch over La Défense, the high-rise business suburb; and, perhaps the most debated glass and
steel insect of all, the large, beetlelike, opera house at the Bastille; all these would be open and
waiting on July Fourteenth.[6] In addition to the architectural props, a fierce climate of
commercialism (bearing with it everything from guillotine earrings to tricolor bread), together
with active political discussion surrounding elections for the European Parliament, a major
economic summit in Paris, and potential revolution in China provided a lively backdrop for the
celebrations themselves. While the world may not have appeared in Paris for the occasion in the
form of exposition exhibits, it did arrive embodied in its political leaders and their entourages.
Between rival Conservative and Socialist guest lists, the army of summit participants, and a
timely tour by Mikhail Gorbachev, the city saw a lengthy parade of dignitaries, hurried to and
fro amid police escorts. Metal railings to control crowds and small squadrons of traffic police
filled the streets, while local and international news merged in media interviews.

The months of June and July in Paris saw the main crescendo of celebration and protest,
as mounted by the French state, together with groups positioned within, around, and against
it. The sheer volume of events was almost overwhelming; here I will describe only the most
public displays. Of these, six seem particularly relevant to issues at hand, four large nighttime
outdoor gatherings and two museum exhibits. Moving between personal memories and
official reports, I will offer a short sketch of each in chronological order.

The first event was held at the edge of one of Paris' two large parks, on June 10th. A protest
concert sponsored by S.O.S. Racisme, the French antiracist coalition movement, it drew some
300,000 people and lasted all night.[7] As an eclectic array of bands performed in front of the
Chateau de Vincennes, crowds milled about before the sprawling stage, speaker stacks and
video screens. Along one side a midway of booths sold refreshments and distributed political
literature, including the official program.

"The Concert of Equality," the brochure announces above a colorful image of dancing
figures, and includes an article about the abolition of slavery as well as a schedule of the
evening's entertainment. Just inside the cover is an editorial written by the movement's leader,
Harlem Desir, dedicating the concert to the Revolutionary Haitian leader Toussaint
L'Ouverture, and relating the memory of him to contemporary events, including the upheaval
in China. Beginning with a reference to the revolutionary ideals of liberty and equality for Man,
it calls for a widening of them to include all people: ". . . France is only the country of the Rights
of Man when it realizes the Rights of Man for those who are excluded from them."[8]

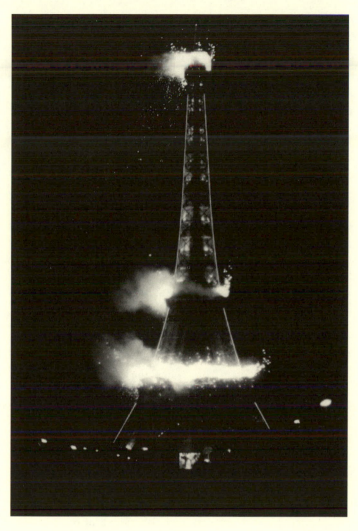

"The Tower of all Cultures."

A week later, the conservative mayor of Paris, Jacques Chirac, sought to upstage the coming state celebrations with a *fête exceptionelle* of his own, a lavish birthday party for the Eiffel Tower. Before seven hundred invited guests, and a surrounding crowd of five to six hundred thousand, the tower turned chameleon with the aid of ample lighting and fireworks. Packed along the Champs-de-Mars, site of the original Centennial fair, people chatted, drank, ate and watched. The mood contained a family tone, the smaller children drooping before the final crescendo, a rendering of "Happy Birthday," sung in English by all on stage, including special guest Ronald Reagan. In the flickering light of video screens, thousands of *citoyens* and *citoyennes* sang along, breaking into greater applause than they had for the rendering of *La Marseillaise* that had opened the evening.[9]

The official program for the occasion opens with a statement by Chirac himself. Calling the Eiffel Tower a "symbol of the communication between men," he underscores that the extravaganza is a "present that Paris offers to those who love it," born out of generosity and a "spirit of fraternity." It proceeds to describe the different scenes of the show and explain their significance. Just before the closing birthday number, comes a section entitled "The Tower of All Cultures," describing the singers' voices rising as a hymn to the Eiffel Tower, and to "universal brotherhood." The musical sequence is provided by the blind, African-American musician, Stevie Wonder.[10]

The 8th of July, just a few days prior to the inauguration of the new Opera house, saw another protest concert, this one overrunning the Bastille. Led by the French singer Renaud (with backing from the Communist party and independent left groups), the organizers decried debt (of Third to First World nations), apartheid and colonialism.[11] Most directly, their newsprint flyer objected to the vast expense of the state and city Bicentennial celebrations, and the segregation between rich and poor nations at the summit meetings. Beneath a banner depicting a Jacobin version of "hear no evil, see no evil, speak no evil" draped above the Opera entrance, a crowd of one hundred thousand listened to music and political exhortations. A small number of concertgoers managed to climb onto the monumental column marking the site of the ancient fortress, but they were quickly dislodged by police. Dressed in a Revolutionary *sans-culotte* outfit, Renaud called the summit meeting "an insult to the collective memory."[12]

And then, finally, it was not merely *the* year, but also *the* day, July 14th, 1989. Following the same path as the now-traditional morning military parade, "*La Marseillaise*," the enormous media ball depicted in *Newsweek*, wound its way towards the Place de la Concorde, former site of the guillotine, before a million spectators, and the assorted cameras of the world. On television the images were remarkably chaotic, figures looming out of darkness; on the street they were even more so, firecrackers, shouts, the shifting crowd and—there—a distant float. As the crowning moment, Jessye Norman, the African-American opera singer, dressed as a living French flag, delivered the great Revolutionary anthem itself.

"The triumph of the Revolution," proclaimed the headline of the conservative paper *Le Figaro* the next day. "The Revolution continues," announced that of the Communist *l'Humanité*. "Grand, our 14th of July," added the more neuter *France-Soir*, over a color photo spread matching Jessye Norman with a tank. "Encore!" applauded the leftist *Libération*, next to a black Florida A & M drummer. Each publication offered its summary, a last salvo in the media barrage.[13] The following Monday *Libération* put out a final supplementary section. On page ten we find a photograph of a bare-breasted African woman, staring straight, perhaps seductively, into the camera. The caption beneath focuses on neighboring images from the parade, explaining their symbolic commemoration of Tiananmen square.[14]

On a quieter note, French museums offered hundreds of special exhibits during the summer and throughout the year, two of which are particularly worthy of exploration. The Musée d'Orsay recalled "1889," presenting an account of the Centennial World's Fair and the building of the Eiffel Tower. On the gallery floor one found a layout of the fair, the spatial arrangements carefully reproduced in miniature. On the walls were drawings of tower plans and the stages of its construction, as well as of theme exhibits from the fair. On a lower level, a continuous slide show presented black and white images of the fair and tower. In retrospect, one of these images in particular stands out: two figures before a grass hut, a bare-breasted black woman and a dark-suited white man sharing a light. We find the photograph again on the front of the journal catalogue of the exhibit, where the caption reads "Strange encounter."[15]

Meanwhile, over on the Right bank, the Centre Georges Pompidou and the Grande Halle at La Villette presented a joint exhibition entitled *Magiciens de la Terre*, or "Magicians of the Earth." Beyond the variety of its individual displays, the presentation's most remarkable feature may have lain in its very self-presentation:

> First global exhibition of contemporary art, bringing together around a hundred artists
> in a worldwide selection, from both modern and traditional cultures. An extensive

"Strange Encounters."

research process was undertaken across every continent, Africa, the Americas, Australia, Asia, Europe . . . to discuss with artists and to select works for the exhibition . . . the artists's [*sic*] works are exhibited individually and not in order to represent their culture. The time has come to look again at the categories as well as the geographical and cultural boundaries which have divided and prejudiced opinions on the relations between different cultures in the world. While clearly respecting the differences between the significations and the practices of art in each country, the exhibition intends to show the universality of the creative act by exhibiting artists from the entire world.[16]

Researched and collected by a team of specialists, "ethnologues, anthropologists, historians, and critics," the exhibit sought to display as art, material extending beyond "imposed, preconceived Western notions . . ." (Applefield 1989: 1, 5).[17] And so, split between a refurbished exhibit hall and the shrine of Paris modernism, newer and older meanings of that elusive term would combine—*culture*—the plural, the ethnic, transmuting back into the high, the human.

Four spectacles outside, two indoors. What to make of all of this? Do these different spaces, different moments share some things in common? How to describe the Bicentennial in general terms? Certain threads of universalism, of difference do seem suggestively common. *Liberté, Egalité, Fraternité*, the Revolutionary triad marches on. Yet, after two hundred years we find "liberty" hushed, "equality" dangling the most open political question mark, and variants of "fraternity" loudly proclaimed by official left, right and center. The French revolution is emphatically presented as a world affair, an inheritance extending beyond immediate kin to a united and colorfully global brotherhood. But this ancient metaphor of kin identity also extends back from a vision of unity into questions of difference.[18] Once inside a family circle, do some brothers appear older, others younger? Where do sisters fit around the table? To underscore shades of difference within the Family of Man, let us turn to a time when colonialism and imperialism were stated terms of foreign policy, and fall through the exhibit on 1889 into 1889, midway between more recent celebrations and the sacred date they would commemorate.

The Centennial

The French flag is the only one to have a staff a thousand feet tall.
—Gustave Eiffel [19]

There's all *they* know about the empire—the belly dance.
—Jules Ferry[20]

Itself born in the aftermath of the disastrous Franco-Prussian war and the bitter defiance of the Paris Commune, France's Third Republic faced the centennial of the Revolution with some hesitation and much argument. The practice of regularly celebrating Bastille day had just been initiated in 1880, while the *Marseillaise* had become the national anthem only the year before. Both carried with them far more open overtones of contentious politics than they do today, as indeed did the concept of Republicanism itself (Almavi 1984; Vovelle 1984).[21] Ultimately, the government would choose to diffuse much of the revolutionary imagery and lessen the sense of political memorial surrounding the affair. "1789 was a historic date in economics as well as politics, and it is to examine the world's economic situation that all nations are invited," read the prospectus of a government committee studying the coming celebration in 1885. The official commemoration, they suggested, would have the task of "summing up what freedom of work has produced in terms of progress during the past hundred years" (Harriss 1976: 8). The result was the largest world's fair to that date, the first French one to include a substantial colonial exhibit, and the one that produced the most enduring monument of all ephemeral celebrations, the Eiffel Tower.

It was an era rich in empire and exhibition. The latter part of the nineteenth century and the first half of the twentieth saw both the greatest expansion of Western imperialism, and also the rise of world's fairs as a prime means of national and civic celebration and self-promotion in Western Europe and the United States. Under the leadership of Jules Ferry, France had just acquired new possessions in Indochina and Africa to add to its colonial network, ranked second only to that of Britain. This expanding imperial role, it is important to note, was not universally popular in France, nor were strains of assimilation asserted (if sporadically implemented) under its rule (Girardet 1972; Lewis 1962).[22] The world's fairs, on the other hand, while ideologically contested, held more immediate mass appeal. In a period before the electronic transmission of images or large-scale tourism, the exhibition of exotic goods and foreign structures within a confined space offered a glimpse of the globe to a mass audience, presenting a popular panorama of human geography and history blended through entertainment and science.[23]

The European tradition of universal expositions also served as a gauge of national struggles to define a distinctively modern ethos of progress. In describing the nation itself the focus was on artifice not nature (Benedict 1983: 5). The largest pavilion in the fair of 1889 was that reserved for the gallery of machines, containing the technology of industrialized nations.[24] Yet this technology was also displayed within competing visions of society, varieties of social engineering infusing that of the literal sort. As well as being about machines, the exhibits were about workers, health, and progress. The preceding series of exhibitions in France had felt the influence of engineer, sociologist, and reformer Frédéric Le Play, the Commissioner-General of the 1867 fair. Despite the intervening change of regime, the 1889 version carried on this tradition (Rabinow 1989: 93, 175–83). Two exhibits dealt with human life and evolution, a history of human habitation and an exposition of labor and the Anthropological sciences, and yet another centered on social institutions. At the same time, as part of these narratives the fair offered an encapsulated look at France's place in the world, including its grip on parts of the globe. France's Empire was laid out in miniature on the Esplanade des Invalides, attached by an umbilical cord of pavilions to the main exhibit at the Champ-de-Mars. The overall organization of space was strikingly clear: at the center the Eiffel Tower, below it the great gallery of machines, and then, physically separate, the collected colonies, fittingly next to the Palace of War. The symbolic relationship of separate parts was further underscored in technological terms; the two sectors being connected by a train.[25]

Let us explore the Centennial via a closer look at its extremes, the colonial exhibition and the Eiffel Tower. Quoting an original bulletin, the Museé d'Orsay exhibit catalogue describes the 1889 exhibition in terms of science fiction made real, and the foreign brought to life:

> "Jules Verne dreamed of the voyage around world in 80 days. We will realize it, in 1889, on the Esplanade and on the Champ-de-Mars, in 6 hours!" On the Esplanade des Invalides, what disorientation! Minarets, cupolas, pagodas, galleries and colonnades, buildings of raw earth, huts of thatch or bamboo, surround the *grand palais* of the French colonies in foreign shapes and colors . . . (Musée d'Orsay 1989: 102)

It goes on to chronicle the encounter between the French and the visiting colonial peoples from both an intended, and possibly an unintended point of view, the march of progress against the loss of magic:

> Structures and villages were inhabited by their native peoples, as the Ministry of Colonies had wished, in order to "put into direct contact with our civilization those populations which it is our duty to win to our ideas." In fact, this world confrontation was a source of inspiration and reflection for the visitors from the Occident, won over by the melancholy of attending the departure of this "humanity from beyond a dream with its theaters and its dances, its palaces and its princes, its temples and its gods." (Musée d'Orsay 1989: 117)[26]

Here we have human future and progress, positioned opposite human heritage and the past. Though one might intend to reshape the other, it ends up seduced by it—at least as long as the other appears vanquished, rare and vanishing. Hints of nostalgia in an age of high imperialism. The fair's colonial exhibition, it is reported, attracted large crowds.[27]

At the other end of the fair, rising supremely above it, stood Europe's latest, and tallest monument. In his remarkable essay on the Eiffel Tower, Roland Barthes calls the structure "the symbol of Paris, of modernity, of communication, of science or of the nineteenth century, rocket, stem, derrick, phallus, lightening rod or insect, confronting the great itinerary of our dreams, it is the inevitable sign . . ." (Barthes 1979: 4). Quintessentially useless, yet constructed along the most functional of lines, in its most physical semiotics the tower represents an engineering feat. Not only does it rise to remarkable heights, it also foils resistance, the very open, exposed design allowing gales to whistle harmlessly through. As historian Joseph Harriss points out, "the real strength of the tower is in its voids as much as its iron" (Harriss 1976: 63).

During its construction the tower was often compared to that other, less successful, attempt to build to heaven, the tower of Babel. "Slavery: the tower of Babel/Liberty, Progress: the tower of Eiffel!" ran the most concise and hopeful couplet (Musée d'Orsay 1989: 204). The comparison offers temptations beyond its rhyme, Babel representing a mythic origin of difference, Eiffel a symbolic closure. At the fair we would then find Babel on the ground, amid the collected tongues and dust of the world, all shadowed by abstract reason, pure and open against the sky. Colonialism, slavery below, liberty, progress above: a division realized by the iron power of technological truth. And at the summit of everything, floating freely—blue, white, and red—the Republic, France.

Over the ensuing century the tower has become an emblem of tourism, part of "the universal language of travel . . ." (Barthes 1979: 4). Where once the world came to it, Eiffel's tower now goes out to the world, on poster and postcard, and the world returns again to see a form it already knows. In 1989 the tower's deepest shadow would seem to fall quite evenly around its base, a souvenir in every language. "We are all citizens of the Eiffel Tower," a former critic would once write.[28] *Souvenir*, of course, relates to memory, and the way postcards must look similar to prove their authenticity. At the beginning of his essay Barthes points out that one must take "endless precautions" to avoid seeing the tower in Paris. It is omnipresent. At the end he notes that, once upon the structure, ". . . one can feel cut off from the world and yet owner of a world" (Barthes 1979: 3, 17). It inspires separation from the real, inclusion of domain. One remembers everything and nothing there, all of progress, no confusion. After a move from church and manor to office high-rise, what better site for conservative commemoration of modern ethos?

1889: A fair and a monument, one that would vanish far more quickly and painlessly than the empire, the other endure well after it. In both, the chaos of revolution fades behind expansion and industry, leaving a shadow of gradual progress, not immediate emancipation. Yet a promise of the future is clearly made: though mechanical and social technology, the well-conceived Nation will lead itself, and the Empire, out of archaic dreams and forward in prosperity. Old fears of either stasis or change, memories of terror can be all cast aside; this Republic, we are reminded, is to be a Republic of locomotives, not of guillotines.

The Bicentennial Revisited

> The Republic no longer intends to make distinctions in the human family.
> —Proclamation of 1848[29]

In a book containing over three hundred pages, the official commission in charge of the French Bicentennial attempts to present all celebrations and exhibitions relating to that occasion throughout 1989. Extending from Paris throughout France, provinces and possessions, and finally across the world, it covers commemorations of 1789 from Madagascar to Iceland. Both the scope of events and the scope of their inscription are remarkable; here a concert of revolutionary hymns in Nancy, there a school competition in New Caledonia (winners sent to visit the Metropole), there again an exhibit on Danton and Robespierre in Columbia, each, however large or small, recorded with appropriate addresses, times, and a graphic symbol to identify its universal type.[30] The commemoration of history is itself prepared for history: one could count, map, or chart the celebrations, with even the humblest receiving a line. Though its great sweep might fail, faltering in some tropical heat to miss a poem or mislabel a march, the eye of Paris seeks to take in the globe. A vast catalogue of emptiness, an empire of museums, perhaps, its gaze nonetheless hints at universal heritage, of the Revolution as panhuman experience, of a history for all. Tellingly, the French commission's very title ties it, as loudly as possible, not just to 1789, the Revolution, but also 1789 the Declaration, of rights for Citizens, and for Man. Whisper and shout echo the same: deep down unity has triumphed over difference.

What has changed since 1889? On the one hand, we see an exhibit on Anthropology and Labor, an exhibit on the history of human habitation, and on the other *Magiciens de la Terre*. The colonial is taken out of anthropology, out of evolution, out of science, and transferred into art. Once in the culture of progress, cultures must be saved from progress. Meanwhile, where the world's fair avoided the national past, the Musée d'Orsay commemorates the world's fair, while references to the Revolution fill every kiosk. The past and difference, orphaned by imperialism, are then adopted by museums. Some elements remain—the organization, timing, and control of crowds, for example—but the layout displays snares, tangles and diffusion. Space is not so neatly ordered; where the skyline rose to a jarring central tower, it now stretches around a number of vying shapes. No longer do we find graphic colonial segregation laid out along the Seine, only *de facto* political segregation of First and Third World leaders at the summit. Liberty at home has become a representational assumption. As well as official celebration, there is also official protest. At the Chateau de Vincennes we hear talk of slavery past and racism present. A month later the Bastille is retaken, this time to fight debt and apartheid. And on the right, the retired American monarch blesses Eiffel's creation, and the progressive harmony of technology.

Simultaneously the entire world is anthropologized, sent down the Champs Elysées, under the shadow of the arch of Napoleonic triumphs, and, now looming behind it, that of capitalist enterprise. Self and Other, after all, can fill the same screen. "Liberté, Égalité, Fraternité . . . Unité!" in the words of the editor of *National Geographic* (Garrett 1989). Indeed many of the visuals seem framed by that magazine's eye—hoop dress, breasts, the Eiffel tower all; indeed, the entire Marseillaise parade could almost be from an issue gone mad, a collage of cultural costumes, a map, co-ordinates forgotten.

Still, is it only an ironic footnote that this great Socialist world parade followed the same route as the military review? Is only the one, cavalry, legionnaires in close array, tanks with muzzles lifted high, jets in tight formations, is only one a real exercise in symbolic power? Between Napoleon's triumphal arch and the former site of the guillotine, along a mighty boulevard, the tribes of the world marched before crowd and camera, turning neither left nor right.

Spectacles, Modernity and Anthropology

In imagining what a historic beginning might be like, the modern imagination has turned back again and again to the events of the French Revolution. This historic rupture, more than any other, has assumed for us the status of modern myth.
—Paul Connerton[31]

It is safest to grasp the concept of the postmodern as an attempt to think the present historically in an age that has forgotten to think historically in the first place.
—Fredric Jameson[32]

Having set picture and frame, let us now stand back for critique. Where to fit the French Bicentennial? As an ethnographic festival, an example of political ritual? If so, what kind? Would *Newsweek*'s "first postmodern patriotic festival" and "spectacle in the style of irrelevance" hold up in any sense as analytic categories? A potential parallel case might be found in an academic discussion of modern political ritual in France, written by one of France's leading anthropologists. In a 1988 article, Marc Abélès examines two rituals performed by the French president François Mitterand, an inauguration of a train station and a pilgrimage to a significant hill top, one of official origin and one personal. He finds enough similarity between these two events in modern France and mingled categories of religion and politics found in the rituals of traditional society to declare that they do not differ in kind. Rather, modern rituals exhibit the additional characteristics of allowing for personal invention and the transmission of particular messages, while remaining a most effective "historic form of legitimacy" (Abélès 1988: 398). Abélès provides us with a another mirror for Bicentennial Man, that of the traditional simple society, as reconstructed by a modernist science compensating for distinctions born out of other separate modernist social sciences. Alongside the modern/postmodern divide of *Newsweek* describing spectacle we have the modern/traditional divide of a returned native anthropologist describing ritual. Where then to fit the Bicentennial?

Let us first approach the question through the term "spectacle," as applied to a particular form of visual display and social ritual. Spectacle, Festival, Ritual, and Modern each describe a complicated analytic knot; the threads between the first and last may best unravel a patch of the Bicentennial. In the name of analytic clarity, John MacAloon offers an etymology and definition for the term "spectacle," linking it to an emphasis on the visual, on dynamism, and on an audience. In addition, and in opposition to its relative, the "festival," a spectacle can carry connotations of awe as much as joy. Contemporary society's confusion of image and reality, MacAloon suggests, infuses such modern spectacles such as the Olympic games, reflecting an attempting an attempt to control "diffuse cultural themes and anxieties" (MacAloon 1984: 243–50, 273).[33]

In modern spectacle then, we might see a corollary to traditional visual ritual, a transitory moment of separation and reintegration, a glimpse of an underlying social framework and the sacred edges of the profane. Ritual in traditional societies, spectacle in modern societies, each are portrayed as important events. Their importance is recognized by their audience and explicated by their interpreter. From such a perspective Abélès' analysis of Mitterand's activities fits well in the mold. Minor ceremonies become incorporated into larger political strategies, in this case that of an individual, modern politician. Through innovative twists and conscious messages, ceremonial moments continue to reinforce the outlines of modern society.

The formula "festival=culture" is, of course, a time-honored one in anthropology. The collected ethnographic catalogue of ritual moments is impressively large, and includes a more than ample array of fairs and parades. Let us then take this formula seriously, return to our examples, simplify 1889 to its fair, 1989 to its parade, and apply the analysis. Clearly these are ceremonial moments, set apart from everyday life. An emphasis on visual display seems central. The Eiffel Tower is a sight, its postcard even more so. Yet the scope and means of each spectacle involves expanded notions of audience; the limits of the village grow unclear, for the community boundaries are neither fixed nor singular. The exhibition of 1889 was not simply a fair, but a *world's* fair, self-consciously French and imperial, bringing together people and objects otherwise far-flung. Here the means of presentation lay closely allied with the means of transportation. The tribal march of 1989 was not a simple parade, but a choreographed, designed, televised extravaganza. Viewed from the street it appeared as chaos, viewed from the camera, it appeared as a merely puzzling collage. Here the means of presentation lay closely allied with the means of communication. Each event was available to a wide audience, the first largely national in scope, the second international. For such a wide audience many elements drop away on a purely technological level. In the first case the technological limit is physical transportation: an exhibit in a world's fair must be easily loaded, unloaded and labeled. In the second case the limit is electronic transmission: smell, touch and taste are left behind in television's translation of image and surrounding sound. In both, however, the process of transmission and reception of meaning in ritual involves either symbols of increasingly universal value, or increasing shades and variants of symbolic understanding.

Thus while analogy to traditional ritual suggests something important about political order, it fails to ask two additional questions about spectacles increasingly important in modern and possible postmodern variants: Who is the audience? And does the audience (or all of it) care? This last question suggests another point of difference between Centennial and Bicentennial, and highlights a peculiarity of the latter. An Eiffel Tower or an exotic pagoda might inspire "awe" in 1889, but does a Funky Chicken in 1989? Despite filling many magazines, the French Bicentennial filled few hearts. An opinion poll in *Paris Match* found 70% agreeing that too much was being made of the whole affair.[34] The majority of people I talked to in France downplayed the Bicentennial. "I can understand how it might interest foreigners," they would begin, "but . . . " A good number of Parisians, their parking curtailed, pointedly left town. One old woman told me she never goes out on July 14th anyway, as "these days it's only Arabs dancing in the streets." The latest commemoration: a nuisance, an inconvenience, something to be downplayed, derided, only for foreigners or threatening aliens—can one get further from awe?

As an alternative to anthropological models of ritual, Jonathan Crary offers a more immediately historical genealogy of spectacle, after first wondering whether "one can still well ask if the notion of spectacle is the imposition of illusory unity onto a more heterogeneous field." Drawing on Jean Baudrillard, Walter Benjamin, and T. J. Clark, he links spectacle to nineteenth-century bourgeois life and the growth of consumer society, before citing Guy Debord and offering an alternative coupling to the twentieth-century rise of television and sound cinema. Spectacle, then, could be either a term of modern industry or postmodern media (Crary 1989: 97–107).

Here we have a definition that might account for both 1889 and 1989, or rather a definitional diad, one for each century in question. Twin versions of spectacle, but fraternal, not identical in relation. As a first step this pairing would appear promising: where the Centennial could represent a "traditional" modern spectacle, the Bicentennial would represent a postmodern variant. Turning away from categories of ritual we encounter the other side of modernity, the horizon which seeks to reinvent, not identify or overcome tradition. To be a tribe is no longer to be uncivilized but rather to have culture, and thus identity. In the modern festival America can be represented by a threshing machine, in a postmodern one by Reagan and the Florida A & M marching band. But just what sort of spectacles are these? If a traditional ritual, or time out of time, reflects the possibility of different orders before resolving in communitas, what would a world's fair or a festival of the planet's tribes reflect? And how might they relate to the French Revolution?

Memory, History and Commemoration

The memory of a society extends as far as the memory of the groups composing it.
—Maurice Halbwachs[35]

There are *lieux de mémoire*, sites of memory, because there are no longer *milieux de mémoire*, real environments of history.
— Pierre Nora[36]

As another step into audiences and issues of the past in the present, let us open the term "commemoration," and examine festivals of remembering and their relations to history and social memory. In his influential study, *The Collective Memory*, Maurice Halbwachs lays the groundwork for discussions of memory extending beyond the scope of an individual subject, placing individual memory into matrix of socially constructed time and space.[37] The other axis of his argument involves distinguishing collective forms of memory from that other social record of the past, history. He sees in each an opposite focus; history concerning itself with cataloguing change, collective memory primarily with recalling resemblances (Halbwachs 1980: 84). History, in some senses then, is an illusion: a universal shroud cast over disparate collective traditions; general history starts when social memory fades and living groups dissolve. While historians eagerly seek to chronicle disruptions with precision, the collective memory resists impressions of change, maintaining illusions of continuity in the face of revolution. "Even when institutions are radically transformed, and especially then, the best means of making them take root is to buttress them with everything transferable from tradition" (Halbwachs 1980: 78, 82).

Here we have description of a sense of the past as it might operate in societies with collective memory (i.e., traditional) and societies with written chronological history (i.e., modern). While such a division may partly obscure the historical dimensions of the traditional,[38] let us make it to distinguish the concept of social memory, and move from Halbwachs to the French historian Pierre Nora in an effort to trace the potential uniqueness of modern pasts more fully. After all, neither the Centennial nor the Bicentennial are simply rituals of culture and evocations of a past event for different presents, but also expressly rituals of timed culture, times out of time set in chronological time. Nora describes the trajectory of the Western experience in terms of the erosion of memory into history, memory being "life . . . the secret of so-called primitive and archaic societies," where history is reconstruction, the means through which "our hopelessly forgetful modern societies, propelled by change, organize the past" (Nora 1989: 8). He suggests that this process has revealed a new form of the past in the present, the *lieux de mémoire*, or "sites of memory." Struck by the historical amnesia of modernity, France's *lieux de mémoire* have become exposed amid the draining of its traditional memory. These *lieux* include "Museums, archives, cemeteries, festivals, anniversaries, treaties, depositions, monuments, sanctuaries, fraternal orders," which "mark the rituals of a society without ritual; integral particularities in a society that levels particularity; signs of distinction and of group membership in a society that tends to recognize individuals only as identical and equal" (Nora 1989: 12).

Here again, history and memory are seen in opposition, with the *lieux de mémoire* filling a curious, perhaps modern, perhaps increasingly postmodern void between them. In some senses the Bicentennial would seem a prime example of such a concept: a national anniversary, a year simultaneously full and empty of meaning, an occasion born of history but not historical. Something betwixt, between, material, symbolic, functional, yet for all its historicity separated from historical reality: the commemoration of the French Revolution becomes a site of recall for post-memory France. Nora adds a certain measure of subtlety by cautioning that *lieux de mémoire* may not be a single category, but rather plural and contested, specifically featuring an opposition of the official against the popular. The first variety of *lieux*, he suggests, are imposed from above, "spectacular and triumphant," yet displaying the "coldness and solemnness of official ceremonies," such that one "attends them rather than visits them." The second kind, on the other hand, are "places of refuge, sanctuaries of spontaneous devotion and silent pilgrimage," places where "one finds the living heart of memory" (Nora 1989: 23). The Revolution, then, could be simultaneously remembered from more than one site, and in more than one way.

But, some might continue to ask, was memory ever so full, now so lost, history so empty, and now so complete? Are the two so directly opposed? The *lieux de mémoire* concept offers an attractive knot of connections through which to explore the Bicentennial assemblage, but threads between the collected events become rather slippery. Where lay the "living heart of memory" amid the jostle and noise? On some side street? In a village or an immigrant neighborhood? In an Italian castle among surviving nobility, mourning the day?[39] Among the Parisians who left the city? Those parts of the assembled crowds who paid little attention? All those, French or otherwise, who did not know what day it was? Is opposition only found in form of silent pilgrimage, or might one also look within official spectacle? Recalling the summer's counter-celebrations, it would appear that not all planned spectacle comes down from the top, or at least not uniformly from the same part of the top. History, perhaps, is also constructed sideways, or at a number of angles up and down. The events of the Bicentennial may have shared a common moment, but they did not all enter or leave it in exactly the same direction.

Extending the metaphor of memory a bit further only adds another cautionary note, if we recall that not all present reworkings of the past are equally distant or cold. Renato Rosaldo's discussion of "imperialist nostalgia" provides another window through which to examine the Bicentennial and its relations to the Centennial, one with a view over postmodernism to colonialism. Rosaldo suggests that the curious blend of memory and romanticism found under the term "nostalgia" largely describes a recent Western development, a modern gaze back at the traditional. Faced with a spate of recent films depicting the colonial past with a wistful touch, he observes that the West now mourns that which it has actively destroyed, and curiously enough, it is often the very agents of this destruction, such as colonial officials and missionaries, who feel the loss most keenly (Rosaldo 1989: 109). Moments after triumph afford the victors the luxury of wistfulness, regret, guilt, and glorification. Thus from atop the Eiffel tower huts below appear quaint and picturesque; thus from within the Pompidou Center worldwide display appears equally artful and magical.[40]

Colonialism and Difference

Jacobinism, indestructible devourer of differences.

— *L'Événement du jeudi*, special edition
on minorities in France[41]

And now back to that difficult image, the "strange encounter" of 1889. In one frame the imperial welter of race, gender, sexuality, and civilization. An odd image for the hundredth anniversary of the French Revolution, but, then again, not so odd really: civilized man and primitive woman share a light, coming together in empire and progress. The Centennial woman focuses on her cigarette, culturally bare—proper without clothes, and yet lacking propriety because of it. The Centennial Man also focuses on *his* cigarette, bowing slightly to accommodate their differences in stature. The meeting might be described as exchange, perhaps of knowledge for inspiration, or less nobly, of vice for vice. Here the Revolution would promise not Terror but Enlightenment; here the primitive would become more *risqué* than threatening.[42]

Where then to go in 1989? Time has worked some changes; the uniformed European male has vanished, as has the grass hut in the background, though some dark suits and bare breasts remain. Yet right up at the top of the symbolic pyramid, as the Republic incarnate, towers Jessye Norman, official ghost of the official parade. The *tricolore* singing the *Marseillaise*, the clear voice of Liberty rising in the air. France has often been a she, but American, and black? Before the assembled leaders of the world?

In describing the growth of female symbols in nineteenth-century American parades, Mary Ryan notes that "their status as the quintessential 'other' within a male-defined cultural universe made them perfect vehicles for representing the remote notions of national unity and local harmony." She compares the early French and American republics, whose assumptions "created a feminine, depoliticized cultural field for the abstract symbols around which the republic could seek ideological unity" (Ryan 1989: 150). A central allegorical figure for both nations was the Goddess of Liberty. "Liberty," Lynn Hunt reminds us, "was an abstract quality based on reason. She belonged to no group, to no particular place" (Hunt 1984: 62). And yet here, in 1989, is this same abstract liberty, portrayed by a clearly particular individual, from a clearly particular place: Jessye Norman, serving as Marianne, difference now acknowledged at the very mouth of unity. Might, however, some of Ryan's thesis still carry through? Replace the national with the international, add in another strand of harmony—ethnic, racial. It would seem that the polity is now the world, and France's nationalism (in some official versions) tied to its internationalism, where it was once tied to its colonialism. The world, its divides threatening to fracture that universal, Man, must somehow be contained, brought into the very representation of national identity, made to sing universality back to difference.

Much has been written about traditional festivals of inversion, ritual glimpses of social worlds turned upside down, and their relation to revolutionary change. In the Bicentennial too, everyday relations are transformed, if through varieties of official commemoration more than popular festival; even the counter-celebrations are forms of organized protest, not popular religion. Certain parameters are shared by both left and right, certain elements accepted as needing to be addressed. While one side may emphasize the Revolution, the other the Eiffel Tower, all acknowledge some heritage, something to be extended or protected. Agreement reigns about the human brotherhood, the debate lying, rather, in terms of the relationship and the terms of equality. In this sense the world is not here inverted, or even levelled, but rather flattened and distanced. All humans have culture. All share History, especially the Revolution, and most especially the nicer parts of it. The future should be different and better, however mourned the past. The glimpse is of a social horizon, universal and very far.

For another thing links Jessye Norman, *les Magiciens*, and Stevie Wonder, the potentially threatening shades of savagery and sexuality. Are these not beings and images at a remove? Dark skins from America, a drum from China, art from all over the world—what has happened to the Empire of 1889? Where is the map of the colonies? Could not an immigrant from Algeria or Senegal play Marianne? Could not a performer from Madagascar or Vietnam serenade the Eiffel Tower? No, difference is veiled, even as it is unveiled. France is part of the world—generally speaking. This time, no emphasis on the most intimate ties, no unpleasant family history. Rather, along similar lines that external colonialism covered national domination within Europe in the 1880s, now internationalism covers tensions of an uneasy home. The official celebrations acknowledge difference, but suggest, elliptically, that it has also been resolved, at least in Paris; slavery is a musical legacy from America, magic is universally aesthetic, and the Chinese are trying to follow the French. Color on the streets, in museums, reworks the portrait, quickly, easily. By expanding Western history universally, and presenting Western "tribes," all can experience equality—the flat, distant equality of being the same.

In 1937, the commissioner-general of that year's fair could write, in a remarkable mixture of colonial longing and Machiavellian advice:

> We need festivals, and above all popular festivals . . . civilization has hardened us . . . we no longer know how to divert ourselves, we no longer know how to relax, we no longer know how to laugh . . . The spontaneity of the people itself is exhausted, worn out. Motion finds refuge on cinema screens, spirit in the metallic throat of loud speakers. These are the machines which live in our place. It is dismal. Our daughters and our sons ask for some American Negro music—a crude vigor often admirable in another place— or some Apache rhythms, to shake a little their boredom . . . A wise government—and let not the tyrants have a monopoly on wisdom—gives festivals to its people. One 14th of July a year does not suffice us. In the desert of difficult times that we are crossing, expositions are like oases. It was enough, moreover, to wander through the [Colonial]

Exposition of 1931 to understand that grand fairs retain all of their glamour for the masses . . . That year, the French learned a little geography. That year, "the child enamored with maps and stamps," who dozes in the heart of every adult, could feast his eyes on thousands of marvels about which he had dreamed once, bent over adventure books and travel stories. Curiosity is a popular virtue. It is an educable virtue, a virtue that we can turn towards real grandeur, towards grace, towards beauty. We are neglecting too much the cultivation of it. For lack of care, it degenerates; it becomes corrupted. Let us not accuse the people, let us accuse their masters. (Bloch and Delort 1980: 11–12)

A hundred years after the heady days of empire and the colonial exhibit on Invalides, fifty years after the colonial exhibit at Vincennes,[43] no one speaks of white men with burdens. Yet notes of the civilizing mission echo in calls for extending the Revolution around the globe. And a sense of nostalgia has only increased: if the entire world has lost the traditional, perhaps both colonizer and colonized can at last safely play at being tribes.

1889—The world, lining the Seine in spatial order, mapped out by theme and place, its core exhibits on machines, its periphery clusters of colonies, a fair beneath the shadow of its tower. 1989—The world, in motion, monuments dispersed, its past bared in museums, its center gaudy celebration, its margins organized concerts. Postmodern? The *Newsweek* account is not unconvincing. *Lieux de mémoire*? Rarely, if ever, have some version of memory and history seemed so simultaneously present and absent, so concentrated and so self-preoccupied. Still a century has not transformed everything. To argue an easy equation between these commemorations would distort a confusion of pasts in the past and pasts in the present into something too cleanly opposed; clothes do change, along with faces, words, and maps, however many hints of Man linger on. Here we arrive at a final question of time and organization, that of origin and change. For whether postmodern or modern, Centennial and Bicentennial both appeal to the same source, the same ancestor for their identity.

Commemoration of Revolution

The initial day of a calendar serves as a historical time-lapse camera. And, basically, it is the same day that keeps recurring in the guise of holidays, which are days of remembrance. Thus the calendars do not measure time as clocks do; they are monuments of a historical consciousness of which not the slightest trace has been apparent in Europe in the last hundred years. In the July revolution an incident occurred which showed this consciousness still alive. On the first evening of fighting it turned out that the clocks of the tower were being fired on simultaneously and independently from several places in Paris. An eye-witness, who may have owed his insight to the rhyme, wrote as follows: "*Qui le croirait! On dit qu'irrités contre l'heure/ De nouveaux Josués au pied de chaque tour,/ Tiraient sur les cadrans pour arrêter le jour.*" ["Who would have believed it! We are told that the new Joshuas at the foot of every tower, as though irritated with time itself, fired at the dials in order to stop the day."]

—Walter Benjamin[44]

When, and at what point do things start to count? Or the more direct question: what *does* link the dates 1789, 1889 and 1989? Are centuries quintessential examples of empty, arbitrary signs; does a wrap of chronology leave no marks at all? Certainly it would be easy to answer in the affirmative. After all, what remains of the Centennial? The Eiffel tower, and now and then a temporary museum exhibit. And as for the Bicentennial, what will remain of it? The Opera and its hulking brethren (a true *fraternité*?)—surely they will join the tower, perhaps slightly more functional, most certainly less dominating, fading into a similar series of postcard shots. The T-shirts, papers, and videotape can but melt in air, at least until recalled by ghosts of exhibits future. Yet, despite the indifference, a Parisian aversion to non-Parisian crowds and noises, a city overrun by Americans, Germans, Japanese, ex-Colonials, and assorted Provincials, France is an undeniably chronological society, where measurement itself has meaning. Even if many were not transported by the displays, few questioned them, or more accurately, questioned the fundamental significance of the date. A distinctive technology of time governs modern commemoration. Rather than a similarity of season or situation, standardized measurement schedules the ritual moment.

Could it be otherwise? Could there be memories of modern revolution, brought on by shifting winds, or a rise in temperature? One might consider the events of 1989 in Eastern Europe as an appropriate reminder of dramatic social change. Certain actions are taken, crowds gathered, or statues toppled, along lines described before. The sudden shock of possibility, a break in the coverage, wavering images, old language reborn. No invitations went out before the collapse of the Berlin Wall; vacations weren't planned with it in mind. Or, keeping within a stricter ethnographic lineage, consider May, 1968, when Paris saw its most recent reflection of revolutionary threat. Pried from beneath the pavement, cobblestones rose again in barricades, physical reminders of the ways of rebellion past. All eyes turned towards France, the fragility of its social body exposed again before open chaos in the street. Here, perhaps, we might see another form of collective memory, the restless movements of a mob, the traditional gestures of conflict.[45] Rituals of revolution, as it were, actions of the past reflected through the actors of the present. Barricades, the *Marseillaise*, Jacobin dress—even chaos can have its formulas, its laws, and even change re-call its ancestry, perhaps remembering its way back to structure, perhaps reinforcing earlier patterns.[46]

Holding such moments against the Bicentennial, we do see at least one similarity: the centrality of crowds, of outdoor gatherings in which certain norms are suspended. People did turn out for the described events in large numbers—laughing, shouting, and throwing fire crackers. Of course, this was a sanctioned gathering, not a riot. The masses focused on entertainment and festivities more than on destruction or physical transgressions. All groups met at specified times, in ordered fashion to witness an event, even if each contained many individuals who seemed remarkably indifferent to official proceedings and pronouncements. The organs of control were omnipresent; battalions of police arrayed behind barricades— mobile metal these, not cobblestone. Occasionally, there were hints, moments, surges against the lines and anger at crowd control, as the long black cars slipped through straining wedges of frustrated would-be pedestrians. But only a flicker. The Bastille was taken again, but this time released back to the Opera the next day.

Could cloaks of festival and spectacle create and blanket crowds, prevent historical drama by providing official theater? In a popular history of Parisian fairs, Jean-Jacques Bloch and Marianne Delort suggest as much:

> Who knows . . . if that atmosphere of liberty and festivity which reigned in Paris in 1968, that rarest of times when strangers challenged each other joyously in the street, did not mark (all claims aside) the place unoccupied by the laughter of a universal exposition which had not taken place. (Bloch and Delort 1980: 12)

Official commemoration may thus simultaneously celebrate and smother change, back along the lines of Turner's (1969) ritual process.

But is there not another level at which change can be subverted? Is not the constant flow of measured time a subtler illusion than a world's fair? Its units are equally empty, but sometimes some are named. Certain events in Paris become "the French Revolution," they become singular, an it—*the* Revolution, a model, a guide, an ancestor, for all other radical moments in France.[47] And, as such, it can serve as author, an origin for the Republic, or a range of ideologies. Once this revolution, once *the* Revolution, becomes tied to "July 14th, 1789," it becomes, in

Nora's sense, an identified site of history: official and filled with significance, entered in schoolbooks, inscribed on monuments, noted on calendars. But also, and perhaps as significantly, forever named as the past.[48]

The obvious is not uninteresting. Historian Donald Wilcox suggests that the very perception of time as absolute and linear defines our experience in ways subtle but deep:

> We are so accustomed to apply absolute time to the quotidian details of life that we do not readily appreciate the extent to which it changes the focus of identity, depersonalizing historical realities and removing them from immediate contact with life . . . As a means of measuring the intervals between concrete events in terms of these primary qualities, the absolute dating system is implicitly subversive of traditional notions of personal identity. (Wilcox 1987: 255)

As Benjamin suggests with regard to calendars and clocks, in order to endure a revolutionary consciousness would have to re-inscribe time itself, rewriting a pattern of days, holidays, and memories.[49] The Jacobins, of course, tried, but the Bicentennial remembers 1789, not - III. An older rationalization of time lives on, reinforced by celebration.[50] In this sense the program of the Eiffel Tower celebration, the Hollywood history of the right, speaks most tellingly. "*Rendez-vous* in a hundred years!" it proclaims on its final page, before closing with an advertisement for a large, dark Citroën.[51]

Anthropology and Commemorative Spectacle

> . . . [m]odern thought is one that moves no longer towards the never-completed formation of Difference, but towards the ever accomplished unveiling of the Same . . . what is revealed at the foundation of the history of things and of the historicity proper to man is the distance creating a vacuum in the Same, it is the hiatus that disperses and regroups it at the two ends of itself. It is this profound spatiality that makes it possible for modern thought still conceive of time—to know it as succession, to promise it to itself as fulfillment, origin, or return.
>
> —Michel Foucault[52]

In efforts to describe universal human behavior by cataloguing cultural difference, practitioners of anthropology have done a great deal to fill out the category of traditional. However, when ethnography actually confronts the modern at home, it all too frequently fails to recognize it as other than that which it has imagined home from far afield. Paris is neither a village, nor wholly French. The translation of scales and measures requires more than transportation or expansion. For while the commemorative spectacles of 1889 and 1989 are modern analogies to anthropological categories of political ritual, and the modern indeed shares with the traditional, it shares by intentional comparison and distancing, not uniformity. When anthropology gazes at the present, eye to camera, it must also watch frame and focus, present and past. In a modern and international world, images near and images far have different backgrounds and resolutions; when the camera itself builds spectacle, smell and touch diminish, while image, transmission and reconstruction blur in bites of sight. Moving or still, film brings everything closer, from farther away.[53]

Perhaps it is the same with certain memories. Imagine, for a moment, that as well as "imperialist" nostalgia there is also "revolutionary" nostalgia, the mask of dated histories recalling and forgetting memories of change. When can one mourn what one destroys, except as it vanishes, and when can one celebrate what one might fear, but as it crosses the stage, carefully timed? The French Bicentennial, then, would mark an intersection of nostalgias: colonialism finding a museum, culture returning to art, and the *tricolore* to a coffee cup.

Of course, nostalgia may not always have the last word. Yes, postmodern festivals are different from modern festivals and traditional ones. But in recognizing a category that seeks to describe the complexity of contemporary existence, it is important to remember that this variety of complexity does not simply eradicate prior complexities. Postmodern does not erase modern, any more than modern erases traditional. In a Europe now disturbed by its own tribes, some reborn from beneath the mantle of modern socialism and carrying guns, the Bicentennial parade in the City of Light cannot suggest that either revolution or empire are quite beyond memory, or forgetting.

Notes

A previous version of these observations was presented at the Berkeley Symposium on Visual Representation in March 1990. In addition to the conference organizers, reviewers of VAR, *U.C. Berkeley, and the Camargo Foundation, the author must thank Susanna Barrows, Arthur Chandler, Pamela Cheek, John Leedom, Jono Mermin, Richard Price, Paul Rabinow, Marc Redfield, Randy Starn, Lucien Taylor, Silvia Tomásková, and Brackette Williams for different assistance, comments, and encouragement along the meandering way. The author also wishes to thank the Réunion des musées nationaux and the Bibliothèque Historique de la Ville de Paris for their permission to reproduce the image "Strange Encounters" on page 327.*

1.   However debatable their definitions, I will employ these terms, conserving the ethnographic convention which accepts categories used by native speakers, in this case the language of assorted contemporary international journals, newspapers, and pamphlets. Relevant informants on the "traditional, modern, postmodern" triad here include Clifford (1988), Fabian (1983), Hebdige (1986), and Jameson (1991). In the gray overlap between social and artistic varieties of "modern" and "postmodern" modernity, I informally invoke public architecture as the best scale model for the commemorative festival. This invocation is one between lived experience, visual image, and textual representation of visual image, such as that sometimes found in descriptions of landscapes and structures. Here the architecture in question is a French one, or rather an international national French one, as viewed by an American reading French and American views; moreover it is also an architecture of time, a ritual monument to chronological history, and the heritage of universal counting, as viewed by one of the inheritors.

2.   Other historical comparisons could be found in the tradition of festivals during the Revolution itself, especially the Fête de la Fédération on the first anniversary of Bastille Day, and the Festival of the Supreme Being in 1794, both held (like the later world's fairs) on the Champ-de-Mars. Other fairs, especially the Colonial Exposition of 1931 and the "Cinquantenaire" festival of 1937, would offer further comparative possibilities. Considerations of scope and space dictate these events beyond the central margins. For more on revolutionary festivals and culture see Hunt (1984), Ozouf (1988), and Schama (1989). For more on world's fairs see Benedict (1983), Bloch and Delort (1980), Hodeir (1987), Rabinow (1989) and *Le livre des expositions universelles 1851–1989* (1983).

3.   From "Un entretien exceptionnel avec le Président de la République française, François Mitterand." *Le Courrier de l'UNESCO* (6 June 1989): 6.

4.   The first two themes of the fair were to be *Les Chemins de la Liberté* (liberty seen emerging out of a historical ground provided by the Enlightenment, recovering from the challenge of fascism, and just welcoming young nations fresh from the margins of history) and *La Solidarité Humaine* (a unity which diverse human societies must recognize as both fact and absolute necessity in the face of world problems). To round out the futuristic focus there would be two other sections as well: *La Biologie* (concentrating on genetics, human blood, and the brain) and *Construction d'un quartier de l'an 2000* (depicting problems and progress in urban life less through technology than in terms of general living conditions). The ultimate stated goal of the project was to underline the problems confronting the modern world, and to help inspire a genuine mobilization of the youth of France, Europe, and the Third World. See *Projets pour l'exposition universelle de 1989 à Paris: livre blanc,* (1985): 11, 30–35.

5.   Between 1986 and 1988 socialist Mitterand occupied the presidency, while conservative Chirac was prime minister.

6.   For a concise summary of the various architectural projects, see Robert Hughes, "Paris à la Mitterand," *Time* (18 September, 1989): 88–92.

7.   For an official account, see Dannielle Rouard, "Les « potes » de Pékin," *Le Monde* (13 June, 1989): 24.

8.   Pamphlet "Le Concert de l'Égalité." (Paris: S.O.S. Racisme, 1989).

9. For a synopsis see Anne Giudicelli, "On ne badine pas avec la Tour," *Libération* (17–18 June, 1989): 29.

10. See pamphlet "Paris 89: Programme Officiel" (Paris: 1989). A not uninteresting pun lies imbedded in the translation of *Tour* to Tower—for English speakers this could suggest a cultural tour, the world's fair still haunting the iron structure. However, if the reader will permit a dry observation, this particular program was remarkably expensive.

11. *"Dette, apartheid, colonies, ça suffat comme çi!"* ran the slogan. See pamphlet "Bienvenue à la manifestation et au concert du 8 Juillet, Ça suffat comme çi!" (Paris: 1989).

12. See article "Ça suffat comme çi," *L'Humanité* (14 July, 1989): 11.

13. See *Le Figaro* (July 15–16, 1989): 1; *L'Humanité* (15 July, 1989): 1; *France-Soir* (15 July, 1989): 24; and *Libération* (15–16 July): 1.

14. See *Libération* (17 July, 1989): 10.

15. See "1889. La Tour Eiffel et l'Exposition universelle," *Le petit Journal des grandes Expositions*, 1989, 196. The image is also reproduced in the more lavish exhibit catalogue, *1889, La Tour Eiffel et l'exposition universelle*, 117.

16. From the short bilingual brochure *Magiciens de la Terre*, (Paris: Centre Georges Pompidou/La Grande Halle-La Villette, 1989), translation in text.

17. For more on the exhibition see the full version catalogue *Magiciens de la Terre* (1989) and comments in Bhabha and Burgin (1992), as well as Applefield (1989).

18. The term "difference" can sprawl analytically vague, yet for all its theoretical currency it retains an everyday tone in its abstraction. For this reason I choose to employ it, generalities displayed but undissected.

19. Quoted in Harriss (1976), 140.

20. Reportedly said while passing a sideshow of the colonial exposition. See Wright (1987), 300.

21. The 1880s marked the first decade of the Republic in which its existence might be said to be taken as given, immediate, post-Commune monarchist threats having receded. Even so, the elections of 1885 saw a resurgence of anti-republican right, and in 1889 itself the maverick candidacy of General Boulanger hinted the possibility of a new authoritarian regime (Wright 1987), 230–52. The essays in Nora (1984), provide fuller histories for a number of elements of republican ritual.

22. Indeed, it can be argued that the empire was not the clear product of any conscious, consistent expansionist government policy (Wright 1987), 240–41, 299–300.

23. Not surprisingly, parallels can be made with the growth of anthropology as a discipline, and the introduction of similar colonial themes within the academy. George Stocking opens his history of Victorian anthropology with an image of the Crystal Palace of 1851, the first great world's fair (Stocking 1987), 1.

24. For an inventory of some of the exhibited items see *Reports of the United States Commissioners to the Universal Exposition of 1889 at Paris* (1890).

25. For the fair's layout see illustrations in Bloch and Delort (1980), 83 and Musée d'Orsay, (1989), 254–69. For a richer account of changing and conflicting context of social and spatial visions expressed in French world's fairs see Rabinow (1989).

26. The quotations are taken from Archives Nationales F12 3760 and Melchior de Vogüe, *Remarques sur l'Exposition du Centenaire*, 165.

27. The exhibition's allure is perhaps allegorically described by an anecdote told by its *commissaire spécial* himself, a mocking tale about a "working girl" and an "Annamite" [Indochinese] man who fall in love, only to be foiled by French laws on bigamy. A view from the top: worker, woman, colonial—conjoined by desire, separated by the state. Bloch and Delort (1980), 95. For a remarkable collection of quotations surrounding the 1889 colonial exhibit, see *Le livre des expositions universelles 1851–1989*, (1983), 90–91 (sources p. 347).

28. See Mary Blume, "Eiffel Tower, at 100, Has Defeated Its Critics," *International Herald Tribune* (5 June): 16.

29. Quoted in Charles-Robert Ageron, "L'Exposition coloniale de 1931," in Nora (1984).

30. See *Programme des manifestations du Bicentenaire de la Révolution Française*, (Paris: Mission de la Bicentennaire de la Révolution Française et des Droits de l'Homme et du Citoyen, 1989), esp. 130, 236, 283.

31. Connerton (1989), 6.

32. From Jameson (1991), ix.

33. Much of MacAloon's model flows out of the work of Victor Turner, especially *The Ritual Process* (1969). Both emphasize social control as the political ends of "experiences of unprecedented potency," or "awe,"

though Turner applies his model universally, while MacAloon examines "modern" society as a special case.

34. See *Time* 134, (24 July, 1989 134): 15.

35. From Halbwachs (1980), 82.

36. From Nora (1989), 7.

37. Connerton (1989) provides a more general review of social memory, dividing it into commemorative ceremonies (ritual) and bodily practices (habit). This essay, while privileging the former of his categories, ultimately involves both in its special case of chronological celebration. Middleton and Edwards (1990) offer a collection of essays on memory and forgetting, from a perspective of politics, communication, and social psychology.

38. A resurgence of interest in the historical sensibilities of purportedly non-historical peoples has marked anthropology in recent years, cautioning against overly facile distinctions. See for example Price (1990).

39. A rather remarkable Paris TV news story on Channel 2, on Sunday, July 16th, reported a counter-celebration of the nobility, organized by a relation of Mussolini and protesting, among other things, the "materialistic" tendencies of modern society.

40. One could consider a long list, from aristocrats to witchcraft, of things that might seem cozier from a distance. The point in questioning nostalgia is not to remove either rejoicing or regret as possible reactions to social change, but rather to uncover a wider, and deeper range of memories and histories. See also Davis and Starn (1989) and Lowenthal (1985).

41. From Labro (1989), 68.

42. However, the image could also be read the other way, as repression of veiled fears. Neil Hertz (1985) follows several examples, text and image, of a "recurrent turn of mind: the representation of what would seem to be a political threat as if it were a sexual threat." The prime source is Revolutionary Paris, 1848 and Commune editions, the prime threat, a castrating woman. Our strange encounter would then hint at another exchange of fire, that of seduction and domination, covering fears of castration, or—as bad or worse—decivilization, the loss of clothes, culture, Empire and History.

43. In 1931 an entire exposition devoted to colonialism was held at the Bois de Vincennes in Paris (See Chandler 1989). In addition, the "Cinquantenaire" festival of 1937 also featured a large colonial exhibit.

44. From Benjamin, "Theses on the Philosophy of History," in Benjamin (1969), 261–62 [trans. in text].

45. For more description and analysis see the journal *Pouvoirs* 39 (1986), a special issue on May '68 as well as Vigier (1988), 52–57.

46. Recall Marx's lines witnessing the erosion of the Second Republic into the Second Empire: "And just when they [the living] seem engaged in revolutionizing themselves and things, in creating something that has never yet existed, precisely in such periods of revolutionary crisis they anxiously conjure up the spirits of the past to their service and borrow from them their names, battle cries and costumes . . ." (Marx 1975: 15). The comparisons with Halbwach's formulation of change and tradition are not uninteresting: for both opposed terms representing different ends of time join at transformatory moments. In the face of the future, memory of the past becomes indispensable.

47. Simon Schama suggests that the "French Revolution" *per se* (as opposed to the series of its events) only came into being in 1830, when, as a memory, it helped to reconstruct the political landscape (Schama 1989: 7).

48. No chronological date, after all, can be identical to any other. Thus when one is frozen in significance, that particular significance is then denied to the present; time is both distinctly marked *and* separated.

49. This rewriting could come in the form of replacement rather than opposition. See Connerton (1989: 41–48) regarding relations between National Socialist festivals, Christian and pagan calendars.

50. Regarding the Revolutionary calendar see Hunt (1984: 70–71), and Bronislaw Baczko, "Le Calendrier Républicain," in (Nora 1984: 38–79). Regarding shifts in historical pedagogy away from chronology, and the issue of French school children not knowing the dates of the Revolution, see Lowenthal (1985: 222–23). After 1989, one would imagine, a greater number might pass the test.

51. Pamphlet "Paris 89: Programme Officiel" (Paris: 1989).

52. Foucault (1973: 340).

53. Film also affects perception of time. See Pinney (1990) for further discussion of the moving, the still and representation in anthropology.

References

Note: short pamphlets and articles referenced in the notes have been omitted.

1890. *Reports of the United States Commissioners to the Universal Exposition of 1889 at Paris.* Washington, D.C.: Government Printing Office.

1983. *Le livre des expositions universelles 1851–1989.* Paris: Union Centrale des Arts Décoratifs.

1985. *Projets pour l'exposition universelle de 1989 à Paris: livre blanc.* Paris: Flammarion.

1989a. *Magiciens de la Terre.* Paris: Centre Georges Pompidou/La Grande Halle—La Villette.

1989b. *Programme des manifestations du Bicentenaire de la Révolution Française.* Paris: Mission de la Bicentenaire de la Révolution Française et des Droits de l'Homme et du Citoyen (1989): 130, 236, 283.

Abélès, Marc. 1988. "Modern Political Ritual: Ethnography of an Inauguration and a Pilgrimage by President Mitterand." *Current Anthropology* 29, 3: 391–404.

Adler, Jerry , and Christopher Dickey. 1989. "Les Jours de Gloire." *Newsweek,* (24 July, 1989): 20–23.

Amalvi, Christian. 1984. "Le 14-Juillet." In *Les Lieux de mémoire I: La République.* ed. I. P. Nora 421–71. Paris: Gallimard.

Applefield, David. 1989. "Art Protest, Protest Art . . ." *Free Voice XII,* No. 5 (June): 1, 5.

Baczko, Bronislaw. 1984. "Le Calendrier Républicain." In *Les Lieux de mémoire I: La République* I, ed. P. Nora, Paris: Gallimard.

Barthes, Roland. 1979. *The Eiffel Tower and Other Mythologies.* New York: Hill and Wang.

Benedict, Burton. 1983. *The Anthropology of World's Fairs.* Berkeley: Lowie Museum of Anthropology and Scolar Press.

Benjamin, Walter. 1969 (1955). *Illuminations.* Ed. H. Arendt. New York: Schocken Books.

Bhabha, Homi and Victor Burgin. 1992. "Visualizing Theory." *Visual Anthropology Review* 8, 1: 71–80.

Bloch, Jean-Jacques and Marianne Delort. 1980. *Quand Paris allait "à l'Expo."* Paris: Librairie Arthème Fayard.

Chandler, Arthur. 1989. "Empire of the Republic: The *Exposition Coloniale Internationale de Paris, 1931.*" Unpublished manuscript.

Clifford, James. 1988. *The Predicament of Culture.* Cambridge, Mass.: Harvard University Press.

Connerton, Paul. 1989. *How Societies Remember.* Cambridge: Cambridge University Press.

Crary, Jonathan. 1989. "Spectacle, Attention, Counter-Memory." *October* 50: 97–107.

Davis, Natalie Zemon and Randolph Starn, eds. 1989. "Introduction: Memory and Counter-Memory." *Representations* 26 (Spring): 1–6.

Fabian, Johannes. 1983. *Time and the Other: How Anthropology Makes its Object.* New York: Columbia University Press.

Foucault, Michel. 1973 (1966). *The Order of Things.* New York: Vintage Books.

Garret, Wilbur E. 1989. "Liberté, Egalité, Fraternité . . . Unité!" *National Geographic* 176 (July): 3–5.

Girardet, Raoul. 1972. *L'idée coloniale en France.* Paris: La Table Ronde.

Halbwachs, Maurice. 1980 (1950). *The Collective Memory.* New York: Harper & Row.

Harriss, Joseph. 1976. *The Eiffel Tower.* London: Paul Elek.

Hebdige, Dick. 1986. "Postmodernism and 'The Other Side'." *Journal of Communication Inquiry* 10 (2):78–98.

Hertz, Neil. 1985. "The Medusa's Head: Male Hysteria Under Political Pressure." *The End of the Line: Essays on Psychoanlysis and the Sublime.* New York: Columbia University Press.

Hodeir, Catherine. 1987. "La France d'Outre-Mer." In *Cinquantenaire: de l'Exposition internationale des arts et des techniques dans la vie moderne,* 284–93. Paris: Institut Fraçaise d"Architecture/Paris-Musées.

Hughes, Robert. 1989. "Paris à la Mitterand." *Time* (18 September, 1989): 88–92.

Hunt, Lynn. 1984. *Politics, Culture, and Class in the French Revolution.* Berkeley: University of California Press.

Jameson, Frederic. 1991. *Postmodernism: Or, the Cultural Logic of Late Capitalism.* Durham, North Carolina: Duke University Press.

Labro, Michel. 1989. "Et nos minorités hexagonales?" *L'Événement du jeudi* 244 (6–12 July).

Lewis, Martin Deming. 1962. "One Hundred Million Frenchmen: The 'Assimilation' Theory in French Colonial Policy." *Comparative Studies in Society and History* 4, 2: 129–53.

Lowenthal, David. 1985. *The Past is a Foreign Country.* Cambridge, England: Cambridge University Press.

MacAloon, John J. 1984. "Olympic Games and the Theory of Spectacle in Modern Society." In *Rite, Drama, Festival, Spectacle,* ed. J. J. MacAloon, 241–80. Philadelphia: Institute for the Study of Human Issues.

Marx, Karl. 1975 (1852). *The Eighteenth Brumaire of Louis Bonaparte.* New York: International Publishers.

Middleton, David and Derek Edwards, eds. 1990. *Collective Remembering.* London: Sage Publications.

P.
Redfield

Musée d'Orsay. 1989. *1889: La Tour Eiffel et l'Eposition universelle*. Paris: Éditions de la Réunion des Musées Nationaux.

Nora, Pierre. 1984. *Les lieux de mémoire I: La République*. Paris: Gallimard.

————.1989. "Between Memory and History: Les Lieux de Mémoire." [Trans. Marc Roudebush] *Representations* 26 (Spring): 7–25.

Ory, Pascal. 1984. "La Centenaire de la Révolution Française." In *Les Lieux de mémoire I: La République*, ed. P. Nora, 523–39. Paris: Gallimard.

Ozouf, Mona. 1988. *Festivals and the French Revolution*. Cambridge: Harvard University Press.

Pinney, Christopher. 1990. "The Quick and the Dead: Images, Time and Truth." *Visual Anthropology Review* 6, 2 (Fall): 42–54.

Price, Richard. 1990. *Alabi's World*. Baltimore: Johns Hopkins University Press.

Rabinow, Paul. 1989. *French Modern: The Norms and Forms of the Social Environment*. Cambridge: M.I.T Press.

Rosaldo, Renato. 1989. "Imperialist Nostalgia." *Representations* 26 (Spring):107–22.

Ryan, Mary. 1989. "The American Parade: Representations of Nineteenth-Century Social Order." In *The New Cultural History*, ed. L. Hunt, Berkeley: U.C. Press.

Schama, Simon. 1989. *Citizens: A Chronicle of the French Revolution*. New York: Alfred A. Knopf.

Stocking, George. 1987. *Victorian Anthropology*. New York: The Free Press.

Turner, Victor. 1969. *The Ritual Process*. Chicago: Aldine Publishing Co.

Vigier, Philippe. 1988. "Le Paris des barricades (1830–1968)." *L'Histoire* (113): 52–57.

Vovelle, Michel. 1984. "La Marseillaise." In *Les Lieux de mémoire I: La République*, ed. P. Nora. Paris: Gallimard.

Wilcox, Donald J. 1987. *The Measure of Times Past: Pre-Newtonian Chronologies and the Rhetoric of Relative Time*. Chicago: University of Chicago Press.

Wright, Gordon. 1987. *France in Modern Times*. 4th ed. New York: W.W. Norton & Co.

Simulations of Postmodernity
Images of Technology in
African Tourist and Popular Art

Bennetta Jules-Rosette

Introduction

ＡNOH ACOU IS STARVING. IN THE SMALL BEACH RESORT OF GRAND BASSAM, CÔTE D'IVOIRE, once a holiday retreat for French colonial administrators, Anoh now sells carvings of wooden suits, radios, and telephones at a roadside stand. He works in an *atelier* with another Ivoirian carver, Koffi Kouakou, who specializes in postmodern images. Koffi is the image-creator who is assisted by Anoh and several apprentices. In 1990, Koffi's next project was a wooden computer. Bewildered and distressed, Anoh wrote to me during the same year complaining of declining sales. When I returned to the atelier two years later, I found that the market for carved shoes and suits had expanded to tap small-scale consumers. Koffi had started to carve baseball caps, Coca-Cola bottles, toothpaste tubes, and wooden packets of Marlboros, creating an African "pop" tourist art. Innovative images of technology and Western material culture attract curiosity seekers, but the market for these works is not stable. Anoh and Koffi's dilemma stems from the types of artistic themes that attract tourists. Images of an idyllic Africa "that never was" are exotic souvenirs. As a result of deliberately ignoring popular trends and stereotypes by focusing on modern images, artists like Anoh and Koffi are at risk. Although these tourist artists claim to produce objects that appeal to Westerners, interpretations of what Westerners like are often based on stereotypes, distortion, and outdated marketing trends (cf. Mount 1974: 39–41).

V. Y. Mudimbe (1988: 12) emphasizes that African "art" is, in part, an artifact of the Western imagination. He considers African art to be a historical product of "the meta-morphosis of concrete realities into abstract categories" (Mudimbe 1986: 3). Since many African languages lack a global term for "art," and these expressive cultural objects are used for the purposes of ceremony and trade, Mudimbe refers to "African art" as a question mark, a categorical invention. According to Mudimbe, tourist art is an extreme manifestation of the the link between cultural signs and their economic manipulation. From the point of view of the producers of tourist art and its images, however, Mudimbe overlooks crucial processes and motivations. Through an aesthetics of communication, these image-creators have transformed their work into "art" and have molded a self-identification as artists. Artistry is embedded in the repetitive, commercial features of their productions evident in the commodification of indigenous cultural categories.

Tourist artists reverse Mudimbe's historical equation by transforming abstract categories of what they perceive to be art into concrete objects for display and sale to cultural outsiders. Commercial art in Africa is not an evolutionary mutation of invented traditions. It is a form of intercultural communication. Much of the recent debate concerning tourist art as an empty, or ghost, category revolves around its commodification and quality (cf. Vogel 1991: 10–11; Kasfir 1992: 62–66). Artists use commodification and mass production as means of saturating the tourist market and identifying their consumers. Thus, mass production may be examined most effectively from a sociological perspective as a strategy for artist-audience communication rather than as a criterion for evaluating the quality of art works.

By assuming that an ethnography of tourist art in Africa is possible, I am arguing for developing avenues through which the voices of the artists may be heard and the innovations of their works seen and valued. This objective differs in critical respects from Trinh Minh-ha's method of "reassemblage" in which knowledge of the cultural Other is possible primarily through a montage of one's own internal experiences in confrontation with other cultures (Penley and Ross 1986: 93). By the same token, my emphasis is not placed on the European derivation of Africanist discourses and imagery (Miller 1985: 14–22). I am proposing a process related to these approaches, yet quite distinct from them. Tourists artists, I contend, manipulate European images of an idyllic Africa to devise a new and subtle communicative code, an aesthetics of communication. Whether or not they accept these images is unimportant. They use them in a cycle of symbolic and commercial exchange that results in intercultural communication. The fact that tourist art is market-driven and that it lends itself to commodification are points in its favor as a protean form of communication between African artists and their audiences (cf. Kasfir 1992: 63–64). In terms of content, tourist art is dominated by neither inherently African nor Western idioms. Nevertheless, its message structure—which is fluid, incorporative, and open—is characteristic of communicative styles found across the African continent. Therein lies the Africanity, the originality, and the resiliency of tourist art as an expressive cultural form that is accessible for ethnographic speculation.

Resembling the cargo cults of postwar New Guinea, Anoh and Koffi's art promises the powers that technology bestows without any of its limitations. Wooden telephones and radios do not need to be repaired. Carved suits remain neatly pressed and on display for all to see. Images of technology, however, have troublesome connotations in tourist art. Technological signs have different meanings in local African and foreign art markets. They evoke the world of work from which the tourist has escaped (cf. MacCannell 1989: 55–56). Technology conjures up the phantoms of history, for it is through the tools of technology that colonial domination was achieved.[1] The specter of technology in Africa raises unpleasant personal and collective memories for foreign consumers of tourist art. For local consumers, however, technology holds the promise of progress and the reversal of domination. As responses to foreign influences, images of technology are handled in contrasting ways in tourist and popular art. Since tourists artists seek mass commercial appeal for their works, they avoid controversial representations of modernity. Ironically this avoidance is coupled with a mechanization of the workplace influenced by industrial, assembly-line procedures. Popular artists, who often work in the same manner, incorporate explicit criticisms of Western technology into their creative products.

Although tinged with pathos and a sense of lack, certain images of technology, such as Koffi's carved suits, are designed to convey an aura of progress and change. In most tourist art, the surface image is soothing and nostalgic. These antiseptic images reflect artists' perceptions of Western preferences and audience demand.[2] For example, monument paintings, which are a subgenre of the idyllic landscape among Zairian artists in Lusaka, exhibit interesting thematic variations. Paintings of Victoria Falls and Mount Kilimanjaro represent natural African monuments. They contrast with paintings of modern industrial monuments such as Kariba Dam and the mines of the Copperbelt. Juxtaposition of natural and manufactured monuments contains a hidden message about the destruction of an idyllic Africa. The artists manipulate ambivalent messages to appeal to different consumer audiences. Nevertheless, the meanings convey political overtones. Tourists in Europe and the United States expect to visit modern sights and industrial monuments, but these sights do not mesh with an idyllic view of Africa. Discrepancies, however, abound between audience taste and artists' perceptions. Jean-François Lyotard (1984: 76) considers the gap in perception characteristic of the tourist art trade to be a general feature of postmodern consumer cultures worldwide.

When I asked Toto, one of the landscape painters in the Kanyama artists' circle of Lusaka, why industrial monuments were not more popular, he replied with a description of market demand.

> Toto: The paintings of Gécamin [i.e., the bombers over the copper mines of Shaba] show the history of the wars in Katanga. No one would understand them here.
> BJ-R: But why aren't there paintings of Lusaka? Or paintings of other cities here?
> Toto: Ah, you see that, well, if one begins to con . . . to do the construction of buildings [i.e., tall buildings in town], whatever it is, then someone could say that, automatically, that one is doing European art. And the Europeans don't like us, the Africans, to do European art.

This statement elucidates the overwhelming preponderance of the idyllic landscape genre. Several artists with whom I discussed this genre emphasized that it was readily saleable. The primary market toward which it is directed, they said, is that of European tourists. Lusengu Kalala, another Zairian painter, qualified that local expatriates are not as interested in the idyllic landscape as outsiders. This landscape genre has several variations that reflect a particular intentionality. An attitude that beckons toward a return to an imaginary past is evoked by the static landscapes painted in blues and greens with a background of thick forest, often with birds flying past. Closely related to this genre are the waterscapes. These paintings depict a lonely helmsman as he steers a canoe across a calm river. The two positive portrayals of the village and forest contrast with what might be termed the threatened landscape. In this variation, either the village or the forest is depicted in reds, browns, and oranges as it goes into flames. Although the artists themselves are initially reluctant to interpret this genre negatively, there is little doubt that the entire village's destruction reflects more than the

Fig. 1. *Victoria Falls* by Mpinda Joseph, Kanyama Painters' Circle, Lusaka, Zambia, is an example of a painting of a natural monument. Photo: Bennetta Jules-Rosette.

seasonal changes of slash-and-burn agriculture. As towns grow and modernize, the idyllic, isolated village has become a nostalgic myth. In an aesthetically pleasing way, the flames forecast the ultimate results of these changes.

Landscape paintings contrast with the far smaller output of contemporary scenes. While paintings of industrial monuments glorify modernity, they do so with extreme caution. These depictions are copied from postcards and are almost photographic in their realism. The ambiance of calm and the muted colors presented in the idyllic landscape are replaced by the harsh lines of the superhighway and the dam. An implicit lament about the destruction of the idealized old and peaceful way of life is communicated on each canvas. A contrast may be drawn between the idyllic rendition of Victoria Falls and a painting of Kariba Dam. In the first, the water falls gracefully with reflections of sunlight laced through it. In the latter, the water is harnessed under the dam, and the harsh lines of the superhighway that crosses the dam are emphasized. The negative connotations of the dam as an obstruction of nature are indicated subtly. They emerge through color and contour when the dam is juxtaposed to the sunlit waters of Victoria Falls.

The narrative structure of tourist art involves a quest for an ideal and untouched Africa. A similar quest is reflected in some of the poetry of the *négritude* literary movement of the 1950s and 1960s and the early films of African cinematographers such as Ousmane Sembène.[3]

Fig. 2. *Kariba Dam* by Mpinda Joseph, Kanyama Painters' Circle, Lusaka, Zambia, exemplifies the modern monument in which the forces of nature are harnessed. Photo: Bennetta Jules-Rosette.

The use of idyllic themes in contemporary African painting and carving was promoted by the colonial art schools founded in the 1940s and 1950s. Themes and styles prevalent in the art academies are modified and simplified by many tourist artists. Popular artists transform these themes in order to convey political messages.

An interesting play upon history occurs in popular paintings. The landscapes are used as a backdrop to evoke an ancestral past. Among the most dramatic renditions of historical events in Zairian popular painting are the images of *wakati ya wa Belges* (the time of the Belgians). Also referred to as the genre of *colonie belge*, these paintings depict floggings and mutilations believed to be suffered at the hands of Belgian colonizers and their African lackeys. In their classification of popular Zairian paintings, Ilona Szombati-Fabian and Johannes Fabian (1976: 5–6) place *colonie belge* within a larger genre of "things past." *Colonie belge* has no parallels in tourist art because of the specificity of its historical and political points of reference. Although dated from 1885 to 1959, *colonie belge* nonetheless transcends time and space by using explicit historical and regional symbols to invoke the present. The appearance of African lackeys in military garb to inflict punishment catapults us into a neocolonial present. Specific dates often situate these paintings as representing a condition that existed over a century ago. Protected under the cloak of history, these paintings actually criticize present injustices (Fig. 3).

Integrating Technology into Neotraditional Art

The case of tourist art illustrates that Western influences do not always take the form of direct representations of objects associated with European cultures but instead rely on an imagined notion of what is perceived to be popular in the West. Artistic syncretism is a complex and continuous process in which external influences constitute a subtle overlay on indigenous art forms. This process is evident in the images of technology that appear in Africa's continuing artistic traditions, or neotraditional art. Within these artistic traditions, individuals often assume the role of the cultural Other even though they do not perform for outsiders. A fascinating instance of the incorporation of foreign influences into neotraditional art and ritual performances is the case of the *Mami Wata* spirit. Mami Wata, or the mermaid figure, which is a totalizing symbol in Zairian popular painting, remains the object of worship in West Africa. Generally represented as a foreign woman of Mediterranean or Indian origin, Mami Wata has her roots in traditional beliefs about water spirits.

Contemporary Mami Wata images in Côte d'Ivoire, Togo, and Nigeria are adorned with artifacts of Western technology: watches, Western jewelry, mirrors, automobile spare parts, and sunglasses. She appears accompanied by a snake into which she materializes when the sacred contract of absolute devotion to her is broken. Mami Wata epitomizes the simultaneous fear of and attraction to the wealth issuing from Western technology. Although the Mami Wata figure may be used to elucidate the deep-seated ambivalence toward computers and other new technologies in African nations, from the perspective of aesthetics and ritual performance, she links traditional forms of worship to technology and the new arts (cf. Jules-Rosette 1990: 229–31). Henry Drewal (1988: 160–85) describes the spirit possession rituals, dreams, and visions of Mami Wata devotees in Nigeria, Togo, and Zaire. According to Drewal, new technologies have been integrated into the ritualized communications with Mami Wata. Drewal (1988: 181) explains:

> In Zaire, paintings of the mermaid . . . are frequently covered with texts describing the artist's conversations with the spirit . . . and, in Nigeria and Togo, Mami Wata worshippers write notes to their spirit and receive messages in the same form. Writing has thus become a ritual act, part of Mami Wata performance. Other means of communication are drawn from newer Western technology—the telephone, airplane, and motorcar help to connect the great distances between Mami Wata's abodes in the oceans and on African soil.

Blending of the old and new is not a facile combination that symbolically resolves the conflicts inherent in cultural change. Devotion to Mami Wata and to her iconic representation leaves the question of technology's influence unanswered. Although the treasures that Mami Wata brings are indeed highly valued, enslavement to her is feared, and there are those who do not dare utter her name.[4]

Technological Transformation in Tourist and Popular Painting

Mami Wata is the ultimate outcome of merging the past, the present and the utopian future. But this figure evokes mixed emotional reactions and does not propose a symbolic resolution to the dilemmas that it reflects. We might more productively speculate that images of technology do not refer exclusively to specific objects, such as watches, airplanes, telephones, or concrete states of affairs but, instead, to a narrative complication in an unfolding series of images. None of these images requires a fixed reference point in social history or local culture. Instead, they make sense in terms of the contexts of their artistic production and exchange. These images simulate hypothetical realities that arise in the cycle of artistic exchange. The artistic sign becomes a valued imaginary object, for what it

Fig. 3. *Colonie belge* by Zairian painter Tshibumba Kanda-Matulu, Lubumbashi, Zaire, circa 1977. Photo courtesy of the collection of Bogumil Jewsiewicki.

represents no longer exists, or perhaps never existed (cf. Baudrillard 1981: 10–12). Moreover, the artistic sign in tourist art engenders an ideal image of Africa and sustains a commercial relationship between the senders and receivers of artistic expression. Blurred genres that contextualize these signs are a consequence of changes in the patterns of communication between artists and their audiences (cf. Gombrich 1960: 234–41; Geertz 1983: 29–33).

It is now possible to examine three typical tourist paintings—the idyllic landscape, the burning village, and the industrial monument as a narrative sequence. In the idyllic landscape, modern technology is an anachronism. Anonymous peasant women appear pounding corn, and fishermen are shown casting their nets. These simple technologies bestow a folkloric quality on the pristine landscape and show an untouched Africa, often represented by two or three palm trees that fade into the horizon. In the burning village, this harmonious ideal is consumed by flames, but the beholder sees neither charred trees nor destroyed homes and fields. The flames appear innocent and decorative. The abandoned village, another variation on the idyllic landscape, shows empty houses that blend into the foliage behind them. Paintings of the burning village and the abandoned village carefully avoid the fate of the inhabitants. No one mourns the loss of the village or returns to its charred debris. Although images of technology do not appear in these paintings, technology is the tacit antisubject that causes destruction without confrontation (cf. Greimas and Courtés 1979: 369–70).

A third element in this narrative sequence is the industrial monument. The idyllic landscape is domesticated and transformed. From the debris of charred villages arises the industrial monument with its clean and severe lines. Although we never see the human forces and technologies that construct the monument, the dam itself is a technological tool used to generate electricity for the villages and cities that surround it. (Fig. 2) When the dam is viewed alone as a single framed image, no sense of loss or threat surrounds it. The industrial monument is a symbol of progress. When it is placed in a narrative sequence, the industrial monument is the outcome of change and warns us of the fate of the village in flames.

The cultural narrative that I propose places these paintings in an interpretive context. Although I have witnessed artists paint all three subgenres of the landscape in the idyllic, burning, and monument variations, they sell them to contrasting audiences and display them in different locales. This narrative sequence unites the subgenres through which painters encode their artistic messages (cf. Eco 1976: 273–75). Every artist "knows" the public meanings that these paintings convey and the ironic messages that are withheld for cultural insiders. Popular painters bring these hidden messages into the foreground and make incisive statements about technology's role in their society.

Narrative structure in popular painting is complex. Each narrative is condensed into a single painting in which subject and antisubject are juxtaposed (cf. Brett 1986: 96–100). In some of these paintings, the idyllic landscape forms a backdrop on which events inscribed in collective memory are depicted. Szombati-Fabian and Fabian (1976: 13–16) deal with this problem by classifying paintings into staggered semiotic systems that serve as codes for interpreting the iconic signs in popular paintings.[5] In order to elucidate genres for scholars and collectors, they classify the idyllic landscape and its offshoots as "things ancestral" and place paintings of historical subjects such as the Arab slave trade and the time of the Belgians in "things past." There is no genre that represents "things falling apart." Close scrutiny of the paintings classified in this manner reveals, for example, that Arab slave traders conduct their business in idyllic villages with chiefs cloaked in leopard skins. Ancestral things overlap with the past. Police outposts for the prisoners depicted in *colonie belge* paintings are surrounded by the thatched houses of the ancestral village. Bombs dropped on these calm villages exploding the landscape into the flames of deadly civil wars appear in the "things present" genre.

Similarities in the background and styles of these paintings are not fortuitous. Tshibumba Kanda-Matulu and Kalema, painters from Lubumbashi whose works are contained in several collections of Zairian popular art, often produced simultaneously in different genres.[6] Other artists who devote their attention more intensively toward the tourist trade also paint for popular and gallery audiences.[7] Often a painter spends an entire week producing idyllic landscape backdrops, some of which are sold expediently in their original form while others are embellished with popular themes. Thus, the production process partially explains the overlap in content across genre classifications. This ethnographic explanation of production, however, does not account for successive iterations and reinterpretations of the landscape within each painting genre.

In the Arab slave trade paintings, the idyllic landscape is a background for the decline of tradition triggered by external contact and exploitation. The landscape serves a similar purpose in the *colonie belge* paintings. In an intriguing painting by Tshibumba depicting an attack on Shaba in March of 1977, a village represented by four homes is bombed by the Zairian Air Force. Two jet bombers descend on the village. (Fig. 4) A bomb drops on the most traditional round thatched house while the three rectangular houses remain intact. The foreground of the painting depicts a woman with a baby on her back turned away from the viewer as she flees the village. Kneeling next to her is a traditional chief with a white beard whose body resembles that of a female. The chief's head is turned backward at a 180° angle while his body crawls forward. In this case, the idyllic landscape is destroyed by the negative technological forces of war. This painting does not need to be juxtaposed in a narrative sequence for its significance to emerge. The burning village, which tourist artists depict in

Fig. 4. *Attempt to ward off the first attack on Shaba* by Tshibuma Kanda-Matulu, Lubumbashi, circa 1977. Photo courtesy of the collection of Bogumil Jewsiewicki.

flames without identifying the source, has been bombed in Tshibumba's painting. Deadly forces annihilate the ancestral landscape.

Popular painters hurl us into the vertigo of mixed messages. These artists invoke the stability of the past and cast it aside with the violence of the present and the precarious future. They are less concerned with representing facts about modernity and the postmodern future than they are with developing an aesthetic model that generates a dialogue between political events and art. Jean Baudrillard alludes to this process of model and image creation when he describes the simulation of violence in mass media broadcasts. Baudrillard (1981: 31–32) states:

> Simulation is characterized by a *precession of the model*, of all models around the merest fact —the models come first and their orbital circulation . . . constitutes the genuine magnetic field of events. Facts no longer have any trajectory of their own, they arise at the intersection of the models . . . This anticipation, this precession, this short circuit, this confusion of the fact with the model . . . is what allows each time for all possible interpretations, even the most contradictory . . . in a generalized cycle.

This generalized cycle in popular art includes technology as part of the painter's model. Technology is the source of interpretation and the agent of change. Popular painters evaluate and criticize technology's role in the political order. In contrast, tourist artists represent technology with decorative embellishment, allusion, and indirect reference. These contrasting strategies emerge through the themes appearing in the works of tourist carvers and painters.

Engraving Technology: The Case of Tourist Carving

Introduction of taxation and the monetary economy that accompanied colonial domination coincided with the widespread diffusion of images of modern technology on the coins used for tax payments.[8] Coins minted between 1929 and 1931 in the former Belgian Congo bore engraved images of automobiles and biplanes. (Fig. 5) After paying their taxes, villagers wore these coins around their necks as symbols of administrative conformity. When they received the coin, individuals who had never seen an airplane were exposed to its image in association with colonial wealth and control. This form of commercial art has a long history in Africa. As early as the fifteenth century, cowrie shells exchanged in trade with the Portuguese at the Bight of Benin were highly prized for the aesthetic qualities (cf. Polanyi 1968: 294–95). Taxation coins, however, differed from earlier forms of combined commercial and artistic exchange because they were engraved with modern Western technologies that embodied a direct and immediate association with colonial domination.

Contemporary carvers embellish their works with images of modern technology. They carve automobiles, airplanes, telephones, suits, and even computers. Although many of these carvings are made to meet consumer demand, they are also recycled as cult objects for use in ritual performances. Drewal (1988: 171–83) notes the presence of modern technological artifacts on the altars of Mami Wata cultists in Nigeria. It is not uncommon to find a carved pole with a string attached, representing the telephone line used by Mami Wata to communicate with her worshippers. John Nunley (1988: 108–12) notes the placement of modern technological artifacts on the transformed Yoruba hunters' masks used among the Ode-lay secret societies in Freetown, Sierra Leone. These innovations do not dilute conventional art forms. Neotraditional artists use images of technology as a way of controlling and dominating the modern world. Yet, the fabrication of modern artistic representations does not provide a major source of income from tourists. Among tourist carvers, it is more common to find airplanes and automobiles made and sold to fill orders for specific clients. The production of carved technological images for a restricted market is prevalent among the Kamba carvers of Kenya.

In the manner of the tourist painters, whose attitudes are reflected in Toto's pragmatic response, Kamba carvers shy away from direct images of modern technology. They produce for outsiders without reproducing Western images. Even the more innovative carvers, such as Safari Mbai, who has entered the gallery trade, express reluctance to become technological critics. In an extended interview, Safari explained his carving and marketing strategies as pitched toward tourists. He asserts:

> Tourists want to have a feeling that they have actually been in Africa . . . [T]hey don't want to see me in a tie. That they can see in their own country. That's why they are more impressed here by the Samburu and the Masai, and also the animals. They are especially interested with the elephant and most of the animals which are not available in their country.

Safari, who is a regular contributor to the Africa Arts Gallery in Nairobi, is not merely a souvenir carver. His works include abstract and experimental pieces. In order to have the freedom to experiment, however, Safari continues to carve for the tourist art market and to gauge its fluctuations in style, taste, and preference. When I found a carving of an airplane in Safari's studio, he explained that the carving had been ordered by a British client for his son's birthday. Safari distanced himself from the piece and professed no interest in experimenting with carvings of technological objects. In his own way, Safari has taken as many artistic risks as Koffi Kouakou of Côte d'Ivoire. Safari's marketing strategies, however, have been geared toward the Kenyan tourist art trade.

Although the carvers and sculptors of pieces intended for the tourist trade work primarily in contemporary urban settings, they do not draw upon their immediate environment as an inspiration for artistic themes. A market-driven analysis might provide a simple explanation. Carvings of technology are not profitable. At least, the artists do not think so. Their efforts to create touristic authenticity lead to the reproduction of variations within the idyllic landscape genre. Yet the artists manipulate the ideal of authenticity as a referential illusion within the cycle of symbolic and economic exchange that characterizes tourist art.[9] The urban environment is a fertile ground for innovation and exchange among tourist artists, but it is not a source of their artistic representations.

Reproduction of traditional figures masks an artistic *alter ego*. Postcolonial artists may wear

Fig. 5. Engraved coin minted in 1929 and worn as a sign of annual tax payment in the Belgian Congo. Photo: D. Ponsard, Musée de l'Homme Collection, M. H. X. 985.10.

ties and sell art works in a complex local and international market (cf. Bhabha 1987: 8–10). These artists, however, believe that widespread commercial acceptance of their works requires simplification of themes and designs along with the rejection of their postcolonial identities. Safari intones: "... they don't want to see me in a tie." Although most of the tourist carvers embrace modern production technologies and marketing methods, they carefully insulate their creative works from these influences. Their artistic themes emerge out of an imagined past that, in turn, shapes their professional and cultural identities. Anoh and Koffi, who bravely deviated from this path, found themselves alone and starving. (Figs. 6 & 7)

Parallels exist between the psychology of masking in traditional African ritual performances and the protection of professional identity by tourist artists. Simon Ottenberg (1975: 11–12) points out that putting on a mask among Afikpo ritual performers in Nigeria transforms the dancers into spirits. Tourist artists employ their signatures as masks in a dialectical exchange with various audiences. Some artists whom I interviewed had as many as

Fig. 6. *Simulated Suits*. Carvings of modern Western apparel in the latest styles from the atelier of Koffi Kouakou and Anoh Acou, Grand Bassam, Côte d'Ivoire model postmodernity. Photo: Bennetta Jules-Rosette.

five different signatures for their works. They often used their given names for gallery expositions and partial names or pseudonyms for the tourist trade. Michel Foucault (1984: 123–24) points out the imaginary power of the artistic signature. Artistic presence is embodied in the signature. Artists are aware of the diverse roles that they play in a postcolonial society, and they manipulate their masks for both creative inspiration and profit. In this regard, a distinction may be drawn between the artists' performances *for* the West and *as* international artists. This distinction offers a potentially productive schema for the reclassification of neotraditional, tourist, and popular art works with reference to the artists' intentionality and perceptions of consumer demand.

Representations of Technology in Tourist Painting

In contrast to the tourist carvers, painters work in a variety of genres. Zairian painter Diouf Kabamba (also known as Moussa), founder of the Kanyama artists' circle in Lusaka, expressed concerns about the audience for and social meanings of his artworks. With the exception of one painting of a guitar player, most of Diouf's works do not contain images of Western objects. (Fig. 8) In both tourist and gallery formats, Diouf painted the burning village without

Fig. 7. Carved computer by Koffi Kouakou at the Grand Bassam atelier, Côte d'Ivoire. Photo from the collection of Bennetta Jules-Rosette.

a depiction of the source of violence. Nevertheless, he ventured a political interpretation of the burning village by expressing his view that it resulted from mismanagement by the neocolonial state. Diouf's dilemma involves a conflict between his intended and actual audiences (cf. Jules-Rosette 1984: 171–73).[10] In an early interview, Diouf questioned the relationship between artistic production and perceived audience demand. He explained:

> Granted, it's the Europeans who buy our art, but we don't produce for the Europeans. We want our own people to understand what we produce. But that's a delicate problem.

Diouf's dilemma pertains to the impact of Western technology on the dissemination of contemporary African art. In his interview, Diouf compared painters and writers. He argued that African writers are able to publish their works in Europe, but that painters are caught in a more difficult marketing situation in which the audience for their work is primarily local. During his lifetime, Diouf traveled to Belgium, France, the United States, and Canada to exhibit his art works. In 1982 he died an exile in Zambia. Diouf incorporated the styles of Kuba carving, impressionism, and cubism into his new figuratist work and led his circle to follow suit. Yet, Diouf was torn between internationalism and localism in his painting, between the desire to be a politically committed artist and the necessity to sell his paintings anonymously on the tourist art circuit. As part of his lifelong artistic project, Diouf strove to develop an international audience for his school of painting while remaining firmly rooted on African soil.

Lusengu Kalala was originally one of Diouf's followers and is now an established painter and head of the Palette d'Or Studio in Kinshasa. He led the Kanyama circle in technological innovation. To Lusengu, innovation meant the use of appropriate technological resources for artistic experimentation. Lusengu guided the circle in its experimentation with the palette knife and introduced the use of white typewriter correction fluid for highlighting paintings and pastel drawings (cf. Jules-Rosette 1979: 117–30). Lusengu explained his highlighting technique to me during an instructional session.

> On black and white, I begin working with a candle . . . A small demonstration should help you. After having worked with the candle on white and black I begin to paint, with pastel . . . With blanco [white typewriter correction fluid], I emphasize the highlights, the highlights . . . I continue to give the trees movement in the picture, for example, and all of that. Well, that's truly my technique, my little trick of white and black.

This method is based upon the use of a simple innovation that recycles Western technological by-products. Lusengu's resourcefulness is not uncommon among tourist artists who prepare bedsheets to be employed as canvases and strip old water heaters for copper to be used in relief carvings. While Picasso used found materials to effect primitivism, contemporary African artists adopt these materials out of necessity and thereby transform technological waste into an artistic statement.

Conclusions: Contemporary Art and the Technological Promise in Africa

Processes of artistic production in tourist and popular art are shaped by technological invention and experimentation. Carving cooperatives and painting studios imitate the industrial assembly line by reproducing large quantities of apparently identical objects through coordinated production procedures. Individuals mechanize their own work by the repetitive production of painted landscapes, backdrops, and carved templates that glut the tourist art market. Industrial technology is a leitmotif of tourist art production in Africa. Artists, however, insulate their identities and output from their production procedures. Toto and Safari emphasize the psychological distance between their identities as contemporary artists and the idyllic images that they produce. Lusengu uses technological innovation to create ancestral landscape images. This paradox is part of the postmodern condition in which images of a nonexistent idyllic past haunt contemporary artists who employ the latest available methods of production. Chemical dyes, acid solutions, and shoe polish are used to simulate ancient objects. Contemporary African art ceases to be Mudimbe's question mark and becomes the driving force in a new form of symbolic and economic exchange. Understanding of these symbolic processes is enriched by seeking the artists' explanations of their work and environment.

While the painters and carvers imitate industrial methods of production, high technologies have reached African urban centers already. Young computer professionals and trainees experiment with computer graphics and laser reproductions. The object of one computer programming session that I observed in Nairobi was the production of a set of art works for an official government visit. Computer students were as proud of their "art" as they were of their technological mastery. From the ranks of these young computer trainees, some of Africa's new commercial artists may emerge.

Simulation of the past and its projection into the future is a technique of postmodern representation that is used by tourist and popular artists. The reproduction of postmodern culture in Africa, however, does not rely on the growing presence of high technology.

Fig. 8. *The Guitar Player* by Zairian artist Diouf Kabamba. This painting is one of the few works by Diouf containing an object of Western origin. Photo courtesy of Ibongo Gilunga, National Museum of Zaire.

trainees experiment with computer graphics and laser reproductions. The object of one computer programming session that I observed in Nairobi was the production of a set of art works for an official government visit. Computer students were as proud of their "art" as they were of their technological mastery. From the ranks of these young computer trainees, some of Africa's new commercial artists may emerge.

Simulation of the past and its projection into the future is a technique of postmodern representation that is used by tourist and popular artists. The reproduction of postmodern culture in Africa, however, does not rely on the growing presence of high technology. Incorporative systems of representation arise in continuing ritual and performance traditions, as the Mami Wata cults and Ode-lay sects suggest. By appropriating technology as a sign, artists and local consumers possess its powers. Technological signs, including the Mami Wata and the computer, simulate progress, wealth, and mastery. Ambivalence toward these signs masks technology's presence under the antiseptic images of tourist art. This ambivalence provokes a re-examination of the audiences for the artistic images and for the technologies. Will technology in art resemble the colonial taxation coin destined to be returned to its foreign producers or will it become an integral part of aesthetic expression and production in contemporary African art? In my view, technological signs illustrate the incorporative capacities of the living African arts. These signs also demonstrate the extent to which contemporary African artists working in tourist and popular idioms have irrevocably entered a postmodern world culture of artistic production and exchange.

Notes

1.   The association of technology with colonial domination and external control is an economic reality. Walter Rodney (1972: 35) expresses this view when he states:

> The capitalist countries are technologically more advanced and are therefore the sector of the imperialist system which determined the direction of change. A striking example to this effect is the fact that synthetic fabrics manufactured in the capitalist metropoles have begun to replace fabrics made from raw material grown in the colonies. In other words, (within certain limits) it is the technologically advanced metropoles who can decide when to end their dependence on the colonies in a particular sphere. When that happens, it is the colony or neo-colony which goes begging cap in hand for a reprieve and a new quota. It is for this reason that a formerly colonized nation has no hope of developing until it breaks effectively with the vicious circle of dependence and exploitation which characterizes imperialism.

2.   The tourist art system involves both symbolic and economic exchange. Artists respond to perceived audience demand as it is mediated to them through middlemen and culture brokers. The tourist art system is a vehicle for intercultural communication. The messages communicated, however, are often ambiguous and inexact. The results of these communications include overproduction of unpopular items and glutting of the tourist art market with certain objects that display little stylistic variation or innovation (cf. Bascom 1976: 306–308; Jules-Rosette 1984: 18–22). If the tourist art system is viewed as a process of communication and exchange rather than a system of artistic classification, new trends in art production may be readily examined and incorporated into the system.

3.   The early writings of the *négritude* movement reflect an idyllic image of Africa that resembles the perspective of tourist artists. Léopold Senghor's poem "Congo," for example, evokes a natural Africa, untouched by colonial intervention and technology (Senghor 1948: 168–70). This image of Africa appeals to a mixed audience because of its nostalgic qualities. It also reflects the influence of European perceptions of a nostalgic ideal type (cf. Mudimbe 1988: 83–85).

4.   Ronald M. Wintrob (1970: 143–57) describes the distress and psychological disorders that befall individuals who believe they have broken contracts with the Mami Wata spirit or are being pursued by her. Belief in the Mami Wata spirit is undoubtedly a cultural and historical result of foreign contact. She is thought to be so dangerous that many members of indigenous cults and religious sects forbid the mention of her name or the possession of images of her.

5.   Staggered semiotic systems propose that a metalanguage unites various levels of expression and

Jewsiewicki (1985: 60–66). The reproductions of Tshibumba's paintings in this paper have been made available courtesy of Jewsiewicki's collection.

7.   Many painters and carvers working in the tourist art idiom do so in order to support themselves financially while they prepare more experimental works for gallery expositions and international sale. Some of these artists sign their tourist and gallery pieces with different names in order to protect their artistic reputations (cf. Jules-Rosette 1984: 142–44).

8.   These taxation coins have been photographed for Musée de l'Homme collection M.H.X. 985.10 by D. Ponsard. Figure 4 is reproduced with permission from the Musée de l'Homme. The coins illustrate the intersection of art, commerce and modern technology. Images appearing on the coins reinforced the relationship between modern technology and colonial domination.

9.   Tourist artists create a reality effect by copying traditional genres and styles in order to convey an illusion of authenticity (cf. Barthes 1974: 271). Artificial aging and modification of pieces sustain this illusion.

10.   Since Diouf's death in 1982, a small collection of his paintings has been located by Ibongo Gilunga in the Modern Art Section of the National Museum of Zaire. Figure 8 is reproduced from the National Museum's collection. Diouf's impact was widespread, and much research remains to be done on his works. In a previous study, I discussed Diouf's attempts to create a balance between the local and international audiences for his school of painting (Jules-Rosette 1984: 142–73).

B.
Jules-
Rosette

References

Bascom, William. 1976. "Changing African Art." In *Ethnic and Tourist Arts: Cultural Expressions from the Fourth World*, ed. Nelson H. H. Graburn, 303–19. Berkeley: University of California Press.

Barthes, Roland. 1967. *Elements of Semiology*. Trans. Annette Lavers and Colin Smith. London: Jonathan Cape.

———. 1975. "An Introduction to the Structural Analysis of Narrative." *New Literary History* 6, 2: 237–72.

Baudrillard, Jean. 1981. *Simulacres et Simulation*. Paris: Éditions Galilée.

Bhabha, Homi. 1987. "Interrogating Identity." *ICA Documents* 6: 5–11.

Brett, Guy. 1986. *Through Our Own Eyes: Popular Art and Modern History*. Philadelphia: New Society Publishers.

Drewal, Henry. 1988. "Performing the Other: Mami Wata Worship in Africa." *The Drama Review* 32, 2 (Summer): 160–85.

Foucault, Michel. 1984. "What Is an Author?" In *The Foucault Reader*, ed. Paul Rabinow, 113–38. New York: Pantheon Books.

Geertz, Clifford. 1983. *Local Knowledge: Further Essays in Interpretive Anthropology*. New York: Basic Books.

Gombrich, E. H. 1960. *Art and Illusion: A Study in the Psychology of Pictorial Representations*. New York: Pantheon Books.

Greimas, Algirdas Julien and Joseph Courtés. 1979. *Sémiotique: Dictionnaire Raisonné de la Théorie du Langage*. Paris: Librairie Hachette.

Jewsiewicki, Bogumil. 1985. "La Mémoire et l'Imaginaire." In *Le Quotidien, Entre la Mémoire et l'Imaginaire*, ed. Bogumil Jewsiewicki with François Mathieu, 60–66. Québec, Canada: Université Laval.

Jules-Rosette, Bennetta. 1979. "Technological Innovation in Popular African Art." *Journal of Popular Culture* 13: 116–30.

———. 1984. *The Messages of Tourist Art: An African Semiotic System in Comparative Perspective*. New York: Plenum Publishing Corporation.

———. 1990. *Terminal Signs: Computers and Social Change in Africa*. Berlin: Mouton de Gruyter Publishers.

Kasfir, Sidney L. 1992. "Taste and Distaste: The Canon of New African Art." *Transition* 57: 52–70.

Lyotard, Jean-François. 1984. *The Postmodern Condition: A Report on Knowledge*. Trans. Geoff Bennington and Brian Massumi. Minneapolis, Minnesota: University of Minnesota Press.

MacCannell, Dean. 1989. *The Tourist: A New Theory of the Leisure Class*. New York: Schocken Books.

Miller, Christopher L. 1985. *Blank Darkness: Africanist Discourse in French*. Chicago: University of Chicago Press.

Mount, Marshall Ward. 1974. *African Arts: The Years Since 1920*. Bloomington, Indiana: Indiana University Press.

Mudimbe, V.Y. 1986. "African Art as a Question Mark." *African Studies Review* 29, 1 (March): 2–4.

———. 1988. *The Invention of Africa: Gnosis, Philosophy, and the Order of Knowledge*. Bloomington, Indiana: Indiana University Press.

Nunley, John. 1988. "Purity and Pollution in Freetown: Masked Performance." *The Drama Review* 32, 2 (Summer): 102–22.

Ottenberg, Simon. 1975. *Masked Rituals of Afrikpo: The Context of African Art*. Seattle, Washington: University of Washington Press.

Penley, Constance and Andrew Ross. 1986. "Interview with Trinh T. Minh-ha." *The New American Filmmakers Series* 32: 87–103.

Polanyi, Karl. 1968. *Primitive, Archaic, and Modern Economies*. Compiled by George Dalton. Garden City, New York: Anchor Books.

Rodney, Walter. 1972. *How Europe Underdeveloped Africa*. London: Bogle-L'Ouverture.

Senghor, Leopold Sedar. 1948. "Congo." In *Anthologie de la Nouvelle Poésie Nègre et Malgache de Langue Française*, ed. Léopold Sédar Senghor, 168–70. Paris: Presses Universitaires de France. This poem also appears in Senghor, Léopold Sédar. 1956. *Éthiopiques*. Paris: Éditions du Seuil.

Szombati-Fabian, Ilona and Johannes Fabian. 1976. "Art, History, and Society: Popular Art in Shaba, Zaire." *Studies in the Anthropology of Visual Communication* 3, 1 (Spring): 1–21.

Vogel, Susan. 1991. "Foreword." In *Africa Explores: Twentieth-Century African Art*, ed. Susan Vogel, 8–13. New York: The Center for African Art.

Wintrob, Ronald M. 1970. "Mammy Water: Folk Beliefs and Psychotic Elaboration in Liberia." *Canadian Psychiatric Association Journal* 15: 143–57.

The Photograph as an Intersection Of Gazes The Example of National Geographic

Catherine Lutz and Jane Collins

Aᴸᴸ ᴘʜᴏᴛᴏɢʀᴀᴘʜꜱ ᴛᴇʟʟ ꜱᴛᴏʀɪᴇꜱ ᴀʙᴏᴜᴛ ʟᴏᴏᴋɪɴɢ. ᴀꜱ ᴘᴀʀᴛ ᴏꜰ ᴀ ʟᴀʀɢᴇʀ ᴘʀᴏᴊᴇᴄᴛ ᴛᴏ ᴇxᴀᴍɪɴᴇ the *National Geographic* magazine's photographs as cultural artifacts from a changing twentieth century American scene, we have been struck by the variety of looks and looking relations that swirl in and around them.[1] These looks—whether from the photographer, the reader, or the person photographed—are ambiguous, charged with feeling and power, and are central to the stories (sometimes several and conflicting) that the photo can be said to tell. By examining the "lines of sight" evident in the *Geographic* photograph of the "non-Westerner," we can see that it is not simply a captured view of the other, but rather a dynamic site at which many gazes or viewpoints intersect. This intersection creates a complex and multi-dimensional object; it allows viewers of the photo to negotiate a number of different identities both for themselves and for those pictured; and it is one route by which the photograph threatens to break frame and reveal its social context. Some of the issues raised in this chapter are particular to this specific genre of photograph while many others illuminate photographic interpretation more generally.

We aim here to explore the significance of "gaze" for intercultural relations in the photograph, and to present a typology of seven kinds of gaze that can be found in the photograph and its social context. These include (1) the photographer's gaze (the actual look through the viewfinder), (2) the institutional, magazine gaze (evident in cropping, picture choice, captioning, etc.), (3) the readers' gaze, (4) the non-Western subjects' gaze, (5) the explicit looking done by Westerners who are often framed together with locals in the picture, (6) the gaze returned or refracted by the mirrors or cameras that are shown, in a surprising number of photographs, in local hands, and (7) our own, academic gaze.

The Gaze and Its Significance

The photograph and the non-Western person share two fundamental attributes in the culturally tutored experience of most Americans; they are objects at which we *look*. The photograph has this quality because it is usually intended as a thing of either beauty or documentary interest and surveillance. Non-Westerners draw a look, rather than inattention or interaction, to the extent that their difference or foreignness defines them as noteworthy yet distant. A look is necessary to cross the span created by the perception of difference, a perception which initially, of course, also involves looking. When people from outside the Western world are photographed, the importance of the look is accentuated.[2]

A number of intellectual traditions have dealt with "the gaze," looking or spectating as they occur in photography and art. Often these types of analysis have focused on the formal features of the photograph alone, excluding history and culture. While we are critical of several of the perspectives on gaze that we review below, to view photographs as having a certain structure can be consistent with an emphasis on an active and historical reader. In other words, we will argue that the lines of gaze perceptible in the photograph suggest the multiple forces at work in creating photographic meaning, one of the most important of which is readers' culturally informed interpretive work. One objective of our research has been to test the universal claims of certain of these theories about gaze by looking at actual cases of photographs being taken, edited, and read by individuals in real historical time and cultural space. Nonetheless, the interethnic looking that gets done in *National Geographic* photos can be conceptualized by drawing on a number of the insights of these analyses.

Feminist film theory, beginning with Mulvey (1985), has focused on the ways in which looking in patriarchal society is, in her words, "split between active/male and passive/female. The determining male gaze projects its phantasy on to the female figure which is styled accordingly" (1985: 808). The position of spectator, in this view, belongs to the male and allows for the construction of femininity. John Berger (1972) has also treated the gaze as masculine. He points out that contemporary gender ideologies envisage men as active doers and define women as passive presence, men by what they do to others, women by their attitudes towards themselves. This has led to women's focus on how they appear before others and so to a fragmentation of themselves into two parts—"the surveyor and the surveyed . . . One might simplify this by saying: *men act* and *women appear*. Men look at women. Women watch themselves being looked at . . . [and] the surveyor of woman in herself is male" (1972: 46–47; see also Burgin 1986).

Mulvey and Berger alert us to how the position of spectator has the potential to enhance or articulate the power of the observer over the observed. Representations produced by the artist, the photographer, and the scientist in their role as spectators have permanent, tangible qualities and are culturally defined as quasi-sacred. Both Mulvey and Berger point out that it is the social context of patriarchy, rather than a universal essential quality of the image, that gives the gaze a masculine character.

Recent critiques of these views take issue with the simple equation of the gaze with the masculine, with the psychoanalytic emphasis of this work and its concomitant tendency to universalize its claims and to ignore social and historical context, as well as its neglect of race and class as key factors determining looking relations (e.g., de Lauretis 1987; Gaines 1988; Green 1989; Jameson 1983; Tagg 1988; Traube 1992; Williams 1987). These critiques make a number of proposals useful for our examination of *National Geographic* photographs. They suggest, first, that the magazine viewer operates within a racial system in which there are taboos on certain kinds of looking, for example, black men looking at white women. Gaines (1988) forcefully suggests that we need to rethink ideas about looking "along more materialist lines, considering, for instance, how some groups have historically had the license to 'look' openly while other groups have 'looked' illicitly" (1988: 24–25). She also argues that those who have used psychoanalytic theory claim to treat looking positions (viewer/viewed) as distinct from actual social groups (male/female) even while they are identified with gender and in so doing, "keep the levels of the social ensemble [social experience, representational systems, and so on] hopelessly separate."

Work on women as spectators suggests that viewers may have several possible responses to images, moving toward and away from identification with the imaged person, and sometimes "disrupt[ing] the authority and closure of dominant representations" (Williams 1987: 11; compare Burgin 1982). This research suggests that looking need not be equated with controlling; Jameson argues that there may be legitimate pleasures in looking at others which are not predicated on the desire to control, denigrate, or distance oneself from the other. More broadly, we can say that the social whole in which photographers, editors, and a diversity of readers look at the non-Western world allows no simple rendering of the spectator of the magazine, including the spectator's gender.

Several critiques have centered on the program advocated by a deconstructionist approach to the viewer. From this latter perspective, the goal is to de-center the viewing subject and subvert the attempt to find a coherent object at the end of the gaze. But as de Lauretis points out, "the Western bourgeois spectator-subject [no more than] the spectator addressed by radical (non-feminist) avant-garde film practices, and the deluded, divided, or diffuse subject of poststructuralist and anti-humanist discourse" are understood "as simply human, that is to say, male and white" (1987: 123) and, we can add, Western. Similarly, Julien and Mercer (1988) note that the announcement of the "end of representation" has not been accompanied by consideration of the possibility of the "end of ethnocentrism."

Much feminist analysis of the power of gaze has drawn on the psychoanalytic theorizing of Lacan (1981). While it carries the dangers of a universalizing focus, Lacan's view of the gaze can be helpful as a model for the *potential* effects of looking. Lacan speaks of gaze as something distinct from the eye of the beholder and from simple vision: it is that "something [which] slips . . . and is always to some degree eluded in it [vision]" (1981: 73); it is "the lack." The gaze comes from the other who constitutes the self in that looking, but the gaze the self encounters is "not a seen gaze, but a gaze imagined by me in the field of the Other" (1981: 84). Ultimately, however, the look that the self receives is "profoundly unsatisfying" because the Other does not look at the self in the way that the self imagines it ought to be looked at. The photograph of the non-Westerner can be seen as at least partially the outcome of a set of psychoculturally informed choices made by photographers, editors, and caption writers who pay attention at some level to their own and the other's gaze. Their choices may be made in such a way as to reduce the likelihood of the kind of disappointment Lacan mentions. What can be done in the photograph is to manipulate, perhaps unconsciously, the gaze of the other (via such processes as photo selection) so that it allows us to see ourselves reflected in their eyes in ways which are comfortable, familiar and pleasurable. Photographs might be seen as functioning in the way Lacan says a painting can, which is by pacifying the

C.
Lutz &
J.
Collins

viewer. What is pacified is the gaze, or rather the anxiety that accompanies the gap between our ideal identity and the real. This taming of the gaze occurs when we realize that the picture does not change as our gaze changes. In Lacan's view, we are desperate for and because of the gaze, and the power of the pictorial representation is that it can ease that anxiety. Photos of the ethnic Other can help relieve the anxiety provoked by the ideal of the Other's gaze and estimation of us.[3]

Homi Bhabha, on the other hand, argues that the gaze is not only crucial to colonial regimes, but that a tremendous ambivalence and unsettling effect must accompany colonial looking relations because the mirror which these images of the other hold up to the colonial self is "problematic, for the subject finds or recognizes itself through an image which is simultaneously alienating and hence potentially confrontational (29). There is always the threatened return of the look" (1983: 33). From this perspective, which borrows from Lacan and Freud, colonial social relations are enacted largely through a "regime of visibility" in which the look is crucial both for identifying the other and for raising questions of how racist discourse can enclose the mirrored self as well as the other within itself. The photograph and all its intersections of gaze, then, is a site at which this identification and the conflict of maintaining a stereotyped view of difference occurs.[4]

Foucault's analysis of the rise of surveillance in modern society is also very relevant to understanding the photographic gaze, and recent analyses (Green 1984; Tagg 1988) have sharply delineated ways in which photography of the other operates at the nexus of knowledge and power that Foucault identified. Foucault pointed to psychiatry, medicine, and legal institutions as primary sites in which control over populations was achieved. His novel contribution was to see these institutions as exercising power not only by coercive control of the body but by creating knowledge of the body and thereby forcing it "to emit signs" or to conform physically and representationally to the knowledge produced by these powerful institutions. The crucial role of photography in the exercise of power lies in its ability to allow for close study of the Other, and to promote, in Foucault's words, the "normalizing gaze, a surveillance that makes it possible to qualify, to classify and to punish. It establishes over individuals a visibility through which one differentiates them and judges them" (1977: 25).

In the second half of the nineteenth century, photography began to be used to identify prisoners, mental patients, and racial or ethnic types. According to Tagg, its efficacy lies not so much in facilitating social control of those photographed but in representing these others to an audience of "non-deviants" who thereby acquire a language for understanding themselves and the limits they must live within to avoid being classed with those on the outside. Foucault's analysis might suggest that the gaze of the *Geographic* is part of the "capillary system" of international power relations allowing for the surveillance, if not the control, of non-Western people. The magazine's gaze at the Third World operates to represent it to an American audience in ways which can but do not always shore up a Western cultural identity or sense of self as modern and civilized. The gaze is not, however, as singular or monolithic as Foucault might suggest. In itself, we might say, a look can mean anything, but lines and types of gaze, in social context, tend to open up certain possibilities for interpreting a photograph and foreclose others. They often center on issues of intimacy, pleasure, scrutiny, confrontation, and power.[5]

A Multitude of Gazes

Many gazes can be found in any photograph in the *National Geographic*. This is true whether the picture shows a landscape devoid of people; a single person looking straight at the camera; a large group of people, each looking in a different direction but none at the camera; or a person in the distance whose eyes are tiny or out of focus. In other words, the gaze is not simply the look given by or to a photographed subject. It includes seven types of gaze.[6]

The Photographer's Gaze

This gaze, represented by the camera's eye, leaves its clear mark on the structure and content of the photograph. Independently or constrained by others, the photographer takes a position on a rooftop overlooking Khartoum or inside a Ulithian menstrual hut or in front of a funeral parade in Vietnam. Photo subject matter, composition, vantage point (angle or point of view), sharpness and depth of focus, color balance, framing and other elements of style are the result of the viewing choices made by the photographer or by the invitations or exclusions of those being photographed (Geary 1988).

C. Lutz & J. Collins

Sontag argues that photographers are usually profoundly alienated from the people they photograph, and may "feel compelled to put the camera between themselves and whatever is remarkable that they encounter" (1977: 10). *Geographic* photographers, despite an often expressed and fundamental sympathy with the third world people they meet, confront them across the distances of class, race, and sometimes gender. Whether from a fear of these differences or the more primordial (per Lacan) insecurity of the gaze itself, the photographer can often make the choice to insert technique between self and his or her subjects, as can the social scientist (Devereux 1967).

Under most circumstances, the photographer's gaze and the viewer's gaze overlap. The photographer may treat the camera eye as simply a conduit for the reader's look, the "searchlight" (Metz 1985) of his/her vision. Though these two looks can be disentangled, the technology and conventions of photography force the reader to follow that eye and see the world from its position.[7] The implications of this fact can be illustrated with a photo that shows a Venezuelan miner selling the diamonds he has just prospected to a middleman (August 1976; see Fig. 1). To take his picture, the photographer has stood inside the broker's place of business,

Fig. 1. The gaze of the camera is not always exactly the same as the gaze of the viewer, but in most *Geographic* photographs the former structures the latter in powerful ways. In this August 1976 photograph of a Venezuelan diamond transaction, the viewer is strongly encouraged to share the photographer's interest in the miner rather than in the broker. Photo: Robert Madden, © National Geographic Society.

shooting out over his back and shoulder to capture the face and hands of the miner as he exchanges his diamonds for cash. The viewer is strongly encouraged to share the photographer's interest in the miner, rather than the broker (whose absent gaze may be more available for substitution with the viewer's than is the miner's), and to in fact identify with the broker from whose relative position the shot has been taken and received. The broker, like the North American reader, stands outside the frontier mining world. Alternative readings of this photograph are, of course, possible; the visibility of the miner's gaze may make identification with him and his precarious position more likely. Ultimately what is important here is the question of how a diverse set of readers respond to such points-of-view in a photograph.

THE MAGAZINE'S GAZE

This is the whole institutional process by which some portion of the photographer's gaze is chosen for use and emphasis (Lutz and Collins 1993: Chapters 2 and 3). It includes (1) the editor's decision to commission articles on particular locations or issues; (2) the editor's choice of a small number of pictures from the voluminous number (11,000 on an average assignment) the photographer has taken; and, (3) the editor's and layout designer's decisions about cropping the picture, arranging it with other photos on the page to bring out the desired meanings, reproducing it in a certain size format to emphasize or downplay its importance, or even altering the picture. The reader, of course, cannot determine whether decisions relating to the last two choices are made by editor or photographer. The magazine's gaze is more evident and accessible in (4) the caption writer's verbal fixing of a vantage on the picture's meaning. This gaze is also multiple and sometimes controversial, given the diverse perspectives and politics of those who work for the *Geographic*.

THE MAGAZINE READER'S GAZES

As Barthes has pointed out, the "photograph is not only perceived, received, it is *read*, connected more or less consciously by the public that consumes it to a traditional stock of signs" (1977: 19). Independently of what the photographer or the caption writer may intend as the message(s) of the photo, the reader can imagine something else or in addition. The reader, in other words, is "invited to dream in the ideological space of the photograph" (Tagg 1988: 183). Certain elements of composition or content may make it more likely that the reader will resist the photographic gaze and its ideological messages or potentials. These include whatever indicates that a camera (rather than the reader's eye alone) has been at work—jarring, unnatural colors, off center angles, and obvious photo retouching.

What *National Geographic* subscribers see is not simply what they each get (the physical object, the photograph), but what they imagine the world is about before the magazine arrives, what imagining the picture provokes, and what they remember afterwards of the story they make the picture tell or allow it to tell. The reader's gaze, then, has a history and a future, and it is structured by the mental work of inference and imagination, provoked by the picture's inherent ambiguity (Is that woman smiling or smirking? What are those people in the background doing?) and its tunnel vision (What is going on outside the picture frame? What is it, outside the picture, that she looks at?). Beyond that, the photo permits fantasy ("Those two are in love, in love like I am with Stuart, but they're bored there on that bench, bored like I have been in love." or "That child. How beautiful. She should be mine to hold and feed."). Such differences between the reader's gaze and that of the magazine led us to investigate the former directly by asking a number of people to interpret the pictures (Lutz and Collins 1993).

The reader's gaze is structured by a large number of cultural elements or models, many more than those used to reason about racial or cultural difference. Cultural models that we have learned help us interpret gestures such as the thrown back shoulders of an Argentinean cowboy as indicative of confidence, strength and bravery. Models of gender lead to a reading of a picture of a mother with a child as a natural scenario, and of the pictured relationship as one of loving, relaxed nurturance; alternatively, the scene might have been read as underlaid with tensions and emotional distance, an interpretation that might be more common in societies with high infant mortality. There is, however, not one reader's gaze; each individual looks with his or her own personal, cultural, and political background or set of interests. It has been possible for people to speak of "the [singular] reader" only so long as "the text" is treated as an entity with a single determinate meaning that is simply consumed (Radway 1984) and only so long as the agency, enculturated nature, and diversity of experience of readers are denied.

The gaze of the *National Geographic* reader is also structured by photography's technological form, including a central paradox. On the one hand, photographs allow participation in the non-Western scene through vicarious viewing. On the other, they may also alienate the reader by way of the fact that they create or require a passive viewer and that they frame out much of what an actual viewer of the scene would see, smell, and hear, thereby atomizing and impoverishing experience (Sontag 1977). From another perspective, the photograph has been said (Metz 1985) to necessarily distance the viewer by changing the person photographed into an object—we know our gaze falls on a two dimensional object—and promoting fantasy. Still, the presumed consent of the person to be photographed can give the viewer the illusion of having some relationship with him or her.

Finally, this gaze is also structured by the context of reading. Where and how does the reader go through the magazine—quickly or carefully, alone or with a child? In a less literal sense, the context of reading includes cultural notions about the magazine itself—as high middlebrow, scientific, and pleasurable. The *National Geographic* sits near the top of a socially constructed hierarchy of popular magazine types (e.g., highbrow, lowbrow) that runs parallel to a hierarchy of taste in cultural products more generally (Levine 1988). Readers' views of what the photograph says about the subject must have something to do with the elevated class position they can assume their reading of *National Geographic* indicates. If I the reader am educated and highbrow in contrast to the reader of *People* magazine or the local newspaper, my gaze may take on the seriousness and appreciative stance a high-class cultural product requires.

THE NON-WESTERN SUBJECT'S GAZE

There is perhaps no more significant gaze in the photograph than that of its subject. How and where the photographed subject looks shapes the differences in the message a photograph can give about intercultural relations. The gaze of the non-Westerner found in *National Geographic* can be classified into at least four types; she or he can confront the camera, look at something or someone within the picture frame, look off into the distance, or not look at anything at all.

The gaze confronting the camera and reader comprises nearly a quarter of the photos that have at least some non-Western locals in them.[8] What does the look into the camera's eye suggest to readers about the photographic subject? A number of possibilities suggest themselves.

The look into the camera must at least suggest acknowledgement of photographer and reader. Film theorists have disagreed about what this look does, some arguing that it short circuits the voyeurism identified as an important component of most photography: there can be no peeping if the subject meets our gaze. The gaze can be confrontational: "I see you looking at me, so you cannot steal that look." Others, however, have argued that this look, while acknowledging the viewer, simply implies more open voyeurism: the return gaze does not contest the right of the viewer to look and may in fact be read as the subject's assent to being watched (Metz 1985: 800–801).

This disagreement hinges on ignoring how the look is returned and on discounting the effects of context inside the frame and in the reader's historically and culturally variable interpretive work. Facial expression is obviously crucial. The local person looks back with a number of different faces, including friendly smiling, hostile glaring, a vacant or indifferent glance, curiosity, or an ambiguous look. Some of these looks, from various ethnic others, are unsettling, disorganizing, and perhaps avoided. In *National Geographic*'s photos, the return look is, however, usually not a confrontational or challenging one. The smile plays an important role in muting the potentially disruptive, confrontational role of this return gaze. If the Other looks back at the camera and smiles, the combination can be read by viewers as the subject's assent to being surveyed. In 38% of the pictures of locals where facial expressions are visible (N=436), someone is smiling (although not all who smile are looking into the camera), while a higher 55% of all pictures in which someone looks back at the camera include one or more smiling figures.

The camera gaze can also establish at least the illusion of intimacy and communication. To the extent that *National Geographic* presents itself as bringing together the corners of the world, the portrait and camera gaze are important routes to those ends. The non-Westerner is not distanced, but characterized as approachable; the reader can imagine someone is about to speak to him or her. The photographers commonly view the frontal shot as a device for cutting across language barriers and allowing for intercultural communication. The portrait is, in the words of one early *Geographic* photographer, "a collaboration between subject and photographer" (National Geographic Society 1981: 22). In published form, of course, the photographed person is still "subjected to an unreturnable gaze" (Tagg 1988: 64), in no position to speak.

The magazine's goal of creating intimacy between subject and reader contradicts to some extent its official goal of presenting an unmanipulated, truthful slice of life from another country. Virtually all the photographers and picture editors we spoke with at the *National Geographic* saw the return gaze as problematic and believed that such pictures ought to be used sparingly because they are clearly not candid, and potentially influenced by the photographer. They might also be "almost faking intimacy," one editor said. Another mentioned that the use of direct gaze is also a question of style, suggesting more commercial and less "gritty" values. The photographer can achieve both the goals of intimacy and invisibility by taking portraits which are not directly frontal, but in which the gaze angles off to the side of the camera.

To face the camera is to permit close examination of the photographed subject, including scrutiny of the face and eyes which are in common sense parlance the seat of soul, personality or character. Frontality is a central technique of a "documentary rhetoric" in photography (Tagg 1988: 189); it sets the stage for either critique or celebration, but in either case evaluation of the other as a person or type. Editors at the magazine talked about their search for the "compelling face" in selecting photos for the magazine.

Racial, age, and gender differences appear in how often and how exactly the gaze is returned and lend substance to each of these perspectives on the camera gaze. To a statistically significant degree, women look into the camera more than men, children and older people look into the camera more often than other adults, those who appear poor more than those who appear wealthy, those whose skin is very dark more than those who are bronze, those who are bronze more than those whose skin is white, those in native dress more than those in Western garb, those without any tools more than those using machinery.[9] Those who are culturally defined by the West as weak—women, children, people of color, the poor, the tribal rather than the modern, those without technology— are more likely to face the camera, the more powerful to be represented looking elsewhere. There is also an intriguing (but not statistically significant) trend towards higher rates of looking at the camera to occur in pictures taken in countries that were perceived as friendly towards the United States.[10]

To look out at the viewer, then, would appear to represent not a confrontation between the West and the rest, but the accessibility of the latter. This interpretation is supported by the fact that historically the frontal portrait has been associated with the "rougher" classes, as the Daumier print points out (see Fig. 2). Tagg (1988), in a social history of photography, argues that this earlier class-based styling was passed on from portraiture to the emerging use of photography for the documentation and surveillance of the criminal and the insane.

Camera gaze is often associated with full frontal posture in the *National Geographic*; as such, it is also part of frontality's work as a "code of social inferiority" (Tagg 1988: 37). The "civilized" classes, at least since the nineteenth century, have traditionally been depicted in Western art turning away from the camera and so making themselves less available.[11] The higher status person may thus be characterized as too absorbed in weighty matters to attend to the photographer's agenda. Facing the camera, in Tagg's terms, "signified the bluntness and 'naturalness' of a culturally unsophisticated class [and had a history which predated photography]" (1988: 36).

These class coded styles of approach and gaze before the camera in gestures have continued to have force and utility in renderings of the ethnic other. The twist here is that the more civilized quality imparted to the lighter skinned male in Western dress and to adult exotics who turn away from the camera is only a relative quality. Full civilization still belongs, ideologically, to the Euro-American.

C.
Lutz &
J.
Collins

Fig. 2. A gaze toward the viewer, in *National Geographic*'s photographs, appears to represent the accessibility of the photographic subject. Historically, frontal portraits have been associated with low-class status, as suggested by this 1853 Daumier print, "Pose de l'homme de la nature" and "Pose de l'homme civilisé."

Whether these categories of people have actually looked at the camera more readily and openly is another matter. If the gaze toward the camera reflected only a lack of familiarity with it, then one would expect rural people to look at the camera more than urban people. This is not the case. One might also expect some change over time, as cameras became more common everywhere, but there is no difference in rate of gaze when the period from 1950 to 1970 is compared with the later period. The heavy editorial hand at the *Geographic* argues that what is at work is a set of unarticulated perceptions about the kinds of non-Westerners who make comfortable and interesting subjects for the magazine. *National Geographic* editors select from a vast array of possible pictures on the basis of some notion about what the social/power relations are between the reader and the particular ethnic subject being photographed. These aesthetic choices are outside explicit politics but encode politics nonetheless. A "good picture" is a picture which makes sense in terms of prevailing ideas about the other, including ideas about both accessibility and difference.

In a second form of gaze by the photographed subject, the non-Westerner looks at someone or something evident within the frame. The ideas readers get about who the Other is are often read off from this gaze which is taken as an index of interest, attention, or goals. The Venezuelan prospector who looks at the diamonds as they are being weighed by the buyer is interested in selling, in making money, rather than in the Western viewer or other compatriots. The caption supplies details: "the hard-won money usually flies fast in gambling and merry-making at primitive diamond camps, where riches-to-rags tales abound." And in a 1966 picture showing Ferdinand and Imelda Marcos happily staring at their children, the audience is thereby assured of their family-oriented character.

A potential point of interest in many photographs is a Western traveler. In 10% of these latter pictures, at least one local looks into the camera. Yet in 22% of the pictures in which only locals appear, someone looks into the camera. To a statistically significant degree, then, the Westerner in the frame draws a look away from those Westerners beyond the camera, suggesting both that these two kinds of Westerners might stand in for each other, as well as indexing the interest they are believed to have for locals.

Third, the Other's gaze can run off into the distance beyond the frame. This behavior can suggest radically different things about the character of the subject. It might portray either a dreamy, vacant, absent-minded person or a forward looking, future-oriented, and determined one. Compare the October 1980 photo of three Argentinean gauchos as they dress for a rodeo with the November 1980 shot of a group of six Australian Aborigines as they stand and sit in a road to block a government mining survey team. Two of the gauchos, looking out the window at a point in the far distance, come across as thoughtful, pensive, and sharply focused on the heroic tasks in front of them. The Aboriginal group includes seven gazes, each heading off in a different direction and only one clearly focused on something within the frame, thus giving the group a disconnected and unfocused look. It becomes harder to imagine this group of seven engaged in coordinated or successful action; that coordination would require mutual planning and, as a corollary, at least some mutual gaze during planning discussions. Character connotations aside, the out-of-frame look may also have implications for viewer identification with the subject, in some sense connecting with the reader outside the frame (Metz 1985: 795).

Finally, in many pictures, no gaze at all is visible, either because the individuals in them are tiny figures lost in a landscape or in a sea of others, or because the scene is dark or the person's face is covered by a mask or veil. We might read this kind of picture (14% of the whole sample) as being about the landscape or activity rather than the people or as communicating a sense of nameless others or group members rather than individuals. While these pictures do not increase in number over the period, there has been a sudden spate of recent covers in which the face or eyes of a non-Western person photographed are partly hidden (November 1979, February 1983, October 1985, August 1987, October 1987, November 1987, July 1988, February 1991, December 1991). Stylistically, *National Geographic* photographers may now have license to experiment with elements of the classical portrait with its full-face view, but the absence of any such shots before 1979 can also be read as a sign of a changing attitude about the possibilities of cross-cultural communication. The covered face can tell a story of a boundary erected, contact broken.

In its articles on the non-Western world, the *National Geographic* has frequently included photographs that show a Western traveler in the local setting covered in the piece. During the post-war period, these Western travelers have included adventurers, mountain climbers, and explorers; anthropologists, geographers, botanists, and archaeologists; U.S. military personnel; tourists; and government officials or functionaries from the U.S. and Europe from Prince Philip and Dwight Eisenhower to members of the Peace Corps. These photographs show the Westerners viewing the local landscape from atop a hill, studying an artifact, showing a local tribal person some wonder of Western technology (a photograph, mirror or the camera itself), or interacting with a native in conversation, work or play. The Westerner may stand alone or with associates, but more often is framed together with one or more locals.

C. Lutz & J. Collins

These pictures can have complex effects on viewers for they represent more explicitly than most the intercultural relations it is thought or hoped obtain between the West and its global neighbors. They may allow identification with the Westerner in the photo and, through that, more interaction with, or imaginary participation in, the photo. Before exploring these possibilities, however, we will speculate on some of the functions these photographs serve in the magazine.

Most obviously, the pictures of Westerners can serve a validating function by proving that the author was there, that the account is a first-hand one, brought from the field rather than from the library or photographic archives. In this respect, the photography sequences in *National Geographic* articles resemble traditional ethnographic accounts, which are written predominantly in the third person but often include at least one story in the first person that portrays the anthropologist in the field (Marcus and Cushman 1982). For this purpose, it does not matter whether the Westerner stands alone with locals.

To serve the function of dramatizing intercultural relations, however, it is helpful to have a local person in the frame. When the Westerner and the other are positioned face-to-face, we can read their relationship and natures from such features as Goffman (1979) has identified in his study of advertising photography's representation of women and men—their relative height, the leading and guying behaviors found more often in pictured males, the greater emotional expressiveness of the women and the like.[12] What the Westerners and non-Westerners are doing, the relative vantage points from which they are photographed, and their facial expressions give other cues to their moral and social characters.

The mutuality or non-mutuality of the gaze of the two parties can also tell us who has the right and/or need to look at whom. When the reader looks out at the world through this proxy Westerner, does the other look back? Here we can look at the February 1960 issue showing two female travelers looking at an Ituri Forest man in central Africa (see Fig. 3). Standing in the upper left hand corner, the two women smile down at the native figure in the lower right foreground. He looks towards the ground in front of them, an ambiguous expression on his face. The lines of their gaze have crossed but do not meet; because of this lack of reciprocity, the women's smiles appear bemused and patronizing. Their smiles are neither returned friendly greetings nor can we discern any reason for their smiles in the man's behavior. In its lack of reciprocity, the gaze *is distinctly colonial*. The Westerners do not seek a relationship but are content, even pleased, to view the other as an ethnic object. The composition of the picture, structured by an oblique line running from the women down to the man, shows the Westerners standing over the African; the slope itself can suggest, as Maquet (1986) has pointed out for other visual forms, the idea of *descent* or decline from the one (the Western women) to the other.

A related function of this type of photo lies in the way it prompts the viewer to become self-aware, not just in relation to others, but as a viewer, as one who looks or surveys. Mulvey (1985) argues that the gaze in cinema takes three forms—in the camera, the audience, and the

Fig. 3. Photographs in which Western travelers are present encode complete messages about intercultural relations. The nonreciprocal gazes in this February 1960 picture encode distinctly colonial social relations. Photo: Lowell Thomas, Jr., 1954.

characters as they look at each other or out at the audience. She says that the first two forms have to be invisible or obscured if the film is to follow realist conventions and bestow on itself the qualities of "reality, obviousness, and truth." The viewer who becomes aware of his or her own eye or that of the camera will develop a "distancing awareness" rather than an immediate unconscious involvement. Transferring this insight to the *National Geographic* photograph, Mulvey might say that bringing the Western eye into the frame promotes distancing rather than immersion. Alvarado (1979/80) has also argued that such intrusion can reveal contradictions in the social relations of the West and the rest that are otherwise less visible, undermining the authority of the photographer by showing the photo being produced, showing it to be an artifact rather than an unmediated fact.[13] Whether or not Westerners appear in the picture, we *are* there, but in pictures that include a Westerner, we may see ourselves being viewed by the Other, and we become aware of ourselves as actors in the world. The act of seeing the self being seen is antithetical to the voyeurism which many art critics have identified as intrinsic to most photography and film (Alloula 1986; Burgin 1982; Metz 1985).

This factor might best account for the finding that Westerners retreat from the photographs after 1969 (see Fig. 4). Staffers in the photography department said that pictures including the article's author came to be seen as outdated and so they were eliminated. Photographer and writer were no longer to be the stars of the story, we were told, although text continued to be written in the first person. As more and more readers had traveled to the exotic locales of their articles, the *Geographic* staff saw that the picture of the intrepid traveler no longer looked so intrepid. While the rise in international tourism may have had this effect, other social changes of the late 1960s contributed as well. In 1968, popular American protest against participation in the Vietnam War reached a critical point. Massive anti-war demonstrations, the police riot at the Democratic Convention, and especially the Viet Cong's success in the Tet Offensive convinced many that the American role in Vietnam and, by extension, the Third World, would have to be radically reconceptualized. The withdrawal or retreat of American forces came to be seen as inevitable, even though there were many more years of conflict over how, when and why. American power had come into question for the first time since the end of World War II. Moreover, the assassinations of Malcolm X and Martin Luther King, and the fire of revolt in urban ghettoes, gave many white people a sense of changing and more threatening relations with people of color within the boundaries of the United States.

C.
Lutz &
J.
Collins

Most of the non-*Geographic* photos now considered iconic representations of the Vietnam War do not include American soldiers or civilians. The girl who, napalmed, runs down a road towards the camera; the Saigon police chief executing a Viet Cong soldier; the Buddhist monk in process of self-immolation—each of these photographs, frequently reproduced, erases American involvement.

The withdrawal of Americans and other Westerners from the photographs of *National Geographic* may involve a historically similar process. The decolonization process accelerated in 1968 and led Americans (including, one must assume, the editors of *National Geographic*) to see the Third World as a more dangerous place, a place where they were no longer welcome to walk and survey as they pleased. The decreasing visibility of Westerners signaled a retreat from a Third World seen as a less valuable site for Western achievement and as a place of more difficult access and control. The decolonization process was

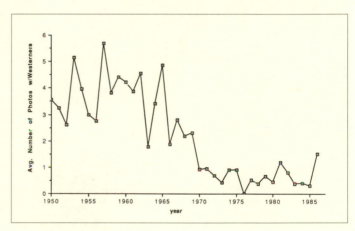

Fig. 4. Average number of photos per article containing Westerners, 1950–86.

and is received as a threat to an American view of itself. In Lacan's terms, the Other's look could threaten an American sense of self-coherence and so in this historical moment the Westerner—whose presence in the picture makes it possible for us to see ourselves being seen by that Other—withdraws to look from a safer distance, behind the camera.

THE REFRACTED GAZE OF THE OTHER: TO SEE THEMSELVES AS OTHERS SEE THEM

In a small but nonetheless striking number of *National Geographic* photographs, a native is shown with a camera, a mirror or mirror equivalent in his or her hands. Take the photograph in which two Aivilik men in northern Canada sit on a rock in animal skin parkas, one smiling and the other pointing a camera out at the landscape (November, 1956). Or the picture that shows two Indian women dancing as they watch their image in a large wall mirror. Or the picture from March of 1968 that shows Governor Brown of California on Tonga showing a group of children Polaroid snapshots he has just taken of them (March, 1968).

Fig. 5. A surprising number of *Geographic* photographs feature mirrors and cameras, with Westerners offering third-world peoples glimpses of themselves. In this August 1956 picture, a staff artist in what was then French Equatorial Africa shows a woman "her look-alike." Photo: Volkmar Kurt Wentzel, © National Geographic Society.

Mirror and camera are tools of self-reflection and surveillance. Each creates a double of the self, a second figure who can be examined more closely than the original—a double that can also be alienated from the self, taken away, as a photograph can be, to another place. Psychoanalytic theory notes that the infant's look into the mirror is a significant step in ego formation because it permits the child to see itself for the first time as an other. The central role of these two tools in American society (for example, its millions of bathrooms have mirrors as fixtures nearly as important as their toilet) stems at least in part from their self-reflective capacities. For many Americans, self-knowledge is a central life goal; the injunction to "know thyself" is taken seriously.

The mirror most directly suggests the possibility of self-awareness, and Western folktales and literature provide many examples of characters (often animals like Bambi or wild children like Kipling's Mowgli) who come upon the mirrored surface of a lake or stream and

Fig. 6. This February 1925 photograph is captioned "His first mirror: Porter's boy seeing himself as others see him," suggesting that self-awareness comes with Western contact and technology. Photo: Felix Shay, © National Geographic Society.

see themselves for the first time in a kind of epiphany of newly acquired self-knowledge. Placing the mirror in non-Western hands makes an interesting picture for Western viewers because this theme can interact with the common perception that the non-Western native remains at least somewhat child-like and cognitively immature. Lack of self-awareness implies a lack of history (Wolf 1982); he or she is not without consciousness but is relatively without self-consciousness. The myth is that history and change are primarily characteristic of the West and that historical self-awareness was brought to the rest of the world with "discovery" and colonization.[14]

In the article "Into the Heart of Africa" (August 1956), a magazine staff member on expedition is shown sitting in his Land-Rover holding open a *National Geographic* magazine to show a native woman a photograph of a woman of her tribe (see Fig. 5). Here the magazine serves the role of reflecting glass, as the caption tells us: "Platter-lipped woman peers at her look-alike in the mirror of *National Geographic*." The *Geographic* artist smiles as he watches the woman's face closely for signs of self-recognition; the fascination evident in his gaze is in the response of the woman, perhaps the question of how she "likes" her image, her own self. An early version of this type of photo a quarter of a century earlier shows an explorer in pith helmet who, with a triumphant smile, holds up a mirror to a taller, native man (see Fig. 6). He dips his head down to peer into it and we, the viewers, see not his expression but a redundant caption: "His first mirror: Porter's boy seeing himself as others see him." By contrast with the later photo, the explorer's gaze is not at the African but out towards the camera, indicating more interest in the camera's reception of this amusing scene than in searching the man's face for clues to his thinking. It also demonstrates the importance of manipulating relative height between races to communicate dominance. In the same genre, a Westerner in safari clothes holds a mirror up to a baboon (May 1955). Here as well, the *Geographic* plays with the boundary between nature and culture. The baboon, like Third-World peoples, occupies that boundary in the popular culture of white Westerners (see Haraway 1989); its response to the mirror can only seem humorously inadequate when engaged in the ultimately human and most adult of activities, self-reflection.

The mirror sometimes serves as a device to tell a story about the process of forming national identity. National self-reflection is presumed to accompany development, with the latter term suggesting a process that is both technological and psychosocial. The caption to a 1980 picture of a Tunisian woman looking into a mirror plays with this confusion between the individual and the nation, between the developing self awareness of mature adults and historically emergent national identity: "A moment for reflection: Mahbouba Sassi glances in the mirror to tie her headband. A wife and mother in the village of Takrouna, she wears garb still typical of rural women in the region. Step by step, Tunisia has, by any standards, quietly but steadily brought herself into the front rank of developing nations."

Cameras break into the frame of many *National Geographic* photographs. In some, a Westerner is holding the camera and showing a local group the photograph he has just taken of them. Here the camera, like the mirror, shows the native to himself. Frequently the picture is shown to children crowding happily around the Western cameraman. Historically it was first the mirror and then the camera that were thought to prove the superiority of the Westerner who invented and controls them (Adas 1989). In many pictures of natives holding a mirror or camera, the magazine plays with what McGrane (1989) identifies with the nineteenth-century European mind, that is, the notion "of a low threshold of the miraculous [in the non-Western native], of a seemingly childish lack of restraint" (1989: 50).

In other pictures, the native holds the camera. In one sense, this violates the prerogative of the Western surveyor to control the camera as well as other means of knowledge production. From an early point in the history of photography, its users recognized that the camera was a form of power. In an analysis of photographs of Middle-Eastern women, Graham-Brown (1988) provides evidence that colonial photographers were motivated to keep local subjects "at the lens-end of the camera" (61), and quotes one who, in 1890, complained, "It was a mistake for the first photographer in the Pathan [Afghanistan] country to allow the natives to look at the ground glass screen of the camera. He forgot that a little learning is a dangerous thing" (1988: 61). The camera could be given to native subjects only at risk of giving away that power.

Suggesting little peril, however, the pictures in *National Geographic* which place the camera in other hands create an amusing or quaint scene. A broad smile graces the face of the Aivilik man above who uses the camera lens to view the landscape with a companion (November 1956). At least one caption suggests that, although the subject goes behind the camera—in 1952 a young African boy looking through the viewfinder—what he looks out at is the imagined self at whom the Western photographer has been looking moments before: "Young Lemba sees others as the photographer sees him."

Such pictures were more common in the 1950s. We can detect a change, as decolonization proceeded, in the simple terms with which the problem is depicted in an amazing photograph

Fig. 7. A rare picture from August 1982 draws attention to the presence of the camera by photographing people being photographed for pay. Photo: O. Louis Mazzatenta, © National geographic Society.

from August 1982 (see Fig. 7). It sits on the right hand side of the page in an article entitled "Paraguay, Paradox of South America." The frame is nearly filled with three foreground figures—a white female tourist standing between an Amerindian woman and man, both in indigenous dress, both bare-chested. The three stand close together in a line, the tourist smiling with her arm on the shoulder of the sober-faced native woman. The tourist and the man, also unsmiling, face off slightly towards the left where a second camera (in addition to the one snapping the photo that appears in the magazine) takes their picture. The poses and the caption ask us to look at the natives as photographic subjects: "Portraits for pay: A tourist poses with members of the Maca Indian tribe on Colonia Juan Belaieff Island in the Paraguay River near Asunción. The Indians charge 80 cents a person each time they pose in a photograph . . . "

This rare photograph invites us into a contradictory, ambiguous, but in any case, highly charged scene. It is not a pleasant picture, in contrast with more typical *Geographic* style, because it depicts the act of looking at unwilling subjects, suggesting two things in the process. The first is the voyeurism of the photograph of the exotic. The camera gaze is *doubled* in this picture, not the native subject as in the photos above where the camera enters the frame in some explicit sense, and this doubling underlines that Western gaze. The picture's ambiguity lies in its suggestion that we are seeing a candid shot of a posed shot, and that we are looking at the subject look at us though in fact the Indian gaze is diverted 20 degrees from ours. This unusual structure of gaze draws attention to the commodified nature of the relationship between looker and looked-at. The Indians appear unhappy, even coerced; the tourist satisfied, presumably with her catch. Here too an apparent contradiction—the diverted gaze and its candid appearance suggest that the *National Geographic* photographer took this picture without paying, unlike the tourists; the caption suggests otherwise.

The photograph's potentially disturbing message for *National Geographic* readers is muted when one considers that the camera has not succeeded so much in representing the returned gaze of indigenous people as it has in taking the distance between Western viewer and non-Western subject one step farther, and in drawing attention to the photographer (and the artifice) between them. A symptom of alienation from the act of looking even while attention is drawn to it, this photo may exemplify a principle which Sontag says operates in all photography: "The photographer is supertourist, an extension of the anthropologist, visiting natives and bringing back news of their exotic doings and strange gear. The photographer is always trying to colonize new experiences, to find new ways to look at familiar subjects—to fight against boredom. For boredom is just the reverse side of fascination: both depend on being outside rather than inside a situation, and one leads to the other" (1977: 42). Avoiding boredom is crucial to retaining readers' interest and membership as well.

One could also look at the photograph from a 1990 issue on Botswana showing a French television crew—in full camera and sound gear and from a distance of a few feet—filming two Dzu men in hunting gear and "authentic" dress. The Frenchmen enthusiastically instruct the hunters in stalking posture, and the caption critiques them, noting that they have dressed up the natives (who otherwise wear Western clothing) for the benefit of European consumers. While this photograph is valuable in letting the reader see how images are constructed rather than found, its postmodern peek behind the scenes may also do what Gitlin notes contemporary journalism has done: engaged in a demystifying look at how image-makers control the face political candidates put forward, they encourage viewers to be "cognoscenti of their own bamboozlement" (1990).

Ultimately the magazine itself is a mirror for the historical, cultural, and political economic contexts of its production and use. That context is reflected in the magazine's images themselves, but not in a simple reflective way, as either the objectivist myth of the nature of cameras and mirrors or as the Althusserian notion of a "specular," or mirror-like ideology (in which the subject simply recognizes him or herself) would have it. It is perhaps more in the form of a rippled lake whose many intersecting lines present a constantly changing and emergent image.

THE ACADEMIC SPECTATOR

In one sense, this gaze is simply a sub-type of the reader's gaze. It emerges out of the same American middle class experiential matrix with its family of other cultural representations, its formal and informal schooling in techniques for interpreting both photograph and cultural difference, and its social relations. We read the *National Geographic* with a sense of astonishment, absorption, and wonder, both as children and, in a way that is different only some of the time, as adults. All of the looks embedded in the pictures are ultimately being filtered for you the reader through this, our own gaze. At times during this project, we have looked at an American magazine reader who is looking at a photographer's looking at a Western explorer who is looking at a Polynesian child who is looking at the explorer's photographed snapshot of herself moments earlier. While this framing of the seventh look might suggest that it is simply a more convoluted and distanced voyeurism, it can be distinguished from other kinds of readers' gazes including the voyeuristic and the hierarchic by both its distinctive intent and the sociological position (white, middle class, female, academic) from which it comes. Its intent is not aesthetic appreciation or formal description, but critique of the images in spite of, because of, and in terms of their pleasures. We aim to make the pictures tell a different story than they were originally meant to tell, one about their makers and readers rather than their subjects.[15] The critique arises out of a desire "to anthropologize the West," as Rabinow (1986) suggests we might, and to denaturalize the images of difference in the magazine in part because those images and the institution which has produced them have historically articulated too easily with the shifting interests and positions of the state. The strong impact of the magazine on popular attitudes suggests that anthropological teaching or writing purveys images which, even if intended as oppositional (certainly not always the case), may simply be subsumed or bypassed by the *National Geographic* view of the world.

C.
Lutz &
J.
Collins

In addition, a suspicion of the power of images is here, as they exist in a field more populated with advertising photography than anything else. The image is experienced daily as a sales technique or as a trace of the commodity. That experience is, at least for us, and perhaps for other readers, transferred to some degree to the experience of seeing *National Geographic* images. Even if we are simply "invited to dream" in the photograph, we are also invited to forget and to be lost in it.

Our reading of theory has also tutored our gaze at the photographs in distinctive ways, told us how to understand the techniques by which they work, how to find our way to something other than an aesthetic or literal reading, suggesting that we view them as cultural artifacts. It also suggested that we avoid immersion in the many pleasures of the richly colored and exotically peopled photographs, as in Alloula's reading of Algerian colonial period postcards. He notes his analytic need to resist the "aestheticizing temptation" (1986: 116) to see beauty in those cards, a position predicated in part on a highly deterministic view of their hegemonic effect.[16] Alternatively, more positive views of the political implications of visual pleasure exist, a view which Jameson (1983) and others argue is achieved in part by unlinking a prevalent disdain for popular culture products from the issue of pleasure. Validating both seemingly contradictory views, however, would seem to be the fact that the seductiveness of the pictures both captures and instructs us. We are captured by the temptation to view the photographs as more real than the world or at least as a comfortable substitute for it—to imagine at some level a world of basically happy, classless, even noble, people in conflict neither with themselves nor with "us." These and other illusions of the images we have found in part through our own vulnerability to them. The pleasures are also instructive, however. They come from being given views, without having to make our own efforts to get them, of a world different, however slightly, from the American middle class norm. The considerable beauty with which those lives are portrayed can potentially challenge the latter, as well.

Concluding Remarks

The many relations of looking represented in all photographs are at the very foundation of the kinds of meaning that can be found or made in them. The multiplicity of looks is at the root of a photo's ambiguity, each gaze potentially suggesting a different way of viewing the scene. Moreover, a visual "illiteracy" leaves most of us with few resources for understanding or integrating the diverse messages these looks can produce. Multiple gaze is the source of many of the photograph's contradictions, highlighting the gaps (as when some gazes are literally interrupted) and multiple perspectives of each person involved in the complex scene. It is the root of much of the photograph's dynamism as a cultural object, and the place where the analyst can perhaps most productively begin to trace its connections to the wider social world of which it is a part. Through attention to the dynamic nature of these intersecting gazes, the photograph becomes less vulnerable to the charge or illusion that it masks or stuffs and mounts the world, freezes the life out of a scene, or violently slices into time. While the gaze of the subject of the photograph may be difficult to find in the heavy crisscrossing traffic of the more privileged gazes of producers and consumers, contemporary stories of contestable power are told there nonetheless.

Notes

1. This essay, which appeared originally in *V.A.R.*, is drawn substantially from a book (Lutz and Collins 1993) that examines the production and consumption of *National Geographic* photographs of the "non-Western" world in the post World War II period. That book and this essay is in part based on an analysis of 600 photographs from that period; on several visits to the Washington headquarters where the magazine is produced and interviews conducted there with a number of photographers, picture editors, caption writers, layout and design people, and others; and on interviews with 55 individuals from upstate New York and Hawaii who "read" a set of Geographic photographs for us. The present essay benefits extensively from the coding and analytic help of Tammy Bennington, and from the stimulating comments on earlier drafts by Lila Abu-Lughod, Tamara Bray, Phoebe Ellsworth, John Kirkpatrick, Daniel Rosenberg, Lucien Taylor and anonymous reviewers for *V.A.R.*
    The term "non-Western" which bounds the project is awkward but represents our focus on the world outside the boundaries of the United States and Europe and our interest in how these powerful world areas (which include almost all of the magazine's readers) have constructed and construed other peoples. Our analysis here and elsewhere suggests that, despite some important distinctions which these readers can and do make within the category of the "non-Western," there is a fundamental process of identity formation at work in which all "exotics" play the primary role of being not Western, not a white, middle class reader.

2. The same of course can be said for other categories of people who share a marked quality with the non-Westerner, including physical deviants (Diane Arbus' pictures, for example), the criminal (Tagg 1988), and, most commonly, women (e.g., Goffman 1979).

3. The differences between painting and photography are also important. The gaze cannot be altered at will or completely to taste, and so the looks that are exchanged in *National Geographic* photographs can be seen as more disappointing and less pacifying than are, for example, Gauguin's pictures of Polynesian women.

4. This analysis resembles the less psychoanalytically freighted work of Sider on the stereotype in Indian-white relations. Sider frames the problem as one of "the basic contradiction of this form of domination—*that is cannot both create and incorporate the other as an other*—thus opening a space for continuing resistance and distancing" (1987: 22).

5. Ellsworth's research (e.g., 1975) on gaze in natural and experimental contacts between people (conducted in the United States) has been central in making the argument for a thoroughly contextual view of looking relations in the discipline of psychology.

6. An early typology of the gaze from a colonial and racist perspective is found in Sir Richard Burton's accounts of his African expeditions, during which he felt himself to be the victim of "an ecstasy of curiosity". Wrote Burton: "At last my experience in staring enabled me to categorize the infliction as follows. Firstly is the stare furtive, when the starer would peep and peer under the tent, and its reverse, the open stare. Thirdly is the stare curious or intelligent, which generally was accompanied with irreverent laughter regarding our appearance. Fourthly is the stare stupid, which denoted the hebete incurious savage. The stare discreet is that of Sultans and greatmen; the stare indiscreet at unusual seasons is affected by women and children . . . Sixthly is the stare flattering—it was exceedingly rare, and equally so was the stare contemptuous. Eighthly is the stare greedy; it was denoted by the eyes restlessly bounding from one object to another, never tired, never satisfied. Ninthly is the stare peremptory and pertinacious, peculiar to crabbed age. The dozen concludes with the stare drunken, the stare fierce or pugnacious, and finally the stare cannibal, which apparently considered us as articles of diet." (Burton in Moorehead 1960: 33). One can imagine a similarly hostile categorization of white Westerners staring at "exotics" over the past centuries.

7. Some contemporary photographers are experimenting with these conventions (in point of view or framing) in an effort to undermine this equation. Victor Burgin, for example, intentionally attempts to break this down by making photographs that are "'occasions for interpretation' rather than . . . 'objects of consumption'" and that thereby require a gaze which more actively produces itself rather than simply accepting the photographer's gaze as its own. While one can question whether any *National Geographic* photograph is ever purely an object of consumption, the distinction is an important one and alerts us to the possibility that the photographer can encourage or discourage, through technique, the relative independence of the viewer's gaze.

8. This figure is based on 438 photographs coded in this way, 24% of which had a subject looking at the camera.

9.   These analyses were based on those photos where gaze was visible, and excluded pictures with a Westerner in the photo. The results were, for gender (N=360) x^2=3.835, df=1, p<.05; for age (N=501) x^2=13.745, df=4, p<.01; for wealth (N=507) x^2=12.950, df=2, p<.01; for skin color (N=417) x^2=8.704, df=3, p<.05; for dress style (N=452) x^2=12.702, df=1, p<.001; and for technology (N=287) x^2=4.172, df=1, p<.05. Discussing these findings in the Photography Department, we were given the pragmatic explanation that children generally are more fearless in approaching photographers, while men often seem more wary of the camera than women, especially when it is wielded by a male photographer.

10.   In the sample of pictures from Asia in which gaze is ascertainable (N=179), "friendly" countries (including the PRC after 1975, Taiwan, Hong Kong, South Korea, Japan, and the Philippines) had higher rates of smiling than "unfriendly" or neutral countries (x^2=2.101, df=1, p=.147). Excluding Japan, which may have had a more ambiguous status in American eyes, the relationship between gaze and "friendliness" reaches significance (x^2=4.14, df=1, p<.05).

11.   Tagg notes that the pose was initially the pragmatic outcome of the technique of the Physiono-trace, a popular mechanism used to trace a person's profile from shadow onto a copper plate. When photography took the place of the Physionotrace, no longer requiring profiles, the conventions of associating class with non-frontality continued to have force.

12.   For example, Goffman (1979) draws on ethological insights into height and dominance relations when he explains why women are almost always represented as shorter than men in print advertisements. He notes that "so thoroughly is it assumed that differences in size will correlate with differences in social weight that relative size can be routinely used as a means of ensuring that the picture's story will be understandable at a glance" (*ibid.*: 28).

13.   The documentary filmmaker Dennis O'Rourke, whose films *Cannibal Tours* and *Half Life: A Parable for the Nuclear Age* explore Third World settings, develops a related argument for the role of reflexivity for the imagemaker (Lutkehaus 1989). He consistently includes himself in the scene, but distinguishes between simple self-revelation on the part of the filmmaker and rendering the social relations between him and his subjects, including capturing the subject's gaze in such a way as to show his or her "complicity" with the filmmaker. O'Rourke appears to view the reader's gaze more deterministically (for example, as "naturally" seeing the complicity in a subject's gaze) than do the theorists considered above.

14.   Compare the pictures of natives looking into a mirror with that of an American woman looking into the shiny surface of the airplane she is riveting in the August 1944 issue. It is captioned, "No time to prink [primp] in the mirror-like tail assembly of a Liberator." The issue raised by this caption is not self-knowledge (Western women have this), but female vanity, or rather its transcendence by a woman who, man-like, works in heavy industry during the male labor shortage period of World War II. Many of these mirror pictures evoke a tradition of painting in Western art in which Venus or some other female figure gazes into a mirror in a moment of self-absorption. Like those paintings, this photo operate "within the convention that justifies male voyeuristic desire by aligning it with female narcissistic self-involvement" (Snow 1989: 38).

15.   Our interviews with readers show that they do not always ignore the frame, but also sometimes see the photograph as an object produced by someone in a concrete social context.

16.   Alloula seems not to broach the possibility of alternative kinds of pleasure (or, more broadly, positive effects or readings) in the viewing because the photos are seen to have are singular ends and because of his fear of what he terms an "intoxication, a loss of oneself in the other through sight" (1986: 49).

C.
Lutz &
J.
Collins

References

Adas, Michael. 1989. *Machines as the Measure of Men*. Ithaca: Cornell University Press.

Alloula, Malek. 1986. *The Colonial Harem*. Minneapolis: University of Minnesota Press.

Alvarado, Manuel. 1979/80. "Photographs and narrativity." *Screen Education* (Autumn/Winter): 5–17.

Barthes, Roland. 1977. "The Photographic Message." In *Image-Music-Text*, trans. Stephen Heath. Glasgow: Fontana/Collins.

Berger, John. 1972. *Ways of Seeing*. London: British Broadcasting Corporation and Penguin Books.

Bhabha, Homi K. 1983. "The Other Question: Homi K. Bhabha Reconsiders the Stereotype and Colonial Discourse." *Screen* 24 (6): 18–36.

Burgin, Victor, ed. 1982. *Thinking Photography*. London: Macmillan.

———.1986. *The End of Art Theory: Criticism and Post-modernity*. Houndsmills, Basingstoke, Hampshire: Macmillan.

de Lauretis, Teresa. 1987. *Technologies of Gender: Essays on Theory, Film, and Fiction.* Bloomington: Indiana University Press.

Devereux, George. 1967. *From Anxiety to Method in the Behavioral Sciences.* The Hague: Mouton.

Ellsworth, Phoebe. 1975. "Direct Gaze as Social Stimulus: The Example of Aggression." In *Nonverbal Communication of Aggression,* ed. P. Pliner, L. Krames, and T. Alloway. New York: Plenum.

Foucault, Michel. 1977. *Discipline and Punish: The Birth of the Prison.* New York: Pantheon Books.

Gaines, Jane. 1988. "White Privilege and Looking Relations: Race and Gender in Feminist Film Theory." *Screen* 29 (4): 12–27.

Geary, Christraud M. 1988. *Images from Bamum: German Colonial Photography at the Court of King Njoya, Cameroon, West Africa, 1902–1915.* Washington, D.C.: Smithsonian Institution Press.

Gitlin, Todd. 1990. "Blips, bites and savvy talk." *Dissent* 37: 18–26.

Goffman, Erving. 1979. *Gender Advertisements.* New York: Harper and Row.

Graham-Brown, Sarah. 1988. *Images of Women: The Portrayal of Women in Photography of the Middle East, 1860–1950.* London: Quartet Books.

Green, David. 1984. "Classified Subjects." *Ten-8* 8 (14): 30–37.

———.1989. "Burgin and Sekula." *Ten-8* 26: 30–43.

Haraway, Donna J. 1989. *Primate Visions: Gender, Race, and Nature in the World of Modern Science.* London: Routledge.

Jameson, Fredric. 1983. "Pleasure: A Political Issue." In *Formations of Pleasure,* ed. F. Jameson, 1–14. London: Routledge and Kegan Paul.

Julien, Isaac and Kobena Mercer. 1988. "Introduction: De Margin and De Centre." *Screen* 29 (4): 2–10.

Lacan, Jacques. 1981. *The Four Fundamental Concepts of Psychoanalysis.* New York: Norton.

Levine, Lawrence W. 1988. *Highbrow/Lowbrow: The Emergence of Cultural Hierarchy in America.* Cambridge: Harvard University Press.

Lutkehaus, Nancy C. 1989. "'Excuse me, Everything is Not Alright': On Ethnography, Film, and Representation. An Interview with Filmmaker Dennis O'Rourke." *Cultural Anthropology* 4: 422–437.

Lutz, Catherine and Jane Collins. 1993. *Reading National Geographic.* Chicago: University of Chicago Press.

Marcus, George E. and Dick Cushman. 1982. "Ethnographies as Text." *Annual Review of Anthropology.* 11: 25–69.

Maquet, Jacques. 1986. *The Aesthetic Experience.* New Haven: Yale University Press.

McGrane, Bernard. 1989. *Beyond Anthropology: Society and the Other.* New York: Columbia University Press.

Metz, Christian. 1985. "From The Imaginary Signifier." In *Film Theory and Criticism: Introductory Readings,* 3rd ed., ed. Gerald Mast and Marshall Cohen, 782–802. New York: Oxford University Press.

Moorehead, Alan. 1960. *The White Nile.* New York: Harper & Brothers.

Mulvey, Laura. 1975. "Visual Pleasure and Narrative Cinema." In *Film Theory and Criticism: Introductory Readings,* 3rd ed., ed., Gerald Mast and Marshall Cohen, 803–16. New York: Oxford University Press.

National Geographic Society. 1981. *Images of the World: Photography at the National Geographic.* Washington, D.C.: National Geographic Society.

Rabinow, Paul. 1986. "Representations are Social Facts: Modernity and Post-Modernity in Anthropology." In *Writing Culture,* ed. J. Clifford and G. Marcus, 234–61. Berkeley: University of California Press.

Radway, Janice. 1984. *Reading the Romance.* Chapel Hill: University of North Carolina Press.

Sider, Gerald. 1987. "When parrots learn to talk, and why they can't: domination, deception, and self-deception in Indian-White relations." *Comparative Studies in Society and History* 29: 3–23.

Snow, Edward. 1989. "Theorizing the Male Gaze: Some problems." *Representations* 25: 30–41.

Sontag, Susan. 1977. *On Photography.* New York: Dell/Delta.

Tagg, John. 1988. *The Burden of Representation.* Amherst: The University of Massachusetts Press.

Traube, Elizabeth G. 1992. *Dreaming Identities: Class, Gender, and Generation in 1980s Hollywood Movies.* Boulder, CO: Westview Press.

Williams, Anne. 1987. "Untitled." *Ten-8* 11: 6–11.

Wolf, Eric. 1982. *Europe and the People Without History.* Berkeley: University of California Press.

BBC Domesday
The Social Construction
of Britain on Videodisc

Alan Macfarlane

I N THE 1980S THE TWO MEDIA, TELEVISION AND COMPUTING, AIDED BY LASERS, BECAME UNIFIED into a new medium, interactive videodisc. This article will describe the most ambitious project in this field up to the present, namely the two "Domesday" videodiscs made by the British Broadcasting Corporation in the years 1984–1986. This project used the latest techniques in information retrieval and data storage to lay down, in electronic form, a portrait of British society in the 1980s. The scheme cost several million pounds and involved more than a million "authors." By examining from the inside how it was made, we can learn something about the potentials and limitations of a medium which, either in the form of videodisc or compact disc, is likely to be the most important technological development for visual anthropology of the next few years.

Precedents

Nine hundred years ago the Domesday Survey attempted to describe in two volumes the landholding system of most of England. It is nearly all concerned with property relations. The present survey by the British Broadcasting Corporation is not limited to what would now be classified as one section of "The Economy." The BBC has attempted to cover a much wider area, including the Environment, Society and Culture. Perhaps the closest precedent, which combined visual and textual materials and attempted to give a portrait of a society, was a series of beautifully illustrated books produced by Collins in the 1940s, collectively known as "Britain in Pictures." Yet this series, as well as other anticipations, such as Tom Harrison's "Mass Observation" project, only provide weak precedents for the BBC Domesday Videodisc Project.

A New Medium and a New Message

It is conventional when describing videodisc to single out its central feature as the marriage in the early 1980s of two technologies. On the one side the development of television, combined with advances in laser techniques, made it possible for the first time to inscribe and store pictures in a new way. It is now possible, on a disc the size of a gramophone record, to store up to 108,000 still visual images. There are also two tracks available to store sound or digitally encoded information. A little more than 300 megabytes of information (the equivalent of over one thousand normal floppy discs) can be held on each of the two sides of the disc. Put in the startling sales talk of the industry, this would mean that the text and illustrations of the *Encyclopedia Britannica* could be stored three times over on one videodisc. It is estimated that the whole of the Library of Congress, if stored in this form, would fit into a large sitting room. The medium will hold still photographs, moving films, graphics, texts, statistics and sound recordings.

This large quantity of material would be virtually unusable without a second development, namely in computing. There have been hardware advances which have led to a range of cheap and powerful micro-computers which can be linked to the videodisc. These are made particularly useful by the new information retrieval systems which have emerged from work on database systems and artificial intelligence The Domesday Discs make available to a much wider public a combined system which has the storage and searching power of a large mainframe computer, but are filled with data which no conventional computer could hold, sound and pictures, as well as statistics and texts.

That we are stepping away from previous media is indicated by attempts to speculate on what a videodisc really is. Peter Armstrong, the inspiration and general editor of the BBC Discs, goes through the possibilities. It is a sort of electronic book, and yet it is not really a book because one has random access to it. We might add that it is also different from a book both in scale and because the link to a microcomputer makes it possible to manipulate data in a new way. An interactive book is a new kind of book. Is it then an encyclopedia? Up to a point, but not entirely because it is not split into fixed "articles," nor is it attempting encyclopedic coverage. Is it a database with pictures and sound? It is indeed this, but this makes it different from all previous computerized databases. Armstrong argues that it is most helpful to think of the Discs as a kind of "electronic exhibition." He writes that this exhibition "tries to reflect many aspects of life today in just the same way that . . . the Great Exhibition of 1851 or the 1951 Festival of Britain did for their times . . . the visitor to the electronic exhibition can wander around freely, focusing on those elements that catch the eye."[1]

It would be fashionable, and to a limited extent helpful, to liken the Domesday Discs to other powerful images of our time, the mysterious secret library in Umberto Eco's *The Name of the Rose*, or the labyrinths which Borges has constructed. Indeed, to those familiar with the description of the finite yet infinite library described in Borges' account of "The Library of Babel," the Domesday Discs seem to be playing with the same paradox. It has been estimated that for someone working through it for forty hours a week, fifty weeks a year, sequentially, "it would take you about seven years to call up and examine all the material on the two discs."[2] Yet this is a limited way to search. Once one starts to compare, investigate, go down the diverging tracks, re-examine material, the library, archive or exhibition is endless.

An Open Audience

A. MacFarlane

It has been a characteristic of previous types of communication that they have to be aimed at a certain audience in time and space. For instance a book could be written for children living in the 1980s, or, more precisely, for upper middle-class, educated, English children. Even exhibitions have to be planned with a fairly delimited set of viewers in mind. Because of the strange nature of this medium, it can claim to address the world, present and future. Armstrong argues that the advantage of an electronic exhibition is that it can claim to be for everyone.[3] Although the promotional literature may turn out to be over-ambitious, it is worth noting the sort of audiences envisaged for the Discs. It will be of use in "Schools and colleges," "Libraries," "Commercial organizations," "Tourism and travel organizations," "Land and estate agents," "Courier and distribution services," "Local and national government offices," to "Writers and journalists," "Film and television companies," and "Regional Development agencies." It is difficult to think of any book, film, or even exhibition which could be addressed to such a diverse potential audience. There is also the later possibility of private use. It is not only directed to different interest groups, but different ages. Parts of the discs assume a reading age of only eight or nine, other parts assume full maturity and university education. One can go into them at almost any level.

It is open in another way in that it is consciously designed not only for the present, but also for the future. In origin, and largely in execution, the discs were "primarily intended as historical records," "it was this idea of the creation of a multi-media record of our times for use in the future that was the primary motivation in the creation of the Domesday Discs . . ." Thus "if the exhibition stands the test of time, it can equally be visited in the coming centuries by those who want to look back at what we thought, how we looked, what we did in the 1980s, and also—for what we decided to include in the exhibition—what we thought important."[4] It is not yet clear how long a disc will last; some say many centuries, others only a few years. If the optimists are right, then the discs may in the future be a major source for twentieth-century British history. My chief role on the editorial board was as a historian; it was my job to imagine what people in the future would like to know about and to make sure that at least some of the subjects were recorded and recoverable.

The Contents of an Electronic Exhibition

There are two discs. One is the "Community Disc," which is based on a geographical classification, the other the "National Disc" which is principally organized by topic. The "Community Disc" is meant to be a view from below, largely compiled by more than a million citizens of Great Britain; the "National Disc" is preponderantly compiled from official statistics and national sources. On the "Community Disc" the country was divided into 23,000 three by four kilometer squares. These were assigned to schools and other groups. They were asked to write a twenty-page essay, to supply three photographs, and to undertake a land use survey and amenities count in the assigned square. In the event, some 9,000 squares were covered, constituting the majority of the more densely populated parts of Britain, but large areas of moorland were not described. More than 20,000 photographs and 200,000 screen pages of information have been produced, which can be combined with the surveys and with a complete set of the latest Ordnance Survey maps at four levels, down to the 1:10,000 scale. The country is split onto the two sides of the Disc, as North and South. A unified gazetteer with 250,000 names allows one to find any place.

The schools and other groups were deliberately not told what to write about beyond suggesting that it should be a portrait of an area, "what people do there, what kind of environment it is. What do people there currently talk and think about? What are their hopes and fears?"[5] Consequently the photographs and texts are very varied. The headings for one rural parish (Dent in Cumbria) can be given as an example of what is covered. We have short pieces on the Town of Dent, farming, a typical child's day in 1985, the primary school, employment, inns, shops, arts and crafts, cobbled streets, Adam Sedgwick, the river Dee, flowers, sporting events, St. Andrew's Church, housing, changes during living memory, needs for the future. An example of what is written can be taken from a day in the life of a twelve-year-old boy in a suburb of Newcastle who starts "I get up at 6:15 a.m. to do my paper round. My dad has been unemployed now for two years, so I am the only wage earner in the family . . . (after school) . . . I'm off down to the woods with my friends. We have a secret den down there but it won't be secret any more now that I've told you! Sometimes we go chasing rabbits with dogs . . . "

The National Disc is divided in two. One side contains some sixty minutes of moving film, consisting of about 120 short clips arranged into montages for each of the years between 1980 and 1986. Almost all of these are news or sporting events. For instance, for 1983, the subjects included are: the Waldorf shooting, the launch of breakfast T.V., the Scotland vs. Wales rugger match, the People's march for jobs, Sebastian Coe winning a race, the Conservative landslide election victory, the hottest July for three hundred years, the Maze prison break out, Kinnock elected leader of the Labour Party, Cecil Parkinson resigning, the arrival of Cruise missiles, Torvill and Dean ice skating, three shot in Armagh Chapel, and the I.R.A. bomb at Harrods. At present it is only possible to select a year and then watch it through, in continuous play.

On the other side of the disc there are several sets of data. There are some 22,000 photographs divided into 512 picture sets. These include thirty portfolios by leading British photographers, about 5,000 photographs selected from entries in a national competition run by the BBC under headings such as "Work," "Leisure," "Home Life," and the rest chosen from photo archives and specialist collections. These cover "all those aspects of life in Britain in the 1980s that were felt to be essentially visual: contemporary art, street fashion and wildlife are obvious examples."[6] There are also nine sets of several hundred photographs taken by moving through a house or landscape and snapping every few feet in various directions. These "surrogate walks," round a council flat, a stone cottage, Brecon town centre and a Scottish pine forest, are an experiment to simulate moving through an area in any direction. Thus it is hoped that a future historian might be able to prowl round a number of houses, occasionally going up very close to examine the contents of a drawer or the ornaments on a shelf.

A second major data set consists of extended texts. There are 45 specially commissioned and signed essays. For instance, I was asked to cover "Customs and Traditions in the 1980s" in about two thousand words. At a more specific level, there are about two thousand articles from newspapers, journals, Government reports, press hand-outs, the ephemeral sheets of small organizations and other sources. Their inclusion is to cover two needs, in some cases to provide useful information, for instance on how the magistrate's courts work, in others to show a lively debate in progress, for instance over nuclear disarmament.

A third set of materials consists of some six thousand data sets, "each containing up to ten thousand cell values." This material was drawn from government reports and surveys and from the 1981 Census and General Household Survey, from specialist archives, from Universities. For instance, it has made available many of the most interesting data sets at the ESRC Survey Archive, at Birkbeck College, and at the Centre for Urban and Regional Development Studies at Newcastle. There are two major types of statistical data, mappable and tabular. As instances of the former, one can plot onto national, regional, county or even smaller areas certain types of mortality statistics, the distribution of types of footwear and clothing, the consumption of alcoholic drinks and the number of women in penal institutions. The 3,600 tabular data sets include topics such as attitude surveys, criminal sentencing patterns in 1983, the readership of daily morning papers over a ten-year period, the natural radioactivity in diet. Some 340 of the data sets have been specially prepared from material which was not machine-readable. Many of the data sets can now be compared because the project has reprocessed the raw statistics down to a common square-kilometer standard.

Finding and Examining Exhibits

There are several different ways to find one's way around this exhibition. One is the "gallery" concept which follows the idea of the electronic exhibition further, building on earlier work at the Massachusetts Institute of Technology. A simulated three-dimensional gallery has been created on the National Disc, again echoing Eco and Borges with a flavor of Lewis Carroll. This provides access to the visual materials on the disc, and some of the more general texts. One moves into a room, say "Popular Arts and Crafts" and finds iconic pictures on the wall, doorways apparently leading out into towns and houses, large signs with "Defence" or "Health" written on them. Using the cursor, one can go up to one of these and, by pointing, go "through" the icon, door, or label into the set of pictures, an essay, or surrogate walk.

A second way is to search down through hierarchical indexes. There are two main kinds. There is a geographical index whereby one can start at the whole of Britain, and then proceed by pointing to a specific area and go on down and down through layers of maps, sometimes ending at the street or even individual building level. When the right map is found it is possible to examine it in various ways, for instance find the exact grid reference of places on it, measure distances, or draw lines round an area and compute the surface area in the appropriate unit of miles, kilometers, yards or meters.

The other hierarchical index, on the National Disc, is by subject rather than by place. All the data sets are stored in a five-level hierarchy. Thus one might start by choosing one of the four top-level categories, say "Culture" rather than "The Economy," "Environment" or "Society." This would give a list of twelve second-level headings, for instance "Arts and Entertainment," "Beliefs and Attitudes," "Consumption," "Language" and so on. Each of these is further divided into a list of particular data sets, indicating pictures, films, maps and tables. This branching process enables a user to narrow down a general interest, or to group together material in a general field. The concepts of branching hierarchies, of a sort of segmentary system, based on computer notions of trees and nodes, is an important part of the conceptual system that the discs will teach.

The third searching system is through a keyword retrieval method. This is largely based on information retrieval experiments in Cambridge in the 1970s. A user is asked what topic or subject he or she is interested in and can type in a single word or string of words. One could type in a broad category such as "Crime" and obtain several hundred data sets, or narrow it down by something more specific such as "Magistrates" when one will be presented with a few. A string of words may be typed in, either in the grammatical form "The use of trawlers in North Sea fishing," or as a string of key words "Fishing North Sea Trawlers." Both of these are treated in the same way. All words are reduced to their stems. Thus queries for fishing, fishes, fish, fisheries, will produce the same list. Very common and general words with little meaning are ignored; thus, "the," "use," "of," "in" would be stripped out in the query above. The computer program then looks through for matches, starting with "perfect" matches, where all the terms occur in a data-set title. These are presented at the top of a list, which then goes on through the data-set titles presenting them in order of decreasing similarity. Thus if only one term out of four is missing, that title is listed next and so on. There is a good deal of flexibility and serendipity in the system, and lower down a list a user may well find an unexpectedly apposite data set. One often finds some very odd inclusions because of the multiple meanings of words combined with the stripping to stems. On the "National

Disc," the system is searching the titles of the thousands of data sets. On the "Community Discs," the schools were asked to provide four keywords or key phrases for each page of text. These were to be of a fairly general kind such as "traffic," historic houses," "vandalism" or "fishing." Each photograph on the "Community Disc" was also captioned with key words. These keywords and captions can be accessed through the search program.

The main refinement in the analysis of material, apart from the mapping programs already mentioned, is the use of the power of the microcomputer to present statistical data in a variety of graphical forms. The displays that are drawn on the screen are not merely prearranged patterns like the graphs or maps one might find produced in a book or exhibition. "The basic philosophy of Domesday is to give you access to the raw data you need to construct your own displays of the data and enable you to draw your own conclusions about its meaning. Therefore, the data on the disc is stored as raw values and there are ways to display these actual numbers."[7] Suppose one is interested in a mappable data set, one can control the maps produced from the raw values in various ways. One can select the area to be covered, for instance the population in institutions, for the whole country, for a specific county, or for other delimited areas. On the map one can alter the interpretation by altering the scale on which the data is plotted, large blocks or very tiny squares, one can change the class intervals of the data, one can change the coloring and meaning of colors. Through the manipulation of these and other techniques one can work out correlation coefficients between different maps. Perhaps it was hardly surprising to find a correlation for England of 0.948 between maps of ethnic minority households and a map of all foreign-born households. But more adventurous associations could be attempted. It is also possible to overlay maps onto a background to show visually to what extent values overlap, where both the variables are present in one place, and where they occur independently.

The analysis of tabular data sets gives the user other tools. The data is first presented as a graph with two axes, for instance the number of members of different religions in Britain on the vertical scale, the type of group plotted along the horizontal scale, Anglican, Roman Catholic, Spiritualist, Muslim, Sikh and so on. This is first presented as a bar chart. By pointing at the relevant bar we can discover that over the three census points, 1975, 1980 and 1985, there were a total of, for instance, 162,000 members of spiritualist churches, 256,000 Jehovah's Witnesses. In this particular case, the variable of year can be changed and the computer can re-plot the data of any or all of these years. From this, for instance, we find that Anglican membership declined from 2,272,000 in 1975 to 2,508,000 in 1985, while Muslim membership increased in the same period from 400,000 to 900,000, and Mormons similarly increased from 80,000 to 102,000. Naturally, it is necessary to look at the text which is provided to see what is meant by "Membership," "Spiritualist churches," the source of the surveys and so on. This is a relatively simple table, though the possibilities of manipulating it, for instance putting together several religious groups and re-plotting, or of altering the vertical axis to bring out more detail, are already considerable. Furthermore, the display may more conveniently be looked at as a bar chart, a pie chart, a back-to-back bar chart, as a line graph, or as a loop bar. The last of these runs through the data by a certain variable, for instance displaying religious membership in 1975 for ten seconds, then moving through each year in turn and so on back to the beginning. This helps the eye detect trends. In other tables one can change a string of variables and sub-select small populations. For instance, if one were examining the "informal economy" and its effects on morality one might look at the table on the numbers of those who confessed to fiddling their expenses at work. This can be re-plotted for five-year age groups, for marital status, for each of ten standard regions of England, and for the age at completing full time education.

As a result of the assembly and access systems, it is "worth bearing in mind as you build a Domesday data map that you are accomplishing in a few minutes what would take a professional cartographer or statistician perhaps weeks of work by conventional means. In fact, you will often be producing data displays which have never been seen before, simply because of the prohibitive amount of work required."[8] The Disc contains general and specific warnings about the danger of mistaken inferences by those who do not understand basic statistics, and a useful short introduction in the Guide to statistical techniques.

A.
Macfarlane

If one has found or created an interesting data map or table, what can one do with it? There are three options. The "bookmark" system allows one to save all the workings and outcome of those workings to date and then to do another calculation on a different data set, returning after this to the first at exactly the point at which one left off. This is not merely a matter of taking a photograph of the scholar's desk and presenting him with the papers in the same place on the desk when he returns. The computer makes it possible to store all the stages, all the manipulated information up to that point in time, so that one can proceed from exactly where one left off. This is important when comparing two data sets. The second option makes it possible to save these or other subsets of the statistical or textual data by writing them to floppy discs. There are naturally copyright constraints on what is downloaded in this way, but it will make it possible to manipulate data sets using computers and programs that are not in the present system. It is also possible with certain microcomputers and a suitable printer to make a hard copy of the graphs and maps that have been constructed.

Learning to use the BBC Domesday discs, to understand the nature of the material it contains and its omissions, to master the access and data manipulation systems and the practical matters of pointers, of menu-bars, of levels of information, of icons and other matters, is not easy. It is likened in the accompanying *Guide* to learning to drive a car. That seems about the right analogy. It is possible to step into the system and immediately to find some interesting things, one's village, a photograph set, a moving film. Yet it requires many new skills to be able to move with assurance and to interrogate the material in a novel and interesting way. It would take several hours a day, spread over a number of weeks, to be able to master it properly. This is not time wasted, however, because the Domesday disc not only provides access to a very large amount of information, but learning to use the system provides a crash course in elementary statistics, in theories of information retrieval using computers, in graphics, in geographical grid systems, in the phrasing of meaningful questions. Hence it is important not merely for what it contains but also for the methods used to interrogate the data.

Finite Resources for an Infinite Task

Borges never discussed who made his infinite library, how long they had, how much money they spent, what political pressures they were under or what classification schemes they had in mind. A future historian or contemporary user who wishes to understand the value and limitations of the material on the Discs, or to examine them as a social construction made by and of a society, needs to know all these things. We need to know as much as possible about the constraints and pressures on the making of the discs and how these affected the choices that had to be made.[9]

One overriding pressure was shortage of time. The original idea for the project was developed into a proposal by Peter Armstrong in a week in May 1984. Conventional video-discs were already being published by that date, but Armstrong saw that the BBC celebration of the 900th anniversary of Domesday could be widened using this new medium in a new way. By the time funding was assured and a team assembled, there were just two years to complete the project. The anniversary of Domesday could not be moved back; the drawbridge on data collection, on the development of software and hardware, had to be drawn up earlier than one would have liked. But Parkinson's Law undoubtedly operated and the deadline concentrated the mind and smoothed over difficulties. There was a sense of euphoria and of a struggle against impossible odds, throughout the project.

Shortage of time was complicated by financial constraints. The initial sum raised, a million pounds from BBC Enterprises, half a million from the ministry of Education and a million from Philips Electronics, may sound a large amount. Given the scale of the operation, which included seven man-years of computer programming, the development of a new computer and videodisc player, as well as the data gathering and processing, it was not enough. Only some supplementary funding from E.S.P.R.I.T. made it possible to complete the task properly, and this was in doubt until very near the end. The financial and time difficulties were affected by much wider market forces. An example of this was the changing partnership with Acorn computers. Originally as manufacturers of the BBC micro, Acorn were to produce not only the new hardware, but also to write the software. Early in the project Acorn collapsed and was only saved by Olivetti. It was necessary to start much of the software development over again with a new software team, "Logica." One day the full story of the relationship between Philips, Acorn and the BBC will need to be told for it has had profound consequences on the project and in particular on the cost of the system. Originally it was envisaged that the whole system would cost under £1,500, and that it might be cheaper for schools which already had the "Model B" micro. As the project proceeded the system became tied to a new BBC micro, the "Master" series, and to a much more expensive player. The result is that even for schools, who obtain large discounts, the price is about £3,000 for the full system, for others it is nearer £4,000. This puts it out of the reach of many buyers.

Another constraint was the need both to invent the medium and the message. In producing an encyclopedia or a television series, one can concentrate on the content and presentation. In this case it was never certain until the last minute that the project, and in particular the ability to produce laser discs which contained both pictorial and digital information, could be done at all, let alone in time. Even a month before the final launch in November 1986, there were still very grave technical problems.

The fact that this was a new medium posed another problem which set limits to what could be done; this was the question of copyright. Copyright law is currently in the middle of complete revision in order to cope with the new problems caused by photocopying, computers, and television. Here was a medium which incorporated all those problems and many others as well. Where did the copyright in the thousands of data sets lie and how could it be cleared and protected? This legal nightmare became more apparent as the project proceeded. Indeed it was only halfway through that copyright clearance was obtained for many of the central datasets. Two small examples of the problems can be given. In the case of the many thousands of schools it became necessary to obtain the consent and signatures of hundred of thousands of pupils, their parents or guardians, before the material could be used. In the case of moving films it was impossible to include excerpts from drama, music, advertisements and other important classes of television held in the BBC archives because of the copyright problems. Thus it is restricted to "news." Although most organizations, for instance the Ordnance Survey, the Office of Population Census and Statistics, and many companies and institutions were very generous in providing material, there is no doubt that the time and difficulty of obtaining permission limited what could be assembled.

Another background pressure caused by the nature of the medium was the question of censorship. With a film or book one can take risks in including borderline material for two reasons. Firstly, if it is aimed at a limited audience, for instance middle-aged men in macintoshes, explicit pictures can be included which would not be suitable for nine-year-old schoolchildren. The discs were aimed at everyone, and hence had to avoid affronting anyone. This difficulty was compounded by a second. If a film is made it is submitted to the Board of Film Censors and they need only see it through to decide if there are difficulties. The cutting of the final film can be done quite quickly. To submit the two videodiscs to this process is another matter. If they take seven years to read through, and if any change means extended changes in indexes and classification, there would be no chance of meeting the Anniversary date. It was therefore necessary to avoid anything that could be considered to be on the borderline, whether libelous, possible pornographic, inciting to racial hatred, or giving classified information. Since a user could go straight to a photograph, statistical set, or page of text, while ignoring the context, caption or source, it was particularly necessary to be vigilant.

A final background pressure was political. One of the avowed aims of the project was to contribute to public awareness and information. Peter Armstrong makes this point forcefully. The previous Domesday Book was gathered by the center to give it greater control and to lay the foundation for the growing power of the Normans in England. "With the new Domesday, by contrast, the intention is not to affirm a centralizing power by the centralization of information. Instead our hope is that it will help to democratize information. The people help provide and the people can call up information; and, crucially, the people can themselves see whatever patterns in British life become visible when disparate fragments are brought together." In a more personal way Armstrong says the same by dedicating the discs to the memory of his father, William, Lord Armstrong of Sanderstead. "It is from his lifelong work in the Civil Service that I have learned whatever insight I have brought to the Domesday Project about the importance for our national life of information that is detailed, impartial and freely available."[10]

Thus one of the most important innovations of the project was that it put into the hands of the general public a mass of data which had hitherto, to all intents and purposes, been inaccessible. All the material had, in theory, been in the public domain and there is no "secret" information included. Yet the difficulty of finding and then of making sense of much of this material had inhibited most of the population from even making the attempt.

I must admit that there were paranoid moments when I expected to hear that copyright permission would not be given for large sets of data, that other material was drying up, or that the whole project had quietly been shelved for one reason or another. This was avoided in a number of ways. By keeping Members of Parliament, the House of Lords, the Queen and the Prime minister informed of what was going on, while not actively involving them in a way that could lead to pressure, the project walked the tightrope between collusion and opposition with some success. It was fortunate to have the negotiating skills of one of its Board members, Sir John Boreham, the retiring head of the Central Statistical Office, to help in this. Yet the project could at any time have turned sour, especially towards the end which coincided with difficulties between the BBC and the government in power over questions of bias and objectivity.

The final self-portrait of Britain has many strengths, but also many weaknesses. Yet it cannot be accused of being as systematically biased as some other attempts to provide a self-portrait of a civilization. When NASA decided to leave 118 pictures in a space capsule on the Voyager interstellar project in order to give extraterrestrials some idea of what our planet and its inhabitants were like, much discussion took place as to what should be included. In the end the pictures included such things as the Sydney Opera House, a factory production line, some pictures from "The Family of Man" and the *National Geographic*. The interested extraterrestrials could only be given a diagram of a nude man and pregnant woman because NASA "had vetoed the photograph of them taken from a medical text, which might have aroused an adverse public reaction." They would have seen a picture of a string-quartet, but not have been aware of certain other matters because the NASA authority "reached a consensus that we shouldn't present war, disease, crime and poverty."[11] Self-censorship has undoubtedly been exercised on the Domesday Discs, but hardly on this grand scale.

Making History

We have seen that the initial and primary aim of the Domesday Project was to lay down a time capsule for future historians to be used alongside other historical sources. A second aim was to provide as accurate and rich a portrait of Britain as possible for contemporary citizens.

A third aim was to democratize information, to be as open and explicit as possible. All these aims overlap and they all reinforce the need to document as openly and explicitly as possible how the discs were compiled. A future historian or a present user will benefit much more from the discs if he can gain a picture of how it was made and in particular the criteria for the selection and exclusion of material.

This need for self-documentation was recognized by the project and led to a number of decisions to provide information for present and future users. Tamsin Willcocks, a doctoral student, supervised by a member of the Board, was present as an observer at seven or eight meetings and intends to write a sociological analysis of the making of the discs. A full list of credits gives the names of all those who were involved in the numerous committees, the sources of the data sets are carefully recorded.

Although these topics may be covered in a projected book by the general editor Peter Armstrong and a major data coordinator and member of the Board, Professor Howard Newby, as yet a number of other suggestions made at editorial Boards to document the editorial process have not been followed up. The minutes of the Editorial Board (February 1986) note that it was suggested "that the minutes of the Editorial Board, and a profile of Board Members and senior members of the Domesday team should also be included on the disk—this will be needed by historians to interpret material on the disk." This does not seem to have been done.[12] To have done so would have been evidence of both great confidence and a demonstration of that openness that the project was attempting to promote. This essay is partly an attempt to redress this omission. It is also an attempt to make a start on another task that was minuted at the same meeting. "The Editorial Board should consider producing a document 'In Retrospect'. This would highlight problems in the collection and dissemination of data—especially problems of access to data that does not exist, and more importantly, the lack of data in some areas."

This can only be a personal view, and it comes from a particular vantage point. The making of the discs was a very large project and decisions were arrived at by individuals and by a number of Committees, the Education Committee, Software Committee, Technical Liaison Committee, Marketing Committee, Consultative Committee and so on. But, as Armstrong describes it, "The Central Committee (choosing my phrase carefully) was the Editorial Board . . . The Board met monthly in order to resolve the policy issue of what should be put on the discs and how this could best be achieved."[13] Membership of the Editorial Board gave a circumscribed yet privileged view of some of the background to the making of the discs.[14]

A clear statement of "Editorial Policy" is made by Peter Armstrong. "It was clear to all of us that balance and objectivity of the kind the BBC demands of its programs would be equally important for the discs. It could not be a picture of the UK from a single viewpoint." Yet it "was equally clear that this was going to be very difficult to achieve. Although there was room for a mass of material, everything still had to be selected by someone."[15] The Editorial Board was to act as an enabling, guiding, body, but "not a centralized operation by a group of people with strong ideas about British life and how it should be reflected. Our role has been rather to gather and shape all the material . . ."[16] The word "shape," however, highlights the ambiguity and responsibility facing both the Editorial Board and all others involved in the Project. How can one combine objectivity with the need to select, how distance oneself and obtain some overview of such a vast subject?

The explicit aim of the board to avoid foisting their own prejudices onto the material conflicted head on with the need for some criteria by which the seamless web of material could be broken up, some being included, the rest excluded. Any anthropologist knows that he must have some theories, some frame of questions, otherwise he will be drowned. As the huge scale of the project began to become apparent to those who had to select statistical data sets, this problem emerged at an explicit level on the Editorial Board. It seemed clear that the National Disc could not be merely "data-driven," for there was too much material. One solution, falling back on academic experience, was to take themes, problem areas, or as they were called "storylines," which would guide the selection process.

Some members of the Editorial Board suggested that one solution would be to take certain themes which could be used as a means of organizing and selecting the data. These would for the most part remain implicit rather than explicit, an agenda for choice. But they would formalize what would otherwise be a very *ad hoc* and unsystematic, not to say unprincipled, choice of materials. The sort of "storyline" that might be considered would be "the economic restructuring of Britain in the 1980s," the "Changing Urban and Regional System," "The Changing World of Women," "Structured Social Inequality." Other themes to do with the North-South divide etc. were also considered. This would also have the advantage of overcoming some of that timeless, synchronous approach which has already been noted.

On the other hand, it put much more power into the hands of the data providers, and as was evident from the storylines chosen, could well be interpreted as being a particular and possibly slanted view of what was important. Others might be interested in other things, like "The Changing World of Children," or "Ethnic Restructuring," which might thus be partially excluded. It was decided (March 1985) not to adopt this approach, but rather that data supply "should be index driven, although this may result in large volumes of data, which would be pruned at a later stage." Re-affirming this later, "the meeting decided not to work to fixed storylines at this stage, or to include these on disk," although "striking, contrasted storylines, reflecting the personal views of their authors, would be provided at a later stage on paper or floppy disk and would build upon data already on the video disk rather than drive its selection." Thus the principle of a very loose direction from the center was maintained.

Another version of a similar pressure towards implicit or explicit themes was resisted in April 1985 when considering the relations of the Videodisc project to the television series on England since Domesday. As with all television series, this had to have a thematic-*cum*-narrative approach and there was a discussion as to whether the Domesday Discs should try to organize itself along similar themes. The Board decided that "it must be the case that the disk drives the series, and also that data must be seen to be neutral, and not to be structured specifically towards the series." Consequently there was no formal overlap in approach.

An Index-Driven Approach

What then did the Board mean by "index-driven" as an alternative to "theme" driven? It meant that what was to be created was a very long list of topics that should be covered if possible. This list was created from numerous different sources, from United Nations publications on cultural data, for example, from dictionaries, from *Notes and Queries on Anthropology*, from Benn's Press *Directory of Periodicals*, from guides and handbooks, from the expertise of subject specialists and from the obvious and available data. As the lists of topics grew longer, there were attempts by individuals and the various committees to see what was missing and what overlapped. Although the result is perhaps less elegant and internally consistent than a more intellectual, centralized, planned approach, it is clear that this piecemeal, cumulative, common sense, and somewhat random approach has ended up with a more interesting, diverse, and less biased set of data than a directed arrangement. So many cooks have made this broth with so many ingredients that no single recipe or viewpoint could dominate. Quirkiness, the unexpected, the original have been allowed space.

The dual pressures towards balance and openness are shown if we examine some of the major categories of material collected. The guidance for the schools, as we have seen, was very open. They were asked to give "an informative and revealing portrait of your area: what people do there, what kind of environment it is. What do people there currently talk and think about? What are their hopes and fears?" It must not be either too local, nor too general, the guiding principle being whether it would interest someone in another part of the country or in a hundred years time. It should be about the present rather than the past. There should be a rough overview of the whole block on the first page, and then "What goes on the second and subsequent pages is up to the group." They should select some titles and write round these. Negatively, "there should be little need to get too much involved with deeply controversial matters or to include personal details of individuals. In particular, personal names must not be included in your group's entry, except in reference to public officers or well-known personalities. Comments of a personal nature should also be avoided." Further guidance was given on how to create keywords, but here again no specific topics or approaches were suggested. It was only in the land-cover survey and amenities survey that the schools were given a list of things to look out for. It is difficult to envisage a more open approach.

In relation to photographs there was the same open invitation. The schools photographs were left up to the schools; they were to send in four on any subject, taken by themselves or others they could obtain, and three would be chosen. Photographic sets on major themes were to be collected in an attempt to fill in as many of the major topics suggested by the general index as possible. But to prevent this becoming exclusively the product of professional photographers, a national competition was organized. Some guidance was needed here since it is unlikely that a competition merely saying "Send your best snaps" would have produced interesting results. But the themes chosen were wide: "in the '80s," they were "Street life," "Country life," "Faces," "Leisure," "Work," "Home." This produced five thousand very interesting photographs for the National Disc, about half of those submitted being chosen.

An area where the open index-driven approach is most clearly shown is in the choice of texts. The first idea was to commission several hundred experts in various fields to give an overview/state of the art summary of the position in the 1980s. This approach remained at the more general level essays such as Peter Townsend on "Social Welfare," Gerald Priestland on "Religion," Alan Tomlinson on "Sport and Games," or William Brass on "Population." The instructions given writers of these 2,500 word essays indicate the approach. As to the audience, "We can think of the typical reader of this essay as someone who comes into a public library (either in this century or the next) wanting to know something about this topic. We can assume interest, but no particular knowledge . . . Perhaps the level of the popular encyclopedia or Sunday Colour supplement is what we should aim for." As for "Style," the directions are revealing. "The essay should be factual rather than theoretical or hortatory. We are looking for a balanced overview rather than a statement of personal opinion. Of course, many issues will be controversial, but our aim here should be to report all sides rather than point to a particular conclusion . . . Accurate and lively writing should be the aim." The same point was restated again under the heading "BBC Balance." Contributors were told: "You will appreciate that, as with all BBC Publications, Domesday Discs should reflect all shades of opinion in this country without leaning overall either to the right or to the left. Clearly, total objectivity is a chimaera, but our aim should be to achieve a reasonable overall balance." In the discussions at the Editorial Board as to who should be selected to write the forty-five essays, a conscious attempt was made to choose people who represented various shades of opinion.

Such essays give an overview. But they are rather equivalent to asking the referee to describe the game. For future historians in particular, as well as for current users, just to fill the videodisc up with hundreds of academic assessments seemed a missed opportunity. It seemed that it would be interesting to supplement this by collecting together a wide range of "ephemera" of the 1980s, which had been written by the players, in the heat of the game, rather than by the referee looking back over it. It was agreed (July 1986) to do this, and the result in the shape of more than two thousand articles, is on the disc. There is at least the chance of local, unusual, from-the-bottom upwards, flavor.

Opening the medium out to include articles in papers, journals, speeches, fly-sheets and so on is, of course, a risky process. Apart from the original selection, editorial control is being delegated away from the centre. This is explicitly recognized by Armstrong and the

Board. Thus in the *User Guide*, Armstrong writes: "These articles do not represent any one person's views, they are from all points on the political and ideological spectrum. On a controversial topic we have tried to include contrasted pieces on the same theme. Nor are these articles offered with any guarantee of accuracy. The source is carefully recorded and it is up to you to accord to them whatever credibility you choose."[17] Or again, "Do not assume that any one piece of text carries our imprimatur—each is a fragment of how this society wrote about itself."[18] The inclusion of such material will certainly heighten the historic value of the compilation.

As to how the two thousand pieces were selected, there was still a considerable problem. Having stated the need for balance as between sides in an argument, the need to provide a "colorful mixture on the major topics of our time," and a list of areas of particular interest given by the index of subjects (which had already emerged at this stage) there was still an enormous sea of publications out of which only a few could be selected: ". . . it is out of the question to include more than a tiny fraction of the mass of material that is published in Britain even in a single week." Only a certain amount could be used since everything had to have copyright clearance, be re-typed and checked. With the assistance of subject specialists and under the scrutiny of the Board, the "text editor (Madeleine Kingsley) has tried . . . to produce a varied and readable, as well as authorative collection of text that reflects most of the issues in the forefront of our concern in the 1980s." Only very careful research will identify any serious omissions. Some natural but unnecessary obsessions were noted by the Board; for instance dozens of articles about the weather and climate have been cut out, but each of us is likely to find something we consider important either passed over or treated in a way which will make us argue.

Drawing Boundaries

Nowhere on the videodisc is it explained in any explicit way how the general boundaries were drawn round the data. Three self-imposed limits are worth noting. The first is in time. It appears that the project as originally envisaged was intended to be much more historical, one of the seven major sections was "History." By a decision (March 1985) the seven sections were reduced to five; "History" was one of those that disappeared. It was explicitly decided to take the years 1985–86 as the period to concentrate on, and move outward from that. Materials for all of the 1980s would be treated as relevant, and as minuted (September 1985) "most material will be from the 1980s with 1970s material included only for comparisons." This means that while texts and statistics often refer back a few years the concentration is on the present. The view is simply expressed in the *Survey Guide* which was prepared for teachers and children writing accounts of their areas. They were reminded that they were writing for future historians "the guiding principle is to bear the general reader in mind at all times asking the question, 'would someone in a different part of the country or a hundred years in the future be interested in reading this?'," but they were not to do so by writing the history of their area. "We all need to bear in mind that the information we are compiling concerns life today, in the 1980s, rather than history. We find it tempting to describe our areas in terms of the past, but that is not the idea of Domesday."[19] Thus memories and ideas of change are to be found, but not antiquarian local history.

It is a defensible decision in view of the size of the material, but it is important to recognize that it leads to a certain distortion. Taken by itself, the discs would tend to give a rather timeless and foreshortened view of Britain. Traces of the history of the country are present in every photograph and every essay, but it is only through subtle work that a future observer will be able to discern some of the side effects of long-term, structural, changes.

A second boundary is in geographical space. Through satellite imagery, Domesday goes high into the sky, but it resolutely refuses to follow most of the many webs that lead out from Britain. One day there may be a European or even global Domesday. This particular first attempt is much more circumscribed. The Editorial Board discussed the question of how much material from outside Britain, or about Britain's links with the Commonwealth and the rest of the world should be included. This discussion was summed up in the decision at the September 1985 Board that "Britain will also be viewed as an island: there will be no information relating Britain to other countries, or on other countries" views of Britain unless it is very relevant." This may seem very isolationist, exemplifying a "Little Britain" attitude which should make any self-respecting anthropologist blush. The problem is, of course, that once one relaxes this boundary to accommodate reality, almost everything in the world becomes relevant, from Hong Kong, the Falklands, British tourism throughout the world, British investments throughout the world, the views of the British throughout the world and so on. We all know that we live in a world system, and that this is particularly true of an old imperial nation like Britain. Yet it is also clear that the Discs recognized a shift in power and perception during the last twenty years. The Great Exhibition of 1851, or even "Britain in Pictures" devoted much space to "Britain and her Empire." Here we were deliberately concentrating on an artificial boundary. This was symbolically expressed by the maps. The widest level map on the discs is that of Great Britain. There is no map of Europe as a whole, let alone the world. It is "this island now."

This does not mean that there is nothing to be found about the relations of the British and the rest of the world. In the texts, in the discussions of language, in the many tables on countries of origin and ethnic groups, in the photographs of life-styles, in the economic data on trade and investment, there is a wealth of material for a future historian to estimate how deeply involved the country is with America, Europe and the rest of the world. Yet is it also important for such an observer to know that a decision was taken only to include material from abroad if it was "very relevant." Again we have the problem of the bounded anthropological community, the Pacific island or Himalayan valley, artificially disembodied in order to make it comprehensible.

A third boundary is more difficult to specify, but it might be said to be that between "information" and "knowledge." We have already seen that it was early recognized that it would neither be possible nor advisable to produce an "Encyclopedia." For instance, it is stated that "The Domesday Discs are emphatically not encyclopedias and make no claim to systematic coverage of human knowledge . . . Domesday is an exhibition of life as it was lived in the 1980s—what we did, how we looked, what we owned and so on."[20] The distinction can be shown quite simply if we take the first two entries in the famous eleventh edition of the *Encyclopedia Britannica* that deal with subjects in the field of theoretical knowledge. These are the letter "A" and its derivation, "Abatement," "Abbey," "Abbreviation," "Abduction," "Abdication," "Aberration," "Abeyance," "Abhidhanna" (a Buddhist term), "Abhorrers." None of these would appear except very accidentally, on the Domesday Discs. One might learn how many Hindus or Muslims there were, but little about what they believed; one could learn about science policy or funding, but not the principles of chemistry or biology; one would have examples of recent poetry and prose, but nothing on recent developments in literary criticism and so on. In other words the material and external manifestations of thought are documented, but the contents are largely omitted.

Such a decision was not taken lightly. For a long time there were five sections, not the present four. The fifth was called "Science and Technology" and it was envisaged that under "Science" might be included scientific knowledge. Thus one might commission essays on recent and important developments in astronomy, particle physics, molecular biology, or other interesting fields. Finally this idea was rejected and the section disappeared (June 1985). It became clear that to make a useful contribution even within biology, chemistry, or physics would mean that the discs would have to take on a very large educational role, teaching basics and whole disciplines before the specialized articles could be understood at all. It was also asked why "science" should be privileged in this way. If there were articles on the natural sciences, why not on medical knowledge, on economics, on archaeology, on history, on literature, on anthropology, and so on? This would have turned the discs into something very different and stretched the budget and time, not to mention the competence, of the makers well beyond the agreed limits. There is thus some evidence about abstract thought here, but a future historian would have to be aware that the main contents of specialist thought and belief, the special preserve of academic life, is largely missing. It does not provide the equivalent of Open University degree information, though it will no doubt provide much useful material.

A. Macfarlane

Censorship and the Underside of Life

A confrontation that faces every artist in constructing a picture of life is that between honesty, accuracy and detail on the one hand, and the desire not to wound, give offense or end up in prison, on the other. This was obviously writ large in such an enormous undertaking. We were particularly keen that as honest an account as possible be given. Just as we treasure the few revealing insights into the Elizabethan, Georgian or Victorian underworld given in the works of pamphleteers, artists like Hogarth, or certain diaries, so the future will want to know about what life was really like in the 1980s. Yet it would also be unbalanced to concentrate merely on problems—AIDS, Violence, Unemployment—without remembering that much of life is humdrum and fairly cosy.

How far is it possible to create an electronic exhibition that allows people, now and in the future, to see below the surface, to turn over the stones? If we regard the Discs as a vast electronic exhibition we have available a medium where we can wander around, ask questions, get out exhibits we want to look at and make the associations we wish to make. We can go back to the stores and look in the storage boxes, rather than being confined to the pre-arranged thematic arrangements of a curator's or author's mind. But we are still left with the question of how much has been deliberately omitted from the boxes.

These omissions can be sub-divided into various kinds. Firstly there is the omission of very extreme and subversive material: a statement of the aims of the I.R.A., of the Animal Liberation Front, or the National Front, made by the organizations themselves, are not on the Disc. All three will be dealt with indirectly through texts, statistics and photographs. But without much formal discussion, it was decided implicitly that the disc could not become a platform for "extremist" groups. This is a loss to historians, but the question of how far intolerance can be tolerated is very prominent when a medium which will be used in schools is being devised. Thus political "extremism" is circumscribed.

Another circumscription is in criminal matters. Of course there is a vast amount on crime on the disc; there are extraordinary statistics illustrating everything from levels of fear of assault and the incidence of punishment, to petty thieving. But honest and direct accounts of criminal networks, of how massive fraud is organized in big companies, of the inside workings of the arms trade, of the dimensions of drug dealing, could not, of course, be included. Historians will have to allow for this. There is a tendency towards the law-abiding, even though the photographs and statistics also show another side. In particular, the large area of twilight activity, the "informal" or "black economy," where the stated rules of morality are subverted under economic pressures can only be approached indirectly. Again there are some clues for a future historical detective.

A third circumscription is linked to this in the borderlines between crime and immorality. The huge industry linked to prostitution, pornography, drugs, is of course visible in various ways through the disc. But again it is difficult to give future historians much idea of this. Inside accounts of these topics by the practitioners, explicit films and photographs which are, of course, circulating through the bedrooms and playgrounds of Britain, have to be ignored.

A final limitation is in relation to what are considered to be "secrets of State." The Discs were made in a period of particular nervousness over state secrets and, in particular, information about the very large defence establishment in Britain. A belief that the enemy know very little and might welcome information from the disc to plot military or other installations is widespread. A disgorging of official statistics, a million schoolchildren tramping about the countryside asking questions and taking photographs, all this could well have disclosed something that the Government felt should not be in the public domain. A tacit agreement not to encourage this to happen, in return for an unprecedented access to government-held information, seems to have been part of the Faustian compact which the disc makers have made. Future historians also need to know this.[21]

These guidelines were in a sense so obvious and so unassailable that they were not openly discussed, except in asides and hints, for the most part at the Editorial Board level. They were furthermore largely self-imposed. There was no government or other committee or Board through which the material had to be filtered. In only one area did the project formally set up a sort of censorship and this was in relation to the community surveys. In that case, having warned the schools to avoid personal and libelous material, it was openly stated that "Your group's material will be reviewed prior to recording it on the Domesday Discs . . ."[22] It was reported that in order to retain spontaneity and local flavor "contributions were not edited, except for legal considerations. Even spelling was not corrected . . ." and that "over-all" the quality of the contributions was a "tribute to the British educational system."[23]

The Manipulation of Statistics

The attempt to be open, within limits, in the collection of texts and photographs so that present and future users could see a portrait that was largely the product of the population of Britain, not the construct of an Editorial Board and a few BBC committees, is also evident in the way in which the statistical datasets have been handled. We have already seen that what is held on the discs is not a set of graphs and maps prepared from the original figures, but rather the "raw" values themselves, held in as disaggregated a form as possible. It is then up to the user to manipulate these and to test hypotheses and draw inferences. It was apparent that a combination of very large sets of "raw" data from many different sources, with some quite sophisticated statistical programs, put into the hands of the general public an exciting, but potentially explosive tool. It was minuted (January 1986) that "Those meeting were concerned that users should not be allowed to draw spurious correlations from the data on the discs. Measures will be taken to prevent this although it cannot be stopped entirely. These included a note on the album cover, a warning included in the picture essay on Domesday, and also in the manual . . ." No warning was included on the cover, indeed there is nothing at all on either cover. But the warnings in the other two places are worth noting, since they again illustrate the mixture of caution and innovation that characterized the construction of the discs.

In the *User Guide*, the public is warned that the statistical data as sets of data is patchy, that there are "imbalances and gaps." "For example, there is a very large number of statistics on employment from the currently intense activity by government and researchers in this area. A similar depth of statistical area, such as natural history, is harder to achieve."[24] In relation to specific data sets, users are advised to read the text which can be called up in relation to each data set before drawing any conclusions because "All surveys have anomalies, as well as particular methods and aims." A brief but helpful summary of some principles of statistical analysis is then given in two pages, warning of "skewness in data" and so on.[25] Under "Some Statistical Warnings" in the Domesday essay, users are warned against "the possibility of wrong-headed conclusions, if users are not aware of the limitations of some of these techniques." "In particular we would wish to warn you about three possible traps. First, subdividing a data set may produce such a small sample that no wide-ranging conclusion would be drawn from it. Second, when using rates, ratios or percentages, you must ensure that the numerator is genuinely a subset of the denominator. Third, ratios calculated and mapped for a geographical area may not be true for any part of the area. These warnings are explained in detail in the text accompanying the relevant data sets." The tension between wanting to provide people with access to information and the possibility of finding out something new, and yet wanting to prevent abuse of such information which we found in each category of information is here too. The passage ends by warning that "some of our critics have expressed fears about making raw data and statistical software available to untrained members of the public. So our message must be—enjoy experimenting with the data on the disc, but be cautious in the conclusions you draw from it."[26]

Fact, Truth, Inference, and Error

We have seen that in each case the Board has taken a calculated risk. It has put its general authority behind a category of data, from schools, essays, statistics, maps. But in each case it warns the users that they cannot necessarily assume that the data is "true," it is merely one way of looking at things. This raises one of the most interesting questions in relation to the disc, the relation between fact and fantasy. Susan Sontag's observations on photography are also true of this new medium, it "trades simultaneously on the prestige of art and the magic of the real," the videodiscs contain "clouds of fantasy and pellets of information."[27]

It is essential that users should realize this, yet it is not something that is self-evident or widely understood. The videodisc is simultaneously providing a huge amount of reputable information, "teaching," and at the same time warning people to be wary. The pictures in the exhibition are often two-way mirrors, they have surface and latent messages, they are distorting.

Now most of us most of the time do not exercise such a wary attitude. While accepting, if formally asked, that the media may deceive, it is probably the case that people believe much of what they "read" in papers, television, radio and in books. In particular, they believe what the BBC has to say. One reaction to the community disk that I have already encountered is an incredulous, and slightly hurt one, by people who are able to compare their own knowledge and perception of a local area with the very brief account by some schoolchildren. They do not usually find gross errors, but a sense that this is a very partial and perhaps one-sided coverage from a point of view that is very different from their own. Yet the account seems to come with the full backing of the BBC and the power of the "truthful" medium, the TV screen. The idea that one must distinguish between lies and omissions, that one can be "economical" with the truth and yet not lie, that one can tell the truth, but not the whole truth and nothing but the truth, that there are a variety of truths and none absolutely right, all these very relativistic messages, familiar to anthropologists, are being brought home by the videodiscs. In essence the discs bring home to a wider public the loss of innocence, the end of positivism, which, for instance was one of the central messages of the Renaissance and was later incorporated into what Collingwood called the Copernican revolution in history, "the discovery that so far from relying on an authority other than himself, to whose statements his thought must conform, the historian is his own authority and his thought autonomous, self-authorizing, possessed of a criterion to which his so-called authorities must conform and by reference to which they are criticized."[28] Again and again in the *Guide* and elsewhere the user is advised to think for himself, to be his own authority, not to accept the statement on the disc as authoritative.

In general this is one of the most genuinely educational and innovative parts of the videodisc. If it can help many people to see that the borderline between fact and opinion, between "hard" data and inference, is a very thin one, that statistics, photographs and even factual descriptions can be manipulated, this will be to all our advantages. Yet we need to be aware that the disc is treading on dangerous ground. It is simultaneously using the powerful authority of the BBC, of powerful communications techniques, of illustrious authors etc., and at the same time teaching people to question authority. In this respect it has faith in an open and unhierarchical world. But this faith is unlikely to go unchallenged.

A separate but related question is that of palpable error. With such a huge amount of data being processed in complex ways in such a short time, there are likely to be problems of error.

These may be at three levels. Firstly, the original data may be wrong. Clearly it was beyond the resources of the project to check every piece of information, every one of the 9,000 local accounts, the 2,000 texts from magazines, the thousands of maps and so on, in any detail. Obvious slips and internal inconsistencies might be noted. But even if they were, it was questionable as to whether they should be corrected. Indeed it is the case that, as with the decision not to correct spelling, it was the policy not to correct data. This was part of the point of the warning that people had to be wary of the factual accuracy; this was a disc about what people said and wrote about Britain, their representations, rather than an attempt at including only verifiable and verified facts.

The next level at which errors might creep in was in the often complex set of stages of transfer from the original through re-typing and computerized sorting, into the final product. Such errors have little heuristic value for historians, except those interested in typing skills, and were to be kept to a minimum.

The third possible source of error lay in the difficulties of making a multimedia and multi-data presentation. Basically, it was necessary to be able to set millions of cross-links between maps, photographs, texts, statistics. With even one mis-numbering or false link, very gross errors would be shown to the user. For instance, if the alignment between maps and their overlays was not correct, the whole sophisticated mapping routines would be useless.

The steps taken to check the data needed to be specified in detail and placed in the archive. As they were reported to the Board in November 1986, three weeks before the final launch, they were as follows. All maps had been checked and the relationship of pictures and text to maps on the Community Disc. On the National Disc pictures and captions had been thoroughly checked, as had film and text. Not every word of text had been re-read and corrected, but first and last pages were checked against the title. The Gallery and software had received thorough checking. All this enormous amount of work seems in order.

The real problem lay in the tabular and mappable data. It will be remembered that there are some 6,000 data sets, some of them very large. Unlike texts and maps and photographs, the figures are in themselves meaningless. It only needs the slip of a typewriter key, or a small bug in the software, to produce garbage figures which would be difficult to locate. We need to know more clearly how much error there is likely to be, not in the original figures which no doubt have errors built into them, but extra errors created during the re-processing into new formats and placing the materials on the disc. At an Editorial Board meeting (November 1985) it was minuted that "CURDS are concerned about the errors in the data: they will check a sample of data before it is supplied to the project, but would prefer that all data is checked once it is on the disk. Newcastle and Birkbeck are to consider how the data, once on the disk, should be checked." In the light of this premonition the report to the Board that in this area "checking had been much more selective . . . Birkbeck had also done some checking of data" needs to be amplified. The implications of the report that "the thesaurus and index had been checked selectively, at about 10% in extent" also needs further elaboration. What error rate is likely?

We were aware that there were likely to be errors at all these levels and it was minuted that "the Board suggested that at the Launch it was made clear that checking was an enormous task and that further errors should be reported back to the Domesday office." It will be interesting to see the file of *addenda* and *corrigenda* for such a large-scale project.

Classification, Keywording and the Attempt at Neutrality

As an unusual map of how a group of people in the 1980s classified and named their social world, the Domesday discs will be of considerable interest. For future historians, for instance, in examining what was grouped with what, the boundaries between topics, the taboos, ambiguities, mental boundaries, common assumptions, obsessions, and prejudices will become clearer. It should therefore be noted that many of the Editorial Board meetings were taken up with detailed discussions of the classification schemes which were constantly being altered. These many discussions are not recorded in detail except in the large files of papers documenting month by month the growing thesaurus.

One example of a set of decisions, in relation to "Culture" at the meeting in September 1985, will show the sort of additions and rearranging that was taking place throughout the project. It was noted that the following new categories were to be added: "Under consumption, shopping and toys. Under arts and entertainment, festivals. Under leisure and recreation, leisure policy. Under mass communication, media issues." "The categories Jargon, and Slang, have been amalgamated." "The Category Literature and Poetry, under arts and Entertainment, is to be extended to include popular publishing." "Under Consumption, Furniture is to be included within Durable Household Goods." Then there was some discussion on the topics within the category "Beliefs and Attitudes." It was suggested that attitudes to work and to old age are included, that gender roles and sexuality are combined, and morality added as a separate class. "Depending on the topic of opinion poll data available, some reclassification may be necessary." Earlier that year it had been decided to make the following changes (April 1985): "Local history has been dropped. Religion and Ethnicity has been changed to Religion and Philosophy, and Race and Ethnicity. Social Welfare has been divided into Social Welfare and Health." In re-drawing such classificatory maps we change the data we collect and how it is perceived and found by users.

The real problem, of course, is that there is no unique and satisfactory classification of the real world. It is all imposed and merely more- or less-satisfactory. No preexisting Linnean Classification of the whole of Society, Economy, Culture, and Environment for an advanced industrial nation was available. Library and museum classification schemes were not appropriate as a whole, though parts of them could be used. So, along with everything else, the Boards, subject specialists, and particularly David Lee, the expert on indexing, were working out a comprehensive classification scheme and thesaurus. It is possible to short-circuit this by direct searches which avoid moving down through the hierarchy. Yet the way in which the final classification was made does necessarily impose limits on the data. As we have seen, data collection was to be "index-driven"; thus, to a certain extent, what was observed to be relevant was the result of the classifying principles of those involved. The net they wove inevitably affected the fish they caught. Only careful research will reveal some of the ways in which this classification scheme is less than satisfactory.

Once a set of material had been located as worth including another problem had to be faced, which was the question of labeling. There were two aspects to this problem. One was the implications for data retrieval by keyword. The way in which a text or photograph was keyworded would determine whether it was ever found by a searcher, with what else it was grouped by computer searches, and so on. Explicit instructions on this were given to the schools who were asked to keyword their contributions so that users could make a "subject" search. It was pointed out that "unfamiliar keywords will actually hide information from eventual users," for instance a user looking for "cars" or "traffic" would not find it if it had been indexed under "vehicular transport." Information would also be hidden if the keywords were too specific. A stately home would only be found, if given by name, by those who already knew that the place exists. The guidance given was that "in all cases the keyword should be one step more general than the specific topic written about. The important question to ask is, 'I've written about . . ., but what is it an example of?'" In the case of schools, some uniformity was imposed by asking that one of the four keywords per page was chosen from the list of thirty-six general terms such as "Armed Forces," "Arts and Crafts," "Attitudes," etc. The other three were to be chosen by the schools.[29] One assumes that similar principles were used with the national data sets, but it would be helpful for historians to have a description of the method included with the documentation of the project in the archives.

The choice of keywords is a subjective matter. For instance, with what more general class is the particular to be joined? What indeed, is it an example of? Again future historians will look at the relationship between the contents and the keywords and learn a good deal about patterns of thought in the 1980s. They will do this with the local disc, and also the national disc. They will wonder to what extent the constructors of keywords were self-consciously aware of the choices they were making. The answer is that although it was clearly impossible to tread a neutral path in all cases, keyworders were aware that labeling is a very tricky business and that the most innocent decision can have considerable implication.

Just as in classification, the decision to put "AIDS" under "Medicine," "Morals," or "Sex" would have obvious implications, so the way a data set is termed can show bias. As Armstrong observed, "In fact the keywords themselves often turned out to be more sensitive than the things they referred to. An article about inner city violence, for example, might be balanced in itself, but should it be referred to as 'riots', with all that that implies, or 'social deprivation', with its alternative view?"[30] Sometimes it was impossible to avoid making a choice. If possible, however, the aim was to be as neutral and objective in the keywording as possible. Just as in level, one went from the particular to the general, so in partisanship, one went from the committed to the even-handed. A few serious blunders here might mean that the whole project was dismissed by one extreme or the other as partisan and worthless. There were many discussions of these matters, but only a few are minuted. One of these rare instances occurred at the meeting in January 1986. "The meeting was concerned about the handling of certain sensitive subjects—riots, Northern Ireland, ethnicity and color etc. Ideally these should be put into classes as generalized as possible, but as the system tends towards specificity, this is not really possible. Extensive use of cross referencing and careful choice of keywords should minimize the problem. The meeting then discussed the possibly inflammatory nature of keywording and their use by readers of the Domesday discs." This gives a clue to future historians as to what were perceived by the makers as the areas of particular sensitivity, and their strategy for minimizing the difficulties, but their realization that there is no complete solution.

Choices had to be made, however, and one example of a set of re-labeling decision in relation to "Society" will give a flavor of what was happening. At a Board meeting in September 1985 "Legislature is to be renamed Parliament. Political Development is to be renamed Political Issues . . . News Events is to be renamed News Stories. Inventions is to be renamed Innovations." In the absence of a tape recorder it would be difficult to recall the detailed argument put forward for each of these changes, or for changing "Ecology" to "Wildlife," "Industry" to "Extractive Industry" and "Landscape" to "Land Use and Landscape" at the same meeting. An unusually long and fierce argument, whose details completely escape me, led in July 1985 to the decision to divide "Sports, Leisure and Recreation" into "Sports and Culture," "Leisure and Recreation."

Future Developments and Lessons from the Project

In looking back it is often helpful to look forward. One of the frustrations of any piece of work, even on this scale, is that one knows that there is always more material and more interesting ways of using it, if only one had more time and money. What could be and should be done in the future and what has one learned from this project?

One area for likely future improvements is in the searching software. What is on the discs is a very great advance beyond what has ever been attempted or done before on videodisc or elsewhere, but it is clear that it is still at an early stage. We have seen that the material can be retrieved through an hierarchical search, through keyword matching, and through an iconic gallery. Other modern types of search could not be developed in time. Boolean searching which would enable a user to be much more precise, is not supported. The system of likelihood searching with "full relevance feedback" pioneered by Dr. Martin Porter, which would allow much more interaction between the database and the user, is not present. In general, the whole field of "intelligent systems," causing such a stir in the computing world, could contribute a great deal here. This is one of the areas where the BBC has earmarked funds to do further research.

A useful area for software development will be in enabling the user to manipulate the data sets more flexibly. The *Guide* for instance envisages customized discs, using Basic, which will enable a user to rearrange picture sets, add titles and captions, make their own programs from the data, using it as a kind of archive. "We also plan to release software which will allow you to read a sequence of video-disc moves onto a floppy disc. This can be played subsequently and will control the video-disc player just as if someone were operating it. A synchronized commentary can be recorded on an audio cassette."[31] The "storylines" which before were excluded for fear of distorting data collection can now be reintroduced, but only as an explicit, added, layer. Thus one would know that one was being taken round Ken Livingstone's London, or Edwina Currie's Health Service. More sophisticated packages to allow the user to unload data from the disc and examine it are promised, and other software to enable a user to add his won data-sets to the archive, held on computer storage. Thus "we anticipate a cottage industry growing up around Domesday as more and more applications are developed for the mass of material which they contain."[32]

A.
Macfarlane

A second and related area lies in questions as to how such huge data sets will be held in the future. Two thoughts may be mentioned here. The first assumes that personalized, distributed, archives of this kind will become more common as stand-alone systems. If they are to do so, and particularly if they are not to become stranded in a few institutions, they must become cheaper. The discs themselves, £200 for the pair, are within many people's reach and given what is on them, amazing value. But we have seen that the system has grown inexorably in price, fulfilling the law of most building, defence and other projects that the final product will cost at least twice the amount that the makers originally promised. This law has one major exception nowadays, and that is in computing and video technology. Ingenuity and competition should bring the price down.

One way in which this may happen is through separating the pictorial and the textual/statistical aspects of the disc. Basically, to have a player that will read both digital and visual information is, at present, very expensive, though who knows how soon other firms, particularly in Japan, will bring out cheaper players. If they do, well and good. In the meantime, as the problem became obvious to the Board, there was much discussion of a long-term alternative. This was to store pictures on a picture disc, which could be played on an ordinary, relatively cheap, player, and to store the data on another medium. For smallish data-sets this could be on a computer hard-disc, but with over 300 megabytes, the solution appeared to be CD-ROM and, hopefully, one day CD-RAM (and very soon CD-I). Once again, this is not a straightforward matter and one only had glimpses on the Editorial Board of some of the difficulties. Among these was the fact that the technology was changing very fast, but international standards were not agreed, and the fact that one of the partners, Philips, having invested a good deal in a certain system would be rather unhappy at a simultaneous launch of an alternative, much cheaper, system. But the subject was kept alive throughout the last year of the project during which this new possibility emerged. In November 1985, the Board was told that "Philips have increased the price of the video disk player to such an extent that it is now felt to be out the range of the markets at which it was originally aimed: it is presently estimated at about £2,500 for schools, and £3,500 for home users. In view of this, the project has decided to publish not only on LV ROM, as originally planned, but also to publish the data on CD ROM. This will mean that conventional video and compact disk players can be used in combination, at a cost of c. £1,500. In using CD ROM technology, there may be problems with transparent overlays, also the project will not be able to utilize other advantages such as the greater storage capacity (600 mb) and the possibilities for use of sound, in order to maintain compatibility with the LV ROM version. However, the meeting approved this development."

Having approved the development, what became of it? At the next meeting we were told that "Philips have agreed in principle to the use of CD ROM technology in the Project but the

BBC are investigating costs to see whether it is justified or not." In January, "the use of compact disc in the system is being actively explored." In February, "The CD ROM approach is still being investigated at a probable cost of c. £1,500." At the next meeting, in May, it was reported that "The CD ROM option for assessing (*sic*) the digital material on the disk only has yet to be agreed: we await agreement on CD ROM formats internationally." That was the last time that CD ROM was explicitly mentioned. A possible reason for its disappearance may be seen at the minute at the last meeting of the Board where it was "reported that the possibility of a disc with access to a limited amount of material on Domesday was still being considered, and technical requirements were being examined . . . there was some feeling in Enterprises that sales of the first product should not be hindered by reference to a cheaper, if less useful, alternative." But the matter needs further thought now, for it had clearly been understood that the CD ROM option (and it is not clear that this minute refers to that) would be decidedly cheaper, but not necessarily less useful, and that in the light of the worrying increase in costs, both the Board and Philips had agreed to pursue this for the future.

As regards the technological side, a further area for reflection lies in the more general question of whether such large data sets are best stored in this form. There can be little doubt that for historical purposes, to give a finite, encapsulated, and storable image of Britain, the decision was right. This is the ultimate time-capsule and it will be widely distributed, and not "updatable or erasable," by future groups wishing to rewrite history. Armstrong believes that they were produced in this way "because they are primarily intended as historical records," "as a historical record, they are designed to be laid down like wine, gaining value with age."[33] On the other hand, if they are seen as principally giant databases for use by organizations, whether private or public, then this may not be the way things will go. "The giant databases of the future will probably have to be held centrally, with all the problems and costs of on-line access which that implies." There will also be other problems. Armstrong thinks that "the biggest problem in achieving the Encyclopedia Galactica will . . . not be technical, but a legal one—copyright."[34] An equally grave one in a system that has the virtue of being updatable is that it will be much easier to erase, and alter the record. The Orwellian nightmare of a present that is constantly rewriting the past, based on Stalin's Russia, is much easier to envisage when most of the information on a society is held at the center and one small computer program can delete a year, a movement, or a point of view.

This may seem a trivial problem, but it is already present in a small way with this Disc. It is well known to historians that it is the victors who tend to write history, and it should be equally obvious that the process of selection which the Domesday team have exercised has already in a subtle way rewritten the past. To take a tiny example, I asked myself and some colleagues what they remembered of national significance for the year 1983. They were unable, though intelligent and with good memories, to remember correctly a single event in that year. You might try the test yourself. I then told them of the twelve events included as film extracts on the Domesday Disc. They remembered them well when reminded, and the Disc reinforced their memory. I myself, having watched "1983" several times, could reel off twelve things that happened in that year, even the months in which they occurred. They are, of course what the editors chose as representative of that year. If the disc was widely successful, hundreds of thousands of citizens would share those few images, and find it difficult, without consulting diaries and newspapers in libraries, to remember anything else. Supposing the disc was on a medium to which data could be added and erased, it is not difficult to see how a whole population could be easily persuaded about a certain selection of events in their recent past. As anthropologists know, the borderline between myth and history is confused and permeable. Future databanks may well provide the ideal tool to weave changing myths of the past with which to guide and control the present. It may then seem a bitter irony that the Domesday Disc was conceived in 1984.

Apart from the software and technical aspects, other ideas have been put forward to make discs on other themes. These implicitly show how the medium is perceived to be useful. One limitation, as we have seen, is in the cramped national boundaries. Other countries were reported to be interested in undertaking their own Domesday surveys to commemorate anniversaries, for instance the discovery by the west of Australia (1988) or the French Revolution (1989), though I do not know if anything has come of these. One assumes that the Japanese and Americans may wish to do something. In January 1986 possible future discs were discussed: these included a second pressing of the Domesday discs in Autumn 1987, to incorporate corrections but no new data; a 1990 edition of the Domesday disc "not called Domesday but a home information system about Britain"; a global disc, provisionally entitled "The Blue Planet"; and a number of more specialized discs, for instance, a disc based around the Kenneth Clark series *Civilization*, with additional stills and walks, an Ecology disk and so on. All these plans were dependent for funding on the success of the first Domesday project.

A. Macfarlane

The mention of a "home information system" brings us to a last point. The strength and the weakness of the first Domesday Disc was that it was trying to do everything. Its software had to be very general, and hence while good at most things was not excellent in any particular area. Its audience was of all ages and backgrounds and this led to various compromises and decisions as has already been explained. It was initiated as a project of a historical kind, and retained this flavor. Yet its commercial success depended very much on it being of use to the present. It was an educational venture, originally targeted at schools and drawing very heavily on the enthusiastic participation of schoolchildren and teachers. Yet it was made at a time when the combination of the most serious teacher's strike in modern times, uncertainties over educational funding, the rising cost of the system, and a refusal to commit funds to its widespread use in schools began to make it look as if its main market would *not* be in schools. It was pulled towards many users—government, business, and so on, as well as the educational and historical. It is to its credit that it never abandoned its first educational and historical aims. But it is important that historians should know that the project was always looking over its shoulder, not only in order to avoid being accused of being biased or partisan, but also because the future of individual makers and of the whole approach would to a large extent be tested by the market. This was not a philanthropic, government-funded, or academic project which could proceed without considering the political and financial implications of decisions. Although the editorial Board took its decisions largely free from direct pressures, they were always there, and future historians will soon detect them as they unravel the complex garment that has been made to clothe a nation.

Notes

This paper is intended to provide the factual background which is necessary in order to understand the BBC Domesday Videodisc project. It does not consider the parallel series of films presented by Michael Wood. I am most grateful to Sarah Harrison and Julian Jacobs for their comments on earlier drafts.

1.   Peter Armstrong and Mike Tibbetts, *Domesday Video-Disc User Guide* (BBC Publications, 1986), 16. Hereafter cited as Armstrong, *Guide*.

2.   Armstrong, *Guide*, 17.

3.   Armstrong, *Guide*, 16.

4.   Peter Armstrong, "The Domesday Project: An Overview of the Production of the Domesday Discs," on Side A of the "National Disc," 42 (hereafter Armstrong, "Domesday"); Armstrong, *Guide*, 16.

5.   *The Domesday Project Survey Guide* (1985), 11.

6.   Armstrong, *Guide*, 131.

7.   Armstrong, *Guide*, 169.

10.   Armstrong, *Guide*, 175.

11.   Limited to a few thousand words, I can only make a brief start on this large and important topic.

10.   Armstrong, "Domesday," 44–45.

11.   Cited and quoted in Halla Beloff, *Camera Culture* (Blackwell, 1985), 21.

12.   It is true that this was merely a suggestion and not further discussed. But if there had been reasons

for not following up the suggestion because it was impracticable or impossible, we were not informed of them. Probably it was just forgotten. Dates in brackets refer to Editorial Boards held on those months.

13. Armstrong, "Domesday," 13–14.

14. For the record, the Editorial Board first met in October 1984 and there were twenty meetings in all. I was present on the Board from June 1985 to November 1986, attending eleven of the twelve Board meetings during that time.

15. Armstrong, "Domesday," 15.

16. Armstrong, "Domesday," 8.

17. Armstrong, *Guide*, 141.

18. Armstrong, "Domesday," 30.

19. *The Domesday Survey Guide* (1985), 12 (hereafter cited as *Survey*).

20. Armstrong, *Guide*, 116.

21. I am not in a position to know whether the government departments held back on any of their materials because of their sensitivity. We would need a report from those who assembled the data sets at Essex, Birkbeck, Newcastle to find out about this. For instance, they could perhaps throw light on the report at the December 1985 Editorial Board that "OPCS are also able to supply a tape containing vital statistics, but not including statistics on ethnicity, marriage, divorce or migration as these are not readily available."

22. *Survey*, 13.

23. *Survey*, 18,19. It was agreed (September 1985) that "the guidelines as to what has had to be edited are to be included on the local disk." This has not yet been done and should be included as the next edition of the disc as it would increase the historical value of the material.

24. Armstrong, *Guide*, 163.

25. Armstrong, *Guide*, 197–98.

26. Armstrong, "Domesday," 35.

27. Susan Sontag, *On Photography* (Penguin, 1979), 69.

28. R.G. Collingwood, *The Idea of History* (Oxford, 1961), 236.

29. *Survey*, 15–16.

30. Armstrong, "Domesday," 12

31. Armstrong, *Guide*, 239–41.

32. Armstrong, *Guide*, 239.

33. Armstrong, "Domesday," 42; Armstrong, *Guide*, 241.

34. Armstrong, "Domesday," 42.

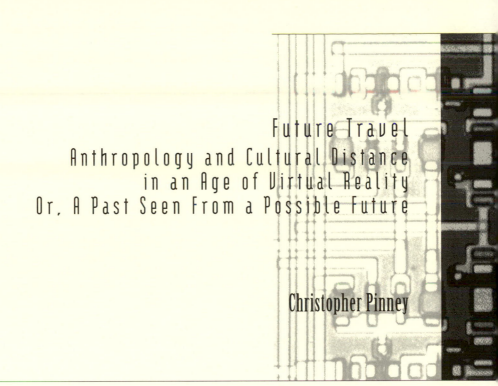

Future Travel
Anthropology and Cultural Distance in an Age of Virtual Reality
Or, A Past Seen From a Possible Future

Christopher Pinney

[The Year is 2029 in instruction unit 47,
London subsection C of the Citizenship Foundation.]

I AM HONORED TO BE ABLE TO ADDRESS YOU ON THE OCCASION OF MY RETIREMENT. IT GIVES me even greater pleasure to record that next week I shall be leaving for Reforestation Zone 27 of the Himalayan foothills where I will be able to spend my last years in quiet solitude and contemplation. When the time comes my ashes will be taken to Kashi where they will be cast into the holy River Ganges. You will all be aware that had I had the misfortune to have retired ten years ago, in 2019, I would have, on this occasion, presented a brief Cryogenic Suspension De-inauguration Lecture after which I would have been frozen pending further scientific breakthroughs. This reversal of fortune is remarkable and it is this change with which I will be concerned here. It is this reinvention of the world we lost, and our reattainment of our nonsubjectivities which I want to examine in this talk.

Until 2020 Virtuality consumers were largely Western and metropolitan and—as we will all be painfully aware—the world's wealth was increasingly consumed within a parallel world of virtuality. The merging of the Nintendo and Fujitsu Corporations with what was left of IBM in 1998 lead to a proliferation throughout the capitalist world of millions of "journey program units" and "teledildonic units." These immobile devices with head mounted visual displays and full body data-gloves (later known as "senso-sheaths") allowed cyberspace foreign holidays in real and imaginary locations[1] and sexual encounters with imaginary or real persons. By the following year three million head-mounted displays and senso-gloves were privately owned in the USA alone.

Tourism, a major source of Third World income, collapsed. Travellers were reluctant to contract Delhi-belly when they could experience the subcontinent pain-free through a virtuality journey program. Disease-free "teledildonics" ("interactive tactile tele-presence[s]"—Rheingold 1991: 348) made sex an increasingly sterile pursuit. This finally limited the spread and mortality from AIDS, but the care of a residual and aging population became an increasing economic burden.

Given over to the simulatory pleasures of immediate and unlimited gratification, this world came to care even less for the agony of the non-metropolitan world.[2] Global food sources were secured, but the punitive measures required to maintain these and their cheap labor supplies became (even more) invisible, lost in a world of simulation which no longer required a veneer of humanity in which to ensconce its exotic holiday locations. The process of periphero-cide apparent throughout the fifteenth to twentieth centuries was obscenely intensified, taken to the point of destruction. By 2004 the Fujitsu syndicate had sold 18 million Personal Virtual Worlds—the new lightweight data suits that produced perfect resolution personal worlds. Two years after this the Global Cyberspace Foundation was established and in the next 15 years a further 450 million Personal Virtual Worlds were sold. Throughout this period we dissidents struggled uselessly for the rights of the non-Virtual world. But what did the Virtual world care when it could experience anything at the touch of a button?

Between 2015 and 2025 this situation began to change however. Across all of Global Zone A there were popular movements in support of debt cancellations and tariff agreement changes to benefit the Southern Global Zone. Citizen migration controls were abolished, huge transfers of wealth arranged and massive restitution and unilateral movements of cultural and historical collections were undertaken.

Younger members of my audience may be amazed to reflect on the fact that only forty years ago when I delivered a paper on the subject of cyberspace[3] I had to explain to the audience in very basic terms what this technology involved. Indeed, younger members of this audience will find it hard to perceive the circumstances of that seminar. It had taken me two hours to travel a mere sixty miles to work that morning and during that journey I saw over 10,000 private motor cars. The sky above London was full of aeroplanes carrying non-Governmental personnel. The audience's only experience with Virtual Reality was a crude device in a local amusement arcade and the academics had still to accept Walter Benjamin's attempt of fifty years previous in his Arcades Project to "bridge the gap between everyday experience and traditional academic concerns, to achieve [a] phenomenological hermeneutics of the profane world" (Buck-Morss 1989: 3). When I gave that seminar it was [still] only eight years since the writer William Gibson had introduced the term cyberspace in his execrable novel *Neuromancer*. There he had described it as:

> Cyberspace. A consensual hallucination experienced daily by billions of legitimate oper-ators, in every nation . . . A graphic representation of data abstracted from the banks of every computer in the human system. Unthinkable complexity. Lines of light ranged in the nonspace of the mind, clusters and constellations of data. (Gibson 1986: 67)

Five years after this the Fujitsu Laboratories—one of the future central corporations in the

Global Cyberspace Foundation—pronounced that: "What Mankind Can Dream, Technology Can Achieve" (Fujitsu Laboratories *Research and Development*, 1989; cited in Rheingold 1991: 291).

In the 1990s the world was posed on the brink of "Virtuality," a technological world of simulation made possible by "Virtual Reality"(VR).[4] This technological apotheosis of man in his role as *Homo depictor* allowed the cybernetic creation of complete simulatory environments communicated to the body via three-dimensional glasses/headsets and body suits.[5] The Japanese Ministry of International Trade and Industry had already organized a "virtual reality study commission" at the beginning of the 1990s which met monthly (Rheingold 1991: 310), and by 1992 some British schoolchildren were learning languages through immersion in a foreign "virtual city."[6] At that time critical responses tended to emphasize its role as future entertainment (or "edutainment"), as a "teledildonic"[7] or glorified video game, and there had been almost no consideration of the implications of this new form of travel and cultural experience for either anthropology or even mass tourism. In any event, those few analyses which had appeared by that stage showed no prescience of coming changes.

At the time I gave the seminar in 1992 I was able to report that Virtual Reality already had a practical utility in the field of medical research. Technology pioneered at the University of North Carolina (Chapel Hill) already allowed wearers of head-mounted displays (the headgear which produces the visual experience of Virtual Reality) to examine three-dimensional molecular structures. Enormously complex mathematical models of, say, human protein dihydrofolate reductase were transformed into structures that the VR traveller could walk around and through. Primitive ARMs (Argonne Remote Manipulator— a Virtual Reality glove) had just begun to generate "haptic" (tactile and propriocentric) forces that permitted the traveler to physically manipulate the molecular structures, searching for new patterns, new possibilities.[8] Similarly architects' plans could by that date be explored and lived in before expensive mistakes were made in their construction.

It was already believed in the 1990s that the increasing military use of VR might also have practical benefits.[9] As Rheingold observed, "war games in cyberspace . . . use less petroleum and create fewer conditions for fatal accidents" (Rheingold 1991: 361). But it had still not been realized that VR would come to displace some "real" wars into the bargain. At that time people were still incensed by Baudrillard's claim that THE GULF WAR [OF 1990] [HAD] NOT TAKE[N] PLACE. Many people's unwillingness to subsume the charred bodies of 150,000 Iraqi conscripts under "simulation"[10] blinded them to the correctness of Baudrillard's claim that it was television (whose interests ran parallel to a recession hit military machine) which made it necessary. The whole technological apparatus impelled the resolution (to be adjudicated microscopically via a million cathode ray tubes) of the questions:

"Am I beautiful enough, am I operational enough, to take my place in the history of warfare?"

Virtual Reality however—as we now know—took this full circle and provided a cyberspace where such suturing can be produced without recourse to death and destruction. When cyberspace became (perceptually and sensually) more "real" than reality it was this— peopled merely by electronic shadows—which became the arena for the resolutions and terminations of politicians and armaments manufacturers.

The *Shape* of Things to Come

Virtual Reality was soon used in anthropology, at first as a teaching instrument—students were able to "visit" (via a "senso-sheath") renowned field sites in cyberspace. Data collected in the field, together with satellite-mapped cartographic data formed the basis of Virtual Reality programs that allowed wearers of the "senso-sheath" to walk through Zandeland or Tikopia and converse with informants through speech interface programs, observe ritual—

do all the things "real," pre-virtuality anthropologists used to do. Although this technology was perfected in 2015, it was founded on work started in 1991—the Fujitsu "Neuro-Drummer" project which developed neural network software—"self-modifying networks of connections, similar to the way some 'neural nets' in the human brain process information" (Rheingold 1991: 295) and the Carnegie-Mellon University's successful attempts to endow artificial cyberspace characters with "personalities" (Rheingold 1991: 308).

Because of the magnitude of the changes which have occurred over the last forty years and particularly the last ten—it is easy to forget how different things were when I started in anthropology. Younger listeners may well be amazed by parts of my narrative. The immediate origin of senso-anthropology can be traced to the coincidence of two factors, both occurring in 2008. The first of these was the Universal distribution by the World-wide Virtual Reality Corporation of senso-sheaths to all Full Citizens of Global Zone A with access to all journey programs for accredited experts. The second, announced only two months later was the restriction of all air travel to Global Government Officers, Forestation Directors and Ozone Technographers. All bulk sea traffic which intersected whale restocking zones had of course ceased three years before.

The situation facing what was then known as "social" anthropology appeared grave. The drift towards studies in Europe at the end of the last century had already been completely stopped by the total ban on anthropological research by the Federation of Warring European Fascist Statelets. For a few years many anthropologists were employed in the post-AIDS rehabilitation and repopulation programs, but this too soon came to an end. Understandably therefore the ban on air travel, even for optimally appraised social investigators caused great anguish and discontent among Division A, B and C anthropologists. In the middle of 2008 therefore the Global Governance Secretariat downgraded nearly all employed anthropologists who were then allocated social and ethical instruction programs for Non-Cerebral Cleansing Workers. A few, who had practiced a "senso" anthropology within their "social" anthropology were retained to train the new generation of "senso"-anthropologists. These were previously underemployed and inexperienced D and E class anthropologists who showed a determination to forge a new science of "senso-anthropology."

By 2012 the print-reading students of the 1990s had been replaced by the experienced consumers of the Nintendo Corporation's "Culture-Travel" programs who had spent their childhood in the "Fujitsu-Disney Cyberpark" (Rheingold 1991: 288). Disappeared worlds of the type which anthropologists from Malinowski[11] to Lévi-Strauss had always mourned were preserved in cyberspace, immune from the depredations of visiting anthropologists.

Some young senso-anthropologists have proclaimed that their science is completely new, a rupture from past practice. Apart from the special case of the radical mutations introduced by the Pandora virus[12] in 2020 this is an exaggeration for much of their experiences are grounded in pre-Virtual anthropology. Most Journey Programs have, however distantly, an origin in the pre-Virtual anthropology monographs written in the last century. These formed the basis for many early programs and the topography and geo-cultural configurations owe much to them.

Heidegger and Cartesian Perspectivalism

The sorry story which I will relate is that of what a German philosopher of the last century—Martin Heidegger—termed "the age of the world picture." It is the history of this and its destruction by Virtual Reality about which I shall speak. It has been argued by some that Virtual Reality was first created in the "anamorphic" rock paintings of the Upper Paleolithic (Rheingold 1991: 380–381). It is claimed that these anamorphic representations were "painted in a precisely distorted manner on natural protuberances and depressions in the limestone in order to give the rendering a three dimensional appearance when viewed from the proper light and angle" (ibid). How interesting that the cavemen of Lascaux should have prefigured the contemporary activities of our contemporary global Cyberspace Foundations.

And how interesting that, in the intervening thirty thousand years, this Virtual Reality could be so effectively suppressed. It is the history of this suppression about which I shall also tell.

Heidegger traced a homology between the bounded visuality of Renaissance and post-Renaissance representations and the Cartesian objectification of the world on which its exploitation by science depended. It is from this stage that "human capability . . . is given over to measuring and executing, for the purpose of gaining mastery over that which is as a whole" (Heidegger 1977: 132). Science, rooted in mathematical knowing in advance, is concerned with the projection of objects within a spatiotemporal field of certainty. "We first arrive at science as research when the Being of whatever is, is sought in such objectiveness" (Heidegger 1977: 127). In a similar vein, Pierre Bourdieu described the "pernicious" effect of the anthropologist "taking up a point of view on the action, withdrawing from it in order to observe it from above and from a distance" (Bourdieu 1977: 2).

C.
Pinney

Heidegger argued that although Plato's stress on *eidos* (1977: 131) prefigured later developments, it is Enlightenment rationalism—manifested through what Martin Jay was later to call Cartesian perspectivalism (1988: 4)—that truly begins to view the world as picture—"the fact that the world becomes a picture at all is what distinguishes the modern age" (1977: 130). Whereas for Parmenides "man is the one who is looked upon by that which is" (1977: 131), in the modern age "that which is . . . come[s] into being . . . through the fact that man first looks upon it, in the sense of a representing that has the character of subjective perception" (*ibid*). In the modern age man sets himself *before* and also *against* nature and the world is "placed in the realm of man's knowing and of his having disposal" (1977: 130). There begins, Heidegger argues,

> that way of being human which mans the realm of human capability as a domain given over to measuring and executing, for the purpose of gaining mastery over that which is as a whole. (1977: 132)

It is an easy matter to trace parallel developments in the practice and theory of Western travel in which, as the world entered the modern period, travel became increasingly systematized and rule-bound. *One important function of this methodization occurring in the sixteenth century was to produce the object of travel as a pictorial surface and the outward and return journey as parts of the picture frame.*

The magnitude of the transformation of the spatial imagery of travel can be conceived through the opposition of the earlier pilgrim's view of the world centered on the Holy Land or Rome with a later stress on a grid of equivalent sites each of which should be surveyed from the highest vantage point so as to immediately perceive the terrain as a whole—what Kenneth Littlejohn termed the "hodological" approach. We may recall the opposition he drew between Temne conceptions of the landscape—a poetics of space—and Western surveying grounded in a massive "dequalification" of this poetic character. European determinations of space, he argued:

> are responsible for an initial dequalification of any landscape they take over. Surveying rests on this initial dequalification, space being reduced to "points" which are all alike. The best method of surveying is by beacons—"points of light"—on hilltops at night, when the qualities of intervening landscape are totally blotted out. (Littlejohn 1967: 335)

In the earlier view the Holy Land is the *axis mundi*, a cosmological and cosmogonic center in which, as Mary W. Helms remarked, to travel through space is also to travel through time back to *illud tempus* (1988: 34ff). This, as Fabian noted, is an incorporative and concentric vision of "circles of proximity to a center in real space and mythical Time, symbolized by the cities of Jerusalem and Rome" (Fabian 1983: 26).

In the sixteenth century—although, as Justin Stagl argued, the travellers' world remained "qualitatively heterogeneous" (1990: 321)—major transformations are apparent.[13] Chief among these is the development of a "formal doctrine of travel" by Zwinger, Turler,

Pyrckmair and Blotius, all working under the influence of Ramist methodology.[14] Joan-Pau Rubies i Mirabet has described this process as "teaching the eye to see" (n.d.). As Stagl noted the terms they used to describe their doctrine—*ars apodemica* or *prudentia peregrinandi*—remained in use until the eighteenth century (the "art of travel," *Reisekunst*—1990: 316), and survived until the end of the twentieth century in the form of anthropological fieldwork, "the most archaic scientific method [then] in existence" (1990: 328).

Stagl studied 300 treatises—manuals for proper and correct travel—published during the sixteenth century and it is clear that their advice mirrors the more general process described by Heidegger in which:

> to represent [*vor-stellen*] means to bring what is present at hand [*das Vorhandene*] before oneself as something standing over against, to relate it to oneself, to the one representing it, and to force it back into this relationship to oneself as the normative realm. (1977: 131)

Thus the new "true" travelling (*peregrinari*) was privileged over the older "aimless and useless rambling (*vagari*)." Movement through space was now justified in terms of education and "useful knowledge" although Stagl suggested that the methodizers were also arguing against those who associated travel with pilgrimage (which had been discouraged during the Reformation) and rising states eager to restrict the freedoms of their subjects (1990: 317).

The *ars apodemica* provided instructions on what and how to observe, on the posing of suitable questions and the recording and evaluation of information (1990: 320). They urged the traveller to "ascertain interesting facts from everywhere and everyone":

> he should communicate with people of all estates and trades . . . and be as persistent as possible without becoming irksome or suspicious to them. There is . . . advice on how to enter into conversation, to pose questions and to elicit information from people, without them noticing it. (1990: 320)

In addition to systematizing the method of encounter with other societies, the manuals also gave advice—some of it based on earlier traditions (1990: 318), concerning behavior at the end of one's travels:

> After returning the traveller should resume his native dress and customs, not show off with foreign expressions or despise old friends, but should remain in epistolary contact with his new won friends abroad. (1990: 318)

Stagl's complex argument then went on to describe the decay of the "art of travel" in the face of rigorous specialized expedition methodologies (such as Degerando's[15]) which in turn produced a reaction in the form of "sentimental journeys"—in which travels in the outer world were merely the pretext for the author's "inner experiences" (Stagl 1990: 326–7).

What was clear here is *the importance of the journey*—of a movement through space—regulated by the appropriate rules in which the full, embodied traveller could practice his "art." Although this is emphasized even more after 1800, even in this early empiricism Stagl noted that great importance was placed on the relative invisibility of the traveller to those among whom he travelled. Appropriate native dress and disguise were recommended which did not arouse the suspicions of local peoples. In the later period of rigidly methodized travel one can perhaps detect the intensification of the perspectival voyage and the subjectivity (predicated precisely on the requirements of *objectivity*) it engendered. As Heidegger wrote:

> Science as research is an absolutely necessary form of this establishing of self in the world; it is one of the pathways upon which the modern age rages to fulfillment of its essence with a velocity unknown to its participants. (1977: 135)

World as Picture, and Simulation

Writing in 1887, Sir John Lubbock (author of *The Origin of Civilization and the Primitive Condition of Man* etc.) claimed in an address on the subject of "The Pleasures of Travel" that:

C.
Pinney

> We may have read the most vivid and accurate description, we may have pored over maps and plans and pictures, and yet the reality will burst on us like a revelation . . . like everyone else, I had read descriptions of the Pyramids. Their form is simplicity itself. I do not know that I could put into words any characteristic of the original for which I was not prepared. It was not that they were larger; it was not that they differed in form, in color, or situation. And yet, the moment I saw them, I felt that my previous impression had been but a faint shadow of the reality. The actual sight seemed to give life to the idea. (1887: 117–8)

This claim is interesting only because it runs so directly counter to the consensus of most pre-Virtuality travelers that the places to which they traveled could only really be judged in terms of their simulatory reference to the expectations created by "maps and plans and pictures."[16] Lubbock's stance is however only provisional and temporary, for having praised "reality" over its faint representational shadows, he then also acknowledged that representations of other places could "help us to see much more than we should perhaps perceive for ourselves" (1887: 119):

> It may even be doubted whether some persons do not derive a more correct impression from a good drawing or description, which brings out the salient points, than they would from actual but unaided, inspection. The idea may gain in accuracy, in character, and even in detail, more than it misses in vividness. (1887: 119)

The manner in which European travelers to the Middle East mediated the real by means of simulation has been brilliantly discussed by Timothy Mitchell. Marx noted that man "raises his structure in imagination before he erects it in reality" (cited in Mitchell 1988: 21) and Mitchell—as also Linda Nochlin has done—unearths ample evidence of this in travelers' responses to the Orient—what was, ostensibly, an external reality—the "great signified." As products of a representational world they were unable to grasp the real except when conceived as an exhibition, a painting, a photograph—"a picture world set apart from its observer" (1988: 23).[17]

One means to this was the adoption of what was termed the "point of view," "a position set apart and outside." Lane for instance sketched Cairo and its suburbs in 1825 from the summit of a large hill used for military telegraphing, echoing the advice given in 1642 by James Howell that upon encountering a strange city the true traveler should ascend the highest summit in order to "gain a general impression of the place and to make a quick drawing" (Stagl 1990: 320).[18]

This clearly exemplifies that Cartesian need to see things as "a whole," as a picture, but this adoption of the bird's eye view also suggests a striving by the imperial cartographer for a divine omniscience for a "point of view" which, prior to the invention of the aeroplane could only have been available to divine vision.[19] This totalization made possible by a lofty and encompassing stance is recognized by the Earl of Ronaldshay in his *India: A Bird's-Eye View* (1924). Here he wrote that:

> man . . . with his varied outlook upon the universe demands a picture of more than the mere outward appearance of things. The bird's-eye view which he requires is a *mosaic* of diverse pieces—a *composition* of historical, pictorial, statistical and ethnographical *vignettes*. (1924: vi; *emphasis added*)

Henry B. T. Somerville of the British Royal Navy who was involved in the hydrographic survey of the Pacific between 1889 and 1900 and recorded his impressions of the Solomon Islands with the help of *Notes and Queries in Anthropology* (Poignant 1980: 16) drew a striking aerial metaphor. In a talk illustrated with lantern slides in 1928 entitled "Surveying in the South Seas" he commented that:

> My title of "Surveying" may refer to two separate things; one technical, as appertaining to hydrography, or chart-making; the other to the wide outlook that may be made, *as from some kind of moral aeroplane*, over the affairs of mankind, and the places he inhabits. (Somerville 1928: 1; *emphasis added*)[20]

Within twentieth-century non-Virtual anthropology what were almost literally birds'-eye views were surprisingly common. Evans-Pritchard credits the Royal Air Force for an air view of the Nuong village in his classic monograph *The Nuer* (1940: plate XVI). Edmund Leach used a similar view to illustrate "the surroundings of Pul Eliya" in his 1961 monograph *Pul Eliya* (1961: plate 1). Marcel Griaule developed a well-known penchant for aerial photography which he himself ascribed to his experiences during his first job as an air force navigator. "Perhaps," he wrote, "it is a quirk acquired in military aircraft, but I always resent having to explore unknown terrain on foot. Seen from high in the air, a district holds few secrets" (cited by Clifford 1988: 68).

Mitchell's argument that "the Orient was something one only ever rediscovered" certainly also holds good for nineteenth- and twentieth-century descriptions of India which were also frequently "reoccurrence[s] of a picture one had seen before, a map one already carried in one's head, as the reiteration of an earlier description" (Mitchell 1988: 30). These "representational" metaphors perhaps have their roots in the great Orientalist Sir William Jones' proclamation in 1773. Here—to quote from Max Muller's later account—Jones is to be imagined "standing lone on the deck of his vessel and watching the sun diving down in to the sea—with memories of England behind him and hopes of India before him":

> I found one evening, on inspecting the observations of the day, that *India* lay before us, *Persia* on our left, whilst a breeze from *Arabia* blew nearly on our stern . . . It gave me inexpressible pleasure to find myself in the midst of so noble an amphitheater, almost encircled by the vast regions of Asia. (cited by Muller 1919: 32)

One hundred years later, in 1873, Edward Lear commented on the "impossible picturesqueness" of his first encounter with Bombay and Sir Richard Temple (one-time Governor of Bombay) noted in his *A Bird's-Eye View of Picturesque India* (1898) that:

> when entering on the field of Indian picturesqueness I feel like one who looks on some vast collection of beautiful Objects, say the National Gallery or Kew Gardens, and knows not where to begin his survey. (1898: 17)

In 1915, Norah Rowan Hamilton records in her *Through Wonderful India and Beyond* that she "had stepped into one of the tales of Haroon Al Raschid" (1915: 16), and in 1921 E.V. Lucas commented:

> It is difficult for a stranger to India, especially when paying only a brief visit, to lose the impression that he is at an exhibition—in a section of a World's Fair. How long it takes for this delusion to wear off I cannot say. All I can say is that seven weeks are not long enough. (1921: 5)

's perception of the world as exhibition even extended in some cases to the experience journey. The Sanskritist Monier Williams interpreted the crew of the *Venetia* which

415

transported him to India in 1875 as possible objects of an academic display:

> The whole company would well have illustrated a lecture on the ethnology of the world. At any rate they formed a singularly picturesque and interesting line of 132 specimens of the human species, methodically arranged for inspection around the quarter deck of the ship. The mixed crowd of passengers . . . ranged round them like animals in a zoological show—offered quite as curious an exhibition of diversified humanity in their own way . . . (1879: 11–12)

The most striking evidence, however, of this "framing" of India was the bestowal of an actual gateway. This was erected in Bombay in in the 1890s in the form of an iron gazebo on Apollo Bunder in Bombay. When George V visited for the Delhi Durbar the gazebo had been replaced by a white plaster triple arch surmounted by a large dome. The Emperor entered and departed the colony through this door. In 1927 the present structure known as the Gateway of India was completed—this being a basalt edifice in the Indo-Saracenic style, a style which Luytens condemned as "mere wall paper" which committed the sin of "capturing Indian details and inscribing their features like hanging pictures on a wall" (Metcalf 1984: 42).[21]

The Rise of the Frame

A once fashionable but now little read French philosopher named Jacques Derrida once posed this question:

> imagine the damage caused by a theft which robbed you only of your frames, or rather of their joints, and of any possibility of reframing your valuables or your art-objects. (Derrida 1987: 18)

From the perspective of 2029 it is quite clear that Virtual Reality performed such a theft of our own frames—of our "World Picture"—but the thirty thousand years between Lascaux and the Global Cyberspace Foundation of the twenty-first century has to be accounted for. We need to account, in other words, for the rise of the "frame" which transformed earlier virtual realities into mere "pictures" for so long.

To raise the possibility of the "picture" is to presuppose a frame. The nature of this frame is necessarily problematic, poised as it is between the inside and the outside. John Berger, an art historian-turned-professional French peasant of the last century, once made a convincing argument concerning the historical role of the frame and the migration of value in European painting. What Berger also stressed—and subsequent events demonstrated the veracity of this—is that the values defined within painting came also to determine the wider philosophical and political values of society. During the period between Van Eyck and Ingres, he argued:

> the framed easel picture, the oil painting, was the primary art product. Wall painting, sculpture, the graphic arts, tapestry, scenic design, even many aspects of architecture were visualized and judged according to a value system which found its purest expression in the easel picture. For the ruling and middle classes the easel picture became a microcosm of the whole world that was virtually assimilable: its pictorial tradition became the vehicle for all visual ideals. (1972b: 213)

What Berger also noted was the manner in which the oil painting permitted the "imitation" of nature in a manner that convinced and pleased the Cartesian mind. Within this system of Cartesian perspectivalism, "nature was predestined for man's use and was the ideal object of his observation" (1972b: 214). For Berger, as for Heidegger and also Lévi-Strauss,[22] European techniques of representation as exemplified and moulded by oil-painting, "refer to the experience of taking possession":

Just as its perspective gathers all that is extended to render it to the individual eye, so its means of representation render all that is depicted into the hands of the individual owner-spectator. Painting becomes the metaphorical act of appropriation. (1972b: 215)

Berger stressed the importance of the ability of oil paint to "render the tangibility, the texture, the luster, the solidity of what it depicts"(1972a: 88), and his argument concerning the depiction of mobile wealth in Holbein's *The Ambassadors* (1533) is still remembered. Within this representational appropriation, however, value was also articulated with reference to the frame. Berger noted how the positioning of the owner-spectator changed. Whereas in earlier paintings the commissioner of a crucifixion or nativity might have been depicted *within* "standing at the foot of the cross or kneeling around the crib" (1972b: 216), this tactic was later made redundant "because physical ownership of the painting guaranteed their immanent presence within it."

This journey of the spectator-owner from the inside to the outside is formalized by a parallel migration of *gold*—a literal signifier of value—from the surface of the picture to the frame. The use of gold picture-grounds had been singled out for particular criticism by Alberti in his treatise on painting written in 1435–6. For Alberti, a rigorous system of linear perspective (in which "vision makes a triangle. The base . . . is the quantity seen and the sides are those rays which are extended from the quantity to the eye"—1966: 47) also involves a mode of portraying light and shade which the use of gold within the picture disrupts. He complained about those who used gold in "their *istoria*" believing that this literal signifier of value would give "majesty." Alberti by contrast advocated its removal to the periphery of the base of the visual pyramid:

Even though one should paint Virgil's Dido whose quiver was of gold, her golden hair knotted with gold, and her purple robe girdled with with pure gold, the reins of her horse and everything of gold, I should not wish gold to be used, for there is more admiration and praise for the painter who imitates the rays of gold with colors. [However] I would not censure the other curved ornaments joined to the painting such as columns, carved bases, capitals and frontespieces even if they were of the most pure and massy gold. (1966: 85)

The gold leaf used by medieval painters (Berger 1972a: 99) is displaced onto the gilded oblongs which—Baroque hiccups aside[23]—formalized the post-Renaissance hegemony of the rectangular world as picture:

Ideally the easel picture is framed. The frame emphasizes that within its four edges the picture has established an enclosed, coherent and absolutely rigorous system of its own. The frame marks the frontier of composition and the picture's illusory but all-pervasive three-dimensional space constitutes the rigid laws of this order. (1972b: 219)

The framed world as picture was also seen by the traveler as the ideal, as a letter home from Flaubert in Cairo[24] in 1850 illustrates:

What can I say about it all? What can I write you? As yet I am scarcely over the initial bedazzlement . . . each detail reaches out to grasp the whole. Then gradually all this becomes harmonious and the pieces fall into place of themselves, in accordance with the laws of perspective. (cited by Mitchell 1988: 21)

Within anthropology over the last several centuries there have clearly been similar migrations of value and—until recently—a parallel reliance on the frame. "Strangeness" and "⸺erence"—anthropology's signifiers of value—have been increasingly pushed to the ⸺where, although they continued to play the same indispensable and constitutive role, their strategic function had changed. Within twentieth-century ethnography "remoteness" (inexplicability/strangeness) was not permitted *within* the frame, just as for Alberti "in a plane panel with a gold ground . . . some places shine that ought to be dark and are dark that ought to be light" (1966: 85). The anthropologist tabooed strangeness (the value created by "difference") within the frame—for it was also a part of his professional competence to make the "strange" familiar and coherent. But, located now along the edges of his account— conceptualized in terms of the "remoteness" of the place or society described through the journeyings to and fro—the value of strangeness was permitted, indeed required.[25]

A Poussin and Claude in Every Back-Yard

Rheingold observed that the first teledildonic experiences would be *communications* with other senso-sheath wearers (over the telephone) rather than experiences with artificial bodies. The frequency of such communications—as we now know—altered previous estimates of value and: "the physical commingling of genital sensations [came] to be regarded as a less intimate act than the sharing of the data structures of [our] innermost self-representations" (Rheingold 1991: 352).

Further fundamental shifts and transformations of notions of value rooted in an earlier scarcity also occurred. Lévi-Strauss once argued that both Poussin and the Impressionists projected the "same amount of beauty" (Lévi-Strauss 1969: 136) onto their subjects.[26] The difference between them was that the access to the subjects depicted had changed:

> The ennoblement and aesthetic promotion of suburban landscapes can be explained perhaps by the fact that they, too, are beautiful, although this had previously not been recognized, but it is mainly a consequence of the fact that the great landscapes which had inspired Poussin were no longer available. (Lévi-Strauss 1969: 136)

Cyberspace threw this process—the progressive beautification of the mundane—into reverse and triggered the decay of the once elegant. The democratization of the previously scarce instituted ever-receding foci of value as the landscapes of Claude and Poussin became common-place scrublands, despised because of their omnipresence.

Chorology in the Brain

The incarnated viewer of the world as picture fused easily with a longer Western tradition of chorology through which a mythic cultural self-presence was instituted. From classical times onward *the travel account* has emerged from the geographic vanishing point to incarnate society and its individuals. Michel de Certeau identified the standard form of such accounts in Montaigne's essay "On Cannibals":

> First comes the outbound journey: the search for the strange, which is presumed to be different [by] the place assigned it in the beginning by the discourse of culture. This *a priori* of difference, the postulate of the voyage, results in a rhetoric of distance in travel accounts. It is illustrated by a series of surprises and intervals (Monsters, storms, lapses of time, etc.) which at the same time substantiate the alterity of the savage, and empower the text to speak from elsewhere and command belief. (de Certeau 1986: 69)

From the perspective of 2029 it is easy to see the Journey Programs of cyberspace as the culmination of two millennia of human traveling. From its origins as a sacred journey, travel has come—via various epochs that have moulded it differently—finally in this age of cyberspace to reside in the brain—a neurological chorology. As Paul Virilio wrote many years ago, "from now on everything will happen without our even moving, without us even having to set out" (Virilio 1989: 112). We are by now used to this proposition, we have spent the last two decades never having even to set out. As Virilio noted we have replaced the ascendancy granted in the nineteenth and twentieth centuries to distance/time with the ascendence of the *"distance/speed* of the electronic picture factories" (Virilio 1989: 112).[27]

But this *intensification* and *culmination* is in no sense grounded in a continuity with these earlier modes. Rather this intensification and increasing speed of the journey has involved a transformation. Exceeding the speed of light, for instance, cannot be comprehended simply in terms of its supercession of speeds less than that of light. There is *a going beyond, a rupture* which must be comprehended. The bullock cart, the steam railway engine and the head-mounted display of the visual component of cyberspace from one perspective suggest obvious affinities, but beyond these lie more significant chasms. Such was understood by Virilio even in the late 1980s:

> If automobile vehicles, that is, all air, land and sea vehicles are today also less "riding ani-mals" than *frames* in the optician's sense, then it is because the self-propelled vehicle is becoming less and less a vector of change in physical location than a means of repre-sentation, the channel for an increasingly rapid optical effect of the surrounding space. (Virilio 1989: 114)

Space has been detemporalized.[28] In other words, travels in cyberspace have permitted "cannibals" without the "monsters, storms, [and] lapses of time."

The Frame of the Other

De Certeau suggested that the Other always figured as a form of vanishing point whose converging lines were the "accounts of the outward journey and the return." (de Certeau 1986: 69) The journey—the setting off and returning—also constituted the historical "frame" of the "picture of a new body" (the Other) which assured the "strangeness of the picture." The parallels with Heidegger's disparaged World as Picture are striking, for here also distance marks the separation of the world from those who should be living *within* it. Travel accounts support this view of the *journey* as the "frame" of the other. This is made most explicitly clear in Augustus Klein's *Among the Gods* (1895) in which he refers to India and Ceylon as "the picture" and the Indian Ocean as "the frame." He describes the passage across the Indian Ocean:

> All through the glowing hours of sunlight the mind reposes in a delightful inactivity, reveling in a dreamy sense of having left far behind all the complicated problems and the intricate life of the land, and of having floated forth into boundless freedom where space and time are not . . .
> Long, long ago the shores of the Western lands sank down beneath the horizon. They are like some far-off dreamland now, and what was once the land of dreams will soon rise up from the sea, and will prove itself, for many months to come, brilliantly and dazzlingly real.
> But we have had enough of the frame. Let us come to the picture itself. (1895: 3–5)

It is now forty years since UNC researchers commenced their work on the possibility of ultrasound images accessed via a head-mounted display which would allow them to "see directly into the living tissue" (Rheingold 1991: 26). Today we are all familiar with the huge range of such diagnostic technology, but there is a more important metaphorical sense in which inside and outside came to lose their fixity. In the short term Virtual Reality dramatically intensified the metropolitan world's oppression of, and indifference to, the "Third World" but it contained within it the seeds of its own destruction. Virtuality was uniquely different from other forms of representation inasmuch as it is "unframed." Unlike paintings, photographs, books, fruit machines, and the cinema, it had no apparent frame, or window. Now, at least, the experiencer of Virtuality does not spectate, but is immersed within, and part of, the visual and experiential field. There had of course been Virtuality journey programs which permitted the traveler to remain an invisible presence, but these were destroyed by the Pandora virus which by a series of complex and brilliant mutations transformed invisible travelers into the visible.[29]

With no window, with no "framing," what were the consequences for cyber-anthropology to be? These possibilities were anticipated in Flaubert's letter from Cairo of 1850, referred to above:

> What can I say about it? What can I write you? As yet I am scarcely over the initial bedaz-zlement . . . each detail reaches out to grip you; it pinches you; and the more you con-centrate on it the less you grasp the whole. Then gradually all this becomes harmonious and the pieces fall into place of themselves, in accordance with the laws of perspective. But the first days, by God it was such a bewildering chaos of colors. (cited by Mitchell 1988: 21)

Flaubert's initial disorientation is manifested as "an absence of pictorial order." During the period of bedazzlement, "each detail reaches out to grip you; it pinches you . . . " (1988: 21). As Timothy Mitchell noted, there is insufficient distance between the viewer and the view and hence the eyes are "reduced" to organs of touch—"without a separation of the self from a picture moreover it becomes impossible to grasp 'the whole'" (1988: 22).

Cultural Distance Without Distance; or Arriving Without Setting Out

Mark Poster had also presciently suggested some of the possible consequences of this in 1990 when he observed that electronic writing[30] would "destabilize the figure of the subject . . . the Cartesian subject who stands outside the world of objects in a position that enables certain knowledges of an opposing world of objects . . ." (1990: 99). Similarly Howard Rheingold had hinted—via a brief New Age excursion into anthropology—at such a possibility and argued that Virtuality might well become the avenue to a recasting of the familiar buccaneering cogito. The thirty-thousand-year-old "anamorphic" paintings in the Lascaux cave may have strived for Virtuality effects through the use of "special theatrical rituals and light-and-sound spectacles intended to alter . . . consciousness" (Rheingold 1991: 382). In the Pueblo *kiva* the pre-Socratic intent is even clearer:

> [M]an is ever reminded that he lives in the whole of the immense and naked universe. And he is constantly made aware of the psychic universal harmony which he must help to perpetuate by his ceremonial life. (Frank Water, cited by Rheingold 1991: 383)

Until representation through cyberspace became the dominant mode however, modern Western selves—as we have already suggested—consolidated themselves through an accumulating externality, an ineluctable accretion of possessions—presences—which effaced (through a displacement) the absence of the very self they purported to reflect.[31] Gayatri Spivak suggested that the self was "always a production rather than [a] ground"(1987: 212), a conclusion that subsequent events amply demonstrated. To recapitulate, among the most important of these possessions for the nineteenth- and twentieth-century bourgeoisie (the most secured selves in history) were representations such as oil paintings (Berger 1972 a & b) and the immanent historicity produced by photographic portraiture (Trachtenberg 1985). Critical to these representations' complicity in producing Western selves was their "framing," their ability to set themselves up as bounded objects against which the self produces its illusion of presence. The frame secures the converging lines which institute the vanishing point which is "the anchor of a system which *incarnates* the viewer."[32]

As the visual and haptic qualities of the medium were refined virtuality quickly came to exceed the reality-effects offered by the non-virtual world. The simulation of, for instance, the 1990s was always largely metaphoric, a world hallucinated by French professors slumped in front of their American TV sets with two six-packs. For most people it was a world whose perceptual seamlessness was always liable to be ruptured by the shaking hand that holds the photograph, the cough from the back row of the cinema auditorium. The imaginary worlds of Virtual Reality by contrast are only "framed" through physical insertion into the "senso-sheath" and the ability to finance it. In the 1990s, many people were arguing that cyberspace would always be "framed" socioeconomically, technologically, and culturally.[33] This was in many ways true, but phenomenologically the Virtual and non-Virtual were blurred. The technology of VR must of course always be consciously entered but once within—especially for the addict—*there is no turning back, no turning away.* There is none of the distance engineered by the frame.

The frame that Virtual Reality lost, however, was not only visual. It is clear that cyberspace worlds could no longer be viewed as pictures. But in addition a *temporal* frame was also shed. The frame imposed by the voyage, the journey, was also lost. In Paul Virilio's words the traveler arrived *without having to set out* and one result of this was that cultural distance came to shed its temporal aspects. Retrospectively we can see that the *temporal* framing provided by the journey was crucial to the framing of certain Western subjectivities. As James Clifford presciently noted, "a journey *makes sense* as a 'coming to consciousness'; its story hardens around an identity. (*Tell us about your trip.*)" (1988: 167; *emphasis added*). There is an intimate connection here between journeying and what Homi Bhabha described as the *depth* of Enlightenment identity. He wrote of "that *dimension of depth* that provides the language of identity with its sense of 'reality'; a measure of the 'me' which emerges from an acknowledgement of my inwardness, the depth of my character . . . "(1987: 6).

Perhaps one can see the efforts of the sixteenth-century authors of the *ars apodemica* as attempts to enforce this *depth* through their stigmatization of *vagari*—mere aimless wandering. To wander aimlessly—for pleasure, not education—suggested openness to chance encounters and to new knowledge. This was the sort of traveling that many states actively discouraged in the sixteenth century as also in Thomas Moore's *Utopia* of 1515 (Helms 1988: 6) for fear of the new and subversive ideas which might thereby be introduced. "Methodized" travel however, to use Stagl's term, positioned the traveler as the apex of the visual cone which mirrored the vanishing point on the other side of the image. The rigorous, "true" traveler, sitting, like James Howell upon the nearest vantage point acquired *depth* through this "point of view." There was no chance here, to echo Flaubert, of anything "gripping you" or "pinching you."

Subjective identities themselves were grounded in narrational journeys as the sagacious neurologist Oliver Sacks observed. Writing in the 1980s about a patient who criss-crossed hundreds of different personae in his daily existence, Sacks mused thus:

> Each of us *is* a singular narrative, which is constructed, continually, unconsciously, by, through, and in us . . . We must recollect ourselves, recollect the inner drama, the narrative, of ourselves. A man *needs* such a narrative, a continuous inner narrative, to maintain his identity, his self. (1986: 105–106)

Since 1839 ever increasing numbers of the world's population have come to construct these narratives and recollect their histories through photographic reproductions, isolated pictures organized in frames that were usually called "albums." Sack's patient who lacked such "a quiet, continuous, inner narrative" was driven to a "narrational frenzy":

Unable to maintain a genuine narrative or continuity, unable to maintain a genuine inner world, he is driven to the proliferation of pseudo-narratives, in a pseudo-continuity, pseudo-worlds peopled by pseudo-people, phantoms. (1986: 106)

Our experience of Virtual Reality has shown that this causality can operate in reverse—the phantom-worlds and pseudo-worlds of cyberspace could also destroy (have also destroyed) the quiet inner narrative on which the nineteenth- and twentieth-century self was built.

In only forty years Virtual reality made "distance-travel" a reality while "time-travel" has remained the domain of science fiction. Some of today's distance-loop paradoxes are as remarkable as any time-loop paradox dreamt up by Ray Bradbury or the makers of *Terminator*. As Constance Penley argued, one of the fascinations of the time-loop paradox was the possibility of observing the "primal-scene" (parental intercourse—one's own conception) and of assuming the identity of one's own father or mother.[34] The collapse of space and distance has been almost as cognitively disorienting as the possibilities offered by the time-loop paradox. The removal of the outward journey and the return—the removal of the frame and the incarnated viewer—have indeed threatened the "entire gridding of the system [which presupposes] that there is a *place* for every *figure*" (de Certeau 1986: 70). Whereas time travel blurred parent and child, Virtual Reality's distance-travel has blurred self and other.

Conclusion

How surprised should we be by the remarkable changes of recent years? Is it a consequence of certain formal features of this new means of representation (and specifically its detemporalization of space) or is it the result of some as yet completely unknowable factor such as the diffusion of the Pandora computer virus?

The contemplative thinker could perhaps have known what would happen without any direct experience of Virtual Reality. Heidegger's litany of complaints about Cartesian perspectivalism concluded with a prescient glimpse of future change. He noted that science as research effloresced in what he termed "giganticism":

everywhere and in the most varied forms and disguises the gigantic is making its appearance. In so doing, it evidences itself simultaneously in the tendency toward the increasingly small. We have only to think of numbers in atomic physics. The gigantic presses forward in a form that actually seems to make it disappear—in the annihilation of great distances by the airplane, in the setting before us of foreign and remote worlds in their everydayness, which is produced at random through radio by the flick of the hand. (1977: 135)

Today the flick of a hand produces worlds not merely conjured by the crackle and static of international radio stations, but seamless three-dimensional worlds peopled by casts of millions and all characterized by an absorbing and hypnotic intensity.

Yet for Heidegger this giganticism—at first apparently the triumph of the world as picture—also came to exist as the "invisible shadow that is cast around all things everywhere when man has been transformed into *subjectum* and the world as picture" (*ibid.*). This "shadow," Heidegger suggested, "extends itself into a space withdrawn from representation" [i.e., from the world as picture] and—he concluded somewhat mysteriously—it may lead to "genuine reflection" (1977: 136). Heidegger's obscurity however is dispensable for there are other and much clearer prefigurations of what has happened over the last forty years.

The first of these dates from 1764, when Oliver Goldsmith published his poem *The Traveler; Or, A Prospect of Society* in which the vantage point, or the "point of view," meets its nemesis. In the poem a traveler sits among the Alps and looks down upon the various countries whose boundaries meet underneath his gaze. As he looks down "where an hundred realms appear" (line 34) he reaches the relativistic conclusion presaged in his dedicatory foreword that "there may be equal happiness in states that are differently governed from our own; that every state has a particular principle of happiness" (1906: 4). Denied a vantage point over a singular terrain the wanderer is faced with a plural multiplicity of worlds whose equal merits he is forced to recognize.[35]

It was precisely this fecundity of worlds and perspectives which would later engage theorists considering the role of narrative in cinematic film. Anticipating the displacements created by Virtual Reality, film theorists—such as Stephen Heath—highlighted the role of narrative in assuring "that the subject positioning brought about by perspective will not be undone by the movement of the film" (Carroll 1988: 162). It was "narrative" and its ability to restore equilibrium which subdued and restored the disruptions created by character and camera movement and editing. It sutured the potentially destabilizing effects of the contradictory lines of force unleashed by devices such as shot/reverse shot sequences.[36] Narrative restores the frame:

> . . . the spectator is situated by a constant renewal of perspective. Thus organized [by narrative], the frame imposes a coherence and continuity, forestalling the risk of textual and subjective chaos. Indeed "the narrative is the very triumph of framing." (Lapsey and Westlake 1988: 139, referring to Stephen Heath)

However, in much the same way that a vantage point which permits more than one simultaneous "prospect" negates the subject's power and control, it has also become evident that the absence of narrative within Virtual Reality has also undercut the position of the subject. Located within cyberspace this subject is not only a participant—rather than simply a spectator poised at the apex of converging lines of vision—but has also lost the temporal frame. In previous epochs this was provided by the narrative of the journey referred to by de Certeau. Today it is gone. We always arrive without setting out, and we are catapulted— disorganized, unpositioned, and *split*.

The second prefiguration of the changes which have occurred recently has an even earlier point of reference. Forty years ago when I gave the talk on this subject in London[37] any one of the audience could have strolled down to the newly constructed Sainsbury wing of what was then the National Gallery and viewed Hans Holbein the Younger's *The Ambassadors*. Now of course they could not because it's in the Museum of New World Art at Delhi. Had they done so, they would have seen the foretelling of everything I have just said. As Homi Bhabha wrote at the time—partly paraphrasing Jacques Lacan:

> The two still figures stand at the center of their world, surrounded by the accou- trements of *vanitas*—a globe, a lute, books and compasses, unfolding wealth [and, he might have added, the signs of travel]. They also stand at that moment of temporal instantaneity where the Cartesian subject emerges—in the same figural time—as the subjectifying relation of geometrical perspective . . . the *depth* of the image of identity. But off-center, in the foreground [. . .] there is a flat spherical object, obliquely angled . . . the disc is a skull; the reminder (and remainder) of death, that makes visible, nothing more than the alienation of the subject, the *anamorphic ghost*. (1987: 7; *emphasis added*)

Perhaps then in addition to Rheingold's list of the cave paintings at Lascaux, and the Pueblo *kivas*—the pre-technological manifestations of Virtual Reality—we need to add Holbein's anamorphic skull. This signifies the death of the subject, and also the death of the traveler. What we have learned is that if I can arrive without ever having to set out, that self-same "I" ceases to exist.

Notes

The latter section of this title is intended to indicate my indebtedness to arguments made many years ago by John Berger (see Berger 1972b). Other recent considerations of Virtual Reality which may be of interest include Cornell (1991); Brown (1991); D'Amato (1992).

1.   A trend which had been forecast as early as the 1980s in the film *Total Recall* (Dir. James Cameron, based on the Philip K. Dick novel).

2.   VR's capability as a sedative or hallucinogen was much touted in the early 1990s. Rheingold suggested that "in a world of tens of billions of people, perhaps cyberspace is a better place to keep most of the population relatively happy, most of the time." A global system which was not prepared to provide food for half its population proved unwilling, however, to provide (greatly more expensive) cyberspace.

3.   This was given on 17th February 1992 in the Department of Anthropology and Sociology, School of Oriental and African Studies, University of London. I would like to thank all surviving seminar participants, particularly Kit Davis, Tim Screech, David Parkin, Claire Harris & Lisa Croll for their kind suggestions. I am also grateful to Chris Wright, Lucien Taylor and an anonymous reviewer for *VAR* for their help.

4.   The subject of Howard Rheingold's fascinating book, *Virtual Reality*, Summit Books, $22.05; Secker and Warburg, £16.99.

5.   "Embedded in the inner surface of the suit, using a technology that does not exist, is an array of intelligent sensor-effectors—a mesh of tiny tactile vibrators of varying degrees of hardness, hundreds of them per square inch, that can receive and transmit a realistic sense of tactile presence" (Rheingold 1991).

6.   This was a project funded by the British Department of Employment in West Denton School, Newcastle upon Tyne but at that stage involved merely the use of desktop color monitors rather than VPL Eyephones and Datagloves (*The Guardian*, 16.1.92.: 35).

7.   A term first coined in 1974 by Theodor Nelson to describe How Wachspes's patent for the conversion of sound into tactile sensation (Rheingold 1991: 345).

8.   Rheingold 1991: 26–7. Most of Rheingold's book was given over to a survey of contemporary research in the USA and Japan (with brief excursions to France and Britain).

9.   Although just as many analyses stressed its origins as a form of military technology. Had a talk such as this been written in the 1990s without the benefit of hindsight it would very probably have been attacked for its effacement of its own "logistics of perception" to use Virilio's term. Other critics—unable to see what has actually occurred—might have derided its mock-apocalyptic tones as the kind of futurology which might well have revealed itself to be McLuhanism part-two—a critical frenzy which demonstrated the critic's distance from the quotidian inertias which always scupper the logics of "innovation." However, had they said any of these things, time would have proved them wrong.

10.   Baudrillard argued that it was a "televisual subterfuge," a simulacral contest in which "what was at stake was not political or territorial domination, but the very status of war itself, its meaning and its future" (Gilbert Adair, 'Fading of the Looking Glass War', *The Guardian* 11.7.91).

11.   "Ethnology is in the sadly ludicrous, not to say tragic, position that at the very moment when it begins to put its workshop in order, to forge its proper tools, to start ready for work on its appointed task, the material of its study melts away with hopeless rapidity. Just now, when the methods and aims of scientific field ethnology have taken shape, when men fully trained for work have begun to travel into savage countries and study their inhabitants—these die away under our very eyes" (Malinowski 1922: xv).

12.   This still remains a virus of great mystery. It is currently believed that this remarkable and elusive creature was devised by disaffected software engineers from the Southern Global Zone. Among its chief interventions was its embodying and rendering visible of all Virtuality travelers in whatever programs they inhabited. Until 2020 a sizeable part of the mass Virtuality market used voyeuristic and masturbatory programs which permitted their own invisibility in cyberspace. After the ineradicable corruptions following the global spread of the Pandora virus this was no longer possible.

13.   I do not wish to overstate this however. Stagl notes that although the *ars apodemica* represented the "secularization of pilgrimage," they retained certain aspects of an earlier genre—directions for pilgrims (1990: 317). Readers are recommended to refer to Stagl's original and important research.

14.   According to the "practically oriented universal method for all arts and sciences" (Stagl 1990: 312) developed by Petrus Ramus (1515–1572).

15.   Joseph-Marie Degerando prepared a "method for the observation of savage people" for Baudin's expedition in 1800. See Degerando (1969).

16. Perhaps some sense of the process of textual recuperation and generation centered on travel is given by Boswell's remark that he made journeys only "in order to keep a journal" (Carter 1988: 47). There are clearly also profound and formative links between the concepts of travel, writing and authorship which (to coin a phrase) *space* does not permit me to *pursue*.

17. Mitchell also notes that Lane's *Account of the Manners and Customs of the Modern Egyptians* (1835) an early piece of written para-ethnography, had originated as part of a larger visual record of Egypt made with a *camera lucida*. This was abandoned after Lane was unable to find a publisher who could reproduce "the minute and mechanical accuracy of the drawings" (1988: 23).

18. Mitchell cites Herman Melville's complaint during a visit to Constantinople: "Perfect labyrinth. Narrow. Close, shut in. If one could but get *up* aloft" (1988: 32).

19. However, it should be noted that in the sixteenth century Zwinger had described travel by air, referring to the "examples of Daedulus and of the Angels" (Stagl 1990: 316).

20. I am grateful to Roslyn Poignant for directing my attention to this.

21. The "gateway" was also occasionally a "door" as in Norah Rowan Hamilton's comments in 1915 on a sweet alluring smell as she approached the coast of Bombay on the steamer "Persia" concluding that "the door had been left ajar into the conservatory of the world" (1915: 14). A study of the relationship between the visual framing, and India's "essence" conceived of as perfume remains to be done. A good place to start would be with Pasolini's account of his trip with Moravia to Bombay, *L'Odore dell' India* (1974, English translation *The Scent of India*, 1984).

22. Berger wrote that "significantly enough" it was an anthropologist (Lévi-Strauss) who first came close to recognizing the "analogy between *possessing* and the way of seeing which is incorporated in oil painting" (1972a: 83).

23. See Jay (1988: 16) for comments on Christine Buci-Glucksmann's assessment on the "explosive power of baroque vision."

24. Appropriately, Flaubert was on a photographic mission with Maxime du Camp.

25. See Ardener (1987) for the view that his "remoteness" was not an exclusive function of geography.

26. Sasha Markovic has pointed out the fallaciousness of the argument here, given that Poussin's landscapes were "imaginary." Lévi-Strauss would have done better to cite an artist such as Constable.

27. Similarly, Mark Poster when anticipating the decentering effects of "computer writing" in 1990, stressed its antecedents in the forms of earlier conventional transport systems which "increase the speed with which bodies move in space." (1990: 128). This however suggests a false continuity, a continuum which the ruptures of recent years have invalidated. See below.

28. See Soja (1989).

29. Pandora's roots can be traced as far back as the Michelangelo virus which corrupted vast amounts of corporate software on 6th March 1992.

30. He was referring here to word-processor inscribed text.

31. See C.B.MacPherson (1962) and James Clifford's interesting use of this (1988: 217–18).

32. Norman Bryson (1983: 106) cited by Rotman (1987: 14). Bryson makes an evolutionary distinction between the "glance" and the "gaze," the "vanishing point" and the "punctum," and a corporeal and disembodied spectator (see Rotman 1987: 32–33). Among the various representational modalities discussed by Rotman, it is perspectival painting coded by the vanishing point ("founded on a fiction of a framed portion of nature, a detached fragment of some prior visual 'reality,' being represented with truth and accuracy" 1987: 40) which most clearly parallels the realist strategies of travel and anthropological accounts. The distinctions drawn by commentators such as Bryson, Alpers and Jay between various forms of subject positioning and perspective contingent on specific historical moments and movements in Western artistic and other representation do not, I believe, overturn the general trajectory and hegemony of Cartesian perspectivalism described in this talk.

33. One of these people was Lucien Taylor, the then editor of *V.A.R.* (personal communication).

34. Thus in *The Terminator* a character called John Connor chooses Kyle Reese to travel back from 2010 to prevent the Terminator (a killer cyborg) from exterminating Sarah Connor, the future mother of John ("the man who will lead the last remnants of humanity to victory over the machines that are trying to rid the world of humans.") A photograph of Sarah (with "a faraway look on her face and a sad smile") causes Kyle to fall in love with her; they make love; he is killed; she destroys the Terminator; and then gives birth to her son shortly after the photograph—of her thinking about Kyle—is taken by a Mexican boy with a

polaroid. As Penley notes, "cause and effect are not only reversed but put into a circle: the later events are caused by the earlier events, and the earlier by the later" (1989: 127). John Connor gets to choose his own father and "within the narrative logic of this film it is Kyle who is the motherfucker" (1989: 129).

35. Travelling without ever reaching his goal—his vanishing point:

> My fortune leads to traverse realms alone,
> And find no spot of all the world my own.

—the wanderer desolately ascends the mountains only to discover the reasons for his own rootlessness and lack of placed-ness—the misrule of his own country and the migration of villagers:

> Forced from their homes, a melancholy train,
> To traverse climes beyond the western main.

36. A pair of shots, each of which represents "from a more or less oblique angle, one endpoint of an imaginary 180-degree line running through the scenographic space" (Jean Pierre Oudart, cited by Carroll 1988: 183).

37. See footnote 4.

References

Alberti, Leon Batista. 1966. *On Painting*. Trans. John R. Spencer. New Haven: Yale University Press.

Ardener, Edwin. 1987. "Remote Areas: Some Theoretical Considerations." In *Anthropology at Home*, ed. A. Jackson. ASA 25. London: Tavistock.

Berger, John. 1972a. "Past Seen from a Possible Future." In his *Selected Essays and Articles: The Look of Things*. Harmondsworth: Penguin.

————. 1972b. *Ways of Seeing*. Harmondsworth: Penguin Books and BBC Publishing.

Bhabha, Homi. 1987. "Interrogating Identity." In *Identity*, ed. Homi Bhabha, London: Institute of Contemporary Arts.

Bourdieu, Pierre. 1977. *An Outline of Theory of Practice*. Cambridge: Cambridge University Press.

Brown, Paul. 1991. "Metamedia and Cyberspace: Advanced Computers and the Future of Art." In *Culture and Technology in the Late Twentieth Century*, ed. Philip Hayward. London: John Libbey.

Bryson, Norman. 1983. *Vision and Painting: The Logic of the Gaze*. London: Macmillan.

Buck-Morss, Susan. 1989. *The Dialectics of Seeing: Walter Benjamin and the Arcades Project*. Cambridge, Mass.: MIT Press.

Carroll, Noel. 1988. *Mystifying Movies: Fads and Fallacies in Contemporary Film Theory*. New York: Columbia University Press.

Carter, Paul. 1988. "Invisible Journey: Exploration and Photography in Australia, 1839–1889." In *Island in the Stream: Myths of Place in Australian Culture*, ed. Paul Foss. Leichhardt (NSW): Pluto Press.

Clifford, James. 1988. "Tell Me About Your Trip: Michel Leiris." In his *The Predicament of Culture: Twentieth-Century Ethnography, Literature and Art*. Cambridge: Harvard University Press.

Cornwell, Regina. 1991. "Where is the Window? Virtual Reality Technologies Now." *Artscribe* (January): 52–54.

Cuignon, Charles. 1983. *Heidegger and the Problem of Knowledge*. Indianapolis: Hackett Publishing Co.

D'Amato, Brian. 1992. "The Last Medium: the Virtues of Virtual Reality." *Flash Art* XXV, 162 (Jan–Feb): 96–98.

De Certeau, Michel. 1986. "Montaigne's 'Of Cannibals': The savage 'I'." In his *Heterologies: Discourse on the Other*. Manchester: Manchester University Press.

Degerando, Jean-Marie. 1969. *The Observation of Savage Peoples*. London: Routledge.

Derrida, Jacques. 1987. *The Truth in Painting*. Chicago: Chicago University Press.

Evans-Pritchard, Edward. 1940. *The Nuer*. Oxford: Clarendon Press.

Fabian, Johannes. 1983. *Time and the Other: How Anthropology makes its Object*. New York: Columbia University Press.

Gibson, William. 1986. *Neuromancer*. London: Grafton (first published 1984).

Goldsmith, Oliver. 1906. *The Traveler and The Deserted Village*. Ed. W. Murison. Cambridge: Cambridge University Press.

Hamilton, Norah Rowan. 1915. *Through Wonderful India and Beyond*. London: Holden and Hardingham.

Heidegger, Martin. 1977. "The Age of the World Picture." In his *The Question Concerning Technology and Other Essays*. New York: Harper Torchbooks.

Helms, Mary W. 1988. *Ulysses' Sail.* Princeton: Princeton University Press.

Jay, Martin. 1988. "The Scopic Regimes of Modernity." In *Vision and Visuality*, ed. Hal Foster. Seattle: Dia Press.

Klein, Augustus. 1895. *Among the Gods: Scenes of India—With Legends Along the Way.* Edinburgh: William Blackwood.

Lapsey, R. & M. Westlake. 1988. *Film Theory: An Introduction.* Manchester: Manchester University Press.

Leach, Edmund R. 1961. *Pul Eliya: A Village in Ceylon.* Cambridge: Cambridge University Press.

Lear, Edward. 1953. *Indian Journal: Watercolours and Extracts from the Diary of Edward Lear, 1873–1875.* Ed. R. Murphy. London: Jarrolds.

Lévi-Strauss, Claude & Charbonnier, Georges. 1969. *Conversations with Claude Lévi-Strauss.* London: Cape.

Littlejohn, Kenneth. 1967. "The Temne House." In *Myth and Cosmos*, ed. J. Middleton. New York: Natural History Press.

Lubbock, John. 1887. "The Pleasures of Travel." In his *The Pleasures of Life.* London: Macmillan.

Lucas, E.V. 1924. *Roving East and Roving West.* London: Methuen.

Macpherson, C.B. 1962. *The Political Theory of Possessive Individualism.* Oxford: Oxford University Press.

Malinowski, Bronislaw. 1922. *Argonauts of the Western Pacific.* London: Routledge.

Metcalf, Thomas. 1984. "Architecture and the Representation of Empire: India 1860–1910." *Representations* 6: 37–65.

Mitchell, Timothy. 1988. *Colonizing Egypt.* Cambridge: Cambridge University Press.

Muller, Max. 1919. *India: What Can it Teach Us?* London: Longmans, Green and Co.

Pasolini, Pier Paolo. 1984. *The Scent of India.* London: Olive Press.

Penley, Constance. 1989. "Time Travel, Primal Scene, and the Critical Dystopia." In her *The Future of an Illusion: Film, Feminism and Psychoanalysis.* London Routledge.

Poignant, Roslyn. 1980. *Observers of Man.* London: Royal Anthropological Institute

Poster, Mark. 1990. *The Mode of Information: Poststructuralism and Social Context.* Oxford: Polity.

Rheingold, Howard. 1991. *Virtual Reality.* New York: Summit Books.

Ronaldshay, Earl of. 1924. *India: A Bird's Eye View.* London: Constable.

Rubies i Mirabet, Joan-Pau. n.d. "Teaching the Eye to See." Unpublished ms.

Sacks, Oliver. 1986. *The Man Who Mistook His Wife for a Hat.* London: Picador.

Soja, Edward. 1989. *Postmodern Geographies: The Reassertion of Space in Critical Social Theory.* London: Verso.

Somerville, Henry B.T. 1928. "Surveying in the South Seas." Unpublished ms. [Photographic Collection. Royal Anthropological Institute, London].

Spivak, Gayatri Chakravorty. 1987. "Subaltern Studies: Deconstructing Historiography." In her *In Other Worlds: Essays in Cultural Politics.* London: Methuen.

Stagl, Justin. 1990. "The Methodising of Travel in the 16th Century: A tale of three cities." *History and Anthropology* 4 (2): 303–338.

Trachtenberg, Alan. 1985. "Albums of War: On Reading Civil War Photographs" *Representations* 9: 1–32.

Williams, Monier. 1879. *Modern India and the Indians.* London: Trubner's Oriental Series.

Virilio, Paul. 1989. "The Last Vehicle." In his *Looking Back on the End of the World*, ed. Dietmar Kamper & Christoph Wulf. NY: Semiotext(e).

four

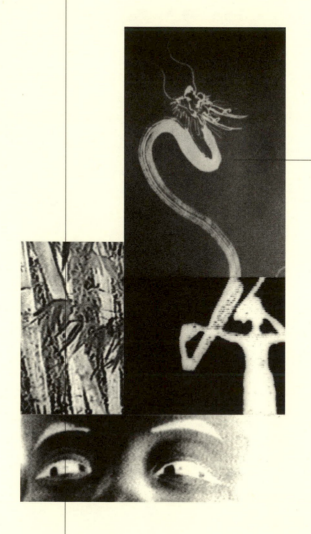

Visualizing Theory: "In Dialogue"

Speaking Nearby

Nancy N. Chen and Trinh T. Minh-ha

Nancy N. Chen: *One of the most important questions for myself deals with the personal. In your latest film* Shoot for the Contents *Clairmonte Moore refers to himself as "a member of the residual class" which is a euphemism for "living underground, for living outside the norm, and for living outside of the status quo." Then another character Dewi refers to having the "pull" of being here and there. I think that this reflects on the personal and I would like to ask how your family background or personal experience has influenced your work.*

Trinh T. Minh-Ha: Although the ideology of "starting from the source" has always proved to be very limiting, I would take that question into consideration since the speaking or interviewing subject is never apolitical, and such a question coming from you may be quite

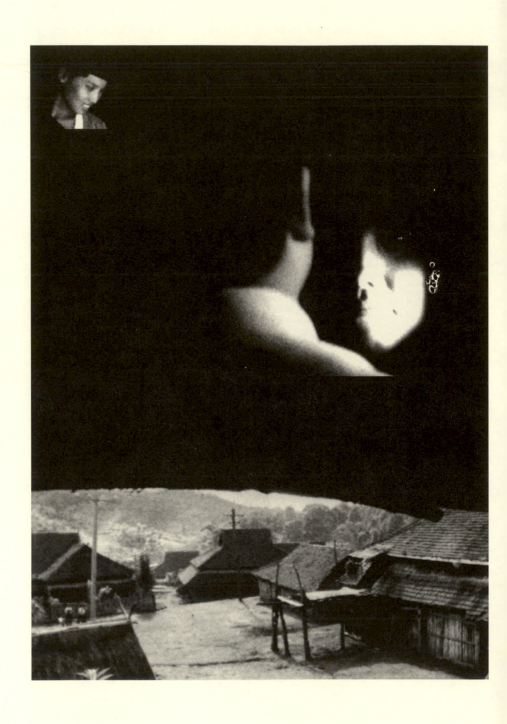

Images from *Shoot for the Contents*, Trinh T. Minh-ha.

differently nuanced. There is not much, in the kind of education we receive here in the West, that emphasizes or even recognizes the importance of constantly having contact with what is actually within ourselves, or of understanding a structure from within ourselves out. The tendency is always to relate to a situation or to an object as if it is only outside of oneself. Whereas elsewhere, in Vietnam, or in other Asian and African cultures for example, one often learns to "know the world inwardly," so that the deeper we go into ourselves, the wider we go into society. For me, this is where the challenge lies in terms of materializing a reality, because the personal is not naturally political, and every personal story is not necessarily political.

In talking about the personal, it is always difficult to draw that fine line between what is merely individualistic and what may be relevant to a wider number of people. Nothing is *given* in the process of understanding the "social" of our daily lives. So every single work I come up with is yet another attempt to inscribe this constant flow from the inside out and outside in. The interview with Clairmonte in SHOOT FOR THE CONTENTS is certainly a good example to start with. His role in the film is both politically and personally significant. In locating himself, Clairmonte has partly contributed to situating the place from which the film speaks. The way a number of viewers reacted to his presence in the film has confirmed what I thought might happen when I was working on it. Usually in a work on China, people do not expect the voice of knowledge to be other than that of an insider—here a Chinese—or that of an institutionalized authority—a scholar whose expertise on China would immediately give him or her the license to speak about such and such culture, and whose superimposed name and title on the screen serve to validate what he or she has to say. No such signpost is used in SHOOT; Clairmonte, who among all the interviewees discusses Chinese politics most directly, is of African rather than Chinese descent; and furthermore, there is no immediate urge to present him as someone who "speaks as . . ." What you have is the voice of a person who little by little comes to situate himself through the diverse social and political positions he assumes, as well as through his analysis of himself and of the media in the States. So when Clairmonte designates himself literally and figuratively as being from a residual class, this not only refers to the place from which he analyzes China—which is not that of an expert about whom he has spoken jokingly, but more let's say that of an ordinary person who is well versed in politics. The designation, as you've pointed out, also reflects back on my own situation: I have been making films on Africa from a hybrid site where the meeting of several cultures (on non-Western ground) and the notions of outsider and insider (Asian and Third World in the context of Africa) need to be re-read.

This is where you talk about the intersubjective situation in your writings.

Right. I have dealt with this hybridity in my previous films quite differently, but the place from which Clairmonte speaks in SHOOT is indirectly linked to the place from which I spoke in relation to Africa. Just as it is bothersome to see a member of the Third World talking about (the representation of) another Third World culture—instead of minding our own business (*laughter*) as we have been herded to—it is also bothersome for a number of viewers who had seen SHOOT, to have to deal with Clairmonte's presence in it. And of course, the question never comes out straight; it always comes out obliquely like: "Why the Black man in the film? Has this been thought out?" Or, in the form of assumptions such as: "Is he a professor at Berkeley?" "Is he teaching African Studies or Sociology?"

In some ways those questions indicate there's a need for authenticity. My question about Clairmonte concerns what he said about identity and I think that the issue of identity runs throughout all of your work. You've often talked about hyphenated peoples and I'm interested if in any way that notion stems from your personal experience. Have you felt that people have tried to push you, to be a Vietnamese-American or Asian-American, or woman-filmmaker? All of these different categories is what Clairmonte points out to. In your works and writings you distinctly push away that tendency. I think you are quite right in pointing out earlier that there is a very strong tendency to begin with a psychological sketch like "What are your primary influences . . ." (laughter) *I would be very interested in learning about your particular experiences in Vietnam. Could you talk more about that?*

I will. But again, for having been asked this question many times, especially in interviews for newspapers, I would link here the problematization of identity in my work with what the first chapter of *Woman, Native, Other* opened on: the dilemma, especially in the context of women, of having one's work explained (or brought to closure) through one's personality and particular attributes. In such a highly individualistic society as the one we belong to here, it is very comforting for a reader to consume difference as a commodity by starting with the personal difference in culture or background, which is the best way to escape the issues of power, knowledge and subjectivity raised.

My past in Vietnam does not just belong to me. And since the Vietnamese communities, whether here in the U.S. or there in Vietnam, are not abstract entities, I can only speak while learning to keep silent, for the risk of jeopardizing someone's reputation and right to speech is always present. Suffice it to say that I come from a large family, in which three different political factions existed. These political tendencies were not always freely assumed, they were bound to circumstances as in the case of the family members who remained in Hanoi (where I was born) and those who were compelled to move to Saigon (where I grew up). The third faction comprised those involved with the National Liberation Front in the South. This is why the dualistic divide between pro- and anti-communists has always appeared to me as a simplistic product of the rivalry between (what once were) the two superpowers. It can never even come close to the complexity of the Vietnam reality. All three factions had suffered under the regime to which they belong, and all three had, at one time or another, been the scapegoat of specific political moments. As a family however, we love each other dearly despite the absurd situations in which we found ourselves divided. This is a stance that many viewers have recognized in Surname Viet Given Name Nam, but hopefully it is one that they will also see in the treatment of Mao as a figure and in the multiple play between Left and Right, or Right and Wrong in Shoot.

How I came to study in the States still strikes me today as a miracle. The dozen of letters I blindly sent out to a number of universities to seek admission into work-study programs . . . It was like throwing a bottle to the sea. But, fortunately enough, a small school in Ohio (Wilmington College) of no more than a thousand and some students wanted a representative of Vietnam. And so there I was, studying three days of the week and working the other three days at a hospital, in addition to some other small odd jobs that helped me to get through financially. As an "international student," I was put in contact with all other foreign students, as well as with "minority" students who were often isolated from the mainstream of Euro-American students. It was hardly surprising then that the works of African American poets and playwrights should be the first to really move and impress me. By the sheer fact that I was with an international community, I was introduced to a range of diverse cultures. So the kind of education I got in such an environment (more from outside than inside the classroom) would not have been as rich if I had stayed in Vietnam or if I had been born in the States. Some of my best friends there, and later on at the University of Illinois (where I got an M.A in French Literature and Music; a Master of Music in Composition; and a Ph.D in Comparative Literatures) were Haitians, Senegalese and Kenyans. Thanks to these encounters, I subsequently decided to go to Senegal to live and teach.

When I planned for university education abroad, I could have tried France (where financially speaking, education is free) instead of the United States. I decided on the United States mainly because I wanted a rupture (*laughter*) with the educational background in Vietnam that was based on a Vietnamized model of the old, pre-1968 French system. Later on, I did go to France after I came to the States, in a mere university exchange program. It was one of these phenomena of colonialism: I was sent there to teach English to French students (*laughter*).

During this year in France I didn't study with any of the writers whose works I appreciate. Everything that I have done has always been a leap away from what I have learned, and nothing in my work directly reflects the education I have had except through a relation of displacement and rupture as mentioned. While in Paris, I studied at the Sorbonne Paris-IV. It was the most conservative school of the Sorbonne. But one of the happy encounters I made was with noted Vietnamese scholar and musician Tran Van Khe, who continues until today to shuttle to and fro between France and Vietnam for his research, and with whom I studied ethnomusicology. That's the part that I got the most out of in Paris. So you go to Paris, finally to learn ethnomusicology with a Vietnamese (*laughter*).

This throws my question about intellectual influences or ruptures the question (laughter). *In all your works, but particularly your writings on anthropology, ethnography and ethnographic films, there's a critique of the standard, the center of rationality, the center of TRUTH. I think that critique is also shared by many anthropologists, especially those in the post-structuralist tradition. Do you think that there is more possibility in ethnography if people use these tools? What do you think would be possible with reflexivity or with multivocality?*

Anthropology is just one site of discussion among others in my work. I know that a number of people tend to focus obsessively on this site. But such a focus on anthropology despite the fact that the arguments advanced involve more than one occupied territory, discipline, profession and culture seems above all to tell us where the stakes are the highest. Although angry responses from professionals and academics of other fields to my films and books are intermittently expected, most of the masked outraged reactions do tend to come from Euro-American anthropologists and cultural experts. This, of course, is hardly surprising. They are so busy defending the discipline, the institution and the specialized knowledge it produces that what they have to say on works like mine only tells us about themselves and the interests at issue. I am reminded here of a conference panel years ago in which the discussion on one of my previous films was carried out with the participation of three Euro-American anthropologists. Time and again they tried to wrap up the session with dismissive judgements, but the audience would not let go of the discussion. After over an hour of intense arguments, during which a number of people in the audience voiced their disapproval of the anthropologists' responses, one woman was so exasperated and distressed, that she simply said to them: "the more you speak, the further you dig your own grave."

If we take the critical work in REASSEMBLAGE for example, it is quite clear that it is not simply aimed at the anthropologist, but also at the missionary, the Peace Corps volunteer, the tourist, and last but not least at myself as onlooker. In my writing and filmmaking, it has always been important for me to carry out critical work in such a way that there is room for people to reflect on their own struggle and to use the tools offered so as to further it on their own terms. Such a work is radically incapable of prescription. Hence, these tools are sometimes also appropriated and turned against the very filmmaker or writer, which is a risk I am willing to take. I have, indeed, put myself in a situation where I cannot criticize without taking away the secure ground on which I stand. All this is being said because your question, although steered in a slightly different direction, does remind me indirectly of another question which I often get under varying forms: at a panel discussion in Edinburgh on Third Cinema for example, after two hours of interaction with the audience, and of lectures by panelists, including myself, someone came to me and said in response to my paper: "Oh, but then anthropology is still possible!" I took it both as a constructive statement and a misinterpretation. A constructive statement, because only a critical work developed to the limits or effected on the limits (here, of anthropology) has the potential to trigger such a question as: "Is anthropology still a possible project?" And a misinterpretation, because this is not just a question geared toward anthropology, but one that involves all of us from the diverse fields of social sciences, humanities and arts.

Whether reflexivity and multivocality contribute anything to ethnography or not would have to depend on the way they are practiced. It seems quite evident that the critique I made

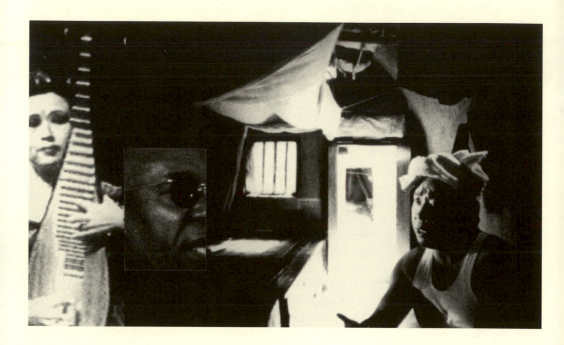

of anthropology is not new; many have done it before and many are doing it now. But what remains unique to each enterprise are not so much the objects as the relationships drawn between them. So the question remains: how? How is reflexivity understood and materialized? If it is reduced to a form of mere breast-beating or of self-criticism for further improvement, it certainly does not lead us very far. I have written more at length on this question elsewhere ("Documentary Is/Not a Name," *October* No. 52, 1990) and to simplify a complex issue, I would just say here that if the tools are dealt with only so as to further the production of anthropological knowledge, or to find a better solution for anthropology as a discipline, then what is achieved is either a refinement in the pseudo-science of appropriating Otherness or a mere stir within the same frame. But if the project is carried out precisely at that limit where anthropology could be abolished in what it tries to institutionalize, then nobody here is on safe ground. Multivocality, for example, is not necessarily a solution to the problems of centralized and hierarchical knowledge when it is practiced accumulatively—by juxtaposing voices that continue to speak within identified boundaries. Like the much abused concept of multiculturalism, multivocality here could also lead to the bland "melting-pot" type of attitude, in which "multi" means "no"—no voice—or is used only to better mask the Voice—that very place from where meaning is put together. On the other hand, multivocality can open up to a non-identifiable ground where boundaries are always undone, at the same time as they are accordingly assumed. Working at the borderline of what is and what no longer is anthropology one also knows that if one crosses that border, if one can depart from where one is, one can also return to it more freely, without attachment to the norms generated on one side or the other. So the work effected would constantly question both its interiority and its exteriority to the frame of anthropology.

This goes back to your previous point that being within is also being without, being inside and outside. I think this answers my next question which is about how if naming, identifying and defining are problematic, how does one go about practicing? I think that you are saying that it also opens up a space being right on that boundary. I would now like to turn from theory to filmmaking practice. Your writing has often been compared to performance art. Could you say that this is also true of your filmmaking as well in the four films that you have made so far?

I like the thought that my texts are being viewed as performance art (*laughter*). I think it is very adequate. Viewers have varied widely in their approaches to my films. Again, because of the way these films are made, how the viewers enter them tells us acutely how they situate themselves. The films have often been compared to musical compositions and appreciated by people in performance, architecture, dance or poetry for example. So I think there is something to be said about the filmmaking process. Although I have never consciously taken inspiration from any specific art while I write, shoot or edit a film, for me, the process of making a film comes very close to those of composing music and of writing poetry. When one is not *just* trying to capture an object, to explain a cultural event, or to inform for the sake of information; when one refuses to commodify knowledge, one necessarily disengages oneself from the mainstream ideology of communication, whose linear and transparent use of language and the media reduces these to a mere vehicle of ideas. Thus, every time one puts forth an image, a word, a sound or a silence, these are never instruments simply called upon to serve a story or a message. They have a set of meanings, a function, and a rhythm of their own within the world that each film builds anew. This can be viewed as being characteristic of the way poets use words and composers use sounds.

Here I'll have to make clear that through the notion of "poetic language," I am certainly not referring to the poetic as the site for the consolidation of a subjectivity, or as an estheticized practice of language. Rather, I am referring to the fact that language is fundamentally reflexive, and only in poetic language can one deal with meaning in a revolutionary way. For the nature of poetry is to offer meaning in such a way that it can never end with what is said or shown, destabilizing thereby the speaking subject and exposing the fiction of all rationalization. Roland Barthes astutely summed up this situation when he remarked that "the real antonym of the 'poetic' is not the prosaic, but the stereotyped." Such a statement is all the more perceptive as the stereotyped is not a false representation, but rather, an arrested representation of a changing reality. So to avoid merely falling into this pervasive world of the stereotyped and the clichéd, filmmaking has all to gain when conceived as a performance that engages as well as questions (its own) language. However, since the ideology of what constitutes "clarity" and "accessibility" continues to be largely taken for granted, poetic practice can be "difficult" to a number of viewers, because in mainstream films and media our ability to play with meanings other than the literal ones that pervade our visual and aural environment is rarely solicited. Everything has to be packaged for consumption.

With regard to your films you've always been able to show that even what one sees with one's eyes, as you say in your books, is not necessarily the truth. My next question concerns Laura Mulvey's comment on language where any tool can be used for dominance as well as empowerment. Do you think that this is also true of poetic approaches to film?

Oh yes. This is what I have just tried to say in clarifying what is meant by the "poetic" in a context that does not lend itself easily to classification. As numerous feminist works of the last two decades have shown, it is illusory to think that women can remain outside of the patriarchal system of language. The question is, as I mentioned earlier, how to engage poetical language without simply turning it into an estheticized, subjectivist product, hence allowing it

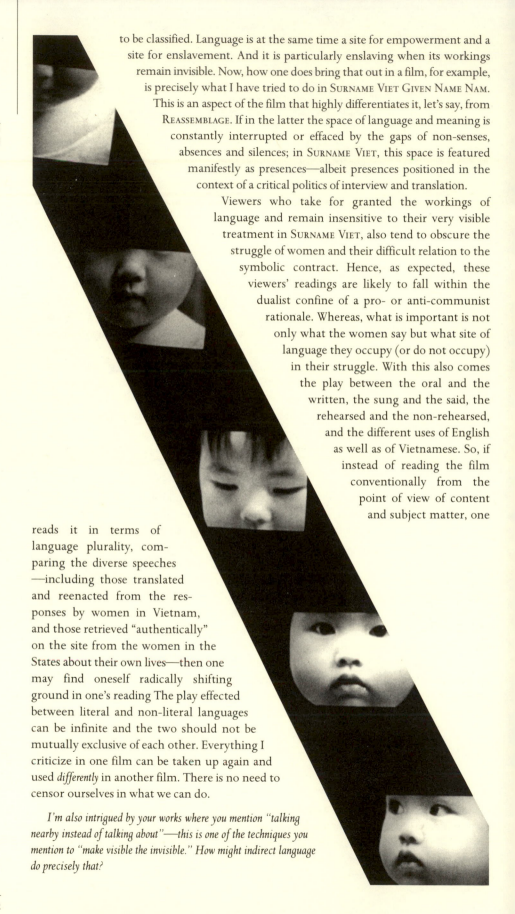

to be classified. Language is at the same time a site for empowerment and a site for enslavement. And it is particularly enslaving when its workings remain invisible. Now, how one does bring that out in a film, for example, is precisely what I have tried to do in Surname Viet Given Name Nam. This is an aspect of the film that highly differentiates it, let's say, from Reassemblage. If in the latter the space of language and meaning is constantly interrupted or effaced by the gaps of non-senses, absences and silences; in Surname Viet, this space is featured manifestly as presences—albeit presences positioned in the context of a critical politics of interview and translation.

Viewers who take for granted the workings of language and remain insensitive to their very visible treatment in Surname Viet, also tend to obscure the struggle of women and their difficult relation to the symbolic contract. Hence, as expected, these viewers' readings are likely to fall within the dualist confine of a pro- or anti-communist rationale. Whereas, what is important is not only what the women say but what site of language they occupy (or do not occupy) in their struggle. With this also comes the play between the oral and the written, the sung and the said, the rehearsed and the non-rehearsed, and the different uses of English as well as of Vietnamese. So, if instead of reading the film conventionally from the point of view of content and subject matter, one

reads it in terms of language plurality, comparing the diverse speeches —including those translated and reenacted from the responses by women in Vietnam, and those retrieved "authentically" on the site from the women in the States about their own lives—then one may find oneself radically shifting ground in one's reading The play effected between literal and non-literal languages can be infinite and the two should not be mutually exclusive of each other. Everything I criticize in one film can be taken up again and used *differently* in another film. There is no need to censor ourselves in what we can do.

I'm also intrigued by your works where you mention "talking nearby instead of talking about"—this is one of the techniques you mention to "make visible the invisible." How might indirect language do precisely that?

The link is nicely done; especially between "speaking nearby" and indirect language. In other words, a speaking that does not objectify, does not point to an object as if it is distant from the speaking subject or absent from the speaking place. A speaking that reflects on itself and can come very close to a subject without, however, seizing or claiming it. A speaking in brief, whose closures are only moments of transition opening up to other possible moments of transition—these are forms of indirectness well understood by anyone in tune with poetic language. Every element constructed in a film refers to the world around it, while having at the same time a life of its own. And this life is precisely what is lacking when one uses word, image, or sound just as an instrument of thought. To say therefore that one prefers not to speak about but rather to speak nearby, is a great challenge. Because actually, this is not just a technique or a statement to be made verbally. It is an attitude in life, a way of positioning oneself in relation to the world. Thus, the challenge is to materialize it in all aspects of the film—verbally, musically, visually. That challenge is renewed with every work I realize, whether filmic or written.

The term of the issue raised is, of course, much broader than the questions generated by any of the specific work I've completed (such as REASSEMBLAGE, in which the speaking about and speaking nearby serve as a point of departure for a cultural and cinematic reflection). Truth never yields itself in anything said or shown. One cannot just point a camera at it to catch it: the very effort to do so will kill it. It is worth quoting here again Walter Benjamin for whom, "nothing is poorer than a truth expressed as it was thought." Truth can only be approached indirectly if one does not want to lose it and find oneself hanging on to a dead, empty skin. Even when the indirect has to take refuge in the very figures of the direct, it continues to defy the closure of a direct reading. This is a form of indirectness that I have to deal with in SURNAME VIET, but even more so in SHOOT. Because here, there is necessarily, among others, a layered play between political discourse and poetical language, or between the direct role of men and the indirect role of women.

That leads me to some questions that I had about your latest film because you choose Mao as a political figure and he is also one who plays with language. There is a quote in the film: "Mao ruled through the power of rhymes and proverbs." I think this is a very apt statement about the scope of the film. I'm curious as to "Why China?" You mentioned before about how your next project or your next film is a rupture from the previous one. So was going to China just a complete change from SURNAME VIET?

It's not quite a rupture. I don't see it that way. Nor do I see one film as being better than another; there is no linear progress in my filmic work. There is probably only a way of raising questions differently from different angles in different contexts. The rupture I mentioned earlier has more to do with my general educational background. So why China? One can say that there is no more an answer to this question than to: "Why Africa?" which I often get, and "Why Vietnam?" (*laughter*), which I like to also ask in return. Indeed, when people inquire matter-of-factly about my next film in Vietnam, I cannot help but ask "why Vietnam?" Why do I have to focus on Vietnam? And this leads us back to a statement I made earlier, concerning the way marginalized peoples are herded to mind their own business. So that the area, the "homeland" in which they are allowed to work remains heavily marked, whereas the areas in which Euro-Americans' activities are deployed can go on unmarked. One is here confined to one's own culture, ethnicity, sexuality and gender. And that's often the only way for insiders within the marked boundaries to make themselves heard or to gain approval.

This being said, China is a very important step in my personal itinerary, even though the quest into Chinese culture has, in fact, more to do with the relation between the two cultures—Vietnamese and Chinese—than with anything strictly personal. The Vietnamese people are no exception when it comes to nationalism. Our language is equipped with numerous daily expressions that are extremely pejorative toward our neighbors, especially toward Chinese people. But Vietnam was the site where the Chinese and Indian cultures met, hence what is known as the Vietnamese culture certainly owes much from the crossing of these two ancient civilizations.

Every work I have realized was designed to transform my own consciousness. If I went to Africa to dive into a culture that was mostly unknown to me then, I went to China mainly because I was curious as to how I could depart from what I knew of Her. The prejudices that the Vietnamese carry vis-à-vis the Chinese are certainly historical and political. The past domination of Vietnam by China and the antagonistic relationship nurtured between the two nations (this relationship has only been normalized some months ago) have been weighing so heavily on the Vietnamese psyche that very often Vietnamese identity would be defined in contradistinction to everything thought to be Chinese. And yet it merits looking a bit harder at the Vietnamese culture—at its music, to mention a most explicit example—to realize how much it has inherited from both China and India. It is not an easy task to deny their influences, even when people need to reject them in order to move on. An anecdote whose humor proved to be double-edged was that, during my stay in China, I quickly learned to restrain myself from telling people that I was originally from Vietnam—unless someone really wanted to know (precisely because of the high tension between the two countries at the time). The local intellectuals, however, seemed to be much more open vis-à-vis Vietnam as they did not think of Her as an enemy country but rather, as a neighbor or "a brother." This, to the point that one of them even told me reassuringly in a conversation: "Well you know it's alright that you are from Vietnam; after all, She is a province of China." (*laughter*)

So it reifies that power relationship . . .

Yes, right . . . (*laughter*). On a personal level, I did want to go further than the facades of such a power relationship and to understand China differently. But the task was not all easy because to go further here also meant to go back to an ancestral heritage of the Vietnamese culture. I've tried to bring this out in the film through a look at politics via the arts.

I think Wu Tian Ming's commentary in the film gives a very good description of the present state of the arts in China. I have another question. In your book When the Moon Waxes Red *there is a chapter on Barthes and Asia. This is where you talk about his notion of the void and how it is important not to have any fixed notions of what Asia is supposed to be about. You've stated that* Shoot for the Contents *is precisely about that void, but one of the difficulties about creating a space where there can be a void is the fact that some people are unnerved by it; there is also the possibility of reifying stereotypes, of reifying the notion of Asia as other or as exotic, or feminine, or mysterious. Do you think that this was something you had thought about carefully in making your film or in the process of making your film did this issue come up?*

It always does, with every single film that I have made. And the risk of having viewers misread one's films through their own closures is always there. The only consistent signs that tell me how my films may have avoided falling into these ready-made slots is the controversial and at times contradictory nature of the readings they have suscitated. But to say the space of the Void can reify stereotypes is already to reify the Void. Perhaps before I go any further here with Shoot, I should ask you what in the film makes you think that people could fall right back on a stereotyped image of China?

Possibly when there are different scenes of China. In the film one cuts from one location to another, so you see scenes that are in northern China and then the next few frames you see Xishuanbana from southern China and they are all conflated as one image or representation of China. I saw this film with several China scholars and they were very concerned with the image of China as being enigmatic, as a space that is a void which cannot be defined, and the possible reification of China as a mystery.

Are these scholars from here in the States or from China?

These aren't Chinese friends.

Maybe that is one difference worth noting, because as I mentioned earlier, there is no speaking subject that is apolitical, and sometimes I have had very different readings of my

男

女

man

Woman

earlier films from Africans than from African-Americans for example; not to mention Euro-Americans . . . although generalizations are never adequate, and you will always have people who cross the lines. First of all, to take up the point you make about conflating the images from different cultures across China: the film has a structure that momentarily calls for this deliberate violation of internal borders, but other than that, this structure is devised precisely so as to emphasize the heterogeneity of Chinese society and the profound differences within it—hence the impossibility to simply treat China as a known Other. If you remember, it is at the beginning of the film, when Mao's concept of The Hundred Flowers is being introduced that you see a succession of images from different places in China. This is the very idea of the hundred flowers which the visuals indirectly evoke. But as the film progresses, the cultural differences that successively demarcate one region from another are sensually and politically set into relief, and never do any of these places really mix. The necessary transgression and the careful differentiation of cultural groupings have always been both structurally very important in my films, in SHOOT, as well as in the three previous ones.

As far as the Void is concerned, the comment certainly reveals how people understand and receive the Void in their lives. For some, "void" is apparently only the opposite of "full." As absence to a presence or as lack to a center, it obviously raises a lot of anxieties and frustrations because all that is read into it is a form of negation. But I would make the difference between that negative notion of the void, which is so typical of the kind of dualist thinking pervasively encountered in the West, and the spiritual Void thanks to which possibilities keep on renewing, hence nothing can be simply classified, arrested and reified. There is this incredible fear of non-action in modern society, and every empty space has to be filled up, blocked, occupied, talked about. It is precisely the whole of such an economy of *suture* (*laughter*), as film theorists calls it, that is at stake in this context of the Void.

Nobody who understands the necessity of the Void and the vital open space it offers in terms of creativity, would ever make that comment (which is mystifying in itself as it equates void with enigma and mystery), because the existence of everything around us is due to the Void. So why all this anxiety? What's the problem with presenting life in all its complexities? And, as we have discussed earlier, isn't such a reaction expected after all when the authority of specialized or packageable knowledge is at stake? Among other possible examples, I would also like to remind us here, that when the film opens with a remark such as "Any look at China is bound to be loaded with questions," that remark is both supported and countered by the next statement, which begins affirming "Her visible faces are miniscule compared to her unknown ones," but ends with the question: "*Or is this true?*" As in a throw of the dice, this casual question is precisely a point of departure for the film and the reflection on the arts and politics of China. It is later on followed by another statement that says "Only in appearance does China offer an everchanging face to the world." So the knowable and unknowable are never presented as being mutually exclusive of one another.

A distinction that may be useful here is the one theorists have made between a "radical negativity" and a negation. The negation is what the negative, dualistic reading of the void points to; while a radical negativity entails a constant questioning of arrested representations—here, of China. This is where Barthes' statement on the stereotyped being the antonym of the poetic, is most relevant. There are a few immediate examples that I can mention (although specific examples never cover the scope of the issue raised, they just tell you about the single problem involved in each case) in terms of the choices I made in the film to prevent its readings from closing off neatly within the knowable or unknowable categories. Again, the question of language: the dialogue between the two women narrators features not only a difference in ideology but also a difference in the modes of speaking. Both modes can easily be mis/identified: one as the illogical, elliptical and metaphorical language of poetry, and the other as the logical, linear and dogmatic language of political discourse. If the film is entirely done with only one of these two languages, then the risk of it falling into the confines of one camp or the other is very high. But in SHOOT, you have both, and the narrators'

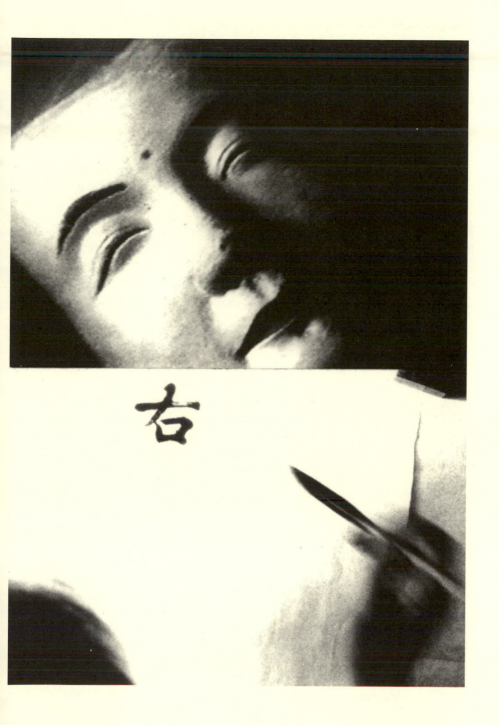

dialogue is also punctured all along by the direct speeches of the interviews, or else by songs which offer a link between the verbal and the non-verbal.

Also by the text itself where you have English and Chinese characters as well as Confucius and Mao . . .

Exactly. Sometimes, it is strategically important to reappropriate the stereotypes and to juxtapose them next to one another so that they may cancel each other out. For example the fact that in the film, the "Great Man" can be both Confucius and Mao, makes these two giants' teachings at times sillily interchangeable. Such a merging is both amusing and extremely ironical for those of us who are familiar with China's history and the relentless campaigns Mao launched against all vestiges of Confucianism in Chinese society. The merging therefore also exposes all wars fought in the name of human rights as being first and foremost a war of language and meaning. In other words, what Mao called "the verbal struggle" is a fight between "fictions." The coexistence of opposite realities and the possible interchangeability of their fictions is precisely what I have attempted to bring out on all levels of the film, verbally as well as cinematically. If the only feeling the viewer retains of SHOOT is that of a negative void, then I think the film would just be falling flat on what it tries to do; it would be incapable of provoking the kind of vexed, as well as elated and excited reactions it has so far.

You mention the viewer quite often, and in another interview you once said that audience-making is the responsibility of the filmmaker. Can you talk about who your viewers are, what audience, or for whom are you making a film, if such a purpose exists?

There are many ways to approach this question and there are many languages that have been circulated in relation to the concept of audience. There is the dated notion of mass audience, which can no longer go unquestioned in today's critical context, because mass implies first and foremost active commodification, passive consumption. Mass production, in other words, is production by the fewest possible number, as Gandhi would say (*laughter*). And here you have this other notion of the audience, which refuses to let itself be degraded through standardization. For, as Lenin would also say, and I quote by memory, "one does not bring art *down* to the people, one raises art *up* to the people." Such an approach would avoid the levelling out of differences implied in the concept of the "mass" which defines the people as an anonymous aggregate of individuals incapable of really thinking for themselves, incapable of being challenged in their frame of thought, and hence incapable of understanding the product if information is not packaged for effortless and immediate consumption. They are the ones who are easily "spoken for" as being also smart consumers whose growing sophisticated needs require that the entertainment market produce yet faster goods and more effectual throwaways in the name of better service. Here, the problem is not that such a description of the audience is false, but that its reductive rationale reinforces the ideology in power.

The question "for whom does one write?" or "for whom does one make a film?" was extremely useful some thirty years ago, in the 60s. It has had its historical moment, as it was then linked to the compelling notion of "engaged art." Thanks to it, the demystification of the creative act has almost become an accepted fact: the writer or the artist is bound to look critically at the relations of production and can no longer indulge in the notion of "pure creativity." But thanks to it also, the notion of audience today has been pushed much further in its complexities, so that simply knowing for whom you make a film is no longer sufficient. Such a targeting of audience, which has the potential to change radically the way one writes or makes a film, often proves to be no more than a common marketing tool in the process of commodification. Hence, instead of talking about "the audience," theorists would generally rather talk about "the spectator" or "the viewer." Today also, many of us have come to realize that power relationships are not simply to be found in the evident locations of power—here, in the establishments that hold the means of production—but that they also circulate

among and within ourselves because the way we write and make films is the way we position ourselves socially and politically. Form and content cannot be separated.

Furthermore, in the context of "alternative," "experimental" films, to know or *not* to know whom you are making a film for can both leave you trapped in a form of escapism: you declare that you don't care about audience; you are simply content with the circulation of your work among friends and a number of marginalized workers like yourself; and you continue to protect yourself by remaining safely within identified limits. Whereas I think each film one makes is a bottle thrown into the sea. The fact that you always work on the very limits of the known and unknown audiences, you are bound to modify these limits whose demarcation changes each time and remains unpredictable to you. This is the context in which I said that the filmmaker is responsible for building his or her audience.

So of importance today, is to make a film in which the viewer—whether visually present or not—is inscribed in the way the film is scripted and shot. Through a number of creative strategies, this process is made visible and audible to the audience who is thus solicited to interact and to retrace it in viewing the film. Anybody can make REASSEMBLAGE for example. The part that cannot be imitated, taught, or repeated is the relationship one develops with the tools that define one's activities and oneself as filmmaker. That part is irreducible and unique to each worker, but the part that could be opened up to the viewer is the "unsutured" process of meaning production. With this, we'll need to ask what accessibility means: a work in which the creative process is offered to the viewer? Or a work in which high production values see to it that the packaging of information and of fiction stories remain mystifying to the non-connoisseur audience—many of whom still believe that you have to hold several millions in your hand in order to make a feature of real appeal to the wide number?

You've answered on many levels but your last point draws attention to the state of independent art and experimental film here in the U.S. Could you comment on your experience with or interactions with those who try to categorize your work as documentary, as ethnographic, as avant-garde feminist, as independent? Could you talk about the process of independent filmmaking instead of more mainstream films?

Independent filmmaking for me is not simply a question of producing so-called "low-budget" films outside the funding networks of Hollywood. It has more to do with a radical difference in understanding filmmaking. Here, once a film is completed, you're not really done with it, rather, you're starting another journey with it. You cannot focus solely on the creative process and leave the responsibilities of fundraising and distribution to someone else (even if you work with a producer and a distributor). You are as much involved in the pre- and the post- than in the production stage itself. Once your film is released you may have to travel with it and the direct contact you have with the public does impact the way you'll be making your next film. Not at all in the sense that you serve the needs of the audience, which is what the mainstream has always claimed to do, but rather in the sense of a mutual challenge: you challenge each other in your assumptions and expectations. So for example, the fact that a number of viewers react negatively to certain choices you have made or to the direction you have taken does not necessarily lead you to renounce them for the next time. On the contrary, precisely because of such reactions you may want to persist and come back to them yet in different ways.

In my case, the contact also allows me to live out the demystification of *intention* in filmmaking. With the kind of interaction I solicit from the viewers—asking each of them actually to put together "their own film" from the film they have seen—the filmmaker's intention cannot account for all the readings that they have mediated to their realities. Thereby, the process of independent filmmaking entails a different relationship of creating and receiving, hence of production and exhibition. Since it is no easy task to build one's audiences, the process remains a constant struggle, albeit one which I am quite happy to carry on. Viewers also need to assume their responsibilities by looking critically at the representative place from which they voice their opinions on the film. Ironically enough, those who inquire about the audience of my films often seem to think that they and their immediate peers are the only people who get to see the film and can understand it. What their questions say in essence is: We are your audience. Is that all that you have as an audience? (*laughter*). If that is the case, then I think that none of us independent filmmakers would continue to make films. For me, interacting with the viewers of our films is part of independent filmmaking. The more acutely we feel the changes in our audiences, the more it demands from us as filmmakers. Therefore, while our close involvement in the processes of fundraising and distribution often proves to be frustrating, we also realize that this mutual challenge between the work and the film public, or between the creative gesture and the cinematic apparatus is precisely what keeps independent filmmaking alive.

Freud's essay 'Family Romances' is about the fantasy that one's family is not one's real family. 'The commonest of these imaginative romances', he writes, is 'the replacement of both parents or of the father alone by grander people'. The family romance however is almost infinitely various: 'its many-sidedness and its great range of applicability enable it to meet every sort of requirement.'

virtual

A nostalgia for the relational world of earliest childhood is at the root of family romances. In the eyes of the child its parents are all-powerful. The 'grander people' apparently substituted for the father or mother in later fantasies are merely these same parents as they originally appeared to the child.

scenes

Maturity brings the knowledge that one's parents are not omnipotent. Their idealised images however are not abandoned but displaced. National leaders and other figures in positions of authority or caring may be unconsciously identified with the ideal parents. As such expressions as 'motherland' and 'fatherland' imply, nationalism itself is a beneficiary of feelings originally directed towards the parents.

I dentification with the perfect parents in an international arena underlies the 1955 photographic exhibition *The Family of Man*. Prevalent opinion in the US during the immediate post-war years saw the country as being in a tutelary position of benevolent authority towards the rest of the world. Appropriately, the particular version of 'the family' which this exhibition projected into every part of the globe was the domestic ideal of the Eisenhower years.

played

Lovers (heterosexual), marriage-ceremonies, pregnancies and birth are the subjects of the large black-and-white photographs in the entrance to *The Family of Man* exhibit, and at the beginning of the exhibition catalogue. (The very first image, with a caption from the bible, is of a sunrise—or sunset—over an ocean.) A common biology is offered as guaranteeing what the curator's introduction calls 'the essential oneness of mankind throughout the world'.

between

Yet another variation on the family romance might be seen in *The Family of Man* exhibition, one rooted in earliest experience. The infant does not initially distinguish itself from its (m)other, the difference has to be learned. Failure to adequately separate self from other may result in others being seen merely as a more or less disguised reflection of oneself. In the ensuing misrecognition an erroneous 'understanding' takes the place of *tolerance* of an unbridgeable difference.

Rodgers and Hammerstein based their Broadway musical *South Pacific* on two romantic episodes from James Michener's book *Tales of the South Pacific*, in turn founded on Michener's experiences as a US officer on a 'French' Pacific island during World War II. Publicity for the 1958 20th Century Fox screen version of *South Pacific* emphasised its dual virtues as spectacle (it was shot using the TODD-AO wide-screen process) and as 'family entertainment'.

virtual

One story tells of the love between a young Navy nurse and a middle-aged French plantation-owner. She fears that her lack of sophistication will disqualify her from entry into his world, while he is afraid that she will prefer younger men to him. She rejects his proposal of marriage however only when she learns of his previous marriage to a native Polynesian woman. She subsequently overcomes her racial prejudice and accepts him and his children.

characters

Much the same problems of race and class differences within sexual relations trouble the other romance in *South Pacific*, that between a young Navy lieutenant and a native Polynesian girl. He—WASPy, wealthy and Ivy League—first rejects marriage to her, worrying how it would be received by his Philadelphia family. He later resolves to follow his heart, but dies in the course of a combat mission before he is able to tell her.

As was normal in the 1950s, *South Pacific*—like the *The Family of Man* exhibition—depicts sexual relations as purely biologically determined. Love is assumed to be exclusively heterosexual and to ineluctably issue in marriage and children. Historian John Diggins records, 'By 1957 an incredible 97 percent of Americans "of marriageable age" had taken the vows'. When Allen Ginsberg turned up in San Jose to continue a homosexual affair with Neal Cassady he was shown the door by Cassady's wife.

in

Nellie, the Navy nurse, says to Emile, the planter: 'I'll show you a picture of a Little Rock fugitive… I got this clipping from my mother today'. Emile reads aloud, 'Ensign Nellie Forbush, Arkansas' own Florence Nightingale…' The film of *South Pacific* appeared shortly after an actual image from Little Rock had appeared in newspapers world-wide. It shows fifteen-year old Elizabeth Eckford trying to enter Little Rock's Central High School. She is prevented from doing so by the Arkansas National Guard and a mob of jeering Whites.

virtual

Class identifications were never strong in the US. No history of feudalism had drawn clear distinctions between the masses and a ruling elite. Little of the US Socialism which had nevertheless developed into the1930s survived the Soviet invasion of Hungary in 1956. The Korean war—ostensibly a UN intervention but fought mainly at the instigation of, and by, the US—was a war against communism. Unsurprisingly, *South Pacific* was able to represent class conflict only in ethnic terms.

spaces

Ethnic, sexual and other forms of 'identity politics' were becoming the alternative to national party politics in the disunited states at the same time that ethnic rivalries were proving stronger than proletarian union in the soviet socialist republics. Throughout the world ethnic conflicts and solidarities alike nevertheless remained subordinate to nationalism. In spite of mutating distributions of ethnic populations within nations, increasing displacements of populations between nations, and space-contracting technologies, the fantasy of 'nation' remained the most powerful form of the family romance.

Visualizing Theory

Homi Bhabha and Victor Burgin

V.A.R. *presents work by theorists, image-makers and those who are both. What follows are discussions of two "visual" works by Victor Burgin produced for the different sites of the gallery and the street. The first of the discussions is from an edited transcript of a public conversation between Homi Bhabha and Victor Burgin, with interventions from the audience, which took place at the* INSTITUTE OF CONTEMPORARY ARTS, *London, in April, 1991. The second is an edited extract from a talk given by Burgin during a residency at* FILM IN THE CITIES, *St. Paul, in the Summer of 1989.*

Family Romance (1990)

Homi Bhabha: *In his book* BETWEEN,[1] *Victor writes about being between theory and practice, between different art practices, and between different theories. Looking at the work in that book, and at some of the new work, I thought that 'between' is a very interesting place of enunciation, because it's also the place 'in the midst of'. It's not only between two polar positions, it is also in a new place—formed when those two positions somehow ignite, incite and initiate something that, in my own work, I've called a "third space." One of the characteristics of this place 'in between' is that there is always that moment of surprise, that moment of interrupting something. I think Victor's work catches that quality precisely. The gaze that he tries to work through is always a gaze which has been interrupted. But from that moment of interruption emerges something new, something different, a displacement. Victor's work has always, for me, very productively questioned the notion of* the private and the public. I would wager that his use of psychoanalysis has been a way of questioning what is the private in the public, and what is the public in the private. Not merely as a way of saying that those practices, or those peoples, or those minorities who have constituted in some ideological sense a private sphere, should now be brought more into the public sphere. Not simply that, so much as Victor actually questions the boundary itself: why do we, in a certain historical moment, define something as private, or as public? I think this is a very different kind of practice than one that says something like, "we should draw hidden histories out into the public." This, certainly, is very valuable, but I think Victor is doing something different. Then there is another question, I think, which Victor's "betweenness," reveals: the question of the interdisciplinarity of practices. It is not only a question of being between preconstituted disciplines, but of translating those preconstituted disciplines into something else, into a practice that through that interdisiplinarity changes our concept of culture.

Victor Burgin: Homi suggested we begin with some slides of a recent work—FAMILY ROMANCE.[2] In my book, BETWEEN, I spoke about the way I conceived of the gallery as the "negative of the cinema." In the cinema we sit in darkness; in the gallery, generally, everything is light. In the cinema we sit still and the images move; in the gallery the images sit still and we move. In the cinema the sequence of images, the sequence of the reading, is determined for us; whereas in the gallery we determine the sequence and the duration ourselves. In the cinema it is the speech of the actors which is dominant, in the gallery the "inner speech" which accompanies spectatorship is heard more clearly. As in previous works—like THE BRIDGE, which made references to Hitchcock's VERTIGO—I'm interested more in the movie we remember than the one we see on the screen. I'm also interested in the way we may "remember" a film we never saw except through such things as reviews, posters, trailers and television clips, synopses, illustrated books, and so on. My interest in actual films shows in the element of sequentiality and *mise-en-scène* in my work. I generally use the space of the gallery to show one work, consisting of several separate parts, and introduced by some sort of contextualizing panel of writing. This panel is not intended to offer an explanation, it rather gives a few fragments from the environment in which I conceived of the work. For example here, on the right of the contextualizing panel for FAMILY ROMANCE, there is a vertical line of iconograms. I put those there by way of allusion to the horizon of expectations within which I was working at that time, some nine months before the Gulf War broke out. I used a computer to originate the work, and all the production was done by silk-screen printing. One result of using the silk-screen process is that the half-tone images in the right-hand panels are made up of a cross-hatching pattern of straight lines: so, the production process begins with a modern technology—film; it goes through a postmodern technology—digitization; and ends by echoing pre-modern technologies—the medieval wood-cut, or steel-engraving. The computer screen image itself, of course, is composed as a mosaic—which has its roots in classical antiquity.

Each panel is seven feet by three feet in size; the shape of the panel is derived from the shape of the Cinemascope format in which the film *South Pacific* was first shown. To be precise, it was first shown in Todd-AO, but it had its widest distribution in Cinemascope. As I've said, the images are put together on the screen of my computer. You'll notice in the images on the right that what you see in the background is always the same. This is the very first image in *South Pacific*. It's the image you see when the movie first appears on the screen, out of the darkness of the cinema; before the orchestra swells into the first notes of the theme, "Bali-Hi"; before even the title—"South Pacific"—comes out at you in Cinemascope, in what was probably the first use of those massive, chunky, "3-D" letter forms. Even before all that, you first see this silent sunset, or sunrise—we don't know, as there's not that much action taking place—over what, presumably, is the Pacific. That very first image in the film is the background image in all of the sections. Now, no figures actually appear in front of that image in the film, nor do these characters appear together; or, on the rare occasions when some do appear together, they don't appear together in the same way. What I've done, watching SOUTH PACIFIC unroll on the screen of my computer rather than on the cinema screen, is I've

been able to disarticulate the film, inspired by the notion that the film has a manifest content, a manifest face—the public face of the film, turned towards us—but that there is always, escaping in that fleeting afterimage, the sense of something which *might* have taken place in the film. There is a "latent content," another film, other films, inscribed in the manifest film. So I was using that classic Freudian distinction between manifest and latent, and also that classic sense of the latent as that which is repressed, that which only symptomatically appears, in the margin, flickering briefly on the edge of your apprehension. And then you're sucked back into the forward movement of the filmic narrative as it's dictated to you in the cinema. SOUTH PACIFIC is a manifestly heterosexual film, if not a hetrosexist film. It is centered, absolutely squarely, on the family—on sexuality contained within the family: heterosexual reproductive sexuality. And all the time there are these homoerotic undertones, in fact they are often very much overtones—to the point, certainly for us today, of cliché, with all these sailors living together on this island. But there are lots of other things going off, such as age differences and, certainly, racial differences. Someone who has a centrally marginal, or marginally central, rôle in the film—who acts as a sort of catalyst, as someone around whom much of the action turns, is "Bloody Mary." The very name denigrates her. She's shown as very much the "mother earth" figure around whom the lovers turn, but at the same time denigrated. I coupled her together with the romantic hero of the film, but in a very different relationship from that which you find in the film.

In the left-hand panel, there's a series of words printed horizontally, and in each case there is a letter blanked out. It's easy for anyone with a grasp of English to reconstruct the words. "s"-blank-"XUALITY"; hey, what's that? It's no big puzzle. We can easily reconstruct the words: "sexuality," "class," "gender," "nation," "family," "color," "creed." They're all words that represent components of an identity. In many discourses they're represented as the very ground of identity. For example, I remember very well the days when one could comfortably ascribe one's identity to one's class origin and one's 'class position.' I think we're now all aware that we live in a world where we're much more sensitive to the fact that these grounds of identity are plural, disparate, and refuse to come together comfortably to form a unified solid ground. We're continually hopping from one ground to another. The blanked-out letters, if you put those together, spell "romance." Again there's a play with manifest and latent. There's the manifest but disturbed, interrupted, word which represents that item, that "hook," upon which you're supposed to hang your identity. That item is shown, but it's shown as disturbed. There's something there that's been obliterated. But when you read across the line of those elisions you find that what is spelled out there is not on the side of what is supposed to be stable, not on the side of the Law, the symbolic order, but on the side of the Imaginary, on the side of Desire: that which continually escapes through the space of those elisions, slips through those cracks, to speak—inscribing itself precisely in the blank space. Then there's the other word, leaping between the poles of the Northern and Southern hemispheres: "exile," "stranger," "alien," "refugee," etc. This gestures towards some of the postcolonial problematics which have troubled recent politics and theory, and which, if I can return a compliment, have been so marvelously articulated in Homi's work.

I thought that you had been so perceptive about the homoerotic, which is there in this film certainly, but also more generally in the American imagination—MOBY DICK also came to mind. In the pairings, I thought you had rearticulated something about cultural difference which was attempting to say that the whole thing works on a kind of repressed paranoia. It did seem to me to be a very striking innovation, not only in your reading of the film, but also in terms of the whole question of cultural difference. What I thought was so interesting was precisely the way in which you made me rethink the problem through this work.

One of the ways I can relate the work to the theme of paranoia, now you've mentioned it, is in the element of the combinatory in Freud on paranoia. He goes through the various paranoiac forms—delusional jealousy, persecutory paranoia, and so on—and finds that each

form can be expressed as a grammatical reformulation of the negation of the proposition "I love him," the various forms in which this "I love him" can be denied. In the form of persecutory paranoia, as you know, "I love him," goes through the intermediary of "No, I hate him" to become "He hates me." In delusional jealousy "I love him" becomes "She loves him." So the various forms which paranoia takes can be reduced—here Freud appears very much as a structuralist *avant la lettre*—to a combinatory. That's the way that I started to deconstruct the film. The panels on the right rearticulate relationships between primary subjects in the film, displace these relationships, shift the relationships between subjects in different ways according to a sort of combinatory.

So that in fact the work, against the film itself, which is trying to talk about cultural pluralism, and so on, and multi-culturalism, which is such a popular political move now in institutions in complex Western societies . . . the work is really saying, you can't deal with the problem of cultural difference just by saying, you know, if we all get drunk together and dance with Bloody Mary . . . you know, that kind of, "You wear my sari, I'll wear your sarong," doesn't really work.

Precisely. When this work was first shown it attracted a very angry attack in the L.A. paper *Artweek*. The writer thought SOUTH PACIFIC was a marvellous film, and that I'd somehow fallaciously claimed that it failed to talk about racism. This wasn't my point. My point was that the humanist version of the problematic of racial difference proposed by this film, and by the *Family of Man* exhibition of the same time, isn't sufficient for us now.

We've being talking a certain kind of language, but I now want us to step back a moment, because I've been looking at some of the reviews. What about people who would say, and have indeed said to you, that this kind of language, this kind of citing of theory . . . Citing in three ways: the work cites theory, stages it, upstages it. When you talk about your work you cite theory in that way; for example, the reference to paranoia, the reference to Freud, etc., in your work and then somehow when you look at the work, one of the great pleasures of the work, is you try—and I think very successfully in some ways—to visualize, to make specular, make pleasurable, a certain kind of theoretical position. But what about people who say, "Must we know all this before we look at that work?" What would you say about that? Do we need to know all this in some kind of intellectual sense?

I've been through a number of positions on this. In that volume, BETWEEN, I begin by showing some of the earlier poster pieces—for example, the "possession" poster—which were out on the street as a sort of populist gesture of making something that anybody could understand. But of course what you find out—empirically, through the interviews that were conducted on the streets of Newcastle at the time—is that "anybody" doesn't understand. Or that, rather, everybody understands, but they understand very different things. That was really about the time that I was starting to get interested in psychoanalysis, and I was starting to see that the populist ambition to make work that would be commonly understood was fundamentally wrong-headed. I tried various strategies, and I finally decided, "Well, you can't please everyone, so you might as well please yourself." I realized that one's audience is always imaginary. I suppose, classically, we begin by working to please our parents, and there's a certain extent to which those imagos are still present when any of us work, if only in the background. But in the foreground, in the 1970s, when I was doing most of the work in BETWEEN, I was thinking, "Well, I don't know who goes into the galleries anymore. All I do know is that there are a lot of people who subscribe to the same magazines I subscribe to. So I'm going to work for them." So I was working for people who read *Screen*, who read *m/f*... there's a whole period in which I was working for them. Now they, I don't think, ever went into the galleries. I think there were very few people in SoHo, in New York, doing the Saturday round of the galleries with a copy of *Ideology & Consciousness* in their Gucci handbag. So there was a displacement involved—from the site of the imaginary audience to the actual physical site of the gallery. Now, I think that displacement was echoed in the work itself. Because, clearly, when theory itself is cited—cited with a "c" now—in the gallery, then its site of address is different. When you encounter theory on the gallery wall, as a fragment, it's coming at you from somewhere else. And the addressee is also different, so there is then that element of presenting theory itself as a spectacle. I'm thinking now of these works from the mid-'70s—such as Zoo, the piece I made in Berlin—where I would occasionally insert a little summary of, for example, Foucault on panopticism. I had to write in what used to be called a "lapidary" style, the style developed for inscribing monuments. You didn't want to have to chisel away for too long, you had to say things succinctly. I tried to compress a theoretical idea into a few terse lines, for inscription into the photographic emulsion. In the form of an inscription, they were completely lifted out of the context of the academy, in which they were naturalized as the lingua franca of academic discourse. In a way, it was like isolating ideas behind the glass of a display case, but also trying to get them to work in some different way. Eventually, more people who did read those theory magazines began coming into the gallery, and a different sort of art was being produced. But by then I had started to think about "reasonable expectations": I don't know who comes into the gallery, but I know what they reasonably expect, and they reasonably expect something pleasurable to look at. So then, in the wake of Laura Mulvey's "Visual Pleasure and Narrative Cinema"[3]—the author is here tonight, and I hope she'll forgive me for invoking that essay yet again—but having been led by Laura to think about pleasure as a political issue, and having first attempted a rather severe and stoic work, I then tried to bring back some "visual pleasure," but differently . . .

I like this notion of "bringing back." I think it creates a kind of temporal interruption, which has nothing to do with bringing something back in its old form. It's part of this thing I started off by talking about, this interruption and then reinscription, the something new produced in between, in the midst of the surprise. You said these images started off in a late-1950s American romance-based film, then you said that your various processes with these images brought back a kind of medieval mode of production of representation. There are two interesting things here: the way in which this destroys the notion of the present of the work, and indeed the presence of the

work, as a plenitude, in a simple pleasurable identification. In another way, I feel what goes on here is both a critique of cultural pluralism, which is different cultural practices in the same time, in the same temporal schema. And it's also a critique of cultural relativism, different cultural practices in the same space. You know, Magiciens de la Terre—I'm just relating this work to the idea of the larger international exhibitions we've had—"So long as we put them all in the same space, all at the same time, then the problem of inequalities and discriminations, all this disappears." I know—because I was involved a little bit in the Magiciens de la Terre thing—that that was their idea: if you took bits from everywhere, gave them, as indeed they did, the same kind of modular boxes, the same spaces, gave them the same rooms then, you know, "we've done our bit." People can then decide what they like and what they don't like. Of course, my point was it's precisely the between that is important. From that point of view, I think, you've problematized something very important in both the inside and the outside of the image in culture and of cultural difference; and indeed, the private and the public, the popular and the theoretical, and you've actually performed the problem.

I like the idea of the performance of a problem, it almost suggests a new game show.

Well let's have it, shall we drag someone in from the audience....?

Man in Audience: *You say your images are produced digitally, could you speak a bit about that, and about how it's changed your practice?*

Let's say I'm in New York, and I decide to go the Metropolitan Museum to look at a Titian. I'll take a cab, or the subway, and on the way I'll see ads, newspaper photographs and various other images. Back home, in the evening, I'll maybe watch the news on TV, and then go out to the cinema. At any moment during the day, what I'm actually seeing can be overlaid by recollection and anticipation of other images, from other moments. The computer allows me to construct analogs of the way these image-fragments—Freud used the expression, "the day's residues"—work together in the mind. The virtual space of the computer screen comes to represent the psychical space of mental processes such as fantasy and memory. My previous practice was to use photography. One of the things I liked about photography was that it allowed me to put everything in the environment on a common basis, on film. In a photograph, The Arc de Triomph or a matchbook cover can occupy the same amount of space in the frame, and through double-exposure they can occupy the same space at the same time. Similarly, what I like about digitization is that it brings everything onto a common ground. But the computer is a much more powerful tool for what I try to do because it can more easily accept a wide range of inputs—scanned images, live video, tape, video-disk, and so on—and it's much faster, and infinitely more versatile, in combining them.

Woman in Audience: *What would be the difference for you between showing this work in a gallery, or museum, and showing it in the street?*

It's a bit like the difference between writing for an academic journal and writing advertising copy. There's no question of putting the same text into two different contexts. It's rather a question of writing for a specific location. I have made works for the street, but this isn't one of them. When the question you just asked gets raised it's often to valorize street work over gallery work. But I don't think it's that simple. For example, take that whole issue of "working outside the gallery," you know, breaking out of the gallery and taking to the street. The gallery space, in principle, is a space like many others—like this space we're in now, like the space of the seminar room, or the space of the cinema. If there's any "struggle" it's for what goes on in that space, what gets talked about, what gets said in that space. And then, obviously, what is then taken out of that space—the seminar room, the cinema, the gallery—into everyday social and political relations. That's what I think is important. There's no difficulty involved in breaking out of the gallery and taking art into the streets—it's by now a thoroughly familiar and venerable form of activity. But you have to be careful, because what usually happens in the process is not that art is taken to "the people," it's rather that the street is turned into a museum.

Man in Audience: *Could you say something about the use of color in this work?*

The film SOUTH PACIFIC got quite a lot of press at the time it came out because of the work of the cameraman, Leon Shamroy. Shamroy used a technique of passing colored gels in front of the lens to heighten the drama of particular moments. So the screen would suddenly go all orange, or violet. At the time the film was released this was considered a great advance in the art of cinema-photography. Shamroy subsequently found the technique to be an embarrassment, and he disowned it. But what it reminded me of was that common corpus of colors which characterizes 1950s design in general. When I was researching the work I came across an ad in *Life* magazine, for refrigerators, where the image of the same refrigerator was reproduced in a range of colors very similar to the range of gels used in the film. So, in retrospect, Shamroy's use of gels evokes domestic U.S.A. in the midst of the ostensibly distant and Other location of the film.

Laura Mulvey: *You haven't actually talked about the vertical words: "exile," "stranger," "alien," "refugee" . . . I wondered if you could just say something about those particular words. And then, otherwise, I was really struck by the relationships between the figures in the frame, and by the relationships between physiognomy, figure and frame.*

First, there's a fixed grid of words reading horizontally—"family," "gender," "class," and so on—and that's repeated. Next, there's that which crosses and disturbs that grid, in the form of the elisions, and the implied word "romance"—and that is repeated too. So I wanted something else, to serve as a counterpoint, which would change between images. So while the grid speaks of solidarity—with class, race, gender, and so on; these are convergent concepts, representing the ground on which subjects are brought together—the vertical words speak to divergence, to the impossibility of making things join. So "exile," "stranger," and so on, were words which spoke of diaspora. To connect this with your second point, the form of the vertical words echo the form of the reflections of the sun on the ocean. The decision was, in every panel except one, to keep that reflection as a bar separating the figures in the frame: they're always deployed one to each side of that bar.

What I was wondering about was the way in which "stranger"—"exile," "alien" and so on—is a sign of diaspora, and also it's what's repressed in the creation of a citizen of the United States, where the concept of the national identity involves the erasure of all of those things. I was thinking of how these things come out, emerge from, these images.

Those things here have something to do with "site-specificity": in the microcosm, to do with the initial exhibition of this work in Los Angeles, but coming out of the sort of debates I'm involved in at the University of California, Santa Cruz—which is on a hill overlooking the Pacific. In the macrocosm, it's to do with being situated in the U.S. in general, where I'm, myself, a "resident alien"—a far-flung fragment of a "somewhere else." So there was, as Homi put it very well, that "performance" of a problem, perhaps even an "acting out," of a situation that's at once geographical, intellectual and emotional—"psychogeographical," if I can apply that Situationist word, in a rather different way, to the condition of exile.

Those words—"exile," "alien," and so on—reiterate the condition of U.S. nationality, and then, looking at the image of the three sailors, I was particularly struck by the "triumph" of racial difference in the U.S., the subordination of ethnic differences to racial difference.

Yes, one of my references in the "context panel," in fact, is to the attempted subordination of racial and ethnic differences to nation—which, again, I was very much aware of in the context of the growing nationalist rhetoric which accompanied the build-up to the Gulf War.

And, just one more thing, I was thinking about what you said about the background, about not being able to tell whether the sun is setting or rising, and I thought that, in the context of American cinema, and American mythology, the sun has to be setting—because the American odyssey is always towards the West. And what I see in these images, also, is some of the anxiety of having reached the limit of that quest.

Notes

1. *Between*, Oxford and New York, Basil Blackwell/ICA, 1986.

2. Reproduced in full, and in color, in *Digital Dialogues: Photography in the Age of Cyberspace*, ed. A. Cameron, T. Druckrey and T. Ziff. Birmingham, *Ten-8*, 1991; and in, V. Burgin, *Passages*, Musée d'art moderne de la Communauté Urbaine de Lille, Villeneuve d'Ascq, 1991.

3. Laura Mulvey, "Visual Pleasure and Narrative Cinema" (1975), in *Visual and Other Pleasures*, London, Macmillan, 1989.

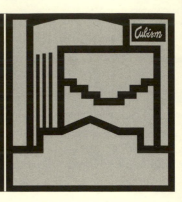

Minnesota Abstract (1989)

Victor Burgin: Psychoanalytic theory is the critical tool I use most often. Freud's original discovery—the foundation stone of psychoanalysis—was that thoughts we find painful, or otherwise cause us anxiety, may be repressed and become unconscious. I'm increasingly interested in the idea that we encounter the symptomatic *return* of the repressed not only in the speech, actions and dreams of individuals, but also in the anonymous cultural productions of nations. The histories of many nations contain painful and discreditable facts. Great Britain, at the end of the nineteenth-century, at the height of its power and prestige, preferred not to remember the extent to which its great wealth had been derived from the slave trade. A painful fact of American history is that the United States is founded on an act of expropriation, in which the indigenous peoples of the north American continent were systematically deprived of their lands. It was perhaps inevitable that this fact should come to my mind when I visited Minneapolis. Here, I encountered an environment in which the repressed images and names of Native Americans constantly return: on the labels of products on supermarket shelves, in corporate logos, on automobiles, and so on.

Shortly after I arrived in Minneapolis, the Sunday July 23 edition of the local *Star Tribune* newspaper carried a story headed, "Historian finds names of Minnesota's forgotten Indians." Although it was a local story, concerning the Twin Cities, the story came from an outside agency—Associated Press. It was based on information supplied by Virginia Rogers, working for the Minnesota Historical Society in St. Paul. The part of the story which caught my attention read:

> The US government created the 837,120 acre White Earth Reservation in 1867, intend-
> ing that all Chippewa Indians be relocated there. As enticement, the government
> offered 40 acres of land for every 10 acres cultivated . . . for nearly 20 years the Chippewa

who relocated to White Earth fulfilled government expectations, farming quite successfully. In 1885, however, white settlers on adjoining Red River Valley lands adopted a resolution demanding that the reservation be opened to white settlers . . . For the next two years, Episcopalian Bishop Henry Whipple lobbied Congress and the administration on behalf of White Earth Indians. All of Whipple's efforts were in vain: By 1982, just 1,952 acres remained in trust.

The name "White Earth" reminded me of the name "Little Earth"—a Federal-sponsored "HUD" housing development in the Twin Cities occupied mainly by Native Americans. Since the project was built, the care invested in it by the people who live there, together with a changed market situation, has turned what was originally assumed to be a strictly non-commercial housing project into an attractive, potentially profitable, "investment opportunity." Today, official mismanagement of Little Earth has brought it to the point where the project is in danger of being taken from the people who now live there, and sold to private interests— and this in spite of the scandal over alleged massive frauds perpetrated by HUD officers during the Reagan administration. The *Star Tribune* story about White Earth concludes: "White Earth prospered until people outside the reservation realized that the Indians had rich resources in trees and farm land . . . Then they legislated the reservation nearly out of existence." It seemed that history was threatening to repeat itself: what had happened then to White Earth could happen now to Little Earth.

The famous "first rule" of psychoanalysis is to say whatever comes to mind. I try to apply that rule when I work. I work mainly through attention to what Freud called "condensation." A dream image, or a fragment of the analysand's speech, may represent a site where several paths of thought merge. In this work, the image in the central panel condenses elements derived from logotypes which make reference to Native Americans: *Mutual of Omaha; Detroit Bank and Trust; Continental Airlines.* The following buildings are cited, in St. Paul: *Minnesota World Trade Center; Cathedral of St. Paul; Minnesota State Capitol; in Minneapolis: IDS Center Tower; Piper Jaffray Tower; Normandy Inn Best Western.* For me, new to the Twin Cities, these are the buildings which give a distinct signature to the skylines. My drawings of them evolved into a form which reminded me of the work of Stuart Davis. I was living near the Walker Art Center. On one of my visits to the museum I checked to see if they had a Stuart Davis painting in the collection—they did; the title, COLONIAL CUBISM, was a gift. Western European colonialism advanced through the building of forts, followed by cities—literally cementing itself into place. Davis' painting is unusual in that it does not contain the element of *writing* he usually incorporated into his work. I therefore "forged" the words in the title of Davis' painting in his own characteristic style. The colors? "Legally"-expressed market relations were the alibi which turned "expropriation" of Native American lands into the more respectable "purchase." In 1803, through the "Louisiana Purchase," the United States bought almost 900,000 square miles of land from France. A few square miles of this parcel, lying west of the Mississippi River near its confluence with the "St. Peters" (later, "Minnesota") River, later became part of the Twin Cities. For this reason the colors of my panels quote the red, white and blue of "Old Glory" in a format which more directly evokes the "*Bleu, blanc, rouge*" of the French *tricolore*—much in evidence in this Bicentennial Year of the Declaration of the Rights of Man.

The historical parallel to be drawn between "White Earth" and "Little Earth" seemed worth pointing out in public. I took the central graphic element in MINNESOTA ABSTRACT and combined it with a text—set in parallel columns—based on the *Star Tribune* story and what I had learned about the HUD housing project. Through the agency of a friend, I asked a Native American organization to check my text, changed it in line with their suggestions, and submitted the finished design for their approval. This piece was made for the street rather than for the gallery—designed in black and white so it could be cheaply reproduced on a photocopy machine. I asked the organization which had invited me to Minneapolis to help me print and distribute the "flyer." They declined, worried about embroiling themselves in a controversy that might affect their funding (this was the summer of the Helms/Mapplethorpe furore). The Minneapolis critical monthly journal *Artpaper* had already offered me their back-cover, and I had designed the piece to fit their "tabloid" format—it appeared in the *October* issue. *Artpaper* ran off extra copies of the page for posting in the streets.

MUTUAL TRUST

THEN & NOW

White Earth, an 837,120 acre reservation, was the result of an 1867 treaty between the US government and the White Earth Anishinabi people. Those who relocated to White Earth met government demands: abandoning traditional ways to become successful farmers.

In 1885 white settlers on adjoining lands demanded that White Earth be opened to them. Bishop Henry Whipple lobbied Congress on behalf of the Anishinabi, but in vain. By 1982 only 1,952 acres of White Earth remained in trust.

Little Earth is a Twin Cities HUD project occupied mainly by Native Americans. In the years since it was built, the care invested in Little Earth by the people who live there has turned it into an attractive 'investment opportunity'—ripe for picking.

Today, the HUD mismanagement of Little Earth has brought it to the point where the homes of Native Americans are again in danger of being sold to speculators chasing private profit. **Now with Little Earth, as then with White Earth, the powers-that-be are putting greed before need.**

GREED BEFORE NEED

Visualizing Theory

Contributors

Homi Bhabha is Lecturer in English at the University of Sussex. He is the author of *Nation and Narration* and *Location of Culture*, both published by Routledge.

Marc Blanchard is Professor of French and Comparative Literature, and Director of the Critical Theory Program at the University of California, Davis. Among his publications are *In Search of the City: Engels, Baudelaire, Rimbaud* and *3 Portraits de Montaigne: Essai sur la représentation à la Renaissance*.

Victor Burgin teaches in the Art History and History of Consciousness programs at the University of California, Santa Cruz. He is the author of *Passages*, and a contributor to the volume *Interpreting Contemporary Art*.

Nancy N. Chen teaches Anthropology and Sociology at Tufts University. She is currently working on a film on popular healing practices in China.

Jane Collins is Associate Professor of Sociology and Women's Studies at the University of Wisconsin at Madison. Her most recent book, co-authored with Catherine Lutz, is *Reading National Geographic*.

Hal Foster is Professor of Art History and Comparative Literature, Cornell University, and editor of the journal *October*. His publications include *Recodings: Art, Spectacle, Cultural Politics* and *Compulsive Beauty*.

Martin Jay is Professor of History at the University of California, Berkeley. Among his books are *Fin-de-siècle Socialism* and *Force Fields*.

Ludmilla Jordanova is Professor of History at the University of York, England. Her publications include *Languages of Nature*, and *Sexual Visions: Images of Gender in Science and Medicine Between the Eighteenth and Twentieth Centuries*.

Bennetta Jules-Rosette is Professor of Sociology at the University of California, San Diego. Her last book, entitled *Terminal Signs: Computers and Social Change in Africa*, deals with the effects of new technologies and computerization in Africa. She is currently writing a new book entitled *Parisianism and Universalism: African Writing and Identity in France*.

Catherine Lutz is Professor of Anthropology at the University of North Carolina, Chapel Hill. Most recently, she has co-authored *Reading National Geographic* with Jane Collins.

Dean MacCannell is Professor of Applied Behavioral Sciences at the University of California, Davis. He is Co-Editor of *American Journal of Semiotics* and author of *The Tourist: A New Theory of the Leisure Class* (with Juliet F. MacCannell).

David MacDougall's recent ethnographic films include *Photo Wallahs* (co-directed with Judith MacDougall), about photography as a medium of both desire and evidence in a north Indian hill station, and *Tempus de Baristas*, about social change and personal identity in eastern Sardinia.

Alan Macfarlane is Professor of Historical Anthropology at Cambridge University, and Fellow of the British Academy. His most recent publications include *Marriage & Love in England: Modes of Reproduction 1300–1840* and *The Culture of Capitalism*.

George Marcus teaches in the Department of Anthropology at Rice University. His books include *Anthropology as Cultural Critique*, co-edited with Michael M. J. Fischer, and *Writing Culture*, co-edited with James Clifford.

Henrietta Moore is Lecturer in Social Anthropology at the London School of Economics. She is author of *Space, Text and Gender* and *Feminism and Anthropology*.

Rachel Moore is writing a doctoral dissertation on film as modern ritual for the Cinema Studies department at New York University called *Savage Theory*.

Bill Nichols teaches in the Department of Cinema at San Francisco State University. His recent books include *Representing Reality: Issues and Concepts in Documentary*.

Christopher Pinney is Lecturer in South Asian Anthropology at the School of Oriental and African Studies, University of London. His main fieldwork was concerned with temporal notions among industrial workers in Madhya Pradesh; later work has focused on Indian popular photography and ritual images.

Peter Redfield is writing a doctoral dissertation in anthropology at the University of California, Berkeley, which examines relations between technology and nature in French efforts to develop French Guiana, penal colony through space center.

C. Nadia Seremetakis is the author of *The Last Word: Women, Death and Divination in Inner Mani*. She is currently working on a visual ethnography of recent immigrant populations in urban Greece.

Paul Stoller is Professor of Anthropology at West Chester University. His books include *The Cinematic Griot: The Ethnography of Jean Rouch* and *Embodying Colonial Memories*, forthcoming from Routledge.

Marilyn Strathern is Professor of Anthropology at Cambridge University. Her books include *The Gender of the Gift, Partial Connections*, and *After Nature: English Kinship in the Late Twentieth Century*.

Susan Rubin Suleiman is Professor of Romance and Comparative Literatures at Harvard University. Her most recent books include *The Female Body in Western Culture: Contemporary Perspectives* and *Subversive Intent: Gender, Politics, and the Avant-Garde*.

Michael Taussig is Professor in the Department of Anthropology at Columbia University. His two most recent publications are *The Nervous System* and *Mimesis and Alterity: A Particular History of the Senses*, both published by Routledge.

David Tomas teaches in the Department of Visual Arts at the University of Ottawa. His most recent videotape is *Rum and Coca-Cola*.

Eliot Weinberger's most recent book is *Outside Stories*, published by New Directions.

Annette Weiner is Kriser Distinguished Professor of Anthropology and Dean of the Graduate School of Arts and Sciences at New York University. She is also President of the American Anthropological Association. Her most recent book is *Inalienable Possessions: The Paradox of Keeping-While-Giving*.

Picture Credits

Foreword, Lucien Taylor: (x) *Sight and Might,* photo by Lucien Taylor.

The Camera People, Eliot Weinberger: (7) *Grass,* film by Merien Cooper and Ernest Schoedsack, courtesy of Milestone Film & Video; (9) *Chang,* film by Merien Cooper and Ernest Schoedsack, courtesy of Milestone Film & Video; (11) "Dani victory celebration" from *Dead Birds,* a film by Robert Gardner, copyright Film Study Center, Harvard University; (12) "New Guinea Warrior Shouts at the Enemy" from *Dead Birds,* a film by Robert Gardner, copyright Film Study Center, Harvard University; (13) "An Arrow is Removed from a Wounded Warrior" from *Dead Birds,* a film by Robert Gardner, copyright Film Study Center, Harvard University; (15) *The Nuer,* a film by Hilary Harris and George Breidenbach, copyright Film Study Center, Harvard University; (16) from *Lorang's Way,* a film by David & Judith MacDougall, courtesy of University of California Extension Center for Media and Independent Learning; (17) from *The Wedding Camels,* directed by David & Judith MacDougall, courtesy of University of California Extension Center for Media and Independent Learning; (19) "Bororo maiden choosing the most perfect male dancer at the Garawal ceremony," from *Deep Hearts* by Robert Gardner, copyright Film Study Center, Harvard University; (20) "Boatman, The Ganges, Benares, India," photo by Jane Tuckerman, from *Forest of Bliss* by Robert Gardner, copyright Film Study Center, Harvard University; (23) "Boatman with Dead Child; Benares, India," photo by Christopher James, from *Forest of Bliss* by Robert Gardner, copyright Film Study Center, Harvard University; (24) "Zulay Facing the 21st Century," by Jorge Mabel Preloran.

Whose Story Is It?, David MacDougall: (29) Images from *V.A.R.* 7:2, Fall 1991.

Trobrianders on Camera and Off, Annette Weiner: All photos by Annette Weiner. (55) "Buying film before the next cricket performance," *V.A.R.* 8:1, Spring 1992; (56) "Time out at a cricket performance at Gateshead," *V.A.R.* 8:1, Spring 1992; (57) "Leaving Gateshead fairgrounds for their hotel after a long day of cricket playing and dancing," *V.A.R.* 8:1, Spring 1992; (58) "Dressing for a dance performance, Flora Gardette fastens her Trobriand skirt before removing her Western skirt," *V.A.R.* 8:1, Spring 1992.

The Ethnographer's Tale, Bill Nichols: (63) from *Dead Birds* by Robert Gardner, copyright

Film Study Center, Harvard University; (70) from *Reassemblage* by Trinh T. Minh-ha, courtesy of Women Make Movies, Inc.; (73) from *Surname Viet Given Name Nam* by Trinh T. Minh-ha, courtesy of Women Make Movies, Inc.; (77) from *Surname Viet Given Name Nam* by Trinh T. Minh-ha, courtesy of Women Make Movies, Inc.

Artaud, Rouch, and the Cinema of Cruelty, Paul Stoller: (85) from *Les Maîtres Fous* by Jean Rouch; (86) from *Les Maîtres Fous* by Jean Rouch; (89) from *Jaguar* by Jean Rouch; (90) from *La Pyramide Humaine* by Jean Rouch; (91) from *La Pyramide Humaine* by Jean Rouch; (92) from *Petit à Petit* by Jean Rouch; (93) from *Petit à Petit* by Jean Rouch; (94) from *Petit à Petit* by Jean Rouch; (95) from *Petit à Petit* by Jean Rouch.

Cannibal Tours, Dean MacCannell: (101, 106) Images from *Cannibal Tours* by Dennis O'Rourke, copyright Direct Cinema Ltd.

Trinh T. Minh-ha Observed: Anthropology & Others, Henrietta Moore: (119) Trinh T. Minh-ha, courtesy of Women Make Movies, Inc.

Between the Street and the Salon: The Dilemma of Surrealist Politics in the 1930s, Susan Suleiman: (146) Plate 8 in *Nadja.* "No: not even the extremely handsome, extremely useless Porte Saint-Denis . . . ," *V.A.R.* 7:1, Spring 1991; (148) Plate 17 in *Nadja.* "The Humanité bookstore," *V.A.R.* 7:1, Spring 1991; (151) Plate 26 in *Nadja.* "The Sphinx Hôtel, Boulevard Magenta," *V.A.R.* 7:1, Spring 1991; (152) Luis Buñuel, *L'âge d'or,* "Parfois le dimanche . . . ," *V.A.R.* 7:1, Spring 1991; (155) Luis Buñuel, *L'âge d'or.* "J'ai blasphémé peut être . . . ," *V.A.R.* 7:1, Spring 1991.

Exquisite Corpses, Hal Foster: (161) Fig. 1. from *Variétés,* March 15, 1929, "Le mannequin-élégant dans les rues de Paris," photo by A. Dubreuil/"Hommes-sandwich à la foire de Leipzig," anonymous, *V.A.R.* 7:1, Spring 1991; (162) Fig. 2. from *Variétés,* Oct. 15, 1929, "Masque de clinique," anonymous/ "Danseur thibétain," photo by Meshrapom-Russ, *V.A.R.* 7:1, Spring 1991; (163) Fig. 3. from *Variétés,* Oct. 15, 1929, "Children's Corner," photo by Herbert Bayer/"Masque servant à injurier les esthétes," photo by E.L.T. Mesens, *V.A.R.* 7:1, Spring 1991; (164) Fig. 4. from *Variétés,* Oct. 15, 1929, "Voir ou entendre," anonymous, *V.A.R.* 7:1, Spring 1991; (165) Fig. 5a. from *Variétés,* Jan. 15, 1930, "Man Ray: Le penseur," anonymous/ "Brancusi: Enfant," anonymous, *V.A.R.* 7:1, Spring 1991; (165) Fig. 5b. from *Variétés,* Jan. 15, 1930, "Sophie

Arp-Taeuber: Les soldats," anonymous/ "L'automate d'acier R. U. R. qui accomplit au commandement les mouvements humains," anonymous, *V.A.R.* 7:1, Spring 1991; (166) Fig. 6. from *Variétés*, Jan. 15, 1930, "La protection des hommes," anonymous, *V.A.R.* 7:1, Spring 1991; (167) Fig. 7a. from *Variétés*, Jan. 15, 1930, "Cinéma," anonymous/"Théâtre," Russphoto, *V.A.R.* 7:1, Spring 1991; (168) Fig. 7b. from *Variétés*, Jan. 15, 1930, "Trafic," anonymous/"Peinture," anonymous, *V.A.R.* 7:1, Spring 1991; (170) Fig. 8. from *Minotaure*, 1933, "Cluster of 5," *V.A.R.* 7:1, Spring 1991; (171) Fig. 9. from *Minotaure*, 1933, "Cluster of 6," *V.A.R.* 7:1, Spring 1991.

The Disenchantment of the Eye: Surrealism and the Crisis of Ocularcentrism, Martin Jay: (177) Photo by Man Ray; (180) Photo by Man Ray, published in *Minotaure* in 1935, and referred to in footnote 64; (191) Still from *Un chien andalou*, Luis Buñuel and Salvador Dali; (192) Still from *Un chien andalou*, Luis Buñuel and Salvador Dali.

The Memory of the Senses, C. Nadia Seremetakis: (217–26) All photographs courtesy of C. Nadia Seremetakis.

One-Legged Gender, Marilyn Strathern: (244) "An informal demonstration of how one-legged figures are used to prod initiates on the back," photographer unknown; (245) "An initiation dance with a one-legged figure," photographer unknown; (247) Untitled, photographer unknown.

The Hand, Ludmilla Jordanova: (257) p. 58, Chapter III, "The Comparative Anatomy of the Hand," in Sir Charles Bell, *The Hand, Its Mechanisms and Vital Endowments as Convincing Design*. London: William Pickering, 1834. 3rd ed.

Post-Bourgeois Tattoo: Reflections on Skin Writing in Late Capitalist Societies, Marc Blanchard: (289) Original drawing by John White, engraved by de Bry, Virginia c. 1589; (293) Untitled, *V.A.R.* 7:2, Fall 1991.

Remembering the Revolution, Forgetting the Empire: Notes After the French Bicentennial, Peter Redfield: (325) "The Tower of all Cultures," *V.A.R.* 8:2, Fall 1992; (327) "Strange Encounters," *V.A.R.* 8:2, Fall 1992.

Simulations of Postmodernity: Images of Technology in African Tourist and Popular Art, Bennetta Jules-Rosette: (348) *Victoria Falls* by Mpinda Joseph, Kanyama Painters' Circle, Lusaka, Zambia, is an example of a natural monument,

photo by Bennetta Jules-Rosette; (349) *Kariba Dam* by Mpinda Joseph, Kanyama Painters' Circle, Lusaka, Zambia, exemplifies the modern monument in which the forces of nature are harnessed, photo by Bennetta Jules-Rosette; (351) *Colonie belge* by Zairian painter Tshibumba Kanda-Matulu, Lubumbashi, Zaire, circa 1977, photo courtesy of the collection of Bogumil Jewsiewicki; (353) *Attempt to ward off the first attack on Shaba* by Tshibumba Kanda-Matulu, Lubumbashi, 1977. Photo courtesy of the collection of Bogumil Jewsiewicki; (355) Engraved coin minted in 1929 and worn as a sign of annual tax payment in the Belgian Congo, Phototèque du musée de l'homme, cliché D. Ponsard, ; (356) Simulated Suits, carvings of modern Western apparel in the latest styles from the atelier of Koffi Kouakou and Anoh Acou, Grand Bassam, Côte d'Ivoire model postmodernity, photo by Bennetta Jules-Rosette; (357) Carved computer by Koffi Kouakou at the Grand Bassam atelier, Côte d'Ivoire, photo from the collection of Bennetta Jules-Rosette; (359) *The Guitar Player* by Zairian artist Diouf Kabamba. This painting is one of the few works by Diouf containing an object of Western origin, photo courtesy of Ibongo Gilunga, National Museum of Zaire.

The Photograph as an Intersection of Gazes: The Example of National Geographic, Catherine Lutz & J. Collins: (367) Fig. 1. August, 1976, photo: Robert Madden, © National Geographic Society; (371) Fig. 2. "Pose de l'homme de la nature" and "Pose de l'homme civilisé," Honoré Daumier, 1853; (374) Fig. 3. February, 1960, photo: Lowell Thomas, Jr., 1954; (375) Fig. 4. Average number of photos per article containing Westerners, 1950–86; Fig. 5. (376) August, 1956, photo: Volkmar Kurt Wentzel, © National Geographic Society; (377) Fig. 6. February, 1925, photo: Felix Shay, © National Geographic Society; (379) Fig. 7. August, 1982, photo: O. Louis Mazzatenta, © National Geographic Society.

Speaking Nearby, Nancy Chen & Trinh T. Minh-ha: (433–51) All images from *Shoot for the Contents* by Trinh T. Minh-ha.

Visualizing Theory, Homi Bhabha & Victor Burgin: (452–67) Images from *V.A.R.* 8:1, Spring 1992.